The Web Warrior Guide to
Web Design Technologies

Don Gosselin
Ruth Guthrie
Luis A. Lopez
Joel Sklar
Matt Slaybaugh
Louise Soe

THOMSON
―――＊―――™
COURSE TECHNOLOGY

Australia • Canada • Mexico • Singapore • Spain • United Kingdom • United States

THOMSON

COURSE TECHNOLOGY

The Web Warrior Guide to Web Design Technologies
by Don Gosselin, Ruth Guthrie, Luis A. Lopez, Joel Sklar,
Matt Slaybaugh, and Louise Soe

Executive Editor:
Jennifer Locke

Acquisitions Editor:
Bill Larkin

Developmental Editor:
Ann Shaffer

Editorial Assistant:
Christy Urban

Associate Product Manager:
Janet Aras

Production Editor:
Jeanne R. Busemeyer
Hyde Park Publishing Services

Cover Designer:
Joseph Lee
Black Fish Design

Compositor:
GEX Publishing Services

Manufacturing Coordinator:
Laura Burns

Senior Marketing Manager:
Angie Laughlin

Disclaimer
Course Technology reserves the right to revise this publication and make changes from time to time in its content without notice.

ISBN 0-619-06460-9

BRIEF Contents

TABLE OF

Contents

CHAPTER FOURTEEN
JavaScript: Part II   513

CHAPTER FIFTEEN
JavaScript: Part III   549

Preface

The *Web Warrior Guide to Web Design Technologies* provides a survey of the languages and tools used to author Web pages. If you are a beginning Web page author, this book introduces you to the basics of HTML/XHTML and Cascading Style Sheets (CSS) and explains how to develop basic Web pages using the Macromedia Dreamweaver Web authoring tool. You also learn how to create and manipulate images and animation by using Adobe Photoshop, Adobe ImageReady, Macromedia Fireworks, and Macromedia Flash. You will also examine the JavaScript scripting language and Dynamic Hypertext Markup Language (DHTML), which you can use to add interactivity to your Web pages.

This book assumes no prior knowledge of HTML, XHTML, or any of the other languages and tools it discusses. Each chapter provides clear, nontechnical explanations of the important concepts and techniques. The focus, however, is on learning by doing as you complete typical Web authoring tasks, such as designing Web pages using XHTML and CSS. In the tasks, Hands-on Exercises, and Web Design Projects throughout the book, you create many different applications ranging from simple Web pages that link to other Web pages, animations that run within a Web page, and JavaScript programs that interact with visitors to a Web site.

The Approach

This book introduces a variety of languages and tools, focusing on what you need to know to start creating Web pages. In each chapter, you perform tasks that let you use a particular Web technology to build and create entire Web pages or parts of a Web page (such as images and animation). In addition to step-by-step tasks, each chapter includes a Chapter Summary, Review Questions, Hands-on Exercises, and Web Design Projects that highlight major concepts and let you practice the techniques you learn. The Hands-on Exercises are guided activities that reinforce the skills you learn in the chapter and build on your learning experience by providing additional ways to apply your knowledge in new situations. At the end of each chapter are three Web Design Projects that let you use the skills you learned in the chapter to create a Web page on your own.

Overview of This Book

The examples, steps, exercises, and projects in this book will help you achieve the following objectives:

- Understand Web page authoring using HTML and XHTML
- Use Macromedia Dreamweaver to create Web pages
- Control the appearance of your Web pages by using Cascading Style Sheets (CSS)
- Create and edit images using Adobe Photoshop and Adobe ImageReady
- Design animations using Macromedia Flash
- Create and edit images using Macromedia Fireworks
- Add interactivity to your Web pages with JavaScript
- Make your Web pages dynamic with DHTML

This book is divided into eight parts, each of which covers a particular language or tool. **Chapters 1** and **2** cover XHTML, a language that provides the basic building blocks for creating Web pages. Chapter 1 discusses the differences between HTML and XHTML, introduces the basic parts of both languages, and explains how to link and validate your Web pages. Chapter 2 focuses on XHTML and discusses how to work with text and images, create lists, work with frames, create tables, and build forms. Because HTML and XHTML are required for most types of Web pages, you should read Chapters 1 and 2 first. All the other chapters in the book assume you have read these two chapters.

Chapters 3 and **4** teach how to use Macromedia Dreamweaver to create Web pages in a visual environment. Chapter 3 introduces the basic features of Dreamweaver, including how to edit and control text, create links, create and control page properties, design tables, and work with images. Chapter 4 examines more advanced Dreamweaver capabilities, including how to use tools and functions, use multimedia content, set up style sheets, and create simple DHTML animations. **Chapters 5** and **6** explain how to create, edit, and save images for the Web by using Photoshop and ImageReady. Chapter 5 introduces Photoshop's tools for creating, editing, saving, and optimizing images. Chapter 6 teaches advanced Web graphic techniques with ImageReady, including how to animate images, create rollover effects, design image maps, and slice images. **Chapters 7** and **8** show how to use Flash to add animation to your Web pages. Chapter 7 introduces the Flash environment and explains how to draw strokes and paint fills, select and modify objects, and create and manipulate text. Chapter 8 teaches topics related to animation, including working with frames and layers in a Flash document's timeline; using symbols in a document's library; creating frame-by-frame and tweened animations; creating a mask layer and a motion guide layer; and creating buttons with simple actions and sounds. **Chapters 9** and **10** discuss how to create, edit, and save images for the Web using Macromedia Fireworks. Chapter 9 explains how to create and edit images, use Fireworks tools, work with color and other effects, and export and optimize an image for the Web. Chapter 10 teaches how to create image maps, slice and optimize images, create buttons and rollovers, create exportable menus and pop-up menus, and create animated graphics for the Web by using frames and tweening. **Chapters 11** and **12** introduce how to control the appearance of your Web pages using CSS. Chapter 11 discusses the basics of CSS, including syntax, style rules, and CSS selectors. Chapter 12 examines how to work with CSS properties, which are used for controlling the formatting aspects of elements on a Web page, including the appearance of text, margins, borders, and color. **Chapters 13**, **14**, and **15** introduce the JavaScript programming language, which is used for adding interactivity to Web pages. Chapter 13 examines the basics of JavaScript, including how to add JavaScript to a Web page, work with variables, define and call functions, and work with events. Chapter 14 examines the JavaScript data types and the operations that can be performed on them. Chapter 15 looks at decision-making and flow-control statements, which allow you to determine the order in which statements execute in a program. **Chapter 16** teaches how to make Web pages dynamic with DHTML, which is actually a combination of JavaScript, HTML, CSS, and the Document Object Model. Before reading Chapter 16, you should already be familiar with JavaScript, HTML, and CSS.

The *Web Warrior Guide to Web Design Technologies* is a superior textbook because it also includes the following features:

- **Chapter Objectives**: Each chapter begins with a list of objectives so you know the topics that will be presented in the chapter. In addition to providing a quick reference to topics covered, this feature provides a useful study aid.

- **Step-by-Step Methodology**: As new concepts are presented in each chapter, step-by-step instructions allow you to actively apply the concepts you are learning.

- **Tips**: These notes provide practical advice and proven strategies related to the concept being discussed. Tips also provide suggestions for avoiding or resolving typical problems.

- **Cautions**: These notes warn the student about problematic issues.

- **Chapter Summaries**: Each chapter concludes with a summary that recaps the concepts and techniques covered in the section. This feature provides a concise means for you to review your understanding of the main points in each chapter.

- **Review Questions**: This end-of-chapter assessment consists of 15 multiple-choice review questions that reinforce the main ideas introduced in each chapter. These questions ensure that you have mastered the concepts and understand the information you have learned.

 Hands-on Exercises: Each chapter includes five Hands-on Exercises designed to provide you with practical experience. They guide you through the major techniques introduced in each chapter as you create Web pages, images, and animations.

Web Design Projects: Each chapter concludes with three Web Design Projects designed to help you apply what you have learned to real-world situations. They give you the opportunity to independently synthesize and evaluate information and design potential solutions.

Teaching Tools

The following supplemental materials are available when this book is used in a classroom setting. All of the teaching tools available with this book are provided to the instructor on a single CD-ROM.

Electronic Instructor's Manual. The *Instructor's Manual* that accompanies this textbook includes:

- Additional instructional material to assist in class preparation, including suggestions for lecture topics.
- Solutions to all end-of-chapter exercises.

ExamView®. This textbook is accompanied by ExamView, a powerful testing software package that allows instructors to create and administer printed, computer (LAN-based), and Internet exams. ExamView includes hundreds of questions that correspond to the topics covered in this text, enabling students to generate detailed study guides that include page references for further review. The computer-based and Internet testing components allow students to take exams at their computers; they also save the instructor time by grading each exam automatically.

PowerPoint Presentations. This book comes with Microsoft PowerPoint slides for each chapter. These are included as a teaching aid for classroom presentation, to be made available to students on the network for chapter review, or to be printed for classroom distribution. Instructors can add their own slides for additional topics that they introduce to the class.

Data Files. Data files containing all of the data necessary to perform the steps in the chapters, exercises, and projects are provided through the Course Technology Web site at **www.course.com**. They are also available on the Teaching Tools CD.

Solution Files. Solutions to steps within a chapter and end-of-chapter exercises are provided on the Teaching Tools CD-ROM and may also be found on the Course Technology Web site at **www.course.com**. The solutions are password protected.

Distance Learning. Course Technology is proud to present online courses in WebCT and Blackboard, as well as MyCourse 2.0, Course Technology's own course enhancement tool, to provide the most complete and dynamic learning experience possible. When you add online content to one of your courses, you are adding a lot: self-tests, lecture notes, a grade book, and, most of all, a gateway to the twenty-first century's most important information resource. Instructors are encouraged to make the most of the course, both online and off-line. For more information on how to bring distance learning to your course, contact your local Course Technology sales representative.

Acknowledgments

All of the authors would like to thank the reviewers who provided insights for the chapters and helped to shape this book, including Adeleye Bamkole, Passaic County Community College; Al Beddow, Spokane Falls Community College; Amy Berger, San Diego State University; Ayad Bou Diab, Georgia Perimeter College; Bonnie Gauthier, New Brunswick Community College; Chang T. Hsieh, The University of Southern Mississippi; Brenda Jacobsen, Idaho State University; Brian Johnson, Forest Hills Northern High School; Cliff Kettemborough, The University of California Irvine; Christopher King, Maryland State Department of Education; Bernie Kirkey, University College of the Cariboo; Jeanine Meyer, Purchase College; Amy K. Saenz, Harford Community College; Craig Shaw, Central Community College; J. Rene Tubilleja, DeVry Institute in New York; Jamie Weare, Santa Fe Community College; and Carol Welch, University of Maine.

My sincere thanks to my co-authors for their hard work on this project, along with Ann Shaffer for giving the book a common voice. I am extremely grateful to Jeanne Busemeyer and her staff for turning this book into a reality. My thanks also go to Bill Larkin for his patience with me during a very busy year. A very special thanks goes to Margarita Leonard for all of the schedules you've adjusted, fires you've put out, and challenges you've faced with me during the years we've worked together. We'll miss you Margarita!

Don Gosselin

In addition to the production and editorial staff at Course Technologies, I would like to thank my sisters Kate Poaster and Winnie Larson for all their words of encouragement and support. The chaos of life is easier when you have a sister to talk to.

Ruth Guthrie

I would like to thank all of the people at Course Technology, especially Bill Larkin and Margarita Leonard, for their support of my contributions to this book. I also want to thank Ann Shaffer, Developmental Editor, for her guidance and encouragement. Finally, I want to thank my wife Gloria and our daughter, Alyssandra. My work on this book would not have been possible without their love and support.

Luis A. Lopez

To my girls, Diana and Sam, and to my little buddy Jake.

Joel Sklar

I would like to acknowledge the support of my students and colleagues at Cal Poly Pomona, who have motivated me to keep learning about new technologies, such as Dreamweaver MX, and their uses. Of course, I recognize the continuing support of my husband, Christian Soe, and my children, Rowena, Nils, and Erik.

Louise Soe

Thanks to Murad Mirzoyev for permission to use the photographs in Chapters 5 and 6.

Matt Slaybaugh

Read This Before You Begin

The following information will help you as you prepare to use this textbook.

TO THE USER OF THE DATA FILES

To complete the steps and projects in this book, you will need data files that have been created specifically for this book. Your instructor may provide the data files for you. You also can obtain the files electronically from the Course Technology Web site by connecting to www.course.com and then searching for this book title. Note that you can use a computer in your school lab or your own computer to complete the Hands-on Exercises in this book.

The data files for this book are organized in folders named Chapter.*xx*, where *xx* is the chapter number.

Using Your Own Computer

This book is suitable for use with either a Windows or Macintosh computer. To use your own computer to complete the steps, exercises, and projects, you will need the following software and hardware.

Software: All of the chapters in this book assume you are using one of the following operating systems: Windows 2000, ME, 98, or XP or Macintosh OS X. You will also need Internet Explorer 6 or later, or the most recent version of Netscape Navigator. The following list explains the additional software required to complete each chapter.

- **Chapters 1 and 2**: A text editor, such as Notepad, which is installed as part of all of the Windows operating systems or TextEdit, which is included in Mac OS X.

- **Chapters 3 and 4**: Macromedia Dreamweaver MX, which is included on the CD accompanying this book. Note that the version provided on the CD is a 30-day trial version, so you should not install it until you are ready to begin these chapters.

- **Chapters 5 and 6**: Adobe Photoshop 7 and Adobe ImageReady 7, which are included on the CD accompanying this book. Note that the versions provided on the CD are 30-day trial versions, so you should not install them until you are ready to begin these chapters.

- **Chapters 7 and 8**: Macromedia Flash MX, which is included on the CD accompanying this book. Note that the version provided on the CD is a 30-day trial version, so you should not install it until you are ready to begin these chapters.

- **Chapters 9 and 10**: Macromedia Fireworks MX, which is included on the CD accompanying this book. Note that the version provided on the CD is a 30-day trial version, so you should not install it until you are ready to begin these chapters.

- **Chapters 11 through 16**: A text editor, such as Notepad, which is installed as part of all of the Windows operating systems or TextEdit, which is included in Mac OS X.

Hardware: Your computer should meet the hardware requirements necessary to run the operating systems mentioned earlier. In addition, your computer should have a modem with a dial-up connection or some other method of connecting to the Internet. Before installing the software on the CD accompanying this book, check for any hardware requirements listed in the CD's Read Me file.

Data Files: You will not be able to complete the chapters and projects in this book by using your own computer unless you have the data files. You can get the data files from your instructor, or you can obtain the data files electronically from the Course Technology Web site by connecting to www.course.com and then searching for this book title.

Visit Our World Wide Web Site

Additional materials designed especially for this book might be available for your course. Periodically search **www.course.com** for more details.

1

XHTML: PART I

In this chapter you will:

♦ Learn about HTML and XHTML

♦ Work with XHTML DTDs

♦ Study elements and attributes

♦ Work with basic body elements

♦ Link your Web pages

♦ Validate your Web pages

Hypertext markup language, or **HTML**, is a simple language used to design the Web pages that appear on the World Wide Web. Web pages are also commonly referred to as **HTML pages**. HTML by itself has about the same formatting and design capabilities as a word-processing program, such as Microsoft Word. As the Web has grown in popularity, so has the demand for more interesting and visually pleasing Web pages. In order to answer this demand, various kinds of tools and technologies have been developed to aid in the creation of Web page documents and to enhance the capabilities of HTML.

The goal of this book is to introduce the fundamentals of popular Web page design tools and technologies. Entire books are usually devoted to the various tools and technologies discussed here. This book does *not* provide comprehensive coverage of any one tool or technology. Rather, we attempt to provide a survey of popular Web design tools and technologies. Along with descriptions and brief reference materials, this book provides step-by-step exercises that walk you through some basic tasks in each technology. The goal is to help you get started in your own Web design efforts. Use the chapters in this book to gain a solid understanding of the popular Web design technologies. Later, you can dive deeper into any of the subjects that interest you.

Course Technology publishes a number of excellent books (several of which are written by authors who contributed to this book) devoted to the study of each of the individual tools and technologies that you will learn about in future chapters. You can search for books devoted to the Web design subjects that interest you on Course Technology's Web site at www.course.com. In this book, you will only create and work with Web pages on your local computer. If you would like to learn how to publish your Web pages on a Web server, refer to *Creating Web Pages with XHTML*, published by Course Technology.

Web page design, or **Web design**, refers to the creation and visual design of the documents that display on the World Wide Web. Many businesses today have Web sites, and in the future many more businesses will probably have a presence on the Web. To attract and retain visitors, Web sites must be exciting and visually stimulating, which is where quality Web design comes in. Web design is an extremely important topic. However, keep in mind that this book is *not* about Web design, although you will certainly learn many Web design concepts and techniques along the way. Instead, it is a book about the various tools and technologies that you need to employ when designing a Web page. This is a subtle, but important distinction: A book on Web design explains the various visual and graphical design elements you can add to a Web page and lays down precepts for well-designed Web pages (such as the usefulness of bulleted lists and the advisability of animating text).

In contrast, this book teaches the skills required to add design elements to a Web page. (For example, in this book you will learn several ways to animate text in a Web page. This book does not go into the question of when and where animation is appropriate in a Web page.) If you would like to study the topic of Web page design itself, consult a book exclusively devoted to that topic, such as *Principles of Web Design*, published by Course Technology.

 The Web is an ever-changing environment. The tools and technologies discussed in this book are the most popular at the time of this writing. However, new tools and technologies are always being developed, and one or more of them may easily ascend to the top position in terms of popularity. As a Web designer, you should always be on the lookout for new tools and technologies that will assist you in the creation and design of your Web pages.

HTML first became an Internet standard in 1993 with the release of version 1.0. The next version of HTML, 2.0, was released in 1994 and included many core HTML features such as forms and the ability to bold and italicize text. However, many of the standard features that are widely used today, such as the use of tables to organize text and graphics on a page, were not available until the release of HTML 3.2 in 1996. The current version of HTML, 4.01, was released in 1999. HTML 4.01, however, will be the last version of the HTML language because it is being replaced with **extensible hypertext markup language**, or **XHTML**.

Although XHTML is available now, it will take some time for people who write Web pages to adapt to this new language and for all Web browsers to provide complete support for XHTML. In addition, millions of HTML Web pages will continue to exist for a long time to come because it is not worth the time required to convert them to XHTML. Because XHTML is almost identical to HTML, you can easily adapt any of your existing HTML skills to XHTML, and vice versa. The biggest difference between the two languages is that XHTML documents must be well formed (written according to some specific rules) in order for them to actually be considered XHTML documents. This chapter and Chapter 2 are the only ones in this book that are devoted to XHTML. The remainder of the chapters in this book use standard HTML syntax. However, the XHTML skills you will study in this and the next chapter will provide you with enough HTML knowledge to be successful throughout this book.

In this chapter, you will study basic formatting and structural elements that you will use on almost every Web page you build.

INTRODUCTION TO HTML

HTML documents are text documents that contain special instructions, called **tags**, along with the text that is to be displayed on a Web page. HTML tags range from formatting commands that make text boldface and italic to controls that allow user input, such as radio buttons and check boxes. Other HTML tags allow you to display graphic images and other objects in a document or Web page.

 HTML documents must have a file extension of .html or .htm.

An HTML document is also called a **Web page** and is identified by a unique address called the **uniform resource locator**, or **URL**. A URL is also commonly referred to as a **Web address**. Some sample URLs include www.microsoft.com and www.course.com. A URL is a type of **uniform resource identifier (URI)**, which is a generic term for many types of names and addresses on the World Wide Web. The term **Web site** refers to the location on the Internet where Web pages and related files (such as graphic files) that belong to a company, organization, or individual are located. You display a Web page on your computer screen using a program called a **Web browser**. As you probably know, popular Web browsers include Microsoft Internet Explorer and Netscape Navigator.

You probably have experience typing a URL into a browser and then watching as a Web page is displayed in the browser window. However, you may not be familiar with what goes on behind the scenes. When you open a Web page in a browser, the browser requests the Web page from a **Web server**, which is a special type of computer that delivers HTML documents. A Web browser then assembles and formats the document according to the instructions contained in its tags. The process of assembling and formatting an

HTML document is called **parsing** or **rendering**. Within an HTML document, tags are enclosed in brackets (< >); most consist of a starting tag and an ending tag that surround the text or other items they are formatting or controlling. For example, you use two tags to make a line of text boldface: The starting tag for boldface is **<b>** and the ending tag is **</b>**. Any text contained between this pair of tags appears in boldface when you open the HTML document in a Web browser. The following line is an example of how to make text boldface in an HTML document:

```
<b>This text will appear in boldface in a Web browser.</b>
```

 HTML is not case-sensitive, so you can use <B> in place of <b>. XHTML, on the other hand, *is* case-sensitive and requires that you type all tags in lower-case letters. For this reason, all tags are lowercase in this book.

Some tags, however, do not include an ending tag. The **<hr>** tag, for instance, inserts a horizontal rule on a Web page and does not require an ending tag. You simply place the **<hr>** tag anywhere in an HTML document where you want the horizontal rule to appear.

All HTML documents begin with **<html>** and end with **</html>**. These tags tell a Web browser that the instructions between them should be assembled into an HTML document. The opening and closing **<html>...</html>** tags are required and enclose (or contain) all the text and other tags that make up the HTML document. There are literally hundreds of HTML tags and identical XHTML tags, many of which you will use throughout this book. HTML tags are commonly divided into two types: structural tags (which define how a document is assembled) and formatting tags (which define how text will appear when rendered in a browser). Some of the more common structure and formatting tags are listed in Table 1-1.

Table 1-1   Common structure and formatting HTML tags

HTML Tag	Description
`<b></b>`	Formats enclosed text in a bold typeface
`<body></body>`	Encloses the body of the HTML document
` `	Inserts a line break
`<head></head>`	Encloses the page header and contains information about the entire page
`<hn></hn>`	Heading level tags, where *n* represents a number from 1 to 6
`<hr>`	Inserts a horizontal rule
`<html></html>`	Required tags that start and end an HTML document
`<i></i>`	Formats enclosed text in an italic typeface
`<img src="...">`	Inserts an image file
`<p></p>`	Identifies enclosed text as a paragraph
`<u></u>`	Formats enclosed text as underlined

Two important HTML tags are the <head> tag and the <body> tag. The <head> tag defines information about the document and is placed at the start of an HTML document, after the opening <html> tag. Several tags are placed within the <head>...</head> tag pair to help manage a document's content. The <title> tag contains text that is displayed in a browser's title bar and is the only required element for the <head> tag. With the exception of the <title> tag, elements contained in the <head> tag do not affect the rendering of the HTML document. The <head> tag pair and the tags it contains are referred to as the **document head**.

Following the <head> tag is the <body> tag, which contains the document body. The <body> tag pair and the text and tags it contains are referred to as the **document body**. The text and tags you place within the <body>...</body> tag pair control what actually appears in the Web browser. For example, the following code shows a simple HTML document, and Figure 1-1 shows how it appears in a Web browser.

```
<html>
<head>
<title>Hello World</title>
</head>
<body>
<h1>Hello World (this is the heading 1 tag)</h1>
<h2>This line is formatted with the heading 2 tag</h2>
<center>This line is centered</center>
<p>This body text line contains several character formatting tags
including <i>italics</i>, <b>bold</b>, and <u>underline</u>. The
following code line creates a line break followed by a horizontal
rule:</p>
<hr>
<img src="teddybear.gif">This line contains an image.
</body>
</html>
```

You use various parameters, called **attributes**, to configure many HTML tags. Attributes are placed before the closing bracket of the starting tag, and they are separated from the tag name or other attributes with a space. For example, the <img> tag that embeds an image in an HTML document can be configured with a number of attributes, including the src attribute, which specifies the file name of the image file or video clip. To include the src attribute within the <img> tag, you type <img src="mygraphic.gif">.

When a Web browser parses or renders an HTML document, it ignores non-printing characters such as tabs and carriage returns; only recognized HTML tags and text are included in the final document that appears in the Web browser. You cannot use carriage returns in the body of an HTML document to insert spaces before and after a paragraph; the browser recognizes only paragraph <p> and line break <br> tags for this purpose.

Figure 1-1   An HTML document in a Web browser

You can create Web pages in applications (such as Macromedia Dreamweaver) that provide special tools and menus specifically suited for Web page design. Such applications provide a graphical interface in which you can click, drag, and copy the parts of a Web page, much as you would when creating an image in a graphics program. These applications then generate the necessary HTML code for you. However, when you are first learning HTML, it is more instructive to use a simple text editor, such as Notepad, and type the HTML code yourself. You will use a text editor in this chapter and in Chapter 2. Then you can learn to use Dreamweaver in Chapters 3 and 4 of this book.

Next, you will start creating the home page for the Central Valley Farmers' Market Web site. To start creating the home page for the Central Valley Farmers' Market Web site:

1. Start your text editor, and create a new document.

2. Begin the HTML document by typing the opening and closing `<html>` tags, as follows:

```
<html>
</html>
```

It is considered good practice to type the opening and closing tags for a tag pair at the same time in order to ensure that you do not forget to type the closing tag.

3. Add the following between the <html> tag pair. The text within the <title>...</title> tag pair will appear in your Web browser's title bar. Remember that the <title>...</title> tag pair must be contained within the <head>...</head> tag pair. The <title>...</title> tag pair cannot exist outside the <head>...</head> tag pair.

```
<head>
<title>Central Valley Farmers' Market Web</title>
</head>
```

4. Next, add the following body tags above the closing </html> tag:

```
<body>
</body>
```

5. Save the file as **Ch01XHTML01.html** in the Chapter folder for Chapter 1. Keep the file open in your text editor.

XHTML DOCUMENT TYPE DEFINITIONS (DTDs)

Now that you are familiar with basic HTML, you are ready to learn more about XHTML. In order to ensure backward-compatibility with older browsers, you save XHTML documents with an extension of .html or .htm, just like HTML documents. When a document conforms to the rules and requirements of XHTML, it is said to be **well formed**. Among other things, a well-formed document must include a <!DOCTYPE> declaration and the <html>, <head>, and <body> elements. The <!DOCTYPE> declaration belongs in the first line of an XHTML document and determines the XHTML DTD with which the document complies. A **DTD** (short for **document type definition**) defines the tags and attributes that can be used in a document, along with the rules that a document must follow when it includes them. You can use three types of DTDs with XHTML documents: Transitional, Strict, and Frameset. At the end of this chapter, you will learn how to check whether your document is well formed and if it uses the tags and attributes defined in an XHTML DTD.

To understand the differences among the various DTDs, you need to understand the concept of deprecated HTML elements. One of the goals of XHTML is to separate the way the HTML is structured from the way the parsed Web page is displayed in the browser. In order to accomplish this goal, the World Wide Web Consortium decided that several commonly used HTML tags and attributes for display and formatting would not be used in XHTML 1.0. [The **World Wide Web Consortium (W3C)** oversees the development of Web technology standards, including XHTML.] Tags and attributes that are considered obsolete and that will eventually be eliminated are said to be **deprecated**. Table 1-2 lists the elements that are deprecated in XHTML 1.0.

Table 1-2   HTML elements that are deprecated in XHTML 1.0

Element	Description
`<applet>`	Executes Java applets
`<basefont>`	Specifies the base font size
`<center>`	Centers text
`<dir>`	Defines a directory list
`<font>`	Specifies a font name, size, and color
`<isindex>`	Creates automatic document indexing forms
`<menu>`	Defines a menu list
`<s>` or `<strike>`	Formats strikethrough text
`<u>`	Formats underlined text

The three DTDs are distinguished in part by the degree to which they accept or do not accept deprecated HTML elements. This is explained in more detail in the following sections.

Transitional DTD

The **Transitional DTD** allows you to continue using deprecated style tags in your XHTML documents. The `<!DOCTYPE>` declaration for the transitional DTD is as follows:

```
<!DOCTYPE html PUBLIC
"-//W3C//DTD XHTML 1.0 Transitional//EN"
"http://www.w3.org/TR/xhtml1/DTD/xhtml1-transitional.dtd">
```

You should use the transitional DTD only if you need to create Web pages that use the deprecated elements listed in Table 1-2.

Frameset DTD

The **Frameset DTD** is identical to the Transitional DTD, except that it includes the `<frameset>` and `<frame>` elements, which allow you to split the browser window into two or more frames. The `<!DOCTYPE>` declaration for the Transitional DTD is as follows:

```
<!DOCTYPE html PUBLIC
"-//W3C//DTD XHTML 1.0 Frameset//EN"
"http://www.w3.org/TR/xhtml1/DTD/xhtml1-frameset.dtd">
```

You should understand that frames have been deprecated in favor of tables. However, Frameset documents are still widely used, and you need to be able to recognize and work with them in the event that you need to modify an existing Web page that was created with frames.

Strict DTD

The **Strict DTD** eliminates the elements that were deprecated in the Transitional DTD and Frameset DTD. The `<!DOCTYPE>` declaration for the Strict DTD is as follows:

```
<!DOCTYPE html PUBLIC
"-//W3C//DTD XHTML 1.0 Strict//EN"
"http://www.w3.org/TR/xhtml1/DTD/xhtml1-strict.dtd">
```

As a rule, you should always try to use the Strict DTD. This will ensure that your Web pages conform to the most current Web page authoring techniques. Next, you will add a `<!DOCTYPE>` declaration for the Strict DTD to the Central Valley Farmers' Market Web page.

To add a `<!DOCTYPE>` declaration for the Strict DTD to the Central Valley Farmers' Market Web page:

1. Return to the **Ch01XHTML01.html** file in your text editor.

2. Add the following `<!DOCTYPE>` declaration for the Strict DTD as the first line in the document (above the opening `<html>` tag):

```
<!DOCTYPE html PUBLIC
"-//W3C//DTD XHTML 1.0 Strict//EN"
"http://www.w3.org/TR/xhtml1/DTD/xhtml1-strict.dtd">
```

3. Save your changes to the file. Keep the file open in your text editor.

XHTML ELEMENTS AND ATTRIBUTES

In XHTML, you refer to a tag pair and the information it contains as an **element**. You must include both an element's opening tag and closing tag, or the document will not be well formed. Elements that do not include a closing tag are called **empty elements**; you must include a space and a slash before the closing bracket to complete an empty element. The information contained within an element's opening and closing tags is referred to as its **content**. As explained earlier in this chapter, you use various parameters, called *attributes*, to configure XHTML elements. Attributes are placed before the closing bracket of the starting tag, and they are separated from the tag name or other attributes with a space. The value you assign to an attribute must be contained with quotation marks.

Block-Level and Inline Elements

There are two basic types of elements, block-level and inline, that can appear within a document's `<body>` element. **Block-level elements** are elements that give a Web page its structure. Most Web browsers render block-level elements so that they appear on their own line. Block-level elements can contain other block-level elements or inline elements. The `<p>` tag and heading tags (`<h1>`, `<h2>`, and so on) are examples of common block-level elements you have seen so far. Table 1-3 lists the primary block-level elements available in the Strict DTD.

Table 1-3 Primary block-level elements available in the Strict DTD

Element	Description
`<address>`	Address
`<blockquote>`	Block quotation
`<div>`	Generic block-level container
`<dl>`	Definition list
`<fieldset>`	Form control group
`<h1> - <h6>`	Heading-level elements
`<hr>`	Horizontal rule
`<noscript>`	Alternate script content
`<ol>`	Ordered list
`<p>`	Paragraph
`<pre>`	Preformatted text
`<table>`	Table
`<ul>`	Unordered list

Inline elements, or **text-level elements**, are used for describing the text that appears on a Web page. Unlike block-level elements, inline elements do not appear on their own lines, but they fall within the line of the block-level element that contains them. Examples of inline elements include the `<b>` (bold) and `<br>` (line break) elements. You will learn some more inline elements in Chapter 2.

You need to be familiar with block-level and inline elements in order to create well-formed Strict DTDs. In a Strict DTD document, inline elements must be placed inside of a block-level element. Additionally, any text displayed by your document must also be placed within a block-level element. For instance, the following line would not be acceptable in a Strict DTD document, because the text, `<b>` element, and `<br>` element are not contained within a block-level element:

```
This line contains <b>bold</b> text and <br />
a line break.
```

To make the preceding code well formed, you must enclose it within a block-level element, such as the `<p>` element, as follows:

```
<p>This line contains <b>bold</b> text and <br />
a line break.</p>
```

Next, you will edit the Central Valley Farmers' Market Web page to add an inline `<b>` element inside of a block-level `<p>` element.

To edit the Central Valley Farmers' Market Web page and add an inline `<b>` element inside of a block-level `<p>` element:

1. Return to the **Ch01XHTML01.html** file in your text editor.

1

2. Between the two **<body>...</body>** tags, add the following elements and text to the Web page:

```
<p>The <b>Central Valley Farmers' Market</b> offers plenty of
fresh-picked fruits, vegetables, herbs, and flowers. Local
artisans bring wonderful handmade art and crafts. You will also
find lots of baked goods, jams, honey, cheeses, and other
products.</p>
```

In this particular case, do not be concerned if the line breaks in your text editor screen differ from the line breaks shown here.

3. Save the **Ch01XHTML01.html** file, and open it in Internet Explorer. Figure 1-2 displays the Ch01XHTML01.html file with the new paragraph.

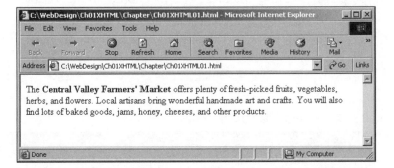

Figure 1-2   The Ch01XHTML01.html file after adding the new paragraph

4. Close your Web browser window, but keep the page open in your text editor.

Standard Attributes

XHTML includes several **standard attributes**, or **common attributes**, that are available to almost every element (with a few exceptions). The standard XHTML attributes are listed in Table 1-4.

Table 1-4   Standard attributes

Attribute	Description
class	Identifies various elements as part of the same group
dir	Specifies the direction of text
id	Uniquely identifies an individual element in a document
lang / xml:lang	Specifies the language in which the contents of an element were originally written
style	Defines the style information for a specific element
title	Provides descriptive text for an element

The `class`, `id`, and `title` attributes are not valid in the `<base>`, `<head>`, `<html>`, `<meta>`, `<param>`, `<script>`, `<style>`, and `<title>` elements; the `dir`, `lang`, and `xml:lang` attributes are not valid in the `<base>`, `<br>`, `<frame>`, `<frameset>`, `<hr>`, `<iframe>`, `<param>`, and `<script>` elements; and the `style` attribute is not valid in the `<html>`, `<head>`, `<title>`, `<meta>`, `<style>`, `<script>`, `<param>`, and `<base>` elements.

Although English is the primary language of the Web, it is certainly not the only language used on the Web. In order to be a considerate resident of the international world of the Web, you should designate the language of your elements by using the `lang` and `xml:lang` attributes. The `lang` attribute is used in HTML documents; the `xml:lang` attribute is used in XHTML–based documents. Because not all browsers support XHTML, you should include both the `lang` attribute as well as the `xml:lang` attribute in your elements for backward-compatibility. In order to specify the language of your entire document, you place the `lang` and `xml:lang` attributes in the `<html>` element.

You assign to the `lang` and `xml:lang` attributes a two-letter code that represents a language. For instance, the language code for English is `en`. Therefore, to assign English as the language for a particular element, you add the attributes `lang="en` and `xml:lang="en` to the element's opening tag. Table 1-5 lists some examples of two letter language codes.

Table 1-5   Examples of two-letter language codes

Code	Language
af	Afrikaans
el	Greek
fr	French
it	Italian
ja	Japanese
sa	Sanskrit
zh	Chinese

If you assign different language codes to the `lang` and `xml:lang` attributes, the value assigned to the `xml:lang` attribute takes precedence.

Another consideration when specifying the original language in which an element was written is the direction that the language reads. Although most Western languages read from left to right, many other languages, including Arabic and Hebrew, are written from right to left. For this reason, you should always include the `dir` attribute along with the `lang` and `xml:lang` attributes. You can assign one of two values to the `dir` attribute: `"ltr"` (for left to right) and `"rtl"` (for right to left). For Western languages such as English, you assign the `dir` attribute a value of left to right, as follows: `dir="ltr`.

The last standard attribute we will discuss here is the `title` attribute, which provides descriptive text for an element similar to the text that appears in a Web browser's title bar. With newer Web browsers, the value assigned to the `title` attribute appears as a ToolTip when you hold your mouse over the element that includes it.

Next, you will add standard attributes to the Central Valley Farmers' Market home page. First, you add the `lang` and `xml:lang` attributes to the `<html>` element to specify that the default language of the page is English and the `dir` attribute to specify that the text direction is left to right. You will also add a paragraph containing an Italian phrase to the Central Valley Farmers' Market home page. You will include in the `<p>` element the `lang` and `xml:lang` attributes to specify Italian as the element's language, along with the `dir` attribute to specify a text direction of left to right. Finally, you will also add a `title` attribute that includes the English translation of the Italian phrase.

To add standard attributes to the Central Valley Farmers' Market home page:

1. Return to the **Ch01XHTML01.html** file in your text editor.

2. Modify the opening `<html>` tag so it includes the `lang`, `xml:lang`, and `dir` attributes, as follows:

   ```
   <html lang="en" xml:lang = "en" dir="ltr">
   ```

3. Next, add the following `<p>` element that contains the Italian phrase just above the closing `</body>` tag. The `<p>` element also includes the `lang`, `xml:lang`, `dir`, and `title` attributes.

   ```
   <p title="What one puts into a dish, one finds!" lang="it"
   xml:lang = "it" dir="ltr"><i>Quello che ci mette, ci
   trova!</i></p>
   ```

4. Save the **Ch01XHTML01.html** file, and open it in Internet Explorer. Figure 1-3 shows how the Ch01XHTML01.html page looks when the mouse is positioned over the Italian phrase. (You may not be able to see the translated phrase if you are working on a Macintosh.)

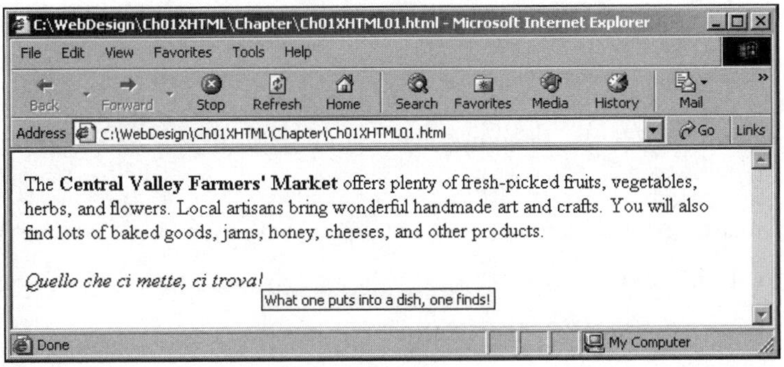

Figure 1-3   The Ch01XHTML01.html file after adding standard attributes

5. Close your Web browser window, but keep the page open in your text editor.

BASIC BODY ELEMENTS

In this section, you will study the following basic body elements:

- Headings
- Paragraphs and line breaks
- Horizontal rules

You have already seen and used several of the elements that you will study in this section, such as the `<p>` and `<br />` elements. However, basic body elements such as these are some of the most commonly used in Web page design. For this reason, you will spend a little more time studying each of these elements. First, you will look at heading-level elements.

Headings

Heading-level elements, or **headings**, are block-level elements that are used for emphasizing a document's headings and subheadings. There are six heading-level elements, `<h1>` through `<h6>`. The highest level of importance is `<h1>`; the lowest level of importance is `<h6>`. The following code shows how to create the six heading-level elements in the document body.

```
<body>
<h1>Heading 1</h1>
<h2>Heading 2</h2>
<h3>Heading 3</h3>
<h4>Heading 4</h4>
<h5>Heading 5</h5>
<h6>Heading 6</h6>
</body>
```

Each heading-level element is a block-level element.

Most Web browsers will render the heading-level elements similar to the output shown in Figure 1-4.

Next, you will add heading-level elements to the Central Valley Farmers' Market Web page.

To add heading-level elements to the Central Valley Farmers' Market Web page:

1. Return to the **Ch01XHTML01.html** file in your text editor.

2. First, add the following `<h1>` and `<h2>` elements as the first elements in the body section:

```
<h1>Central Valley Farmers' Market</h1>
<h2>About the Market</h2>
```

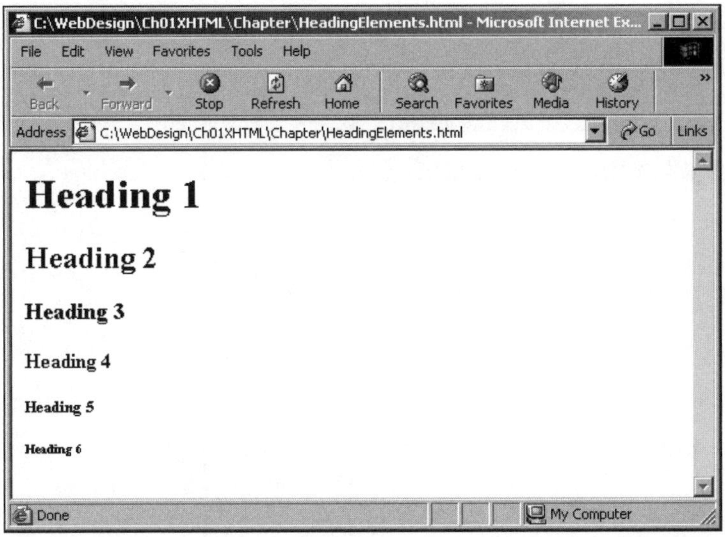

Figure 1-4   Heading-level elements in Internet Explorer

3. Next, add to the end of the body section the following `<h2>` element and paragraph tag that lists the hours of operation:

```
<h2>Hours of Operation</h2>
```

4. Finally, add to the end of the body section the following `<h2>` and `<h3>` elements, which list this week's featured vendors:

```
<h2>Featured Vendor List</h2>
<h3>Big Creek Produce</h3>
<h3>Blue Sky Gardens</h3>
<h3>Maple Ridge Farms</h3>
<h3>Manzi Produce</h3>
<h3>Lee Family Farms</h3>
```

5. Save the **Ch01XHTML01.html** file, and open it in the browser. Figure 1-5 shows some of the new headings in the browser window.

6. Close your Web browser window, but leave the page open in your text editor.

Paragraphs and Line Breaks

The inline paragraph (`<p>`) and line break (`<br />`) elements are the simplest way of adding whitespace to a document. **Whitespace** is an important design element that refers to the empty areas on a page. Whitespace often makes a page more visually pleasing and easier to read. It is tempting for beginning designers to try and pack each page with as much information as possible, but experienced designers know that the presence of whitespace is critical to the success of a page's design, whether you are creating a Web page or a traditional printed page.

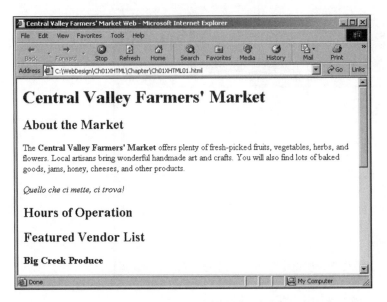

Figure 1-5   Ch01XHTML01.html file after adding headings

You cannot add whitespace to a Web page simply by including spaces or carriage returns in a document. Most Web browsers ignore multiple, contiguous spaces on a Web page and replace them with a single space. Web browsers will also ignore carriage returns. For instance, in the following code, the document body is properly formed because the content is contained within a **\<p\>** element. However, the three lines will be run together on the same line by the browser because the whitespace is ignored, as shown in Figure 1-6.

```
<body>
<p><b>Llamas</b> are from South America,
<b>kangaroos</b> are from Australia,
and <b>pandas</b> are from China.</p>
</body>
```

Figure 1-6   ExoticAnimals.html without line breaks

In order for the line breaks to be rendered by the browser, you must add the <br /> tags as follows. Figure 1-7 shows how the following code is rendered with line breaks in the browser.

```
<body>
<p><b>Llamas</b> are from South America, <br />
<b>kangaroos</b> are from Australia, <br />
and <b>pandas</b> are from China.</p>
</body>
```

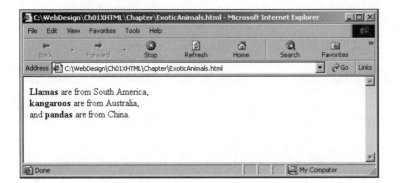

Figure 1-7   ExoticAnimals.html with line breaks

By now, you should understand that the <br /> element only inserts a line break in an existing paragraph. To create separate paragraphs, the content for each paragraph must exist within its own <p>...</p> tag pair. The following code shows a modified version of the Exotic Animals page that includes three separate paragraphs. Figure 1-8 shows the output. Notice that there is more whitespace between the lines when they are enclosed in paragraph elements than when each line ends in a <br /> element. The <br /> element simply wraps the text to the next line, but keeps it as part of the same paragraph. In comparison, the <p> element creates individual paragraphs that are separated by a single line.

```
<body>
<p><b>Llamas</b> are from South America.</p>
<b>Kangaroos</b> are from Australia.</p>
<b>Pandas</b> are from China.</p>
</body>
```

Remember that because the <br /> element is an inline element, it must be placed within a block-level element such as the <p> element.

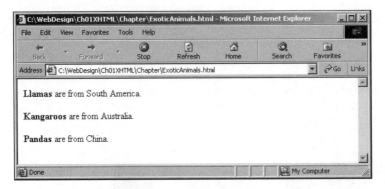

Figure 1-8 ExoticAnimals.html with three separate paragraphs

Next, you will add inline paragraph elements to the heading-level elements you created in the last exercise.

To add inline paragraph elements to the heading-level elements you created in the last exercise:

1. Return to the **Ch01XHTML01.html** file in your text editor.

2. Next, add the inline paragraph shown here in bold beneath the Hours of Operation heading:

   ```
   <h2>Hours of Operation</h2>

   <p>The Central Valley Farmers' Market is held every Tuesday,
   Thursday and Saturday from April through October, then Saturdays
   only in November until Thanksgiving. The Market is open from 7 am
   - 1 pm. <i>The vendors will be there be there rain or
   shine</i>!</p>
   ```

3. Now, add the inline paragraphs shown here in bold for the Featured Vendor List heading and for each individual vendor's <h3> heading element:

   ```
   <h2>Featured Vendor List</h2>

   <p>Be sure to visit this week's featured vendors.</p>

   <h3>Big Creek Produce</h3>

   <p>Offers a diverse selection of produce including restaurant
   quality vegetables and edible flowers. </p>

   <h3>Blue Sky Gardens</h3>

   <p>Grows a variety of organic vegetables including french
   slenderette green beans, spinach, salad greens, squash, pumpkins
   and cherry tomatoes, as well as a vast array of fresh-cut and
   dried flowers.</p>
   ```

1

```
<h3>Maple Ridge Farms</h3>

<p>Specializes in organically grown lettuces, arugula, red
mustard and other greens.</p>

<h3>Manzi Produce</h3>

<p>Hand picks, hand washes, and hand sorts all of their products,
which include nuts, plants, herbs, perennials, flowers, wild
gathered items, meat, fruit, and vegetables.</p>

<h3>Lee Family Farms</h3>

<p>Produces organically-grown traditional Asian vegetables such
as bok choy, lemon grass and hot chili peppers.</p>
```

4. Save the **Ch01XHTML01.html** file, and open it in your Web browser.
Figure 1-9 shows how some of the featured vendor paragraphs appear.

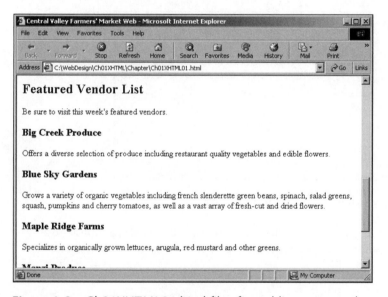

Figure 1-9   Ch01XHTML01.html file after adding paragraphs

5. Close your Web browser window.

Horizontal Rules

The **horizontal rule (<hr>) element** draws a horizontal rule on a Web page that acts
as a section divider. Horizontal rules are useful visual elements for breaking up long documents. Although this element is technically a block-level element, it cannot contain any

content because it is an empty element. However, because it is a block-level element, it can exist on its own line in the document body without being contained within another block element.

HTML included several `style` attributes that you could use to modify the appearance of horizontal rules. However, all of the `<hr>` element's `style` attributes have been deprecated in XHTML in favor of Cascading Style Sheets (CSS). You will learn how to use CSS in Chapters 11 and 12 of this book.

The following document body includes an example of a horizontal rule. The output is shown in Figure 1-10.

```
<body>
<p>The following element is a horizontal rule.</p>
<hr />
</body>
```

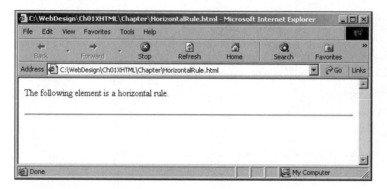

Figure 1-10   Web page with a horizontal rule

Remember that because the `<hr>` element is empty, you must close it by adding a space and a slash before its closing bracket, as follows: `<hr />`.

Next, you will add horizontal rules to the Central Valley Farmers' Market Web page.

To add horizontal rules to the Central Valley Farmers' Market Web page:

1. Return to the **Ch01XHTML01.html** file in your text editor.

2. Add horizontal rules above each of the `<h2>` elements. You should add three `<hr />` elements in all.

3. Save the **Ch01XHTML01.html** file, and open it in your Web browser. Figure 1-11 shows how the horizontal rules appear above the About the Market and Hours of Operating headings.

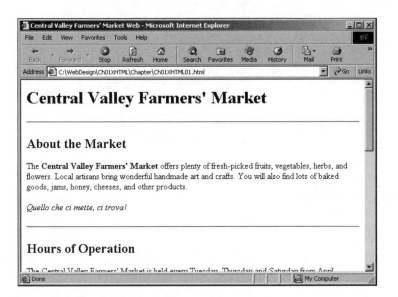

Figure 1-11   Ch01XHTML01.html file after adding horizontal rules

4. Close your Web browser window, but keep the page open in your browser.

LINKING WEB PAGES

Almost every Web page contains **hypertext links**, which are text or graphics that the user can click to open files or to navigate to other documents on the Web. A hypertext link in an HTML document is underlined and is often displayed in a vivid color. In Internet Explorer, blue is the default color for unvisited links; violet is the default color of previously visited links. The target of a link can be another location on the same Web page, an external Web page, an image, or some other type of document. Other types of elements, such as images, can also be hypertext links to other Web pages, images, or files. The text or image used to represent a link on a Web page is called an **anchor**. For example, Figure 1-12 shows a simple Web page that contains two different versions of the same hypertext: one created with text and the other created with a graphic. Clicking either of the links opens the home page for Oracle Corporation.

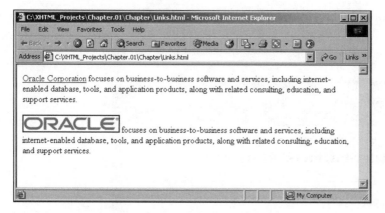

Figure 1-12   Hypertext links in a Web browser

 Although different Web browsers use different default colors for visited and unvisited links (Internet Explorer uses blue and violet), you can change the appearance of the links on a Web page by using CSS.

In the following sections, you will learn how to create hypertext links.

The <a> Element

You create a basic hypertext link by using the **<a> element** (the "a" stands for *anchor*). Although you can use a variety of attributes with the <a> element, the one you will use most is the `href` (for hypertext reference) attribute, which specifies the link's target URL. You can assign either an absolute URL or a relative URL to the `href` attribute. A **relative URL** specifies the location of a file according to the location of the currently loaded Web page. Relative URLs are used to load Web pages located on the same computer as the currently displayed document. If the currently displayed document is located at `http://www.MyWebSite.com/WebPages`, then the following relative URL looks in the WebPages folder for the AnotherWebPage.html file:

```
<p><a href="AnotherWebPage.html">
Another Web Page
</a></p>
```

An **absolute URL** refers to a specific drive and directory or to the full Web address of a Web page. For example, the following code shows how to use the <a> element to create a link to the W3C HTML Validation Service by using an absolute URL of `http://validator.w3.org/`. Figure 1-13 shows how the link appears in Internet Explorer after it has been clicked.

```
<p>To validate your XHTML documents, visit the
<a href="http://validator.w3.org/">
W3C HTML Validation Service</a>.</p>
```

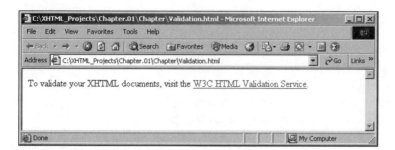

Figure 1-13   Web page with a hypertext link

When you write the descriptive content that will be used as the text for a link, be sure to use something that clearly describes the target of the link. The preceding code, for instances, uses "W3C HTML Validation Service" as the descriptive text for a link. Note that it is considered bad form to use text such as "click" or "click here" as the descriptive text for a link. Therefore, you should avoid creating links with descriptive text such as the following:

```
<p>To validate your XHTML documents, <a
href="http://validator.w3.org/">
click here</a> to visit the W3C HTML Validation Service</p>
```

You can use an image as a link anchor by replacing the content of an `<a>` element with a nested `<img>` element. For instance, the following code creates the image link shown in Figure 1-14. Notice that the link consists of both descriptive text and an image file. Although not actually required when you create an image link, descriptive text can make it easier for your users to identify the image links on your page.

```
<p><a href="Noah.html"><img src="Noah.jpg" height=120 width=120
alt="Photo of a golden retriever." /><br />Click the image to
open Noah's Web page</a></p>
```

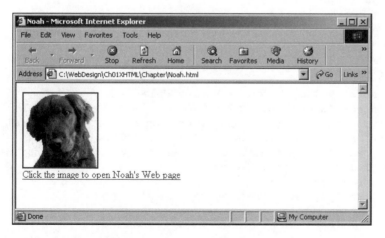

Figure 1-14   Web page with an image link

You will learn more about the `<img>` element in Chapter 2.

Note that the image link displayed in Figure 1-14 includes a border. By default, a border automatically appears around an image link. There will be many times, however, when you will not want your image links to be surrounded by a border because they can draw attention away from the image itself or may not suit your page's overall look. In HTML, you could suppress the border around an image link by using an attribute of `border=0` in the `<img>` element. The `border` attribute has been deprecated in XHTML in favor of CSS and removed entirely from the strict DTD. Therefore, in order for your Web pages to be compliant with the Strict DTD, you must not use the `border` attribute. In order to suppress the image link border in XHTML, you must use CSS. (You will learn about CSS in Chapter 12.)

Next, you will add a new contact information page to the Central Valley Farmers' Market Web site.

To add a new contact information page to the Central Valley Farmers' Market Web site:

1. Verify that you saved your most recent changes to the Central Valley Farmers' Market page, and then create a new document in your text editor.

2. Type the following `<!DOCTYPE>` declaration, along with the opening `<html>` and `<head>` elements:

```
<!DOCTYPE html PUBLIC
"-//W3C//DTD XHTML 1.0 Strict//EN"
"http://www.w3.org/TR/xhtml1/DTD/xhtml1-strict.dtd">
<html lang="en" xml:lang = "en" dir="ltr">
<head>
<title>Contact Info for the Central Valley Farmers'
Market</title>
</head>
```

3. Next, add the following body section to the document. The body section simply contains headings and paragraphs that list the contact information for the Central Valley Farmers' Market.

```
<body>
<h1>Central Valley Farmers' Market</h1>
<h2>Contact Information</h2>
<p>If you have any questions or concerns about the Central Valley
Farmers' Market, please call (908) 626-3764.</p>
<p>You can also send mail to the Central Valley Farmers' Market
at the following address:</p>
<p>P.O. Box 135<br />
Central Valley, CA 94359</p>
```

4. Type the following statement that creates a relative link back to the home page for the Central Valley Farmers' Market:

```
<p><a href="Ch01XHTML01.html">Home</a></p>
```

5. Finish the document by typing the following tags to close the `<body>` and `<html>` elements:

```
</body>
</html>
```

6. Save the file as **Ch01XHTML02.html** in the Chapter folder for Chapter 1 and close it.

Next, you will add the Contacts Web page to the Central Valley Farmers' Market home page.

To add the Contacts Web page to the Central Valley Farmers' Market home page:

1. In your text editor, open the file named **Ch01XHTML01.html** from the Chapter folder for Chapter 1.

2. Click after the closing `</h1>` tag, press **Enter**, and then type the following statement that creates a link to the Contacts.html document:

```
<p><a href="Ch01XHTML02.html">Contact Information</a></p>
```

3. Save the **Ch01XHTML01.html** file, and then open it in Internet Explorer. Figure 1-15 shows how the new link appears.

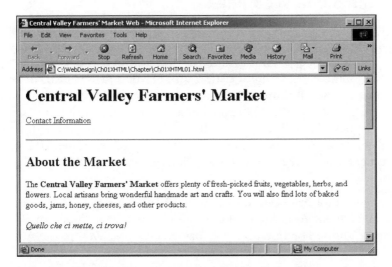

Figure 1-15   Ch01XHTML01.html after adding the Contact Information link

4. Click the **Contact Information** link. The Ch01XHTML02.html file should open in your browser window, as shown in Figure 1-16.

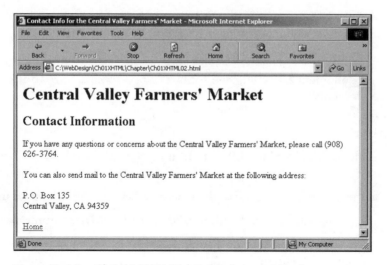

Figure 1-16   Ch01XHTML02.html in Internet Explorer

5. Click the **Home** link to return to the home page for the Central Valley Farmers' Market.

6. Close your Web browser window, but keep the page open in your text editor.

Linking Within the Same Web Page

The `<a>` element can create a link to an external document or to a bookmark inside the current document. This can be particularly effective in helping users navigate through a long Web page. For instance, examine the Web page shown in Figure 1-17, which contains the W3C's home page for information on HTML and XHTML development. If you visit the page and scroll through the document, you will see that it is quite long. In Figure 1-17, you can see a group of text links at the bottom of the browser window that begin with the "news" link. Many of the links in this group, including the news and recommendations links, do not link to external documents but to other locations within the current document. This makes it much easier for visitors to the Web page to navigate through its contents.

Earlier in this chapter, you learned about the standard **id** attribute, which uniquely identifies an individual element in a document. Any element that includes an **id** attribute can be the target of a link. For instance, you may have a long Web page with an `<h2>` element that reads "Summary of Qualifications" near the bottom of the document. To create the element with an **id** attribute of **"sq1"**, you use the following statement:

```
<h2 id="sq1">Summary of Qualifications</h2>
```

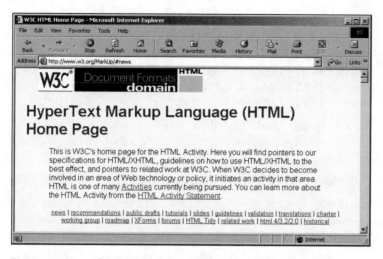

Figure 1-17   The W3C's home page for HTML activity

To create a link to a bookmark, you assign to the **href** attribute of an **<a>** element an **id** value, preceded by the # sign. For instance, to create a bookmark within the same document to the **<h2>** element with the **id** of **"sq1"**, you use the following statement:

```
<p><a href="#sq1">
Read the Summary of Qualifications</a></p>
```

The **id** attribute replaces the **name** attribute that was used in HTML. One problem is that many older browsers do not recognize the **id** attribute. In order to solve this problem, the **name** attribute was deprecated in almost every element except for the **<a>** element. In order to ensure that your links are valid with older browsers, you use both the **id** and **name** attributes inside an **<a>** element, and assign both attributes the same value. To create a bookmark to any other element, including heading-level elements, you nest an **<a>** element inside another element. For example, you use the following statement to create the Summary of Qualifications **<h2>** element as a bookmark that will function in both older and new browsers:

```
<h2><a id="sq1" name="sq1">
Summary of Qualifications</a></h2>
```

Next, you will add links to the Central Valley Farmers' Market home page that jump to the heading level 2 elements.

To add links to the Central Valley Farmers' Market home page that link to the heading level 2 elements:

1. Return to the **Ch01XHTML01.html** file in your text editor.

2. Click after the closing `</p>` tag in the statement that creates the Contact Information link, press **Enter**, and then add the following links to the document's level 2 heading elements:

```
<p><a href="#am1">About the Market</a></p>
<p><a href="#ho1">Hours of Operation</a></p>
<p><a href="#fvl1">Featured Vendor List</a></p>
```

3. Modify the About the Market heading-level element as follows so it includes an `<a>` element with the same `name` and `id` attributes that will bookmark the element:

```
<h2><a id="am1" name="am1">About the Market</a></h2>
```

4. Modify the Hours of Operation heading-level element as follows so it includes an `<a>` element with the same `name` and `id` attributes that will bookmark the element:

```
<h2><a id="ho1" name="ho1">Hours of Operation</a></h2>
```

5. Modify the Featured Vendor List heading-level element as follows so it includes an `<a>` element with the same `name` and `id` attributes that will bookmark the element:

```
<h2><a id="fvl1" name="fvl1">Featured Vendor List</a></h2>
```

6. Save the **Ch01XHTML01.html** file, and then open it in your Web browser; test the links. Figure 1-18 shows how the new links appear in Internet Explorer

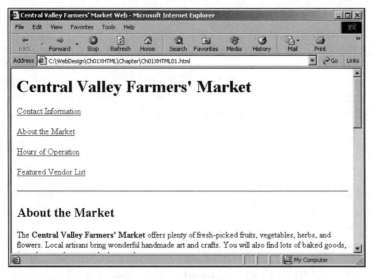

Figure 1-18   Ch01XHTML01.html after adding links to bookmarks

7. Close your Web browser and the text editor.

VALIDATING WEB PAGES

1

In order to ensure that your XHTML document is well formed and that its elements are valid, you need to use a validating parser. A **validating parser** is a program that checks whether an XHTML document is well formed and whether the document conforms to a specific DTD. The term **validation** refers to the process of verifying that your XHTML document is well formed and checking that the elements in your document are correctly written according to the element definitions in a specific DTD.

Several XHTML validating services can be found online. One of the best available is W3C Markup Validation Service, a free service that validates both HTML and XHTML. The W3C Markup Validation Service is located at http://validator.w3.org/. The main Web page for the service allows you to validate a Web page by entering its URI and selecting various options in the form shown in Figure 1-19.

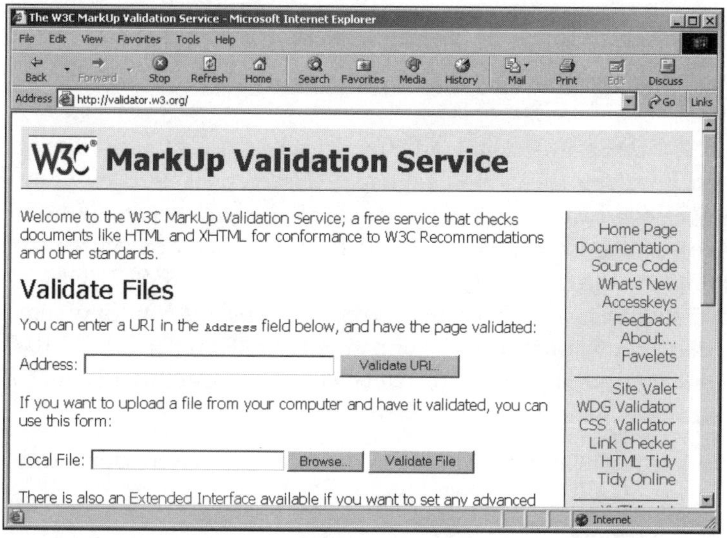

Figure 1-19   W3C MarkUp Validation Service

The form shown in Figure 1-19 is located at the bottom of the W3C Markup Validation Service page, so you may need to scroll down in order to see it.

The W3C Markup Validation Service also includes a separate page that you can use to validate XHTML files by uploading them from your computer. You can open the upload files page of the W3C Markup Validation Service by clicking the Extended Files Upload Interface link at the bottom of the main page or by entering the following Web address: http://validator.w3.org/file-upload.html. Figure 1-20 shows an example of the upload page of the W3C Markup Validation Service.

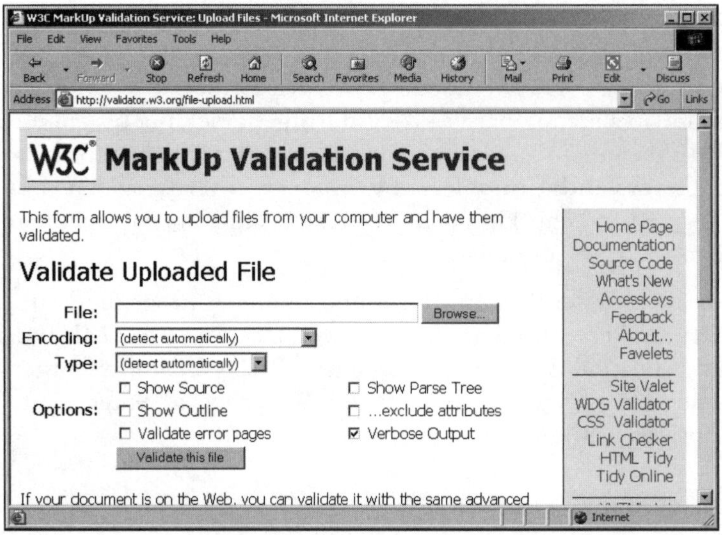

Figure 1-20   Upload page of the W3C MarkUp Validation Service

You click the Browse button in the upload page to select the file you want to validate. In the Encoding list box, you select the language character set used by your Web page. English and many Western languages use the iso-8859-1 character set, although you can select from a variety of other character sets in the Encoding box. For example, if the page you are creating is written in Greek, you can select iso-8859-7 (which represents the Greek character set) from the Encoding box. The Type list box is where you select the type of DTD that you want to use to validate your HTML or XHTML. The check boxes in the Options section allow you to select how your document will be displayed in the browser after it has been validated by the service.

Next, you will validate the Central Valley Farmers' Market Web page using the W3C Markup Validation Service.

To validate the Central Valley Farmers' Market Web page:

1. Start your Web browser, and enter the Web address for the upload page of the W3C Markup Validation Service: **http://validator.w3.org/ file-upload.html**.

2. Click the **Browse** button to display the File Upload dialog box. In the File Upload dialog box, locate the **Ch01XHTML01.html** file. (By default, you should have stored this file in C:\WebDesign\Ch01XHTML\Chapter.) Once you locate the file, double-click it or click it once and select the **Open** button. The drive, folder path, and file name should appear in the File text box on the upload page. In the Encoding list box, select **iso-8859-1 (Western Europe)**. Because the document type is select with the **<!DOCTYPE>** declaration, you can leave the Type list box set to its default setting of *(detect automatically)*. Leave the display option check boxes unselected, and click the **Validate this file**

button. The W3C Markup Validation Service validates the document and returns the results displayed in Figure 1-21. If you receive any errors, fix them, and then revalidate the page.

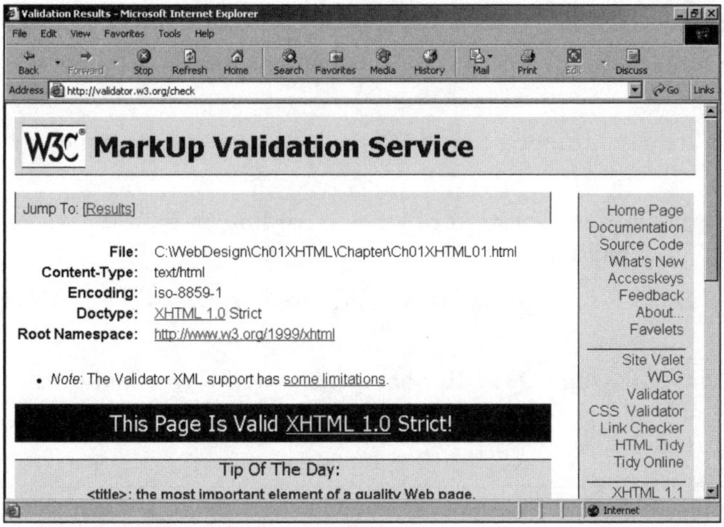

Figure 1-21   Validation results for the Central Valley Farmers' Market page

3. Close your Web browser window and text editor.

CHAPTER SUMMARY

- Hypertext markup language, or HTML, is a simple language used to design the Web pages that appear on the World Wide Web.

- Web page design, or Web design, refers to the creation and visual design of the documents that display on the World Wide Web.

- HTML 4.01 will be the last version of the HTML language because it is being replaced with extensible hypertext markup language, or XHTML.

- HTML documents are text documents that contain formatting instructions, called tags, along with the text that is to be displayed on a Web page.

- The process through which a Web browser assembles and formats an HTML document is called parsing or rendering.

- The <head> tag pair and the tags it contains are referred to as the document head.

- The <body> tag pair and the text and tags it contains are referred to as the document body.

❑ The `<!DOCTYPE>` declaration belongs in the first line of an XHTML document and determines the XHTML DTD with which the document complies.

❑ In XHTML, you refer to a tag pair and the information it contains as an element.

❑ Block-level elements are elements that give a Web page its structure.

❑ Inline, or text-level, elements are used for describing the text that appears on a Web page.

❑ Hypertext links are used to open files or to navigate to other documents on the Web.

❑ A relative URL specifies the location of a file according to the location of the currently loaded Web page.

❑ An absolute URL refers to a specific drive and directory or to the full Web address of a Web page.

❑ In order to ensure that your XHTML document is well formed and that its elements are valid, you need to use a validating parser.

REVIEW QUESTIONS

1. URL stands for _____.
   a. Unique Requirements List
   b. Unnamed Rendering Loop
   c. Uniform Resource Locator
   d. United Repetition List

2. The process through which a browser assembles and formats an HTML document is called parsing or _____.
   a. refreshing
   b. painting
   c. rendering
   d. compiling

3. With which tag pair should all HTML documents begin and end?
   a. `<body>...</body>`
   b. `<head>...</head>`
   c. `<html>...</html>`
   d. `<xml>...</xml>`

1

4. Which element is required in the `<head>` element?

   a. `<hr>`

   b. `<meta>`

   c. `<body>`

   d. `<title>`

5. What must you place on the first line of an XHTML document?

   a. an `<html>` tag

   b. an `<xhtml>` tag

   c. a `<title>` tag

   d. a `<!doctype>` declaration

6. DTD stands for _____.

   a. Data Transfer Display

   b. Digital Technology Definition

   c. Decimal Type Determinant

   d. Document Type Definition

7. Which XHTML DTD(s) allows you to continue using deprecated elements?

   a. XML

   b. XHTML

   c. Strict

   d. Frameset

8. Which of the following closes the empty `<hr>` element in an XHTML document, thus making it backward-compatible with older browsers?

   a. `<hr\>`

   b. `<hr \>`

   c. `<hr/>`

   d. `<hr />`

9. The information contained within an element's opening and closing tags is referred to as its _____.

   a. content

   b. data

   c. attribute

   d. meta information

10. _____ elements give a Web page its structure.

    a. XHTML

    b. Block-level

    c. Inline

    d. Meta

11. _____ is used for describing the text that appears on a Web page.

    a. XHTML

    b. Block-level

    c. Inline

    d. Meta

12. Which of the following elements is a block-level element?

    a. `<html>`

    b. `<p>`

    c. `<br>`

    d. `<b>`

13. You should designate the language of your elements using the _____ and `xml:lang` attributes.

    a. `country`

    b. `local`

    c. `lang`

    d. `language`

14. Which standard attribute can you use to create a ToolTip for an element?

    a. ToolTip

    b. Description

    c. Help

    d. Title

15. What is the correct syntax for creating a bookmark that is compatible with both older and newer browsers?

    a. `<h3 name="mt1">Management Team</h3>`

    b. `<h3 id="mt1" name="mt1">Management Team</h3>`

    c. `<h3><a name="mt1">Management Team</a></h3>`

    d. `<h3><a id="mt1" name="mt1">Management Team</a></h3>`

HANDS-ON EXERCISES

Exercise 1-1

In this exercise, you will create a Web page that displays an invitation to a graduation party.

1. Create a new document in your text editor, and type the `<!DOCTYPE>` declaration, opening `<html>` tag, header information, and the opening `<body>` tag. Use the Transitional DTD and "Graduation Party" as the content of the `<title>` element. Your document should appear as follows:

```
<!DOCTYPE html PUBLIC "-//W3C//DTD XHTML 1.0 Transitional//EN"
"http://www.w3.org/TR/xhtml1/DTD/xhtml1-transitional.dtd">
<html lang="en" xml:lang = "en" dir="ltr">
<head>
<title>Graduation Party</title>
</head>
<body>
```

2. Next, add the following text and elements for the body of the invitation:

```
<center>
<h1>Graduation Party</h1>
<p><i>It's time to celebrate!</i><br />
Join us for a party in honor of</p>
<h2>Monica's Graduation</h2>
<p>Saturday, June 22, 2003<br />
at 2:00 pm</p>
<p><b>The Cohen Residence</b><br />
876 Blackbird Road<br />
R.S.V.P. 555-1212</p>
</center>
```

3. Type the closing `</body>` and `</html>` tags:

```
</body>
</html>
```

4. Save the file as **Ch01XHTMLEX01.html** in the Exercises folder for Chapter 1.

5. Use the W3C HTML Validation Service to validate the **Ch01XHTMLEX01.html** file, and then open it in your Web browser and examine how the elements are rendered.

Exercise 1-2

In this exercise, you will create a document that uses five heading-level elements to organize the cities within Orange County in both California and Florida (both states have counties named Orange). Although many Web page designers use heading-level elements as a formatting tool, the real purpose of heading-level elements is to provide a way of outlining the content of your document in the same manner that you would create a

legal outline or a table of contents. Generally, most Web pages should only include a single
<h1> element as the main heading for a page. Second-level headings should use the
<h2> element, and additional higher numbered headings should continue to be nested
beneath lower numbered headings.

1. Create a new document in your text editor, and type the <!DOCTYPE> declaration,
   opening <html> tag, header information, and the opening <body> tag. Use the
   Strict DTD and "Heading-Level Elements" as the content of the <title> element. Your document should appear as follows:

   ```
   <!DOCTYPE html PUBLIC "-//W3C//DTD XHTML 1.0 Strict//EN"
   "http://www.w3.org/TR/xhtml1/DTD/xhtml1-strict.dtd">
   <html lang="en" xml:lang = "en" dir="ltr">
   <head>
   <title>Heading-Level Elements</title>
   </head>
   <body>
   ```

2. Add the following <h1> and <h2> elements for North America and the United
   States as follows. This document should contain only one <h1> element for
   North America, but may contain additional <h2> elements for the other two
   countries in North America, Canada and Mexico.

   ```
   <h1>North America</h1>
   <h2>United States of America</h2>
   ```

3. Next, add the following <h3>, <h4>, and <h5> elements for some of the cities
   within Orange County in California:

   ```
   <h3>California</h3>
   <h4>Orange County</h4>
   <h5>Anaheim</h5>
   <h5>Huntington Beach</h5>
   <h5>Irvine</h5>
   <h5>Laguna Beach</h5>
   <h5>Newport Beach</h5>
   ```

4. Next, add the following <h3>, <h4>, and <h5> elements for some of the cities
   within Orange County in Florida:

   ```
   <h3>Florida</h3>
   <h4>Orange County</h4>
   <h5>Azalea Park</h5>
   <h5>Lake Buena Vista</h5>
   <h5>Orlando</h5>
   <h5>Winter Garden</h5>
   <h5>Winter Park</h5>
   ```

5. Type the closing </body> and </html> tags:

   ```
   </body>
   </html>
   ```

6. Save the file as **Ch01XHTMLEX02.html** in the Exercises folder for Chapter 1.

7. Use the W3C HTML Validation Service to validate the **Ch01XHTMLEX02.html** file, and then open it in your Web browser and examine how the elements are rendered.

Exercise 1-3

In this exercise, you will create a list of five technology companies, separated by horizontal rules. The paragraph containing company name will use the `title` attribute to store the company's Web address.

1. Create a new document in your text editor, and type the `<!DOCTYPE>` declaration, opening `<html>` tag, header information, and the opening `<body>` tag. Use the Strict DTD and "Technology Companies" as the content of the `<title>` element.

2. Type the following text and elements. Each company's Web address is assigned to the `title` attribute of the `<p>` element that contains the company name. The paragraphs containing each company name are also separated by horizontal rules.

```
<p title="www.sun.com">Sun Microsystems</p><hr />
<p title="www.microsoft.com">Microsoft</p><hr />
<p title="www.oracle.com">Oracle</p><hr />
<p title="www.siebel.com">Siebel</p><hr />
<p title="www.bea.com">BEA</p><hr />
```

3. Type the closing `</body>` and `</html>` tags:

```
</body>
</html>
```

4. Save the file as **Ch01XHTMLEX03.html** in the Exercises folder for Chapter 1.

5. Use the W3C HTML Validation Service to validate the **Ch01XHTMLEX03.html** file, and then open it in your Web browser and examine how the elements are rendered. Hold your mouse over each company name to see if the Web address assigned to the `title` attribute displays as a ToolTip.

Exercise 1-4

In this exercise, you will create the home page for a shoe repair service.

1. Create a new document in your text editor, and type the `<!DOCTYPE>` declaration, opening `<html>` tag, header information, and the opening `<body>` tag. Use the Strict DTD and "Olde World Shoe Repair" as the content of the `<title>` element.

2. Create the document body shown in Figure 1-22. Be sure to add internal links to the Shoe Repair and Leather Repair headings.

Figure 1-22 Olde World Shoe Repair

3. Add the closing **</body>** and **</html>** tags and save the document as **Ch01XHTMLEX04.html** in the Exercises folder for Chapter 1.

Exercise 1-5

In this exercise, you will add a new Web page to the Olde World Shoe Repair Web site.

1. Return to the **Ch01XHTMLEX04.html** file in your text editor, and add the following **<a>** element after the Leather Repair link but above the horizontal rule:

```
<p><a href="Ch01XHTMLEX02.html">Contact Information</a></p>
```

2. Create a new document in your text editor, and type the opening **<!DOCTYPE>** declaration, header information, and opening **<body>** tag. Use the Strict DTD and "Contact Information" as the content of the **<title>** element. (You will find it easiest to copy the existing elements in the **Ch01XHTMLEX01.html** file and paste them into the new file; then simply change the contents of the **<title>** element.)

3. Add an **<h1>** element that reads "Olde World Shoe Repair" and an **<h2>** element that reads "Contact Information", as follows:

```
<h1>Olde World Shoe Repair</h1>
<h2>Contact Information</h2>
```

4. Add the following contact information to the document:

```
<p>123 Main Street<br />
Anywhere, USA 12345<br />
Phone: (565) 555-1212</p>
```

5. Type the following link that returns to the Olde World Shoe Repair home page, along with the closing **</body>** and **</html>** tags:

```
<p><a href="Ch01XHTMLEX04.html">Home</a></p>
</body>
</html>
```

6. Save the file as **Ch01XHTMLEX05.html** in the Exercises folder for Chapter 1.

7. Use the W3C HTML Validation Service to validate the **Ch01XHTMLEX04.html** and **Ch01XHTMLEX05.html** file, and then open the **Ch01XHTMLEX04.html** file in your Web browser and test the links. Note that because the **Ch01XHTMLEX04.html** file does not contain much text, the Shoe Repair and Leather Repair links will not work unless your browser window is fairly small.

WEB DESIGN PROJECTS

For the following projects, save the files you create in the Projects folder for Chapter 1. Create the files so they are well formed according to the Strict DTD. Be sure to validate the files you create with the W3C HTML Validation Service.

Project 1-1

Create a Book of the Month Club Web site. The home page should describe the current month's selection and include book title, author, publisher, ISBN, number of pages, and so on. Also, create separate Web pages for the book selections for the last 3 months. Add links to the home page that open each of the three Web pages. Save the home page as **Ch01XHTMLDP01.html** and the Web pages for previous months using the name of the month.

Project 1-2

Create the Web site for the Central Valley Pottery Studio. On the home page, describe the studio and explain what it teaches and the different types of classes it offers. Create separate Web pages for the following: Adult Classes, Kids' Classes, and Workshops. Within each Web page, include the following information about each class: day, time, dates, instructor, and cost. Save the home page as **Ch01XHTMLDP02.html**. Save the Adult Classes Web page as **Adults.html**, the Kids' Classes Web page as **Kids.html**, and the Workshops Web page as **Workshops.html**.

Project 1-3

Create the Web site for a bug extermination company. On the home page, describe the company's general services and include links to other pages that contain detailed information on the company's procedures for exterminating different types of bugs. Include pages for cockroaches, fleas, and ticks. Also, include a page that contains information on ordering an inspection. Add links to the inspection Web page to the home page, cockroaches page, fleas page, and ticks page. Save the home page as **Ch01XHTMLDP03.html**. Save the cockroaches page as **Cockroaches.html**, the fleas page as **Fleas.html**, the ticks page as **Ticks.html**, and the inspection page as **Inspection.html**.

2

XHTML: PART II

In this chapter you will:

♦ Work with text-formatting and phrase elements
♦ Add images to your Web pages
♦ Create lists
♦ Work with frames
♦ Create tables
♦ Build forms

In the last chapter, you learned about some of the most basic structural elements that are common to all XHTML documents. However, when you get right down to it, probably the most important part of a Web page is the information it displays. The text and the images displayed in the browser are, from the perspective of visitors to your Web site, the payoff. The way information is laid out on a Web page is important, but the type of information on a Web page, such as paragraphs, headings, and so on, will probably be more important as the Web evolves to other types of user agents. A **user agent** is a device that is capable of retrieving and processing XHTML; it can take the form of a traditional Web browser or be a device such as a mobile phone or personal digital assistant (PDA). User agents such as mobile phones and PDAs do not have the processing power or storage capability of a traditional desktop computer. When you are creating Web pages for these user agents, it is especially important that you use XHTML elements and attributes that can be correctly rendered by them without the need for a lot of extra processing.

In this chapter, you will learn how to work with text and image elements that can be used with various user agents. You will also learn how to use lists, frames, and tables to manage the display of your data and forms that you can use to gather information from visitors to your Web site.

WORKING WITH TEXT

XHTML incorporates two types of inline elements for managing text formatting: formatting elements and phrase elements. **Formatting elements** provide specific instructions as to how their contents should be displayed. The `<b>` element, for instance, instructs user agents to display its contents as boldface text. **Phrase elements**, on the other hand, primarily describe their contents. For instance, the `<em>` element is an emphasized piece of information, similar to a quotation. How the `<em>` element is rendered is up to each user agent, although most current Web browsers display the contents of the `<em>` element by using italics. However, a user agent for the hearing impaired may use the `<em>` element to pronounce the text with more emphasis, in order to get the meaning across to the hearing-impaired visitor to the Web site.

Text-Formatting Elements

Generally, you should strive not to use text-formatting elements at all and only use CSS to manage the display of elements on your Web pages. However, because several of the basic formatting elements are so commonly used, they are not deprecated in the Strict DTD. The text-formatting elements that are available in XHTML Strict are listed in Table 2-1.

Table 2-1   Text-formatting elements

Element	Description
`<b>`	Formats text in a bold typeface
`<big>`	Formats text in a larger font
`<i>`	Formats text in an italic typeface
`<small>`	Formats text in a smaller font
`<sub>`	Formats enclosed text as subscript
`<sup>`	Formats enclosed text as superscript
`<tt>`	Formats enclosed text as teletype of monospaced text

 As mentioned in Chapter 1, several elements that were popular in HTML, including the `<basefont>`, `<center>`, `<font>`, `<s>`, `<strike>`, and `<u>` elements, are deprecated in XHTML Strict in favor of CSS.

Next, you will create a simple Web page that uses the text-formatting elements listed in Table 2-1.

To create a simple Web page that uses text-formatting elements:

1. Start your text editor, and create a new document.

2. Type the opening `<!DOCTYPE>` declaration, header information, and opening `<body>` tag. Use the Strict DTD and "Working with Text" as the content of the `<title>` element. Your document should appear as follows:

```
<!DOCTYPE html PUBLIC "-//W3C//DTD XHTML 1.0 Strict//EN"
"http://www.w3.org/TR/xhtml1/DTD/xhtml1-strict.dtd">
<html lang="en" xml:lang = "en" dir="ltr">
<head>
<title>Working with Text</title>
<meta http-equiv="content-type"
content="text/html; charset=iso-8859-1" />
</head>
<body>
```

3. Add the following statements that use each of the text-formatting elements:

```
<p><b>Bold text</b>,
<big>Big text</big>,
<i>Italicized text</i>,
<small>Small text</small>,
<sub>Subscripted</sub> text,
<sup>Superscripted</sup> text,
<tt>Teletype text</tt></p>
```

4. Finish the document by typing the following tags to close the `<body>` and `<html>` elements:

```
</body></html>
```

5. Save the file as **Ch02XHTML01.html** in the Chapter folder for Chapter 2.

6. Open the **Ch02XHTML01.html** file in your Web browser. Figure 2-1 displays the Web page in Internet Explorer.

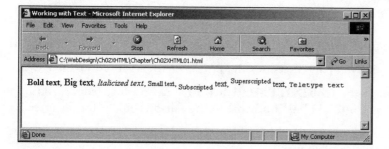

Figure 2-1   Web page with text-formatting elements

7. Close your Web browser window, but keep the page open in your text editor.

Phrase Elements

Although text-formatting elements are commonly used and work perfectly well for displaying text with a specific formatting style, it is much better to format the text on your Web pages by using a phrase element that more adequately describes its content. This helps ensure that your Web pages are compatible with user agents that may not be capable of handling formatting elements. Thankfully, current Web browsers use similar conventions for displaying the content of phrase elements. For instance, most Web browsers render the <em> element in italics. Table 2-2 lists the phrase elements that are available in XHTML, explains how each element is rendered by most Web browsers.

Table 2-2   Phrase elements

Element	Description	Renders As
<abbr>	Specifies abbreviated text	Default text
<acronym>	Identifies an acronym	Default text
<cite>	Defines a citation	Italics
<code>	Identifies computer code	Monospace font
<dfn>	Marks a definition	Italics
<em>	Defines emphasized text	Italics
<kbd>	Indicates text that is to be entered by a visitor to a Web site	Monospace font
<q>	Defines a quotation	Italics
<samp>	Identifies sample computer code	Monospace font
<strong>	Defines strongly emphasized text	Bold
<var>	Defines a variable	Italics

 Tip Phrase elements are preferred over text-formatting elements for handling simple types of formatting (such as bold and italics) on a Web page. However, as you will learn in Chapters 11 and 12, CSS is an even better option for managing the display of elements on your Web pages.

Next, you will create a simple Web page that uses the phrase elements listed in Table 2-2.

To create a simple Web page that uses the phrase elements listed in Table 2-2:

1. Return to the **Ch02XHTML01.html** file in your text editor, and immediately save it as **Ch02XHTML02.html** in the Chapter folder for Chapter 2.

2. Replace the text-formatting elements in the <body> section with the following phrase elements:

```
<p><abbr>Abbreviation</abbr>,
<acronym>Acronym</acronym>,
<cite>Citation</cite>,
```

```
<code>Code</code>,
<dfn>Definition</dfn>,
<em>Emphasis</em>,
<kbd>Keyboard</kbd>,
<samp>Sample</samp>,
<strong>Strong</strong>,
<var>Variable</var></p>
```

3. Save the **Ch02XHTML02.html** file, and then open it in your Web browser. Figure 2-2 displays the Web page in Internet Explorer.

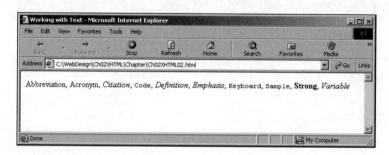

Figure 2-2 Web page with phrase elements

4. Close your Web browser window, but keep the page open in your text editor.

Probably the two most common text-formatting elements are the **<b>** and **<i>** elements. You should use the **<strong>** phrase element in place of the **<b>** text-formatting element and the **<em>** phrase element in place of the **<i>** text-formatting element. This allows user agents other than Web browsers to better understand the meaning of each element, although current Web browsers will still render the **<strong>** element as bold and the **<em>** element in italics.

There are several other types of elements you can use to format text in XHTML, including block-level and quotation elements.

Special Characters

You will often find it necessary to add special characters to your XHTML documents, such as a copyright symbol (©) or a foreign character such as the Latin capital letter E with a circumflex (Ê). The easiest way to add special characters to an XHTML document is to use special sequences of characters called **character entity references**, or **character entities**. You display a character entity by using a descriptive name preceded an ampersand (&) and followed by a semicolon. For instance, the descriptive name for the copyright symbol is "copy". You can display the copyright symbol on a Web page by using a character entity of **©**.

Character entities are case-sensitive. For instance, if you use an uppercase "C" with the copyright character entity, a Web browser will not recognize it as a character entity and will display the text "&Copy;" instead of the copyright symbol.

Table 2-3 lists the character entities for some of the more commonly used special characters.

Table 2-3   Special characters

Character	Description	Character Entity
	Nonbreaking space	` `
¢	Cent	`&cent;`
£	Pound	`&pound;`
¥	Yen	`&yen;`
©	Copyright	`&copy;`
®	Registered trademark	`&reg;`
<	Less than	`&lt;`
>	Greater than	`&gt;`
&	Ampersand	`&amp;`
"	Quotation	`&quot;`

 You can find a complete listing of character entities at www.w3.org/TR/REC-html40/sgml/entities.html.

Next, you will start creating a Web page for the New Millennium Health Club & Fitness Center Web site. You will add a character entity for the ampersand in the health club's name. You will also add a motto for the health club, *À votre santé*, which means "To your health" in French. You will use character entities for the two foreign characters in the phrase. The character entity for the ampersand is `&amp;`, the character entity for the uppercase "A" with a grave accent is `&Agrave;`, and the character entity for the lower-case "e" with an acute accent is `&eacute;`.

To start creating a Web page for the New Millennium Health Club & Fitness Center Web site:

1. Create a new document in your text editor.

2. Type the opening `<!DOCTYPE>` declaration, header information, and opening `<body>` tag. Use the Strict DTD and "New Millennium Health Club Home Page" as the content of the `<title>` element.

3. Add the following elements that contain the company's name and motto. Notice that the `<h1>` element and the motto both use character entities.

```
<h1>New Millennium</h1>
<h2>Health Club &amp; Fitness Center</h2>
<p><strong>Our motto is <em>&Agrave; votre
sant&eacute;</em></strong>.</p>
```

4. Finish the document by typing the following tags to close the `<body>` and `<html>` elements:

```
</body></html>
```

5. Save the file as **Ch02XHTML03.html** in the Chapter folder for Chapter 2, and then open it in your Web browser. Figure 2-3 displays the Web page in Internet Explorer.

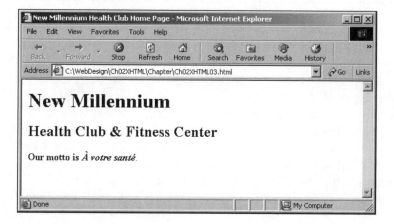

Figure 2-3 Web page with character entities

6. Close your Web browser window, but leave the page open in your text editor.

ADDING IMAGES TO YOUR WEB PAGES

Images are one of the most visually pleasing parts of a Web page. Without images, a Web page is nothing more than a collection of text and hypertext links. Web pages today include images in the form of company logos, photographs of products, drawings, animation, image maps, and other types of graphics. Commerce-oriented Web pages that do not include images will be hard pressed to attract and keep visitors. In the following sections, you will learn how to use the `<img>` element to add images to your Web pages.

The `<img>` Element

You already know the basics of how to add images via the `<img>` element. The `<img>` element is an empty element that must include a space and a slash before its closing bracket in order to be well formed. The `src` attribute specifies the file name of an image file. The `<img>` element also includes other attributes, as listed in Table 2-4.

Table 2-4   Attributes of the `<img>` element

Attribute	Description
src	Specifies the file name of the image file
alt	Specifies alternate text to display in place of the image file
longdesc	Identifies the URL of a Web page containing a long description of an image
width	Defines the width of an image
height	Defines the height of an image
usemap	Identifies an image to be used a client-side image map
ismap	Identifies an image to be used a server-side image map

In order for an XHTML document to be well formed, the `<img>` element must include an `src` attribute. Additionally, an `<img>` element must also include the `alt` attribute. The `alt` attribute, which specifies alternate text to display in place of the image file, is very important for user agents that do not display images, such as the text-based Lynx Web browser and other types of Web browsers that are designed for users of Braille and speech devices. Additionally, alternate text will display if an image has not yet downloaded, if the user has turned off the display of images in their Web browsers, if for some reason the image is not available, and under other circumstances. For instance, the following `<img>` element displays a photo of a father teaching his son how to fly a kite; the element's `alt` attribute is assigned an appropriate value "Photo of a father teaching his son how to fly a kite." If the image has not yet been downloaded or if the user has turned off the display of images in their Web browser, then they will see the alternate text shown in Figure 2-4.

```
<img src="kite.jpg" alt="Photo of a father teaching his son
how to fly a kite." />
```

Figure 2-4   Alternate text displayed in a Web browser

The `alt` attribute also serves another purpose that relates to the `title` attribute (which is one of the standard attributes you learned about in Chapter 1). If an `<img>` element does not include a `title` attribute, the value assigned to the `alt` attribute appears as a ToolTip when you hold your mouse over the image. However, if an `<img>` element does include a `title` attribute, the value assigned to the `title` attribute will appear as a ToolTip instead of the value assigned to the `alt` attribute.

The Chapter folder for Chapter 2 contains an image file named curls.jpg. You will now add this image, along with some alternate text, to the health club Web page.

To add an image with alternate text to the health club Web page:

1. Return to the **Ch02XHTML03.html** file in your text editor.

2. Add the following `<img>` element above the `<h2>` element for the "Health Club & Fitness Center" heading:

   ```
   <p><img src="curls.jpg" alt="Photo of a man and a woman using
   dumbbells to perform bicep curls." /></p>
   ```

3. Save the **Ch02XHTML03.html** file, and then open it in your Web browser. Figure 2-5 shows how the image appears in Internet Explorer, along with the alternate text that appears as a ToolTip. (If you are working on a Macintosh, you may not see the ToolTip.)

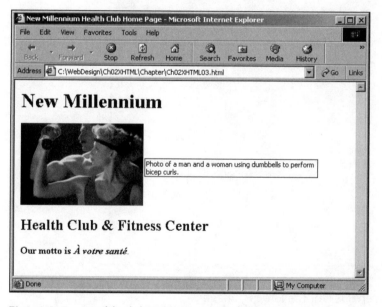

Figure 2-5   Health club Web page after adding an image

4. Close your Web browser window, but leave the page open in your text editor.

Height and Width

The size of an image is measured in pixels. A **pixel** (short for **pic**ture **el**ement) represents a single point on a computer screen. You can think of pixels as millions of tiny dots arranged in columns and rows on your monitor. The number of pixels available depends on a computer monitor's resolution. **Resolution** refers to the number of pixels that can be displayed on a monitor. When you create an `<img>` that only includes the `src` and `alt` attributes, a Web browser needs to examine the image and determine the number of pixels to reserve for it. This can significantly slow down the time it takes for your Web pages to render. However, if you use the `height` and `width` attributes to specify the size of your images, the Web browser will use those values to reserve enough space on the page for each image. This allows the Web browser to render all of the text on the page and then go back and render each image after it finishes downloading. Each image placeholder will display the image's alternative text until the image itself is rendered.

The following code shows an `<img>` element that displays the photo of a father teaching his son how to fly a kite. Notice that the `<img>` element includes the `height` and `width` attributes. Figure 2-6 shows the placeholder that the Web browser reserves for the image.

```
<img src="kite.jpg" alt="Photo of a father teaching his son
how to fly a kite." height="353" width="533" />
```

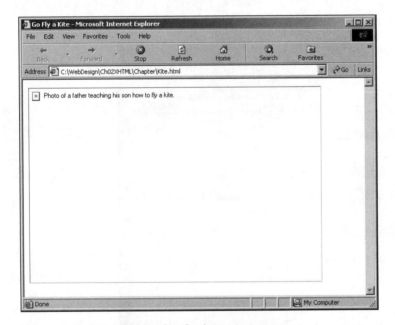

Figure 2-6 Placeholder for the kite.jpg image

 You can find the height and width of an image in pixels by using almost any graphics program such as Adobe Photoshop and Macromedia Fireworks. In Windows, you can also quickly determine the height and width of an image by opening the image in Internet Explorer or Navigator, right clicking the image, and then selecting the Properties command from the shortcut menu. Both browsers display a Properties dialog box that displays the height and width in pixels of the selected image.

A very important point you need to understand is that the values you assign to the **height** and **width** attributes in an **<img>** element should always be the exact dimensions of the original image. In other words, do not use the **height** and **width** attributes in an attempt to resize the image. If you want the image to appear in a different size, use an image-editing program to create a new, smaller version of the image. (Most image-editing programs include commands that automatically reduce the size of an image by a specified percentage or number of pixels.)

Using the **height** and **width** attributes to reduce how an image appears on a Web page will result in a poor quality image. One reason for this has to do with how you calculate the new dimensions of the image. Unless you correctly calculate the proportions for the number of pixels for both the **height** and **width** attributes that will represent the new size of the image, then the image will appear stretched and of poor quality. For instance, Figure 2-7 shows how the kite.jpg image should appear, using the height and width of the original image. Figure 2-8, however, shows the image after the **height** and **width** attributes resized it to a height of 150 pixels and a width of 400 pixels. As you can see, the image in Figure 2-8 is significantly out of proportion from the original.

Figure 2-7   Kite.jpg scaled to its original size

In the following steps, you will add the **height** and **width** attributes to the **curls.jpg** image on the health club Web page. The height of **curls.jpg** is 133 pixels, and its width is 200 pixels.

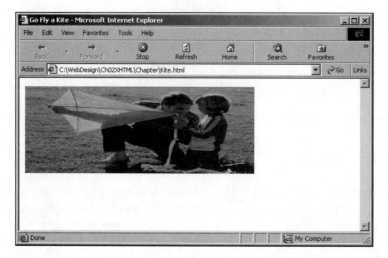

Figure 2-8   Kite.jpg scaled to 150 pixels high by 400 pixels wide

To add the `height` and `width` attributes to an image:

1. Return to the **Ch02XHTML03.html** file in your text editor.

2. Add the `height` and `width` attributes to the `<img>` element as follows:

   ```
   <p><img src="curls.jpg" alt="Photo of a man and a woman using
    dumbbells to perform bicep curls." height="133" width="200"
    /></p>
   ```

3. Save the **Ch02XHTML03.html** file, and then open it in your Web browser. The image should appear the same as it did before you added the `height` and `width` attributes.

4. Close your Web browser window, but leave the page open in your text editor.

CREATING LISTS

You can add three types of lists to a Web page: unordered lists, ordered lists, and definition lists. Table 2-5 lists the elements used to create these lists.

Table 2-5   List elements

Element	Description
`<ul>`	Block-level element that creates an unordered list
`<ol>`	Block-level element that creates an ordered list
`<li>`	Inline element that defines a list item
`<dl>`	Block-level element that creates a definition list

Table 2-5   List elements (continued)

Element	Description
`<dt>`	Inline element that defines a definition list term
`<dd>`	Inline element that defines a definition list item

This section only presents the most basic information on working with lists. In order to change the formatting and appearance of lists, you must use CSS. See Chapters 11 and 12 for more information on working with CSS.

Unordered Lists

An **unordered list** is a list of bulleted items. You nest `<li>` elements within a `<ul>` element to define the items you want to appear in the bulleted list. The following code creates the unordered list shown in Figure 2-9.

```
<h1>Justice Society Of America</h1>
<h2>Founding Members</h2>
<ul>
     <li>The Flash</li>
     <li>The Green Lantern</li>
     <li>The Spectre</li>
     <li>The Hawkman</li>
     <li>Dr. Fate</li>
     <li>The Hour-Man</li>
     <li>The Sandman</li>
     <li>The Atom</li>
     <li>Johnny Thunder</li>
</ul>
```

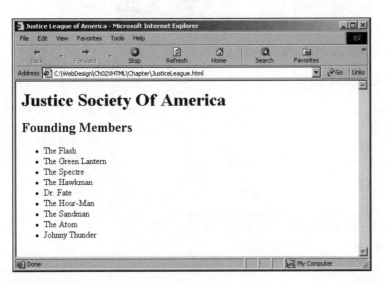

Figure 2-9   Unordered list of superheroes

Next, you will create an unordered employee list.

To create an unordered employee list:

1. Create a new document in your text editor.

2. Type the opening `<!DOCTYPE>` declaration, header information, and opening `<body>` tag. Use the Strict DTD and "Employee Directory" as the content of the `<title>` element.

3. Add the following statements to create the unordered list:

```
<h1>Employee List</h1>
<ul>
    <li>Akahoshi, Lee</li>
    <li>Alansi, Paul</li>
    <li>Alland, Gary</li>
    <li>Armstrong, Bruce</li>
    <li>Asuncion, Linda</li>
    <li>Avery, Janice</li>
</ul>
```

4. Finish the document by typing the following tags to close the `<body>` and `<html>` elements:

```
</body></html>
```

5. Save the file as **Ch02XHTML04.html** in the Chapter folder for Chapter 2.

6. Open the **Ch02XHTML04.html** file in your Web browser. Figure 2-10 displays the Web page in Internet Explorer.

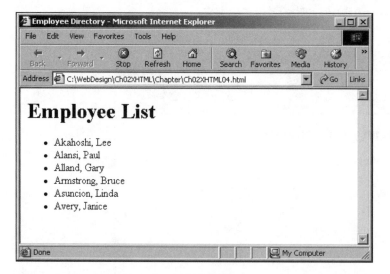

Figure 2-10 Unordered employee list

7. Close your Web browser window.

Ordered Lists

An **ordered list** is a list of numbered items. You nest `<li>` elements within an `<ol>` element to define the items you want to appear in the numbered list. The following code creates the ordered list shown in Figure 2-11.

```
<p>The following actors have played James Bond:</p>
<ol>
    <li>Sean Connery</li>
    <li>George Lazenby</li>
    <li>Roger Moore</li>
    <li>Timothy Dalton</li>
    <li>Pierce Brosnan</li>
</ol>
```

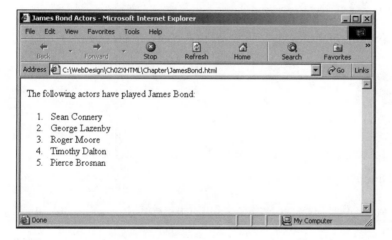

Figure 2-11   Ordered list of James Bond actors

Next, you modify the employee list you created in the last exercise from an unordered list to an ordered list.

To modify the employee list you created in the last exercise from an unordered list to an ordered list:

1. Return to the **Ch02XHTML04.html** file in your text editor.

2. Change the `<ul>` and `</ul>` tags to `<ol>` and `</ol>` tags, as shown in the boldface portion of the following code:

```
<ol>
    <li>Akahoshi, Lee</li>
    <li>Alansi, Paul</li>
...
</ol>
```

An ellipsis that appears in code, as in the preceding example, is used as an abbreviation for additional statements that do not necessarily apply to the current example.

3. Save the **Ch02XHTML04.html** file, and then open it in your Web browser. Figure 2-12 displays the Web page in Internet Explorer.

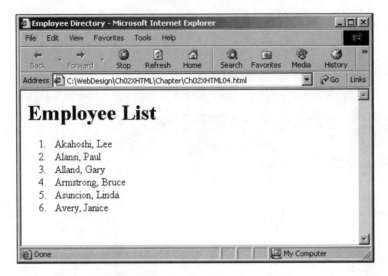

Figure 2-12   Ordered employee list

4. Close your Web browser window, but leave your text editor open.

Definition Lists

A **definition list** is a list of terms and their definitions. Web browsers render each term and its definition on the next line with an indented left margin. You create a definition list by using the `<dl>` element. Within the `<dl>` element, you nest `<dt>` elements for term names and `<dd>` elements for term definitions. The following code creates the definition list shown in Figure 2-13.

```
<h1>Electrical Terms</h1>
<h2>Beginning with the Letter 'O'</h2>
<dl>
     <dt><b>Ohm</b></dt>
     <dd>Measurement unit for electrical resistance
     or impedance.</dd>
     <dt><b>Ohmmeter</b></dt>
     <dd>An instrument used for measuring resistance
     in ohms.</dd>
     <dt><b>Overcurrent</b></dt>
```

2

```
<dd>An electrical current that is in excess of an
appliance's rated current or the ampacity of a
conductor.</dd>
<dt><b>Overload</b></dt>
<dd>A load that exceeds the rating of a system
or mechanism.</dd>
</dl>
```

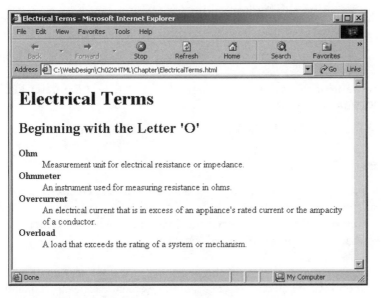

Figure 2-13   Definition list of electrical terms

WORKING WITH FRAMES

The XHTML documents you have created so far have consisted of a single Window object that can hold only one URL at a time. Using frames, you can split a single Web browser window into multiple windows, each of which can open a different URL. **Frames** are independent, scrollable portions of a Web browser window, with each frame capable of containing its own URL. Frames have been deprecated in XHTML. However, they are still widely used and will more than likely continue to be widely used for some time to come. Therefore, this brief section is provided in order to help you recognize and work with frames.

The Frameset DTD

Because frames are still so widely used, the W3C created the Frameset DTD to allow Web page designers to continue using them. As you learned in Chapter 1, the Frameset DTD is identical to the Transitional DTD, except that it includes the `<frameset>` and

`<frame>` elements, which allow you to split the browser window into two or more frames. Although you will use the Frameset DTD in this chapter, you should continue to write the rest of your XHTML code so it conforms to the Strict DTD in order for it to conform to the most current Web page design techniques.

Next, you will start creating a frame-based Employee Directory Web page that lists the first few names in a company's employment directory.

To start creating a frame-based Employee Directory Web page:

1. Create a new document in your text editor.

2. Type the opening `<!DOCTYPE>` declaration and header information. Do *not* include an opening `<body>` tag. Use the Frameset DTD and "Employee List" as the content of the `<title>` element. Be sure to use Frameset DTD in the `<!DOCTYPE>` declaration.

3. Save the file as **Ch02XHTML05.html** in the Chapter folder for Chapter 2.

Creating Frames

You divide a document into frames by using the **`<frameset>` element.** The `<frame>` element is one of the only items that can be placed inside a `<frameset>` element. The Web browser ignores any other text or elements. The `<frameset>` element replaces the `<body>` element that is used in nonframe documents.

Never place a `<body>` element at the beginning of a document containing `<frameset>` tags. If you do, the `<frameset>` element will be ignored, and only the information contained within the `<body>` elements will be visible when the document is rendered by a Web browser.

Frames in an XHTML document can be created in horizontal rows, vertical columns, or both. Two attributes of the `<frameset>` element, `rows` and `cols`, determine whether frames are created as rows or columns. The **rows attribute** determines the number of horizontal frames. The **cols attribute** determines the number of vertical frames. To set the dimensions of the frame, you assign a string to the `rows` or `cols` attribute containing the percentage of space or the number of pixels each row or column should take up on the screen, separated by commas. For example, `<frameset rows="50%, 50%" cols="50%, 50%">` creates two rows, which each take up 50 percent of the height of the screen, and two columns, which each take up 50 percent of the width of the screen.

You must define more than one row or more than one column or your frames will be completely ignored by the Web browser.

It is helpful to use an asterisk (*) to represent the size of frames that do not require an exact number of pixels or exact window percentage. The asterisk allocates any remaining screen space to an individual frame. If more than one frame is sized by using an asterisk, then the remaining screen space is divided evenly. For example, `<frameset cols="100, *">` creates two frames in a column, using pixels to represent one column and an asterisk to represent the other column. The left column will always remain 100 pixels wide, but the right column will resize according to the visible screen space.

The `<frameset>` element creates the initial frames within an XHTML document. The empty **`<frame>` element** is used to specify options for individual frames, including a frame's URL. The `src` attribute of the `<frame>` element specifies the URL to be opened in an individual frame. Frame elements are placed within the `<frameset>` element. Frames can be assigned a name using the **name** attribute; this name can then be used as a target for a hyperlink. You need a separate frame element for each frame in your window. The URLs of frames are opened in the order in which each `<frame>` element is encountered, from left to right and top to bottom.

Next, you will add `<frameset>` and `<frame>` elements to the Ch02XHTML05.html file. The frame elements will create a narrow, column-shaped frame on the left, which will contain the list of employee names. The right frame, a wider column on the right, will display an employee's picture and employment information. This frame should take up the remainder of the screen width.

To add `<frameset>` and `<frame>` elements to the Employee Directory Web page:

1. Return to the **Ch02XHTML05.html** file in your text editor.

2. After the closing `</head>` tag, add `<frameset cols="20%, *">` to start the frame set. The `20%` in the code creates the narrow column on the left; the asterisk creates the wide column on the right.

3. Add the two `<frame>` elements shown here after the opening `<frameset>` tag. The first `<frame>` element opens a Web page named Ch02XHTML07.html, which contains a list of employee names. The second frame opens a Web page named Ch02XHTML06.html, which contains an opening message to display in the right frame. The window containing Ch02XHTML07.html is named "list", and the window containing Ch02XHTML06.html is named "display".

   ```
   <frame src="Ch02XHTML07.html" name="list" />
   <frame src="Ch02XHTML06.html" name="display" />
   ```

4. Type the following lines to close the `<frameset>` and `<html>` elements:

   ```
   </frameset></html>
   ```

5. Save the **Ch02XHTML05.html** file. Before you can open the frame-based Web page, you need to create the Ch02XHTML06.html and Ch02XHTML07.html files.

Next, you will create a Web page that displays an opening message. You will save the Web page as Ch02XHTML06.html. Note that because the Ch02XHTML07.html and Ch02XHTML06.html files are not frames themselves, you will create them by using the Transitional DTD. Note that you are using the Transitional DTD because the `target` attribute (which you will study next) is not available in the Strict DTD.

To create the opening message Web page:

1. Create a new document in your text editor.

2. Type the opening `<!DOCTYPE>` declaration, header information, and opening `<body>` tag. Use the Transitional DTD and "Welcome" as the content of the `<title>` element.

3. Add the following line to instruct the user to click an employee name in the list:

   ```
   <p>Click an employee name in the list to display his or her
   picture and employment information.</p>
   ```

4. Type the closing `</html>` and `</body>` tags:

   ```
   </body></html>
   ```

5. Save the file as **Ch02XHTML06.html** in the Chapter folder for Chapter 2.

Using the `target` Attribute and the `<base>` Element

One popular use of frames creates a table of contents frame on the left side of a Web browser window with a display frame on the right side of the window. The right-hand display frame displays the contents of a URL selected from a link in the table of contents frame. This type of design eliminates the need to open a separate Web browser window when you want the user to be able to display the contents of another URL.

To cause the document for each hyperlink to open in the right frame, you assign to the `target` attribute of the `<a>` element the value you assigned to the frame's `name` attribute. The **target attribute** determines in which frame or Web browser window a URL opens. When you are using the same target window or frame for a long list of hyperlinks, it is easier to use the `<base>` element instead of repeating the `target` attribute within each hyperlink. The **`<base>` element** is used to specify a default target for all links in a document, using the assigned name of a window or frame. You assign to the `<base>` element's `target` attribute the value you assigned to the frame's `name` attribute. Note that the `<base>` element must be placed within the document head, not within its `<body>` section.

The `target` attribute of the `<a>` and `<base>` elements and the `<base>` element are deprecated in the Strict DTD. In order to use the `target` attribute with either of these elements, you must use the Transitional DTD.

Next, you will create the Ch02XHTML07.html file, which contains a list of the employee names in the Employee Directory program.

To create the Ch02XHTML07.html file:

1. Create a new document in your text editor.

2. Type the opening `<!DOCTYPE>` declaration, header information, and opening `<body>` tag. Use the Transitional DTD and "Employees" as the content of the `<title>` element. Also include **`<base target="display">`** in the header section to specify the right frame (named display) as the default target.

3. Add the following links for each employee. Note that instead of opening a Web page in the display window, this code opens .jpg graphic files, each of which contains an employee's photo. (The .jpg files for the employees are located in the Chapter folder for Chapter 2.) Notice that each image includes an `alt` attribute along with the `height` and `width` attributes.

```
<p><a href="Akahoshi.jpg">Akahoshi, Lee</a><br />
<a href="Alansi.jpg">Alansi, Paul</a><br />
<a href="Alland.jpg">Alland, Gary</a><br />
<a href="Armstrong.jpg">Armstrong, Bruce</a><br />
<a href="Asuncion.jpg">Asuncion, Linda</a><br />
<a href="Avery.jpg">Avery, Janice</a></p>
```

Caution

The preceding <a> elements do not include `alt`, `height`, or `width` attributes because they are not available to the <a> element in the Transitional DTD. Although most Web browsers would recognize the attributes if you included them, they would also prevent the document from being well formed.

4. Type the closing `<html>` and `<body>` tags:

   `</body></html>`

5. Save the file as **Ch02XHTML07.html** in the Chapter folder for Chapter 2.

6. Now that you have created the Ch02XHTML06.html file and the Ch02XHTML07.html file, you can open the **Ch02XHTML05.html** file in your Web browser. Click each employee's name to see if the program works correctly. Figure 2-14 shows an example of the file displaying the photo of Linda Asuncion in Internet Explorer.

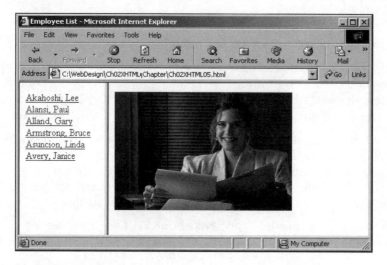

Figure 2-14   Employee directory frame-based Web page

7. Close the Web browser window.

CREATING TABLES

When HTML was first introduced, it provided no means of creating tables, which are essentially rows and columns or tabular data. Tables were introduced in HTML 3.2, and Web designers quickly realized how useful they were. Tables allow you to effectively structure and display information in an organized format that is difficult to achieve by using standard text-formatting elements such as the `<p>` element. Additionally, tables are quickly replacing frames as an essential component of effective navigation systems.

The `<table>` Element

Tables are collections of rows and columns that you use to organize and display data. The intersection in a table of any given row and column is called a **cell**. From your work in word processors and spreadsheets, you are probably more than familiar with traditional tables that organize information in columns and rows. You create tables in XHTML documents using the **`<table>` element**. Within the `<table>` element, you can nest a number of other elements that specify the content of each cell along with the structure and appearance of the table. Table 2-6 lists the attributes of the `<table>` element.

Table 2-6 Attributes of the `<table>` element

Attribute	Description
summary	Provides a detailed summary of a table's structure and content for use in nonvisual user agents
width	Specifies the size of a table
border	Add a border to a table
frame	Specifies which sides of the table should display a border
rules	Specifies which rules should appear in a table
cellspacing	Specifies the amount of space between table cells
cellpadding	Specifies the amount of space between each cell's border and the contents of the cell

Basic Table Elements

Cells are one of the most basic parts of a table. You create a cell within the `<table>` element by using the **`<td>` element**. The content of each `<td>` element is the data that will appear in the table cell. Each `<td>` element essentially represents a column in the table. Table cells are declared within table row elements that you create with **`<tr>` elements**. Each `<tr>` element you include within a `<table>` element creates a separate row.

Table cells can actually contain two types of information: data that you define with the `<td>` element and header information that you define with the **`<th>` element**. Header information usually describes the contents of a single column or multiple columns within a table. The content of each `<th>` element is the data that will appear as the table's header information. User agents will render the contents of a `<th>` element in a distinct manner; most Web browsers will display header information in a bold typeface and align it in the center of the column.

The `<td>` and `<th>` elements can contain plain text, `<img>` elements, and almost any other type of XHTML element.

As an example, consider the table shown in Figure 2-15, which lists the days of the week in English, French, and German.

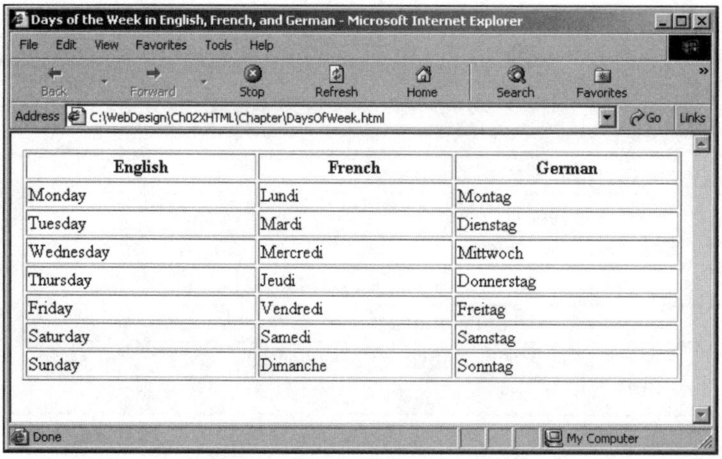

Figure 2-15   Days of the week table

To display the table shown in Figure 2-15, you use the following table elements. Notice that the `<table>` element includes the `width` and `border` attributes.

```
<table width="100%" border="1">
   <tr><th>English</th><th>French</th><th>German</th></tr>
   <tr><td>Monday</td><td>Lundi</td><td>Montag</td></tr>
   <tr><td>Tuesday</td><td>Mardi</td><td>Dienstag</td></tr>
   <tr><td>Wednesday</td><td>Mercredi</td><td>Mittwoch</td></tr>
   <tr><td>Thursday</td><td>Jeudi</td><td>Donnerstag</td></tr>
   <tr><td>Friday</td><td>Vendredi</td><td>Freitag</td></tr>
   <tr><td>Saturday</td><td>Samedi</td><td>Samstag</td></tr>
   <tr><td>Sunday</td><td>Dimanche</td><td>Sonntag</td></tr>
</table>
```

Next, you will create the weekly schedule for a commuter railroad.

To start creating the weekly schedule for a commuter railroad:

1. Create a new document in your text editor.

2. Type the opening `<!DOCTYPE>` declaration, header information, and opening `<body>` tag. Use the Strict DTD and "Metropolitan Commuter Railroad" as the content of the `<title>` element.

3. Add the following heading-level element:

    `<h2>Pleasantville to Coast City</h2>`

4. Now type the following code for a simple table, which only includes the railroad's departure and arrival times from Pleasantville to Coast City:

    ```
    <table width="100%" border="1">
        <tr><th>Depart Pleasantville</th>
            <th>Arrive Coast City</th></tr>
    ```

2

```
<tr><td>6:00 am</td>
     <td>7:00 am</td></tr>
<tr><td>7:00 am</td>
     <td>8:00 am</td></tr>
<tr><td>8:00 am</td>
     <td>9:00 am</td></tr>
<tr><td>4:00 pm</td>
     <td>5:00 pm</td></tr>
<tr><td>5:00 pm</td>
     <td>6:00 pm</td></tr>
<tr><td>6:00 pm</td>
     <td>7:00 pm</td></tr>
</table>
```

5. Finish the document by typing the following tags to close the **<body>** and **<html>** elements:

   </body></html>

6. Save the file as **Ch02XHTML08.html** in the Chapter folder for Chapter 2.

7. Open the **Ch02XHTML08.html** file in your Web browser. Figure 2-16 displays the file as it appears in Internet Explorer.

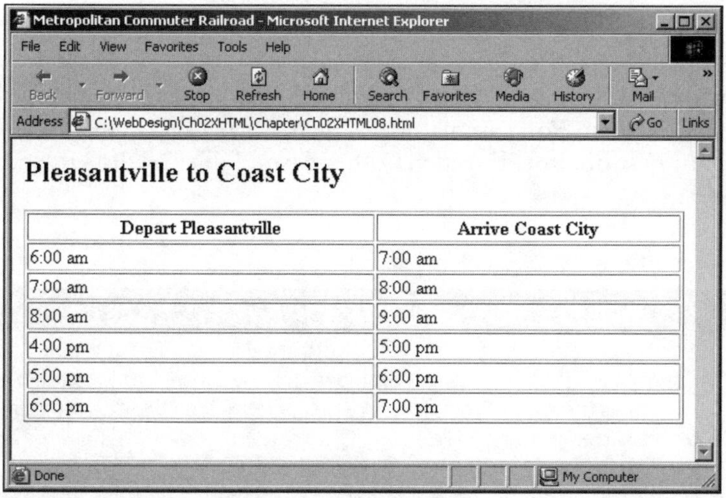

Figure 2-16 Train schedule table

8. Close your Web browser window.

BUILDING FORMS

Many Web sites use **forms** to collect information from users and transmit that information to a server for processing. Forms you may encounter on the Web include order forms, surveys, and applications.

Typically, a Web form works like this: The user enters information in the form and then clicks a button (such as a Submit button) to send the information to a Web server. At that point, a program written in a special language called a **server-side scripting language** processes the user's data. Some of the more popular server-side scripting languages include Common Gateway Interface (CGI), Active Server Pages (ASP), and Java Server Pages (JSP). The programs you create with server-side scripting languages are called **scripts**. Because the main focus of this book is Web page design, you will not study any of the server-side scripting languages used for processing form data that is sent to a server. However, later in this section you will learn how to submit form data to an e-mail address.

 If you would like to learn about some of the server-side scripting languages you can use to process form data, refer to *Web Warrior Guide to Programming Technologies* published by Course Technology.

The <form> Element

The **<form> element** designates a form within a Web page and contains all text and elements that make up a form. You can include as many forms as you like on a Web page. However, you cannot nest one form inside another form. Table 2-7 lists the attributes of the <form> element.

Table 2-7   Attributes of the <form> element

Attribute	Description
action	Required attribute that specifies a URL to which form data will be submitted. If this attribute is excluded, the data is sent to the URL that contains the form. Typically, you would specify the URL of a program on a server or an e-mail address.
method	Determines how form data will be submitted. The two options for this attribute are "get" and "post". The default option, "get", appends form data as one long string to the URL specified by the action attribute. The "post" option sends form data as a transmission separate from the URL specified by the action attribute. Although "get" is the default, "post" is considered the preferred option, because it allows the server to receive the data separately from the URL.
enctype	Specifies the format of the data being submitted. The default value is application/x-www-form-urlencoded.
accept-charset	Specifies a comma-separated list of possible character sets for the form data.

2

The `enctype` attribute specifies an encoding protocol known as multipurpose Internet mail extension, or MIME. Encoding with MIME ensures that data does not become corrupt when transmitted across the Internet. The MIME protocol was originally developed to allow different file types to be transmitted as attachments to e-mail messages. Now MIME has become a standard method of exchanging files over the Internet. MIME types are specified by using two-part codes separated by a forward slash (/). The first part specifies the MIME type, and the second part specifies the MIME subtype. The default MIME type of `application/x-www-form-urlencoded` specifies that form data should be encoded as one long string. The only other MIME types allowed with the `enctype` attribute are `multipart/form-data`, which encodes each field as a separate section, and `text/plain`, which is used to submit form data to an e-mail address.

Next, you will create a subscription form for a newspaper called the *Coast City Gazette*.

To start creating a subscription form:

1. Create a new document in your text editor.

2. Type the opening `<!DOCTYPE>` declaration, header information, and opening `<body>` tag. Use the Strict DTD and "Coast City Gazette Subscription Form" as the content of the `<title>` element.

3. Add the following heading-level element:

   ```
   <h1>Coast City Gazette</h1>
   <h2>Newspaper Subscription</h2>
   ```

4. Add the following two tags to create the form section. In the next exercise, you will add form elements between these tags.

   ```
   <form action="example_script.asp" method="post"
   enctype="text/plain">
   </form>
   ```

5. Finish the document by typing the following tags to close the `<body>` and `<html>` elements:

   ```
   </body></html>
   ```

6. Save the file as **Ch02XHTML09.html** in the Chapter folder for Chapter 2. Do not open the file in a Web browser, because it does not yet contain any form elements.

Form Controls

There are four primary elements used within the `<form>` element to create form controls: `<input>`, `<select>`, `<textarea>`, and `<button>`. The **`<input>` element** creates input fields that users interact with, such as a text box. The **`<select>` element** displays choices in a drop-down menu or scrolling list known as a selection list. The **`<textarea>` element** is used to create a text field in which users can enter multiple lines of information. The **`<button>` element** creates push buttons, submit buttons, and reset buttons. Any form element into which a user can enter data, such as a text box, or that a user can select or change, such as a radio button, is called a **field**.

The `<input>`, `<textarea>`, and `<select>` elements can include `name` and `value` attributes. The `name` attribute defines a name for an element, and the `value` attribute defines a default value. When you submit a form to a Web server, the form data is submitted in "name=value" pairs, based on the `name` and `value` attributes of each element. For example, if you have a text field created with the statement `<input type="text" name="company_info" value="ABC Corp.">`, a "name=value" pair of "company_info=ABC Corp." will be sent to a Web server (unless the default value is changed to something else).

Visitors to your Web page are not required to include a `value` attribute or enter a value into a field before the form data is submitted.

Due to space limitations, this chapter only covers input fields created with the `<input>` element, which creates different types of interface elements to gather information. Table 2-8 lists common attributes of the `<input>` element.

Table 2-8   Common attributes of the `<input>` element

Attribute	Description
alt	Provides alternate text for an image submit button
checked	Determines whether or not a radio button or a check box is selected
maxlength	Sets the maximum number of characters that can be entered into a field
name	Designates a name for the element; part of the "name=value" pair that is used to submit data to a Web server
size	Accepts an integer value that determines how many characters wide a text field is
src	Specifies the URL of an image
type	Specifies the type of element to be rendered; `type` is a required attribute; valid values are text, password, radio, checkbox, reset, button, submit, image, and hidden
value	Sets an initial value in a field or a label for buttons; part of the "name=value" pair that is used to submit data to a Web server

One of the most important attributes of the `<input>` element is the `type` attribute, which determines the type of element to be rendered and is a required attribute. Table 2-9 describes the purpose of each of the valid values for the `type` attribute.

Table 2-9   Valid values for the `<input>` element's `type` attribute

Value	Description
text	Creates a field that accepts a single line of text.
password	Creates a field that is used for entering passwords.
radio	Creates a group of radio buttons from which you can select only one value. To create a group of radio buttons, all radio buttons in the group must have the same `name` attribute. Each radio button requires a `value` attribute. Only one checked radio button in a group creates a "name=value" pair when a form is submitted to a Web server.
checkbox	Creates a check box control that allows users to select whether or not to include a certain item.
reset	Creates a button that clears all form entries and resets each form element to its initial value specified by the `value` attribute.
button	Creates a push button that is similar to the OK and Cancel buttons you see in dialog boxes.
submit	Creates a push button that transmits a form's data to a Web server.
image	Creates a graphical image that transmits a form's data to a Web server. The control performs exactly the same function as the submit value. You include the `src` attribute to specify the image to display on the button.
file	Creates a text box control along with a push button labeled with "Browse" that you can use to upload a file to a Web server. A `<form>` element that contains a file box control must assign a value of "post" to its `action` attribute and "multipart/form-data" to its `enctype` attribute.
hidden	Creates a field that hides information from users. Each character that a user types in a password box appears as an asterisk on the screen, thus preventing anyone near the user from reading the password.

Next, you will add to the subscription form some `<input>` elements for basic customer information.

To add to the subscription form some `<input>` elements for basic customer information:

1. Return to the **Ch02XHTML09.html** file in your text editor.

2. Within the `<form>...</form>` tag pair, add the following `<input>` elements, which gather a customer's name, street address, city, state, zip, e-mail address, and a password to use to manage their account online:

```
<p>Name<br />
<input type="text" name="customer_name" size="50" /><br /></p>
<p>Address<br />
<input type="text" name="address" size="50" /></p>
<p>City, State, Zip<br />
<input type="text" name="city" size="34" />
<input type="text" name="state" size="2" maxlength="2" />
<input type="text" name="zip" size="5" maxlength="5" /></p>
```

```
<p>E-Mail<br />
<input type="text" name="email" size="50" /></p>
<p>Enter a password that you will need to manage your
subscription online<br />
<input type="password" name="password" size="50" /></p>
```

3. Now add the following <input> elements, which create a reset button and a submit button:

```
<p><input type="reset" />
<input type="submit" /></p>
```

4. Save the **Ch02XHTML09.html** file, and then open it in your Web browser. The <input> fields you entered should appear as shown in Figure 2-17.

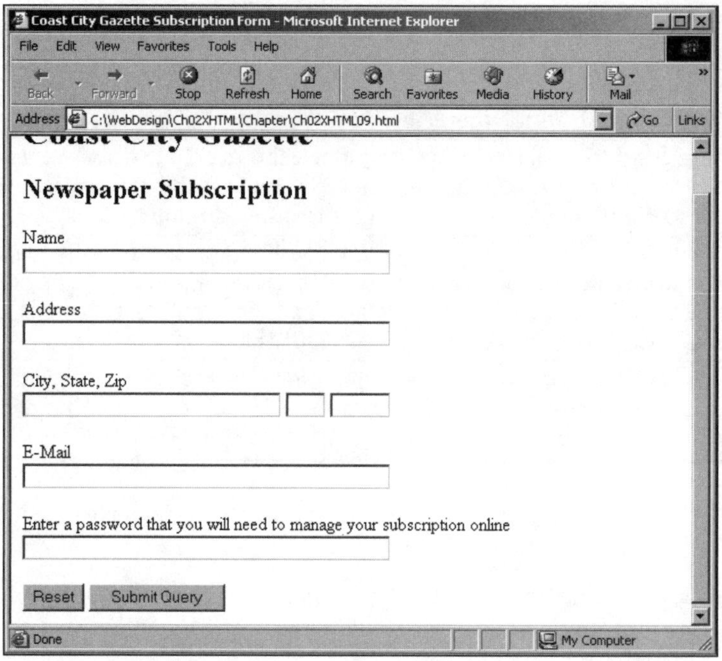

Figure 2-17   Subscription form after adding <input> elements

5. Close your Web browser window.

E-Mailing Form Data

Typically, data from a form is transmitted to a Web server. However, another option is to send the form data to an e-mail address. Sending form data to an e-mail address is a much simpler process than creating and managing a script on a Web server. Instead of relying on a complex script on a Web server to process the data, you rely on the recipient of the e-mail message to process the data. For instance, a Web site may contain an

2

online order form for some type of product. After the user clicks the Submit button, the data for the order can be sent to the e-mail address of whoever is responsible for filling the order. For large organizations that deal with hundreds or thousands of orders a day, e-mailing each order to a single individual is not the ideal solution. However, for smaller companies or Web sites that do not have a high volume of orders, e-mailing form data is a good solution.

To e-mail form data instead of submitting it to a Web server, you replace the Web server script's URL in the `<form>` element's `action` attribute with `mailto:email_address` (where `email_address` is replaced by the e-mail address you want to send the data to). For instance, the following code generates the RSVP form shown in Figure 2-18 for a fictitious wedding planning company. The form's data will be e-mailed to a fictitious e-mail address, rsvp@CentralValleyWeddings.com.

```
<h1>Jose and Melinda's Wedding</h1>
<h2>RSVP Form</h2>
<p><strong>Please send your reply by 3/15/2005.</strong></p>
<form action="mailto:rsvp@CentralValleyWeddings.com"
      method="post" enctype="text/plain">
<p>Your name</p>
<p><input type="text" size="50" /></p>
<p><input type="radio" name="attending"
      value="yes" />Will attend<br />
<input type="radio" name="attending"
      value="no" />Will not</p>
<p><input type="hidden" name="wedding" value="Jose and Melinda"
/></p>
<p><button type="reset">Reset</button>
<button type="submit">RSVP</button></p>
</form>
```

 Notice that the preceding code includes a hidden element that stores the name of the couple whose wedding the RSVP is being returned for.

When you send form data to an e-mail address, use the **enctype** of "text/plain", which ensures that the data arrives at the e-mail address in a readable format. Figure 2-19 shows an example of the e-mail message received by rsvp@CentralValleyWeddings.com after the form generated by the preceding code is submitted. The e-mail message appears in Microsoft Outlook.

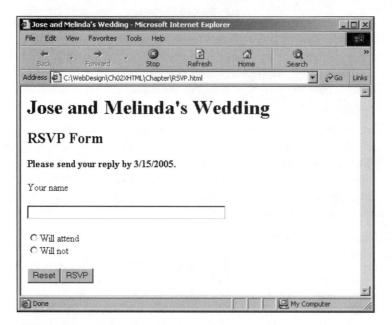

Figure 2-18 RSVP form

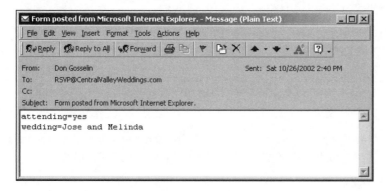

Figure 2-19 Data in Outlook after being e-mailed from a form

The drawback to e-mailing form data is that not all Web browsers support the `mailto:`*email_address* option with the `<form>` element's `action` attribute. In addition, the performance of the `mailto:`*email_address* option is unreliable. Some Web browsers that do support the e-mailing of form data do not properly place the data within the body of an e-mail message. If you write a Web page that e-mails form data, be sure to test it thoroughly before using it.

 When users click the Submit button in order to e-mail form data, they may receive a security warning or be given a chance to edit the e-mail, depending on how their e-mail applications are configured.

Next, you will change the `<form>` element of the subscription form so that the form data is sent to your e-mail address whenever it is submitted.

To change the `<form>` element of the subscription form so that the form data is sent to your e-mail address whenever it is submitted:

1. Return to the **Ch02XHTML09.html** file in your text editor.

2. Modify the opening `<form>` element as follows. Be sure to replace *email_address* with your own e-mail address.

   ```
   <form action="mailto:email_address" method="post"
   enctype="text/plain">
   ```

3. Save the **Ch02XHTML09.html** file, and then open it in your Web browser. Fill in the form fields, and then submit it. Depending on your e-mail configuration, you may see warning dialog boxes or be given a chance to edit the e-mail message.

4. Wait several minutes before retrieving the new message from your e-mail, because transmission time on the Internet can vary. After you receive the e-mail, examine the message to see how the form data appears.

5. Close your Web browser, text editor, and e-mail program.

CHAPTER SUMMARY

- ❏ A user agent is a device that is capable of retrieving and processing XHTML and can include a traditional Web browser or a device such as a mobile phone or personal digital assistant (PDA).

- ❏ Formatting elements provide specific instructions as to how their contents should be displayed.

- ❏ Phrase elements primarily describe their contents.

- ❏ The easiest way to add special characters to an XHTML document is to use a character entity reference, or character entity.

- ❏ In order for an XHTML document to be well formed, the `<img>` element must include an `src` attribute and an `alt` attribute.

- ❏ You use the `height` and `width` attributes to specify the size of your images in order for the Web browser to know how many pixels to reserve on the page for an image.

- ❏ The values you assign to the `height` and `width` attributes on an `<img>` element should always be the exact dimensions of the original image.

- ❏ An unordered list is a list of bulleted items.

- ❏ An ordered list is a list of numbered items.

- ❏ A definition list is a list of terms and their definitions.

❏ Frames are independent, scrollable portions of a Web browser window, with each frame capable of containing its own URL.

❏ Tables are collections of rows and columns that you use to organize and display multidimensional data.

❏ Instead of submitting form data to a Web server, another option is to send the form data to an e-mail address.

REVIEW QUESTIONS

1. Which element should be used in place of the `<b>` element?

   a. `<big>`

   b. `<strong>`

   c. `<bold>`

   d. `<cite>`

2. Which element should be used in place of the `<i>` element?

   a. `<var>`

   b. `<samp>`

   c. `<em>`

   d. `<dfn>`

3. What is the character entity for a quotation mark?

   a. `&q;`

   b. `&quot;`

   c. `&quotation;`

   d. `&qt;`

4. Which of the following elements is used with both unordered and ordered lists?

   a. `<ul>`

   b. `<ol>`

   c. `<li>`

   d. `<dl>`

5. Which of the following elements is used to create frames?

   a. `<begin frame>...</end frame>`

   b. `<frameset>...</frameset>`

   c. `<new frame>...</new frame>`

   d. `<framebuild>...</framebuild>`

6. The size of rows and columns in a frame can be set by using a percentage of the screen size or by using _____.

    a. inches

    b. picas

    c. pixels

    d. a Web browser's internal sizing capability

7. Which is the correct syntax for a `<frame>` element that loads a URL of `MyHomePage.html`?

    a. `<frame href="MyHomePage.html">`

    b. `<frame url="MyHomePage.html">`

    c. `<frame html="MyHomePage.html">`

    d. `<frame src="MyHomePage.html">`

8. The _____ attribute of the `<a>` element determines in which frame or window a URL opens.

    a. `openinwin`

    b. `select`

    c. `goal`

    d. `target`

9. The _____ element is used for specifying a default target for all links in an HTML document using the assigned name of a window or frame.

    a. `<base>`

    b. `<source>`

    c. `<target>`

    d. `<default>`

10. Which of the following elements do you use to create table rows?

    a. `<row>`

    b. `<table_row>`

    c. `<tr>`

    d. `<rt>`

11. What is the default value of the `<form>` element's `enctype` attribute?

    a. `text/plain`

    b. `multipart/form-data`

    c. `application/x-www-form-urlencoded`

    d. `image/gif`

2

12. How is form data submitted to a Web server?

   a. in "value,name" pairs

   b. in "name=value" pairs

   c. as values separated by commas

   d. as values separated by paragraph marks

13. An `<input>` element with a `value` attribute of "text" _____.

   a. displays a static label

   b. creates input fields that use different types of interface elements to gather information

   c. creates a simple text box that accepts a single line of text

   d. creates either a submit or a reset button

14. Each character entered into a password text box appears _____.

   a. with the ampersand (&) symbol

   b. with the number (#) symbol

   c. as a percentage (%)

   d. as an asterisk (*)

15. Which attribute is used to designate a single button in a radio group as the default?

   a. `checked`

   b. `check`

   c. `selected`

   d. `default`

HANDS-ON EXERCISES

Exercise 2-1

In this exercise, you will validate the files you created in this chapter. (You learned how to validate XHTML documents in Chapter 1.)

1. Start Internet Explorer, and enter the URL for the upload page of the W3C HTML Validation Service: validator.w3.org/file-upload.html.

2. Open and validate the **Ch02XHTML01.html** file from the Chapter folder for Chapter 2. If you do receive any errors, fix them, and then revalidate the document.

3. Repeat the validation process for the remainder of the files you created in the Chapter folder for Chapter 2.

Exercise 2-2

In this exercise, you will create a Web page containing a quotation by Mark Twain.

1. Create a new document in your text editor, and type the opening `<!DOCTYPE>` declaration, header information, and opening `<body>` tag. Use the Frameset DTD and "Mark Twain" as the content of the `<title>` element.

2. Add the following statements that contain text-formatting elements:

   ```
   <p><b>Mark Twain said</b><br />
   <i>Everybody talks about the weather, <br />
   but nobody does anything about it.</i></p>
   ```

3. Modify the `<p>` and `<i>` text-formatting elements you added in step 2 to their corresponding phrase elements.

4. Finish the document by typing the following tags to close the `<body>` and `<html>` elements:

   ```
   </body></html>
   ```

5. Save the file as **Ch02XHTMLEX02.html** in the Exercises folder for Chapter 2 and validate it with the W3C HTML Validation Service.

Exercise 2-3

In this exercise, you will create a frame-based Web page with two column frames. The left frame will display some animal names as links. Clicking an animal name will display its picture in the right frame. The image files you need for the exercise are located in the Exercises folder for Chapter 2.

1. Create a new document in your text editor, and type the opening `<!DOCTYPE>` declaration and header information. Do not include an opening `<body>` tag. Use the Strict DTD and "Animals" as the content of the `<title>` element.

2. Add the following `<frameset>` and `<frame>` elements. Notice that, by default, the right frame opens an image file for an element. The image file that opens by default is the first animal in the list that will display in the left frame.

   ```
   <frameset cols="20%,*">
       <frame src="Ch02XHTMLEX03b.html" />
       <frame src="elephant.jpg" name="animal_picture" />
   </frameset>
   </html>
   ```

3. Save the file as **Ch02XHTMLEX03a.html** in the Exercises folder for Chapter 2 and validate it with the W3C HTML Validation Service.

4. Create another document in your text editor, and type the opening `<!DOCTYPE>` declaration, header information, and opening `<body>` tag. Use the Transitional DTD and "Animals" as the content of the `<title>` element. Then, create the

following list of links that will display in the right frame, along with the closing `</body>` and `</html>` elements:

```
<p><a href="Elephant.jpg">Elephant</a><br />
<a href="gazelle.jpg">Gazelle</a><br />
<a href="giraffe.jpg">Giraffe</a><br />
<a href="lion.jpg">Lion</a><br />
<a href="polarbear.jpg">Polar bear</a><br />
<a href="rhino.jpg">Rhino</a><br />
<a href="tiger.jpg">Tiger</a><br />
<a href="zebra.jpg">Zebra</a></p>
</body>
</html>
```

5. Save the file as **Ch02XHTMLEX03b.html** in the Exercises folder for Chapter 2 and validate it with the W3C HTML Validation Service.

6. Open **Ch02XHTMLEX03a.html** in your Web browser and test the links. Figure 2-20 shows the Web page with the giraffe displayed.

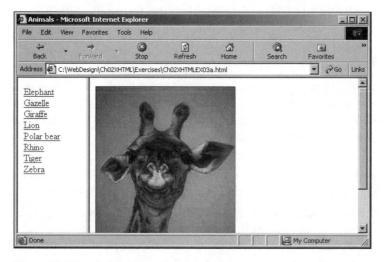

Figure 2-20   Frame-based animal page

Exercise 2-4

In this exercise, you will create a Web page with a table that lists major league baseball players who have 10 or more RBIs (runs batted in) in a single game.

1. Create a new document in your text editor, and type the opening `<!DOCTYPE>` declaration, header information, and opening `<body>` tag. Use the Strict DTD and "10+ RBIs in a Game" as the content of the `<title>` element.

2. Create the table shown in Figure 2-21.

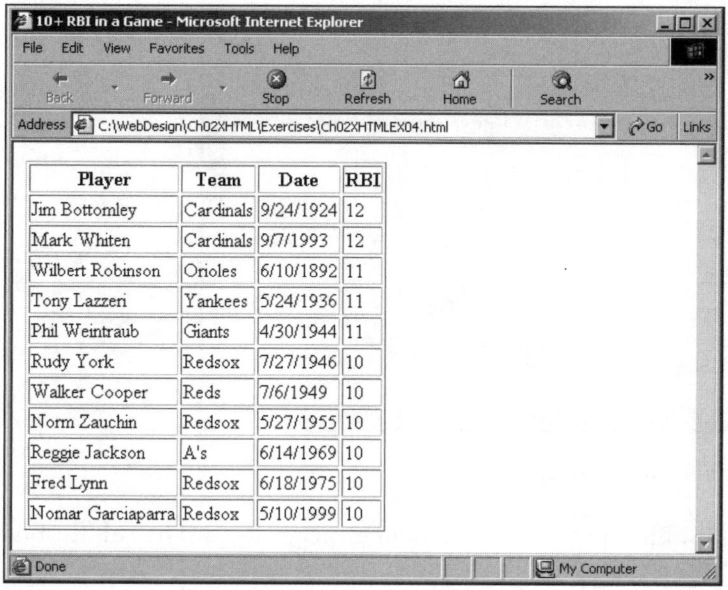

Player	Team	Date	RBI
Jim Bottomley	Cardinals	9/24/1924	12
Mark Whiten	Cardinals	9/7/1993	12
Wilbert Robinson	Orioles	6/10/1892	11
Tony Lazzeri	Yankees	5/24/1936	11
Phil Weintraub	Giants	4/30/1944	11
Rudy York	Redsox	7/27/1946	10
Walker Cooper	Reds	7/6/1949	10
Norm Zauchin	Redsox	5/27/1955	10
Reggie Jackson	A's	6/14/1969	10
Fred Lynn	Redsox	6/18/1975	10
Nomar Garciaparra	Redsox	5/10/1999	10

Figure 2-21 10+ RBIs table

3. Finish the document by typing the following tags to close the `<body>` and `<html>` elements:

```
</body></html>
```

4. Save the file as **Ch02XHTMLEX04.html** in the Exercises folder for Chapter 2 and validate it with the W3C HTML Validation Service.

Exercise 2-5

In this exercise, you will create an airline survey form.

1. Create the airline survey form shown in Figure 2-22. Use the Strict DTD. Design the form using a table and `<input>` elements to create the radio buttons. The `<input>` elements in each row of radio buttons should be assigned the same `name` attribute in order for them to be part of the same group. Assign the appropriate value (Excellent, Good, Fair, Poor, No Opinion) to the `value` attribute for each `<input>` element. For example, you create the radio button for the first "Excellent" button using this statement `<input type="radio" name= "wait_time" value="Excellent" />`.

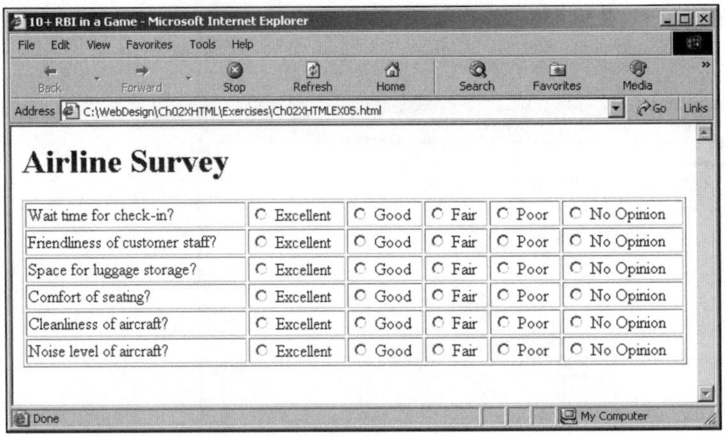

Figure 2-22   Airline survey form

2. Add reset and submit buttons to the airline survey form. The submit button should submit the survey data to your e-mail address.

3. Save the file as **Ch02XHTMLEX05.html** in the Exercises folder for Chapter 2 and validate it with the W3C HTML Validation Service. Once the file is valid, open it in your Web browser. Test the form and submit your data to your e-mail address.

WEB DESIGN PROJECTS

Be sure to validate the files you create in the following projects with the W3C HTML Validation Service.

Project 2-1

Create a document that contains a list of hyperlinks to your favorite recipes. Clicking each hyperlink should open another document, which then displays the selected recipe. Use unordered lists for the recipe ingredients and ordered lists for the preparation instructions. Name the main document **Ch02XHTMLDP01.html**, and name each recipe document according to the recipe name. For example, if you have a recipe for apple pie, name its associated document **ApplePie.html**.

Project 2-2

Create a document with two frames. One frame should take up 200 pixels on the left side of the screen, and the other frame should take up the remainder of the right portion of the screen. Use hyperlinks to create a list of your favorite Web sites in the left frame. When a user clicks a favorite Web site in the left frame, it should open in the right frame. Use the **<base>** element to specify the default target window. Assign to the **src** attribute of the `<frame>` element for the right frame an empty set of parentheses as follows: `<frame src="" name="LinksFrame">`. This tells the Web browser not to display anything in the right frame when the frameset document first opens. Save the main frameset document as **Ch02XHTMLDP02a.html**. Save the links page that will display in the left frame as **Ch02XHTMLDP02b.html**.

Project 2-3

Create a consent form for a school trip. Include fields for information about the trip such as destination, date, and purpose. Also, include fields such as child's name, parent's or guardian's signature, and name, address, and telephone number of child's physician. Use two radio buttons that read "Permission is Granted" and "Permission is NOT Granted" that parents can use to grant or deny permission for the field trip. Save the project as **Ch02XHTMLDP03.html** in the Projects folder for Chapter 2. If you need more help on working with forms, the W3C Web site includes an outstanding online tutorial at www.w3schools.com/html/default.asp.

3

DREAMWEAVER: PART I

In this chapter you will:

- Learn to use the editing features of the Dreamweaver Web authoring tool
- Learn to control text properties to make a page look more appealing
- Create hyperlinks to link pages together on the Web
- Create and control page properties such as colors and backgrounds
- Learn to use tables and table attributes to control layout of Web pages
- Learn to use and manipulate images on your Web pages

Dreamweaver is a Web authoring tool that makes Web development visual, rapid, and easy. It includes a "What You See Is What You Get" (WYSIWYG) interface, which means that your Web pages can look the same in Dreamweaver as they do on the Web; however, you do not have to work with HTML code. As you build a Web page in the WYSIWYG interface, Dreamweaver generates HTML and JavaScript code for you, saving you from the drudgery of coding rollovers or formatting table tags. If you prefer, though, you can choose to edit the code directly. To further improve your productivity, Dreamweaver incorporates templates, libraries, and styles, which are tools that allow you to reuse elements of your work throughout your site. With Dreamweaver, you can develop, manage, test, and automatically update any changes made to your Web site. Dreamweaver is also easily integrated with several other products such as Fireworks (a graphics editing tool) and Flash (a Web animation tool). Given the wide range of technical tasks you can perform in Dreamweaver, it is easy to see why it is one of the most popular Web design tools on the market today. In this chapter, you will learn to create Web pages in Dreamweaver by using a variety of text, tables, and images. You will also learn to create hyperlinks.

THE DREAMWEAVER WORKSPACE

The Dreamweaver workspace enables you to create a Web page that looks, for the most part, identical to the page that later appears in a browser. In this section, you will take a guided tour of the workspace. But first, you need to start Dreamweaver.

To start Dreamweaver:

1. In Windows XP, click **Start** on the Start bar, point to **All Programs**, point to **Macromedia**, and then click **Macromedia Dreamweaver MX**. (If you are working on a Macintosh, open Dreamweaver MX from the Applications folder.) Dreamweaver opens, and the workspace looks similar to Figure 3-1. If you see the Workspace Setup dialog box or the Welcome Window, close them. If your screen looks different from Figure 3-1, do not be concerned. In the remainder of this section, you will learn how to set up your workspace to match Figure 3-1.

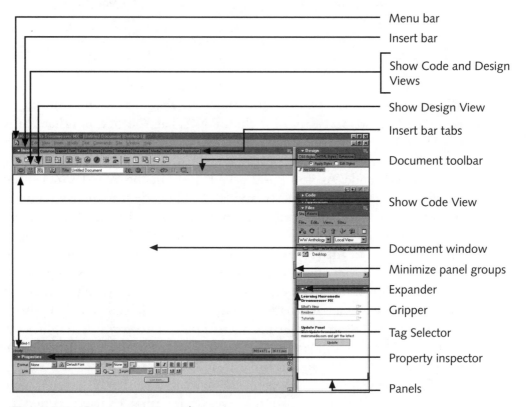

Figure 3-1   Dreamweaver workspace

2. If the Document window is not open on your computer, click **File** on the menu bar, click **New**, and then click **Create**.

Figure 3-1 shows how the Dreamweaver workspace usually looks when you open it for the first time after installation. Your screen might look slightly different, but at the very least you should see the following: an Insert bar, the Document toolbar, the Document window, and panels on the right.

The Document window is where your Web page is displayed. If you see a title bar containing the text "Untitled Document (Untitled −1*)" directly below the Document toolbar, then your Document window is not maximized. You will learn how to change that in a moment. If you see HTML code in the Document window, then your screen is not currently in Design view. You will have a chance to switch to Design view in the next section. For now, ignore it.

The Property inspector and Tag selector should also appear on the bottom of the work area. These two items are the tools that you will use most often to edit your Web page. The Property inspector is the primary tool for formatting text and controlling attributes of objects in Dreamweaver. With it, you can also create and manage hyperlinks, and control the size of images and tables. Several of its icons will already be familiar to you, because they are identical to icons in Microsoft Word. As you can see in Figure 3-1, the Insert bar contains numerous tabs, which you can click to reveal icons used for editing Web pages. For example, by using the Common tab you can insert graphics, tables, and layers. You can also incorporate active elements on a Web page, (such as rollovers), Flash buttons, and text. You will learn more about the Insert bar and the Property inspector as you begin to create a Web page later in this chapter.

The Insert bar and the Property inspector open by default when you start Dreamweaver. You can open any of these windows or panels by clicking Window on the menu bar (at the top of the screen) and clicking the name of the panel you want to open or close. If you prefer, you can use the Ctrl+F2 shortcut keys to open or close the Insert bar and the Ctrl+F3 shortcut keys to open or close the Property inspector. (If you are working on a Macintosh, use the Command key—the one with the Apple on it—instead of the Ctrl key.)

Now turn your attention to the panels on the right side of the screen. The panels provide an easy way for you to add features to your Web pages. You can expand a panel by clicking the white, downward-pointing triangle next to its name. You can shrink a panel by clicking the white, left-facing triangle next to its name. To move a panel, click the gripper in the panel's upper-left corner, and drag the panel to a new location.

As mentioned earlier, the menu bar is at the top of the Dreamweaver workspace. The menu bar commands allow you to perform tasks such as saving files, inserting page elements, and controlling tables and frames. You will become familiar with these as you work with Dreamweaver. Many commands on the menu bar duplicate options available on the Property inspector and the Insert bar. As you gain experience with Dreamweaver, you will develop your own preferences about whether to use the menu bar or the corresponding tools in the workspace.

At the bottom of the work area, you should see a Tag selector, which helps you select specific code elements while working in Design view. When you are working on multiple pages, clicking on the Document tab allows you to move quickly from one page to the next. The window size and download estimate give you an indication of page performance before you publish the page to the Web.

In the following steps, you will have a chance to manipulate elements in Design view. If your screen does not match Figure 3-1 exactly, you can fix that now.

To practice manipulating the elements in Design view:

1. Practice expanding and shrinking the panels on the right side of the screen by clicking the left- and downward-pointing triangles next to the panel names. When you are finished, leave the Design, Files, and Answers panels open, as in Figure 3-1.

2. Use the **Ctrl+F2** shortcut keys to open and close the Insert bar and the **Ctrl+F3** shortcut keys to open and close the Property inspector. (If you are working on a Macintosh, use the Command key—the one with the Apple on it—instead of the Ctrl key.) Then use the Windows menu to perform the same tasks. When you are finished, make sure the Insert bar and the Property inspector are visible.

Throughout the rest of this chapter, if you are running Dreamweaver on a Macintosh, use the Command key—the one with the Apple on it—in keyboard shortcut combinations rather than the Ctrl key.

3. If you a see title bar containing the text "Untitled Document (Untitled −1*)" directly below the Document toolbar in Windows XP, then your Document window is not maximized. Click the **Maximize** button in the Document window title bar. When you are finished, your Dreamweaver title bar (at the top of the Dreamweaver screen) should match the one in Figure 3-1. (If you are working on a Macintosh, drag the bottom-right corner of the Document window to enlarge the Document window. The Document window will remain a separate window, with its own title bar.)

4. Make any other changes necessary to make your screen match Figure 3-1. (Note that on a Macintosh, the Dreamweaver screen will look slightly different from Figure 3-1. For example, you will probably see the Dock at the bottom of the screen.)

CHANGING VIEWS

When you build a Web page in Design view, Dreamweaver generates the necessary HTML and JavaScript code for you. In some cases, you may need to edit that code, in which case you will need to switch from Design view to Code view. Code view displays the HTML source code in a Code window that replaces the Document window. Alternately, you can use Code and Design view, which overlays a smaller Code window on top of the Document window, allowing you to see both the source code and the

WYSIWYG view of your Web page at the same time. In Code and Design view, you can edit the design and the code simultaneously. As you select different elements of the page in Design view, the cursor moves to the relevant line in the source code. Thus, Design and Code view enables you to control exactly what you are editing and see the results of your changes instantly.

You switch from one view to the other by clicking the View icons on the Document toolbar.

To practice switching from one view to another:

1. Position the mouse pointer on the far left side of the Document toolbar, over the icon that looks like empty HTML brackets. A screen tip appears with the words "Show Code View", indicating that you have the pointer positioned over the Show Code View icon. Note that you can rely on screen tips when you are unsure of the name of a toolbar icon.

2. Click the **Show Code View** icon. The Document window displays HTML code.

3. Click the **Show Code and Design Views** icon, to the right of the Show Code View icon. A smaller Code window appears on top of the Document window, as shown in Figure 3-2.

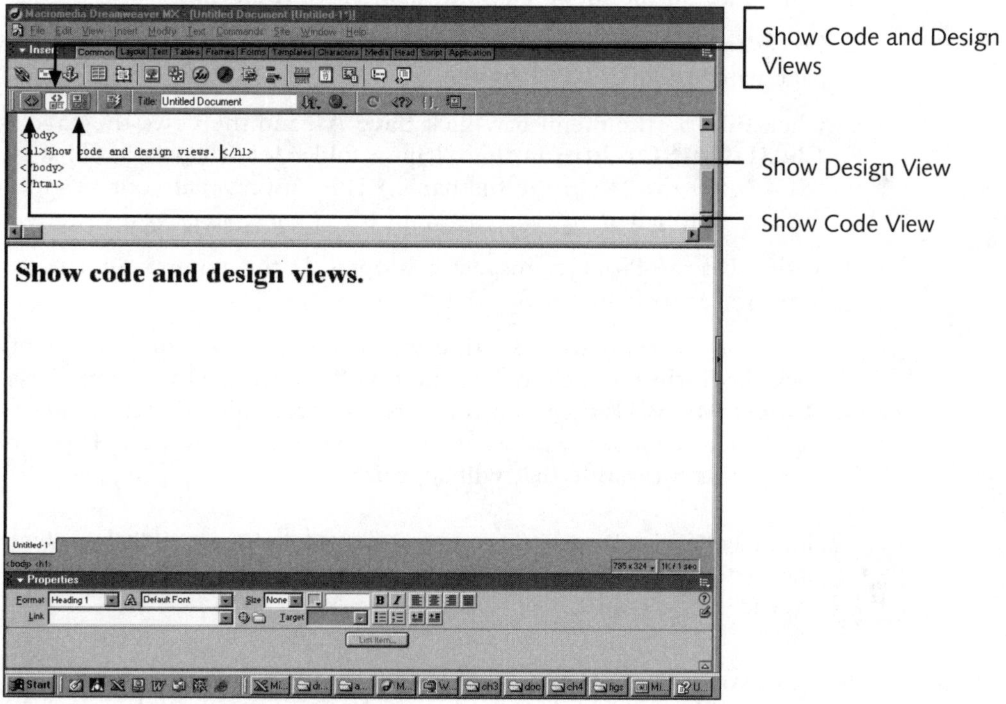

Figure 3-2   Design and Code Views detail

4. Click the **Show Design View** icon to the right of the Show Code and Design Views icon. Your screen returns to Design view. If your screen was not in Design view to begin with, it should be now.

TEXT PROPERTIES

Now that you are familiar with the Dreamweaver workspace, you can use it to create a simple Web page. In this section, you will concentrate on using the Property inspector to create a Web page for a furniture company.

Any element that you add to a Web page is defined by its attributes. For example, a table is defined by attributes such as cell size, color, and borders. The text boxes and toolbar buttons displayed in the Property inspector are relevant to the attributes of whatever part of the Web page is selected in the Document window. For example, if a table is selected, you would see buttons and text boxes that you could use to change the attributes related to tables. However, if you then selected some text, you would see tools that would allow you to change the attributes related to text, such as font, color, and size. You will see how this works in the following steps, as you change the font, color, and size attributes of some text and create a simple list. Working with text in the Property inspector is similar to working with text in a word processor. You will start by opening a file on your data disk.

1. Click **File** on the menu bar and then click **Open**.

2. Navigate to the Chapter folder for Chapter 3 on your data disk, and open the page named **Ch03DW01.htm**.

3. Click **File** on the menu bar, click **Save As**, and then save the page as **Ch03DW01SOL.htm** in the Chapter folder for Chapter 3. (That is, add "SOL" after the "1" in the file name.) This ensures that your original data file remains untouched, in case you want to try these steps again later.

4. Verify that the Property inspector is open. At this point, your screen should look similar to Figure 3-3.

5. Now you are ready to add a title to the Web page. In the Document toolbar, click the **Title** text box, delete the text **"Untitled Document"**, type **Robert Maxx Design** and then press **Enter**. This title will display at the top of your browser window when you view this Web page. If you bookmark a page, this is the title that will appear.

 If you are running Dreamweaver on a Macintosh, keep in mind that any time this text asks you to press the Enter key, you should press the Return key instead.

6. Next, you will change the font for the existing text. Click to the left of the "M" in "Maxx Design" at the top of the Document window, and then drag the mouse down to select all the text in the document.

7. In the Property inspector, the Font list box currently says "Default Font," indicating that the selected text is formatted in the default font. Now you will select a different font. Click the **Font** list arrow and click **Geneva, Arial, Helvetica sans-serif**.

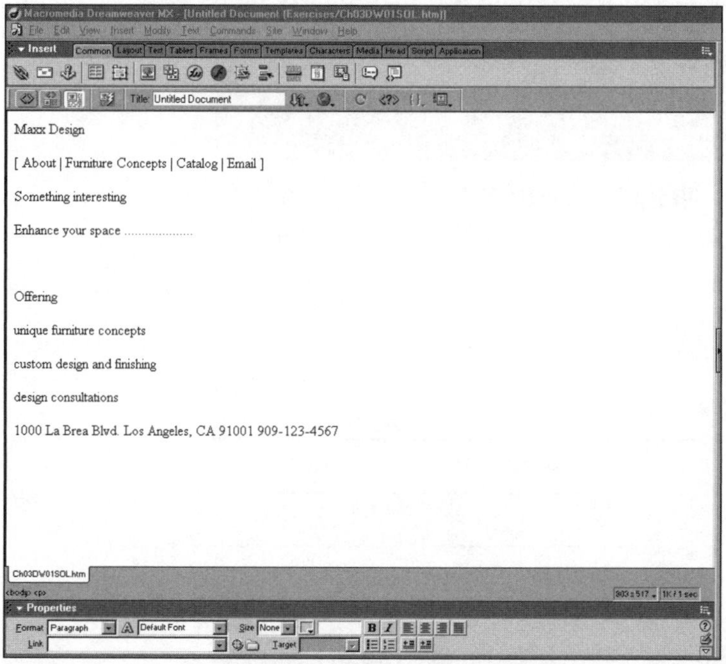

Figure 3-3   Open document Ch03DW01SOL.htm

8. Select the text **Maxx Design** at the beginning of the page. In the Property inspector, click the **Format** list arrow and click **Heading 1**. Click the **Size** list arrow in the Property inspector, scroll down the Size list until you see numbers with plus sign, click **+4**, and then click the **Align Center** icon in the Property inspector. The selected text is now formatted as a centered heading in a new font size. The selected text now appears in the selected font, as shown in Figure 3-4.

Now that you understand how the tools of the Property inspector work, you can use them to further improve the Web page. If you are not sure which buttons are which, remember that you can point to a button to display a screen tip containing the button's name.

To continue working on the Web page:

1. Click anywhere in the Document window to deselect the text.

2. Select the text **[About | Furniture Concepts | Catalog | Email]** and center it by using the **Align Center** icon.

3. Select the text **Something interesting, Enhance your space** (and the dot leader following "space"), click the **Format** list arrow, and click **Heading 3**.

4. Double-click the word **Offering** to select it, and then click the **Bold** icon in the Property inspector. Note that double-clicking text in the Document window selects the text, just as it does in Microsoft Word.

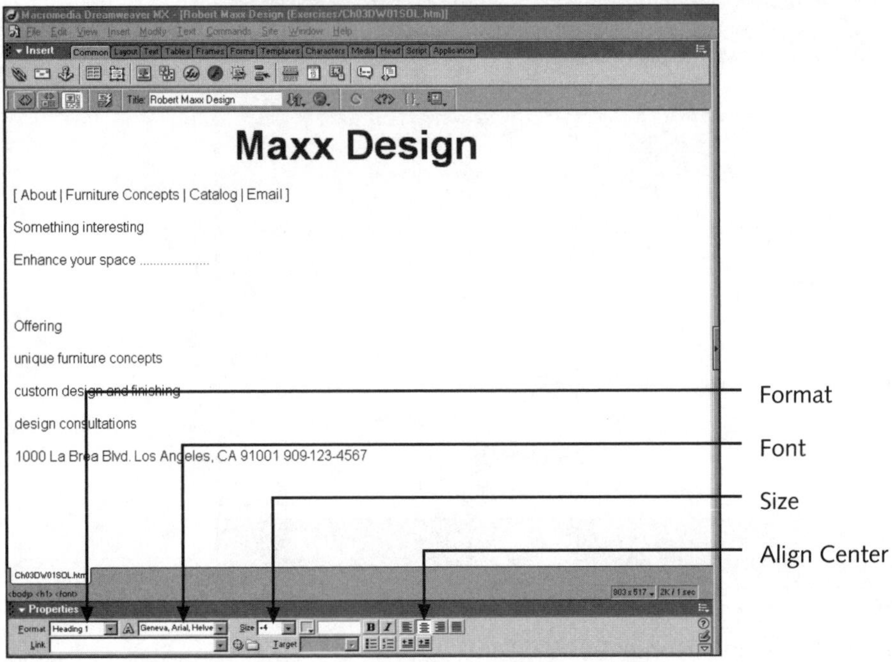

Figure 3-4   Changing text using the Property inspector

5. Use the mouse to select the text **unique furniture concepts, custom design and finishing, design consultations.** Then click the **Unordered List** icon in the Property inspector. The three items are now formatted as a bulleted list.

6. With the list still selected, click the **Text Color** list arrow in the Property inspector, as shown in Figure 3-5. The color palette opens. Drag the mouse over the palette to the brown section in the pinkish brown section along the left side of the palette. Notice that as you drag the mouse, the code corresponding to each color appears at the top of the palette. Point the mouse to the brown whose code is **#993333** as shown in Figure 3-5.

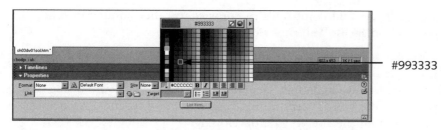

Figure 3-5   Selecting a brown color in the color palette

7. Click **#993333** and then deselect the text in the Document window so that you can see the change. The selected list is now formatted in brown.

8. In the Document window, click between the words "Blvd." and "Los Angeles" and then press **Shift + Enter**. (If you are working on a Macintosh, press Shift+Return.) This inserts a new line without adding a space.

9. Add another line between the ZIP code and the phone number. Select the entire address and center it.

You have finished editing a simple Web page in Dreamweaver. Even though Dreamweaver shows you what your page will look like in a browser, it is still a good idea to check your work in a browser after you finish in Dreamweaver. This is important because some Web page elements (a rollover, for example) will not work in the Dreamweaver application, which means you can only test them in a Web browser. Looking at your page in the browser also lets you resize the browser window and test how the page may look to a user under different conditions.

To preview your page in a browser:

1. Click **File** on the menu bar and then click **Save** to save your changes to the page.

2. With Dreamweaver still open, press **F12**.

3. Close the browser and return to the Dreamweaver interface. (If you are working on a Macintosh, you may need to click the Dreamweaver icon in the Dock to display all the elements of the Dreamweaver interface.)

4. In Dreamweaver, click **File** on the menu bar and then click **Close**. The Document window closes. Your page is no longer open in Dreamweaver, although the rest of the Dreamweaver interface remains open.

HYPERLINKS

Hyperlinks make the Web fun and easy to navigate. People familiar with the Web automatically know that blue underlined text is an invitation to click and visit another page for more information. The simple click navigation method means that users need not remember addresses and commands to connect to other computers. They simply click the hyperlink and access Web sites all over the globe.

As you probably already know, each file on the Internet has a **universal resource locator (URL)**, a unique address consisting of a protocol, domain name, and extension. You can use relative or absolute hyperlinks depending upon what you are trying to accomplish. Usually, an absolute link is used to link to an external site, and a relative link is used to link to a file within the site you are developing.

To implement hyperlinks in Dreamweaver, you select the text you would like to link and type the address of the file you want to link to in the Link text box in the Property inspector. Another method, if you prefer, is to click the Browse for File icon in the Property inspector and select the appropriate file from your directory structure. These are both useful methods because they remove the risk of keying errors and ensure that you get the file name and path name correct.

Making a Link List

In this exercise, you will create a hyperlink list of sites related to the materials you are learning in this book. Because the sites you will link to are corporate sites, external to the page you are developing, you will use absolute addressing for most of them. You will start by opening a new, blank page.

To begin creating a page with a list of links:

1. Click **File**, and then click **New.** The New Document dialog box opens.

2. Click the **General** tab, if necessary, to display it. Click **Basic Page** and then click **Create**. A new, blank page opens in the Document window.

3. In the Document toolbar, replace the current contents of the Title text box with **Web Development Links**.

4. Click in the work area to place your cursor at the top of the page and type **Web Development Links**. Select the text you just typed and change it to **Heading 1** by using the Format list arrow in the Property inspector. Click at the end of the text to deselect it and then press **Enter** to insert a new blank line.

5. Type the following six items, pressing the **Enter** key after each word: **Macromedia, Adobe, JavaScript, WebDeveloper, W3Schools, ASP.** When you are finished, you should have a list of 6 words, aligned on the left side of the Document window. Do not include the commas after each item.

6. Drag the mouse to select the text **Macromedia,** type **http://www.macromedia.com** in the Link text box in the Property inspector, press **Enter**, and then click anywhere in the Document window to deselect "Macromedia". The Macromedia link is now formatted in blue with an underline, indicating that it is now a hyperlink.

7. Repeat Step 6 for the remaining links as follows:

   Adobe: **http://www.adobe.com**

   JavaScript: **http://www.javascript.com**

   WebDeveloper: **http://www.webdeveloper.com/javascript**

   W3Schools: **http://www.w3schools.com/js**

   ASP: **http://www.asp.com**

8. Select all the hyperlinks you created by dragging your mouse over them. Click the **Unordered List** icon in the Property inspector to format the hyperlinks as a bulleted list.

9. Select the hyperlinks for **WebDeveloper** and **W3Schools** by dragging your mouse over only those two. Click the **Text Indent** icon to create a nested list.

10. Save the page as **Ch03DW02.htm** in the Chapter folder for Chapter 3.

11. Press **F12** to preview your page in your browser. Make sure that your Internet connection is active, and then test the links by clicking them. Verify that each link takes you to the correct Web site. Close your browser when you are finished.

12. Close the page in Dreamweaver.

Link List with Relative Links

In the preceding section, you created absolute links—that is, links to sites like Macromedia, http://www.macromedia.com. Next, you will learn how to create a relative link—that is, a link directly to a file in the same directory structure as the page containing the link. You do not need a full URL for a relative link. In the following steps, you will create links to the Web pages you have created so far in this chapter (and to some you will create later in this chapter). You will start by creating a new Web page named Ch03DW03.htm and saving it in the Chapter folder along with the other Web pages you have created so far. Then you will create a list of links on the Ch03DW03.htm page that will link to the other Web pages in the Chapter folder. Because the pages you will link to are located in the same folder as the page containing the links, you can use relative addressing to create the links.

To use relative addressing to create links:

1. Click **File**, and then click **New**. The New Document dialog box opens.

2. Click the **General** tab, if necessary, to display it. Click **Basic Page** and then click **Create**. A new, blank page opens in the Document window.

3. Save your blank document as **Ch03DW03.htm** in the Chapter folder for Chapter 3. It is necessary to save the page first so that the paths to the hyperlinks that the page will ultimately contain work correctly.

4. In the Document toolbar, replace the current contents of the Title text box with **Ch3 Project List**.

5. At the top of the Document window, type **Chapter 3 Project List,** format the new heading as **Heading 2,** click at the end of the text to deselect it, and then press **Enter**.

6. Type the following file names, pressing the **Enter** key after each one: **Ch03DW01SOL.htm, Ch03DW02.htm, Ch03DW04SOL.htm, Ch03DW05SOL.htm.** You should have a list of four items, aligned on the left side of the page. Do not include the commas after each file name.

 If you are familiar with copying and pasting in a word processor, you can use the same techniques to cut and paste text in Dreamweaver. For example, in this case you could use the Edit menu to copy and paste the first file name (Ch03DW01SOL.htm) multiple times, and then edit the copies to create the final list.

7. Use the mouse to select the text **Ch03DW01SOL.htm** and then click the **Browse for File** icon in the Property inspector. The Select File dialog box opens.

8. Navigate the directory structure if necessary, select the file **Ch03DW01SOL.htm**, and then press **Enter** to close the dialog box and create the hyperlink to the file.

9. Use the same technique to select the appropriate file for the **Ch03DW02.htm** link.

You have finished creating the first two links. The next two files in the list have not been created yet. To create links to these as yet nonexistent files, you can either type in the address you expect to use for these files or you can copy an existing link and edit it. In the next set of steps, you will try the latter method.

To edit an existing link:

1. Select the text **Ch03DW04SOL.htm**, and then click the **Link** list arrow to display a list of the links you have created so far. See Figure 3-6.

2. In the Link list, click **Ch03DW01SOL.htm**. The selected link is displayed in the Link text box.

3. Click in the Link text box and edit the link by replacing the 1 with a **4** so that the link now reads **Ch03DW04SOL.htm.** Press **Enter**. The new link, Ch03DW04SOL.htm, appears in the Link text box.

4. Use the same procedure to create a link for **Ch03DW05SOL.htm**.

5. Save your work.

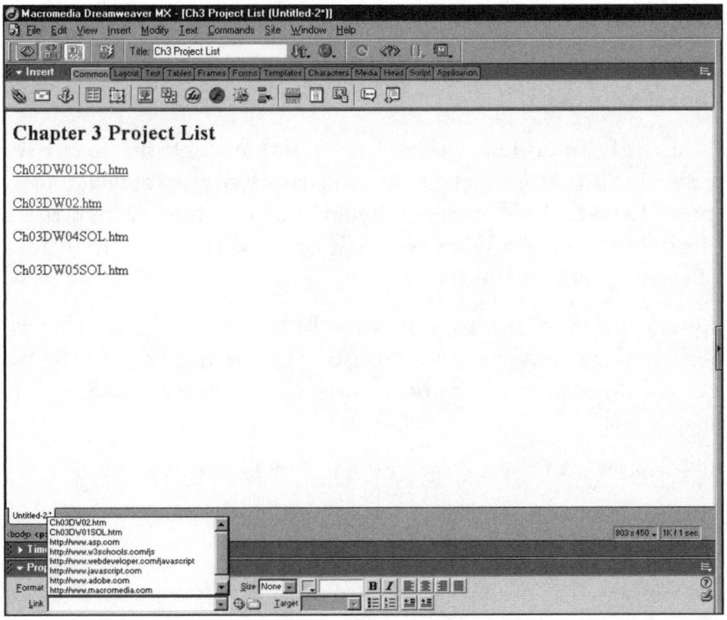

Figure 3-6   Creating relative hyperlinks

6. Press **F12** to view your page in your browser. Verify that the first two links work correctly. If the links do not work, return to Dreamweaver and edit the links to correct them.

7. Close your browser and close the page in Dreamweaver.

Links to E-Mail

So far, you have learned how to create absolute links and relative links in Dreamweaver. In many cases, you will also have to include links to electronic mail in your Web pages. In this section, you will edit the file Ch03DW01SOL.htm (which you created earlier in this chapter) by adding hyperlinks and a link to electronic mail.

To add hyperlinks and an e-mail link to a Web page:

1. Open the file **Ch03DW01SOL.htm** in Dreamweaver.

2. Because you are updating this file, save it as **Ch03DW04SOL.htm** in the Chapter folder for Chapter 3.

3. The second line of the page (the text in brackets) is the text you will transform into a hyperlink menu. Double-click the word **About** to select it, click in the Link text box in the Property inspector, type **about.htm**, and then press **Enter**. Note that the page about.htm does not actually exist. When you test this link later by clicking it in the browser, it will create an error.

4. Create the following links for the next two items in the menu:

Furniture Concepts: concepts.htm

Catalog: catalog.htm

5. Now you are ready to add an e-mail link. Double-click the text **Email** to select it in the Link text box, type the link **mailto:rmdesign@aol.com**, and then press **Enter**. This creates a hyperlink to e-mail. When the user clicks the link, her e-mail application will open with rmdesign@aol.com address as the recipient of the message.

6. Save your work, preview the page in your browser, and verify that your links have been created by moving your mouse over them. The relative addresses you created should appear at the bottom of the browser window even though they are inoperable.

7. Close your browser and then close the page in Dreamweaver.

Creating Named Anchors

In the preceding sections, you created hyperlinks to other Web pages. If a Web page is long, it is sometimes helpful to include links that jump to sections within the same Web page. This makes it easier for users to find sections in a page, allowing them to simply click to get to the information they want rather than having to scroll and hunt for it. Creating hyperlinks to material within a Web page requires two steps. First, you have to mark the location you want to jump to by creating a named anchor. You can think of a **named anchor** as a kind of marker that tells the hyperlink where to jump. The second step, after creating the named anchor, is to create a hyperlink to the section marked by the named anchor.

In the following steps, you will create named anchors and hyperlinks within a resume. You will edit a resume to add named anchors that link to the applicant's qualifications.

To practice creating a named anchor:

1. Open the file **Ch03DW05.htm** from the Chapter folder for Chapter 3 in Dreamweaver.

2. Save the file with the new name **Ch03DW05SOL.htm** in the Chapter folder for Chapter 3.

The second line of the page contains the text you will transform into a hyperlink menu. Each phrase in this line identifies a portion of the resume that requires a link. You will start by creating a name anchor at the beginning of the Objectives section.

3. Click to the left of the heading **Objective** in the third line of the resume, verify that the Common panel is selected in the Insert bar, and click the **Named Anchor** icon in the Insert bar. The Named Anchor dialog box opens. Here you need to enter a name for the anchor.

4. Type **Objective** in the Anchor Name text box and then click **OK**. The Anchor Name dialog box closes, and an Anchor icon appears next to the heading "Objective," indicating that an anchor has been inserted.

You have finished creating the named anchor. Next, you need to create a hyperlink to that anchor. To do this, you need to select the text you want to use as a hyperlink. Then you will drag the Point to File icon (in the Property inspector) up to the anchor you want to link to. In this case, you will drag the Point to File icon up to the anchor you just inserted. You will see how this works in the following steps.

To create a hyperlink to the newly inserted anchor:

1. Select the text **objective** in the second line of the document. (Take care to select the lower case text in the hyperlink menu and not the heading in the third line of the page.)

2. In the Property inspector, click the **Point to File** icon (to the right of the Link text box) and then drag the mouse pointer to the anchor just to the left of the Objective heading. A line appears connecting the anchor with the Point to File icon in the Property inspector. See Figure 3-7.

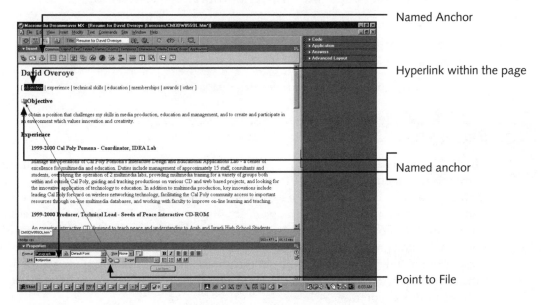

Named Anchor

Hyperlink within the page

Named anchor

Point to File

Figure 3-7   Creating a named anchor

3. Release the mouse button. The text **"#objective"** appears in the Link text box.

Next, you need to create the anchors and hyperlinks for the remaining sections.

To create the anchors and hyperlinks:

1. Use the techniques you learned earlier to create anchors for the following resume headings: **Experience, Technical Skills, Memberships, Awards,** and **Other**. Use **experience, skills, memberships, awards,** and **other** as the anchor names.

2. Use the Point to File icon, as described earlier, to create a hyperlink to the **Experience** heading. The text "#experience" appears in the Link text box.

3. Select the text **Technical Skills** in the hyperlink menu bar on the second line of the page. Although you could use the Point to File icon to create the link, in this case it is easier to enter the link directly into the Link text box. This eliminates the need to scroll while dragging the pointer, which can be tricky.

4. In the Link text box, type **#skills** and then press **Enter**.

5. Use any method you prefer to create the hyperlinks for the **Memberships, Awards,** and **Other** headings. The associated hyperlinks should be as follows: **#memberships, #awards,** and **#other**, respectively.

6. Save your work.

7. Press **F12** to preview your page in your Web browser and verify that the links work correctly.

8. Close your browser and close the page in Dreamweaver.

PAGE PROPERTIES

Earlier in this chapter, you learned how to select individual text items and change their properties. Selecting individual items on a Web page is helpful when you need to make minor individual changes. To make more wholesale changes, you can edit the page properties, which affect the entire page, by using the Page Properties dialog box, shown in Figure 3-8. For example, by using page properties you can change text, positioning, link, and color properties for an entire page at one time. You can also create a wallpaper background and set the page's margin attributes. In the following steps, you will change the page properties for the Maxx Designs page (Ch03DW04SOL.htm), which you created earlier in this chapter.

To practice changing page properties:

1. In Dreamweaver, open the file named **Ch03DW04SOL.htm** from the Chapter folder for Chapter 3 and resave it as **Ch03DW06SOL.htm** in the Chapter folder for Chapter 3. This is the furniture store page to which you added hyperlinks earlier in this chapter.

2. Click **Modify** in the menu bar and then click **Page Properties**. The Page Properties dialog box opens.

3. Click the **Background** text box, type the color code **#000000,** and then press **Tab** twice to move the cursor to the next text box. The color black appears in the black color palette, indicating that you have entered the code for black. See Figure 3-8. Note that you could also click the small arrow on the color palette and select the desired color, rather than typing a code.

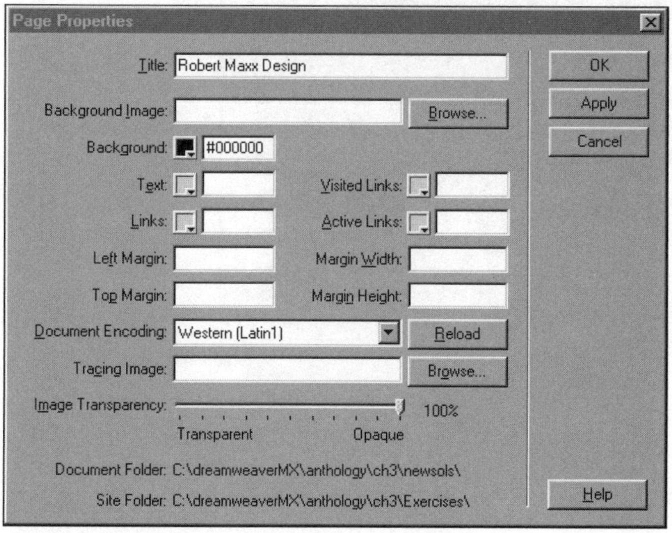

3

Figure 3-8   Page Properties dialog box

4. Enter the following codes:

   Text: **#CC9966** (tan)

   Links: **#FFFF33** (yellow)

   Left Margin: **50** (pixels)

5. Click **OK**. Observe the changes to the page. The page's background is now black.

6. To create a wallpaper background, click **Modify** on the menu bar, click **Page Properties,** click the **Browse** button to the right of the Background Image text box. The Select Image Source dialog box opens. Navigate to the Images subfolder within the Chapter folder for Chapter 3. Select the file named **background.gif** and then press **Enter** to close the Select Image Source dialog box. Press **Enter** again to close the Page Properties dialog box. The selected image is added to the Web page as a wallpaper background, as shown in Figure 3-9.

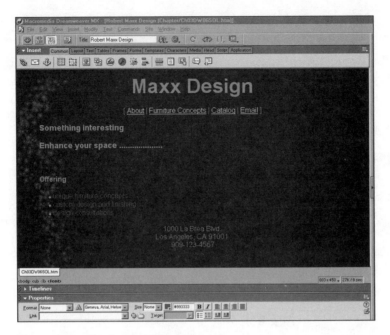

Figure 3-9   Background image

7. Save your work, preview the page in your browser, close your browser, and then close the page in Dreamweaver.

TABLES

Tables are one of the most important aspects of Web design. Without tables, it is very difficult to align text, images, and menus on your Web page. Placing page elements in tables lets you control how the page appears. Figure 3-10 shows two copies of an image with a text description. The first does not use a table and the second does. Notice the difference in layout. The table layout is much more appealing because the text aligns nicely with the image.

To insert tables in Dreamweaver, use the Insert Table tool on the Insert bar. You can also insert a table by selecting the Table command from the Insert menu, or by using the shortcut key sequence Ctrl+Alt+T.

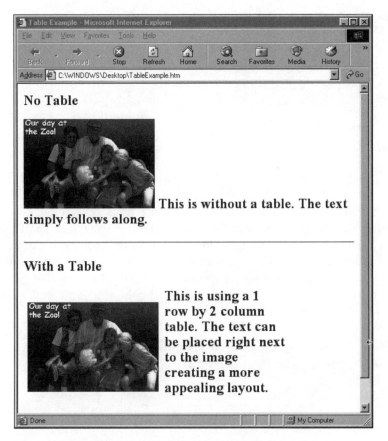

Figure 3-10   Layout without and with table

Any of these options opens the Insert Table dialog box, shown in Figure 3-11. In this dialog box, you are prompted to enter the number of rows and columns that your table will contain. The Cell Padding attribute controls the number of pixels between images and text in the cell and the edge of the cell. The Cell Spacing attribute controls the number of pixels between table cells. You can also indicate a width for the table as a percent of the Web browser window or as a number of pixels. The Border option allows you to set the thickness for the borders of your table. Using a large border gives a nice 3-D effect. A border of zero produces a table with invisible borders. This is useful when you want to align text and graphics neatly on the page. In HTML, you can often use a table to align page elements, creating a more appealing page layout.

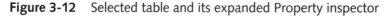

Figure 3-11   The Insert Table dialog box

Once you have created a table, you can change its attributes by using the Property inspector for the table. Figure 3-12 shows a simple 2-row by 2-column table and the Property inspector options that appear when the entire table is selected. (Recall that the Property inspector changes to reflect the item currently selected in the Document window.) When you select a table, small handles appear on the table; you can drag these handles to resize the table. If you have previously resized table rows and columns in a word processor, you will find that resizing Dreamweaver tables in Standard view is no different. By positioning your mouse between rows and columns, you can drag the lines dividing the cells to resize portions of the table.

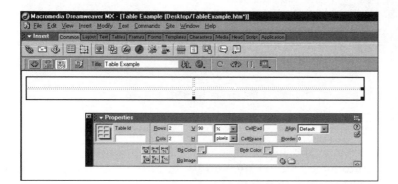

Figure 3-12   Selected table and its expanded Property inspector

Notice that in Figure 3-12 the Property inspector has been moved to a different location on the canvas. Holding your mouse down on any panel gripper will allow you to create a floating panel. You may find this useful when you are working on a particular area of a document with a specific panel.

Table 3-1 lists the options you can control by using the Property inspector for tables.

Table 3-1   Attributes of the Property inspector for tables

Element	Description
Table Name	Allows you to give the table a unique name identifier
Number of Rows	The number of rows in the table
Number of Columns	Number of columns in the table
Width	Width of the table as a percent or pixel number
Height	Height of the table as a percent or pixel number
Space Within Cell	Controls the padding in pixels between the cell walls and text or images contained within the table cell
Space Between Cells	Controls the spacing between cells in the table
Alignment	Controls positioning of the table relative to the browser window
Border Width	Controls the border width in pixels; a border of 0 allows you to control page layout but does not display the table borders
Clear Column Widths	Clears current or modified column widths
Clear Row Heights	Clears current or modified row heights
Convert Table Widths to Pixels	Controls table width in absolute pixel size
Convert Table Heights to Pixels	Controls table height in absolute pixel size
Convert Table Widths to Percent	Controls layout of table widths as a percentage
Convert Table Height to Percent	Controls layout of table height as a percentage
Background Color	Sets the background color for the table
Fireworks Source PNG (background image)	Sets a background image for the table
Border Color	Changes the color of the table border

Individual cells of a table also have properties. When you select an individual cell, the Property inspector displays options for altering individual cells rather than the entire table. The Property inspector for a cell is shown in Figure 3-13. The cell properties are listed in Table 3-2. These properties give you greater control over single cells, columns, and rows of the table, rather than modifying attributes for an entire table.

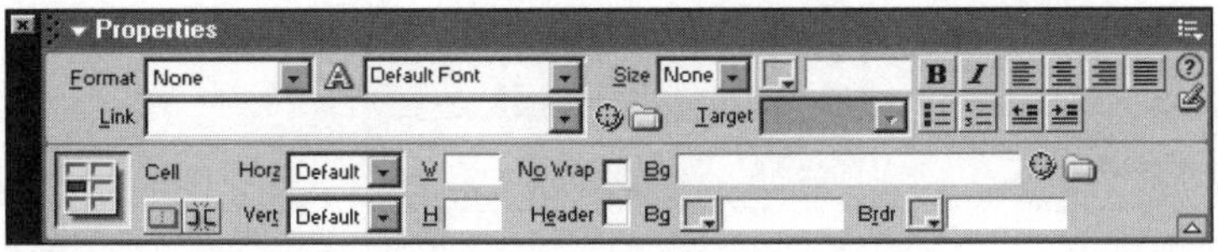

Figure 3-13   Property inspector for a table cell

Table 3-2   Attributes of the Property inspector for cells, rows, and columns

Element	Description
Merges selected cells using spans	Combines two or more table cells
Splits cell into rows or columns	Divides cell into rows or columns
Horizontal alignment of the cell contents	Controls the horizontal alignment of table cell data
Vertical alignment of the cell contents	Controls the vertical alignment of table cell data
Width of cell in pixels or percent	Sets the cell width explicitly
Height of cell in pixels or percent	Sets the cell height explicitly
Do not wrap the contents of the cell	Prevents wrapping, causing the table cell to resize
Makes the cell a header cell	Creates a table header in the specified cell
Background URL of cell	Inserts a background URL of a table cell
Background color	Changes the background color for a cell
Border color of cell	Changes the border color for a cell

In the following steps, you will create a 2-row by 3-column table to align information about airline Web sites.

To create the table:

1. In Dreamweaver, open the file named **Ch03DW07.htm** from the Chapter folder for Chapter 3 and resave it as **Ch03DW07SOL.htm** in the Chapter folder for Chapter 3.

2. Click in the blank line below the first line of blue text ("Comparison of Airline Web Sites").

3. On the Insert bar Common panel, click the **Insert Table** icon. The Insert Table dialog box opens.

4. Enter the following values, using the Tab key to move from one setting to the next: Rows: **2**, Cell Padding: **4**, Columns: **3**, Width: **80** percent, Border: **4**. When you are finished, click **OK**. You can leave Cell Spacing blank. A blank table structure is inserted into the Web page, as shown in Figure 3-14.

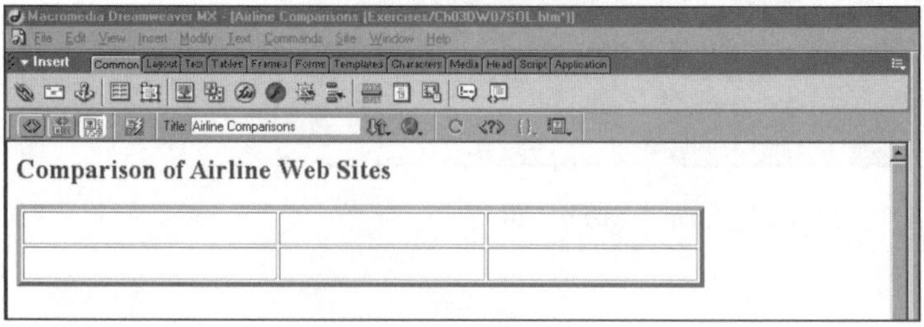

Figure 3-14   2-row by 3-column table of 80% with border of 4

5. Immediately below the table structure, select the hyperlinked text **New Age Airlines**, press **Ctrl+X** to cut it from the document, click in the upper-left cell in the table, and press **Ctrl+V** to paste the hyperlink into the cell.

6. Copy the four items that were originally under the New Age Air hyperlink, and paste them into the bottom cell in the left-most column. When you are finished, your table should look like Figure 3-15.

3

If you make a mistake, press Ctrl+Z to undo your most recent action.

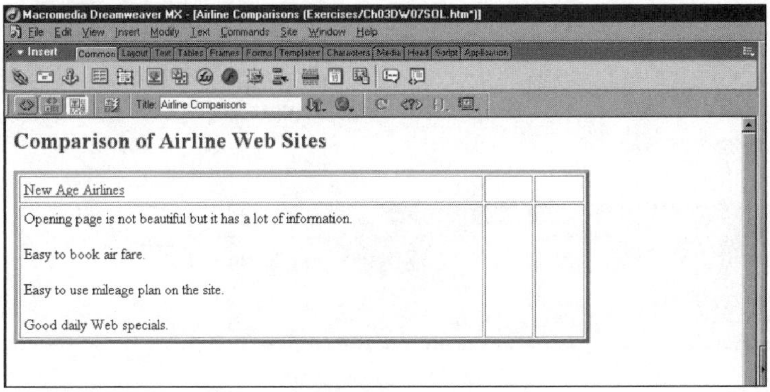

Figure 3-15   Copying data into table cells

7. Repeat step 5, copying the **Java Air** information into column 2 of the table and the **LaVerne Air** information into column 3. The table will resize as you paste the text into it.

8. Click outside the table. The table automatically resizes to a shape that fits within the Web page. If necessary, you can also adjust the table's size by dragging its borders, just as you would in a word processor.

9. Save your work, and preview the table in your browser. Resize the browser window so you can see how the table stretches and shrinks along with the browser window.

10. Close your browser and close the file in Dreamweaver.

IMAGES ON THE WEB

Graphics make the Web more interesting. Pages that display photos and artwork can entice a user to stay at a site longer. **Rollovers**, images that change appearance when the mouse is on top of them, make a Web page more responsive. **Image maps**, graphics with clickable areas that link to other pages, can give a Web site an interesting navigation strategy that users often find more appealing than underlined text links. In this section, you will learn to insert images and edit image properties. You will also create an image map menu bar and rollovers.

To insert images on a page, you use the Image icon on the Insert bar Common panel, as shown in Figure 3-16. You can also insert an image by clicking the Image command on the Insert menu or by using the shortcut key sequence Ctrl+Alt+I. All of these options allow you to browse your local drive and select an image via the Select Image Source dialog box. As with hyperlinks, you can provide absolute or relative names for image files.

 Images on the Web have to be either .jpg or .gif format. The .jpg format is good for photographs or images with complex color patterns. The .gif format is best for line art and graphics with wide areas of the same color. Other image formats such as .png or .bmp cannot display with a Web browser without a Plug-In.

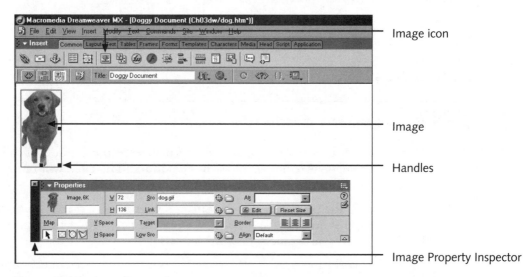

Figure 3-16 Inserting an image

Once the image is on the page, you can resize it in one of two ways. First, you can click the image to select it and then drag its handles until the image is the size you want. A selected image with handles is shown in Figure 3-16. When resizing an image with the mouse, keep in mind that the image will skew (become tall and thin or short and wide) unless you hold down the Shift key while you drag the handles. Holding the Shift key down allows you to resize the image and maintain its proportions. You can also resize an image by using the Property inspector for images, also shown in Figure 3-16. Table 3-3 lists the attributes that you can control using the Image Property inspector.

Table 3-3   Image Property inspector attributes

Element	Description
Image name and memory size	Displays image thumbnail, defined variable name for scripting purposes, and memory size in kilobytes
W and H	Gives image width and height in pixels
Src	Identifies path name (relative or absolute) to image source
Link	Identifies the URL to which the image links; you can type the address or add it using the Point to File or Browse for File icons
Alt	Identifies the text that appears in the browser when the pointer is over the image
Edit	Opens an external graphics editor
Reset size	Resets image size to actual dimensions
Map	Changes image to an image map, gives it a variable name for scripting purposes, and defines image map shapes
V space and H space	Provides horizontal and vertical spacing (in pixels) to set image apart from surrounding text or page content
Target	Indicates the window in which the hyperlinked file is to open
Border	Establishes width of border around image in pixels
Alignment icons	Aligns the selected image along the left or right margins, or centers the image
Hotspot tools	Used to draw specific shapes around areas of a graphic and link them to other Web pages
Low src	Identifies smaller version (in memory) image file that appears until image finishes downloading
Point to file	Inserts a hyperlink using a site map
Browse for file	Opens a Select Image Source dialog box, where you can browse and select a hyperlink file
Align	Used to control image alignment
Help	Links to context-sensitive help
Quick tag editor	Inserts HTML tag manually; a lengthy list of HTML tags is available from a pop-up menu

Alternate text is text that, on some browsers, is displayed in place of a graphic or occurs when the user places a mouse over the image. Every time you add an image to a Web page, you should be sure to specify alternate text for that image. People with vision impairments use electronic readers that allow them to browse the Web by listening. In this situation, alternate text provides a much needed verbal description of an image. In other words, without alternate text, some visitors to your Web page will not be able to hear what your pictures illustrate. Always include Alternate text tags on all of your images.

If you are working on a Web page but do not yet have the file for the image you want to include, you can include an image placeholder by using the Image Placeholder command on the Insert menu. In the Image Placeholder dialog box (shown in Figure 3-17), you can designate a name, size, color, and alternate text for the image prior to inserting it. Later, when the image is available, you can replace the placeholder with the image itself. The image you insert will automatically fit the scale requirements you specified when you created the placeholder image.

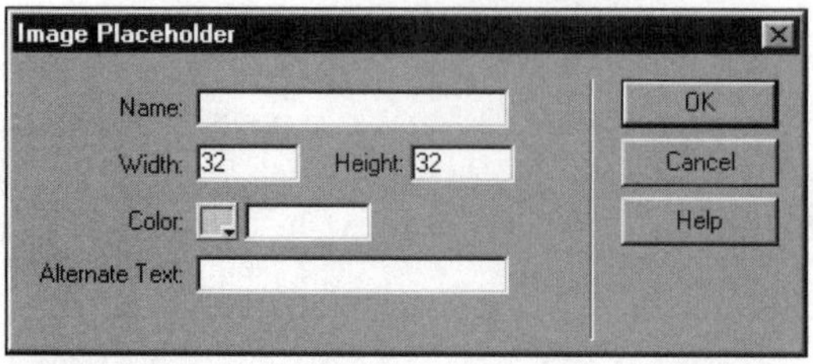

Figure 3-17   Image Placeholder dialog box

Image Maps

An image with several clickable links, called *hotspots*, is called an image map. **Hotspots** are the areas on the image that the user can click to go to another Web page. You can often see good use of hotspots on real estate Web pages, where clicking a portion of a map displays a close-up of a particular area. You can also use image maps as a navigation tool. For example, you may have seen a Web page with navigation tabs at the top of the page. Chances are that all of these tabs make up a single image, which contains one hotspot for each tab. You can replicate such an image map on all the pages of your site, thereby creating a consistent navigation menu.

To create an image map in Dreamweaver, you must first insert an image and then use the Hotspot tools in the lower-left corner of the Property inspector for images. Figure 3-18 shows the Hotspot tools on the Image Property inspector. The shape of the Hotspot tools (rectangle, oval, and polygon) reflects the shape of the hotspot you can create with each of these tools. To use these tools, you click one, and then drag the mouse on the image to draw a hotspot. To link the hotspot, you select the hotspot and then enter the link information in the Property inspector for hotspots. Figure 3-19 shows a circular hotspot drawn over a selected image. The Hotspot Property inspector is also shown with a hyperlink and alternate text. The alternate text displays when the mouse crosses over the hotspot.

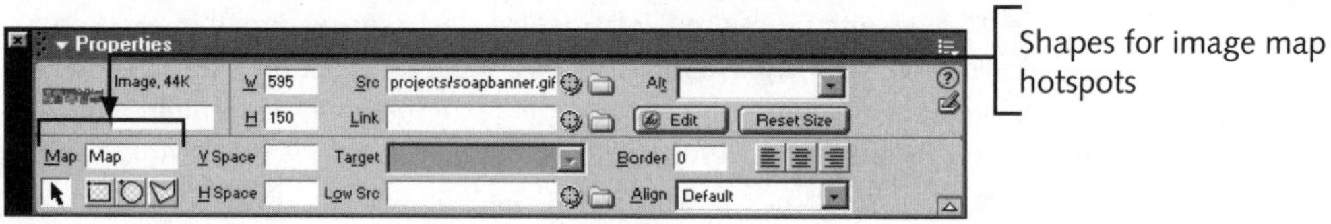

Shapes for image map hotspots

Figure 3-18   Image Property inspector

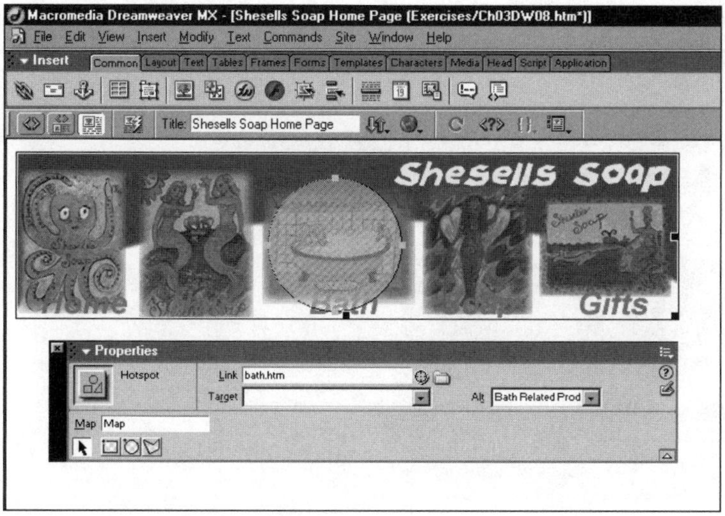

Figure 3-19 Hotspot Property inspector

In the following steps, you will insert an image and then add hotspots to it.

To insert an image with hotspots:

1. Open a blank document in Dreamweaver, and then save it as **Ch03DW08.htm** in the Chapter folder for Chapter 3. It is necessary to save the document first so that the paths to the hyperlinked hotspots can be formed correctly.

2. In the Document toolbar, enter **Shesells Soap Home Page** in the Title text box.

3. Click in the work area to place your cursor at the top of the page and then, in the Insert bar of the Common panel, click the **Image** icon. The Select Image Source dialog box opens.

4. Navigate through your directory structure to select the file **soapbanner.gif** in the Images subfolder within the Chapter folder for Chapter 3, and then press **Enter**. A wide image with 5 rectangular pictures appears in the work area. Make sure the image is selected, as indicated by the handles along its borders. The Property inspector contains the options for editing an image.

5. Click the **Rectangular Hotspot Tool** icon at the bottom left of the Image Property inspector and then move the mouse pointer over the image. The mouse pointer changes into a crosshair.

6. Drag the pointer to draw a rectangle over the Home rectangle on the far left in the Web page. (You may need to scroll your Document window so that you can view the portion of the image where you want to create the hotspot.)

7. Release the mouse button. A shaded rectangle appears on top of the Home rectangle, and the Property inspector displays options for editing a hotspot. See Figure 3-20.

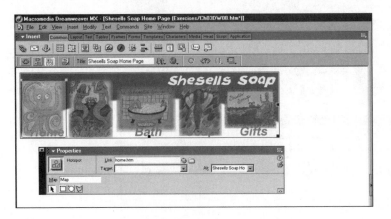

Figure 3-20   Drawing a hotspot

8. In the Hotspot Property inspector, click the **Link** text box, delete the pound sign, and then type **home.htm**. This specifies the page that should open when the user clicks the selected hotspot.

9. Click the **Alt** text box and type **Shesells Soap Home Page**. This text will be used as the alternate text for the hotspot.

10. Draw additional hotspots over the remaining rectangular images, as described in Table 3-4.

Table 3-4   Links for exercise CH03DW08.htm

Location for Hotspot	Link	Alternate Text
Hair rectangle	hair.htm	Hair Products
Bath rectangle	bath.htm	Bath Products
Soap rectangle	soap.htm	Custom Soaps
Gifts rectangle	gifts.htm	Gift Baskets

11. Save your work, preview the page in your browser, move the mouse pointer over the hotspots, and verify that the alternate text appears over the images. Close the browser and then close the page in Dreamweaver.

Do not allow hotspots on an image map to overlap. Overlapping hotspots prevents the links from working properly. Also, note that very small hotspots or hotspots that are drawn too closely together are very difficult for users to identify and click.

Rollovers

Rollovers are images (sometimes text images) that change when the user moves the mouse over them. Rollovers are actually composed of two images that are controlled with JavaScript code that calls a hidden image when the mouse crosses over it. Typically, the image that is visible when the page is first displayed in the browser is called the *up image*; the *over image* is the image that displays only when the mouse moves over the area containing the up image.

Dreamweaver simplifies the task of creating rollovers by allowing you to select files to use for both the up and over images. After you select the images, Dreamweaver automatically generates the JavaScript required to make the rollover function. For example, in a Web site for books, you might include a rollover that shows a closed book (up image) when the mouse is off of the image and an open book when the mouse is over it (over image). Figure 3-21 shows the dialog box you would use to create such a rollover.

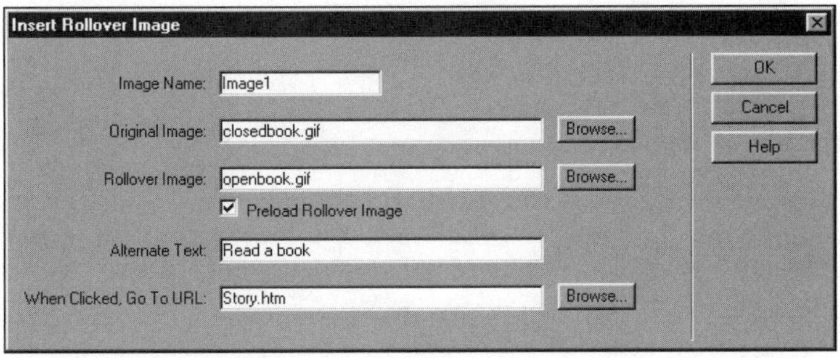

Figure 3-21   Inserting a rollover

In the following steps, you will create rollover images for a Web site called La Bonne Cuisine.

To create rollover images for a Web site:

1. Open a new, blank page and save it as **Ch03DW09.htm** in the Chapter folder for Chapter 3.

2. In the Document toolbar, replace the current contents of the Title text box with **La Bonne Cuisine** and then click in the work area to position your insertion point at the top of the page.

3. On the Insert bar Common panel, click the **Image** icon, select the image **lbclogo.gif** in the Images subfolder, and then press Enter. The image is inserted in the Web page.

4. Click to the right of the image to deselect it.

5. In the Property inspector, set Format to **Heading 1**, type **La Bonne Cuisine** in the work area, and then press **Enter** to move the insertion point to a new line.

6. Click the **Insert Table** icon on the Insert bar Common panel. The Insert Table dialog box opens. Create a table using the following settings: 1 row, 4 columns, 90% width, and a Border value of 0. Delete any settings in the CellPad and CellSpace boxes to leave them blank. Click **OK**. A table consisting of a single row is inserted in the document. Click outside the table to deselect it. At this stage, your page should look similar to Figure 3-22.

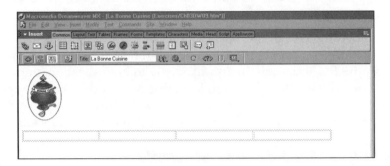

Figure 3-22   Inserting table to lay out graphics

7. Click the table to select it.

8. Click in the left-most cell in the table, and then click the **Align Center** icon in the Property inspector to select it. Click the **Rollover Image** icon on the Common panel. The Insert Rollover Image dialog box opens. Leave the Image name as the default setting (Image2).

9. In the Insert Rollover Image dialog box, the up image is referred to as the Original Image. Click the **Browse** button next to the Original Image text box, select the file **aboutusup.gif** in the Images subfolder within the Chapter folder for Chapter 3, and then press **Enter**. You return to the Insert Rollover Image dialog box.

10. Next, you need to select the over image. In this dialog box, the over image is referred to as the Rollover Image. Click the **Browse** button next to the Rollover Image text box, select the file **aboutusover.gif** in the Images sub-folder in the Chapter folder for Chapter 3, and then press **Enter**. You return to the Insert Rollover Image dialog box.

11. Click the **Alternate Text** text box, type **Learn More About La Bonne Cuisine**, click the **When Clicked Go To URL** text box, type **aboutlbc.htm**, and then click **OK**. The table resizes to accommodate the up image.

Note that rollovers do not work in Dreamweaver. To make sure a rollover works the way you want, you must preview your Web page in a browser. You will do just that in the following steps.

To test your rollover in a browser and continue creating additional rollovers:

1. Save your work, preview the page in a browser, and verify that the rollover works as expected. (When you move the mouse over the image, the text "About Us" should change from red to gold, and the alternate text should appear in a screen tip.)

2. Close the browser.

3. Create three more rollover images on the Web page as described in Table 3–5.

Table 3-5   Images for rollovers

Table Cell	Original (Up) Image	Rollover (Over) Image	Alternate Text	URL
Second from left	consultingup.gif	consultingover.gif	Consulting services	consulting.htm
Third from left	tourup.gif	tourover.gif	Culinary explorations	tour.htm
Right most	trainingup.gif	trainingover.gif	Culinary training	training.htm

4. Save your work, preview the page in your Web browser, verify that the rollovers work as expected, close the browser, and close your page in Dreamweaver.

Misspellings and other errors on a Web page can cause users to leave your site. To avoid such problems, be sure to use Dreamweaver's spell-checker before publishing your page. To access the spell-checker, click Text on the menu bar and then click Check Spelling. You can also press the Shift+F7 key combination.

CHAPTER SUMMARY

❐ Dreamweaver is a WYSIWYG authoring tool that generates HTML and JavaScript code.

❐ The main panels you use to create Web pages are the Insert bar and the Property inspector. You can find other panels on the Window menu on the menu bar.

❐ You use the Property inspector for basic text manipulation such as changing fonts, sizes, justification, and text color. Using the Property inspector, you can also create hyperlinks to other Web pages. The shortcut key for displaying the Property inspector is Ctrl+F3.

❐ The Insert bar is used to insert various elements into a Web site. Several panels in the Insert bar can be viewed by clicking the tabs at the top of the work area. The Insert bar categories are Common, Layout, Text, Tables, Frames, Forms, Templates, Media, Head, Script, ASP, and Application. The shortcut key for displaying the Insert bar is Ctrl+F2.

❏ Using the Common panel in the Insert bar, you can insert images, rollovers, tables, and horizontal rulers. You can also create a hyperlink to an e-mail address and insert Web page elements created by other applications such as Flash, Java, and Fireworks.

❏ To change page attributes, use the Page Properties dialog box, which is available from the Modify menu. You can select and use color swatches for the page attributes, default text, links, and active and visiting links. Additionally, if you want to wallpaper the background of your page, you can browse your hard drive and select and apply a background graphic to create the wallpaper.

❏ Dreamweaver provides easy access to Code and Design views of the Web document as well as split-screen shared Code and Design views.

REVIEW QUESTIONS

1. Which of the following statements about Dreamweaver is true?

   a. Dreamweaver is a WYSIWYG Web authoring tool.

   b. Dreamweaver generates HTML and JavaScript code.

   c. Dreamweaver can be integrated with Fireworks and Flash.

   d. All of the above statements are true.

2. To move a panel to another location in the work area, what tool should you use?

   a. expander

   b. gripper

   c. inspector

   d. none of the above

3. A shortcut key lets you _____.

   a. create hyperlinks within a page

   b. use key sequences to perform common operations more quickly than accessing menus

   c. insert shapes on an image map

   d. do none of the above

4. What is the shortcut key for previewing your Dreamweaver Web page in your browser?

   a. F12

   b. Ctrl+F3

   c. Ctrl+F12

   d. F7

5. Code view lets you _____.

    a. edit code directly

    b. see the design and code at the same time

    c. see how your page will appear in a Web browser

    d. All of the above are true.

6. To edit attributes of elements inserted on your Web page, use _____.

    a. the Insert bar

    b. the Attribute inspector

    c. the Property inspector

    d. the Document toolbar

7. Which of the following is an example of a relative hyperlink?

    a. http://www.coke.com

    b. http://www.coke.com/index.html

    c. index.html

    d. none of the above

8. Which of the following statements is true about the Property inspector?

    a. Attributes of the Property inspector are used to format text.

    b. The Property inspector changes, depending upon the page element selected.

    c. It allows you to make relative and absolute hyperlinks.

    d. All of the above are true.

9. What is the purpose of alternate text?

    a. It marks the code so the programmer can tell what the image file contains.

    b. It can be used by browser readers so that people can hear what the image is.

    c. It forms a hyperlink.

    d. None of the above are true.

10. Named anchors are used to _____.

    a. form menu bars

    b. create a page layout

    c. create hyperlinks within a page

    d. create hyperlinks that open a new browser window

3

11. Setting a table width to 80% causes the table _____.

   a. to be 80 pixels wide

   b. to exceed the browser window

   c. to shrink and grow with the size of the browser window, always maintaining 80%

   d. to shrink and grow with the size of the browser window, always maintaining 80 pixels

12. Which of the following can you do to resize an image?

   a. Edit the image size in the source code.

   b. Select the image and resize it with the mouse.

   c. Use the Property inspector to change the height and width of the image.

   d. All of the above are true.

13. What types of graphics can you use on the Web?

   a. .gif and .jpg

   b. .html and .htm

   c. .bmp and .png

   d. all of the above

14. What does setting a table border equal to 0 do?

   a. It creates an invisible border.

   b. This cannot be done.

   c. It sets the default border to 1.

   d. It creates a white background for the table.

15. If you created a three-rollover menu on a Web page, how many graphics files would be required?

   a. 3

   b. 6

   c. 7

   d. 9

HANDS-ON EXERCISES

Exercise 3-1

In this exercise, you will create an HTML page that links to major soft drink companies. You will also create a title for the page and place the links in a bulleted (unordered) list.

1. Open Dreamweaver if it is not already open, and then open a new, blank document.

2. Save this page as **Ch03DWEX01.htm** in the Exercises folder for Chapter 3.

3. Click Modify and then click Page Properties on the menu bar. Type Soft Drink Links in the Title text box. Change the color of the background to light orange (#FFCC99), the color of the text to dark purple (#330033), the color of the links to blue (#3333FF), and the color of the visited links to dark red (#CC0033). Close the Page Properties dialog box.

4. Click in the work area. In the Property inspector, set Format to Heading 1. Type Soft Drink Links in the work area. Press Enter.

5. In the Property inspector, click the icon to create a Bulleted (Unordered) List.

6. Type the text Coke, Pepsi, Mountain Dew, and Sprite on separate lines to create four bulleted items in the bulleted list. Click and drag to select the entire list and change the Format to Heading 2.

7. Select the text Coke, and type http://www.coke.com in the Link text box in the Property inspector.

8. Create hyperlinks for the other soft drinks: http://www.pepsi.com, http://www.mountaindew.com, http://www.sprite.com.

9. Save your work. Preview your page by pressing F12. Make sure your Internet connection is active, and click the links to see that they operate as expected.

Exercise 3-2

In this exercise, you will create links to famous people's e-mail.

1. Open Dreamweaver if it is not already open, and then open a new, blank document.

2. Save the new page as **Ch03DWEX02.htm** in the Exercises folder for Chapter 3.

3. In the Document toolbar, type Famous People's E-Mail Addresses in the Title text box.

4. At the top of the work area, type E-Mail Addresses of the Rich and Famous and format the new text using the Heading 1 format. Center the heading using the Align Center icon in the Property inspector. Press Enter to create a new blank line.

5. In the Property inspector, click the Align Left icon and then the Text Indent icon. Now the text you type will be aligned on the left and indented.

6. Click the Email Link icon (which looks like an envelope) in the Insert bar Common panel to open the Email Link dialog box. Type Bill Gates in the Text text box and billgates@microsoft.com in the E-Mail text box. Click OK, verify that the e-mail link has been added to the Web page, deselect the link and then press Enter to move the insertion point to the next line.

7. Create additional e-mail links for yourself and for Madonna (madonna@madonna.com), Steven Spielberg (Steve@dreamworks.com), and Jesse Ventura (jesse@minnesota.gov).

8. Format the page to make it attractive.

9. Save your work, preview your page in your Web browser, and verify that the e-mail links work.

10. Close your browser, and then close the page in Dreamweaver.

Exercise 3-3

In this exercise, you will integrate images and text into a table to create a Web page about pet adoption.

1. Open Dreamweaver if it is not already open, and then open a new, blank page.

2. Save the new page as **Ch03DWEX03.htm** in the Exercises folder for Chapter 3.

3. In the Document toolbar, type Adopt a Pet in the Title text box.

4. Click in the work area. Type Adopt a Pet Today and format the new link as Heading 1. Use red (#FF0000) as the text color. Deselect the link and press Enter to move the insertion point to the next line.

5. Insert a new table with two rows and three columns. The table should be 400 pixels wide, with the border set to 0. The table will be very wide. Use the horizontal scroll bar at the bottom of the Document window to scroll from side to side if necessary when completing the remaining steps.

6. In the left-most cell in the top row, insert the image named dog.gif from the Images subfolder in the Exercises folder for Chapter 3. Center the image in the cell.

7. In the left-most cell in the bottom row (beneath the dog image), insert the text I'm adorable and good with kids. Format the new text as Heading 3, and center it in the cell.

8. In middle cell in the top row, insert the image named bird.gif from the Images subfolder in the Exercises folder for Chapter 3. Center the image in the cell.

9. In the cell below the bird image, type the text I sing show tunes and say hello. Format the new text as Heading 3, and center it in the cell.

10. In the right-most cell in the top row, insert the image named cat.gif from the Images subfolder in the Exercises folder for Chapter 3. Center the image in the cell.

11. In the cell below the cat image, type the text A companion that is already house broken. Center the new text in the cell.

12. Save your work, preview the page in your browser, close the browser, and close the page in Dreamweaver.

Exercise 3-4

In this exercise, you will create an image map from a collage of pet images.

1. Open Dreamweaver if it is not already open, and then open a new, blank page.

2. Save the new document as **Ch03DWEX04.htm** in the Exercises folder for Chapter 3.

3

3. In the Document toolbar, type Pet Sites in the Title text box.

4. Click in the work area, type Click to Visit a Pet Site, format the new text as Heading 1, and then press Enter to move the insertion point to the next line.

5. Insert the image named pets.jpg from the Images subfolder in the Exercises folder for Chapter 3.

6. Set the background color (one of the Page Properties) to yellow (#FFFF98).

7. Make sure that the image is selected, as indicated by the selection handles, and then draw a rectangular hotspot over the dog image.

8. Set the following properties for the hotspot: Link:http://www.dogs.com, Alt: Dogs.com, and Target: _blank. The last setting (_blank) will open the hyperlink in a new browser window.

9. Create similar hotspots for the cat and the bird. Set the following properties for these new hotspots:

   ❑ Link: http://www.birds.com, Alt: Birds.com, Target: _blank

   ❑ Link: http://www.cat.com, Alt: Cat.com, Target: _blank

10. Save your work, and preview the page in a browser. Connect to the Internet and verify that the hotspots work correctly.

11. Close your browser, and then close the page in Dreamweaver.

Exercise 3-5

In this exercise, you will create a simple rollover of a person winking.

1. Open Dreamweaver if it is not already open, and then open a new, blank document.

2. Save the new document as **Ch03DWEX05.htm** in the Exercises folder for Chapter 3.

3. In the Document toolbar, type Winky in the Title text box.

4. Create a rollover, using the following files from the Images subfolder in the Exercises folder for Chapter 3: **sageup.jpg** (for the Original file) and **sageover.jpg** (for the Rollover file). Use Find This for the alternate text, and http://www.google.com for the URL.

5. Save your work, preview the page in your browser, and verify that the rollover works as expected.

6. Close your browser, and then close the page in Dreamweaver.

WEB DESIGN PROJECTS

Project 3-1

Create a Web page that contains hyperlinks to your favorite Web sites in three categories: Movies, Music, and Hobbies. Put an appropriate title at the top of the page. Add a blank line, and then add a table with three columns and seven rows. Place three category titles (Movies, Music, Hobbies) in the first row. Use search engines to locate at least six Web sites for each category, and list these Web sites in the appropriate column under the category title. Use descriptive titles in the table cells, and create hyperlinks to each Web site. Add a title to the page and modify the page properties. Choose a background color that you like. Save your page as **Ch03DWDP01** in the Projects folder for Chapter 3.

Project 3-2

Develop a resume in Dreamweaver. Include information such as your name, phone number, e-mail address, home page URL, desired position, education, experience, and technical skills. Insert hyperlinks into logical places in the resume. For example, if you list your school, create a hyperlink to the home page for that school. If you list creating Web pages in Dreamweaver as a skill, create a link to the Macromedia Web site (www.macromedia.com). Enter a page title and modify the page properties by changing the background color to one appropriate for a resume. Save your page as **Ch03DWDP02** in the Projects folder for Chapter 3.

Project 3-3

Develop a storefront for a karate studio. Think about what kinds of information would be useful to customers visiting the page. Design the text and information on the page to emphasize important information. Use a search engine to find links to Web sites that sell karate clothes and equipment. At the bottom of your page, underneath your own karate studio information, add a table that contains at least four links to appropriate Web sites. Include a link to the karate studio owner's e-mail address. At the bottom of the page, include a credit that says, "This page developed by *your name.*" Make your name a hyperlink to your own e-mail address. Enter a page title, and choose a background color appropriate for a karate studio. Save your page as **Ch03DWDP03** in the Projects folder for Chapter 3.

CHAPTER

4

DREAMWEAVER: PART II

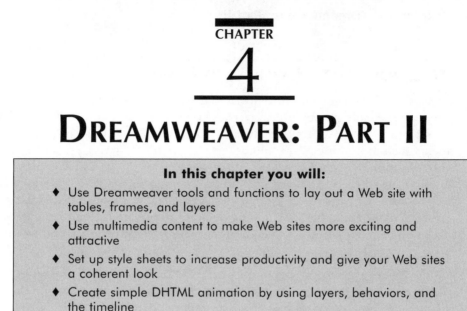

In this chapter you will:

♦ Use Dreamweaver tools and functions to lay out a Web site with tables, frames, and layers

♦ Use multimedia content to make Web sites more exciting and attractive

♦ Set up style sheets to increase productivity and give your Web sites a coherent look

♦ Create simple DHTML animation by using layers, behaviors, and the timeline

Dreamweaver provides excellent tools to help you create and maintain exciting, interactive Web sites. You can either lay out pages by using traditional tables or you can do layout with layers that are converted to tables. You can also use Dreamweaver's Layout view, which is an innovative, flexible, productivity tool. By incorporating multimedia files—images, audio, movies, Flash text, and other animation—you can make a Web site more enticing to visitors. Style sheets that allow you to change the characteristics of existing HTML tags or create custom tags can be applied to multiple documents within a Web site. Dreamweaver also simplifies the process of creating dynamic HTML (DHTML) animation, using layers, behaviors, and the timeline. You will learn more about all of these techniques in this chapter.

Web Site Layout with Layers and Frames

In Chapter 3, you learned how to lay out pages by using tables. You can also organize pages in Dreamweaver by using layers. A **layer** is an extension to HTML that is defined by <layer> tags. The Layer object is an area on an HTML page that can hold elements such as graphics, text, and colors. Layers have *x*- and *y*-coordinates that define their positioning either from the upper-left corner of the HTML page or relative to another layer. Layers can be stacked on top of one another visually, so each layer also has a *z*-coordinate that defines the layer's stacking order. Layers are difficult to control in page layout, because their positioning does not display consistently in different browsers; they also may not adjust to changes in browser size in ways that you intended.

Frames provide an entirely different approach to layout. A **frame** is a small window inside a Web page that contains its own HTML document A **frameset** is an HTML document that holds multiple frames, each of which contains its own HTML document. Frames can be set up with one frame for content that does not change, such as a menu, and another frame whose content changes as you select items on the menu. Dreamweaver helps you create different frame structures and provides tools and commands to help you manage frame content. In the following sections, you will learn how to use different types of layers to lay out a Web page. You will also learn how to use framesets to construct sets of frames containing different HTML documents.

Converting Layers to Tables

The steps in this section show you how to design pages by using layers that Dreamweaver will convert to a table. Note that you can reverse the process and convert a table back to its component layers, and then edit the layout. You can then adjust the layout and reconvert the layers to tables, repeating the process until you are satisfied with the look of your Web page.

Dreamweaver MX provides two different environments for laying out pages. In Standard view, you can insert into a page a table with certain characteristics (such as numbers of rows and columns, 2-pixel wide blue borders, and so forth); alternatively, you can insert a layer into a page. In Layout view, you draw a layer on a page, at which point Dreamweaver inserts a table to hold the layer. You can switch between these Standard and Layout views via the Layout tab of the Insert bar.

In Figure 4-1, Layout view is selected, making the Draw Layout Table and Draw Layout Cell tools available for use. The layout table and layout cell are visible in the document editing window. If Standard view was selected instead, you would be able to insert tables or layers, but Dreamweaver would not automatically draw a table around your layers.

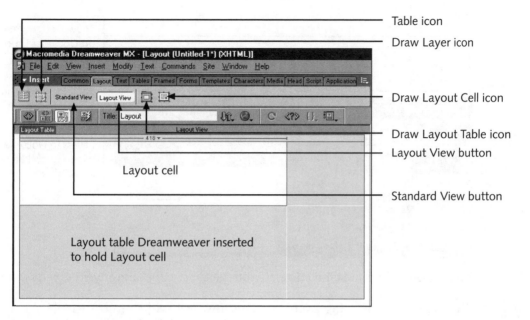

Figure 4-1   Layout tab of the Insert bar

The Property inspector for Layer2 (the one that is selected in Figure 4-2) would display the layer's *x*- and *y*-coordinates (as distance from the left and top of the page in the L and T boxes), as well as the layer's *z*-index or stacking order. Layer2 has a higher z-index than Layer1, which means that it is closer to the viewer when it is displayed in the browser (and so appears to be stacked on top of Layer1). In Figure 4-2, you can see only the part of Layer1 that does not overlap with Layer2, because Layer2 has a higher *z*-index and is, therefore, on top. The Layers panel (which resides in the Advanced Layout panel group to the right of the document editing window) is also shown in Figure 4-2. When you draw layers in Standard view, the layers are listed in the Layers panel, and their stacking order is also displayed.

 Dreamweaver's use of the word *view* may seem confusing. Remember that Standard view and Layout view refer to different approaches to inserting layers and tables. The other views you learned about in Chapter 3, Design view, Code view, and Design and Code view, affect the ways in which you can edit and view pages in the Document window. You can use either Standard view or Layout view in both Design view and Design and Code view. When you work in Code view, you update the HTML code (or other forms of code) by typing, rather than by dragging and dropping objects on the HTML page.

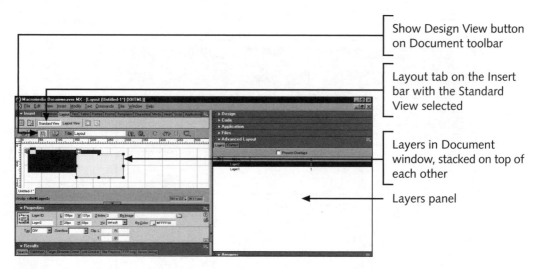

Show Design View button on Document toolbar

Layout tab on the Insert bar with the Standard View selected

Layers in Document window, stacked on top of each other

Layers panel

Figure 4-2 Layers in Standard view, with the Layer panel and Layer Property inspector

To design pages by using layers that Dreamweaver will convert to a table:

1. Start Dreamweaver, open the file named **Ch04DW01.htm** from the Chapter folder for Chapter 4, and then resave it as **Ch04DW01SOL.htm** in the Chapter folder for Chapter 4.

2. If necessary, switch to Design view by clicking the **Show Design View** button on the Document toolbar, as shown in Figure 4-2.

3. Click the **Layout** tab on the Insert bar and then click the **Standard View** button if necessary, as shown in Figure 4-1. Press the keyboard sequences **Ctrl+Alt+R** to show the ruler and **Ctrl+Alt+G** to show the grid, if they are not visible. You will find the ruler and the grid (also shown in Figure 4-2) useful in placing layers on the page that you are editing. The ruler measurements are in pixels.

If you are working on a Macintosh, press the Command key whenever this book tells you to press the Ctrl key.

4. Click the **Draw Layer** icon on the Layout tab of the Insert bar (the icon just to the left of the Standard View button). Then, using the ruler as your guide, position the crosshair mouse pointer 50 pixels from the top and 50 pixels from the left of the page.

5. Drag the crosshair pointer down and to the right. Observe the Window Size box on the status bar (at the bottom of the Document window), and notice how the numbers change to reflect the width and height of the layer you are drawing. (On a Macintosh, look for these values in the Property inspector.)

6. Draw a layer approximately 164 pixels wide by 72 pixels high, and then release the mouse button and move the mouse pointer. After you release the mouse, the Window Size box again reflects the size of the HTML document in the Document window.

7. Click the edge of the layer to select it. Black selection handles appear on the corners and on each side of the layer. Figure 4-3 shows these selection handles. The Property inspector displays options related to editing the selected layer.

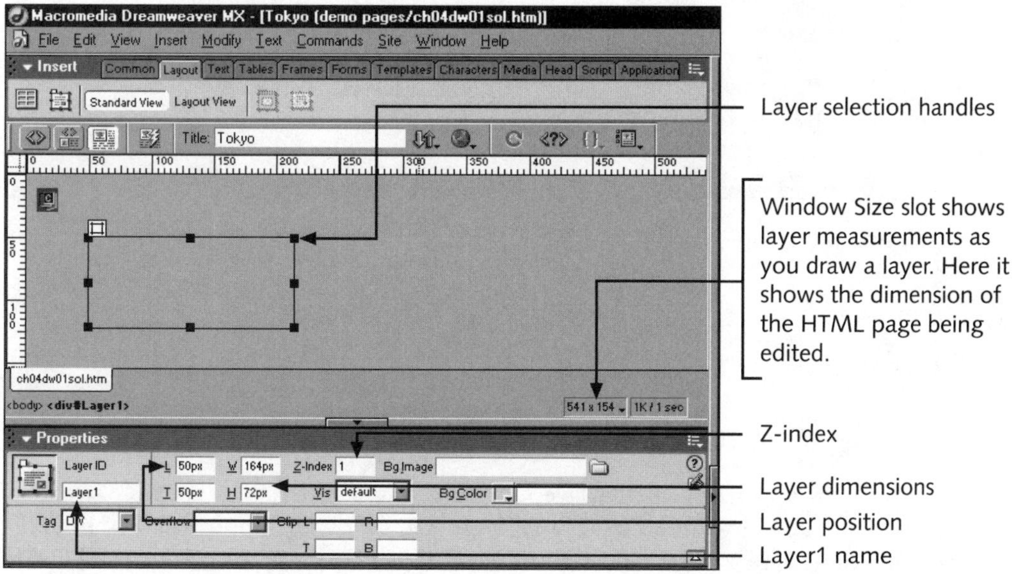

4

Layer selection handles

Window Size slot shows layer measurements as you draw a layer. Here it shows the dimension of the HTML page being edited.

Z-index

Layer dimensions

Layer position

Layer1 name

Figure 4-3 Layer and its Property inspector

8. If necessary, correct the layer height and width in the Property inspector, as shown in Figure 4-3. Notice that Dreamweaver automatically names this layer "Layer1."

To move a layer in any direction, select it and then drag the square handle in the layer's upper-left corner. Alternately, you can select the layer and move it with the directional arrow keys on the keyboard.

9. Create two more layers in the same way. The upper-left corner of Layer2 should be positioned 200 pixels from the top and 200 pixels from the left of the page. This layer should be 130 pixels wide and 161 pixels high. The upper-left corner of Layer3 should be positioned 100 pixels from the top and 400 pixels from the left of the page. This layer should be 180 pixels wide and 107 pixels high. When you are finished, your page should look like Figure 4-4.

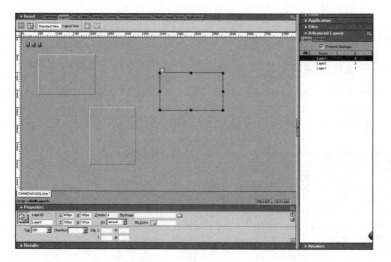

Figure 4-4   Three layers

    Layers cannot overlap or be nested inside each other if you want to convert them to tables.

10. Save your work.

Now that you have created layers in your page, you can insert Web content into them and then convert the layers to a table. In the following steps, you will insert images into your three new layers. One way to accomplish this is to switch to the Common tab on the Insert bar and use the Image icon.

To insert images into the new layers and then convert the layers into a table:

1. Click inside Layer1, click the **Common** tab on the Insert bar, and then click the **Image** icon. Insert the image named **Ch04DW02.gif** from the Chapter folder for Chapter 4.

2. Repeat step 1 for Layer2, inserting the image **Ch04DW03.jpg**. Repeat again for Layer3, inserting the image **Ch04DW04.jpg**.

3. Save your work. At this stage, your page should look like Figure 4-5.

4. Click **Modify** on the menu bar, point to **Convert**, and then click **Convert Layers to Table**. The Convert Layers to Table dialog box opens. The default settings are fine here, so click **OK** to accept them and close the Layers to Table dialog box. Dreamweaver converts your layers into table cells. Your page should look similar to Figure 4-6.

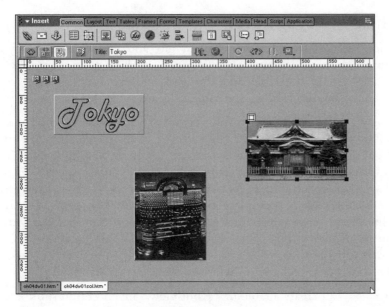

Figure 4-5 Layout with layers

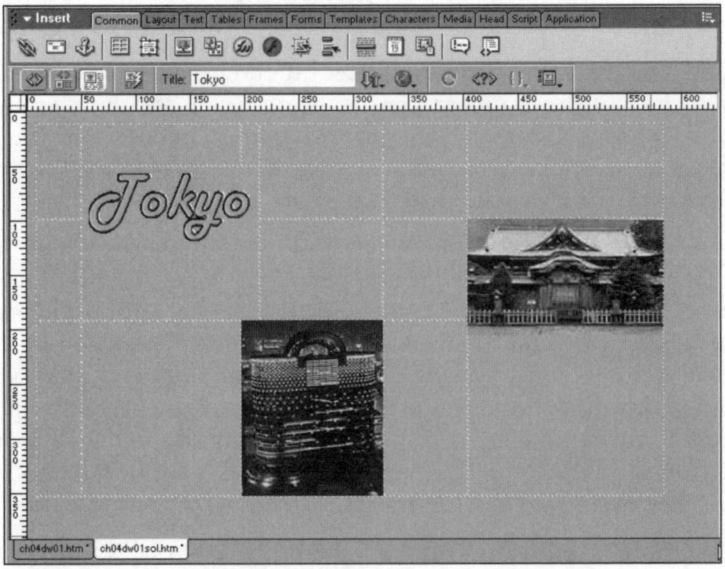

Figure 4-6 Layout after conversion of layers to tables

5. Save your work, and view it in the browser. Close the browser, and close the page in Dreamweaver.

Laying Out Tables in Layout View

In the last section, you switched to the Layout tab, and then used the Layout tab's Standard view to create layers. Layout view allows you to draw tables in an HTML page and then draw cells within the table. In Dreamweaver terminology, tables created in Layout view are called **layout tables**, and table cells are called **layout cells**.

If you draw a layout cell outside an existing layout table, Dreamweaver automatically draws a table around the cell, starting at the left margin of the page and the first free line. This means that if you draw your first layout cell in the lower-right quadrant of an HTML page, Dreamweaver will insert a layout table whose upper-left corner is located in the HTML page's upper-left corner. As you draw table cells, Dreamweaver inserts the necessary columns and rows to complete the table layout. Dreamweaver also inserts spacer cells outlined with faint white lines. You cannot insert content into those spacer cells, but only into the layout cells. Note that you can define one column in the layout table as an **autostretch column**, which means the column will expand and contract to match the table's width to the changing width of the browser window.

In the following steps, you create a table in Layout view. The end result should look similar to that of the preceding sets of steps.

1. In Dreamweaver, open the page **Ch04DW05.htm** from the Chapter folder for Chapter 4, and save it in the same folder as **Ch04DW05SOL.htm**.

2. In the Insert bar, click the **Layout** tab and then click the **Layout View** button (to the right of the Standard View button). If you see the Getting Started in Layout View dialog box, read the information it contains, and then click **OK** to close it. Press the keyboard sequences **Ctrl+Alt+R** to show the ruler and **Ctrl+Alt+G** to show the grid, if they are not visible.

3. Click the **Draw Layout Cell** icon, and then place the insertion point 50 pixels from the top and 50 pixels from the left of the page. Click and drag the insertion point down and to the right to draw a layout cell on the page that is about 164 pixels wide and 72 pixels high. If the dimensions are not exactly correct, you can select the layer by clicking on its border and then typing the height and width in its Property inspector. You can also change the positioning of the layer by dragging it by its handle, or by using the arrow keys on the keyboard. You should see that Dreamweaver creates a layout table to hold your layout cell that extends to the lower-right corner of the HTML document.

4. Create two more layout cells. One cell should be 200 pixels from the top and 200 pixels from the left of the page, with dimensions of 130 pixels wide and 161 pixels high. The second cell should be 100 pixels from the top and 400 pixels from the left of the page, with dimensions of 180 pixels wide and 107 pixels high.

If you find that you do not have enough space in the document editing window to draw the three layers, you may need to close the Property inspector until you get the layer drawn. Then you can open it again to adjust the layer cell dimensions, if necessary. If your document editing window is not wide enough, you can drag the border between the Document window and the panel groups to the right or close the right-side panel groups by clicking the arrow button located on the right border of the Document window.

5. Insert the same images in the layout cells that you inserted in the previous exercise (**Ch04DW02.gif**, **Ch04DW03.jpg**, and **Ch04DW04.jpg**). Your page should look similar to Figure 4-7.

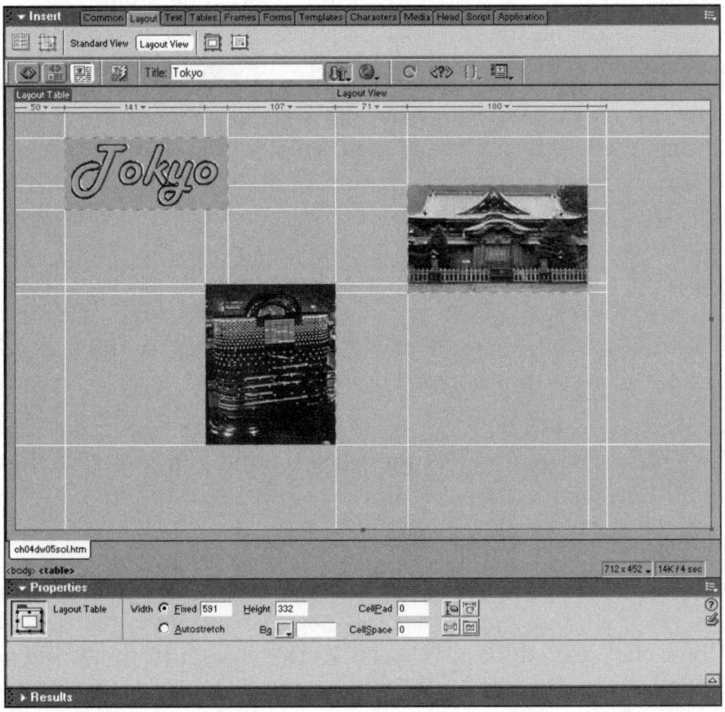

Figure 4-7   Layout View

6. Save your work, and preview the page in the browser. Close the browser, and close the page in Dreamweaver.

As you can see when you review results of the previous two exercises, their output is very similar. In the first, you drew layers and converted them to a table; in the second, you drew table cells, around which Dreamweaver drew a layout table. Both approaches to layout are much easier than using standard tables and give you much more flexibility in arranging elements on your Web page.

Layout with Frames

As mentioned earlier, a frame is a small window inside a Web page that contains its own HTML document. Using frames, which are organized within HTML documents called *framesets*, you can display a group of documents within the same browser window. A frameset differs from other HTML documents because `<frameset>` tags replace the `<body>` tags and define the structure of the frameset in rows and columns. Dreamweaver offers a series of preset frameset structures and tools, such as the Frames panel, to help you manage framesets and frames.

In the following steps, you create and save a frameset and its component frames by creating a new document and choosing Framesets on the General tab of the New Documents window. If you want to turn an HTML document in the Document window into a frameset, you can use the Frames tab on the Insert bar. Dreamweaver then creates a frameset and places the HTML document into the main or largest frame of the frameset.

Framesets and frames can be very confusing at first. To help you, Dreamweaver MX provides tools for creating framesets and frames and for defining how they will appear in the browser (for example, with or without scrollbars or borders). The Frames panel in the Advance Layout panel group makes it easy for you to select the frameset or specific frame that you want to modify. The Save All command on the File menu eases the task of saving framesets and the Frame documents they contain. This command first prompts you for the name of the frameset; it then prompts you for the name of the main frame (the largest one), followed by the names of any other frames. A thick border in the Document window outlines the frame that you are currently saving.

In the following steps, you create a frameset, experiment with different scrollbar and border options, use the Frames panel to select the frameset and component frames, and use the Save All command to save the frameset and the content of the frames within it.

To work with a frameset:

1. Press the **Ctrl+N** key combination to open the New Document dialog box; click the General tab if necessary to display it. Click **Framesets** in the Category list box and then click **Fixed Top, Nested Left** frameset in the Framesets list box. The New Document dialog box displays a preview of the selected frameset, as shown in Figure 4-8.

2. Click **Create** to close the New Document dialog box and create the frameset.

3. Press the keyboard sequences **Ctrl+Alt+R** to hide the ruler and **Ctrl+Alt+G** to hide the grid, if they are visible. Press the **Shift+F2** key combination to open the Frames panel in the Advanced Layout panel group if it is not visible.

4. Replace the contents of the Document window's Title text with **My First Frameset** to give your frameset a title when it appears in the browser window. (The title will also be available to search engines.)

5. This new frameset contains three frames, as shown in Figure 4-9, so you will need to save the frameset and all three frames.

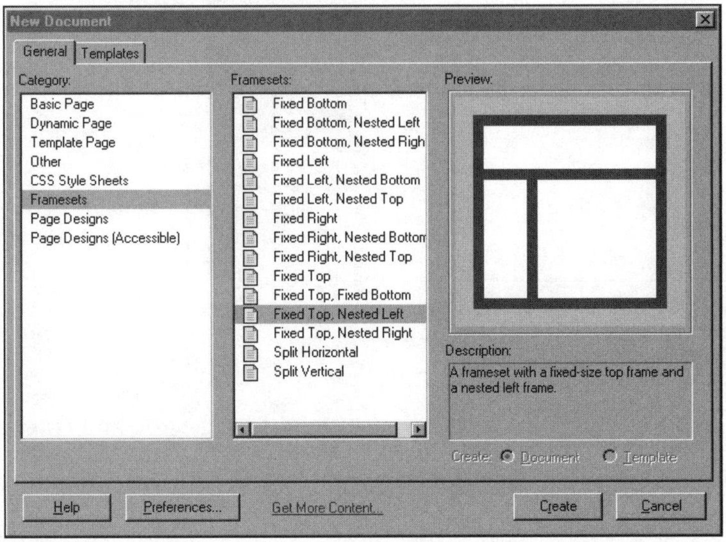

Figure 4-8   Creating a New Document as a frameset

6. Click **File** on the menu bar, and then click **Save All**. The Save As dialog box opens.

7. Navigate to the Chapter folder for Chapter 4, type **Ch04DW06.htm** in the File Name box and click **Save**. Dreamweaver saves the frameset as **Ch04DW06.htm** and displays another Save As dialog box that prompts you for the name of the largest frame. Type **Ch04DW07.htm**, and click **Save** to save that frame. Next, you need to specify a name for the frame on the left. Type **Ch04DW08.htm** in the File Name box, click **Save**, and repeat the process to name the top frame **Ch04DW09.htm**. The frameset in the Document window should appear like the one in Figure 4-9.

8. The default names for the frames within this frameset describe their positions in the frameset: topFrame, leftFrame, and mainFrame. Click anywhere inside the topFrame and type **Top Frame**. Click within the text you just typed, use the Property inspector to **center align** the text, and change its Format style to **Heading 1**. Click within the leftFrame, type **Left Frame**, and format the new text as **Heading 2**. Click in the mainFrame, type **Main Frame**, format the new text as **Heading 2**, and **center align** it.

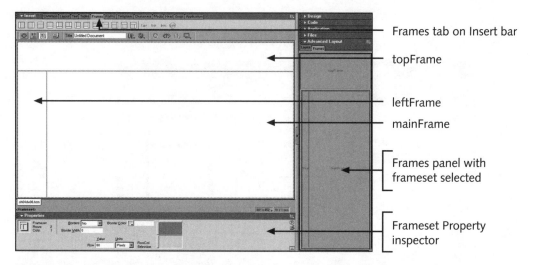

Frames tab on Insert bar

topFrame

leftFrame
mainFrame

Frames panel with
frameset selected

Frameset Property
inspector

Figure 4-9   Frameset with three frames, Frameset Property inspector, and Frames panel

9. Click **File** on the menu bar, and then click **Save All** to save the frameset and its documents. At this point, your frameset should look like Figure 4-10.

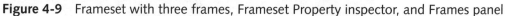

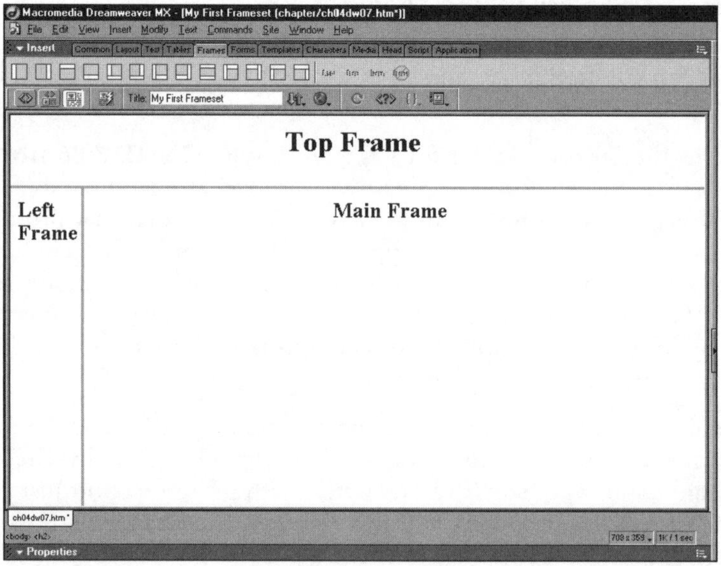

Figure 4-10   Frameset with text in each Frame document

You use the Frames panel in the Advanced Layout panel group to select frames in a frameset. You will see how that works in the following steps, as you select frames and alter them via the Property inspector.

To select and edit frames:

1. Click inside the topFrame in the Frames panel to select it. In the frame's Property inspector, select **Yes** on the Borders dropdown list, and change the border color to red (**#CC0000**). Leave Scroll set to **No**, and leave **No Resize** checked.

2. Click **mainFrame** in the Frames panel to select it. Change the Scroll setting to **Yes**. Vertical and horizontal scrollbars are added to the frame. Click in the mainFrame and then press the **Enter** key 15 times (the Return key on a Macintosh). Type **Bottom of page** to be sure you can use at least the vertical scrollbars when you view the frameset in the browser at the end of these steps.

3. In the Document window, click inside the leftFrame (just to the right of the words "Left Frame"), press the **Enter** key to insert a new line, and type **Red**. Select this text, and type **Ch04DW10.htm** in the Link text box in its Property inspector. Press the **Enter** key to create a hyperlink to a red page in the Chapter folder.

 If you are working on a Macintosh, press the Return key whenever this text asks you to press the Enter key.

4. Next, you need to specify where you want the red page to open when the user clicks the Red link. In this case, you want the page to open in the right-hand mainFrame, so, in the Property inspector with the word Red still selected, click **mainFrame** in the Target dropdown list.

5. Insert another blank line below the Red link, and type **Green**. Select this word, type **Ch04DW11.htm** in the Link text box, and select **mainFrame** in the Target dropdown list in its Property inspector. At this point, your page should look like Figure 4-11.

6. Click **File** on the menu bar, click **Save All,** preview the frameset in the browser, and test the hyperlinks and the vertical scrollbar. Then close the browser, and close the page in Dreamweaver.

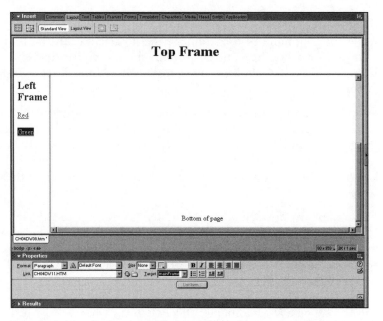

Figure 4-11   Frameset with hyperlinked menu in left frame

DREAMWEAVER SUPPORT FOR MULTIMEDIA

Dreamweaver allows you to incorporate a variety of multimedia content into your Web sites. It generates the HTML tags required to embed different types of multimedia files within Web pages and configures the tags to work in different browser versions. Including multimedia content created in other macromedia applications is easy because of the built-in cross-functionality of macromedia products. However, Dreamweaver also works well with multimedia files developed in nonMacromedia applications.

Dreamweaver tools help with a variety of tasks related to using multimedia on the Web, including the following:

- Inserting multimedia objects through the Common and Media tabs on the Insert bar, the Assets panel, and the Dreamweaver Insert menu.

- Creating HTML tags for different types of multimedia content that work in different browser versions for graphics, audio, video, and Flash files.

- Managing the trade-off between the quality of multimedia objects and their file size and download time. It is possible to edit multimedia objects contained within a page without leaving Dreamweaver by jumping to another application. For example, you can jump to Fireworks to edit and optimize an image to reduce its file size. Once you save the image file in Fireworks,

Dreamweaver replaces the image file with the optimized version on the page open in the Document window.

■ Playing multimedia objects on a page from the Property inspector to be sure they work.

Tools for Inserting Multimedia Files

You can insert multimedia content by using the media icons on the Common and Media tabs on the Insert bar and the Insert dropdown menu. If you have defined a Web site, you can also use the Assets panel, which contains all the multimedia objects within the Web site.

The Common tab provides icons for inserting images, Flash SWF movies, rollover images, navigation bars, and horizontal rules. Flash MX is a Macromedia application for building and compressing (or "shocking") animated movies with sound. Dreamweaver MX produces Flash text files with rollover effects and embedded hyperlinks, and preset Flash buttons that not only have rollover effects and embedded hyperlinks, but also are sometimes animated.

The Media tab provides icons for creating and inserting Flash buttons and text, and for inserting Shockwave files (files that have been compressed using Aftershock). You may already be familiar with the term "plug-in" when it refers to supplementary programs (such as the QuickTime or Flash media player) that can be added to a browser to play non-HTML files that may reside on an HTML page. A browser cannot play the video or audio files on your Web page unless the appropriate plug software has already been installed. In this context, however, the term "plug-in" refers to the multimedia objects themselves. The plug-in object displays not only the movie, but also the controls (such as start, stop, rewind) that the user clicks in order to play the file. When creating a page that will play audio or video files, you insert the audio or video file as a plug-in object in Dreamweaver, and then configure its dimensions and set up parameters (such as automatic starting) that govern how it will be displayed and played. In the end, users who view the page must have an appropriate plug-in application set up in their browsers in order to play your plug-in object.

When you insert a multimedia file into a Web page, you can use the Property inspector to configure properties that govern the appearance of the media file and the plug-in objects. Dreamweaver inserts onto the page a default-size plug-in object that is 36 pixels by 36 pixels. Different media players display different controls (play, stop, pause, rewind) that take up different amounts of space on the page. The default-size plug-in object usually only displays one control—the Play/Stop button. If you enlarge the size of the plug-in object, then you give the viewers of the site more options to control the media file. Although you will not be inserting sound files in this chapter, if you want to experiment with them later you will find that Dreamweaver MX simplifies plug-in configuration on the Web page by using the same tools you use to configure other multimedia files, such as images and Flash movies.

When you are building the Web page, you can test the multimedia files that you have inserted on an HTML page in the Dreamweaver editing window by playing them within Dreamweaver. You can then get some idea of how they will look when your viewers see them in the browser window. To accomplish this, select the file and click the Play button on the Property inspector. If you want to play all multimedia files on an HTML page, press the Ctrl+Alt+Shift+P key combination. Press the Ctrl+Alt+Shift+X key combination to stop playing all multimedia files.

Inserting Multimedia (Image, Flash, Flash Text, Flash Button)

Earlier in this chapter, you inserted images on a Web page. In this section, you update an HTML page by inserting an image, a Flash movie, and by creating and inserting Flash text and a Flash button. You will start by inserting some Flash text.

To insert Flash text into a Web page:

1. Open the page **Ch04DW12.htm** from the Chapter folder for Chapter 4 and resave it as **Ch04DW12SOL.htm** in the same folder. Be sure that Standard view is selected on the Layout tab of the Insert bar.

2. Click the **Media** tab in the Insert bar to open it.

3. Click in the upper-left table cell, and then click the **Flash Text** icon on the Media tab of the Insert bar. The Insert Flash Text dialog box opens.

4. Select an informal font such as **Comic Sans MS** in the Font dropdown list. Type **30** in the Size text box if necessary. Select **center alignment**, type the hexadecimal code **#0000FF** in the Color text box, and **#FF66CC** in the Rollover Color text box.

5. Click in the Text text box, type **Course Technology**, press **Enter**, and type **Presents a New Book**. Verify that the **Show Font** check box is selected, so you can see the text you just typed displayed in the font you selected in step 2.

6. Click the **Link** text box, and type **http://www.course.com/** to create a hyperlink to that URL from the Flash text. This hyperlink is embedded in the SWF (small Web format) file that Dreamweaver creates when you save the Flash text. Select **_self** in the Target dropdown list. Type the hexadecimal code **#FFFF99** in the Bg Color input box to be sure that the background of the Flash text file matches the page background color.

7. You have finished entering all the settings for your Flash text. Now you need to assign a name to the Flash text SWF file. To do this, type **Ch04DW13.swf** in the Save As input box. At this point, your Flash Text dialog box should look like Figure 4-12.

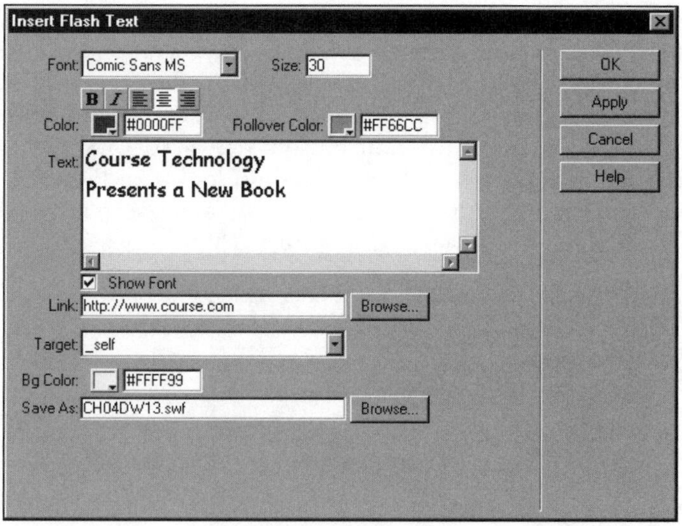

Insert Flash Text

Font: Comic Sans MS   Size: 30

B *I*

Color: #0000FF   Rollover Color: #FF66CC

Text: Course Technology
Presents a New Book

☑ Show Font

Link: http://www.course.com   Browse...

Target: _self

Bg Color: #FFFF99

Save As: CH04DW13.swf   Browse...

OK   Apply   Cancel   Help

4

Figure 4-12   Configuring Flash text

8. Click **Apply** to see the results on the Web page. If you cannot see the Flash text because it is under the Insert Flash Text dialog box, you can drag the dialog box by its status bar to uncover the Flash text.

9. Click **OK** in the Insert Flash Text dialog box to close it and accept the change.

10. Save the page, and preview it in the browser. When you roll the mouse over the Flash text, there should be a rollover color change; when you click the Flash text, the hyperlinked page should open.

Next, you will insert a Flash button. Dreamweaver MX provides a number of preset Flash button styles that you can use to create buttons with rollover effects and embedded hyperlinks. You define the button text when you create the button. Some of the button styles are animated and move when the user rolls the mouse over them. Flash buttons are also saved as SWF files. Flash buttons can make your page much more exciting for the viewer, and they are easy to produce in Dreamweaver.

To add a Flash button to the Web page:

1. Click the right-hand table cell in the top row. Click the **Flash Button** icon on the Media tab of the Insert bar. The Insert Flash Button dialog box opens. Here you can define the Flash button and its hyperlink.

2. Choose **Blue Warper** in the list of button styles. Type **Dreamweaver** in the Button Text text box. Select the font **Arial Black** in the Font list, and set the Font Size to **12**.

You can click the Apply button at any time to preview your Flash button in your Web page. Again, you may have to drag the dialog box if it is covering your Flash button on the Web page.

3. Type **http://www.macromedia.com/dreamweaver/** in the Link text box. Change the background color to the same color as the page (**#FFFF99**) to prevent white edges on the button. Click **_self** in the Target dropdown list to open the hyperlinked page in a new browser window. In the Save As list box, enter the following name for your button: **Ch04DW14.swf**. At this point, your Insert Flash Button dialog box should look like Figure 4-13. If you click the Apply button in the dialog box, Dreamweaver saves the button and displays it on your Web page, as in Figure 4-13.

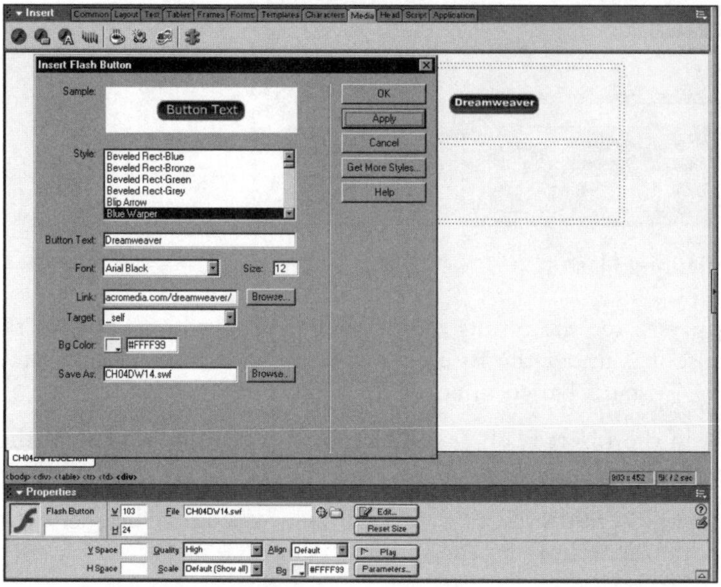

Figure 4-13   Configuring a Flash button

4. Click **OK** to close the dialog box, and view the completed button in your Web page.

In this set of steps, you will insert an image and a Flash SWF movie to complete your multimedia page. You can switch back to the Common tab on the Insert bar, because it is possible to insert both of these multimedia types from that tab.

To insert the image and the Flash movie:

1. Click the **Common** tab in the Insert bar.

2. Click in the left-hand table cell in the bottom row.

3. Click the **Image** icon on the Insert bar, and select the image **Ch04DW15.gif** from the Chapter folder for Chapter 4.

4. Verify that the image (the cover of a Course Technology textbook about Dreamweaver) has been inserted into the table's bottom left-hand cell, and

that the image is selected. In the Property inspector, type **1** in the V Space input box to increase the vertical space above and below the image. Type **4** in the Border input box to place a border around the image. Finally, center the image in the table cell if necessary.

5. Click in the right-hand table cell in the bottom row. Click the **Flash** icon in the Insert bar. The Select File dialog box opens.

6. Select the Flash file **Ch04DW16.swf** in the Chapter folder for Chapter 4, and then click **OK**. A square containing a smaller square which in turn contains the letter "f" (for "Flash") appears in the right-hand bottom table cell. The square is selected, as indicated by square selection handles around its border.

7. In the Property inspector, verify that the **Loop** and **Autoplay** check boxes are selected. These settings will ensure that the Flash movie starts automatically when it is loaded.

8. Now you will test the movie file to make sure it works correctly. Click the **Play** button in the Property inspector. Animated versions of the words "Course Technology," "Web Warrior," and "Dreamweaver!" move up and down in the table cell, accompanied by a short sound clip from a synthesized version of *Country Road*, recorded by Bon Bon Meltdown. The Play button in the Property inspector turns into a Stop button, as shown in Figure 4-14.

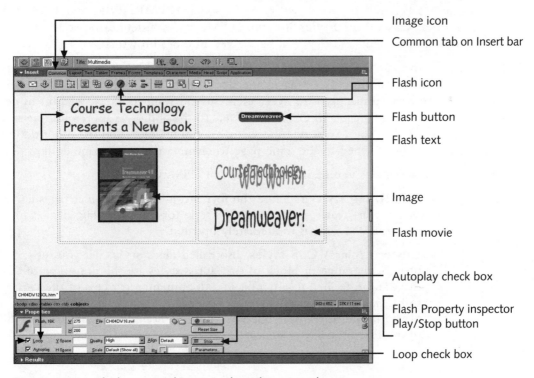

Figure 4-14   Flash movie playing in the editing window

9. Click the **Stop** button in the Property inspector to stop playing the Flash movie.

10. Save your work, then view the page in the browser and check to make sure the Flash movie plays as soon as the page loads. Move the mouse over the Flash text and verify that it changes from blue to pink. Test the Flash text's hyperlink. Also, test the Flash button and its hyperlink.

11. Close the browser, and close the Web page in Dreamweaver.

STYLE SHEETS TO INCREASE PRODUCTIVITY AND GIVE YOUR WEB SITES A COHERENT LOOK

Styles in Dreamweaver are somewhat similar to styles in word-processing applications, and a style sheet could be compared to a word-processing template. Dreamweaver helps you define, change, and apply styles to elements and attributes of Web pages, including font attributes, line spacing, and placement of objects on the page, according to the set of rules contained in a style sheet. You can apply the rules in a style sheet to lines of text, entire pages, or entire Web sites.

Types of Styles

Dreamweaver MX supports two types of styles: **HTML styles** and **CSS styles** (also known as **Cascading Style Sheets**). HTML styles redefine the style of HTML tags within a document, and they can be viewed in older browsers.

One disadvantage of HTML styles is that the redefined tag style needs to be applied to each instance of the HTML tag in the document. Thus, when you change an HTML style, you have to reapply it to every element you want to affect, which can be a lot of work. The term *cascading* in CSS styles refers to the ability to apply multiple style sheets to the same Web page. Two style sheets, one defining colors and the other defining margins, could be attached to the same page to create a particular page design.

Dreamweaver helps you define three types of CSS style sheets:

- **HTML tag styles** redefine the formatting for a particular tag, such as `<h1>`. When you create or change a CSS style for the `<h1>` tag, all text formatted with the `<h1>` tag is immediately updated.

- **Custom (class) CSS styles**, also called **class styles**, let you set style attributes to any range or block of text. Class styles are the only type of CSS style that can be applied to any text in a document, regardless of the tags that control it. All custom (class) styles associated with the current document are displayed in the Apply Style view of the CSS Styles panel and in the CSS mode of the text Property inspector.

- **CSS selector styles** redefine the formatting for a particular combination of tags. For example, <h1> <td> applies to text within <h1> tags that appear inside table cell tags <td>. CSS selector styles also apply to all tags that contain a specific id attribute. If you define a selector style with the value newStyle (id="newStyle"), then it would apply to all tags that contain the attribute-value pair id="newStyle".

Internal style sheets define styles within the <head> tags of an HTML document that apply to the entire document. **External style sheets** exist as separate files that contain style rules. In Dreamweaver, you can export a document's internal style sheet as a separate external style sheet (with the .css file extension). This external CSS file can then be attached to multiple documents to give a Web site a unified appearance. Unlike HTML styles, CSS styles do not have to be applied manually to each instance of the HTML tag on the Web page, but they apply to all instances of the redefined tags, whenever the external style sheet is changed. CSS styles are more complicated to learn, but they can save a lot of manual work once you master their use.

This short discussion of style sheets gives you some idea of how complex this particular tool can be. CSS is discussed much more fully Chapters 11 and 12 of this book. In this chapter, you will complete two exercises that demonstrate how to work with styles in Dreamweaver. These exercises are designed to give you an introduction to the help that Dreamweaver provides in creating and managing style sheets.

What are the advantages of using styles? Suppose you want to format several paragraphs in boldface, red, Arial font. To accomplish this, you could select each paragraph one at a time and alter its properties in the Property inspector. However, it is much faster to change the font type, size, and boldness of the paragraph <p> tag in the HTML Styles panel and then apply those changes to all of the paragraphs in the document. Later, if you want to alter these characteristics, you only need to update the tag style and apply the changes to the paragraphs in the document.

Recall that an internal style sheet defines styles that apply only within a document. Figure 4-15 shows a page displayed in Code and Design views, with HTML code for redefined <H1> and <H2> styles inside the <head> tags of the Web page. These styles apply only to <H1> and <H2> headings on this particular page.

External style sheets are stored in the Cascading Style Sheet (CSS) format and can be attached to or linked to multiple documents. Figure 4-16 shows the HTML code in a document that links to an external style sheet.

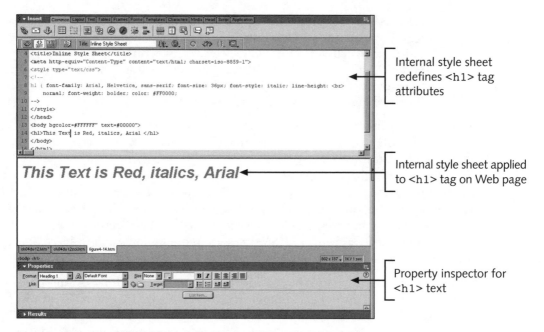

Internal style sheet redefines <h1> tag attributes

Internal style sheet applied to <h1> tag on Web page

Property inspector for <h1> text

Figure 4-15   Redefined internal HTML style in Code and Design view

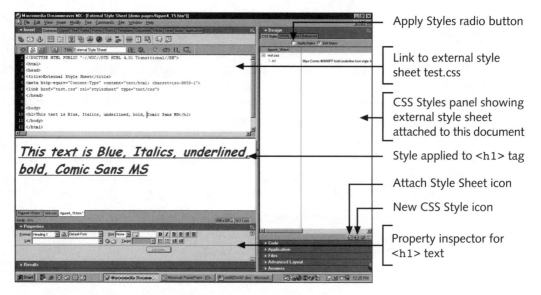

Apply Styles radio button

Link to external style sheet test.css

CSS Styles panel showing external style sheet attached to this document

Style applied to <h1> tag

Attach Style Sheet icon

New CSS Style icon

Property inspector for <h1> text

Figure 4-16   Link to external style sheet

In Dreamweaver, you use the HTML Styles panel to embed defined style formats within existing tags in an HTML document. To open the HTML Styles panel, click the HTML Styles command on the Window menu, or use the Ctrl+F11 key combination.

You can use the New Style dialog box to create a custom style, redefine an existing HTML tag, or use the CSS selector to group tag attributes. The CSS selector lets you group similar tags into a group (for example, all header tags). You can then save the tags internally in the document you are editing or define them in a new or existing external style sheet. You can also export the embedded styles in an HTML document to an external style sheet by clicking Export and then Export CSS Styles on the File menu.

Redefining an HTML Style by Using the CSS Styles Panel

The following steps give you practice redefining an HTML style within a document by using the CSS Styles panel.

To practice redefining an HTML style within a document by using the CSS Styles panel:

1. Open the HTML file named **Ch04DW17.htm** from the Chapter folder for Chapter 4 and resave it as **Ch04DW17SOL.htm** in the same folder. If the CSS Styles panel is not visible on your screen, click **Window** on the menu bar, and then click **CSS Styles** (or press the **Shift +F11** key combination). In the CSS Styles panel, click the **Edit Styles** option button. If the current document contained styles, this would display a hierarchical list of styles in the CSS Styles panel. In this case, the name of the document is displayed, with the words "no styles defined" below it in the CSS panel.

2. In the bottom, right-hand corner of the CSS Styles panel, click the **New CSS Style** icon (shown in Figure 4-16). The New Style dialog box opens.

3. Click the **Redefine HTML Tag** option button. Click the **This Document Only** option button to limit the style's scope to the current document. Click the **Tag** list arrow, and then click **h1**. This indicates that you want to define a new style for all text tagged with the <H1> tag. Click **OK**. The CSS Style definition for h1 dialog box opens.

4. Verify that **Type** is selected in the Category list box, and then select the following attributes: Weight: **bold**; Case: **uppercase**; Color: **#660066** (deep purple).

5. In the Category list box, click **Background** to access a new set of attributes. Type **#00CCCC** in the Background Color text box to change the background color for h1 to turquoise. Click **OK**.

6. Click in the top table cell and type **Happy Fourth of July!** If you are unable to type anything into this table cell, you are probably still in Layout view. In that case, click **Standard View** on the Layout tab of the Insert bar. Click anywhere inside the text and change its Format style to **Heading 1** in the Property inspector. Notice how Dreamweaver applies the redefined h1 style, as shown in Figure 4-17. (Figure 4-17 shows Code and Design view, so you can see the relevant HTML code.)

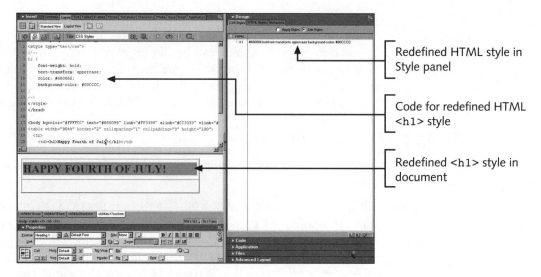

Redefined HTML style in Style panel

Code for redefined HTML <h1> style

Redefined <h1> style in document

Figure 4-17   Redefined <h1> HTML style

7. Preview the page in the browser, close the browser, and close the page in Dreamweaver.

Creating a Style Sheet and Applying Its Styles

In the preceding section, you learned how to create a custom style. After you create a number of custom styles, it is often helpful to save the styles as a separate file, called a *style sheet,* by exporting them. In the following steps, you open a document that has custom styles designed for a resume and export these styles to an external CSS style sheet. You will then attach this style sheet to a second resume and apply its styles to portions of that HTML file.

To export styles to a CSS style sheet:

1. Open the file named **Ch04DW18.htm** (which contains a resume from someone named Joseph) from the Chapter folder for Chapter 4. If necessary, open the CSS Styles panel. The CSS styles that are defined within this document are displayed in the CSS Styles panel. Click the **Edit Styles** option button to see the definitions of the styles that you see in Figure 4-18. Click the **Apply Styles** option button to apply the styles. (Figure 4-18 shows Code and Design view, so you can see the relevant HTML code.)

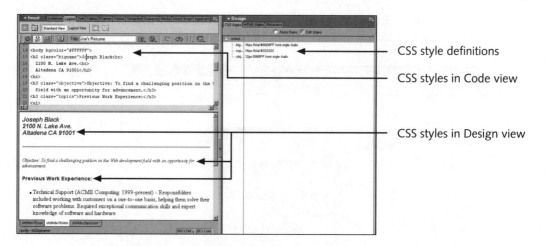

CSS style definitions

CSS styles in Code view

CSS styles in Design view

4

Figure 4-18   CSS styles in Ch04DW18.htm

2. First, you will export these styles in an external CSS file. To do so, click **File** on the menu bar, click **Export**, and then click **CSS Styles**. The Export Styles as CSS File dialog box opens. Here, you need to enter a file name for the CSS style sheet you are creating. Type **Ch04DW19.css** in the File Name text box, verify that the Chapter folder for Chapter 4 is selected in the Save In list box, and then click **Save**.

3. Now you are ready to apply the newly created CSS style sheet to another Web page. You will start by opening the page to which you will attach the style sheet. Open the HTML file named **Ch04DW20.htm** (which contains a resume for someone named Jane) from the Chapter folder for Chapter 4, and resave it as **Ch04DW20SOL.htm** in the same folder.

4. Click the **Attach Style Sheet** icon (shown in Figure 4-16) in the CSS Styles panel to open the Link External Style Sheet dialog box. Use the Browse button to open the Select Style Sheet File dialog box and select the **Ch04DW19.css** file that you just saved, and then click **OK** to close the Select Style Sheet file dialog box and return to the Link External Style Sheet dialog box. Select the **Link** option button, if necessary, and then click **OK**. You should now see the CSS styles you exported from Ch04DW18.htm listed in the CSS Styles panel.

5. Finally, you can apply the styles from the style sheet to sections of Jane's resume. Click the **Apply Styles** radio button (shown in Figure 4-16) at the top of the CSS Styles panel to show the styles that you can apply to sections of this document.

6. Select the first three lines with her name and address and click the **bigname** style in the CSS Styles panel. The style is applied to the selected text.

7. Select the heading **Education:** and click the **topics** style in the CSS Styles panel to apply it, as shown in Figure 4-19.

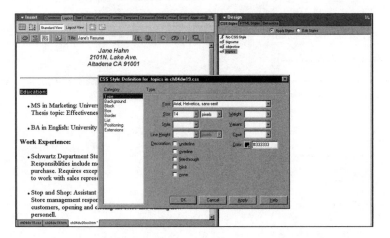

Figure 4-19   Applying external CSS styles to a document

8. Repeat for the headings **Work Experience**, **Skills**, and **Other** lower on the page.

9. Save your work, preview the page in the browser, close the browser, and close the page in Dreamweaver.

SIMPLE ANIMATION WITH DHTML

You can use Dreamweaver tools to quickly animate layers (and layer content). Such animation is one aspect of **dynamic HTML (DHTML)**, a technology that is discussed much more fully later in this book. In the next exercises, you use Dreamweaver commands and tools that generate JavaScript to control the movement of a layer (and its content) on a Web page.

Earlier in this chapter, you worked with layers when you practiced page layout. You typed text and inserted images into layers. In this section, you will use the Dreamweaver Record Path of Layer command to animate a layer containing an image so that the image moves across the Web page. You will also use the Dreamweaver timeline to move several layers across a page.

Animating with the Record Path of Layer Command

In the following steps, you animate a layer containing an image file. You will start by opening the Timelines panel.

To animate a layer containing an image file:

1. Open the HTML file named **Ch04DW21.htm** from the Chapter folder for Chapter 4, and resave it as **Ch04DW21SOL.htm** in the same folder. This page contains an image of an airplane inserted into a layer. You will actually animate the layer, and not the image, but the image is what you will see move on the page.

2. Press the **Alt+F9** key combination to open the Timelines panel. You can close the Property inspector to provide more editing space for your Web page if you need it. As shown in Figure 4-20, the Timelines panel displays a chart with rows for animation channels on the horizontal axis and frames on the vertical axis. Every fifth frame is numbered. Each frame represents a unit of time, the exact size of which depends on the frames-per-second (fps) setting on the timeline. The timeline in Figure 4-20 is set to play 15 fps. The playhead (the red vertical line) is currently positioned on Frame 1. If you leave the playhead where it is when you run the Record Path of Layer command, the animation will begin in Frame 1.

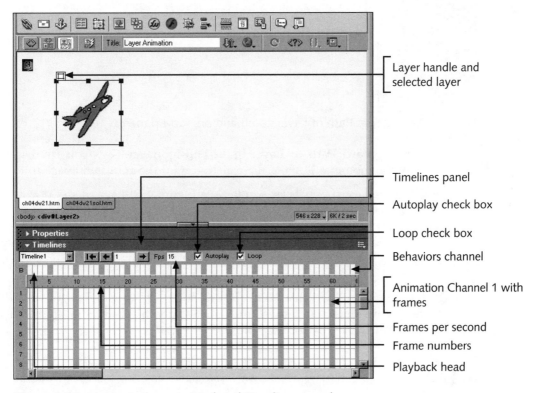

Figure 4-20   Layer to be animated and Timelines panel

3. In the Document window, click the layer's handle, shown in Figure 4-20, to select the layer. A selected layer looks like the one in Figure 4-20. Be sure the image itself is not selected, because you can only animate the layer, not the image.

4. In the Timelines panel, right-click **Frame 1** in Animation Channel 1.(On a Macintosh, Ctrl+Click instead.) This number is highlighted in a red box, because the playhead is currently positioned at Frame 1. A pop-up menu opens, as shown in Figure 4-21.

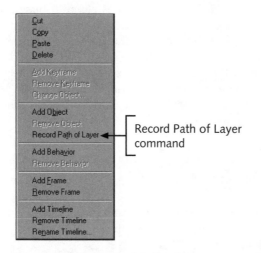

Record Path of Layer command

Figure 4-21   Record Path of Layer command on pop-up menu

5. Click **Record Path of Layer** in the pop-up menu. Now you can drag the layer with the mouse to indicate the path you want the animated image to follow.

6. Drag the layer by its layer handle (see Figure 4-20) across and down the page in a curved line. A dotted line appears, following the trajectory of the mouse pointer. When you release the mouse button, the dotted line turns into a continuous path line, as shown in Figure 4-22. This line indicates the path the image will travel when the browser plays the animation.

7. If you see a dialog box explaining that the Timeline inspector can control layer attributes and that Netscape 4.0 does not process changes to width and height attributes, click the **Don't show me this message again** check box and then click **OK** to close the dialog box.

If your first attempt to record the path of the layer does not work, you may have let go of the layer handle when you started dragging the layer. Try again.

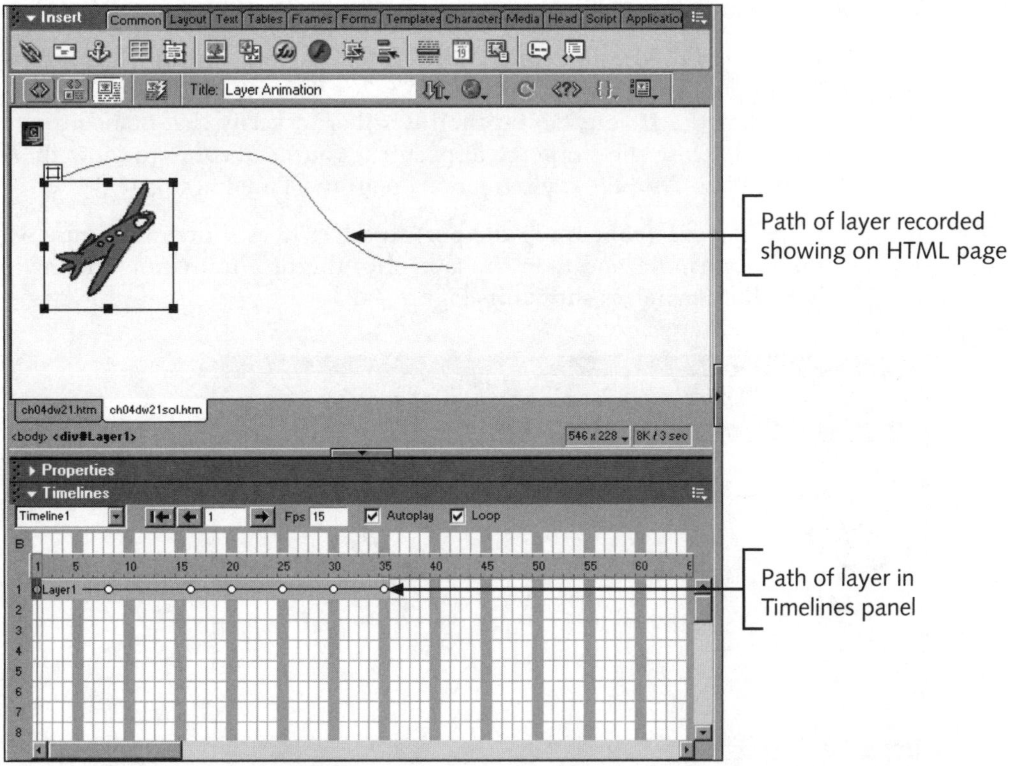

Path of layer recorded
showing on HTML page

Path of layer in
Timelines panel

Figure 4-22 Path line showing path of layer recorded in timeline

The Timelines panel in Figure 4-22 shows a 35-frame timeline for Layer1. At a rate of 15 frames per second, this animation will play for a little over 2 seconds. Your timeline may be longer or shorter, depending on how far you dragged the layer when you recorded its path.

8. To ensure that the animation will begin to play as soon as the page is loaded in the browser, be sure that the **Autoplay** check box is checked in the Timelines panel. Also, verify that the **Loop** check box is selected. This ensures that the animation will play as long as the HTML page is visible in the browser.

9. Save your work, and preview it in the browser. The airplane should fly across the page, following the same path you drew when you dragged the mouse.

10. Close the browser, and close the page in Dreamweaver.

Moving Layers by Using the Timeline

In the following steps, you animate layers using DHTML by dragging two layers into animation channels in the Timelines panel. Then you adjust their positions on the page and the length of their timelines.

To animate layers using DHTML:

1. Open the HTML file named **Ch04DW22.htm** from the Chapter folder for Chapter 4, and resave it as **Ch04DW22SOL.htm** in the same folder. If necessary, click the Layout tab on the Insert bar to verify that Standard view is selected. Close the Property inspector if you need space to view the Timelines panel. (The **Alt+F9** key sequence opens the Timelines panel.)

2. Click **Layer1** (containing the pot) to select it, as shown in Figure 4-23. Grab the layer handle, and drag the layer into the first animation channel in the Timelines panel, as shown in Figure 4-23.

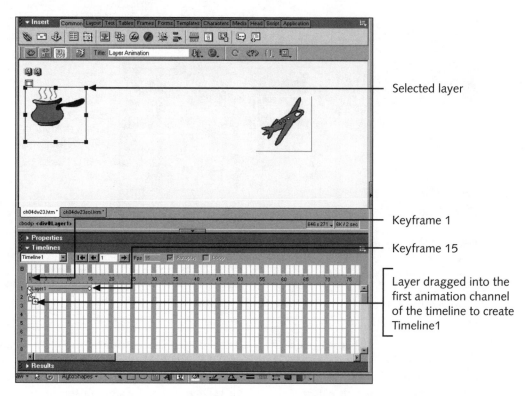

Figure 4-23   Dragging the selected layer into the first Timeline animation channel

3. Timeline1 appears as a light blue line (when not selected) and a dark blue line (when selected) in the first animation channel. It begins in Keyframe 1 and ends in Keyframe 15, which means that at a rate of 15 fps it will play for 1 second. You are going to extend its duration in the next step so that it will play a little longer.

4. Grab the right end of Timeline1 (the blue bar in the first animation channel) in Keyframe 15 and drag it to **Frame 30** of the animation. The playhead (the red vertical line) is now positioned at Frame 30. The animation now will play

for 30 frames at a rate of 15 fps. You can drag the playhead back and forth along the timeline, but the layer does not yet move because its position on the page is constant throughout the timeline. Next you change its position in Frame 1.

5. Open the Property inspector if necessary. To define the layer's beginning position, click in Frame 1 of Timeline1. Select Layer1 again if it is not selected, and type **400px** in the L (left) text box and **100px** in the T (top) text box in the Property inspector. These new coordinates reposition the layer on the page, and an animation guide, indicated by a black line, appears on the screen, as shown in Figure 4-24.

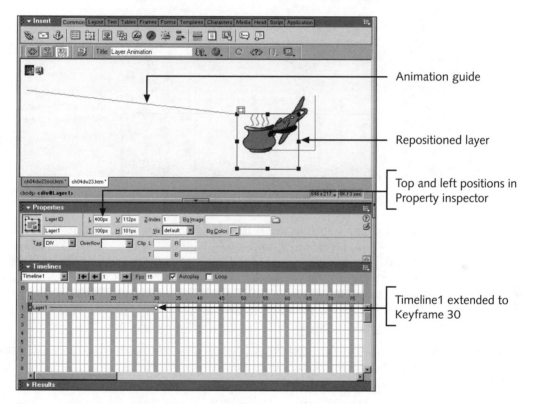

Figure 4-24   Repositioned layer in Keyframe 1 of Timeline1

6. You can play the animation by dragging the red Playback head across the frames in the Timelines panel. As the red Playback head passes over the frames, you should see the layer and its contents move. Figure 4-25 shows the playhead positioned at Frame 12 in the Timelines panel and the position of Layer1 at Frame 12 in the Document window.

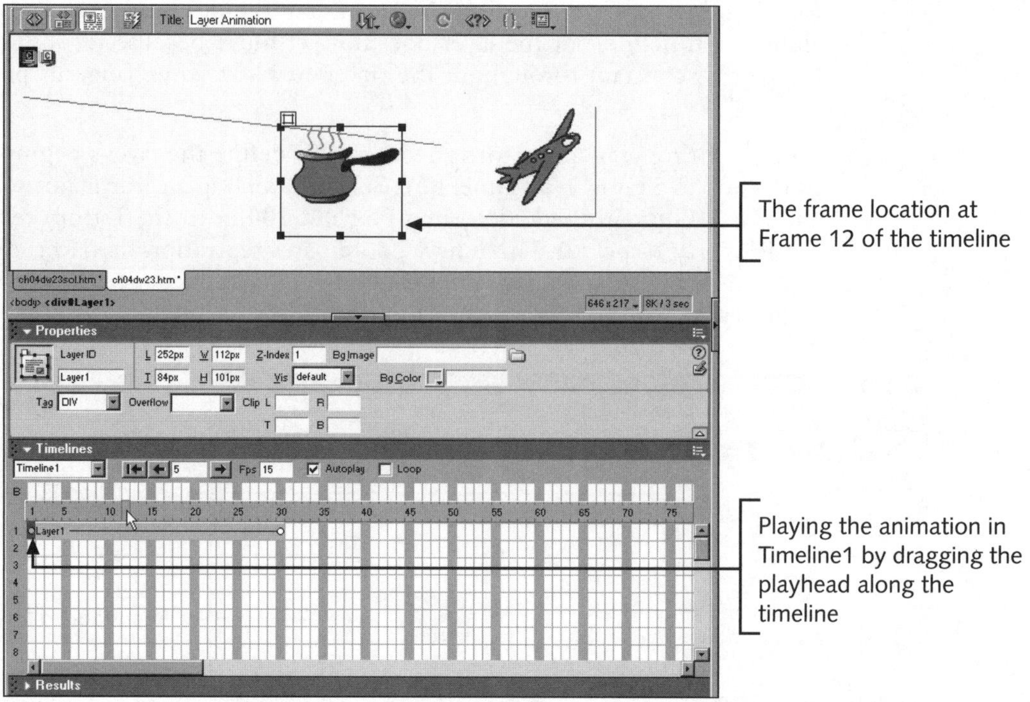

The frame location at Frame 12 of the timeline

Playing the animation in Timeline1 by dragging the playhead along the timeline

Figure 4-25 Using Playback head in the timeline to play layer animation

7. Click **Layer2** with the airplane to select it, and then click its **Layer** tab. Drag and drop the layer into Animation Channel 2. Click the last keyframe of the timeline in Animation Channel 2, and drag the timeline to **Frame 20**. Click the first frame of Animation Channel 2. With Layer2 still selected, in the Property inspector type **200px** in the L text box and **75px** in the T text box. The layer is repositioned in the work area for the first keyframe, and an animation guide appears on the screen.

8. To ensure that the animation plays when the page loads, select the **Autoplay** check box in the Timelines panel.

9. Click **OK** if an information dialog box pops up. The timeline should look similar to Figure 4-26.

10. Save your work, and preview the page in the browser. You should see the two layers move across the page. Layer2 (with the airplane image) stops moving before Layer1, which has a longer timeline. Because you did not select the loop check box, the animation only plays one time and then stops.

11. Close the browser, close the Timelines panel in Dreamweaver, and then close the page in Dreamweaver.

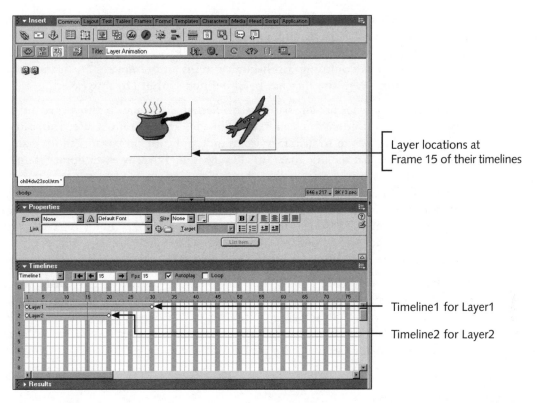

Figure 4-26   Timeline for two animated layers at Frame 15

Advanced Productivity Tools

The following advanced productivity tools in Dreamweaver MX can save you a lot of work: forms, libraries, and templates.

Forms are widely used on the Internet as well as on extranets and intranets. Retail merchants use forms to take customer orders and information. Interactivity makes the Internet very attractive to many companies, because it enables them to do business anywhere, anytime, by using a relatively low-cost communications link with customers and suppliers. Forms are used to gather data, which is then passed to a database for processing.

Two additional productivity tools, libraries and templates, not only increase your productivity, but they can also help you develop and maintain Web sites that are attractive, consistent, and easy for your viewers to navigate and use. Library items and templates allow you to reuse objects and page designs. If one person is responsible for designing a Web site, and if layout is likely to change, then library items provide more flexibility in making page changes. If several developers are collaborating to build a Web site and only one developer has the right to change the design and layout, then templates are a better choice because they give more control to that developer. Dreamweaver recommends against using both library items and templates on the same Web page, because managing both at once is confusing. Both library items and templates are accessible from the Assets panel for a Web site that has been defined within Dreamweaver.

Dreamweaver libraries are repositories of elements for a Web site stored in one place, within a Library folder. You can reuse libraries throughout a site. You can also take changes that you make to a library item and apply (or propagate) those changes to all other Web pages that include that same library item. Dreamweaver library items can contain any element stored within the <body> tags of an HTML page. Libraries actually store the HTML source code that either links to an existing object, such as an image, or defines the characteristics and content of information, such as text. The file extension for a library item is lbi. You cannot edit instances of library items on Web pages unless you detach the instance from the library item. Detached library items are not updated when you modify the library item.

Templates allow you to design a layout for your Web page, save it as a template, and then create multiple pages based on the template. You can also apply (or attach) the template to existing pages. The advantage of templates is that they give a united look and feel to your Web site. You can also change information on all pages on the Web site by changing the template and applying the changes to every page that uses the template.

Chapter Summary

- You can draw layers on a page in Standard view and convert the layers to tables.

- In Layout view, you can draw layout cells. Then you can insert content into the layout cells. Dreamweaver automatically creates layout tables to hold the layout cells.

- The Frames panel helps you define, configure, and manage framesets and the individual Frame windows that a frameset holds.

- The Common tab on the Insert bar allows you to insert images and Flash multimedia content, including Flash movies.

- The Media tab on the Insert bar allows you to embed multimedia content, such as audio and video files, by using the plug-in icon. This tab also allows you to generate Flash buttons and Flash text that change colors as you roll the mouse over them.

- Style sheets provide a coherent, consistent appearance to a Web site. Dreamweaver supports the creation of custom styles and modification of the styles of existing HTML tags. It lets you save them within the document or export them as an external Cascading Style Sheet (with the .css file extension). External style sheets can be reused on multiple pages to provide consistency throughout a Web site.

- Dreamweaver supports DHTML animation by generating JavaScript code that controls the animation of layers (containing text and images) on HTML pages.

❑ Dreamweaver supports other features that increase your productivity in Web site design and development: the creation and management of forms and form objects (such as check boxes and radio buttons); library items that you can reuse on many pages; and templates that store page properties, layout, and content that can be reused on many pages.

REVIEW QUESTIONS

1. If you want to open a hyperlinked page in the mainFrame of a frameset, you choose mainFrame on the _____ dropdown list in the Property inspector.

   a. file name

   b. target

   c. jump to

   d. open file

2. When you use DHTML tools to animate in Dreamweaver, you animate _____.

   a. an image

   b. a table

   c. a layout cell

   d. a layer

3. Selecting the Autoplay check box in the Timeline panel ensures that

   a. The animation plays when the user clicks a button.

   b. The animation plays automatically when the Web page loads in the Web browser.

   c. The animation does not start.

   d. It is not an option.

4. Selecting the Loop check box in the Timeline panel ensures that

   a. Your animation does not play until the viewer clicks a button.

   b. Your animation plays one time and then stops.

   c. Your animation keeps playing until the user loads another page.

   d. None of the above is true.

5. The acronym "DHTML" stands for _____.

   a. Dynamic HyperText Modem Language

   b. Drawing HyperText Markup Language

   c. Dynamic HyperText Markup Language

   d. Drawing HyperText Media Language

6. The acronym "CSS" stands for.

   a. Cascading Style Sheets

   b. Cascading Style Styles

   c. Cover Style Sheets

   d. Critical Style Sheets

7. To play a Flash movie embedded on a Web page from within Dreamweaver Design view, click the _____ button in the Property inspector.

   a. Stop

   b. Play

   c. Forward

   d. Go

8. In order to draw layers that can be converted to tables, you need to switch to the Layout tab and select

   a. Standard View

   b. Layout View

   c. Code View

   d. Document View

9. In order to draw table cells, you need to switch to the Layout tab and select

   a. Standard View

   b. Layout View

   c. Image View

   d. any view

10. A document that holds a group of frames is called a _____.

   a. main frame file

   b. menu file

   c. HTML file

   d. frameset file

11. When you insert Flash text into an HTML page in Dreamweaver, what type of file is saved?

   a. DCR

   b. GIF

   c. SWF

   d. JPG

12. The Dreamweaver command that lets you drag a layer around a page to create an animation is called _____.

    a. DHTML

    b. Timeline

    c. Record Path of Layer

    d. Hide/Show

13. You can export styles from within an HTML document into an external document that has the file extension _____.

    a. htm

    b. css

    c. ftp

    d. ram

14. The panel that lets you animate layers over time is called the

    a. Timelines panel

    b. Behaviors panel

    c. Layers panel

    d. CSS Styles panel

15. The Media tab icon that lets you embed audio or video files in your Web page is called _____.

    a. Flash button

    b. Flash text

    c. a plug-in

    d. Shockwave

HANDS-ON EXERCISES

Exercise 4-1

In this exercise, you will embed a Flash movie in a Web page and adjust its spacing.

1. Open the file **Ch04DWEX01.htm** from the Exercises folder for Chapter 4 and resave it as **Ch04DWEX01SOL.htm** in the same folder. Display the Common tab on the Insert bar.

2. Click on the line below the words "Flash Tour" and then click the Flash icon on the Common tab. Select the Flash movie **Ch04DWEX02.swf** from the Exercises folder for Chapter 4.

3. Use the Property inspector to change the Flash movie attributes and display. Type 5 in the V space and H space text boxes. Play the Flash movie on the page in the Document window by clicking the Play button in its Property inspector.

4. Save your work, preview the page in the browser, verify that the Flash movie plays as soon as the page loads, close the browser, and close the page in Dreamweaver.

Exercise 4-2

In this exercise, you add Flash buttons to a Web page.

1. Open the file **Ch04DWEX03.htm** from the Exercises folder for Chapter 4 and resave it as **Ch04DWEX03SOL.htm** in the same folder. Verify that Standard view is selected in the Insert panel of the Layout tab. Then display the Media tab in the Insert bar.

2. Click in the top table cell. Click the Flash Button icon on the Media tab. In the Flash Button dialog box, choose the StarSpinner style, accept the default font and size, choose _blank in the Target dropdown list, and set the Bg color to #FF9900 to match the color of the page.

The _blank Target setting will open the hyperlinked page in a new browser window.

3. For the button text, type the word Dreamweaver, and then type http://www.macromedia.com/software/dreamweaver/ in the Link text box, and save the new button as **Ch04DWEX03.swf**.

4. Create two new buttons, using the settings specified in step 2. In the second button, the text, Fireworks should link to this page: http://www.macromedia.com/software/fireworks/. Save it as **Ch04DWEX04.swf**. In the third button, the text Book should link to this page: http://www.course.com/. Save it as **Ch04DWEX05.swf**.

5. Save your work, preview the page in the browser, test the Flash buttons, close the browser, and close the page in Dreamweaver

Exercise 4-3

Currently, the Adventure Travel Company has a home page that has a Heading 1 title at the top with the company name. The company's owner thinks this is a boring way to display the company name and wants you to create something more graphically appealing. You decide to create a new title for the company by using overlapping text layers and absolute positioning.

1. Create a new basic HTML page in Dreamweaver. Save this page as **Ch04DWEX06.htm** in the Exercises folder for Chapter 4. In this file, you insert four layers. Three will contain text, and one will contain a colored background.

The layers will overlap to create an appealing title for the Adventure Travel Company home page.

2. Be sure that Standard View is selected on the Layout tab of the Insert bar. Then open the Layers panel (F2), the Property inspector, and the Common tab of the Insert bar.

3. In the Title text box at the top of the work area, enter Adventure Travel. Click in the work area. Click the Draw Layer icon on the Common tab and then click in the work area to insert a layer on the HTML page. The text "Layer1" should appear in the Layers panel, and the layer should be visible in the work area.

4

4. Click Layer1 to select it in the Layers panel. Enter the following properties in the Layer Property inspector: L (left): 24; T (top): 40; W (width): 100; H (height): 100; Bg color: #CC6600 (orange). The layer is repositioned on the screen, displaying new attributes. Click elsewhere in the work area to deselect the layer.

5. Repeat step 3 to create Layer2, with the following properties in the Layer Property inspector: L (left): 57; T (top): 17; W (width): 100; H (height): 100; Bg color: #006633 (green). The layer is repositioned on the screen, displaying new attributes.

6. Repeat step 3 to create Layer3, with the following properties in the Layer Property inspector: L (left): 73; T (top): 52; W (width): 350; H (height): 61. The layer is repositioned on the screen, displaying new attributes.

7. Click in Layer3 so that you can add text. Type Adventure Travel in this layer. Select the text, and enter the following settings in the Property inspector: Size: +4; Font: bold, italic; Text color: #FF9900 (light orange). The text shows in the layer, and the layer is positioned on top of the colored layers.

8. Save your work, preview the page in the browser, close the browser, and close the page in Dreamweaver.

Exercise 4-4

In this exercise, you use HTML styles to format a Web page with the instructions for frying an egg.

1. Open **Ch04DWEX07.htm** from the Exercises folder for Chapter 4, and resave it as **Ch04DWEX07SOL.htm** in the same folder. This page contains plain text with no formatting. Open the HTML Styles panel (Ctrl+F11), if it is not already open.

2. Click the New Style icon at the bottom of the HTML Styles panel. The Define HTML Style dialog box opens. In the Name text box, type Egg Title. Click the option buttons to select Selection and Clear Existing Style. Change the Font Attributes to Font: Arial, Helvetica, sans-serif; Size: +5; Color: #CC6600 (orange); and Style: bold, italicized. Click OK. An HTML style named Egg Title appears in the panel.

3. Select the text Tutorial on How to Fry an Egg, and click Egg Title in the styles list on the HTML Styles panel. Deselect the text, and observe the applied style.

4. Select the text listing the five items needed to fry the egg (Frying Pan, Butter, Eggs, Stove, and Spatula) and click the Unordered List icon in the Property inspector to create a bulleted list.

5. Click the New Style icon at the bottom of the HTML Styles panel to open the Define HTML Style dialog box. In the Name text box, type Egg Subtitle. Click to select the option buttons for Paragraph and Clear Existing Style. Change the Font Attributes to Font: Arial, Helvetica, sans-serif; Size: +1; Color: #FFCC00 (gold); and Style: bold. Click OK. The new style appears in the HTML Styles panel.

6. Select the text Necessary Items: and click Egg Subtitle in the styles list on the HTML Styles panel. Deselect the text, and observe the style applied to the text. Repeat to apply the Egg Subtitle style to the text Directions and "Yum! Yum!"

7. Click the New Style icon in the HTML Styles panel to open the Define HTML Style dialog box. In the Name text box, type Red Text. Click to select the option buttons for Selection and Add to Existing Style. Change the Font Attribute to the Default Font, the Size attribute to None, and make sure the Bold and Italic styles are not selected. Change the text color to #FF0000 (red). Click OK. The new style appears in the HTML Styles panel.

8. Select the bulleted list, and click the style Red Text in the HTML Styles panel. Deselect the text, and observe the red text in the bulleted list. Select the paragraph of text that gives directions for frying the egg, and click the Red Text style again. The paragraph appears with red text.

9. Select the text "Yum! Yum!" and click the style Red Text in the HTML Styles panel. Deselect the text, and observe that the text is red and still has the previously existing style (Arial font with size +1). The Red Text style overlays the Egg Subtitle style.

10. Double-click the Red Text style in the HTML Styles panel to open the Define HTML Style dialog box for Red Text. Click the Clear Existing Style option button to select it. Click OK. Observe that the plus sign on the icon next to the Red Text style disappeared. Select the "Yum! Yum!" text again, and reapply the Egg Subtitle style to the "Yum! Yum!" text by clicking it in the Styles panel.

11. Save your work, preview the page in the browser, close the browser, and close the page in Dreamweaver.

Exercise 4-5

In this exercise, you create a frameset to hold two pages and add another button to the menu page that will open a page in the mainFrame.

1. Create a new document in Dreamweaver, and choose Framesets in the Category window of the New Document dialog box. Choose Fixed Left in the Framesets window. Click Create to create a new frameset.

2. Click File on the menu bar, click Save Frameset, and save the frameset as **Ch04DWEX09.htm** in the Exercises folder for Chapter 4.

3. Click anywhere inside the leftFrame. Click Open in Frame on the File menu. Select **Ch04DWEX03SOL.htm**, the page on which you inserted Flash buttons in an earlier exercise. If the frame is not wide enough to show the entire menu, you can drag the right border of the frame to increase its width.

4. Click anywhere inside the mainFrame. Click Open in Frame on the File menu, and select the file named **Ch04DWEX06.htm** to insert the document in the mainFrame.

5. Click Save All on the Files menu.

6. Click to the right of the Book Flash button in the menu. Press Tab to create another row in the table. Click the Flash Button icon on the Media tab of the Insert bar. The Insert Flash Button dialog box opens. Choose Blue Warper in the list of button styles. Type Egg Recipe in the Button Text text box. Select the font Arial Black in the Font list, and set the Font Size to **12**.

7. Type **Ch04DWEX07SOL.htm** in the Link text box. Change the background color to the same color as the page (#FFFF99) to prevent white edges around the edge of the button. Click _mainFrame in the Target dropdown list to open the hyperlinked page in the mainFrame. In the Save As list box, use the following name for your button: **Ch04DWEX10.swf**.

8. Preview your frameset in the browser, and try the Flash buttons in the leftFrame.

WEB DESIGN PROJECTS

Project 4-1

Create a DHTML page with moving titles and images as an entry page to a business site of your choosing. Place text and images on multiple layers, and use the Dreamweaver timeline to animate the layers. Use different starting and stopping frames for different layers so that they start and stop at different times. Try to design and implement layer animation that enhances the business purpose of the site. Save your page as **Ch04DWDP01.htm** in the Projects folder for Chapter 4.

Project 4-2

Create an HTML resume for yourself in Dreamweaver. Imagine you are applying for a job as a Web site designer. Use different HTML styles to alter the appearance of different titles, subtitles, and sections of your resume. Then imagine you are applying for a job as an accountant, and change the HTML styles to alter the appearance of your resume to suit such a career change. Save your page as **Ch04DWDP02.htm** in the Projects folder for Chapter 4.

Project 4-3

An events company has hired you to create the layout for a Web site that offers information about three types of entertainment: music, movies, and TV. Use a frameset and
your favorite frameset layout structure to design a prototype for the Web site. Choose a
preset Flash button style and create three Flash buttons, **Ch04DWDP03.swf**,
Ch04DWDP04.swf, and **Ch04DWDP05.swf**, to create a menu in one of the frames.
Create a home page and a page for music, movies, and TV with information about your
favorites. Set up the hyperlinks from the buttons so that they load the pages into the
mainframe of your frameset. Save your page as **Ch04DWDP06.htm** in the Projects
folder for Chapter 4.

5

PHOTOSHOP AND IMAGEREADY: PART I

In this chapter, you will

♦ Create images
♦ Edit images
♦ Save and optimize images

Graphics are crucial components of Web sites. Not only do they make pages more interesting, but they often provide information to the reader in a way that text cannot. The most popular program used to create and edit computer graphics is Adobe Photoshop. Adobe also publishes graphics software called ImageReady, which is usually bundled with Photoshop. ImageReady is similar to Photoshop, but it has special features for creating Web-only graphics such as animations, image maps, and rollover buttons. This chapter introduces you to the tools and techniques common to both Photoshop and ImageReady, including creating, editing, and saving images for the Web.

CREATING IMAGES

If you have ever used a painting program (such as Paint, which comes with the Windows operating system), you will be familiar with the idea of creating computer images. Photoshop lets you do far more than just paint, however. It also includes tools for advanced techniques, filters for applying effects across the entire image, layers that allow you manipulate discrete parts of an image, and vector-based tools.

Before you can begin creating images, you need to start Photoshop.

To start Photoshop:

1. Start **Adobe Photoshop 7.0** from the Start menu. (If you are working on a Macintosh, start Adobe Photoshop 7.0 from the Applications folder.) The opening window appears and, after a pause, the Adobe Photoshop window opens, as in Figure 5-1. (Note that yours might look slightly different, depending on what windows are open within Photoshop. If you are working on a Macintosh, your screen will look slightly different than in the figure. For example, you will probably see the Dock at the bottom of the screen.)

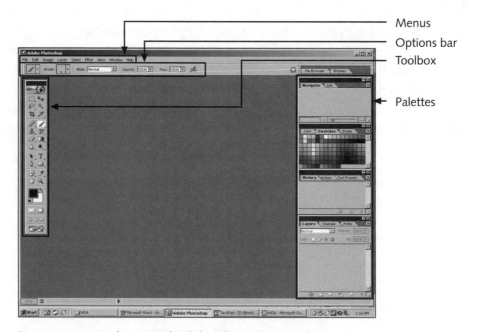

Figure 5-1 Newly opened Adobe Photoshop window

2. If you see windows on your screen that are *not* open in Figure 5-1, close them. If some of the windows in Figure 5-1 do not appear on your screen, simply continue with this chapter. You will have a chance to adjust your screen in the next set of steps.

If you are working on a Macintosh, your screen will look slightly different than Figure 9-1. For example, you will probably see the Dock at the bottom of the screen.

 When starting Photoshop for the first time, you may see dialog boxes appear containing messages suggesting that you reset the primary Scratch volume, customize your color settings, or register Photoshop with Adobe. It is not necessary to do any of these now. Click Cancel or No to close the dialog boxes.

If you or someone else has used your copy of Photoshop, it is possible that your screen will not match Figure 5-1 perfectly. The following steps guide you through the process of setting up your screen to match the figures in this book.

To set up your Photoshop screen:

1. The Photoshop work area contains several palettes, each of which contains sets of tools or commands for working with image files. Click the **Window** menu. You see a list of all available palettes, with checks next to those that are currently visible.

2. The most important palette is the Toolbox, which contains tools such as the Brush tool, the Eraser tool, and the Type tool. These tools allow you to add and remove colors from an image or to add text. If you do not see the Toolbox, click **Window** on the menu bar, and then click **Tools**.

3. If the Toolbox is not already on the left side of the work area, drag it there now. It should snap into place. When a tool is selected in the Toolbox, the Options bar at the top of the Photoshop window displays options for that tool.

4. Click **Window** on the menu bar and make sure that the following palettes are visible as well: **Navigator**, **Swatches**, **History**, and **Layers**.

5. All of the palettes except for the Toolbox are grouped in twos or threes and include tabs that allow you to switch among them. Click the **Color** tab above the Swatches palette. The Color palette becomes visible, covering the Swatches palette.

Using Tools

The Toolbox is the palette containing the tools you use to create images. The Toolbox was shown earlier in Figure 5-1.

Some tools in the Toolbox are actually sets of tools. Sets of tools are differentiated from individual tools by a small triangle below and to the right of the Tool icon. Selecting the icon causes a submenu of the complete set of related tools to appear, as shown in Figure 5-2.

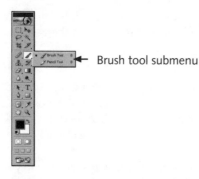

Figure 5-2   The Brush tool submenu

Across the top of the main Photoshop window, just below the menus, you should see the Options bar, shown in Figure 5-3. The Options bar contains settings for each of the tools in the Toolbox. For example, when the Brush tool is selected in the Toolbox (as it is in Figure 5-3), the Options bar displays options for the size and shape of the brush. It also shows more advanced options that control how the colors you add interact with the colors already in the image.

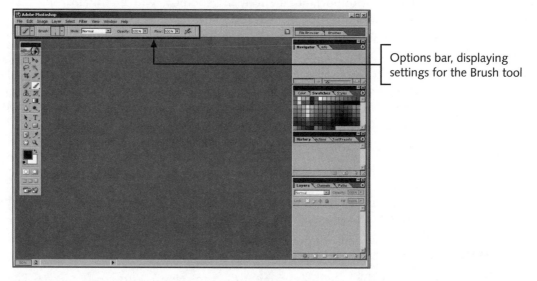

Figure 5-3   The Brush tool settings in the Options bar

In the following steps, you will create an image in Photoshop. The general process goes like this: Drag your mouse diagonally across the Document window to select an area. This **selection area** is outlined with a dashed line called a **marquee**. Then fill the selection area with a solid color or a pattern. The currently selected color is shown as the **foreground color** in the Toolbox (see Figure 5-1). Using tools such as the Brush tool or the Paint Bucket tool results in the foreground color being applied to the open image. Behind the foreground color in the Toolbox is the **background color**. This color is used to augment the foreground color when creating gradients or patterns that fade from one color to another.

To create an image using some of the tools in Photoshop:

1. Click **File** on the menu bar, and then click **New**. The New dialog box opens. In the New dialog box, name the new image, **Autumn Leaves**. Select a Width of **500 pixels** and a Height of **400 pixels**. (You will probably need to use the list arrows to select pixels rather than inches.) Select a Mode of **RGB Color** and select **White** for the Contents. Ignore the other options, and click **OK**. A new window named "Autumn Leaves" appears, containing only white pixels, as shown in Figure 5-4.

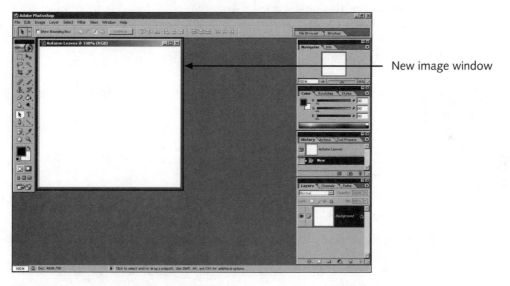

New image window

Figure 5-4   New Autumn Leaves window

2. Click the **Rectangular Marquee** tool in the Toolbox. (This is the icon with the dotted rectangle, in the upper-left corner.) Move the mouse pointer over the image window, and verify that the pointer has changed to a small plus sign. You can use this pointer to draw a selection marquee, but first you need to check the Feather setting, which controls the edge of the selection area.

If you are unsure of the name of a tool in the Toolbox, point to the tool. After a pause, a ToolTip appears with the tool's full name. Throughout this chapter, use this technique to find the tools you need.

3. Verify that the Feather setting in the Options bar is set to **0 px**, and then click and drag the pointer across the upper third of the image window. A dotted rectangle (the selection marquee) appears, indicating the area of the image window that is selected.

4. If you do not see the Swatches palette, click the **Window** menu and then click **Swatches**. The Swatches palette becomes visible. Click one of the dark blue swatches from the Swatches palette.

The Set Foreground Color and the Set Background Color icons in the Toolbox change color to reflect the colors you select in the Swatches palette. When you clicked the dark blue color in step 4, the Set Foreground Color icon turned blue, indicating that your color selection will affect the image's foreground.

5. Select the **Paint Bucket** tool from the Toolbox. The Paint Bucket tool shares space in the Toolbox with the Gradient tool. Hold your pointer down over the Gradient tool to make the Paint Bucket tool visible. Set the Fill to **Foreground** in the Options bar. Click the pointer inside the selected area in the image window. The area fills with blue.

You can reverse any mistakes you make by selecting Undo from the Edit menu.

6. Select the **Rectangular Marquee** tool again, and click outside the selected area. The selection marquee disappears.

7. Click one of the dark green swatches from the Swatches palette. The new color appears as the foreground color in the toolbox.

8. Select the **Paint Bucket** tool again. Set the Tolerance to **0** in the Options bar. (This setting guarantees that only pixels of exactly the same color are affected.) Click the pointer inside the white area in the image window. The area fills with green.

9. Click one of the red swatches from the Swatches palette. The new color appears as the foreground color in the Toolbox.

10. Select the **Brush** tool from the Toolbox. In the Options bar, click the Brush icon. The Brush Preset picker opens. Scroll down the list of brushes, and select the brush that looks like a maple leaf. Set the Master Diameter to **60**, and press **Enter** twice to close the picker. (If you are working on a Macintosh, use the Return key instead of the Enter key.)

In Photoshop and ImageReady, the term picker is often used to refer to a type of dialog box that allows you to make selections, such as color or brush size.

11. Drag the pointer across the green area in the image window. Dozens or hundreds of colored leaves appear. Your image should resemble the one shown in Figure 5-4.

12. Click the **File** menu, and then click **Save As**. The Save As dialog box opens.

13. Select the **Chapter** folder for Chapter 5, name the image **Ch05Photoshop01.gif**, and select the **CompuServe GIF** format. (You will learn the details about selecting file formats later in this chapter in the "Saving and Optimizing Images" section. Until you get to that section, simply select the file format specified in the steps.)

14. Click **Save**. The Indexed Color dialog box appears. Here you need to set how many colors to use in the image.

15. Change the Palette setting to **Local (Perceptual)** and the Colors setting to **64**. Click **OK**. The GIF Options dialog box appears.

16. For most GIF images, the Normal setting is acceptable, so verify that **Normal** is selected and click **OK**. Your completed image should look like the one in Figure 5-5.

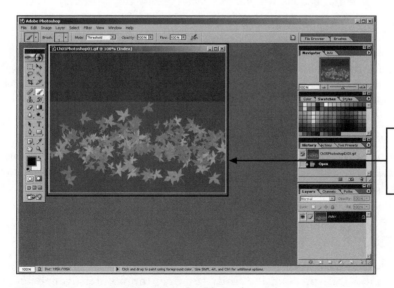

A simple image created with the Brush tool, Paint Bucket tool, and Rectangular Marquee tool

Figure 5-5   An image created with tools

17. Close the image window, but leave Photoshop open. You may be asked to save changes again. Click **No** (or **Don't Save** on a Macintosh).

Using Filters

The tools in the Toolbox are useful for adding color and effects to specific areas of an image. Photoshop also includes many **filters**, available under the Filter menu, that can be used to add graphical effects to entire images or selected areas. The filters are divided into 13 main categories and a few advanced categories. Most of the filter categories recreate the effects of traditional drawing and painting techniques such as watercolor, cross-hatching, and mosaic. Other filters are used to blur, sharpen, or distort the image.

To create an image using some filters:

1. Click the **File** menu, and then click **New**. The New dialog box opens. In the New dialog box, name the new image **Textures**. Select a Width of **400 pixels** and a Height of **500 pixels**. Select a Mode of **RGB Color** and select **Transparent** for the Contents. Ignore the other options, and click **OK**. A new window appears containing a checkerboard pattern, indicating that no pixels are colored.

2. Click one of the blue swatches from the Swatches palette. The new color appears as the foreground color in the toolbox.

3. While pressing the **Ctrl** key (Command Key on a Macintosh), click the white swatch in the Swatches palette. The new color appears as the background color in the Toolbox.

 If the steps in this chapter tell you to select a setting that is already selected by default on your computer, simply verify that the setting is correct and continue with your work.

4. In the Toolbox, select the **Gradient** tool (in the Paint Bucket tool's submenu). In the Options bar, click the **Linear Gradient** icon, set the Mode to **Normal** and the Opacity to **100%**. Drag the pointer from the upper-left corner of the image window to the lower-right corner. The window fills with color, gradating from blue to white.

5. Select the **Elliptical Marquee** tool from the Toolbox. In the Options bar, set the Feather to **0** and the Style to **Normal**. Drag the pointer from near the upper-left corner of the image window to near the lower-right corner. An elliptical selection marquee appears in the image window.

6. Click the **Filter** menu, point to **Render**, and then click **Clouds**. The selection area fills with a simulation of white clouds and blue sky.

7. With the Elliptical Marquee still selected, click outside the selection area to deselect it. While pressing the **Shift** key, drag the pointer over the center of the image. A circular selection marquee appears in the image window.

8. Click **Filter** on the menu bar, point to **Pixelate**, and then click **Crystallize**. The Crystallize dialog box opens. Set the Cell Size to **20** and click **OK**. The selection area takes on the texture of a jewel.

9. Click **Filter** on the menu bar, point to **Distort**, and then click **Spherize**. The Crystallize dialog box opens. Set the Amount to **100%** and click **OK**. The selection area takes on a 3-D effect. The final image should resemble the one shown in Figure 5-6.

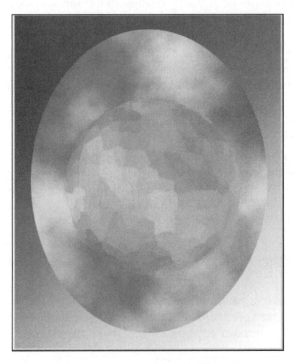

Figure 5-6   Image created with filters

10. Click the **File** menu, and then click **Save As**. The Save As dialog box appears. Select the **Chapter** folder for Chapter 5, and name the image **Ch05Photoshop02.jpg**. Under Format, select **JPEG**. The JPEG dialog box appears. Set the Quality to **6** and click **OK**.

11. Close the image without saving any additional changes.

Using Layers and Vector Shapes

Layers are a Photoshop element that you can think of as sheets of clear plastic. When stacked above one another, they can contain separate image elements. You can edit the contents of a layer without affecting the image elements in the other layers. Using layers makes Web page design easier, and they are a necessary component of animations and rollover effects, which are covered in Chapter 6.

Vector shapes are another kind of element that can be edited without affecting other parts of an image. Web graphics are **bitmap images**, which means they are composed of a grid of pixels, where each pixel can have a different color. When you use tools such as the Marquee tools or Brush tool, you are manipulating the pixels in the bitmap. Vector shapes are composed of lines, rather than pixels, and can be colored with different styles, in addition to solid colors. In Photoshop, you can include vector shapes within your images. This is convenient because you can easily change the shape and size of vector shapes without affecting the rest of the image.

 It is easy to confuse the Shape tools with the Selection tools. Make sure you understand the difference between the Elliptical Marquee tool and the Ellipse tool, and the difference between the Rectangular Marquee tool and the Rectangle tool.

To create an image using layers:

1. Click the **File** menu, and then click **New**. The New dialog box opens. In the New dialog box, name the new image **Layers**. Select a Width of **480 pixels** and a Height of **320 pixels**. Select a Mode of **RGB Color** and select **Transparent** for the Contents. Ignore the other options, and click **OK**. A new window appears containing only transparent pixels.

2. Set the Foreground Color to **red**. Select the **Pencil** tool. In the Options bar, select a brush with a Diameter of **9**. Draw a triangle in the center of the image window.

3. If you do not see the Layers palette, click the **Window** menu and then click **Layers**. The Layers palette appears. Click the **New Layer** icon at the bottom of the Layers palette. A new layer appears in the Layers palette.

4. Set the Foreground Color to **green**. On top of your triangle, draw a circle. The circle appears above the triangle.

5. Click the pointer on the top layer in the Layers palette, named "Layer 2", and drag it below Layer 1. The triangle now appears above the circle.

6. Select the **Eraser** tool from the Toolbox. Select **Layer 1** in the Layers palette.

7. Drag the pointer over the parts of the triangle that cover the circle. The red line disappears, but the green line remains.

8. Select the **Polygon** tool from the Toolbox (in the Rectangle tool's submenu). In the Options bar, set the number of Sides to **3**. Open the Styles palette. Click the **Default Style (None)** style in the upper left of the Style picker (white square with a diagonal red line through it). Set the Foreground Color to **red**. Click in the center of the triangle and drag outward to create a new triangle that matches the old one. A new layer automatically appears in the Layers palette.

9. Select **Layer 1** in the Layers palette. Select the **Ellipse** tool from the Toolbox (in the Rectangle tool's submenu). In the Styles palette click the **Chiseled Sky (Text)** style. Click in the center of the circle you drew and drag

outward to create a new circle that matches the old one. A new stylized circle appears behind the triangle.

10. In the Layers palette, find the Visibility icons to the left of each layer, which look like eyes. Click the **Visibility** icons for Layers 1 and 2. The triangle and circle you drew are now invisible.

11. Click the **Layer** menu, and then click **Flatten Image**. A confirmation box appears. Click **OK**. The layers in the Layers palette merge into one layer, and the transparent background becomes white. The image should resemble the one shown in Figure 5-7.

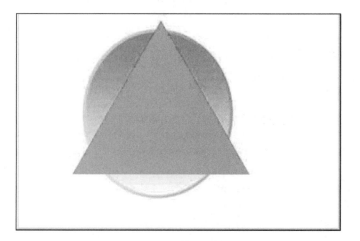

Figure 5-7   Image created with layers

12. Click the **File** menu, and then click **Save As**. The Save As dialog box appears. Select the **Chapter** folder for Chapter 5, and name the image **Ch05Photoshop03.jpg**. Under Format, select **JPEG**. Click **Save**. The JPEG dialog box appears. Set the Quality to **1** and click **OK**.

13. Close the image without saving again.

Using Text

The Type tools in Photoshop are similar to the Shape tools you just used. Both are vector-based, which means type and shapes automatically appear in their own layers. Type can also contain styles independently of other elements in the image. Text in Web graphics often suffers from **aliasing**, which is an effect that causes the edges of the text to appear jagged. Normally you will want to use **anti-aliasing**, a technique that blurs the edges of the text slightly in order to create the appearance of a smooth edge.

To create an image using text:

1. Click the **File** menu, and then click **New**. The New dialog box opens. In the New dialog box, name the new image, **Banner**. Click the **Preset Sizes** menu

and select **468 x 60 web banner**. Select a Mode of **RGB Color** and select **White** for the Contents. Click **OK**. A new image window appears.

2. Set the Foreground Color to **red** and the Background Color to **black**.

3. Select the **Gradient** tool. In the Options bar, click the **Radial Gradient** icon. Drag the pointer from the center of the image to the right side. A gradient appears in the image window that is red in the center and black on the edge.

4. Set the Foreground Color to **white**. Select the **Horizontal Type** tool from the Toolbox. In the Options bar, set the font family to **Times New Roman** or any similar serif font you have installed. Set the font size to **36 px** and set the anti-aliasing method to **Smooth**.

5. Click the pointer in the center of the image. A cursor appears. Type **Welcome to My Web Site!** The text appears as you type it.

6. Select the **Move** tool from the Toolbox. Center the text by dragging it in the image window.

7. Select the **Horizontal Type** tool again. In the Options bar, click the **Create Warped Text** icon. The Warp Text dialog box appears. Select **Flag** as the Style, and use the default settings. Click **OK**.

8. Click the **Layer** menu, point to **Layer Style**, and then click **Drop Shadow**. The Layer Style dialog box appears. Use the default settings, and click **OK**. The text appears to have a faint shadow below and to the right. Notice how the type layer in the Layers palette includes style information.

9. Click the **Layer** menu, and then click **Flatten Image**. Your image should look similar to the one shown in Figure 5-8.

Figure 5-8   Image created with text

10. Click the **File** menu, and then click **Save As**. The Save As dialog box appears. Select the **Chapter** folder for Chapter 5, and name the image **Ch05Photoshop04.gif**. Under Format, select **CompuServe GIF**. Click **Save**. The Indexed Color dialog box appears. Set the Palette setting to **Local (Selective)**. Set the number of Colors to **32** and change the Dither setting to **Pattern**. Click **OK**. The GIF Options dialog box appears. Select **Normal** and click **OK**.

11. Close the image, and do not save.

EDITING IMAGES

Now that you understand the basics of creating images, you are ready to learn how to work with images that you have created and images from other sources. Although you create graphics such as buttons and icons from scratch, photographic images must be scanned or acquired with a digital camera. In this section, you will gain practice with the tools and techniques used to fix problems with scans. You will also learn how to retouch digitized photographs.

Navigating Images

Before you begin manipulating images, you need to be able to find your way around them. One of the tools you will use most often is the **Zoom** tool (also called the Magnifying Glass tool), which lets you increase or decrease the scale of the image window. Photoshop also allows you to change the scale in other ways.

To practice changing the scale in an image:

1. Open the banner image you created in the previous exercise. Notice how the Title bar in the image window displays the name of the file as well as the current magnification, 100%.

2. Select the **Zoom** tool, and click anywhere in the image. The scale doubles, and the Title bar displays the new size, 200%.

3. Double-click the **Zoom** tool icon in the Toolbox. The scale reverts back to 100%.

4. Drag the pointer across a small part of the image. The scale increases so that the area you selected fills the image window.

5. In the lower-left corner of the Photoshop window is a text box that contains the current scale. Type **150** in this box, and then press **Enter**. The scale changes to 150%.

 If you are working on a Macintosh, keep in mind that any time this text asks you to press the Enter key, you should press the Return key instead.

6. While pressing the **Alt** key, click the pointer in the center of the image. The scale decreases to 100%.

7. If you do not see the Navigator palette, click the **Window** menu, and then click **Navigator**. The Navigator palette becomes visible. The Navigator palette includes a thumbnail version of the image, a text box containing the scale, and a slider bar.

8. Drag the slider bar to the right. The scale increases, the image becomes magnified, and a red box around the thumbnail image becomes smaller, indicating which part of the image is visible.

9. Select the **Hand** tool from the Toolbox. Click and drag the pointer across the image. As you drag, the image moves accordingly, and the red box in the Navigator palette changes to reflect the new view.

10. Close the image.

Changing Dimensions

Changing the scale of an image means altering the height and width of how the image is displayed in Photoshop. Changing the scale does not affect the image file and does not affect how the image appears in a browser. Changing the dimensions means changing the actual height and width of an image. In Photoshop, the term **canvas** refers to the dimensions of an image. An image's canvas size is the height and width, in pixels, of the image.

In Photoshop, you alter the image dimensions with the Image Size and Canvas Size menu tools. Image Size lets you stretch or shrink the image; Canvas Size lets you pad or crop the image. **Padding** means adding empty space to the edge of an image in order to make it bigger; **cropping** means removing part of the image in order to make it smaller. Photoshop also includes the Crop tool in the Toolbox and the Trim command under the Image menu.

Practice changing the dimensions of an image:

1. If the banner image is not still open, open it now.

2. Click the **Image** menu, and then click **Image Size**. The Image Size dialog box opens.

3. If the **Constrain Proportions** check box is not selected, check it now. Notice the chain-link icon next to the values in the Image Size dialog box.

4. Type a new Height of **30 pixels**. The Width value automatically changes to match the new height.

5. Uncheck the **Constrain Proportions** check box. Type a new Height of **120 pixels**. Click **OK**. The image is now half as wide and twice as high as it was.

6. Select **white** as the Background Color.

7. Click the **Image** menu, and then click **Canvas Size**. The Canvas Size dialog box opens.

8. Set the Width to **177 pixels** and the Height to **177 pixels**. At the bottom of the dialog box, you see several arrows radiating from a central square. This indicates the anchor, the point from which your changes will pad or crop the image. Set the anchor by clicking the Anchor arrow in the upper-left corner

of the Anchor area in the Canvas Size dialog box. Click **OK**. A warning box appears, asking you to confirm. Click **Proceed**. The image is cropped on the right side and padded on the bottom.

9. Click the **Image** menu, and then click **Trim**. The Trim dialog box appears. Select **Bottom Right Pixel Color** and check all the options under Trim Away. Click **OK**. The image is cropped, trimming away the black area below the image.

10. Select the **Crop** tool from the Toolbox. In the Options bar, set the Width to **300 pixels** and the Height to **400 pixels**. Drag the pointer across the center of the image. Drag the selection area with the pointer to center the selection. Click the **Checkmark** icon in the Options bar to commit the crop operation. The image is cropped based on your selection, and it is automatically resized to the dimensions of 300 by 400 pixels.

11. Close the image.

Fixing Low-Contrast Scans

You are now ready to edit actual digitized photographs in order to prepare them for display on the Web. Often you will find that scanned images have low contrast. That is, the white areas are not truly white, and the black areas are not truly black. Figure 5-9 shows an image with low, normal, and high contrast.

Figure 5-9 Image with different contrast levels

You can solve this problem in Photoshop by using the **Brightness/Contrast** option and the **Levels** option.

To fix a scanned image with low contrast:

1. Click the **File** menu, and then click **Open**. Select the Chapter folder for Chapter 5 and open the file named **Ch05Photoshop05.tif**.

2. Click the **Image** menu, point to **Adjustments**, and then click **Brightness/Contrast**. The Brightness/Contrast dialog box opens.

3. Slide the Contrast slider to the right until the value reads **+85**. Click **OK**. The image now has full contrast.

4. Click the **Edit** menu, and then click **Undo Brightness/Contrast** (to start over).

5. Click the **Image** menu, point to **Adjustments**, and then click **Levels**. The Levels dialog box opens. Notice the graph in the dialog box.

6. Click the **Auto** button and then click **OK**. The levels automatically adjust to optimize the contrast. The image should look like the one shown in Figure 5-10.

Figure 5-10   Image with fixed contrast

7. Click the **File** menu, and then click **Save As**. The Save As dialog box appears. Select the Chapter folder for Chapter 5 and name the image **Ch05Photoshop05SOL.jpg**. Under Format, select **JPEG**. The JPEG dialog box appears. Set the Quality to **6** and click **OK**.

8. Close the image.

Fixing Problem Colors

In addition to the problem of low contrast, scanned images may have colors that do not appear as bright as in the source image. This is a common problem when the source is printed on low-quality paper. You can improve poor color in Photoshop with the **Hue/Saturation** feature.

To fix a scanned image with muddy colors:

1. Click the **File** menu, and then click **Open**. Select the **Chapter** folder for Chapter 5 and open the file named **Ch05Photoshop06.tif**. An image opens with no saturated colors.

2. Click the **Image** menu, point to **Adjustments**, and then click **Hue/Saturation**. The Hue/Saturation dialog box opens.

3. Move the Saturation slider all the way to the left. The colors become completely unsaturated, resulting in a black-and-white image. Move the slider all the way to the right. The colors become oversaturated. Now move the slider so that the Saturation value reads **+75**.

4. Move the Hue slider so that the Hue value reads **+10**. All colors in the image shift slightly, so that reds become more orange, yellows more green, and blues more purple.

5. Move the Lightness slider so that the Lightness value reads **+15**. The image is now slightly lighter.

6. Click **OK**. The image should look like the one shown in Figure 5-11.

Figure 5-11   Scanned image with optimized contrast

7. Click the **File** menu, and then click **Save As**. The Save As dialog box appears. Select the **Chapter** folder for Chapter 5 and name the image **Ch05Photoshop06SOL.jpg**. Under Format, select **JPEG**. The JPEG dialog box appears. Set the Quality to **5** and click **OK**.

8. Close the image.

Retouching with the Brush Tool

Adjusting the brightness, levels, and saturation of an image works well when the entire image has a uniform problem. Sometimes, however, only a certain part of the image needs fixing. Figure 5-12 shows an image with a few blemishes that are probably the result of dust on the image when the photograph was scanned. An easy way to fix small specks like those seen here is with the airbrush capabilities of the Brush tool. Using the normal Brush tool would leave hard edges where you make your edit. The **airbrush capabilities** leaves a smoother line.

Figure 5-12   Image with blemishes

When using the Brush tool, it is necessary to paint with the color that is already in the image. To find this color, select the Eyedropper tool and click the pointer over a pixel in the image. The foreground color will change to the color of that pixel.

To fix a scanned image with small blemishes:

1. Click the **File** menu, and then click **Open**. Select the **Chapter** folder for Chapter 5 and open the file named **Ch05Photoshop07.tif**.

2. Use the **Zoom** tool to magnify the area around the two black specks in the upper-left part of the image.

3. Select the **Eyedropper** tool from the Toolbox. In the Options bar, set the Sample Size to **3 by 3 Average**. Click the pointer near one of the specks. The foreground color changes to a color that is an average of the pixels surrounding the pixel you selected.

4. Select the **Brush** tool. In the Options bar, select a brush with a diameter of **5**. Set the Mode to **Normal**, and the Opacity and Flow to **100%**. Click the pointer over one of the specks. If the color matches, you should see a smooth transition of color. If necessary, undo the operation and try again. You may need to select a new color with the Eyedropper tool.

5. When you are satisfied, remove the second speck in the same way. Your image should resemble the one shown in Figure 5-13.

Figure 5-13   Image with blemishes removed

6. Click the **File** menu, and then click **Save As**. The Save As dialog box appears. Select the **Chapter** folder for Chapter 5 and name the image **Ch05Photoshop07SOL.jpg**. Under Format, select **JPEG**. The JPEG dialog box appears. Set the Quality to **6** and click **OK**.

7. Close the image.

Retouching with the Dust & Scratches Filter

The Dust & Scratches filter is explicitly designed to remove minor blemishes from photographs caused by dust on the camera lens or scanner bed or from scratches in the original photo. This filter works by finding adjacent pixels that are different colors and blurring them.

When using some filters, you will want to apply them to a selected area, rather than to the full image. If you find it awkward to make the selection by using the Elliptical or Rectangular Marquee tools, you can use another type of selection tool, called the **Lasso** tool, which allows you to create a selection area of any shape.

To use the Dust & Scratches filter:

1. Open **Ch05Photoshop08.tif** from the Chapter folder for Chapter 5. You should see a white scratch on the side of the lion.

2. Use the **Zoom** tool to magnify the area.

3. Select the **Lasso** tool from the Toolbox and drag the pointer around the scratch to create a selection marquee.

4. Click the **Filter** menu, point to **Noise**, and then click **Dust & Scratches**. The Dust & Scratches dialog box opens.

5. Set the Radius to **3** pixels and the Threshold to **12** levels. Click **OK**. The scratch disappears. Click the pointer anywhere in the image to make the marquee disappear. The image should resemble the one shown in Figure 5-14.

Figure 5-14   Image with scratch removed

6. Save the image in the Chapter folder for Chapter 5 as a JPEG file with the name **Ch05Photoshop08SOL.jpg**. Use a Quality setting of **6**.

7. Close the image.

Blurring Images

If you do not need to remove particular elements from an image, but only want to de-emphasize the background, you can selectively blur those areas of the image. Blurring reduces color contrast, lightness contrast, and texture contrast by blending adjacent pixels.

If the area you need to select is too irregular for the Lasso tool, you can use the **Magic Wand** tool, which creates a selection area of all pixels that are similar to the color of the selected pixel. Like the Paint Bucket tool, the Magic Wand tool includes a Tolerance setting in the Options bar. Both tools also include a **Contiguous** option. When checked, this option ensures that only similar pixels (which are adjacent to the one you click) are affected.

To de-emphasize the background of an image:

1. Open the file named **Ch05Photoshop09.tif** from the Chapter folder for Chapter 5.

2. Select the **Magic Wand** tool from the Toolbox. In the Options bar, set the Tolerance to **32** and select **Anti-Aliased**. Make sure the Contiguous check box is unchecked. Click the pointer on one of the darker stripes on the blue fabric behind the watch. An irregular selection area appears, containing most of the background and small areas of the foreground.

3. Click the **Filter** menu, point to **Blur**, and then click **Gaussian Blur**. The Gaussian Blur dialog box opens.

4. Set the Radius to **5 pixels** and click **OK**. The background is blurred, and now we need to darken it.

5. With the selection marquee still active, click the Image menu, point to Adjustments, and click Levels. The **Levels** dialog box opens. Set the second Output Level to **200**. Click **OK**. The background is darker. Click the pointer anywhere in the image to turn off the marquee. The image should resemble the one shown in Figure 5-15.

6. Save the image in the Chapter folder for Chapter 5 as a JPEG file with the name **Ch05Photoshop09SOL.jpg**. Use a Quality setting of **6**.

7. Close the image.

Figure 5-15   Image with blurred background

Using Saturation

In addition to blurring the background to de-emphasize it, you can lower its color saturation with the Hue/Saturation dialog box. Adjusting the color saturation of the background can emphasize the foreground and enhance the presentation of the subject. Using the **Sponge** tool has the same effect, but it is more appropriate for making local changes to specific pixels.

To use the Sponge tool:

1. Open the file named **Ch05Photoshop10.tif** from the Chapter folder for Chapter 5. Notice the bright blue and red objects in the background.

2. Select the **Sponge** tool from the Toolbox (in the Dodge tool's submenu). In the Options bar, select a brush with a diameter of **45**. Set the Mode to **Desaturate** and set the Flow to **100%**.

3. Drag the pointer across the bright objects in the background. The background colors become less saturated. The image should look like the one seen in Figure 5-16.

Figure 5-16   Image with desaturated background

4. Save the image in the Chapter folder for Chapter 5 as a JPEG file with the name **Ch05Photoshop10SOL.jpg**. Use a Quality setting of **6**.

5. Close the image.

Replacing Unwanted Elements

Replacing unwanted parts of a photo is one of the most enjoyable aspects of editing images. As you explore the possibilities of this technique, you will realize that photographs can no longer be trusted to be true reproductions of reality. The Clone Stamp tool (also called the *Rubber Stamp tool*) allows you to duplicate specific parts of an image. When you use this tool, you need to specify the brush size, which controls the diameter, in pixels, of the line created when using this tool.

To use the Clone Stamp tool:

1. Open the file named **Ch05Photoshop11.tif** from the Chapter folder for Chapter 5. Notice the yellow date stamp in the lower-right corner, which says '**94 10 12**. (Depending on your monitor, the full date may be hard to read.)

2. Select the **Clone Stamp** tool from the Toolbox. In the Options bar, select a brush of size **35** and then click the **Options** bar to close the Brush picker. Set the Mode to **Normal** and set the Opacity and Flow to **100%**. Select the **Aligned** check box.

3. While pressing the **Alt** key (the Option key on a Macintosh), click the pointer over the cluster of apples in the lower-left corner. This sets the origin point, which sets the source from which you will copy in the next step.

4. Release the **Alt** key and drag the pointer over the date stamp in the lower-right part of the photograph. The area of the picture that you selected as the origin point is copied over the date. The image should look like the one shown in Figure 5-17.

Figure 5-17 Image with unwanted elements removed

5. Save the image in the Chapter folder for Chapter 5 as a JPEG file with the name **Ch05Photoshop11SOL.jpg**. Use a Quality setting of **6**.

6. Close the image.

SAVING AND OPTIMIZING IMAGES

When creating pages for the Internet, you need to factor in the importance of how quickly the pages will load on the user's computer. It is crucial that your pages load quickly. This requires making the file sizes for all the components of a Web page (HTML files, image files, Java applets, Flash movies, and so forth) as small as possible. To make images download quickly on the Web, you must **optimize** them, which means reducing their file size while maintaining the image quality.

You can optimize images by using one of two methods: color reduction or compression. **Color reduction** is appropriate for simple images that contain few colors, such as line graphs. **Compression** is more appropriate for complex images that contain many colors, such as photographs.

Among all the available file formats for bitmap images, only three can be displayed as part of a Web page: GIF, JPEG, and PNG. GIF images can contain a maximum of 256 colors and are optimized through color reduction. GIF images can contain transparent pixels that allow background colors to show through. GIF images also can be animated, as explained in Chapter 6. JPEG images can contain over 16 million colors and are optimized through compression. JPEG images cannot contain transparent pixels and cannot be animated. PNG is a relatively new format that allows both kinds of optimization and can contain transparency. Unfortunately, only the newest browsers are able to display PNG images, so this format is rarely used.

Optimizing GIF Files

When you saved your GIF images in the previous exercises, you used the Save As command, which opened the Indexed Color dialog box. There you were given choices about how to reduce the number of colors in the image. Photoshop includes another command for saving and optimizing images, the Save for Web command. This command gives you more control over the optimization process and allows you to preview your changes. When preparing images for the Web, always use the Save for Web command.

 Remember the difference between the Save As command and the Save for Web command. Only the latter allows you to fully control the optimization of the image.

You optimize GIF images by reducing the number of colors. The maximum number of colors in a GIF image is 256. If you reduce the number of colors by half, to 128, the size of the file will reduce by about half, as well.

Sometimes, reducing the number of colors in an image causes **banding**, an effect in which smooth gradations of colors turn into stripes. One way to fix banded colors is to use **dithering**, which is the technique of adding pixels to an image to break up the boundaries between different colors. Figure 5-18 shows an image at full color, with banded colors, and with dithering.

Figure 5-18   Banded and dithered colors

To optimize a GIF image using color reduction and dithering:

1. Open the file named **Ch05Photoshop12.tif** from the Chapter folder for Chapter 5.

2. Click the **File** menu, and then click **Save for Web**. The Save For Web dialog box appears.

3. Click the **4-Up** tab. The window displays the original image along with three optimized versions. Below each version of the image are the relevant file sizes, modem transfer rates, and optimization settings.

4. A black outline appears around the image in the upper right, as shown in Figure 5-19.

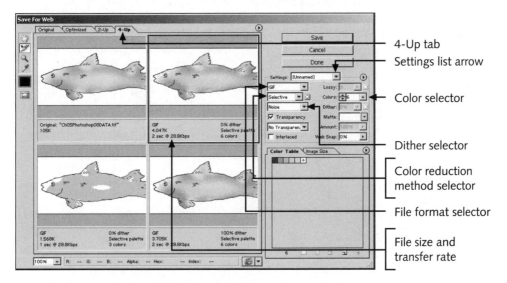

Figure 5-19   Save for Web dialog box

5. Click the **Settings** list arrow, and then select **GIF 32 No Dither**. The file size and transfer rate decrease, and the image shows noticeable color bands. All the colors used in the image are shown in the color table to the right.

6. Click the image in the lower left. A black outline appears around it.

7. In the Settings list, select **GIF 64 No Dither**. The file size and transfer rate increase, and the image shows less noticeable color bands.

8. Click the image in the lower right. A black outline appears around it.

9. In the Settings list, select **GIF 128 No Dither**. Compare the image quality and file sizes of the three optimized versions of the image.

10. Click the image in the upper right again. Click the dither setting list arrow (above the word "Transparency") and select **Noise**. The bands of colors disappear, but the file size increases.

11. In the **Colors** box, click the **Down** arrow to decrease the numeric setting. (Be sure to click the Down arrow, and not the List arrow, which opens a menu of numeric settings.) The number of colors decreases from **32** to **31** and the file size is reduced slightly.

12. Click the arrow several more times until the number of colors used is **6** and watch the image quality change. Reducing the number of colors causes more dithering in the image, resulting in a speckled pattern. Click the **Up** arrow in the **Colors** box several times, and stop when the file size is around **6.5K**. Your screen should resemble the one shown in Figure 5-20.

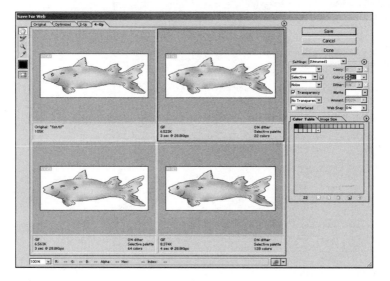

Figure 5-20   Save for Web dialog box with GIF optimization settings

13. Click the **Save** button, and save the image in the Chapter folder for Chapter 5 as **Ch05Photoshop12SOL.gif**.

14. Close the image.

Normally, Web graphics take a few seconds to download from the Web server, and only when the complete file has been loaded does it appear in the Web page. When a GIF is saved with interlaced rows, an incomplete version of the image appears before the complete image has loaded, and the rest of the image appears when the download is complete. To interlace a GIF image, select Interlaced in the Save For Web dialog box.

You can choose which method (Perceptual, Selective, Adaptive, or Web) to use when reducing the colors of an image. The default Color Reduction setting is Selective, and that usually produces the best result. Another option is Web, which favors **Web-safe** colors.

It is not necessary to use Web-safe colors, however, and doing so usually results in lower-quality images.

Similarly, you can optimize GIF images by specifying a certain percentage of **Web Snap**, which controls how many Web-safe colors to use in the image. It is a good idea to leave this setting at 0%, because using a higher setting will result in low-quality images.

It is not necessary to use Web-safe colors when optimizing images.

5

Optimizing JPEG Files

You can also optimize JPEG images in the Save For Web dialog box. The menu options on the right side of the box are different for JPEG images. Compressing a JPEG image is simple. A high Quality setting results in a large image file with no noticeable degradation of the image. A low Quality setting results in a smaller image file that may contain **artifacts**, or areas of texture that are side effects of the compression.

Figure 5-21 shows the possible results of JPEG compression on an image.

Figure 5-21   JPEG compression artifacts

The challenge with JPEG compression is to use as low of a Quality setting as possible while minimizing the artifacts.

Photoshop allows you to blur the image slightly in order to reduce the appearance of artifacts. The effect of blurring an image is often worse than the artifacts themselves, so use this technique sparingly.

Another option when compressing images is to make the image **progressive**, a setting that causes the image to download in stages rather than all at once. A progressive JPEG image is similar to an interlaced GIF image.

To optimize a JPEG image using compression:

1. Open the file named **Ch05Photoshop12.tif** from the Chapter folder for Chapter 5.

2. Click the **File** menu, and then click **Save for Web**. The Save For Web dialog box appears. Click the **4-Up** tab.

3. Click the image in the upper right. From the Settings list, select **JPEG Low**. The file size and transfer rate decrease, and the image shows noticeable artifacts.

4. Click the image in the lower left. From the Settings menu, select **JPEG Medium**. The file size and transfer rate also decrease, and the image shows less noticeable artifacts.

5. Click the image in the lower right. In the Settings list, select **JPEG High**. Compare the image quality and file sizes of the three optimized versions of the image.

6. Click the image in the lower left again. Set the Quality to **27** and the Blur to **0.25**. The file size is low, and the appearance of artifacts is minimized. Your screen should resemble the one shown in Figure 5-22.

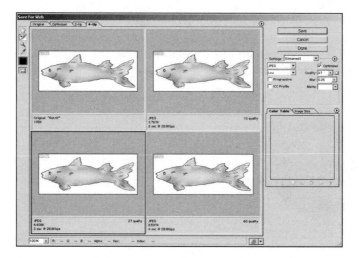

Figure 5-22   Save for Web dialog box with JPEG optimization settings

7. Click the **Save** button, and save the image in the Chapter folder for Chapter 5 as **Ch05Photoshop13.jpg**.

8. Close the image.

Optimizing by File Size

Often Web pages are designed with a fixed total "page weight." For example, in order to make sure the Web page downloads a few seconds or less, you may decide that all the elements of a page must have a combined file size of less than 60KB. If the HTML file itself has a size of 30KB, that leaves another 30KB for all the graphics on the page. It is then convenient to optimize an image based on a fixed file size, rather than just looking at the maximum optimization that does not compromise image quality.

Here you can set certain parameters, and the software finds the best optimization settings for you. First select a target file size for the optimized image in the Desired File Size text field. You will have a good sense of what a reasonable size is after you have optimized several images of different sizes. The target size should depend on the dimensions of the image and the number of colors in it. A small image of 50 by 50 pixels with just a few colors can be optimized to less than 1KB. A 200 by 200 pixel photograph, however, may require at least 20KB. Start with a low number, such as 2KB, and see how the optimization affects the image. If the image quality deteriorates too much, try a larger target size.

To optimize an image by file size:

1. Open the file named **Ch05Photoshop12.tif** from the Chapter folder for Chapter 5.

2. Click the **File** menu, and then click **Save for Web**. The Save For Web dialog box appears. Click the **4-Up** tab.

3. Click the image in the upper right. Click the **Optimize Menu** arrow (the black, right-facing arrow button to the right of the Settings box), and then click **Optimize to File Size**. The Optimize to File Size dialog box appears.

4. Change the Desired File Size to **5K** and select **Auto Select GIF/JPEG**. Click **OK**. The software automatically sets the image to an 11-color GIF image with Diffusion dithering.

5. Click the image in the lower left. Optimize this version by file size, but use a target size of **4K**. The image has noticeable banding and dithering.

6. Select the image in the lower right. Set the format to **JPEG**. Open the **Optimize to File Size** dialog box. Change the Desired File Size to **5K** and select **Current Settings**. Click **OK**. The image is compressed and shows noticeable artifacts.

7. Select the image in the upper right. It should look like the one shown in Figure 5-23. Click the **Save** button, and save the image in the Chapter folder for Chapter 5 as **Ch05Photoshop14.gif**.

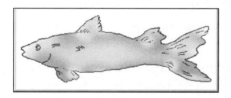

Figure 5-23   Image optimized by file size

8. Close the image.

CHAPTER SUMMARY

- The Toolbox contains all the tools you need to select, draw, and manipulate the image with your mouse.

- Changing the settings in the Options bar can modify the effects of each tool.

- Use filters to change an entire image or the area inside a selection area.

- Layers are like sheets of clear plastic. You can change the elements inside one layer without affecting those in another.

- Text is based on vectors, which means you can edit the text without affecting the rest of the image.

- Use the Zoom tool to magnify the image.

- Use the Image Size dialog box, the Canvas Size dialog box, and the Crop tool to change the dimensions of an image.

- Use the Levels dialog box to fix low-contrast scans.

- Use the Hue/Saturation dialog box to fix problem colors.

- Retouch minor problems with the airbrush capabilities of the Brush tool.

- Repair nicks and specks in an image with the Dust & Scratches filter.

- De-emphasize the backgrounds of images by blurring, darkening, and desaturating them.

- You can smoothly replace areas of an image with the Clone Stamp tool.

- It is crucial to optimize images so that they download quickly.

- In Photoshop, save and optimize images with the Save for Web command.

- Images with few colors, such as graphs, are best saved as GIF images. Images with many colors, such as photographs, are best saved as JPEG images.

- GIF images are optimized through color reduction; JPEG images are optimized through compression.

- Optimizing a GIF image too much can result in banding. Dithering the image can reduce the effects of banding.

- Optimizing a JPEG image too much can result in artifacts. Blurring the image can reduce the appearance of artifacts.

- You can optimize an image by selecting a target file size and letting Photoshop find the best settings.

REVIEW QUESTIONS

1. Which tool would you use to create a selection marquee of any shape?

   a. Lasso tool

   b. Magic Wand tool

   c. Polygon tool

   d. Rectangular Marquee tool

2. Which tool would you use to fill a selection area with a solid color?

   a. Brush tool

   b. Gradient tool

   c. Paint Bucket tool

   d. Rectangle tool

3. What is a layer?

   a. a color gradient

   b. a kind of vector shape

   c. another name for a selection area

   d. like a sheet of clear plastic laid over the image

4. What is anti-aliasing?

   a. a technique that blurs the edges of objects in an image

   b. a technique that lets you create warped text effects

   c. a technique that makes text appear with a jagged edge

   d. a technique that prevents dithering

5. Which of the following allow you to magnify the image display?

   a. Crop tool and Zoom tool

   b. Hand tool and Move tool

   c. Image Size dialog box and Canvas Size dialog box

   d. Zoom tool and Navigator palette

6. Which command or tool would you use to pad the edges of an image?

   a. Canvas Size dialog box

   b. Crop tool

   c. Image Size dialog box

   d. Zoom tool

5

7. When would you use the Levels dialog box?
   a. to blur an image
   b. to change the hue in an image
   c. to change lighting or contrast in an image
   d. to remove scratches from an image

8. What is a measure of the amount of a particular color in an image?
   a. brightness
   b. hue
   c. lightness
   d. saturation

9. Which of the following is *not* a reason to blur part of an image?
   a. to de-emphasize it
   b. to desaturate it
   c. to reduce the appearance of compression artifacts
   d. to reduce texture contrast

10. When would you use the Sponge tool?
    a. to blur part of an image
    b. to copy and paste part of an image
    c. to darken part of an image
    d. to desaturate part of an image

11. When would you use the Clone Stamp tool?
    a. to blur part of an image
    b. to copy and paste part of an image
    c. to darken part of an image
    d. to desaturate part of an image

12. Which file format would probably be best to use for displaying photographs on the Web?
    a. GIF
    b. JPEG
    c. PNG
    d. TIFF

13. What is dithering?
    a. a kind of anti-aliasing
    b. the process of adding individual pixels to an image to reduce color-banding
    c. an artifact of JPEG compression
    d. the appearance of stripes in an image as a result of color reduction

14. What would be the best way to optimize a low-color pie chart image?

    a. banding

    b. color reduction

    c. compression

    d. dithering

15. What term is used to describe a GIF image that loads and displays in stages, rather than all at once?

    a. interlaced

    b. progressive

    c. banded

    d. dithered

5

HANDS-ON EXERCISES

Exercise 5-1

In this exercise, you need to crop a photograph. As you complete the following, take care to choose an appropriate format and optimization method.

1. Open the file named **Ch05PhotoshopEX01.tif** from the Exercises folder for Chapter 5.

2. Select the Crop tool, and select an area around the puppet, centering it. Drag the square handles in the corners of the selection box to adjust the size. When satisfied, double-click inside the selection box. The image resizes to match the selection box.

3. Click the Image menu, point to Adjustments, and then click Levels. The Levels dialog box opens.

4. Click the Auto button. Click OK. The contrast in the image adjusts automatically.

5. Click the Image menu, point to Adjustments, and then click Hue/Saturation. The Hue/Saturation dialog box opens.

6. Select Reds from the Edit menu. Set the Saturation to -30 and the Lightness to -60. Click OK. The red colors in the image are darker and less saturated.

7. Select Save for Web from the File menu. The Save For Web dialog box opens.

8. Click the 2-Up tab to compare multiple optimization settings.

9. Select the image view on the right, and select JPEG Low from the Settings menu. The image shows minimal artifacts.

10. Click Save, and save the image as **Ch05PhotoshopEX01SOL.jpg** in the Exercises folder for Chapter 5.

11. Close the image.

Exercise 5-2

In this exercise, you need to crop a photograph. As you complete the following, take care to choose an appropriate format and optimization method.

1. Open the file named **Ch05PhotoshopEX02.tif** from the Exercises folder for Chapter 5.

2. Select the Crop tool, and select an area around the statue, centering it. Do not include the time stamp in the lower-right corner. Drag the square handles in the corners of the selection box to adjust the size. When satisfied, click the Checkmark icon in the Options bar.

3. Click the Image menu, point to Adjustments, and then click Levels. The Levels dialog box opens.

4. Click the Auto button. The contrast in the image preview adjusts automatically. Slide the center gray slider arrow so that the Input Level is around 2 and the statue's facial features are visible. Click OK.

5. Click the Image menu, point to Adjustments, and then click Hue/Saturation. The Hue/Saturation dialog box opens.

6. Set the Saturation to 50 and click OK. The saturation in the image improves.

7. Select the Sponge tool from the Toolbox. In the Options bar, set the brush size to 45 and set the Mode to Desaturate.

8. Drag the pointer over the brightly colored areas in the background. The background is de-emphasized.

9. Select the Dodge tool from the Toolbox. From the Options bar, set the brush size to 45, set the Range to Shadows, and the Exposure to 50%.

10. Drag the pointer over the dark areas on the statue to make the facial features more visible.

11. Select Save for Web from the File menu. The Save For Web dialog box opens.

12. Click the 2-Up tab to compare multiple optimization settings.

13. Select the Image view on the right, and select JPEG Medium from the Settings menu. The image shows minimal artifacts.

14. Click Save, and save the image as **Ch05PhotoshopEX02SOL.jpg** in the Exercises folder for Chapter 5.

15. Close the image.

Exercise 5-3

In this exercise, you need to optimize a photograph. As you complete the following steps, take care to choose an appropriate format and optimization method.

1. Open image file **Ch05PhotoshopEX03.tif** from the Exercises folder for Chapter 5. Select Save for Web from the File menu.

2. Click the 4-Up tab to compare multiple optimization settings.

3. Select the image preview in the upper-right panel, and select the GIF 32 Dithered preset from the Settings menu.

4. Select the image preview in the lower-right panel, and select the JPEG Low preset from the Settings menu.

5. Compare the two optimized versions with each other and with the original image in the upper-left panel. Both optimized versions look roughly the same.

6. Use the Zoom tool to magnify the image previews. You can see artifacts in the JPEG-optimized image. Increase the Quality to 20.

7. Both optimized images have minimal problems, but the JPEG-optimized image is less than half the size of the GIF-optimized one. Save the JPEG-optimized image as **Ch05PhotoshopEX03SOL.jpg** in the Exercises folder for Chapter 5.

8. Close the image.

Exercise 5-4

Diagrams and charts often use very few colors because they are generated from vector programs and have no anti-aliased edges. In this exercise, you will optimize a low-color graph.

1. Open image file **Ch05PhotoshopEX04.tif** from the Exercises folder for Chapter 5. Select the Save for Web command.

2. Select the 4-Up tab at the top of the screen. This will position the original image on the left of the screen and a test optimized versions on the right and below.

3. Set the image preview in the upper-right panel to the GIF 32 Dithered preset.

4. Set the image preview in the lower-left panel to JPEG Low.

5. Compare the two optimized versions. The JPEG version has a larger file size and several artifacts around the black lines in the image.

6. Reduce the colors in the GIF version to 5 colors and note the file size.

7. Reduce the colors to 4 and check the file size again.

8. Disable dithering. This reduces the file size further, but the red color is lost. Increase colors to 5 again.

9. This is a reasonable optimization. Save the file as **Ch05PhotoshopEX04SOL.gif** in the Exercises folder for Chapter 5.

10. Close the image.

Exercise 5-5

Visual texture conceals banding, dithering, and JPEG artifacts. This means that images with a lot of visual texture can usually be optimized more than other images. In this exercise, you will optimize a drawing.

1. Open file named **Ch05PhotoshopEX05.tif** from the Exercises folder for Chapter 5. Use the 4-Up view in the Save For Web dialog box.

2. Set the upper-right panel to GIF 32 Dithered and the lower-left panel to JPEG Low.

3. The JPEG version shows little degradation. Reduce the Quality to 0, the maximum compression. The image still shows no obvious artifacts.

4. The file size of the JPEG-compressed version is about 7.6. Try optimizing the color-reduced version so that the file size is less than that.

5. Reduce the colors of the GIF optimization to 4 colors. The file size is smaller, but the black color of the tree trunk is missing.

6. Increase the colors to 16, and find the dark green or black color in the Color Table palette. Select the color and lock it by clicking on the Lock icon at the bottom of the palette.

7. Reduce colors to 6. The file size is reduced, but not enough, and the image quality is beginning to degrade.

8. Save the JPEG-compressed version as **Ch05PhotoshopEX05SOL.jpg** in the Exercises folder for Chapter 5.

9. Close the image.

WEB DESIGN PROJECTS

Project 5-1

Use the tools and filters you learned about in this chapter to create a banner advertisement. The image should be 468 pixels wide and 60 pixels high and should include text. Optimize and save the image as **Ch05PhotoshopDP01.gif** in the Projects folder for Chapter 5.

Project 5-2

Locate photographs you have taken with a digital camera, or find print photos and ask your instructor or technical support person to help you scan them. Take the digital images and retouch them, following the techniques covered in this chapter. Optimize and save them as **Ch05PhotoshopDP02a.jpg**, **Ch05PhotoshopDP02b.jpg**, and so on, in the Projects folder for Chapter 5.

Project 5-3

Many sites place a large image on the home page as an introductory graphic. These splash screens are often collages of images related to the topic of the site. Create an image that is 480 pixels wide and 320 pixels high. Take the images you optimized in the second design project and combine them in the new image. Blur the edges to make seamless transitions from one to the other. Add text to introduce your name and the name of your Web site. Optimize and save the image as **Ch05PhotoshopDP03.jpg** in the Projects folder for Chapter 5.

6

PHOTOSHOP AND IMAGEREADY: PART II

In this chapter you will:

♦ Animate images
♦ Create rollover effects
♦ Create image maps
♦ Slice images

Now that you understand how to create, edit, and optimize images in Photoshop, you are ready to use ImageReady to create sophisticated images for Web projects. ImageReady has most of the same features as Photoshop, plus a few tools and palettes specifically designed to help you create animations, rollover effects, image maps, and sliced images.

ANIMATING IMAGES

You can create animation for the Web either by creating a Flash movie or by animating GIF images. To learn how to create Flash movies, see Chapters 7 and 8 in this book. In this section, you will learn how to create animated GIF images.

Optimizing and Saving Animations

ImageReady includes an Optimize palette that has the same features as the Save for Web dialog box in Photoshop. Whereas in Photoshop you must wait until you are ready to save before making your optimization settings, in ImageReady you can select these settings at any time.

Keep in mind that, although a GIF animation contains multiple frames that look like different images, a GIF animation is in fact a single file. Each frame in the animation is optimized with the same settings as the others. The settings you select in the Optimize palette will be applied to all frames in the animation.

Animations can be treated like regular images in a Web page, and no special HTML is needed to display them.

ImageReady allows you to save images using the Save As command or using the Save Optimized As command. The Save As command is only used when saving Photoshop-format (PSD) files when you are in the middle of a project. The Save Optimized As command is used when you are finished with an image and need to save it as GIF or JPG. When saving files in any of the exercises in this chapter, always use the Save Optimized As command, and not the Save As command.

Using the Animation Palette

ImageReady includes an Animation palette that is not available in Photoshop. As seen in Figure 6-1, the Animation palette displays individual frames of animation and contains buttons at the bottom that you can use to create and play back animated images.

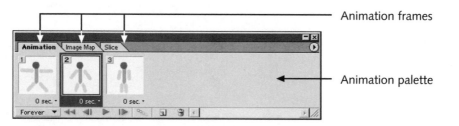

Figure 6-1 The Animation palette in ImageReady

To set the Animation palette and all other palettes to their original positions, click the Window menu, point to Workspace, and then click Reset Palette Locations.

Creating Animations from a Single Layer

The basic element of an animated image is the **frame**. The frames of an animated image all have the same height and width and are displayed one after the other in the same position, just like the frames of film.

The easiest way to create an animated image is by animating a single layer. You can change the position, opacity, and style of a layer from one frame to the next, so that when viewed in succession the layer appears to move.

To create an animation from a single layer:

1. Start **Adobe ImageReady 7.0** from the Start menu. (If you are using Mac OSX, start ImageReady from the Applications folder).

2. Click **File** on the menu bar and then click **New**. The New Document dialog box appears.

3. Name the image **BlinkBall**. Set the width and height to **100** pixels. Under Contents of First Layer, click **Transparent**. Click **OK**. A new image appears.

4. You should see the Animation palette in the lower-left part of your screen and the Layers palette in the lower-right part of your screen. Each palette contains a thumbnail version of the image, as shown in Figure 6-2.

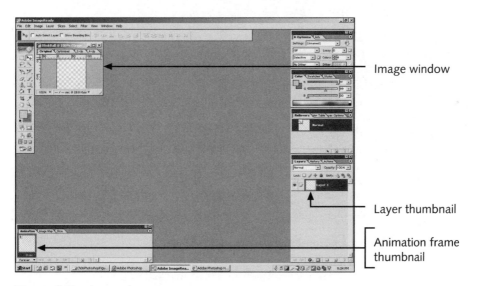

Image window

Layer thumbnail

Animation frame thumbnail

Figure 6-2   A new image

5. In the Color palette, move the **R** slider all the way to the right, the **G** slider to the middle, and the **B** slider all the way to the left. The foreground color in the toolbox should display a bright orange.

6. Select the **Paintbrush** tool. In the Options bar, select a brush of size **35**. Click in the Options bar to close the Brush picker.

7. Click inside the image window, on the left side. An orange circle appears in the image window as well as in the thumbnail versions in the Animation and Layers palettes. The Layers palette shows the contents of the image; the Animation palette shows how the image contents change over time. We only have one frame, so there are no changes yet. Next, you will add a second frame in the Animation palette and change the contents of the image in the Layers palette.

8. Click the **Duplicates current frame** icon in the Animation palette. A second frame appears, identical to the original.

9. Select the **Move** tool in the Toolbox. In the image window, drag the orange disc to the right side of the rectangle. In the Animation palette, the first frame shows the orange ball on the left, and the second frame shows it on the right.

10. Click the **Plays/stops animation** button in the Animation palette. The two frames appear in quick alternation. Click the button again to stop the animation. Your screen should look like that shown in Figure 6-3.

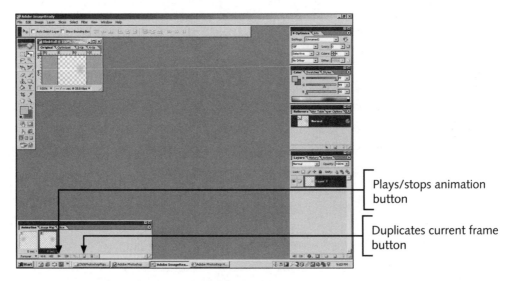

Figure 6-3   A single-layer animation

11. Select appropriate settings in the Optimize palette.

12. Click **File** on the menu bar and then click **Save Optimized As**. Save the image as **Ch06Photoshop01** in the Chapter folder for Chapter 6.

Remember, when saving files, be sure to always use the Save Optimized As command, and not the Save As command.

Tweening

When changing the position, style, or opacity of a layer across multiple frames, you may wish to use tweening as a way to ensure precision and to save time. **Tweening** is a technique in which you decide how the first and last frames of an animation should look, and then allow the software (in this case ImageReady) to create (or *tween*) all the frames in between. The **Tweens animation frames** button is in the Animation palette, as shown in Figure 6-4.

Figure 6-4   The Tweens animation frames button

To create an animation using tweening:

1. Open the file named **Ch06Photoshop02** from the Chapter folder for Chapter 6. Click **File**, click **Save Optimized As**, and then save the file as **Ch06Photoshop02SOL** in the same folder. This file contains an animation with one layer and two frames. Your job is to create a smooth transition between the first and second frame.

2. Click the first frame in the Animation palette. It becomes highlighted to indicate that it is selected.

3. Click the **Tweens animation frames** button. The Tween dialog box appears. Here you can specify which frames to use as your beginning and ending frames via the Tween With list box. This frame currently only contains two frames, so the value of the Tween With setting does not matter here. You can also specify how many frames you want to add between the two existing frames.

4. In the Tween With list box, select **Next Frame**. In the Frames to Add box, select **1** frame. Verify that the **All Layers** option button and the **Position** check box are selected. Click **OK**. A new frame is added to the Animation palette, showing the green disc positioned exactly between the locations in the other two frames.

5. Click the **Plays/stops animation** button in the Animation palette. Verify that the green disc moves up and down as the animation loops. Click the button again to stop the animation.

6. Save your work and close the file.

Creating Animations from Multiple Layers

You can animate the position and opacity of single layers, but to animate other attributes, such as painting, rotation, and text, you need to create multiple layers. Imagine a slide projector displaying the image of a green ball against a screen. By moving the slide projector, you can create the illusion of animation. That is what you did in the previous example. To create more complex animations, however, you might use additional slide projectors, each displaying different images against the screen. In ImageReady, we need to use multiple layers, each containing different images.

Each frame can show the contents of one or more layers, and much of the work in creating animations in ImageReady is deciding which layers to make visible in each frame. As shown in Figure 6-5, the Layers palette contains two layers. To the left of each layer in the palette is a small picture of an eye, called a *visibility icon*. These indicate which layers are visible and which are hidden. In the Animation palette, the second frame is selected. This means that when the animation is played and reaches the second frame, the layer named Welcome! will display, but the layer named Layer 1 will not.

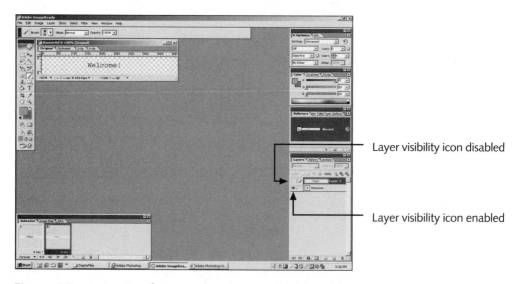

Layer visibility icon disabled

Layer visibility icon enabled

Figure 6-5 Animation frame with only some layers visible

To create an animation from multiple layers:

1. In ImageReady, click **File** on the menu bar and then click **New**. The New Document dialog box appears.

2. Name the image **BannerAd**. Set the Size to **Web Banner (468 × 60)**. Set the Contents of First Layer to **Transparent** and then click **OK**. A new image appears.

3. Save the file as **Ch06Photoshop03** in the Chapter folder for Chapter 6.

4. Use the **Type** tool to write "**Welcome!**" in **24**-pixel, **black**, **Courier** text.

5. Create a new layer in the Layers palette.

6. Select the **Paintbrush** tool. Set the **Foreground Color** to **red**.

7. Drag the pointer over the text to completely cover it with red, as shown in Figure 6-6.

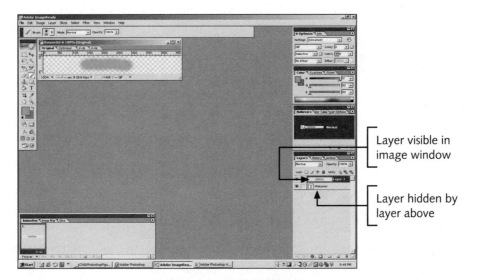

Layer visible in image window

Layer hidden by layer above

Figure 6-6   Text hidden by red paint in new layer

8. Click the **Duplicates current frame** icon in the Animation palette. A new, duplicate frame appears.

9. Click the visibility icon for **Layer 1** in the Layers palette. The layer containing the red paint is now hidden. You see only the image text.

10. Click the **Plays/stops animation** button in the Animation palette. The red stripe blinks quickly, revealing the text beneath.

11. Click the **Plays/stops animation** button in the Animation frame.

12. Select appropriate settings from the Optimize palette.

13. Save your work and close the file.

Creating Animation from Files

In addition to using layers to create animations, you can import multiple files, each of which will become a separate frame of the animation.

To make the thumbnail images in the Layers palette easier to see, click the palette options arrow in the upper-right corner of the palette, click Palette Options, click the largest Thumbnail Size preview, and then click OK.

To create an animation from files:

1. Click the **File** menu, click **Import**, and then click **Folder as Frames**. A dialog box appears where you can select a folder. Within the Chapter folder for Chapter 6, select the subfolder named **Ch06Photoshop03** and then click **OK**. A new image window appears, showing a stick figure with a circular red head. The Layers palette now contains three layers, one for each image in the folder. The Animation palette now contains three frames, one for each layer. When the animation plays each frame, the layer visible in that frame will appear.

2. Click **File** on the menu bar and then click **Save Optimized As**. Save the image as **Ch06Photoshop03SOL** in the Chapter folder for Chapter 6.

3. Click the **Plays/stops animation** button in the Animation palette to preview the animation. The figure's arms and legs move. Click the button again to stop it. To improve the transition from the third frame back to the first, you can add a fourth frame showing the arms held horizontally.

4. Select the second frame, and then click the **Duplicates current frame** button on the Animation palette. The second frame, which shows the arms held horizontally, is duplicated. The Animation palette now contains four frames.

5. Drag the new frame to the right of the right-most frame so that it is the final frame in the animation. Your screen should look like that shown in Figure 6-7.

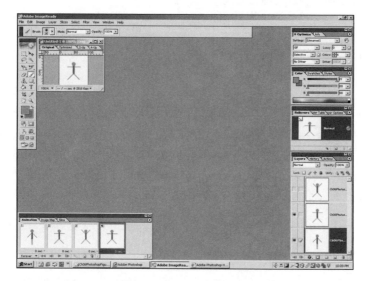

Figure 6-7 Animation created from files

6. Test the animation. The animation now plays smoothly as it loops through the frames.

7. Select appropriate settings from the Optimize palette and save your changes. Close the file.

Although the source files used in this exercise were GIF files, you can use any graphics format as your original images.

Setting the Frame Delay

You have probably noticed that the animations you have seen so far have played back very quickly. You can easily adjust the **frame delay** of each frame to make the animation play more slowly. Unlike film or video, where every frame has the same duration on screen, the frames in a GIF animation can each play for a different amount of time. The default frame delay for animations is zero seconds, which is another way of saying the animation should play back as quickly as the user's computer is able. However, this is usually too fast, and you should select a longer frame delay.

To adjust the frame delay of an animation:

1. Open the .gif file named **Ch06Photoshop04** from the Chapter folder for Chapter 6. An image of a green oval appears in the image window. The four frames of the animation appear in the Layers and Animation palettes.

2. Click the **File** menu and then click **Save Optimized As**. Save the image as **Ch06Photoshop04SOL** in the Chapter folder for Chapter 6. Play the animation and note the speed of playback.

3. For a more realistic preview, click the **Preview in Default Browser** button in the Toolbox. A browser window opens, and the animation plays as it would if it were actually in a Web page. Below the image is the JavaScript and HTML code you would use in the Web page to include this image.

4. Close the browser, return to ImageReady, and note the times listed at the bottom of each frame in ImageReady. Click on the time (**"0 sec"**) of the first frame. The Frame Delay picker appears, as shown in Figure 6-8. Here you can select a different frame delay.

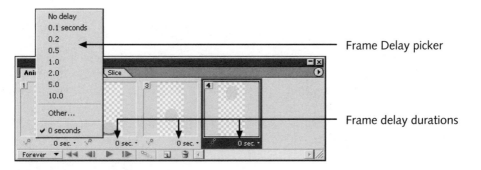

Figure 6-8 Frame Delay picker

5. Click **0.2**. The Frame Delay picker closes.

6. Click the time indicator of the second frame and set the time to **0.1 seconds**.

7. Set the frame delay of the third frame to **0.2**.

8. For the fourth frame, click the time indicator and select **Other**. The Set Frame Delay dialog box appears.

9. Type **0.3** and click **OK**.

10. Preview the animation in the browser again and note the slower playback.

11. Select appropriate settings from the Optimize palette.

12. Save and close the image.

 Always preview your animations in a browser to see them as the user will.

Setting the Loop Count

In addition to controlling the delay of each frame, you can also control how many times the animation **loops**, or plays. When an animation is set to play a finite number of times, it always ends on the last frame. When creating animations that will only loop a finite number of times, make sure that the last frame can act as a stand-alone image.

You set the number of loops in an animation via the Selects looping options menu in the Animation palette.

To adjust the loop count of an animation:

1. Open the file named **Ch06Photoshop05** from the Chapter folder for Chapter 6. An animation with three frames appears.

2. Click the **File** menu and then click **Save Optimized As**. Save the image as **Ch06Photoshop05SOL** in the Chapter folder for Chapter 6.

3. Test the animation to become familiar with how it works.

4. Click the **Selects looping options** list arrow in the lower-left corner of the Animation palette. The current setting, Forever, loops the animation continuously without stopping. The Once setting plays the entire sequence only once.

5. Select **Other**. The Set Loop Count dialog box opens.

6. Type **3** in the Play text box and click **OK**. See Figure 6-9.

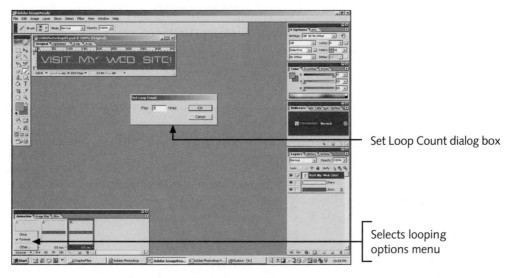

Set Loop Count dialog box

Selects looping
options menu

Figure 6-9   The Selects looping options menu and the Set Loop Count dialog box

7. Play the animation. It should stop on the last frame after looping three times.

8. Select appropriate settings from the Optimize palette.

9. Save and close the image.

CREATING ROLLOVER EFFECTS

By now, you have surely seen rollover effects on the Web, where moving your pointer over an image in a Web page causes the image to change. Although it appears as though a single image changes when the pointer is rolled over it, the effect actually involves multiple images.

Each image used in a rollover effect is called a state. The image that first appears in the Web page is called the Normal state. The other states are described in the following sections.

Rollover effects require JavaScript programming to trigger the switching of images. When you create rollovers in ImageReady, ImageReady creates all the necessary JavaScript coding for you. When you save your rollover images, ImageReady prompts you to save both images and HTML files.

Unlike with animations, where the multiple images in the animation are saved as one file, the images used in a rollover effect are saved as separate files. Note that ImageReady does not allow you to optimize these files separately. To create separate optimization settings for each rollover state, you need to save the rollover files, close them, and then open and optimize each file separately.

ImageReady includes a Rollovers palette where you do most of the work in creating rollover effects. To make the Rollovers palette visible, click Windows on the menu bar and then click Rollovers.

You can create several different kinds of rollovers in ImageReady. First, you can create rollovers from layers, similarly to how you created animations from layers. Next, you can quickly create predesigned rollovers using the new Styles palette. You can also animate your rollovers, creating very sophisticated images.

Creating Rollovers from Layers

In many ways, creating rollover effects in ImageReady is very similar to creating animations. However, the terminology is often different. For example, although the individual parts of an animation are called "frames," each image in a rollover effect is called a **state**. Each state is named for the mouse event that triggers it, as explained in the following list:

- Normal—The image that appears in a given position when the Web page first loads.

- Over—The image that appears when the user's pointer is positioned over the image.

- Down—The image that appears when the mouse button is pressed.

- Up—The image that appears when the mouse button is released. This is usually the same as the Over image.

- Out—The image that appears when the user's pointer is removed from the image. This is usually the same as the Normal state.

- Click—The image that appears when the mouse button is pressed, then released. This is the same as the Down state, and you do not need to use it.

The most common states are Normal, Over, and Out. These three states, respectively, describe the image that first appears in the Web page, the image when the pointer is positioned over the image, and the image after the pointer is removed again.

Just as with animations, rollover effects involve changing which layers are visible over time.

To create a rollover effect from layers:

1. Open the file named **Ch06Photoshop06** from the Chapter folder for Chapter 6. An image of a green rectangle with the text "Home" opens. This image contains two layers.

2. In ImageReady, click the **File** menu and then click **Save Optimized As**. In the Save Optimized As dialog box, choose the name **Ch06Photoshop06SOL** and select the type of **HTML and Images** in the Chapter folder for Chapter 6. ImageReady saves the images and generates the HTML file.

3. The Rollovers palette shows the default Normal rollover state. To make the rollover states more visible, drag the palette tab to the left, as shown in Figure 6-10.

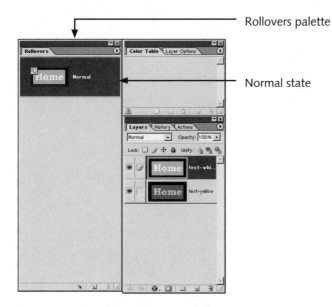

Rollovers palette

Normal state

Figure 6-10   The Rollovers palette

4. Click the **Create layer-based rollover** button in the Rollovers palette. The image is highlighted in the image window, and a new state, the Over state, is added to the Rollovers palette, indented slightly below a "folder" that will contain all the different states. The Over state is like a second frame of an animation, and it can display different layers from the Normal state.

5. Select the **Normal** rollover state. The visibility icons for both layers in the Layers palette are visible.

6. Select the **Over** state. In the Layers palette, click the visibility icon next to the layer named **text-white**. The Over state now shows only the contents from the layer below, named **text-yellow**. The image in the image window reflects the changes. Your screen should resemble that shown in Figure 6-11.

7. Preview the image in the browser and test the rollover. The image should change from light to dark when you move the mouse over it. Moving the mouse off the image causes it to change back. The browser also displays all the HTML and JavaScript code needed to make the rollover effect work in a Web page.

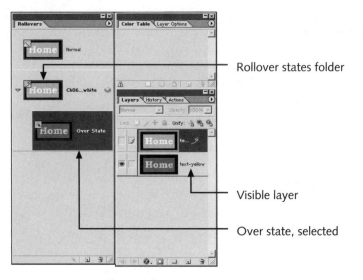

Figure 6-11   Rollover effects

8. Select appropriate settings from the Optimize palette. Unlike animations, rollovers can be optimized and saved in either GIF or JPEG format.

9. Save and close the file.

Creating Rollovers Using Styles

Another way to create rollover effects is by using styles. In ImageReady, **styles** are pre-designed effects that allow you to quickly generate sophisticated-looking images.

Preset styles are available from the Styles palette. To make the Styles palette visible, select Styles from the Window menu. As shown in Figure 6-12, the styles with black triangles in the upper-left corner are rollover styles.

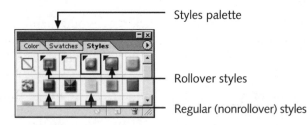

Figure 6-12   The Styles palette

To create a rollover effect using styles:

1. Create a new image with a height and width of **100** pixels.

2. Click the **File** menu and then click **Save Optimized As**. In the Save Optimized As dialog box, choose the name **Ch06Photoshop07.html** and select the type of **HTML and Images** in the Chapter folder for Chapter 6. Set the **Foreground Color** to **black**.

3. Select the **Type** tool. In the Options bar, set the font to **Verdana**, **Bold**, **48 px**.

4. Click on the left side the image window and type the word **Go!** If necessary, use the Move tool to center the text in the image window. Note that the Rollovers palette shows only one state, the Normal state. To create additional rollover states, you simply need to apply a rollover style.

 Recall that you can use the Undo command on the Edit menu to reverse any mistakes and start over.

5. In the Styles palette, move the mouse over the style icons and read the names of the various style names in the screen tips that appear.

6. Click the style named **3-state Gradient**. The black triangle in the upper-left corner of this style's icon tells you that it is a rollover style. The contents of the image window and the Rollovers palette change to reflect your selection.

7. The new states are contained in a "folder" in the Rollovers palette. Click the triangle to the left of the folder to reveal the new states: Over and Down. Some of the other available rollover styles result in only one state being created. Your screen should look like that shown in Figure 6-13.

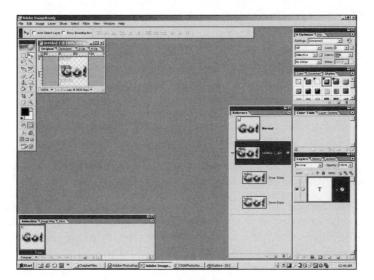

Figure 6-13   Rollover effects created using styles

8. Preview the rollover in the browser and try rolling over and clicking the image.

9. Select appropriate settings from the Optimize palette.

10. Save and close the file.

Using Animation in Rollover Effects

You can combine animation with rollover effects so that moving the mouse triggers an animation to appear. This can be tricky, because you have to keep an eye on the Animation palette, the Rollovers palette, and the Layers palette at the same time. The basic process goes like this: First you set up all the layers you will need. Next you create the necessary rollover states. Then you select each state and, in the Layers palette, specify which layers should be visible during that state. Next, you select the rollover state you wish to animate. Finally, you use the Animation palette to create the frames of animation for that state.

To create a rollover effect that includes animation:

1. Open the file named **Ch06Photoshop08** from the Chapter folder for Chapter 6. An image of a loudspeaker, with three layers, appears.

2. Click the **File** menu and then click **Save Optimized As**. In the Save Optimized As dialog box, choose the name **Ch06Photoshop08SOL.html** and select the type of **HTML and Images** in the Chapter folder for Chapter 6.

3. In the Rollovers palette, create a new **Over** rollover state. Next, you will animate the Over state so that when the user moves the mouse over the image, it is replaced with an animation.

4. Select the **Normal** state. In the Layers palette, turn off the visibility for the layers named **speaker2** and **speaker3**.

5. Select the **Over** state. In the Layers palette, make only the **speaker2** layer visible.

6. We now have a simple rollover. Preview the image in a browser to see the effect.

7. In order to animate the rollover, create a new frame in the Animation palette.

8. With the second frame selected, make the layer named **speaker3** visible in the Layers palette. The Over state changes to indicate that it includes animation. Your screen should resemble that shown in Figure 6-14.

9. Preview the image in your browser. The initial image is the Normal state, which shows the content of the layer named speaker1. Rolling over the image causes the Over state to appear, which you have set to be an animation that alternates between the contents of the layers named speaker2 and speaker3.

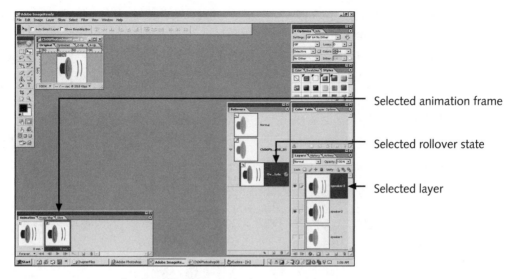

Selected animation frame

Selected rollover state

Selected layer

Figure 6-14   A rollover effect that includes animation

10. Select appropriate settings from the Optimize palette and save and close the file.

CREATING IMAGE MAPS

Image maps are another type of Web graphic. They are usually larger than other images and are often used as **splash screens**, large images used on a Web site's home page.

Any Web graphic can be used as an image map. Typically, a user can click areas of an image map to link to other pages. The linked areas, called **hot spots**, are defined in the HTML file that displays the image. To define the hot spots in an image, you use the Image Map palette. When you save the image map, ImageReady generates all the necessary HTML code.

Creating Image Maps with the Image Map Tools

The Toolbox in ImageReady contains four Image Map tools that you can use to create and select hot spots. Hot spots can be rectangular, circular, or almost any polygonal shape. The Rectangle Image Map tool can create hot spots in either square or rectangular shapes. The Circle Image Map tool can create circular, but not elliptical, hot spots.

To create an image map with the Image Map tools:

1. Open the file named **Ch06Photoshop09** from the Chapter folder for Chapter 6. An image showing a map of Manhattan opens.

2. Click the **File** menu and then click **Save Optimized As**. In the Save Optimized As dialog box, choose the name **Ch06Photoshop09SOL.html** and select the type of **HTML and Images** in the Chapter folder for Chapter 6.

3. To display the Image Map palette, click **Window** on the menu bar and then click **Image Map**.

4. Select the **Rectangle Image Map** tool from the Toolbox. Drag the pointer to draw a rectangle over the area in the image labeled "Upper East Side". A rectangular hot spot area appears, outlined in red. The Image Map palette shows information about the hot spot, as shown in Figure 6-15. The X and Y settings control the x and y coordinates of the pixels in the upper-left corner of the hot spots. The W and H settings control the hot spot's width and height.

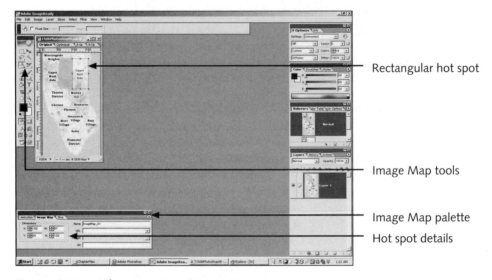

Figure 6-15   A hot spot in an image map

5. Click the **X** down arrow in the Image Map palette. The rectangular hot spot moves to the left.

6. Click the **H** up arrow in the Image Map palette. The hot spot gets longer.

7. Select the **Circle Image Map** tool by clicking and holding your pointer over the Rectangle Image Map tool and selecting **Circle Image Map Tool** from the pop-up selection menu. Drag the pointer over the area named SoHo. Use the **X**, **Y**, and **R** (radius) arrows to adjust the hot spot and center it over the text in the image.

8. Select the **Polygon Image Map** tool. Click the pointer once above the image area named East Village. Click several more times to create a hexagon around the text. Close the shape by clicking on the first point.

9. Select the **Image Map Select** tool. Click and drag the corners of the polygonal hot spot to adjust its size and shape. Your screen should resemble that shown in Figure 6-16.

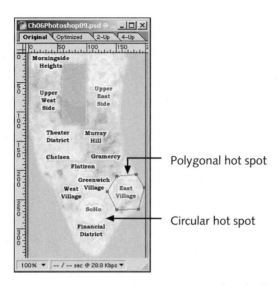

Figure 6-16   An image map created with Image Map tools

10. Select appropriate settings from the Optimize palette and preview the image in a browser. The hot spots you created do not actually link to any other pages, so you cannot test them.

11. Save and close the file.

Controlling Linking Destinations

Each hot spot is a separate link, so you need to define each one with its own Name, URL, Target, and Alt settings. The Name setting is used only for complex images that combine image maps and rollover effects; you can ignore this setting for most image map projects. The URL is the address of the destination Web page (the page you want the hot spot to link to). The Target setting tells the user's browser whether to open the new page in a separate window or frame. The Alt setting specifies the alternate text that displays if the image does not load properly. For more information on these settings, see Chapters 3 and 4. If you do not define this information when creating your hot spots, you can define it later by editing the HTML directly.

To create an image map with the Image Map tools:

1. Open the file named **Ch06Photoshop10** from the Chapter folder for Chapter 6. An image showing the text "Games, Reviews, Music, Tutorials and News" appears. The rectangles containing these words have already been defined as hot spots.

2. Click the **File** menu and then click **Save Optimized As**. In the Save Optimized As dialog box, choose the name **Ch06Photoshop10SOL.html** and select the type of **HTML and Images** in the Chapter folder for Chapter 6.

3. Verify that the Image Map palette is displayed and then select the **Image Map Select** tool.

4. Click the rectangle around the word "Games" to select that hot spot. The Image Map palette displays the hot spot's default name, **ImageMap_01**. Set the URL to **games.html**.

5. Leave the Target field empty and type **Games** as the Alt setting.

6. Click the rectangle around the word "Reviews". Set the URL to **reviews.html** and the Alt setting to **Reviews**.

7. Repeat this process for all the other hot spots, accepting the default name for each. Your screen should resemble that shown in Figure 6-17.

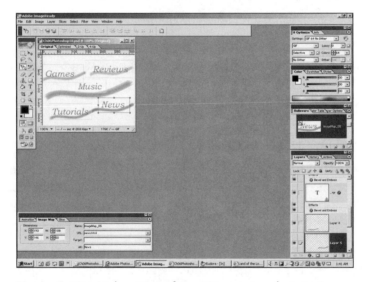

Figure 6-17   Link settings for an image map hot spot

8. Select appropriate settings from the Optimize palette and preview the image in a browser. The links you created go to pages that do not exist, so you cannot test them. Note the HTML code below the image in the browser window. This is the code you would need to include in a Web page in order to make the image map functional.

9. Save and close the file.

Creating Image Maps from Selection Areas

You can also create hot spots that are based on selection areas. You use the Marquee, Magic Wand, or Lasso tools to create the selection areas and then convert them to image map hot spots.

To create an image map from selection areas:

1. Open the file named **Ch06Photoshop11** from the Chapter folder for Chapter 6.

2. Click the **File** menu and then click **Save Optimized As**. In the Save Optimized As dialog box, choose the name **Ch06Photoshop11SOL.html** and select the type of **HTML and Images** in the Chapter folder for Chapter 6.

3. Verify that the Image Map palette is displayed.

4. Select the **Marquee** tool and drag a selection area around the red square in the image.

5. Click **Select** on the menu bar and then click **Create Image Map from Selection**. The Create Image Map dialog box appears.

6. Select **Rectangle** and click **OK**. A new rectangular hot spot appears, with information about it displayed in the Image Map palette.

7. Select the **Magic Wand** tool and click inside the green circle.

8. Click **Select** on the menu bar and then click **Create Image Map from Selection**. The Create Image Map dialog box appears.

9. Select **Polygon** with a Quality of **50** and click **OK**. A polygonal hot spot appears.

10. Select the **Lasso** tool and drag a selection area around the blue X.

11. Click **Select** on the menu bar and then click **Create Image Map from Selection**. The Create Image Map dialog box appears.

12. Select **Circle** and click **OK**. A circular hot spot appears that is large enough to encompass the entire selection area, and even expands beyond the boundaries of the image. Your screen should look like that shown in Figure 6-18.

6

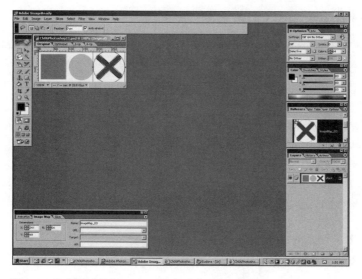

Figure 6-18   Hot spots created from selection areas

13. Select the **Image Map Select** tool and select the hot spot around the red square. In the Image Map palette, type **http://www.course.com/** in the URL text field. Use the same URL for the other two hot spots.

14. Select appropriate settings from the Optimize palette and preview the image in a browser. Clicking within any of the hot spots takes you to the course.com site.

15. Save and close the file.

Creating Image Maps from Layers

You can also create hot spots from the contents of layers. This is convenient when your original image consists of multiple elements, with each element in a separate layer.

To create an image map from layers:

1. Open the file named **Ch06Photoshop12** from the Chapter folder for Chapter 6.

2. Click the **File** menu and then click **Save Optimized As**. In the Save Optimized As dialog box, choose the name **Ch06Photoshop12SOL.html** and select the type of **HTML and Images** in the Chapter folder for Chapter 6.

3. Display the Layers palette if necessary. This image contains two layers. The bottom layer, named Grass, contains an image of the grass by the fox's feet. The other layer, named Fox, contains the image of the fox itself. You will create a hot spot on the fox layer.

4. Select the layer named **Fox**.

5. Click **Layer** on the menu bar and then click **New Layer Based Image Map Area**. A new rectangular hot spot appears, containing almost the entire fox. A smaller rectangular hot spot contains the end of one of the whiskers, which protrudes beyond the larger rectangle.

6. In the Image Map palette, set the Shape to **Polygon**. The hot spots now roughly outline the shape of the fox. In the Image Map palette, change the Quality to **50**. The hot spot now follows the outline of the fox less exactly. Higher Quality settings for polygonal hot spots result in larger file sizes. For most image maps, a Quality setting between 50 and 80 is adequate.

7. Select appropriate settings from the Optimize palette. Your screen should look like Figure 6-19.

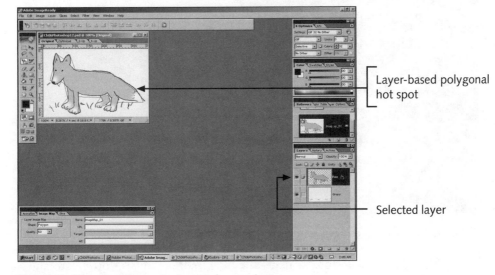

Layer-based polygonal hot spot

Selected layer

Figure 6-19   Creating a hot spot from a layer

8. Save and close the image.

SLICING IMAGES

Sliced images are multiple graphics that are positioned in a Web page to look like a single larger image. Slicing an image into smaller parts, called **slices**, makes the image download faster. It also makes it possible to incorporate multiple features into one image. For example, one sliced image can include multiple rollover effects, animations, and image maps. When you create image slices, each resulting image can be optimized separately, thus allowing the maximum optimization for each area. Also, the separate slices can contain their own animations or rollover effects.

Sliced images are usually used as splash screens on a Web site's home page, but you can use them anyplace where it would make sense to break a graphic into smaller pieces.

ImageReady provides the necessary tools and palettes for creating image slices. You can create slices from layers, or from selection areas.

Creating Slices

Creating sliced images can be tricky, because you quickly end up with several images. The easiest way to get started is by using the Slice tool and the Slice palette, shown in Figure 6-20.

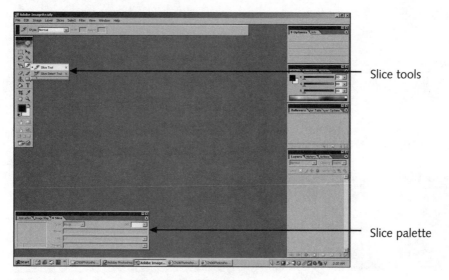

Figure 6-20   The Slice tool and Slice palette

Using the Slice tool results in **user slices**, which are slices you create and can resize. Because slices must always fill a rectangular area, ImageReady then generates **auto slices** to fill in the rest of the image. For example, if you draw a rectangular user slice that takes up the middle third of an image, ImageReady will then draw two rectangular auto slices, one on either side of the user slice, to finish dividing the entire image into slices.

To create a sliced image with the Slice tool:

1. Open the file named **Ch06Photoshop13** from the Chapter folder for Chapter 6.

2. Click the **File** menu and then click **Save Optimized As**. In the Save Optimized As dialog box, choose the name **Ch06Photoshop13SOL.html** and select the type of **HTML and Images** in the Chapter folder for Chapter 6.

3. Click **Window** on the menu bar and then click **Slice** to open the Slice palette.

4. Select the **Slice** tool from the Toolbox.

5. Drag the pointer to draw a rectangle over the word "STOP!". A user slice encloses the text, and four auto slices appear around it. The Slice palette shows information about the new user slice.

6. Select the **Slice Select** tool from the Toolbox.

7. Click the auto slice at the top of the image. Use the Optimize palette to set the slice to **GIF 64 Dithered**. By default, all auto slices are linked and share the same optimization settings; user slices are optimized individually. If you want to select different optimization settings for each auto slice, you need to convert them to user slices. Do this by selecting **Promote to User Slice** from the Slices menu.

8. Select the user slice and optimize it to a setting of **JPEG High**. Your screen should look like Figure 6-21.

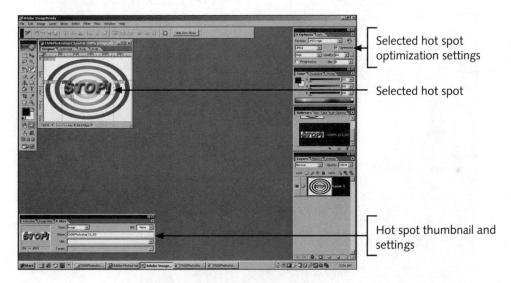

Selected hot spot optimization settings

Selected hot spot

Hot spot thumbnail and settings

Figure 6-21 Creating slices

9. Preview the image in a browser. Although it looks like a single image, it is actually five images positioned together in an HTML table. Below the image you see the details of the image, including a combined file size of around 9K. The original image is around 196K. By slicing the image and optimizing the slices separately, you are able to significantly reduce the time it will take a Web user to download the image.

10. Save and close the file. Each slice is saved as a separate image. Look in the Chapter folder for Chapter 6 to see the new files.

Creating Slices from Selection Areas

As with image maps, you can create slices from selection areas. Once you have some initial slices, you can use additional menu options to divide and align slices.

To create a sliced image with the Slice tool:

1. Open the file named **Ch06Photoshop14** from the Chapter folder for Chapter 6. An image of a flower with stars and the words "Roses," "Tulips," and "Lilies" opens.

2. Click the **File** menu and then click **Save Optimized As**. In the Save Optimized As dialog box, choose the name **Ch06Photoshop14SOL.html** and select the type of **HTML and Images** in the Chapter folder for Chapter 6.

3. Select the **Marquee** tool from the Toolbox. Drag the pointer to draw a rectangle around the gray rectangle and three text links on the left of the image.

4. Click **Select** on the menu bar and then click **Create Slice from Selection**. A new user slice and four auto slices appear, as shown in Figure 6-22.

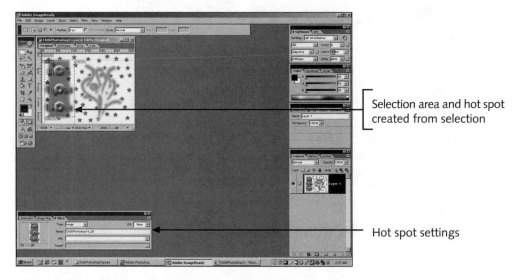

Selection area and hot spot created from selection

Hot spot settings

Figure 6-22   Slices created from a selection

5. Click **Slices** on the menu bar and then click **Divide Slice**. The Divide Slice dialog box appears. Here you can create slices of the same size from a larger slice. It is often easier to create multiple slices this way than by creating them individually with the Slice tool.

6. Check the **Divide Horizontally Into** check box, if not already checked, and uncheck the **Divide Vertically Into** check box. Next to "slices down, evenly spaced", type **3**. Click **OK**. The user slice has been divided into three adjacent user slices.

7. Select the **Lasso** tool. Drag a selection area around the flower on the right of the image.

8. Click the **Select** menu and then click **Create Slice from Selection**. A new user slice and more auto slices appear.

9. Select the **Slice Select** tool. Select each user slice and optimize it as **GIF** with **64** colors. Select one of the auto slices and optimize it as **GIF** with **8** colors.

10. Your screen should look like Figure 6-23. Preview your image in a browser.

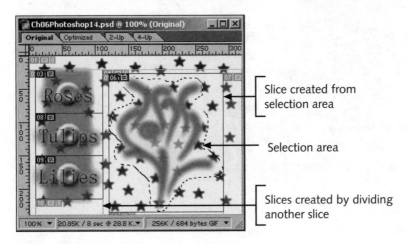

Figure 6-23   Creating slices from selection areas

11. Save and close the image.

Creating Slices from Layers

It can be tricky to slice an image precisely. It is sometimes easier to create slices from layers than it is to use the Slice tool. Creating slices from layers results in **layer-based slices**, which are like user slices, except that changing the contents of a layer automatically changes the related layer-based slice as well.

To create slices from layers:

1. Open the file named **Ch06Photoshop15** from the Chapter folder for Chapter 6.

2. Click the **File** menu and then click **Save Optimized As**. In the Save Optimized As dialog box, choose the name **Ch06Photoshop15SOL.html** and select the type of **HTML and Images** in the Chapter folder for Chapter 6.

3. In the Layers palette, select **Brackets1**.

4. Click **Layer** on the menu bar and then click **New Layer Based Slice**. A new layer-based slice and two auto slices appear, as shown in Figure 6-24. The layer in the Layers palette includes a slice icon.

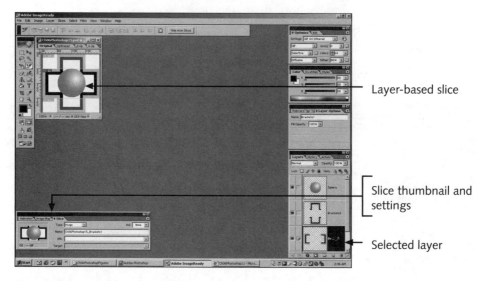

Figure 6-24   A layer-based slice

5. In the Layers palette, select **Brackets2**.

6. Click **Layer** on the menu bar and then click **New Layer Based Slice**. The first layer-based slice subdivides into three, and four auto slices fill the corners of the image.

7. In the Layers palette, select **Sphere**.

8. Click **Layer** on the menu bar and then click **New Layer Based Slice**. You now have 12 layer-based slices.

9. Select the **Move** tool. Drag the sphere layer around the image. The layer-based slices automatically readjust to fit the layer contents. Move the layer until you have a total of only 9 slices.

10. Select each slice with the **Slice Select** tool and select appropriate optimization settings. The slices containing only white or only white, green, and black should look fine when reduced to only 4 colors. The slice containing the sphere should be optimized as JPEG.

11. Your screen should resemble Figure 6-25. Although the image looks the same as it would if you had not sliced it, the combined file size is much smaller than it would be if you had left the image whole.

12. Save and close the file. One HTML file and 9 image files are saved to the Chapter 6 folder.

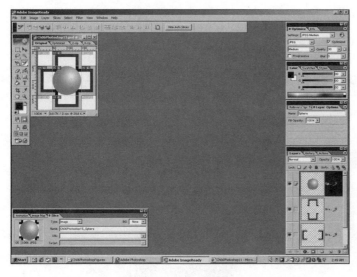

Figure 6-25   Creating slices from layers

Controlling the Display of Slices in HTML

An advantage of slicing images is that you are sometimes able to replace slices with empty space; this means the user will have to download fewer images. The empty space is in fact a table cell defined in HTML, and you can include color and text as you would in any other table.

To create a sliced image with the Slice tool:

1. Open the file named **Ch06Photoshop16** from the Chapter folder for Chapter 6.

2. Click the **File** menu and then click **Save Optimized As**. In the Save Optimized As dialog box, choose the name **Ch06Photoshop16SOL.html** and select the type of **HTML and Images** in the Chapter folder for Chapter 6.

3. Use the **Slice** tool to create a slice around the word "STOP". Make sure that the slice does not include any of the white stripe in the stop sign image.

4. Create another slice around the other text. Again, make sure not to include the adjacent white stripe.

5. Select the **Eyedropper** tool and click the red area in the image. The **Foreground Color** changes to **red**.

6. With the **Slice Select** tool, select the slice containing the word "STOP". In the Slice palette, set the Type to **No Image**. The palette changes to include a box where you can type in text and HTML. Type the following into the box:

```
<div align=center style='color:white; font-size:21pt;
font-weight:bold; font family:arial;'>STOP</div>
```

7. Click the **BG** menu in the Slice palette and then click **Foreground Color**.

8. Select the other slice containing text. Set the Type to **No Image** and set BG to **Foreground Color**. In the text area, type the following:

```
<div align=center style='color:white; font-size:11pt;
font-family:arial;'>Please Read Before You Continue</div>
```

9. Optimize the image slices to **GIF** with **4** colors. Your screen should look like that shown in Figure 6-26.

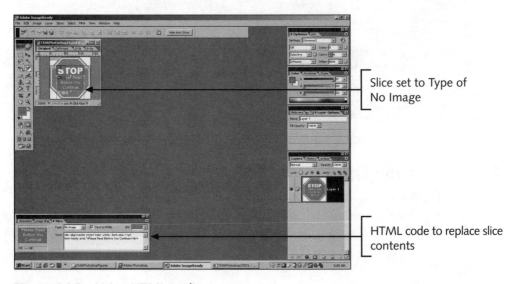

Slice set to Type of No Image

HTML code to replace slice contents

Figure 6-26   Using HTML in slices

10. Preview the image in a browser. It should look like the original image. However, because the text is created in HTML, the image downloads faster. (You would probably only notice this time savings if you were downloading the file over the Web.)

11. Save and close the image.

Using Animation in a Sliced Image

In addition to the ability to optimize parts of an image separately, another advantage to sliced images is the ability to include animation in only a small part of a larger image. If you create animations from entire large images, the files can become prohibitively large. By combining animation and image slices, you can reduce your image's download time.

To use animation in a sliced image:

1. Open the file named **Ch06Photoshop17** from the Chapter folder for Chapter 6.

2. Click the **File** menu and then click **Save Optimized As**. In the Save Optimized As dialog box, choose the name **Ch06Photoshop17SOL.html** and select the type of **HTML and Images** in the Chapter folder for Chapter 6.

3. Select the layer named **Bubbles**, and create a new layer-based slice from it.

4. In the Animation palette, create a new frame.

5. Select the **Move** tool and move the layer contents up about **30** pixels. The layer-based slice expands to include the layer contents in both animation frames.

6. In the Layers palette, set the Opacity to **10%**.

7. Click the **Tweens animation frames** button in the Animation palette. The Tween dialog box appears.

8. Add **3** frames. Select **All Layers** and select all parameters. Click **OK**. The Animation palette now has five frames, showing the bubbles rising and fading away.

9. In the Animation palette, set the Frame Delay of each frame to **0.2** seconds. Set the Loop Count to **Forever**, if necessary. Your screen should look like Figure 6-27.

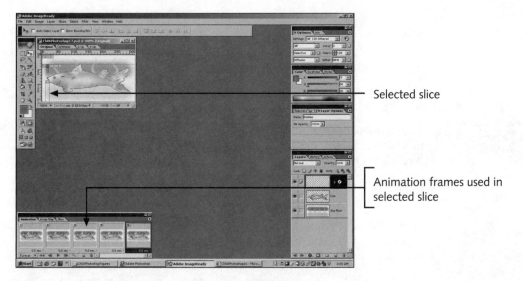

Figure 6-27   Using animation in a sliced image

10. Use appropriate optimization settings for each slice. The slice containing bubbles must be optimized as GIF because it is animated.

11. Preview the image in a browser. Only one of the five image slices is animated. Again, you probably would not notice the time savings this provides unless you downloaded the image over the Web.

12. Save and close the image.

Using Rollover Effects in a Sliced Image

Including rollover effects in a sliced image is similar to adding animation. You select a slice and then add states in the Rollovers palette. Unlike in animation, however, the rollover effects in one image slice can be used to cause another slice to change. You can use this technique to make very sophisticated images, especially if one or more of the slices includes animation as well.

To use a rollover effect in a sliced image:

1. Open the file named **Ch06Photoshop18** from the Chapter folder for Chapter 6.

2. Click the **File** menu and then click **Save Optimized As**. In the Save Optimized As dialog box, choose the name **Ch06Photoshop18SOL.html** and select the type of **HTML and Images** in the Chapter folder for Chapter 6. ImageReady saves all the JavaScript and HTML in one file.

3. Use the **Slice** tool to create slices around each of the text areas. Use the **Slice Select** tool to adjust the size of each user slice in order to include as much of the orange glow as possible, and also to minimize the number of slices—no more than **5**.

4. Select the auto slices that contain only white space. In the Slice palette, set the Type to **No Image**.

5. Select the slice around the word "Home". In the Slice palette, set the Name to **Home**. Select the slice around the word "Articles". Set the Name to **Articles**. Do the same for the slice around the word "About".

6. Drag the Rollovers palette to the left and expand it to make its contents easier to see.

7. Select the slice named **"Home"**. In the Rollovers palette, click the **Create rollover state** button. A new state is created for this slice.

8. In the Layers palette, turn off the visibility for the layer named **glow1**. The new Over rollover state shows the text, but not the glowing background.

9. Select the slice named **"About"**. In the Rollovers palette, click the **Create rollover state** button. A new state is created for this slice. In the Layers palette, turn off the visibility for the layer named **glow2**.

10. Select the slice named **"Articles"**. In the Rollovers palette, click the **Create rollover state** button. A new state is created for this slice. In the Layers palette, turn off the visibility for the layer named **glow3**.

11. Your screen should look like Figure 6-28. Use appropriate optimization settings for each slice.

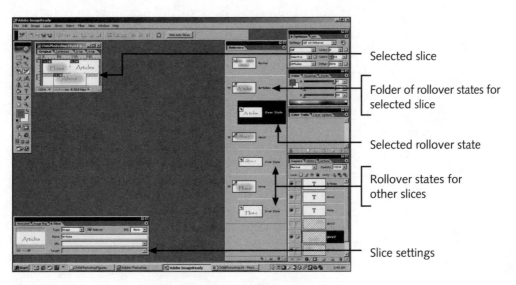

Figure 6-28   Using rollovers in a sliced image

12. Preview the image in a browser. Rolling over each word should cause the orange glow behind the word to disappear.

13. Save and close the file.

CHAPTER SUMMARY

- You can create animations by animating a single layer, changing the visibility of multiple layers, or by importing a folder of image files.

- Tweening lets ImageReady insert new frames between two animation frames and calculate changes in position, opacity, or styles.

- The amount of time a frame is displayed is called the frame delay.

- An animation plays back a specific number of times, as specified by the loop count.

- Rollover effects are JavaScript programs that cause one image to be replaced by another when the user moves or clicks the mouse.

- Rollover effects are created by changing the visibility in layers and can include styles and animation.

- Image maps are normal Web images that can include multiple links.

- Image map hot spots can be rectangular, circular, or polygonal in shape.

❑ Sliced images are multiple images that, when positioned in an HTML table, appear to be one image.

❑ You can use HTML color and text in place of an image slice to reduce file size.

❑ Image slices can include rollover effects and animation

REVIEW QUESTIONS

1. Which type of image must be optimized through color reduction?

   a. animation

   b. image map

   c. rollover effect

   d. sliced image

2. What is tweening?

   a. creating auto slices

   b. creating image maps in between existing hot spots

   c. creating intermediate animation frames

   d. creating rollover states with the Styles palette

3. For which type of image do you *not* need to save an accompanying HTML file?

   a. animation

   b. image map

   c. rollover effect

   d. sliced image

4. Which type of image can be created by using the Styles palette?

   a. animation

   b. image map

   c. rollover effect

   d. sliced image

5. Which type of image requires JavaScript?

   a. animation

   b. image map

   c. rollover effect

   d. sliced image

6. What is not a kind of rollover state?

   a. Click

   b. Down

   c. Normal

   d. On

7. What is not a possible shape for an image map hot spot?

   a. ellipse

   b. pentagram

   c. square

   d. trapezoid

8. Which type of image does not require altering the image, and only needs special HTML to make it work?

   a. animation

   b. image map

   c. rollover effect

   d. sliced image

9. What is not a kind of image slice?

   a. auto slice

   b. user slice

   c. layer-based slice

   d. selection-based slice

10. Image slices are all what shape?

   a. square

   b. rectangle

   c. circle

   d. ellipse

11. Where can you add text and HTML code directly in an image?

   a. animation frames

   b. image map hot spots

   c. image slices

   d. rollover states

6

12. Which image elements can be created from selection areas?

   a. animation frames and image slices

   b. animation frames and rollover states

   c. image map hot spots and image slices

   d. image map hot spots and rollover states

13. Which types of images can contain animation?

   a. image maps and rollovers

   b. image maps, rollovers, and slices

   c. image maps and slices

   d. rollovers and slices

14. Which types of image require multiple image files?

   a. animation and image map

   b. animation and sliced image

   c. image map and rollover effect

   d. rollover and sliced image

15. Which types of image are often used as splash screens?

   a. animation and rollover effect

   b. animation and sliced image

   c. image map and rollover effect

   d. image map and sliced image

HANDS-ON EXERCISES

Exercise 6-1

1. Open the file named **Ch06PhotoshopEX01** from the Exercises folder for Chapter 6, and optimize it and save it as **Ch06PhotoshopEX01SOL** in the same folder.

2. Make the Styles, Layers, and Animation palettes visible.

3. Select the layer named "Ring". Find the style named "Floating Plastic" and apply it to the layer. Apply the same style to the other four layers.

4. In the Animation palette, create three new frames.

5. Select the first frame. Deselect the visibility icons in the layers so that only the layers named "Ring" and "NorthEast" are visible.

6. Select the second frame. Deselect the visibility icons in the layers so that only the layers named "Ring" and "SouthEast" are visible.

7. Repeat for the other two frames and layers, making Ring and SouthWest visible in the third frame and Ring and NorthWest visible in the fourth frame.

8. Set the Frame Delay for each frame to 0.1 seconds.

9. Set the loop count of the animation to 10.

10. Optimize the image using the GIF 64 Dithered setting.

11. Preview the animation in a browser.

12. Save optimized and close the file.

Exercise 6-2

1. Open the file named **Ch06PhotoshopEX02** from the Exercises folder for Chapter 6, optimize it, and save it as **Ch06PhotoshopEX02SOL** in the same folder.

2. Make sure the Rollovers and Layers palettes are visible.

3. In the Rollovers palette, select the Normal state and click the Create rollover state button. A new Over state appears.

4. Click the Create rollover state button again. A new Down state appears.

5. Select the Normal state. In the Layers palette, make only the layers named "house" and "background" visible.

6. Select the Over state. In the Layers palette, make the layer named "smoke" visible.

7. Select the Down state. In the Layers palette, make the layer named "glow" visible.

8. In the Optimize palette, select the JPEG Medium setting.

9. Preview the rollover effect in a browser.

10. Save as optimized and close the file.

Exercise 6-3

1. Open the file named **Ch06PhotoshopEX03** from the Exercises folder for Chapter 6, optimize it, and save it as **Ch06PhotoshopEX03SOL** in the same folder.

2. Make sure the Image Map palette is visible.

3. Select the Magic Wand tool. Set the Tolerance to 50 and make sure the Contiguous check box is *not* selected.

4. Click on one of the red states in the map. All red states are selected separately.

5. Click Select on the menu bar, point to Modify, and then click Expand. The Expand Selection dialog box appears. Type 2 and click OK.

6. Click Select on the menu bar and then click Create Image Map from Selection. The Create Image Map dialog box appears. Select Polygon, and set the Quality to 80 if necessary. Click OK.

7. In the Image Map palette, set the URL to pacific.html.

6

8. Repeat this process for the other three colored areas in the map. Use the following URLs: "mountain.html", "central.html", and "eastern.html".

9. In the Optimize palette, select the JPEG Low setting.

10. Preview the image map in a browser.

11. Save as optimized and close the file.

Exercise 6-4

1. Open the file named **Ch06PhotoshopEX04** from the Exercises folder for Chapter 6, optimize it, and save it as **Ch06PhotoshopEX04SOL** in the same folder.

2. Make sure the Slice palette is visible.

3. Select the Marquee tool. Set the Feather to 0 px if necessary.

4. Select one of the white strips that separates the image content.

5. Click Select on the menu bar, and then click Create Slice from Selection.

6. Select the other white strip and create a slice from the new selection.

7. Select the Slice Select tool and select the first user slice you created.

8. In the Slice palette, set the Type to No Image. Do the same for the other user slice.

9. Select one of the auto slices. In the Optimize palette, select the preset named JPEG Medium.

10. Preview the image in a browser.

11. Save as optimized and close the file.

Exercise 6-5

1. Open the file named **Ch06PhotoshopEX05** from the Exercises folder for Chapter 6, optimize it, and save it as **Ch06PhotoshopEX05SOL** in the same folder.

2. Make sure the Slice and Rollovers palettes are visible.

3. In the Layers palette, turn off visibility for the layers named "Internet Ed arrived on the scen" and "Name: Internet Ed Born: Januar".

4. Select the Slice Select tool. Select the slice containing the word "Bio".

5. In the Rollovers palette, click the Create rollover state button.

6. Double-click the new Over state. The Rollover State Options dialog box appears. Select Down and click OK. The state changes to a Down state.

7. With the Down state selected, turn on visibility for the layer named "Name: Internet Ed Born Januar".

8. Click the Rollovers palette menu and then click Duplicate Rollover State. A new Over state appears. Double-click the new state and change it to Up in the Rollover State Options dialog box.

9. Duplicate the new Up state and change the new state to an Out state.

10. Repeat steps 4 through 9, creating a rollover based on the slice around the word "history". The rollover should display the layer named "Internet Ed arrived on the scen".

11. Select the slices in turn and optimize them. The final set of images should have a total file size of less than 20K.

12. Preview the image map in a browser.

13. Save the optimized version of the image and accompanying HTML file to your Exercises folder with the name **Ch06PhotoshopEX05SOL.html**.

6

WEB DESIGN PROJECTS

Project 6-1

Take the map of the lower 48 American states from Exercise 6-3 and create an image map in which every state is a hot spot that links to a different page. For example, clicking on Missouri should take the user to missouri.html. Save the file in the Projects folder for Chapter 6.

Project 6-2

Create a splash screen that is at least 320 pixels wide and 240 pixels high. Include at least three animated elements, but keep the final total image file size to under 20K. One example would be a house that includes smoke coming out of the chimney, curtains moving in the window, and the front door opening and closing. The three animations should be divided into different slices and have different frame rates. Save the file in the Projects folder for Chapter 6.

Project 6-3

Create a splash screen that is similar to that used in Exercise 6-5, but animate the swapped image. Moving or clicking the mouse over an image should animate the contents of another slice. Save the file in the Projects folder for Chapter 6.

FLASH: PART I

In this chapter you will:

♦ Work with the Flash environment including the Stage, menu bar, Toolbox, panels, and Property inspector
♦ Draw strokes and paint fills using the Flash tools
♦ Select and modify objects
♦ Create and manipulate text

In the early days of the World Wide Web, designers had limited tools and technologies for developing Web sites. Using the available tools, they developed Web pages that conveyed the desired information but did so in a static, mostly text, format. Today, new tools and technologies help designers add more visual excitement to Web sites to attract more visitors and potential customers. One of these tools is Macromedia Flash.

Flash is a Web authoring application that provides Web designers with tools to create interactive, multimedia-rich movies for the Web that incorporate graphics, text, and animations. Using Flash, Web designers can create multimedia Web movies, animated logos, site navigation controls, interfaces, or even entire Web sites. (To see some examples of Flash movies, visit the Macromedia Web site at www.macromedia.com.) Flash movies play on the user's computer using the Flash player that now comes as a standard feature with most major Web browsers and is installed on most new computers. (The Flash player is also available for download from the Macromedia Web site.) The beauty of this arrangement is that you, as the designer, know in advance that your movies will display on the Flash player. Thus you are assured that the user will see exactly what you created.

Another advantage to creating movies in Flash is that Flash movies use vector graphics, as opposed to bitmap graphics, so they are small in size and they scale to the viewer's screen size. Vector graphics are made up of lines and curves and are stored in the form of mathematical equations that tell the computer how to display them. As a result, vector image file sizes tend to be small and can be scaled to different screen sizes without loss of quality. Bitmap graphics, on the other hand, are made up of colored dots called pixels. The color and position information about each pixel has to be stored in the file. As a result, larger images require more pixel information to be stored, resulting in larger files. In addition, bitmap graphics tend to lose their quality when they are scaled to different screen sizes.

In this chapter, you will learn the basic features of Flash. You will see various examples and work through hands-on activities to learn how to use the basic tools in the Flash work environment. You will use the Drawing and Painting tools, Selection and Transforming tools, panels, and the Text tool to create and modify various objects in Flash.

THE FLASH ENVIRONMENT

To get started with the Flash program, you need to become familiar with its work environment. The Flash environment is where you create or import the images, text, sound, and other elements that make up a Flash document. A Flash file is called a **document** while it is being edited. Once you publish the document for viewing in a Web page, the file is called a **movie**. Publishing is covered in the next chapter. The Flash environment may look confusing at first but as you become familiar with each of the main elements, you will see how easy it is to create a Flash document. Key elements of the Flash environment include the Stage, menu bar, Toolbox, panels, Property inspector, and Timeline, as shown in Figure 7-1. The Timeline is used to control animations and will be covered in the next chapter. (Note that on a Macintosh, the screen will look slightly different than in Figure 7-1. For example, you will probably see the Dock at the bottom of the screen.)

Stage

The **Stage** is the large white rectangular area in the middle section of the screen. This is where images are created and modified. The Stage is located within the gray work area. Any image that will be part of the movie must be positioned within the Stage. Images may be placed in the work area, but they will not be displayed in the final movie unless you move them from the work area to the Stage.

Menu Bar

The menu bar is similar to the menu bar in other programs. Using the commands on the Flash menu bar, you can export or publish movies, control the display of the work area, display rulers and gridlines, insert new Flash objects, modify the document properties, test movies, open panels, and open Flash samples and tutorials.

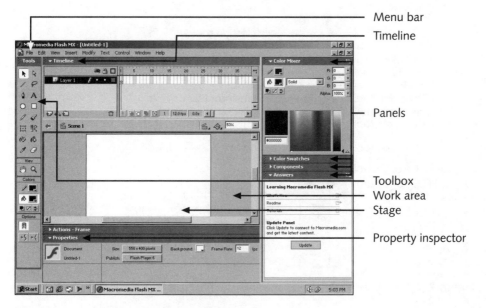

Figure 7-1   Flash work environment

Toolbox

The Toolbox, shown in Figure 7-2, is divided into four areas: Tools, View, Colors, and Options. You can select each of the tools in these areas by clicking the tool or by pressing its keyboard shortcut.

 When you move the mouse pointer over each of the tools, the name of the tool and its keyboard shortcut appear in a small box called a screen tip.

The tools in the Tools area of the Toolbox are used to create and modify the lines, curves, fills, and text that make up the graphic images of a Flash document.

The View area includes the Hand tool and the Zoom tool. These tools are used to change the view of the Stage while working with a Flash document. They do not affect the way the published movie is displayed to the user.

The Colors area includes options for specifying the colors for strokes and fills. **Strokes** refer to lines that you draw or add to an image, and **fills** refer to areas you paint with color. Fills are often enclosed by strokes. The pencil icon and the color box next to it are called the Stroke Color control. The **Stroke Color control** is used to change the stroke color. The paint bucket icon and its color box make up the **Fill Color control**, which is used to change the fill color.

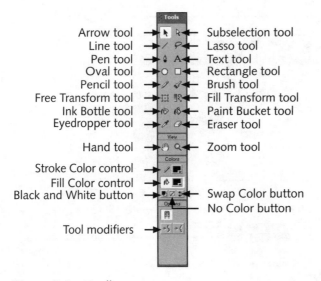

Arrow tool → Subselection tool
Line tool → Lasso tool
Pen tool → Text tool
Oval tool → Rectangle tool
Pencil tool → Brush tool
Free Transform tool → Fill Transform tool
Ink Bottle tool → Paint Bucket tool
Eyedropper tool → Eraser tool

Hand tool → Zoom tool

Stroke Color control →
Fill Color control →
Black and White button → Swap Color button
— No Color button

Tool modifiers →

Figure 7-2   Toolbox

The bottom of this area has three additional buttons. The **Black and White** button is used to change the stroke and fill colors to their default of black and white. The **No Color** button specifies that no color be used. This may be applied to either the stroke or the fill color. The **Swap Colors** button swaps the current stroke and fill colors.

The **Options** area changes to reflect the tool that has been selected. This area shows modifiers that change the way a specific tool works.

Panels

Panels are small windows containing options that give you more control over the various tools in Flash. The panels' default layout displays the Color Mixer, Color Swatches, Components, and Answer panels as well as the Actions panel and the Properties panel, also called the Property inspector. To access other panels, click Window on the menu bar and then click the name of the panel you want to display.

Each panel has a gray title bar displaying its name, as seen in Figure 7-3.

You can expand or collapse a panel by clicking on the collapse arrow on the panel's title bar. Most panels also contain an options menu that you can access by clicking on the options menu control located on the right side of the title bar. Panels can also be repositioned by dragging the icon at the left edge of the title bar. When you place the mouse pointer over this icon, it becomes a four-headed arrow (or a hand on a Macintosh), indicating that the panel can be dragged to a new position.

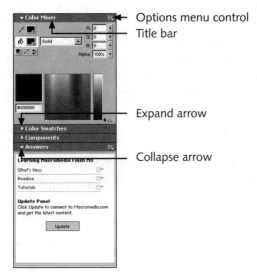

Options menu control

Title bar

Expand arrow

Collapse arrow

Figure 7-3   Panel elements

Press Tab on the keyboard to hide the panels. Press Tab again to redisplay the panels.

Property Inspector

The **Property inspector**, located at the bottom of the screen, provides easy access to the most common attributes of the currently selected tool or object. The contents of the Property inspector change to reflect the tool that is selected. For example, if you select the Arrow tool, the Property inspector displays information about the current document. If you select an object on the Stage such as an oval shape, the contents of the Property inspector change to provide access to the shape's properties such as its color, size, and position.

Starting a New Document

A Flash document can consist of text, images, animations, sounds, and video. In this chapter, you will work on creating and modifying images and text. When you first start the Flash program, you see a blank document with certain default properties. You can change these properties by using the Document Properties dialog box. The properties include the dimensions of width and height, which determine the size of the Stage area. The default dimensions are 550 pixels for the width and 400 pixels for the height. The Document Properties dialog box also includes options that allow you to change the background color, the frame rate (frames per second), and the ruler units.

To change a document's properties:

1. In Windows, start Macromedia Flash from the Start menu. (On a Macintosh, open Macromedia Flash MX from the Applications folder.) The Flash program opens, displaying a new, blank document. If necessary, click **File** on the menu bar, and then click **New** to create a new document. If you see a Welcome window, close it.

2. To set up your screen to look like the figures in this book, click **Window** on the menu bar, point to **Panel Sets**, and then click **Default Layout**. This returns the Flash environment to its original configuration.

3. If necessary, click the **Maximize** button on the Flash program window to expand it to fit the entire screen.

4. To see the document properties, click **Modify** on the menu bar, and then click **Document**. The Document Properties dialog box opens, as shown in Figure 7-4.

Document Properties	
Dimensions:	550 px (width) x 400 px (height)
Match:	Printer Contents Default
Background Color:	
Frame Rate:	12 fps
Ruler Units:	Pixels
Help Make Default	OK Cancel

Figure 7-4   Document Properties dialog box

You can also access some of the document properties in the Property inspector at the bottom of the screen.

5. Type **300** for the Width and **300** for the Height. Do not press Enter (or Return on a Macintosh) and do not click OK yet. Make sure that Ruler Units is set to **Pixels**. The Ruler Units indicate the unit of measurement that will be shown on the rulers.

6. Click the color box next to **Background Color** to display the color palette. Choose a blue color for the document's background.

7. Click **OK**. The Stage becomes smaller, and the background color of the Stage is now blue.

8. To display the Rulers, click **View** on the menu bar and then click **Rulers**. Rulers showing the pixel units appear on the top and left side of the work area.

9. To turn off the rulers, click **View** and then click **Rulers**.

10. Flash can also display gridlines to help you as you work on your document. To see the gridlines, click **View**, point to **Grid**, and then click **Show Grid**. Gridlines appear on the Stage.

11. To turn off the gridlines, click **View**, point to **Grid**, and then click **Show Grid**.

12. To close this document, click **File** on the menu bar and then click **Close**. When prompted to save the document, click **No** (or **Don't Save** on a Macintosh). The document closes, but Flash remains open.

Zoom and Hand Tools

When working with Flash, you can enlarge or reduce the view of the Stage by using the **Zoom tool**. You can also move the view of the Stage to see different areas of your document by using the **Hand tool**. The Hand tool converts the pointer to a hand that can then be dragged to move the view of the Stage. This is also known as panning. Panning is especially useful when you have zoomed in to one part of the image and you want to see another part that is currently out of view. Neither of these tools affects the way the movie is displayed to the user.

To change the view of the Stage:

1. Click **File** on the menu bar and then click **Open**. Browse to the Chapter folder for Chapter 7, select the **Ch07Flash01** file, and then click **Open**. This document contains several sample shapes.

2. Click the **Zoom** tool in the view area of the Toolbox. The pointer changes to a magnifying glass with a plus sign when you move it over the Stage. (If necessary, click the **Enlarge** modifier in the Options area of the Toolbox to display the magnifying glass with the plus sign.) See Figure 7-5.

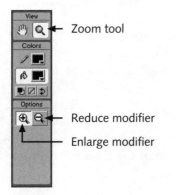

Figure 7-5   Zoom tool and its modifiers

3. Click two times on the **yellow oval** on the left of the Stage. As you click, the Stage is magnified, zooming in to the area where you clicked.

4. To zoom out, first click the **Reduce** modifier in the Options area of the Toolbox. The pointer changes to a magnifying glass with a minus sign.

5. Click three times on the **yellow oval** to zoom out.

 Another way to change the zoom level is by selecting a zoom percentage from the Zoom control drop-down list located at the upper-right corner of the Stage window. You can also enter a value into its text box.

6. Click the **Hand** tool in the Toolbox. The pointer changes to a hand as you move it over the Stage. Drag the pointer on the Stage to move the view of the Stage as shown in Figure 7-6.

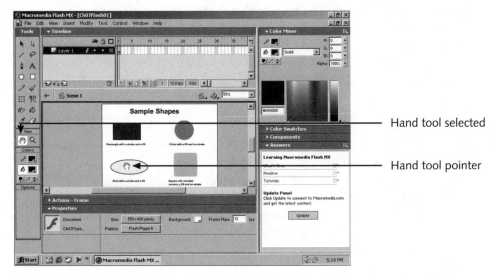

Hand tool selected

Hand tool pointer

Figure 7-6   Using the Hand tool to change the Stage view

 Double-click the Hand tool to zoom out far enough to show all of the Stage. This also centers the view of the Stage.

7. Click **File** on the menu bar and then click **Close** to close the document. If prompted to save changes, click the **No** button (or **Don't Save** on a Macintosh).

Drawing and Painting Tools

The drawing and painting tools include the Line, Pen, Oval, Rectangle, Pencil, and Brush tools. These tools allow you to create the lines, curves, and shapes that make up the images in a Flash document.

Using the Oval and Rectangle Tools

You can use the **Oval tool** to create oval shapes, and you use the **Rectangle tool** to create rectangular shapes. Flash will even help you create perfect circles and squares when **Snap to Objects** is turned on from the View menu. You can also specify the colors of the shapes you create by changing the stroke color and the fill color in the Colors area of the Toolbox. The stroke color is applied to the lines and curves that you draw, and the fill color is applied to the painted areas. When you click the color box next to one of the color controls in the Toolbox, a color palette pop-up window opens. When you move your pointer over the color palette, the pointer changes to an eyedropper. You then click a color on the palette with the eyedropper to select it. You can also enter the color's hexadecimal code in the text box or you can select no color by clicking on the No Color button.

The Rectangle tool also includes an option for creating rectangles with rounded corners. Clicking on the **Round Rectangle Radius** modifier in the Options area of the Toolbox displays a dialog box in which you can specify the number of points by which to round the corners. The higher the number of points, the more rounded the corners will be.

To create ovals and rectangles:

1. Click **File** on the menu bar and then click **New** to start a new document.

2. Click **View** on the menu bar and then click **Work Area** if it is not selected. (It should have a checkmark next to it.) Also, make sure that **Snap to Objects** is selected.

3. Double-click the **Hand** tool to make all of the Stage visible.

4. Click the **Oval** tool in the Toolbox to select it.

5. Click the color box in the **Stroke Color** control in the Toolbox to open the color palette pop-up window. Click the **red** color to make it the stroke color, as shown in Figure 7-7.

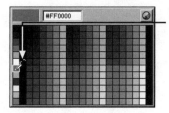 — Eyedropper over red color

Figure 7-7   Color palette

6. Now click the color box in the **Fill Color** control to open its color palette; select **blue** as the fill color.

7. You are now ready to draw an oval. Using the Oval tool you selected earlier, click and drag on the left side of the Stage to create an oval shape. When you release the mouse button, Flash draws an oval with a red stroke and a blue fill.

 Notice that as you drag the pointer, a solid ring sometimes appears next to the pointer. This means that Flash is helping you draw a circle. If you release the pointer when you see the solid ring, Flash will draw a perfect circle. Snap to Objects must be selected for the solid ring to display.

8. Click the **Rectangle** tool to select it. Drag the pointer on the Stage to the right of the oval. Create a rectangle just as you created an oval in Step 7. See Figure 7-8.

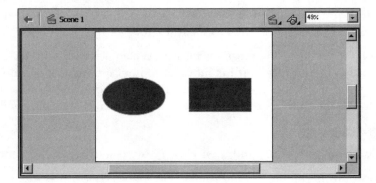

Figure 7-8   Oval and rectangle shapes

 If you make a mistake, click Edit on the menu bar and then click Undo to undo your previous step. By default, Flash has 100 levels of undo, which means you can undo a series of 100 actions.

9. Click the **Round Rectangle Radius** modifier in the options area of the Toolbox. The Rectangle Settings dialog box opens. Enter a value of **20** for the Corner Radius and click **OK**.

10. Drag your pointer on an empty area of the Stage to create a new rectangle with rounded corners.

11. Practice creating more ovals and rectangles using different colors for the strokes and fills.

12. When you are finished practicing, close the document without saving your changes.

Using the Line Tool

The **Line tool** creates straight lines of different lengths and angles. Using the Property inspector, you can specify the line's color and height; you can also select from predefined styles or create your own custom style. To draw a line, you drag the pointer on the Stage. As you drag the pointer, you will sometimes see a solid ring appear next to the pointer when Snap to Objects is turned on. This is Flash's way of helping you draw horizontal or vertical lines, just like it helps you draw perfect circles and squares. The solid ring also appears when you come close to other objects. When this happens, the line you draw will connect to the existing object. Connecting lines allow you to create new objects for your movies.

To draw lines:

1. Click **File** on the menu bar and then click **New** to start a new document.

2. Click the **Line** tool from the Toolbox to select it. In the Property inspector, click the color box in the **Stroke Color** control and then select a **blue** color in the color palette.

3. Move the pointer to the Stage, and watch the pointer change to a crosshair. Drag the pointer from the left side of the Stage to the middle of the Stage. Release the pointer to finish drawing the line. A blue line appears on the Stage.

4. In the Property inspector, use the **Stroke Color** control to change the stroke color to **green.** Then change the Stroke height setting to **4**.

 You can change the Stroke height value by typing a new number or by clicking on the list arrow to display a slider. You then drag the slider up or down to change the value.

5. Click the list arrow for the **Stroke style** setting, which currently displays a solid line. A list of stroke patterns is displayed in the drop-down list. Select the dashed pattern shown in Figure 7-9.

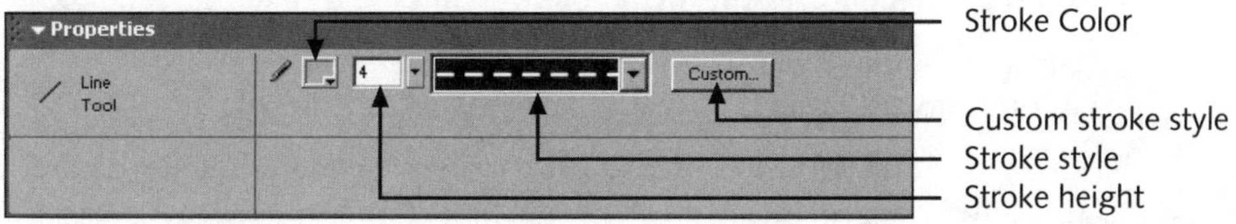

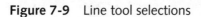

Figure 7-9   Line tool selections

6. Draw several lines on the Stage to see the effects of your stroke settings.

7. Click the **Custom stroke style** button in the Property inspector. The **Stroke Style** dialog box opens.

8. Select **Dotted** from the Type drop-down list and change the Thickness setting to **8**. Click **OK** to close the dialog box.

9. Use the **Line** tool to draw several lines on the Stage using the custom setting.

10. Experiment with the Line tool and the Property inspector settings to create several more lines.

11. Close the document without saving your changes.

Using the Pencil Tool

The **Pencil tool** works in a way similar to the Line tool. However, with the Pencil tool you are not limited to drawing straight lines. The Pencil tool allows you to draw lines and shapes in a freeform way as if you were using a real pencil to draw on paper. The same settings you selected from the Property inspector apply to the Pencil tool. Flash also provides some assistance in drawing with the Pencil tool when you use the **Pencil Mode** modifiers in the Options area of the Toolbox. These modifiers include Straighten, Smooth, and Ink. When the **Straighten** modifier is selected, Flash helps straighten out the lines you draw and even converts your rough drawings of shapes into rectangles or ovals. With the **Smooth** modifier selected, Flash will smooth out the lines and curves you draw. When using the **Ink** modifier, you are on your own; Flash does not help you at all.

To draw with the Pencil tool:

1. Click **File** on the menu bar and then click **New** to start a new document.

2. Click the **Pencil** tool from the Toolbox.

3. Use the Property inspector to set the Stroke style to **Solid** and the Stroke height to **2**. Also, set the Stroke Color to **black**.

4. In the Options area of the Toolbox, click the **Pencil Mode** modifier and, if necessary, click **Straighten** to select it.

5. Move your pointer to the Stage and notice that it looks like a pencil. Draw a rectangular shape, as shown in Figure 7-10. When you release the mouse button, Flash recognizes the shape of your lines and draws a rectangle.

6. Using the same technique, draw an oval shape. Flash also recognizes this shape and transforms your sketch into a nicely rounded oval.

7. Change the Pencil mode to **Smooth**. Draw the same shapes as before. Flash smoothes out the lines you draw, but it does not create rectangles or ovals for you.

8. Change the Pencil mode to **Ink**. Draw the same shapes as before. Note that Flash does not provide any help.

9. Close the document without saving your changes.

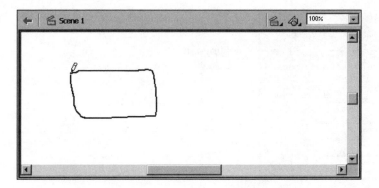

Figure 7-10   Drawing a rectangular shape

Using the Pen Tool

The **Pen tool** is used to draw line and curve segments, also called **paths**, by creating anchor points that connect them. When you select the Pen tool, the pointer changes into a pen icon with a small x next to it, indicating that you are about to start a new line or curve. Clicking on the Stage with the Pen tool creates points that Flash connects with straight lines. To draw curved lines, you click and drag instead of just clicking points. As you drag the pointer, **tangent handles** appear. The length and direction of the tangent handles determine the shape of the curve segment. When you release the pointer, a curved line is drawn. To help you preview the curved lines as you draw, you can click Edit on the menu bar and then click Preferences to open the Preferences dialog box. You then turn on Show Pen Preview in the Editing tab of the Preferences dialog box.

To draw shapes with the Pen tool:

1. Click **File** on the menu bar and then click **New** to start a new document.

2. Click **Edit** on the menu bar and click **Preferences**. (On a Macintosh, click **Flash** and then click **Preferences**.) The Preferences dialog box opens.

3. Click the **Editing** tab and click the **Show Pen Preview** check box to select it, as shown in Figure 7-11.

4. Click **OK** to close the Preferences dialog box.

5. Click the **Pen** tool from the Toolbox.

6. If necessary, use the Property inspector to set the Stroke style to **Solid**, the Stroke height to **2**, the Stroke Color to **black**, and the Fill Color to **red**.

7. Click once on the left side of the Stage to add a point. Move your pointer to the right of the first point and click again to create another point. Flash connects the two points with a straight line.

8. Move the pointer down and click again to add another point. Flash draws another line connecting this point to the previous point.

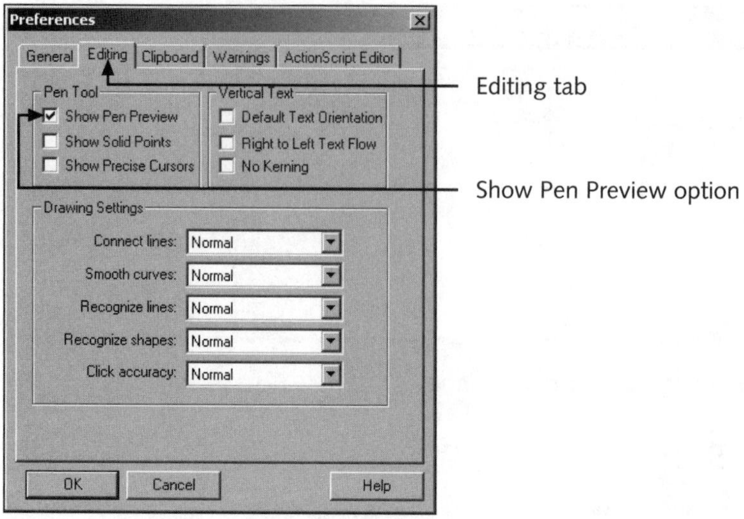

Figure 7-11   Show Pen Preview selected

9. Move the pointer back to your starting point. You see a small hollow circle next to the pen pointer, indicating that the next click will complete your shape. Click when you see this hollow circle. A triangle shape with a red fill appears in the document. See Figure 7-12.

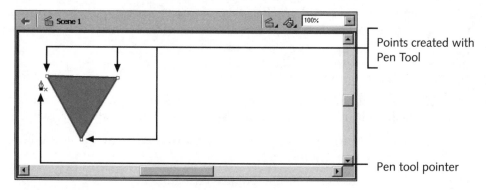

Figure 7-12   Triangle shape created with Pen tool

To complete your line segments without creating a closed shape, double-click wherever you want the end point to appear.

10. In the center of the Stage, click and then drag the pen pointer to the right. Tangent handles appear to help you determine the shape of the curved line. Release the pointer. Now move the pointer down. As you move the pointer, Flash previews the curved line that will be drawn.

11. Click and drag again to the left to create another curved line segment. Release the pointer.

12. Move the pointer back to the starting point. Once the pointer changes to display a small hollow circle next to it, click to complete the curved shape, as shown in Figure 7-13.

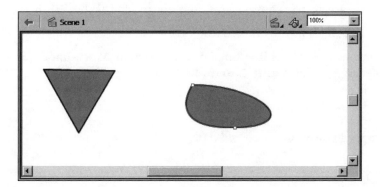

Figure 7-13   Completed curved shape

13. Practice drawing several shapes with the Pen tool, combining straight lines and curved lines.

14. Close the document without saving your changes.

Using the Brush Tool

The **Brush tool** is used to paint fills similar to the way you paint with a real paintbrush. You paint brush strokes that create fills according to the Brush Mode, Brush Size, and Brush Shape. You can choose from the following **Brush Mode** modifiers, which allow you to control how the Brush tool will paint:

- Paint Normal—paint over the strokes and fills

- Paint Fills—paint over the fills only; does not affect the strokes

- Paint Behind—paint "behind" an object

- Paint Selection—paint only the selected object

- Paint Inside—paint only inside the area where the brush stroke is first applied

The Brush Size option changes the size of the brush tip. The Brush Shape option changes the shape of the brush tip. The Lock Fill option is used to lock a gradient or bitmap fill across several objects on the Stage. This means that the gradient or bitmap fill is spread across several objects on the Stage instead of being repeated in each of the objects.

To paint with the Brush tool:

1. Click **File** on the menu bar and then click **New** to start a new document.

2. Select the **Oval** tool from the Toolbox. In the Property inspector, change the Stroke height to **4**, the Stroke Color to **black**, the Fill Color to **blue**, and the Stroke style to **solid**. Draw a large oval on the center of the Stage. You will use this oval to test some of the different modes of the Brush tool.

3. Click the **Brush** tool from the Toolbox to select it.

4. In the Options area of the Toolbox, click the **Brush Mode** modifier and then, if necessary, click **Paint Normal,** as shown on Figure 7-14.

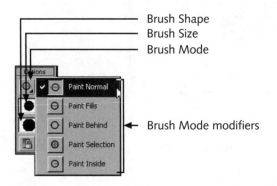

Figure 7-14   Brush tool options

5. Select a paintbrush color by changing the Fill Color to **red** in the Property inspector.

You can also change the paintbrush color by using the Fill Color control in the Toolbox.

6. Use the paintbrush pointer to paint a brush stroke that starts on the left side of the oval, runs through the oval, and ends on the right side of the oval. Notice that the paintbrush paints both the stroke and the fill of the oval.

7. Click the **Brush Mode** modifier in the Toolbox and then click **Paint Fills** to select it. Also, change the Fill Color to **green**.

8. Paint another brush stroke, but this time paint it through a different area of the oval, making sure you paint through the oval's stroke. Notice that now only the oval's fill is painted and not its stroke.

9. Click the **Brush Mode** modifier in the Toolbox and then click **Paint Behind** to select it.

10. Again paint a brush stroke going across the oval, making sure that you start outside of the oval and end on the opposite side. Notice that only the area outside of the oval is painted, giving the effect that you painted "behind" the oval. Actually, there is nothing behind the oval. See Figure 7-15.

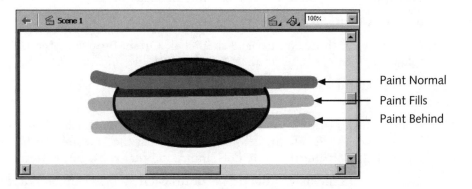

Figure 7-15   Brush strokes using different modifiers

11. Practice painting with the various brush sizes and brush shapes.

12. Close the document without saving your changes.

SELECTING AND MODIFYING LINES, CURVES, AND SHAPES

Once you draw lines, curves, and shapes, you can change their characteristics, but to do this you first need to select them by using the selection tools. The selection tools in the Toolbox include the Arrow, Subselection, and Lasso tools. Once you have selected an object, you can then modify it by using one of the following tools: Free Transform, Fill Transform, Eraser, Ink Bottle, Paint Bucket, and Eyedropper.

Using the Arrow Tool

The **Arrow tool** is used to select lines, curves, or fills and can also be used to select a group of objects. You select objects by clicking on them or by drawing a temporary outline around them called a marquee. Drawing a marquee is useful when you need to select more than one object at one time. When you select an object, Flash covers it with a pattern of tiny dots to indicate that it has been selected. (Some selected objects will display a rectangular outline around them instead of a pattern of dots. These objects have special characteristics that you will learn about in the next chapter.)

Once you have selected an object, you can then modify or move it. The Arrow tool also has several modifiers that may be applied to selected lines and shape outlines. These modifiers include Snap to Objects, Smooth, and Straighten, as described in the following list:

- Snap to Objects—attaches selected objects to other objects when they are moved close together

- Smooth—smoothes the selected line or shape outline

- Straighten—straightens the selected line or shape outline

To modify objects with the Arrow tool:

1. Click **File** on the menu bar and then click **Open**. Browse to the Chapter folder for Chapter 7, select the **Ch07Flash01** file, and click **Open**.

2. Use the **Hand** tool to move the view of the Stage so that the rectangle is in the center.

3. Click the **Arrow** tool to select it. Click inside the blue area of the rectangle located on the left side of the Stage. Notice that the blue area, or fill, of the rectangle has a pattern of tiny dots, indicating that it has been selected.

4. To select both the fill and the stroke, **double-click** anywhere on the rectangle.

5. To deselect the rectangle, click somewhere on the Stage away from the rectangle.

6. Click a point above and to the left of the rectangle and then drag the pointer across and down until a marquee surrounds the entire rectangle, as shown in Figure 7-16. When you release the pointer, both the stroke and the fill of the rectangle will be selected.

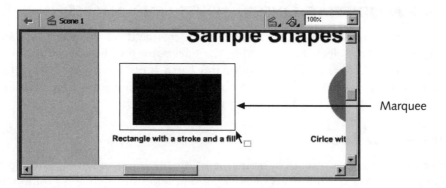

Figure 7-16   Marquee drawn around rectangle

7. Deselect the rectangle and then move the pointer over the right side of the rectangle. When the pointer has a small arc next to it, click once to select the stroke only. One side of the rectangle is selected.

8. Click and drag the selected side of the rectangle to separate it from the rest of the shape.

9. To change the rectangle's shape, move the pointer over the top line segment of the rectangle until you see a small arc next to the pointer. Once you see this arc, click and drag the line up slightly to curve it, as shown in Figure 7-17.

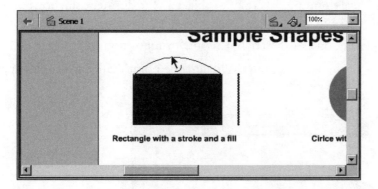

Figure 7-17   Changing the shape of the rectangle

10. Release the mouse pointer. The top line of the rectangle is changed to a curve, and the fill of the rectangle expands to fill the additional area now enclosed by the curved line.

11. Move the pointer over one of the corner points of the rectangle. (Corner points are located where two line segments connect.) When you see a small right-angle icon next to the pointer, click and drag the corner point to change its location. The shape's fill also changes according to the corner's new position.

12. Practice selecting and modifying the other objects on the Stage with the Arrow tool.

13. Close the document without saving your changes.

Using the Subselection Tool

You can adjust the anchor points in lines or curves by using the **Subselection tool**. You can also use this tool to change the angle or length of a straight line and to change the slope and direction of curves. To display the anchor points of a stroke, you click it with the Subselection tool. Strokes that are curved line segments display anchor points and tangent handles. The tangent handles can be used to change the shape of the curve. You can also display the anchor points by clicking on the stroke with the Pen tool.

To modify strokes using the Subselection tool:

1. Click **File** on the menu bar and then click **New** to start a new document.

2. Click the **Oval** tool in the Toolbox. In the Property inspector, set the Stroke Color to **black**, the Stroke height to **4**, the Fill Color to **green**, and the Stroke style to **Solid**.

3. Draw a large oval in the center of the Stage.

4. Click the **Subselection** tool on the Toolbox.

5. Click the oval's outline or stroke to select it. Small square anchor points appear around the oval.

6. Click and drag one of the anchor points to reposition it.

7. Click one of the anchor points. The anchor point's tangent handles appear, as shown in Figure 7-18.

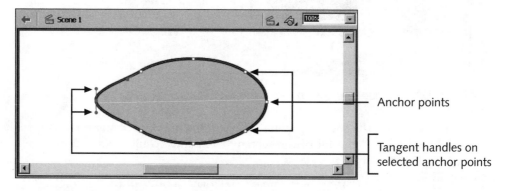

Figure 7-18   Anchor points and tangent handles

8. Click and drag on the ends of the tangent handles to change the slope and direction of the curve.

9. Practice moving the anchor points and adjusting their tangent handles to create a different shape.

10. Create a rectangle and practice adjusting its anchor points.

11. Close the document without saving changes.

Using the Lasso Tool

The **Lasso tool** is used to select irregularly shaped areas by drawing a freeform marquee around them. You can also use the Lasso tool to select a group of objects at one time. You click and drag the pointer to draw a marquee around the areas or objects you want selected, and then you release the pointer to finish the selection. When the

Polygon Mode modifier is selected in the options area of the Toolbox, you can draw a marquee by clicking points around the object (or objects) you want to select.

To select objects using the Lasso tool:

1. Click **File** on the menu bar and then click **Open**. Browse to the Chapter folder for Chapter 7 and open the **Ch07Flash02** file.

2. Double-click the **Hand** tool on the Toolbox to show the entire document.

3. Click the **Lasso** tool on the Toolbox. The pointer takes on the shape of a lasso when you move it over the Stage.

4. Make sure that the **Polygon Mode** modifier in the Options area of the Toolbox is *not* selected.

5. Drag the lasso pointer to create a marquee around two of the buttons. Continue to drag the lasso pointer until you come back to your starting point. Release the mouse button, and then verify that the buttons you selected have blue outlines around them.

6. Click somewhere on a blank area of the Stage to deselect the buttons.

7. Click the **Polygon Mode** modifier in the Options area of the Toolbox.

8. To select buttons 2, 4, and 5 at the same time, click once on the Stage to the left of button 2 to set your starting point. Then click additional points around buttons 4 and 5 to create a marquee around all three buttons, as shown in Figure 7-19.

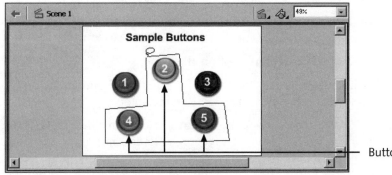

Buttons to be selected

Figure 7-19   Marquee around buttons

9. Double-click at the starting point to end the marquee and to select the objects. Buttons 2, 4, and 5 are now selected.

10. Close the document without saving changes.

Using the Transform Tools

The Flash Toolbox has two transform tools that allow you to modify objects such as lines, curves, shapes, and fills. One of these is the **Free Transform tool**, which can be used to move, rotate, scale, skew, or distort objects. When you select an object with the Free Transform tool, a bounding box with selection handles surrounds the object. You can then drag these handles to transform the object. The pointer changes as you point at or around different corner or edge handles to indicate how the object will be changed when you drag the handles. The handles will also change when one of the modifiers is selected. The modifiers include Rotate and Skew, Scale, Distort, and Envelope. With the **Rotate and Skew** modifier, you can freely rotate an object by dragging a corner handle or you can skew it at a different angle by dragging an edge handle. The **Scale** modifier allows you to change the size of the object. The **Distort** modifier lets you move the corner or edges of an object to change the object's shape. When the **Envelope** modifier is applied to an object, the bounding box displays points and tangent handles. You can then adjust these points or tangent handles to warp or distort the object.

The other transform tool, **Fill Transform**, is used to modify bitmap and gradient fills. A shape such as an oval can have different types of fills. Besides using a simple color as a fill, you can also use a bitmap graphic as a fill. You can also use a gradient, which consists of a blend of two or more colors, as a fill. The Fill Transform tool lets you modify fills that consist of bitmaps or gradients by adjusting their size, direction, or center points.

To modify objects using the Free Transform tool:

1. Click **File** on the menu bar and then click **Open**. Browse to the Chapter folder for Chapter 7 and open the **Ch07Flash01** file.

2. Click the **Hand** tool on the Toolbox and use it to adjust your view of the Stage to display both the blue rectangle and red circle.

3. Click the **Free Transform** tool on the Toolbox.

4. Double-click the blue rectangle to select both its fill and its stroke. A bounding box with selection handles surrounds the rectangle.

5. To rotate the rectangle, click the **Rotate and Skew** modifier. Drag one of the corner handles to rotate the rectangle. Then drag one of the side handles to skew the rectangle. See Figure 7-20.

6. Click the red circle to select it.

7. Click the **Envelope** modifier. The bounding box around the circle displays square points. These points have tangent handles (which are indicated by round points). Drag these points and handles to change the shape of the circle.

8. Practice using the Free Transform tool with its modifiers to change the shapes in this document.

9. Close the document without saving changes.

Dragging the side handle skews the rectangle

Figure 7-20 Modifying the rectangle

Using the Eraser Tool

The **Eraser tool** deletes strokes and fills. With the Eraser tool selected, you drag the pointer over the strokes or fills you want to erase. The Eraser tool erases according to the **Eraser Mode** modifier that is currently selected. These modifiers include the following:

- Erase Normal—erases both fills and strokes

- Erase Fills—erases only the fills and not the strokes

- Erase Lines—erases only the strokes and not the fills

- Erase Selected Fills—erases only fills that have been selected

- Erase Inside—erases fills as determined by the point where you start to erase; does not affect strokes

Other options include the Faucet modifier and the Eraser Shape. The **Faucet modifier** will erase an entire fill or stroke with just one click. The **Eraser Shape** lets you change the eraser to one of several preset sizes of square and oval shapes.

To erase using the Eraser tool:

1. Click **File** on the menu bar and then click **New** to start a new document.

2. Click the **Oval** tool and, if necessary, set the Stroke Color to **black** and the Stroke height to **4**. Also, change the Fill Color to **blue**. Draw a large oval on the Stage.

3. Click the **Eraser** tool in the Toolbox.

4. In the Options area in the Toolbox, click the **Eraser Mode** modifier and, if necessary, click **Erase Normal,** as shown in Figure 7-21. Make sure that the **Faucet** modifier is not selected.

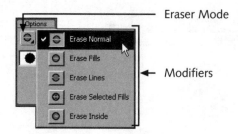

Eraser Mode

Modifiers

Figure 7-21   Eraser Mode modifiers

5. Drag the pointer across the oval, taking care to go across both the stroke and the fill. The Eraser tool should erase both the stroke and fill, just as you would expect an eraser to do.

6. Click the **Eraser Mode** modifier and then click **Erase Fills**. Drag the pointer across a different part of the oval, being sure to go across the stroke and the fill. This time, only the fill is erased and not the stroke.

7. Change the Eraser Mode modifier to **Erase Lines**. Drag the pointer across the oval one more time. This time the fill is not erased, only the stroke. See Figure 7-22.

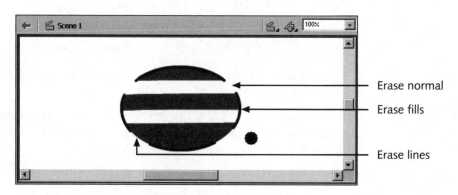

Erase normal

Erase fills

Erase lines

Figure 7-22   Eraser tool applied to oval

8. Click the **Faucet** modifier to select it. As you move the pointer to the Stage area, the pointer changes to a faucet.

9. Click any fill or stroke to erase it.

10. Draw several other shapes to practice using the Eraser tool and its modifiers.

11. Close the document without saving your changes.

Using the Ink Bottle Tool

The **Ink Bottle tool** is used to change the color, size, or style of an existing stroke. It will also add a stroke to a shape that has none. When you select the Ink Bottle tool, the pointer changes to an ink bottle as you move it over the Stage. You then click an object to add or change its stroke based on the color, size, and style settings specified in the Property inspector.

To apply a new stroke to an object:

1. Click **File** on the menu bar and then click **New** to start a new document

 You can also double-click the Eraser tool to erase all the contents of the Stage.

2. In the Colors area of the Toolbox, set the Stroke Color to **black**, if necessary, and the Fill Color to **red**.

3. Click the **Oval** tool and draw a large oval on the left side of the Stage.

4. Click the **Rectangle** tool to select it. Then click the **Stroke Color** control in the Toolbox and click the **No Color** button.

5. Draw a large rectangle to the right of the oval.

6. In the Property inspector, change the Stroke Color to **green**, the Stroke height to **6**, and, on the drop-down list for the Stroke style, select a **dashed line**.

7. Click the **Ink Bottle** tool.

8. Click once on the oval to change its stroke. The stroke should now be a thick dashed green line.

9. Click somewhere on the rectangle to add a stroke. The rectangle now has the same type of stroke as the oval, as shown in Figure 7- 23.

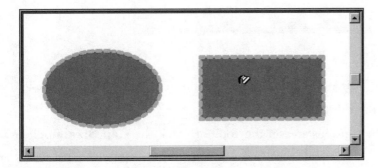

Figure 7-23   Applying a stroke to an existing shape

10. Close the document without saving your changes.

Using the Paint Bucket Tool

The **Paint Bucket tool** fills enclosed areas with color. It also changes the color of an existing fill. The Paint Bucket tool has a Gap Size modifier that allows you to paint areas that are not completely enclosed. The Gap Size modifiers include:

- Don't Close Gaps
- Close Small Gaps
- Close Medium Gaps
- Close Large Gaps

To apply fills with the Paint Bucket tool:

1. Click **File** on the menu bar and then click **New** to start a new document.

2. Select the **Pencil** tool. Click the **Pencil Mode** modifier, and, if necessary, click **Smooth** to select it.

3. In the Property inspector, set the Stroke Color to **black**, set its Stroke height to **1**, and set its Stroke style to **Solid**.

4. Draw several shapes on the Stage similar to those shown in Figure 7-24, making sure you include different size gaps.

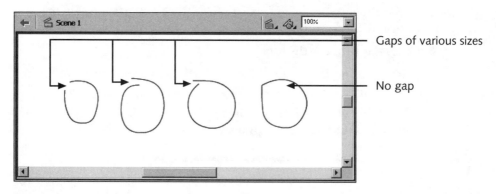

Gaps of various sizes

No gap

Figure 7-24 Shapes

5. Click the **Paint Bucket** tool. The pointer changes to a paint bucket.

6. Change the Fill Color to **blue**.

7. Under the Options area in the Toolbox, click the **Gap Size** modifier and then click **Don't Close Gaps**.

8. Click once inside each of the shapes on the Stage. Only the shapes that are completely enclosed have a blue fill.

9. Change the Fill Color to **yellow** and change the Gap Size modifier to **Close Large Gaps**.

10. Click again inside each of the shapes. This time, both the shapes that are completely enclosed plus those that have a gap contain a yellow fill. (If the gap is too large, no fill is applied.)

11. Experiment with the different gap size options on different shapes that you draw with the pencil.

12. Close the document without saving your changes.

Using the Eyedropper Tool

The **Eyedropper tool** is used to copy the fill or stroke attributes of one object and then apply them to another object. You can also copy the attributes of a text block and apply them to a new text block. A text block is an object that contains text created by the Text tool. The Text tool is discussed in the next section. When you select the Eyedropper tool, the pointer changes to an eyedropper. If you move the eyedropper over a stroke, a small pencil icon appears next to it, indicating that you are about to copy the stroke's attributes. Once you click the stroke, the pointer changes to an ink bottle. You then use the ink bottle to click another object and apply the copied stroke attributes.

You follow a similar process to copy the fill attributes of one object to another. Select the Eyedropper tool, and then move the eyedropper over a fill. A small paintbrush icon appears next to the pointer, indicating that you are about to copy the fill's attributes. When you click the fill whose attributes you want to copy, the pointer changes to a paint bucket. You then use the paint bucket to click another object and apply the copied fill attributes.

To copy stroke and fill attributes:

1. Click **File** on the menu bar and then click **New** to start a new document.

2. Click the **Oval** tool. Set the Stroke Color to **red**, the Fill Color to **green**, and the Stroke height to **4**. Draw a large oval on the left side of the Stage.

3. Click the **Rectangle** tool. Change the Stroke Color to **blue** and the Fill Color to **yellow**. Draw a large rectangle to the right of the oval.

4. Click the **Eyedropper** tool.

5. Click the oval's stroke. The eyedropper pointer changes to an ink bottle, as shown in Figure 7-25.

6. Click anywhere on the rectangle. The rectangle's stroke changes to red, just like the oval's stroke.

7. Click the **Eyedropper** tool again.

8. Click the rectangle's fill. The pointer changes to a paint bucket.

9. Click the oval's fill to change it to **yellow**, just like the rectangle.

10. Close the document without saving your changes.

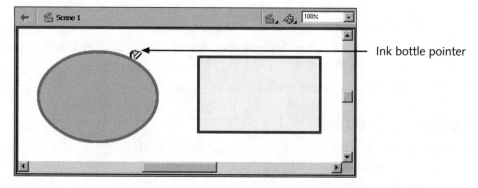

Ink bottle pointer

Figure 7-25 Eyedropper pointer changed to ink bottle pointer

Working with Text

The **Text tool** is used to create text blocks for your documents. There are three types of text blocks: static, dynamic, and input. **Static text** does not change when the user displays your movie. **Dynamic text** is an advanced feature in which text is updated automatically when the movie is being displayed. **Input text** allows for the user to enter text in forms or surveys. Static is the default text type and the type with which you will work most of the time.

To create text, you select the Text tool, click the Stage, and start typing. A text block is created with a round handle on the top right corner, which denotes that the width of the text block will expand as you type. If you drag the round handle to adjust the width of the block, the handle changes to a square, indicating that the width of the block is now fixed. You can also click and drag to create a text block with a fixed width. In this case, the text block displays a square handle on the top right corner, indicating that the width of the text block will remain fixed. As you type text in such a text block, the words wrap around to the next line when you reach the right margin of the block. You can change a fixed-width text block to expand automatically by double-clicking the square handle. The block will then have a round handle.

Once you create a text block, you can move it by using the Arrow tool, and you can also resize, rotate, and skew it by using the Free Transform tool. The font, size, color, and other attributes of the text are determined by the settings in the Property inspector. You can set these attributes before you type the text or you can select existing text and then change its attributes.

To create text blocks:

1. Click **File** on the menu bar and then click **New** to start a new document.

2. Double-click the **Hand** tool to center the view of the Stage.

3. Click the **Text** tool.

4. Using the Property inspector, select a different font of your choice, change the Font Size to **20**, and set the Text (fill) color to **black**. See Figure 7-26.

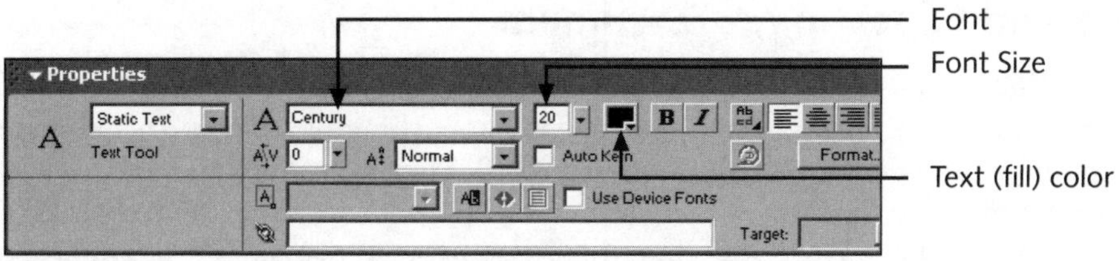

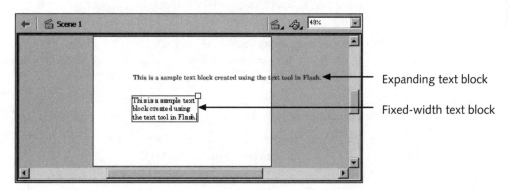

Figure 7-26   Text style settings

If you cannot see all of the options in the Property inspector, separate the Property inspector from the current window by dragging it to a new position.

5. Click once on the Stage and type the following sentence: **This is a sample text block created using the text tool in Flash.** As you type, the text block expands to fit the text.

6. Create another text block on a separate part of the Stage, but this time click and drag to create a fixed text block of about one-third the width of the Stage.

7. Type the same sentence as before into this second block. The text should wrap around to the next line as you reach the right side of the text block. If the text does not reach the end of the block, continue typing until you see the text wrap around to the next line. See Figure 7-27.

Figure 7-27   Text blocks

8. Click the first text block to select it.

9. Adjust the width of the top text block by clicking and dragging its round handle. The handle changes to a square.

10. Close the document without saving your changes.

Printing and Exporting a Document

A Flash document can be printed to obtain a hard copy for reference, and it can also be exported in one of several image formats. As mentioned earlier in this chapter, you can also publish the document as a movie for the Web. You will do this in the next chapter. To print a Flash document, you click File on the menu bar and then click Print to open the Print dialog box. Then you click the OK button to print the document. The printed document is centered on the page.

You can also export a Flash document in one of several image formats, including GIF and JPEG. Once exported, the image file can be opened in another software application or used as part of another file. For example, a document exported as a GIF or JPEG image can be added to a Web page. To export a Flash document, you click File on the menu bar and then click Export Image. You then click the Save as Type list arrow to select an image format, such as GIF. You also assign the image a file name and then click the Save button. Another dialog box opens with adjustable settings based on the image format you selected. For example, if you select the GIF image format, an Export GIF dialog box displays with settings that you can change, such as the image's dimensions and resolution. You can accept the default settings by just clicking the OK button. The document is then exported as an image file, which is a separate file from the Flash document that is saved as a FLA file.

To print and export a Flash document:

1. Click **File** on the menu bar and then click **Open**. Browse to the Chapter folder for Chapter 7, select the **Ch07Flash01** file, and then click **Open**. The document with sample shapes opens.

2. Click **File** on the menu bar and then click **Print**. The Print dialog box opens. If necessary, select the appropriate printer, and then click the **OK** button. The document prints.

3. Click **File** on the menu bar and click **Export Image**. In the Export Image dialog box, type **Sample** as the file name in the File name text box.

4. Click the list arrow for the **Save as type** drop-down list (or the **Format** drop-down list on a Macintosh) and select **GIF Image (*.gif)**. Then click the **Save** button. The Export GIF dialog box opens.

5. Click the **OK** button to accept the default settings in the Export GIF dialog box. The document is exported as a GIF image file.

6. Close the document without saving any changes.

CHAPTER SUMMARY

❑ Flash is a software application that provides Web designers with tools for creating interactive, animated, multimedia-rich movies for the Web. Flash works with vector graphics that consist of lines and curves and are stored as mathematical equations. These files tend to be small compared to bitmap graphics, which consist of pixels and are stored with all of the individual pixel information. Bitmap graphics may be imported into Flash.

❑ Key elements of the Flash environment include the Stage, menu bar, Toolbox, panels, and the Timeline.

❑ The Stage is where images are created, imported, and modified. Whatever is on the Stage will be displayed when the Flash document is published.

❑ The Toolbox contains four areas. The first is the Tools area, which includes the tools to create and modify the graphic objects in a Flash document. The View area has tools used to change the view of the Stage and to zoom in and out. The Colors area has tools to change the stroke and fill colors. The Options area has modifiers for the various tools.

❑ Panels are small windows that contain options for the various tools. Panels may be opened, closed, collapsed, expanded, and positioned as needed. They can also be grouped into windows to be treated as a set. A panel layout may be saved and accessed each time Flash is opened. Panels that are not visible may be accessed through the Windows menu.

❑ The Property inspector is a special panel whose options change depending on which tool or object is selected.

❑ The drawing and painting tools include the Line, Pen, Oval, Rectangle, Pencil, and Brush tools. The selection tools include the Arrow, Subselection, and Lasso tools. The tools used to transform and modify objects include the Free Transform, Fill Transform, Eraser, Ink Bottle, Paint Bucket, and Eyedropper tools.

❑ The Text tool is used to create text blocks. Text blocks may expand automatically as you type or they may be of fixed width. The text attributes are set in the Property inspector.

❑ Flash documents can be printed and can also be exported in several image formats such as GIF or JPEG.

7

REVIEW QUESTIONS

1. Flash gives Web designers the tools to create _____.

   a. interactive movies for the Web

   b. multimedia-rich movies for the Web

   c. small vector graphics

   d. all of the above

2. Vector image files _____.

   a. are stored in the form of pixels

   b. are best for storing photographs with many color tones

   c. tend to be larger than bitmap image files

   d. are stored in the form of equations

3. Images that are to be displayed in the final published movie _____.

   a. must be placed within the gray work area

   b. must be placed on the Stage

   c. must be on the Toolbox

   d. must be placed on a panel

4. The four areas of the Toolbox are _____.

   a. Panels, Stage, View, Colors

   b. Options, View, Paints, Tools

   c. Tools, View, Colors, Options

   d. Tools, Movies, Colors, Options

5. The Line tool is used to _____.

   a. draw straight lines of varying lengths, widths, and colors

   b. draw lines or curves by creating anchor points

   c. draw lines and shapes in a freeform mode

   d. draw filled rectangles

6. The Pencil tool is used to _____.

   a. draw straight lines of varying lengths, widths, and colors

   b. draw lines or curves by creating anchor points

   c. draw lines and shapes in a freeform mode

   d. draw filled rectangles

7. The _____ tool is used to apply color, thickness, and styles to strokes.

   a. Oval

   b. Subselection

   c. Ink Bottle

   d. Lasso

8. Clicking and dragging with the Pen tool will _____.

   a. draw points for smooth, curved lines

   b. select a group of objects

   c. draw points for straight lines

   d. draw fills inside a selected object

9. The term "strokes" refers to _____.

   a. a painted area of an object that may be selected

   b. rectangles with rounded corners that contain fills

   c. irregular shapes that are joined to form other objects

   d. lines and curves that form the outline of an object

10. What are the default dimensions of a new Flash document?

    a. 500 pixels by 300 pixels

    b. 550 pixels by 400 pixels

    c. 500 pixels by 450 pixels

    d. 500 pixels by 400 pixels

11. When drawing with the Oval tool, Flash will help you draw a perfect circle if _____.

    a. the grid lines are displayed

    b. the Snap to Objects is turned on

    c. the Snap to Grid is turned on

    d. the Snap to Guides is turned on

12. The Lasso tool _____.

    a. selects fills only

    b. selects strokes only

    c. selects irregularly shaped objects or a group of objects

    d. selects rope-shaped objects only

7

13. The Eraser tool's Faucet modifier is used to _____ .

   a. add color to an object

   b. erase a fill or a stroke

   c. create faucet-shaped symbols

   d. erase behind selected objects

14. With the Eyedropper tool selected, a small pencil appears next to the pointer when the pointer is moved over a stroke. This means that _____ .

   a. a new line will be drawn

   b. the stroke will be changed to a different color

   c. the stroke will be erased

   d. the stroke's attributes will be copied

15. Text blocks with a small square on the top right corner _____ .

   a. have a fixed width

   b. have an automatically expandable width

   c. have a limit on the number of characters they will hold

   d. have a fixed color

HANDS-ON EXERCISES

Exercise 7-1

1. Start a new document.

2. Click Modify on the menu bar and then click Document to display the Document Properties dialog box.

3. Change the dimensions to 400 pixels wide by 300 pixels high. Change the background color to yellow. Make sure the ruler units are set to pixels. Click OK to close the dialog box.

4. Click View on the menu bar and then click Rulers to turn on the rulers. Also, from the View menu make sure that Snap to Objects is turned on and that Snap to Grid (under Grid) is *not* turned on.

5. Click Window on the menu bar and then click Timeline to close the timeline.

6. Double-click the Hand tool to center the Stage.

7. Select the Line tool. Set the Stroke Color to black, the Stroke height to 1, and the Stroke style to Solid.

8. Starting at a point of 250 pixels from the top of the Stage and 150 pixels from the left of the Stage, draw a horizontal line. Make the line 100 pixels in length. Use the rulers to measure the position and length of your line.

9. Use the Arrow tool to select the line. Click Edit on the menu bar and then click Copy to make a copy of the line. Click Edit and then click Paste to create a duplicate of the line. The duplicate line should display on the middle of the Stage.

 In Windows, you can display the Main toolbar that contains shortcuts to commonly used menu options such as Print, Copy, Paste, and Undo. Display the Main toolbar by clicking Window on the menu bar, pointing to Toolbars, and then clicking Main.

10. With the new line still selected, click Modify on the menu bar, point to Transform, and click Scale and Rotate to open the Scale and Rotate dialog box. Leave the Scale value at 100% and change the Rotate value to 72 degrees. Click OK.

11. Using the Arrow tool, drag the new line's bottom end point. Move the end point of the new line to the left end point of the first line until they snap together.

12. The new line should remain selected in its new position. Now copy and paste this new line. The duplicate of this line is placed on the center of the Stage.

13. Use the Scale and Rotate dialog box as before to rotate the new line by another 72 degrees.

14. Move the new duplicate line by its end point and attach it to the top end point of the second line.

15. Repeat this process to create two more lines to complete your pentagon shape. Be careful not to deselect a new line when it overlaps with another line. Doing so will segment your line when you reselect it.

16. Once you have a pentagon shape, use the Text tool to create a text block that contains your name and the words "Exercise 1".

17. Print the document.

18. Save your document as **Ch07FlashEX01** in the Exercises folder for Chapter 7.

Exercise 7-2

1. Open the **Ch07FlashEX01** file with the pentagon shape created in Exercise 7-1.

2. Close the Timeline panel.

3. Change "Exercise 1" in the text block to "Exercise 2". You can do this by double-clicking the text with the Arrow tool or by clicking the text once with the Text tool.

4. Using the Arrow tool, double-click the pentagon shape to select all of its lines.

5. Copy and paste the shape to create a duplicate pentagon.

6. With the duplicate pentagon still selected, click Modify on the menu bar, point to Transform, and click Scale and Rotate to display the Scale and Rotate dialog box. Set the Scale value to 90 and the Rotate value to 0. Click OK. You should now have a smaller version of the pentagon shape.

7

7. Using the Arrow tool, move the new pentagon shape so that it fits inside the larger pentagon. You can also use the arrow keys on your keyboard to nudge the selected shape into position.

8. Deselect the smaller pentagon shape.

9. Select the Paint Bucket tool and change the fill color to blue.

10. Click once inside the area between the two pentagon shapes to create a blue filled border.

11. Print the document.

12. Save this movie as **Ch07FlashEX02** in your Exercises folder for Chapter 7.

Exercise 7-3

1. Start with a new document.

2. Click Modify on the menu bar and then click Document to display the Document Properties dialog box.

3. Change the dimensions to 300 pixels wide by 300 pixels high. Set the background color to white. Make sure the ruler units are set to pixels. Click OK to close the dialog box.

4. Close the Timeline panel.

5. Double-click the Hand tool to center the view of the Stage.

6. Click View on the menu bar, and make sure that the Rulers and Snap to Objects are turned on. Also, under View and Grid, make sure that Show Grid and Snap to Grid are turned on.

7. Select the Rectangle tool.

8. Set the Stroke Color to black, the Stroke height to 1, the Stroke style to Solid, and the Fill Color to no color.

9. Starting at a grid point close to 100 pixels down and 100 pixels from the left, draw a square by dragging the pointer four grid blocks to the right and four grid blocks down. The pointer will snap to the grid as you drag.

10. Click the Arrow tool and then double-click the square to select all four sides at once.

11. Click Modify on the menu bar and then click Group. Flash will now treat the four lines as one group. The square will turn blue when it is selected.

To modify the individual lines, double-click them. The lines can now be modified individually while in group edit mode. Double-click somewhere else on the Stage to exit the group edit mode.

12. Make sure the square is selected and then copy and paste the square to create a duplicate.

13. Use the Arrow tool to move the duplicate square down and to the right of the original square so that the top left corner of the duplicate square is at the center of the original square. The two squares should overlap.

14. Now use the Line tool to draw a line to connect the top left corner of the first square to the top left corner of the second square. The line should snap to the corners as you draw. Repeat this step to draw lines connecting the other three corners to create a cube.

15. Use the Text tool to create a text block that contains your name and the words "Exercise 3".

16. Print your movie.

17. Save this movie as **Ch07FlashEX03** in the Exercises folder for Chapter 7.

Exercise 7-4

1. From the Exercises folder for Chapter 7, open the **Ch07FlashEX03** file with the cube shape created in Exercise 3.

2. Close the Timeline panel.

3. Change "Exercise 3" in the text block to "Exercise 4".

4. Using the Arrow tool, draw a marquee around the entire cube.

5. Click Modify in the menu bar and then click Group. The entire cube will now be treated as one object. A blue outline surrounds the cube.

6. To reduce the size of the cube, first make sure it is selected. Then click Modify on the menu bar, point to Transform, and then click Scale and Rotate. On the Scale and Rotate dialog box, enter 50 for the Scale value and 0 for the Rotate value. Click OK.

7. Move the cube to the right side of the Stage.

8. Copy and paste the cube to create a duplicate. Move this duplicate to the left side of the Stage.

9. Repeat this process to create three more duplicates of the cube. Place one on the lower left side of the Stage and the other on the lower right side of the Stage and leave another in the center.

10. Click the Free Transform tool. Then click the Rotate and Skew modifier in the Options area of the Toolbox.

11. Click the top left cube. Point to a corner handle and drag it to rotate the cube.

12. Repeat this process to rotate the other cubes in different directions.

13. Print the document.

14. Save this movie as **Ch07FlashEX04** in the Exercises folder for Chapter 7.

7

Exercise 7-5

1. Start with a new document.

2. Click Modify on the menu bar and then click Document to display the Document Properties dialog box.

3. Change the dimensions to 500 pixels wide by 200 pixels high. Change the background color to a light green. Make sure the ruler units are set to pixels. Click OK to close the dialog box.

4. Close the Timeline panel.

5. Double-click the Hand tool to center the view of the Stage.

6. Click View on the menu bar and then Rulers to display the rulers.

7. Click the Text tool on the Toolbox.

8. In the Property inspector, change the Font to Verdana. Also, change the Font Size to 42, the Text (fill) Color to blue, and set the Character Spacing to 10.

9. Click the center of the Stage and type the word "Flash".

10. Click the Arrow tool to turn off the Text tool and to keep the text block selected.

11. Click Modify on the menu bar, point to Transform, and then click Rotate 90° CCW to rotate the text block.

12. Move the text block to the left edge of the Stage.

13. Deselect the text block by clicking on the center of the Stage.

14. Select the Text tool.

15. Change the Font Size to 20, the Text (fill) color to black, and the Character Spacing to 0.

16. This time, create a fixed-width text block by clicking and dragging the pointer starting at about 50 pixels down and 100 pixels from the left. Drag to the right to about the 400 pixel mark. Use the rulers to help you determine the correct position. The text block should be about 300 pixels wide.

17. In this text block, type the following:
    Flash creates movies with graphics, animation, and sound. Flash can be used to create logos, buttons, or even entire Web sites.

18. If you need to adjust the width of the text block, drag its square handle.

19. Now add some ovals, rectangles, lines, or other shapes to your banner to dress it up.

20. Print the document.

21. Save this movie as **Ch07FlashEX05** in the Exercises folder for Chapter 7.

WEB DESIGN PROJECTS

Project 7-1

Create a new logo for your college Web site. The logo should be 300 by 300 pixels in size, should have a background based on your school's colors, and should incorporate the college's name. It should also include various shapes and lines of different sizes and color. Once you have completed the logo, save it as **Ch07FlashDP01** in the Projects folder for Chapter 7. Then export the logo as a GIF image, name it **Ch07FlashDP01.gif**, and accept the default values in the Export GIF dialog box. Finally, print the Flash document.

Project 7-2

Create a navigation bar for use in a company's Web site. The navigation bar should contain four horizontal buttons. Create the buttons on a new document. Set the dimensions of the document to 400 pixels wide by 30 pixels high. To create a rectangular button, use the Rectangle tool with a rounded corner radius of 10 and a gradient fill. Use a gray color for the stroke. Draw the first rectangular button of approximately 100 pixels wide and 30 pixels high. Copy and paste the button to create a duplicate. Move the duplicate to the right of the first button. Create two more duplicates and line all four buttons horizontally. Add text to each button, using white text with an Arial font and a font size of 20. Add text blocks to label the buttons Home, Contact, Services, and Portfolio. Center the text block on each button. Save the file as **Ch07FlashDP02** in the Projects folder for Chapter 7. Export this document as a GIF image with the name of **Ch07FlashDP02.gif**. Accept the default values in the Export GIF dialog box. Print the Flash document.

Project 7-3

Create a banner ad for your favorite music artist. Make the banner 300 pixels wide and 100 pixels high with a background color of your choice. The banner should include text blocks with information about the artist. Rotate one of the text blocks vertically. Add several shapes, such as stars, of different colors. Save the file as **Ch07FlashDP03** in the Projects folder for Chapter 7. Export the banner as a GIF image named **Ch07FlashDP03.gif**. Accept the default values in the Export GIF dialog box. Print the Flash document.

7

8

FLASH: PART II

In this chapter you will:

♦ Learn how frames and layers are used in a Flash document's Timeline to create animations

♦ Learn how symbols are stored in a document's library

♦ Create animations including frame-by-frame and tweened animations

♦ Create a mask layer and a motion guide layer

♦ Create buttons with simple actions and sounds

In Chapter 7, you learned how to create graphics with the basic drawing and painting tools in Macromedia Flash. In this chapter you will learn how to make your graphics come to life with animation. Animation can be used to move objects across the Stage, to make them rotate, or to change their size, shape, or color. You will learn how to use the Library panel, Timeline, layers, and frames to create animations. You will also create buttons with sounds that let the user control the animation, and you will learn how to publish an animated movie for distribution on the Web.

USING THE TIMELINE, FRAMES, AND LAYERS

The Timeline, as shown in Figure 8-1, is used to control and coordinate the frames and layers that make up a Flash document. (Note that if you are working on a Macintosh, your screen will look slightly different than the figures in this book. For example, you will probably see the Dock at the bottom of the screen.) A **frame** represents a particular instant in time and contains the content of the Stage at that instant. Each frame may contain different images or different states of the same image. Frames that contain content that has changed from a previous frame are called **keyframes** and are distinguished from other frames by a dot. As the document's animation is played over time, the frames display in succession, creating the appearance of movement. The rate at which the frames display is determined by the **frame rate**, shown on the bottom of the Timeline. The default frame rate is 12 frames per second. The Timeline is used to coordinate and control the timing of the animation by determining how and when the frames are displayed.

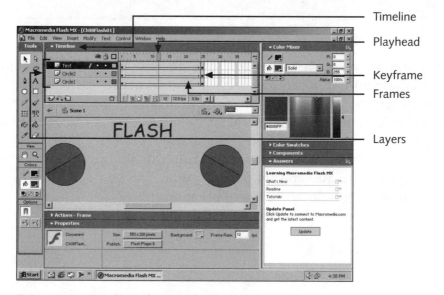

Figure 8-1   Timeline of a sample Flash document

Layers, another part of a document, are also controlled by using the Timeline. **Layers** are displayed on the left side of the Timeline and are used to organize the various graphic objects such as shapes, lines, and text that are part of a document. Each row within the Timeline represents one layer. The frames for each layer are shown on the right side of the Timeline. By default, a new Flash document contains one layer and one frame. As you add more layers, additional rows are inserted into the Timeline. You also add more frames to extend the length of the animation. When you draw on a layer or change something on a layer, the objects on the other layers are not affected. Your changes affect only the contents of the current layer. Placing objects on different layers also allows you to animate them in different ways where the animations occur at the same time. For example, you can place a square shape in one layer and animate it so that it rotates over a certain period of time. Then you can add text to another layer and animate the text so that it fades in over the same period of time. Both of these animations can play at the same time without affecting each other.

Another important element of the Timeline is the playhead. The **playhead** is the red rectangle on the Timeline header that has a red vertical line below it. When you play a document's animation, the playhead moves along the Timeline header. As it moves, the different frames that make up an animation are displayed. You can use the mouse pointer to drag the playhead back and forth through the frames to test the animation. This is known as **scrubbing**.

Using the Timeline to Test an Animation

8

As you learned in Chapter 7, you use Flash to create documents. When you publish the document for use on the Web, the document is referred to as a movie. Technically speaking, documents and movies are two different types of files. A Flash document is contained in a file with a .fla extension, which is the native format for Flash files. The .fla file contains the graphic objects that make up your document and that can be edited within the Flash program. A movie, by contrast, has a .swf file extension and is played by the Macromedia Flash Player. The Flash Player is a plug-in or helper application that works with your browser to display .swf files. The Flash Player comes installed with most new computers and can also be downloaded for free from Macromedia's Web site. The .swf file contains all of the elements in your document in a format that can be recognized by the Flash Player. This file cannot be edited in Flash. Instead, to make changes to the movie you need to edit the .fla file.

After you create a Flash document with animation, you need to test it to make sure it works correctly. To test your document, you click the Play command in the Control menu. This plays the animation within the Flash program window (that is, as a .fla file). Another way to test your document is to click the Test Movie command in the Control menu, which plays the document as a movie (.swf file) in a separate Flash Player window.

To test a document and explore its Timeline:

1. Start **Macromedia Flash MX** from the Start menu. (If you are working on a Macintosh, start Macromedia Flash MX from the Applications folder.) The Flash window opens with a new document.

2. To set up your screen to look like the textbook's figures, click **Window** on the menu bar, point to **Panel Sets**, and then click **Default Layout**. This returns the Flash interface to its original configuration.

3. If necessary, click the **Maximize** button on the Flash program window to expand it to fit the entire screen.

4. Click **File** on the menu bar, click **Open**, and then open the file named **Ch08Flash01** in the Chapter folder for Chapter 8. If necessary, change the zoom level to 100%. A Flash document with two circles and text opens. The document's Timeline displays three layers named Circle1, Circle2, and Text, each with 25 frames.

5. To test the document, click **Control** on the menu bar and then click **Play**. The two circles rotate, and the text moves from above the Stage onto the Stage. Notice how the playhead moves throughout the animation. It moves from one frame to the next until it reaches the end at Frame 25.

6. Click **Control** on the menu bar and then click **Rewind**. The playhead returns to Frame 1.

7. To test the document by scrubbing, drag the playhead back and forth along several of the frames.

8. On the Circle1 layer, click the dot that is under the column with the eye icon. A red X replaces the dot, and the left circle is no longer visible on the Stage. See Figure 8-2. To make the layer visible again, click the red X.

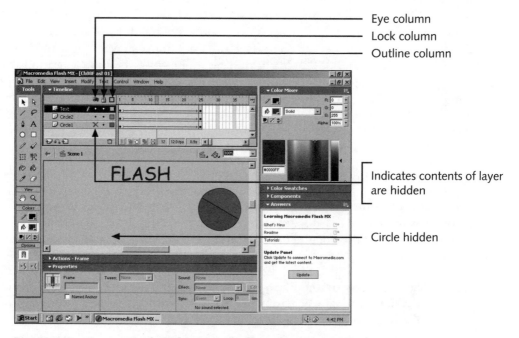

Figure 8-2 Contents of Circle1 layer hidden

9. Click the dot under the Lock column with the padlock icon for the Circle1 layer. A padlock icon appears to indicate this layer cannot be changed. Click the padlock icon to unlock the layer.

10. Click the small square under the Outline column with the square icon for the Circle1 layer. The circle appears in an outline format. Click the small square again to turn off Outline view.

11. Click **File** on the menu bar and then click **Close** to close the document. If prompted to save your changes, click **No** (or **Don't Save** on a Macintosh).

Understanding Symbols and the Library

A **symbol** is a graphic element with special properties that you create in Flash. Symbols are used to create certain types of animations and to add interactive elements to a Flash document. There are three types of symbols: movie clips, buttons, and graphics. **Movie clips** are the default symbol and contain their own Timeline. They operate independently of the Timeline of the document in which they appear. **Graphic** symbols can be either static images or animated images. They operate in sync with the Timeline of the document in which they appear. **Button** symbols have their own four-frame Timeline and may be used to make the published movie interactive. For example, buttons can be added to a movie to allow the user to stop or play the animation.

When you create a symbol, it is automatically stored in the document's library. A **library** is used to store symbols, as well as imported bitmap images and sounds. You can access, organize, and modify symbols in the document's library using the Library panel shown in Figure 8-3. You open the Library panel via the Library command on the Window menu.

8

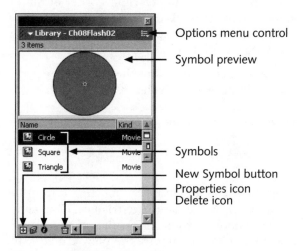

Figure 8-3 Library panel

The Library panel displays the names of all the symbols in the library. Each symbol has an icon to the left of its name to show what type of symbol it is. You can click the name of a symbol to see a preview of it at the top of the Library panel. Within the Library panel, you can also organize the symbols inside of folders.

To use a symbol, you drag it to the Stage from the Library panel. You can either drag the symbol from the preview window or drag it from the list of symbols. Each time you drag the symbol onto the Stage you create an instance of the symbol. An **instance** is a copy of a symbol. Flash stores the symbol only once, so you can insert as many instances of a symbol into a document as you need without greatly affecting the final document's file size. A symbol can be modified by clicking the Edit command on the Library panel's options menu. This places the symbol in symbol-editing mode, which displays the symbol by itself in a separate window so that you can edit it. You can exit symbol-editing mode by clicking the Edit Document command on the Edit menu.

To explore the Library panel and create symbol instances:

1. Click **File** on the menu bar, click **Open**, and then open the file named **Ch08Flash02** from the Chapter folder for Chapter 8. If necessary, change the zoom level to 100%.

2. Save the file as **Ch08Flash02SOL** in the Chapter folder for Chapter 8.

3. Click **Window** on the menu bar and then click **Timeline** to close the Timeline panel. Click **Window** on the menu bar and then click **Library**. The Library panel opens. If necessary, move the Library panel to the right side of the Stage to make the Stage contents visible.

4. In the Library panel, click the symbol named **Circle**. The red circle is previewed at the top of the Library panel.

5. Click the **options menu** control at the upper-right corner of the Library panel to display the options menu. Click **Duplicate**. In the **Duplicate Symbol** dialog box, change the Behavior type to **Graphic** and click **OK**. A duplicate symbol, named Circle copy, is added to the library.

6. To change the name of the duplicate symbol in the Library panel, double-click the name **Circle copy**, type **New Circle**, and press **Enter**.

 You can also change the symbol's name via the Properties command on the options menu.

7. Create an instance of your New Circle symbol by dragging it from the Library panel to the Stage. Position it below the dark blue triangle. Drag another instance of the New Circle symbol from the Library panel and place it to the right of the first instance. Next, you will modify the New Circle symbol.

8. To edit the New Circle symbol, select the symbol in the Library panel, click the **options menu** control and then click **Edit**. The symbol is placed in symbol-editing mode, as shown in Figure 8-4. Now that the symbol is displayed in symbol-editing mode, you can alter its appearance.

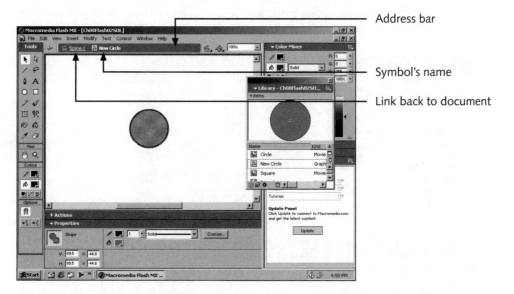

Address bar

Symbol's name

Link back to document

8

Figure 8-4   Symbol-editing mode

9. If necessary, click the **Arrow** tool on the Toolbox. Then click to the right of the New Circle symbol in the Stage to deselect it.

10. Click the **Paint Bucket** tool on the Toolbox. Use the Fill Color control on the Toolbox to change the fill color to **orange**. Click the red area of the circle to change its color to orange.

11. Click **Edit** on the menu bar and then click **Edit Document** to exit the symbol-editing mode and return to the document. Now that you have changed the symbol's color, the two instances of the symbol on the Stage also change color.

As you saw in the preceding steps, when you modify a symbol, all of its instances are also modified. However, you can modify an instance on the Stage in various ways without affecting the symbol or other instances of the same symbol. For example, if you have several instances of a symbol in the same document, you can make one instance smaller than the others, rotate each instance at a different angle, or change the color tint or brightness of one instance without affecting the other instances or the original symbol.

To modify an instance of a symbol:

1. Click the **Arrow** tool and then click the left-most instance of the orange circle.

2. If necessary, click **Window** on the menu bar and click **Properties** to open the Property inspector.

3. From the Property inspector, click the **Color Styles** drop-down list and then select **Tint**.

4. Select a **green** color from the color palette to the right of the Color drop-down list. If necessary, set the Tint Amount to **50%**, as shown in Figure 8-5.

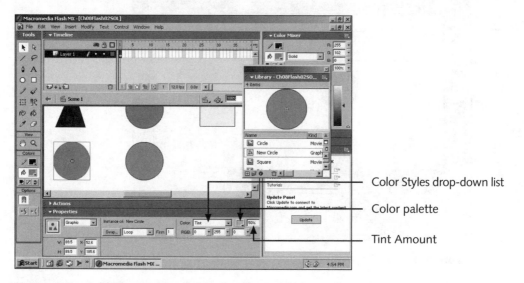

Color Styles drop-down list

Color palette

Tint Amount

Figure 8-5   Selecting a color tint in the Property inspector

5. Now select the right-most instance of the New Circle symbol.

6. Click the **Free Transform** tool from the Toolbox and click the **Scale** button from the options area. Drag one of the corner handles on the circle to increase its size. Notice that the first instance is not affected and neither is the original symbol in the Library panel.

7. Experiment with this document by creating additional symbols and instances. Try modifying existing symbols to see how the symbol's instances are affected.

8. Save your changes to the document and close the file.

WHAT IS ANIMATION?

One of the most exciting features of Flash is its ability to create animation. Changing the content of the Stage from one frame to the next creates the perception of movement that is animation. A frame is like one instant in time. As the document is played one frame at a time, the different content in each frame is displayed. You can create two types of animations in Flash: frame-by-frame and tweened.

Frame-by-Frame Animation

In a **frame-by-frame animation**, you create the content for each frame. If, for example, your document will have 20 frames, then you need to create the content for each of the 20 frames. Some of the content can be repeated in each frame, but other content can be slightly modified so that as the frames are displayed one after the other, the appearance of movement is achieved. Frame-by-frame animations are usually used to build more complex animations, and they tend to produce larger sized files.

To create a frame-by-frame animation:

1. Click **File** and then click **New** to create a new document. Double-click the **Hand** tool on the Toolbox to make all of the Stage visible.

2. Click the **Oval** tool on the Toolbox. Use the Property inspector to set the Stroke color to **black** and the Fill color to **blue**. This circle will be animated to move from the upper-left corner of the Stage to the lower-right corner.

3. Draw a small circle on the top left corner of the Stage. This is the animation's starting point.

4. Now click **Frame 2** of Layer 1 on the Timeline, as shown in Figure 8-6.

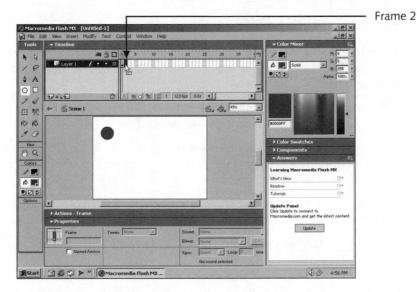

Figure 8-6   Selecting Frame 2 of Layer 1

5. Click **Insert** on the menu bar and then click **Keyframe** to make Frame 2 a keyframe. Recall that a frame must be a keyframe when the content changes from the previous frame.

6. Click the **Arrow** tool, drag the circle slightly down and to the right as shown in Figure 8-7, and then release the mouse button. This is the next position of the circle in the animation.

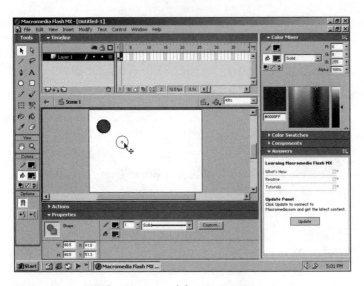

Figure 8-7   Circle positioned for Frame 2

7. Click **Frame 3** and make it a keyframe as you did in step 5. Drag the circle down and to the right again to place it in its next position, closer to the lower-right corner of the Stage.

8. Click **Frame 4** and make it a keyframe. Drag the circle to the lower-right corner of the Stage, which is its final position.

9. You are now ready to test your animation. To do this, click **Control** on the menu bar and then click **Play**. The circle moves from the upper-left corner of the Stage to the lower-right corner.

10. Try adding more keyframes that move the circle to other positions. Test your document to see what your animation looks like with the additional keyframes.

11. Save your file as **Ch08Flash03** in the Chapter folder for Chapter 8. Close the file.

Tweened Animation

Instead of creating the content for each frame to build a frame-by-frame animation, you can let Flash build the content for you in a tweened animation. A **tweened animation** is one in which you create the content for the beginning frame and the ending frame. Flash then creates the in-between frames (hence, the term "tweened"), varying the content evenly in each frame to achieve the appearance of animation. **Tweening** is the process Flash uses to create the individual frames. A tweened animation is easier and quicker to create than a frame-by-frame animation because you only need to create the content for two frames, the one at the beginning of the animation and the one at the end. Each of these two frames is a keyframe.

There are two types of tweened animations: motion tweens and shape tweens. **Motion tweens** are used to create an animation in which an object changes its position, rotates, or even changes in color. You can also create motion tweens to make an object fade in or out. **Shape tweens** are used to change a shape over time. For example, you can create an animation in which a circle shape gradually changes into a square shape.

Motion Tweened Animation

To create a motion tweened animation, you create an object in the first frame and convert the object to a symbol. In order for an object to be animated via motion tweened animation, the object must be a symbol. You then create a keyframe in the frame where the animation will end. In this keyframe, you move the object to a different position or you change its properties. Then you instruct Flash to create a motion tweened animation starting in the first frame. Flash will then create additional frames that contain the different states of the object as it transitions between the first and last frame.

In the next set of steps, you will convert existing triangle shapes into symbols. You will then place each triangle instance on a separate layer so that they can be animated individually.

To create symbols for a tweened animation:

1. Open the file named **Ch08Flash04** from the Chapter folder for Chapter 8, and then save it as **Ch08Flash04SOL** in the same folder. The document contains four triangle shapes, each in its own layer.

2. Double-click the **Hand** tool to make all of the Stage visible.

3. Click the **Arrow** tool on the Toolbox and then click the **green triangle** to select it.

4. Click **Insert** on the menu bar and then click **Convert to Symbol**. In the Convert to Symbol dialog box, change the name to **Green Triangle** and leave the Behavior as **Movie Clip**, as shown in Figure 8-8. Click **OK**.

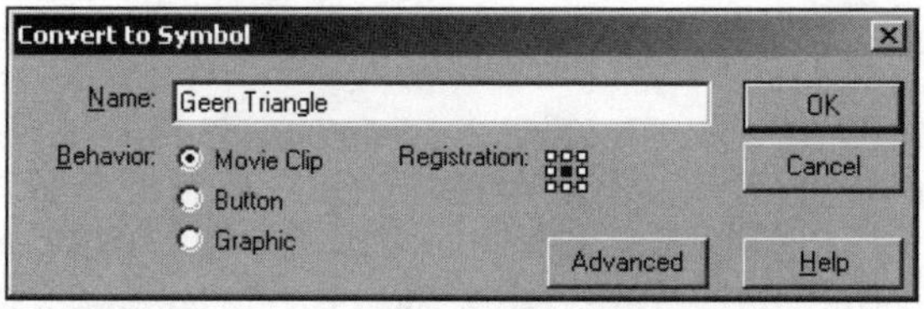

Figure 8-8 Convert to Symbol dialog box

5. Click **Window** on the menu bar and then click **Library** to display the Library panel. The Green Triangle symbol is listed in the library.

6. Click the **yellow triangle** to select it. Click **Insert** on the menu bar and then click **Convert to Symbol** to convert it to a symbol, just as you did with the green triangle. Name the new symbol **Yellow Triangle** and leave the Behavior as **Movie Clip**.

7. Repeat this process for the blue triangle and for the red triangle. You should have four symbols in the library, one for each triangle, as shown in Figure 8-9.

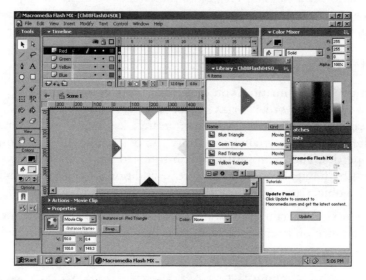

Figure 8-9   Library panel showing triangle symbols

The next step in creating a tweened animation is to add keyframes and to create the tween. In the steps that follow, you will animate each of the triangles so that they move towards the center and form a square. First, notice that the document currently has only one frame. Each of the triangles exists only in Frame 1, within their respective layers. To animate the triangles, you need to add additional frames to each layer. You will start by first adding a keyframe for the Red layer. This keyframe will be added at the end of the animation. The end of an animation depends on the length of time you want the animation to play. For this example, the animation is to play for 2½ seconds, and the frame rate is set at 12 frames per second. Therefore, the animation will end at Frame 30.

To create keyframes and a motion tweened animation:

1. Click **Frame 30** of the Red layer. Then click **Insert** on the menu bar and click **Keyframe**. Frame 30, where the animation will end, is now a keyframe and Frames 2 through 29 are added to the layer. The triangle shape is copied to all the new frames in the layer. Notice that the other triangles disappear. This is because the other triangles only exist in Frame 1 of their respective layers. After you add more frames to the other layers, the triangles will become visible.

2. In Frame 30 of the Red layer, move the red triangle to the middle of the Stage, as shown in Figure 8-10. This is the end position of the triangle where it will form the left part of the final square shape. Frame 1 now contains the start position of the triangle and Frame 30 contains the end position. Next, you instruct Flash to create the in-between frames.

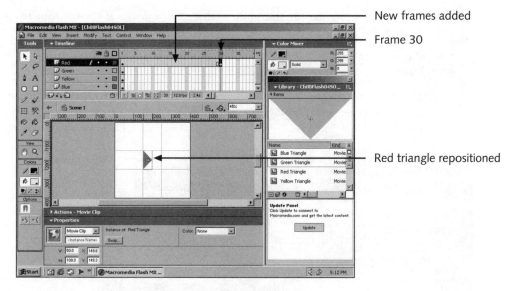

New frames added

Frame 30

Red triangle repositioned

Figure 8-10   Red triangle positioned for Frame 30

3. Click **Frame 1** of the Red layer. Click **Insert** on the menu bar and then click **Create Motion Tween**. The motion tween is represented in the Timeline by a black line and a light-blue background in Frames 1 through 30 of the Red layer.

4. Click **Control** on the menu bar and then click **Play** to test your animation. The red triangle starts at the left edge of the Stage and moves towards the middle. You have finished animating the red triangle. Now you need to do the same for the remaining triangles.

5. Click **Frame 30** of the Green layer. Click **Insert** on the menu bar and then click **Keyframe**.

6. Move the green triangle to the middle of the Stage to form the top part of the final square shape.

 You can use the arrow keys on the keyboard to nudge the triangle into position.

7. Click **Frame 1** of the Green layer. Click **Insert** on the menu bar and then click **Create Motion Tween**. A motion tween is added to the Green layer similar to the Red layer.

8. Test your animation again, this time by pressing **Enter**. (On a Macintosh, use the Return key instead of the Enter key.) The red and green triangles move from the edges of the Stage to the center to form part of the square.

9. Repeat this process for the yellow triangle to make it move from the right side of the Stage to the middle to form the right side of the square.

10. Repeat the process once more for the blue triangle to have it move from the bottom of the Stage to the middle.

11. Test the animation to make sure that all four triangles move at the same time from the edges of the Stage to the middle to form a square, as shown in Figure 8-11.

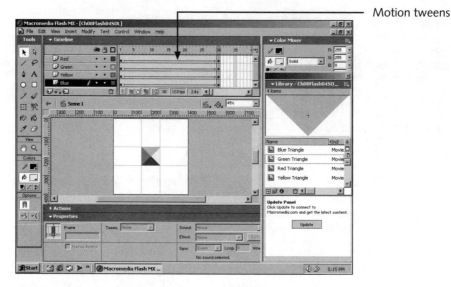

Figure 8-11   Four triangles form a square

12. Save your changes.

In the previous steps, you created a motion tween with several objects in different layers. In addition to moving the triangles from one part of the Stage to another, you can also make the triangles rotate as they move. You can even control how fast the triangles start or end within the animation sequence by changing the **Ease value** in the Property inspector.

To rotate the triangles in the motion tweens:

1. Open the **Ch08Flash04SOL** file, if it is not already open.

2. If necessary, click **Window** on the menu bar and then click **Properties** to display the Property inspector. Double-click the **Hand** tool to make all of the Stage visible.

3. Click the **Arrow** tool, and then click **Frame 1** of the Yellow layer in the Timeline to select it.

4. In the Property inspector, click the **Rotate** drop-down arrow and then click **CW**. Enter **2** for the number of times to rotate.

5. To test your animation, click somewhere on the Stage and then press **Enter**. The yellow triangle should rotate as it moves to the center of the Stage.

6. Click **Frame 1** of the Yellow layer to make it the current frame.

7. In the Property inspector, change the Ease value to **100** by dragging the Ease slider up, as shown in Figure 8-12.

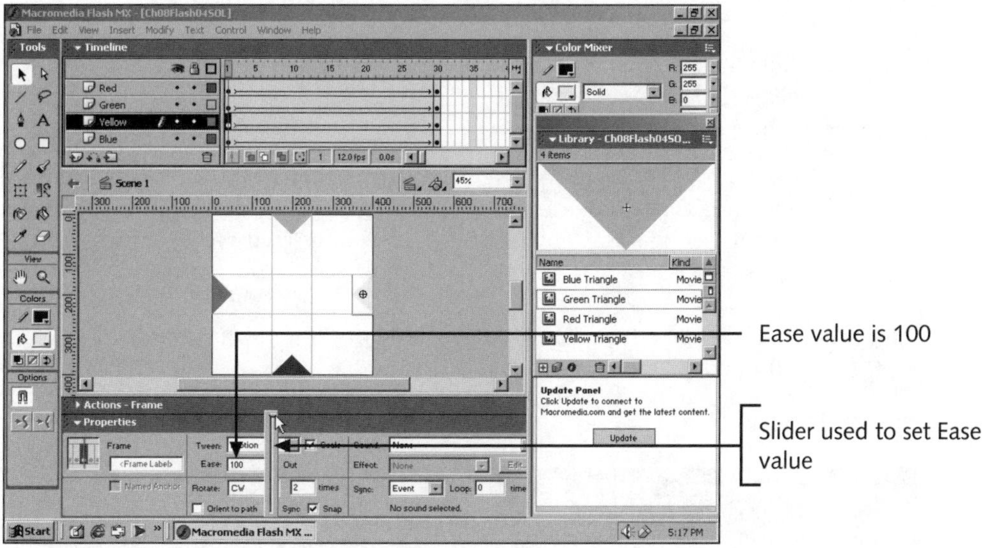

Figure 8-12   Setting the Ease value in the Property inspector

8. Press **Enter** to test your animation again. The yellow triangle slows down as it moves closer to the center of the Stage during the animation.

9. To do the same for the red triangle, click **Frame 1** of the Red layer. In the Property inspector, select **CW** for Rotate, enter **2** for number of rotations, and **100** for Ease.

10. Test your animation again. The red triangle rotates and also slows down as it gets closer to the center of the Stage.

11. Repeat step 9 for the green and blue triangles and test your animation again.

12. Save your work.

In addition to moving and rotating an object, you can also make it fade in or fade out. In the following steps, you will change the Brightness Amount for each of the triangles by using the Property inspector. The **Brightness Amount** affects the relative lightness or darkness for an image. You apply the effect on Frame 1 of each layer by setting the Brightness Amount to 100%. At 100%, the object will be white, which makes it invisible against the white background. Flash will gradually change the Brightness Amount to the default value of 0% by the last frame, making the object gradually become visible (or fade in) during the animation sequence. Note that if the document's background is not white, you can use the **Alpha Amount** setting to create the same effect. An Alpha Amount value of 0% makes the object transparent.

To create a fade-in effect:

1. Open the **Ch08Flash04SOL** file, if it is not already open.

2. If necessary, click **Window** on the menu bar and then click **Properties** to display the Property inspector.

3. Click the **Arrow** tool, if necessary, and then click **Frame 1** of the Yellow layer. Click the yellow triangle on the Stage to display its instance properties in the Property inspector.

4. In the Property inspector, select **Brightness** from the Color Styles drop-down list. Type **100** for the Brightness Amount and press **Enter** or use the slider to set the amount to 100. The yellow triangle becomes white. See Figure 8-13.

Recall that on a Macintosh you need to press Return whenever this book tells you to press Enter.

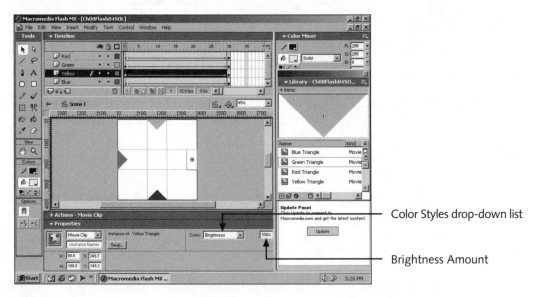

Color Styles drop-down list

Brightness Amount

Figure 8-13   Brightness Amount changed for triangle

5. Click **Control** and click **Play** to test the animation. The yellow triangle fades in as it moves to the center of the Stage.

6. To do the same for the blue triangle, click **Frame 1** of the Blue layer. Click the blue triangle on the Stage and select **Brightness** from the Color Styles drop-down list. Type **100** for the Brightness Amount and press **Enter**. The blue triangle becomes white.

7. Repeat step 6 for the red and green triangles and then test your animation.

8. Save your changes and then close the document.

Shape Tweened Animation

Now that you have learned how Flash helps you create a motion tween, you will see that you can create a shape tween in a similar way. A shape tween occurs when one shape is transformed into another shape. As with a motion tweened animation, you create the content in the beginning and ending frames and then allow Flash to complete the animation by creating the in-between frames. A shape tween is represented in the Timeline by a black line and light-green background for the frames.

Note that the object you plan to animate in a shape tween cannot be a symbol. This is different from creating a motion tween, where you first have to convert an object into a symbol. A shape tween can be applied to fills and lines, and even to text. However, before you can apply a shape tween to text, you need to convert the text to fills. To do this, you use the Break Apart command located in the Modify menu. The Break Apart command converts text into individual text blocks, one for each character. You apply the command a second time to convert the individual characters into fills, which can then be used in a shape tween.

To create a shape tween:

1. Click **File** on the menu bar and then click **New** to create a new document.

2. Save the file as **Ch08Flash05** in the Chapter folder for Chapter 8.

3. If necessary, click **Window** on the menu bar and then click **Properties** to open the Property inspector.

4. Click the **Rectangle** tool on the Toolbox.

5. Click the **Fill Color** control on the Toolbox and click the **No Color** icon (the white square with a diagonal red line through it) below the color controls on the Toolbox. Then click the **Stroke Color** control and, if necessary, use the color palette to set the color to **black**.

6. Draw a rectangle on the center of the Stage.

7. Click **Frame 30** in the Timeline for Layer 1, click **Insert** on the menu bar, and then click **Keyframe** to add a keyframe. New frames are added and the rectangle is copied in all the frames through Frame 30.

8. Click the **Arrow** tool on the Toolbox. Then click somewhere on the Stage outside the rectangle to deselect the rectangle.

9. Move the pointer to the middle of the top line until you see a curve icon next to the arrow. Then drag the line down slightly to change its shape. Release the mouse pointer.

10. Now move the pointer to the upper-left corner of the rectangle until you see a corner icon next to the arrow. Then drag the corner slightly up and to the left to change its position. Release the mouse pointer. The shape of the rectangle changes, as shown in Figure 8-14.

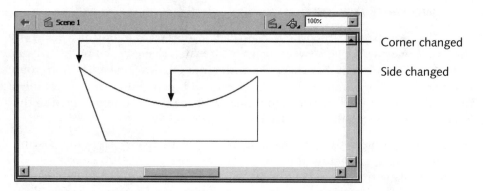

Figure 8-14   Modified shape

11. Click **Frame 1** in the Timeline. In the Property inspector, select **Shape** from the Tween drop-down list. Frames 1 through 30 in the Timeline now have a black line with a light-green background to represent the shape tween.

12. To test your animation, press **Enter**. The rectangle changes gradually into the modified shape of Frame 30.

13. Save your work and close the file.

SPECIAL LAYERS

Flash allows you to create different types of layers. One of these is a **guide layer**, which can serve as a guide as you draw. For example, if you want to draw some graphic elements so that they are aligned diagonally on the Stage you can create a guide layer that contains a diagonal line. Then you can use the line as a guide to align the graphic elements. The contents of the guide layer are not displayed in the final movie.

A special kind of guide layer, called a **motion guide layer**, provides a path for an object to follow when it is used in a motion tween. This is useful when you want to animate an object to move along an irregular path. You draw the path with a tool such as the Pencil tool in the guide layer; in the layer below it, you create the motion tween for the object.

Another kind of layer, a **mask layer**, contains a graphic object, such as an oval shape, through which the contents of one or more underlying layers will show. The content of the underlying layers is only visible when the mask layer's graphic object is over it.

Creating a Mask Layer

When you create a mask layer, the layer below it is hidden, or masked. In other words, the layer below the mask layer is the *masked* layer. An object in the masked layer is only visible when the object in the mask layer is over it. The graphic object in the mask layer can be text or any filled shape.

In the following steps, you will create a circle in a mask layer. You will create a motion tween to have the circle move across the contents of the masked layer. As the circle passes over the masked layer, its contents will become visible.

To create a mask layer animation:

1. Open the file named **Ch08Flash06** from the Chapter folder for Chapter 8 and save it as **Ch08Flash06SOL** in the same folder.

2. Click **Insert** on the menu bar, and then click **Layer** to add a new layer.

3. Select the new layer in the Timeline, click **Modify** on the menu bar, and then click **Layer**. In the Layer Properties dialog box, change the name of the layer to **Circle** and change the layer's Type to **Mask**, as shown in Figure 8-15. Click **OK** to close the dialog box.

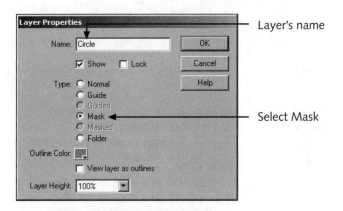

Figure 8-15   Layer Properties dialog box

4. In the Timeline, click the **Text** layer to select it. Click **Modify** on the menu bar and click **Layer** to open the Layer Properties dialog box for the Text layer. Change the Text layer's type to **Masked**. Click **OK** to close the dialog box. In the Timeline, the Text layer is now indented under the Circle layer, as shown in Figure 8-16.

Figure 8-16   Masked Text layer

5. Click **Frame 1** of the Circle layer to select it. Click the **Oval** tool on the Toolbox. Make sure you have a fill color selected. Draw a circle over the first letter "F" in the text block. Make the circle just big enough to cover the letter. Now you are ready to use the circle to create a motion tweened animation. As you will recall, the first step in this process is converting the object into a symbol.

6. Click the **Arrow** tool, and then double-click the circle to select it. Click **Insert** on the menu bar and click **Convert to Symbol**. Name the symbol **Circle** and accept the default Behavior of **Movie Clip**. Click **OK**. The next step is to insert a keyframe in the ending frame of the animation.

7. Click **Frame 25** of the Circle layer in the Timeline. Click **Insert** and then click **Keyframe** to make this frame a keyframe. Frames 2 through 24 are also added automatically. To extend the Text layer through Frame 25, you need to add regular frames.

8. Click **Frame 25** of the Text layer in the Timeline. Click **Insert** and then click **Frame** to add regular frames through Frame 25. The text is also copied through Frame 25.

9. Click **Frame 25** of the Circle layer and drag the circle so that it is over the exclamation point at the end of the text. This is the end position of the circle's animation.

10. Click **Frame 1** of the Circle layer. On the Property inspector, select **Motion** from the Tween drop-down list. Test your animation to make sure that the circle moves from the left to the right of the text. See Figure 8-17.

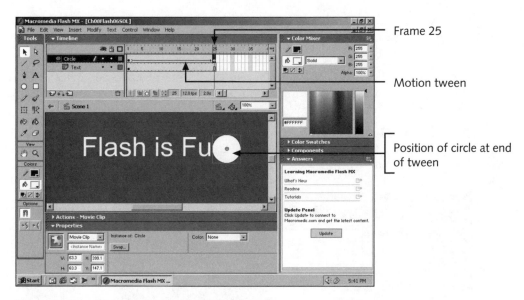

Figure 8-17   Motion tween in Circle layer

11. To see the masking effect, click the Lock column icon on the Timeline to lock both layers. Then press **Enter** to test the animation again. You see a spotlight effect as the circle moves over the text.

12. Save your work and close the file.

Creating a Motion Guide Layer

Another special type of layer, called a motion guide layer, provides a path for an object to follow. You draw a path in the motion guide layer using a tool such as the Pencil tool. You then create a motion tween of an object in the layer below the motion guide layer. This layer is called the **guided layer**. The object in the guided layer follows the path you draw in the motion guide layer.

To create a motion guide layer animation:

1. Open the file named **Ch08Flash07** from the Chapter folder for Chapter 8 and save it in the same folder as **Ch08Flash07SOL**.

2. Double-click the **Hand** tool to make all of the Stage visible. Click **View** on the menu bar and make sure **Snap to Objects** is selected.

3. Click the **Arrow** tool, and then drag a marquee around the basketball on the Stage to select all of the basketball. Click **Insert** on the menu bar and then click **Convert to Symbol**. Name the symbol **Ball**, make sure **Movie Clip** is selected for Behavior, and click **OK**. The basketball is now a symbol and can be used in a motion tweened animation.

4. Click **Frame 30** and click **Insert** on the menu bar. Click **Keyframe** to create a keyframe at Frame 30. This is where the motion tweened animation will end.

5. Click **Frame 1** of the layer. On the Property inspector, select **Motion** from the Tween drop-down list. You now have a motion tween that will be used to move the ball. Next you need to create the motion guide layer.

6. Click **Insert** on the menu bar and then click **Motion Guide**. This adds a new layer above Layer 1 called **Guide: Layer 1**. Layer 1 is indented in the Timeline to indicate that it is now a guided layer, as shown in Figure 8-18.

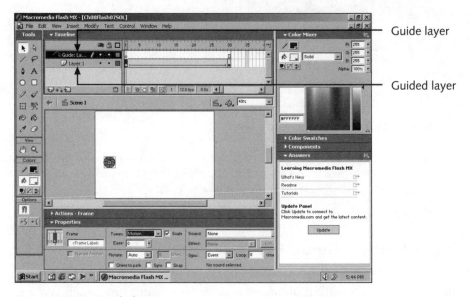

Figure 8-18   Guide layer

7. Click **Frame 1** of Guide: Layer 1.

8. Click the **Pencil** tool on the Toolbox. Click the **Pencil Mode** modifier in the Options area of the Toolbox and select **Smooth**. Draw a curved line on the Stage similar to that shown in Figure 8-19. This line represents the path that the ball will follow.

9. Click **Frame 1** of Layer 1. Click the **Arrow** tool and, if necessary, move the ball so that its center snaps to the starting point of the line you drew.

10. Click **Frame 30** of Layer 1. Move the ball so that its center snaps to the ending point of the line, as shown in Figure 8-20.

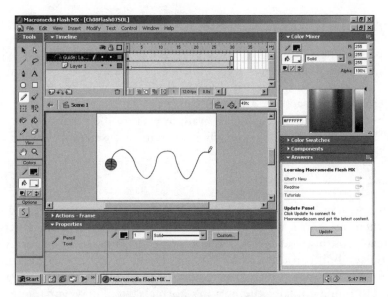

Figure 8-19   Path drawn with the Pencil tool

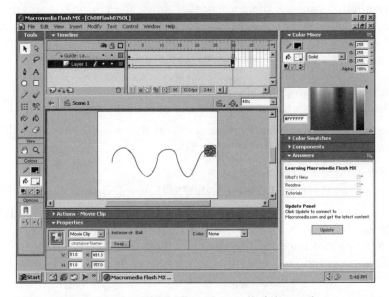

Figure 8-20   Moving the ball to the end of the path

11. Press **Enter** to test your animation. The ball moves along the path. Even though the path is visible while you test the animation, it will not display in the final movie. You can hide the path while testing the animation by clicking the dot under the Eye column for the Guide: Layer 1.

12. Save your work and keep the document open.

USING BUTTONS, ACTIONS, AND SOUNDS

Another of the useful and exciting features of Flash is the ability to make a movie interactive. Adding some interaction draws your audience in because it allows them to control the movie, rather than just watch it. One of the easiest ways to do this is to add **buttons** that perform some action. A button can be in almost any form. For instance, you can create buttons shaped as rectangles, ovals, or even in the form of text. A simple example would be a button that the user clicks to start an animation or one that can stop the animation.

Creating a Button

To create a button, you create a new symbol. As you learned when you created symbols for the library, there are three types of symbol behaviors: **Movie Clip**, **Button**, and **Graphic**. To create buttons, you create symbols with the **Button** behavior. After you create the Button symbol, you then edit the symbol, which will have a Timeline consisting of only four frames, Up, Over, Down, and Hit. Each frame represents a state of the button. The **Up** frame contains the button's normal state. The **Over** frame contains the content that shows what the button will look like when the mouse pointer is moved over it. The **Down** frame contains the content that shows the button's appearance when it is clicked. The **Hit** frame does not affect the appearance of the button. Instead, it represents the clickable area of the button. This is useful when a button is not a solid shape. For example, if you have a button consisting of text, it may be hard for the user to click the text itself, especially if the button is small. To make it easier for the user to click the button, you can draw a rectangle in the Hit frame of the button that is slightly larger than the text. This rectangle then represents the area of the button that the user can click.

In the following steps, you will modify the document that has the moving ball created in the preceding section. You will first create a button.

To create a button:

1. Verify that the file named **Ch08Flash07SOL** is still open.

2. To add a new symbol for a button, click **Insert** on the menu bar and then click **New Symbol**. Name the symbol **Button1** and make sure you select **Button** as the Behavior for this symbol. Click **OK**. The program switches to symbol-editing mode to create the new button. The button's Timeline shows its four frames. See Figure 8-21.

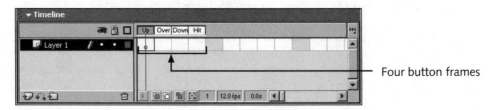

Four button frames

Figure 8-21   Button's Timeline

3. Click the **Rectangle** tool on the Toolbox. Click the **Round Rectangle Radius** modifier on the Options area of the Toolbox to open the Rectangle Settings dialog box. Set the Corner Radius to **10** points and click **OK**.

4. Change the Fill Color to **green** and change the Stroke Color to **No Color**. Now draw the button shape in the middle of the Stage, as shown in Figure 8-22. This button shape represents the normal or Up state of your button.

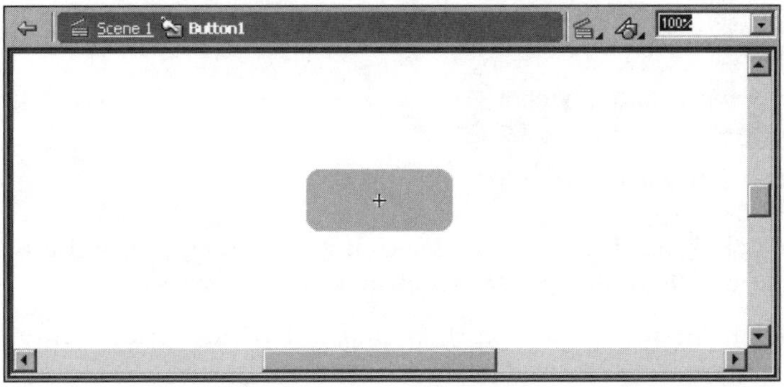

Figure 8-22   Button shape

5. To create an Over state for your button, click the **Over** frame of Layer 1 to select it. Click **Insert** on the menu bar and click **Keyframe** to make this a keyframe. The button shape is copied to the Over frame and remains selected. Change the fill color to **yellow**. The button shape is now yellow.

6. Click the **Down** frame. Click **Insert** on the menu bar and then click **Keyframe** to make this a keyframe. The button shape is copied to this frame and remains selected. Press the **right arrow** on your keyboard 3 times. Then press the **down arrow** 3 times. This moves the shape 3 pixels to the right and 3 pixels down.

7. To exit the symbol-editing mode, click **Edit** on the menu bar and then click **Edit Document**.

8. Click **Window** on the menu bar and then click **Library** to open the Library panel. The Button symbol is listed in the Library panel. Click the **Button1** symbol in the Library panel to select it. See Figure 8-23.

9. Click the **options menu** control on the upper-right corner of the Library panel's title bar to display the options menu. Click **Duplicate** to create a duplicate of the Button1 symbol. In the Duplicate Symbol dialog box, name this symbol **Button2** and click **OK**.

10. Click the **Button2** symbol in the Library panel to select it and then click the **options menu** control to display the options menu. Click **Edit** to edit the symbol.

8

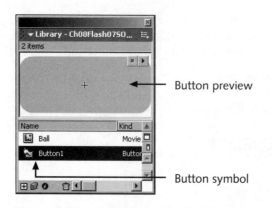

Button preview

Button symbol

Figure 8-23   Button1 symbol in Library panel

11. If necessary, click the **Up** frame to select it. Click once on the button's green fill and then use the color palette to change the color to **red**.

12. Click **Edit** on the menu bar and then click **Edit Document** to return to the document.

When you create a new symbol, such as the buttons you just created, the symbol resides in the document's library. It is not yet on the Stage. As you learned earlier, in order to use the symbol you need to create an instance of the symbol by dragging it onto the Stage. You can create as many instances as you need, and you can change the properties of each instance to make it unique. Each instance on the Stage is a copy of the symbol in the library. In the following steps, you will insert an instance of each of the Button symbols in the library. You will also add text to each of the button instances.

To create instances of the Button symbol:

1. In the Timeline, click the **Guide: Layer 1** to select it.

2. Click **Insert** on the menu bar and then click **Layer**. A new layer is inserted above the motion guide layer. Double-click the new layer's name and change it to **Buttons**.

3. Click **Frame 1** of the Buttons layer to select it.

4. Drag an instance of the **Button1** symbol from the library to the upper-left corner of the Stage. Drag an instance of the **Button2** symbol to the right of the first button instance on the Stage.

5. To test the buttons, click **Control** on the menu bar and then click **Enable Simple Buttons**. This option lets you test the buttons within the Flash program window.

6. Move your pointer over each of the buttons on the Stage to see the rollover effect. Click each button to see how it moves when it is pressed. When you are through testing the buttons, click **Control** on the menu bar and then click **Enable Simple Buttons** to turn this option off.

7. Click the **Text** tool on the Toolbox. In the Property inspector, change the Font Size to **24** and the Text (fill) color to **black**. Click inside the green button instance on the Stage to create a text block on the button. Type the word **Play**. See Figure 8-24.

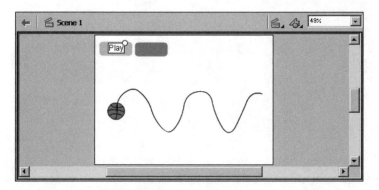

Figure 8-24   Text block on button

8. Now click inside the red button instance to create a text block on this button. Type the word **Stop**.

9. Save your work.

Adding Actions

The buttons you have added to the document do not control anything yet. Before the buttons can control the animation, you need to add actions to them. **Actions** are code elements of Flash's programming language, which is called **ActionScript**. You do not need to learn ActionScript to add actions to your documents because Flash provides many pre-programmed actions that you can access through the Actions panel. The **Actions toolbox**, on the left side of the Actions panel, contains a list of folders that represent different action categories. You click a folder to display additional folders or actions. When you double-click a specific action, its code is entered into a **script pane** on the right side of the Actions panel. When adding actions to buttons, make sure to add them to the button instances on the Stage. Do not add the actions to the Button symbols in the Library panel.

To add Actions to the button instances:

1. Click the **Arrow** tool and then click the green **Play** button on the Stage to select it. Make sure you select the button instance, and not just the text block.

2. Click **Window** on the menu bar and then click **Actions** to display the Actions panel. To view the buttons on the Stage and the Actions panel at the same time, drag the Actions panel from the left side of its title bar. The pointer should change to a four-headed arrow (or a hand on a Macintosh) to indicate that you can drag the panel and reposition it on a different part of the screen. Drag the panel so that you can see the Stage, as shown in Figure 8-25.

8

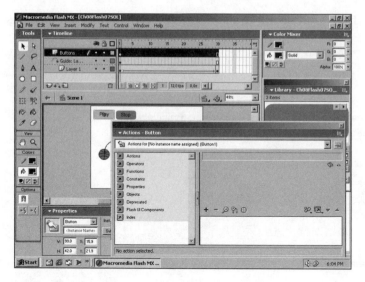

Figure 8-25 Repositioned Actions panel

3. In the Actions toolbox, click the **Actions** folder to display the various action categories available. Then click the **Movie Control** folder to display the list of actions that control a movie. See Figure 8-26.

 If the Movie Control actions look different from those in Figure 8-26, Flash may be in Export Mode. Click the View Options button and then make sure Normal Mode is selected.

4. Double-click **Play** under Movie Control in the actions list to insert the Play action code into the script pane. See Figure 8-27.

5. Click the **Stop** button instance on the Stage to select it.

6. In the Actions panel, double-click **Stop** in the Movie Control actions list to add the Stop action code to this button instance.

Figure 8-26 Actions for movie control

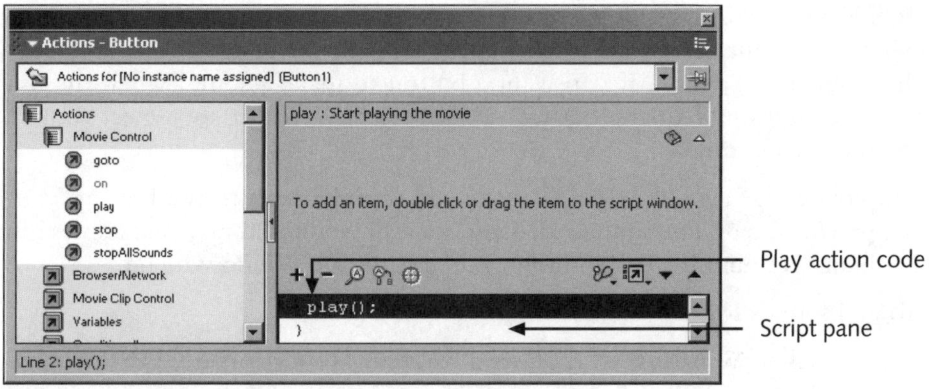

Figure 8-27   Play action code in the script pane

7. Click **Window** on the menu bar and then click **Actions** to close the Actions panel.

8. To test the animation, click **Control** on the menu bar and then click **Test Movie**. A new window opens and the animation plays. Click the **Stop** button to stop the animation. Then click the **Play** button to start it again.

9. Close the test window when you are through testing the animation and the buttons.

10. Save your work.

Adding Sounds

Now that you have created animations and added interactivity to your document with buttons, you can make your document even more interesting by adding sound. You can add sound effects to buttons or you can add sounds that play during certain frames. You cannot create sounds within Flash. Instead you import them using the Import command from the File menu. Sound files that can be imported into a Flash document can be in one of three file formats: WAV, MP3, or AIF. You can also drag a sound from a different document's library to the current document.

After you import a sound into your document, the sound file will reside in the document's library. Recall that the document's library stores not only the symbols you create but also any imported bitmap images and imported sound files. Bitmaps and sounds in the Library panel have different icons to distinguish them from symbols.

To add a sound from the library to a specific frame in your document, create a new layer, select the layer's frame where you want the sound to play, and then use the Sound drop-down list in the Property inspector to select the sound. The frame where the sound will play must be a keyframe.

To add a sound effect to a button, you edit the Button symbol, select the button's frame where you want the sound to play, and then drag the sound from the Library panel to the Stage. For example, if you want a button to make a sound when the user clicks it, you add the sound to the button's Down frame. You can also select sounds using the Property inspector.

The following steps show you how to add sound effects to the buttons you created in the previous steps. The sounds used are from the Sounds library that comes installed with Flash and is found in the Common Libraries in the Window menu.

To add sounds to the buttons' instances:

1. Click **Window** on the menu bar, point to **Common Libraries**, and click **Sounds** to open the Sounds library. The Sounds library displays in the Library panel.

2. If the document's Library panel is not open, click **Window** on the menu bar and then click **Library** to open it. Make sure that the contents of both the document and Sounds libraries are visible.

3. Scroll down the list of sounds in the Sounds library until you see the **Bucket Hit** sound. Drag this sound from the Sounds library into your document's library to make the sound available to your document. See Figure 8-28.

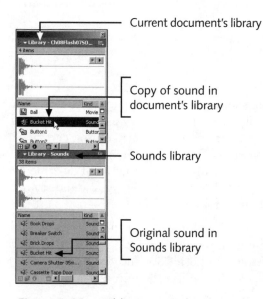

Figure 8-28 Adding a sound to your document's library

4. Scroll to the bottom of the sounds in the Sounds library to find the **Visor Hum Loop** sound. Drag this sound to your document's library.

5. Click the **options menu** control on the Sounds library title bar to display the menu commands. Click **Close Panel** to close the Sounds library.

6. On the document's library, click **Button1** to select it. Then click the **options menu** control and click **Edit** to edit the button.

7. In the Button1 Timeline, click the **Down** frame of Layer 1 to select it. Drag the Bucket Hit sound from the Library panel to the Stage. The Down frame now contains a waveform that represents the Bucket Hit sound, as shown in Figure 8-29.

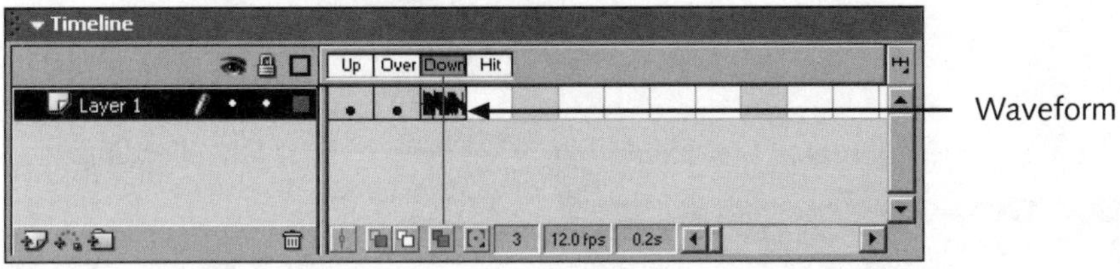

Figure 8-29 Sound's waveform in Button1 Down frame

8. Click **Edit** on the menu bar and then click **Edit Document** to return to the document.

9. Click **Button2** in the Library panel to select it. Then click the **options menu** control and click **Edit**.

10. In the Button2 Timeline, click the **Down** frame of Layer 1 to select it and drag the Bucket Hit sound to the Stage as you did for Button1.

11. Click **Edit** on the menu bar and then click **Edit Document** to return to the document.

12. Click **Control** on the menu bar and then click **Enable Simple Buttons**. If you have your computer's speakers on, you hear a sound when you click either button.

Another way to enhance your document is to add a background sound. You place a background sound in the frame in which you want it to start playing. The frame must be a keyframe.

To add a background sound:

1. Click the **Buttons** layer to select it. Then click **Insert** on the menu bar and click **Layer** to add a new layer. Change the name of this layer to **Sound**.

2. Click **Frame 1** of the Sound layer.

3. In the Property inspector, select the **Visor Hum Loop** sound from the Sound drop-down list. Leave the Effect selection as **None** and the Sync option at **Event**. Enter **2** for Loop to make this sound play twice each time the animation starts from Frame 1. See Figure 8-30.

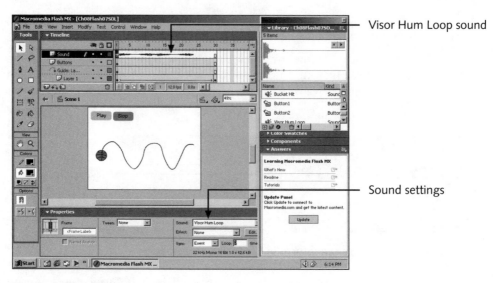

Visor Hum Loop sound

Sound settings

Figure 8-30   Background sound

4. To test your document, click **Control** on the menu bar and then click **Test Movie**. Make sure you have your computer's speakers on so you can hear the movie's background sound. Close this window to get back to the document.

5. Save your work.

6. Click **File** on the menu bar and then click **Exit** to exit Flash. (On a Macintosh, click **Flash** on the menu bar and then click **Quit Flash**.)

Publishing Your Movie

Up to now, you have been testing your documents by using the Play or Test Movie commands under the Control menu. Using the Test Movie command creates a .swf file that is played in a separate Flash Player window. After you finish creating a document, you may want to distribute it for use on the Web. To do this, you publish it so that it will play within an HTML page. Using the Publish Settings dialog box shown in Figure 8-31, you can specify how you want to publish your document. When you click Publish, Flash will create the necessary files, such as the .swf and .html files.

To publish your document to be viewed on the Web, select Flash (.swf) and HTML (.html) in the Publish Settings dialog box. When you click Publish, the program will create a Web page with the HTML code required to embed the .swf file in the page. If Use default names is selected, the .swf and .html files will have the same name as the .fla document. If you prefer, you can use other names for the files. In order to display your movie, the user's Web browser must have the Flash Player plug-in installed. The player comes installed with most browsers today and is also available for free download from the Macromedia Web site (www.macromedia.com).

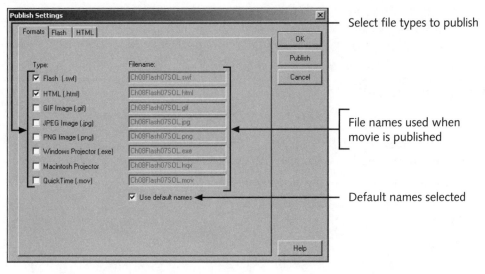

Figure 8-31   Publish Settings dialog box

CHAPTER SUMMARY

❐ Macromedia Flash allows you to create animations by placing different states of an image in different frames and then displaying the frames one after another. A document's frames are coordinated by the Timeline. You can insert frames to extend the document over time. The Timeline's playhead indicates which frame is currently being displayed.

❐ Layers are used to organize the images, animations, and other objects that make up a document. Different objects can be placed in separate layers so that they can be edited or animated individually. Special types of layers include guide layers and mask layers.

❐ Frame-by-frame animations require you to create content for each frame. Tweened animations require you to create the content for the beginning and ending frames, and Flash creates the in-between frames. You can create motion tweened animations where an object moves, rotates, or changes in size or color. You can also create a shape tweened animation where an object changes its shape.

❐ Objects used in motion tweened animations must be converted to symbols. Symbols are stored and organized in the document's library. To use a symbol in a document, you create a copy or instance of the symbol on the Stage. Multiple instances can be created of the same symbol, and you can change an instance's properties without affecting the symbol or other instances of the same symbol. A symbol is stored only once regardless of the number of instances created for that symbol.

❐ Buttons can be added to a document to allow user interaction. Buttons are symbols with their own four-frame Timeline. You can create rollover effects as well as add sound effects to buttons. You can also add actions to buttons to control a movie.

◻ After you finish a document, you can publish it—in other words, make it available on the Web. Movies published for the Web have the .swf file extension. Flash also creates the necessary HTML to play the movie in a browser.

REVIEW QUESTIONS

1. The Timeline is used to _____.

   a. organize a document's symbols and sounds

   b. coordinate a document's frames and layers

   c. control the size of a document's graphics

   d. provide a thumbnail view of a symbol

2. In animation, each _____ in a document is displayed in succession over time.

   a. layer

   b. symbol

   c. frame

   d. keyframe

3. Each _____ is represented as a row in the document's Timeline and may contain different objects.

   a. layer

   b. symbol

   c. frame

   d. keyframe

4. Two special types of layers are _____ layers and _____ layers.

   a. guide, outline

   b. guide, mask

   c. large, small

   d. graphics, mask

5. The document's _____ stores and organizes symbols you create in Flash.

   a. Timeline

   b. panel

   c. frame

   d. library

6. When you drag a symbol onto the Stage, you create a(n) _____ of the symbol.

   a. outline

   b. instance

   c. property

   d. movie clip

7. The three types of symbol behaviors are _____, _____, and _____.

   a. movie clip, instance, picture

   b. movie clip, button, image

   c. instance, button, graphic

   d. movie clip, button, graphic

8. In _____ animation, you create the content for the beginning and ending frames. Flash will then create the content for the in-between frames.

   a. frame-by-frame

   b. tweened

   c. keyframe

   d. loop

9. In _____ animation, you create the content for each frame.

   a. frame-by-frame

   b. tweened

   c. keyframe

   d. loop

10. To make an object move using a motion tween, the object must first be converted to a _____.

    a. layer

    b. frame

    c. circle

    d. symbol

11. To animate four objects at the same time within a document, you should place each object on a separate _____.

    a. layer

    b. frame

    c. library

    d. Timeline

8

12. Changing the _____ amount for an object in a tweened animation will control how fast the object's animation begins or ends.

    a. rotate

    b. alpha

    c. ease

    d. brightness

13. To apply a shape tween to text, you must first _____.

    a. apply the Break Apart command twice to the text

    b. convert the text into a symbol

    c. change the properties of the characters within the text

    d. group the text as one object

14. _____ will allow you to make a document interactive.

    a. Graphics

    b. Movie clips

    c. Buttons

    d. Frames

15. _____ is the native format for Flash document files.

    a. .swf

    b. .fla

    c. .exe

    d. .htm

HANDS-ON EXERCISES

Exercise 8-1

In this exercise, you will create a motion tweened animation that moves the letters of the word "Flash". Each letter will be in its own layer. You will need to convert each letter into a symbol before you can complete the animation. The letters should start at the center of the Stage and move towards the top half of the Stage.

1. Open the file named **Ch08FlashEX01** from the Exercises folder for Chapter 8 and save it as **Ch08FlashEX01SOL** in the same folder. The document contains five layers, each with one letter.

2. Select the letter F on the Stage and convert it into a symbol. Name this symbol F and leave its behavior as Movie Clip. Then select the letter L on the Stage and convert it into a symbol with the Movie Clip behavior. Name the symbol L. Repeat this for the letters A, S, and H. Open the Library panel to see the symbols.

3. Select Frame 25 of Layer F and insert a keyframe. While still in Frame 25, move the instance of the letter F to the upper-left side of the Stage. Use the Transform command in the Window menu to open the Transform panel. Make sure that Constrain is checked so that both the width and height will increase proportionally. Change the width to 300% and then press **Enter** to increase the size of the letter.

4. Repeat the previous step for each of the other letters. Be sure to insert a keyframe in Frame 25 of each layer and then move each letter to a different part of the top half of the Stage. Increase the size of each letter in its ending frame.

5. Create a motion tween in Frame 1 of Layer F by selecting Motion from the Tween drop-down list in the Property inspector. Also, select CW under Rotate and enter 3 for the number of times to rotate.

6. Repeat the previous step for each of the other letters. Do this by selecting Frame 1 of each layer and then selecting Motion from the Tween drop-down list in the Property inspector. Make sure you also select CW for Rotate and 3 for the number of times to rotate.

7. Test your animation. The letters should start at the center and move to the top part of the Stage. They should rotate and increase in size while moving.

8. Save your work and close the file.

Exercise 8-2

In this exercise, you will make the letters of the document you created in Exercise 8-1 fall down to the bottom of the Stage. You will do this by adding another motion tween to each layer.

1. Open the file named **Ch08FlashEX01SOL** from the Exercises folder for Chapter 8 and save it as **Ch08FlashEX02SOL** in the same folder.

2. Select Frame 40 of Layer F and insert a keyframe. With frame 40 still selected, move the letter F to the bottom of the Stage and rotate it using the Free Transform tool on the Toolbox so that it appears to be lying down.

3. Repeat the previous step for each of the other letters, making sure you create a keyframe in Frame 40 of each layer and then reposition each letter in its last frame.

4. Select Frame 25 of Layer F and select Motion from the Tween drop-down list in the Property inspector. Select CCW under Rotate and enter 5 for the number of times to rotate.

5. Repeat the previous step for each of the other letters by creating a motion tween in Frame 25 of each layer, setting Rotate to CCW, and setting the number of times to rotate to 5.

6. Test the document by pressing Enter. The animation matches the one you created in Exercise 8-1, except that at the end the letters fall down to the bottom of the Stage.

7. Save your work and close the file.

Exercise 8-3

In this exercise, you create a shape tweened animation using text. You first have to break apart the text before you can use it in a shape tween.

1. Start a new document and save it as **Ch08FlashEX03** in the Exercises folder for Chapter 8.

2. Select the Text tool and, if necessary, open the Property inspector.

3. In the Property inspector, choose Impact for the Font and set the Font Size to 80. Select blue for the Text Color and set the Character Spacing to 30.

4. In the middle of the Stage, type the word FLASH in all caps.

5. Use the Break Apart command in the Modify menu to convert the text block into individual text blocks, one for each letter. Apply the Break Apart command a second time to convert the letters to fills. You will no longer be able to edit the letters as text.

6. Create a keyframe in Frame 25. In Frame 25, delete the word FLASH and draw an oval in the middle of the Stage at about the same area where you had the word FLASH.

7. In Frame 1, select Shape from the Tween drop-down list in the Property inspector.

8. Test your document. The FLASH letters should change into the shape of the oval through the animation.

9. Save your work and close the file.

Exercise 8-4

In this exercise, you open a partially completed document and add a motion tween and a motion guide layer.

1. Open the file named **Ch08FlashEX04** from the Exercises folder for Chapter 8 and save it as **Ch08FlashEX04SOL** in the same folder. The document contains three layers.

2. Select the boat and convert it into a symbol. Name this symbol Boat and leave its behavior as Movie Clip.

3. Create a keyframe in Frame 30 of the Boat layer. Move the boat across to the right side of the Stage.

4. Create a motion tween in Frame 1 of the Boat layer.

5. To make the water and sun visible throughout the entire animation, insert a regular frame in Frame 30 of the Water layer and then insert a regular frame in Frame 30 of the Sun layer.

6. Test your document. The boat should move in a straight line across the Stage right over the water. Next, to make the boat move in a more natural way, you will add a motion guide layer.

7. Click the Boat layer to select it. Use the Motion Guide command in the Insert menu to add a motion guide layer. This layer should be above the Boat layer in the Timeline and the Boat layer should be indented.

8. Select Frame 1 of the Guide: Boat layer. Click the Pencil tool and, if necessary, select the Smooth Pencil mode modifier. Draw a line from the left side of the Stage to the right that will represent the path the boat should follow. Draw the line above the surface of the water and make sure the line is curved just like the water.

9. Select Frame 1 of the Boat layer. Use the Arrow tool to move the boat so that its center point is snapped to the beginning point of the line. If necessary, first turn on Snap to Objects. You may need to zoom in closer before you move the boat.

10. Select Frame 30 of the Boat layer. Use the Arrow tool to move the boat so that its center point is snapped to the ending point of the line.

11. Test your document. The boat should move along the water from left to right following the path you drew in the motion guide layer.

12. Save your work and close the file.

Exercise 8-5

In this exercise, you apply two motion tweens to an object. The first motion tween should cause the object to grow in size and change in color. The second motion tween should cause the object to go back to its original size and color.

1. Start a new document and save it as **Ch08FlashEX05** in the Exercises folder for Chapter 8.

2. Use the Oval tool to draw a small circle in the middle of the Stage. Use a red fill color and a black stroke color.

3. Using the Arrow tool, double-click the circle to select it and convert it into a symbol. Name the symbol Circle and leave its behavior as Movie Clip.

4. Insert a keyframe in Frame 15 and another one in Frame 30.

5. If necessary, open the Property inspector. Select Frame 15 and click the circle to select it. In the Property inspector, select Tint from the Color drop-down list. Use the color palette to select a pink color.

6. If necessary, open the Transform panel, using the Transform command under the Window menu. Make sure Constrain is not selected. Change the width to 200%.

7. Create a motion tween in Frame 1 and then create another in Frame 15.

8. Save your work.

9. Click File on the menu bar, click Publish Preview, and then click Default - (HTML). The movie opens in your default browser. The circle should expand, change in color, and then go back to its original size and color. Close the browser window when you are finished testing the movie.

10. Close the file in Flash.

8

WEB DESIGN PROJECTS

Project 8-1

Create a new logo for your college that will contain animation. The logo should contain several shapes, the name of the college, and a college slogan (such as "Your Future Starts Here!"). You should also incorporate two motion tweens that occur at the same time. One motion tween should animate one of the shapes in your logo. The other motion tween should animate the name of the college. The college name should fade in throughout the animation. The animation should last for four seconds. Once you have completed your animated logo, save the document as **Ch08FlashDP01** in the Projects folder for Chapter 8. In the Publish Settings dialog box, select Flash (.swf) and HTML (.html). Change the name of the .swf file to **logo.swf** and the name of the HTML file to **logo.html**. Publish the logo. Open the **logo.html** file in your browser to view your animated college logo (**logo.swf**).

Project 8-2

In this project, you will finish a partially completed document by adding motion tweens to move objects and buttons to control the animation. Start by opening the **Ch08FlashDP02** file from the Projects folder for Chapter 8 and save it as **Ch08FlashDP02SOL** in the same folder. Add a motion tween to make the basketball move from its initial position to the upper-right side of the Stage. The motion tweened animation should start in Frame 1 and end in Frame 30. Then add another motion tween to move the baseball from its initial position to the upper-left side of the Stage. It should also end in Frame 30. Extend each of the other layers to Frame 30 by inserting regular frames. Next add a button to play the document's animation and a button to stop it. The buttons should have a rollover effect and a sound effect when clicked. Place the buttons in a new layer. Use the Oval tool to draw a green circle and a red circle next to each other on the bottom of the Stage. Convert each of these circles to symbols, making sure to select Button as their behavior. Edit each of these Button symbols to add keyframes for their Over and Down frames. In the Over frames, change the Fill Color to yellow. In the Down frames, add a sound effect. Use the Plastic Button sound from the Sounds library. Next add the Play action to the green button instance and the Stop action to the red button instance. Test your document to make sure the buttons work. Save the file. Publish your movie for the Web using the file names **banner.swf** and **banner.html**.

Project 8-3

Create a new document with dimensions of 400 pixels in width by 100 pixels in height. You will use a mask layer to display the word FLASH. The letters will mask a rectangle that has a gradient fill; the rectangle will move from the left to the right and back to the left again. Change the name of Layer 1 to Gradient and draw a rectangle on the Stage. Start the rectangle at the top left corner of the Stage and make it about 300 pixels wide and 100 pixels high. Use the green radial gradient for the rectangle's fill. The rectangle should cover about three-fourths of the Stage. Select the entire rectangle and convert it to a symbol. Create a keyframe in Frame 15 and another one in Frame 30. In Frame 15, move the rectangle to the right so that its right side is lined up against the right edge of the Stage. Create a motion tween in Frame 1 and another one in Frame 15. The rectangle should move from the left side of the Stage to the right side and back. Then add a new layer, name it Text, and create a text block with the letters FLASH. Use the Arial font, a Font Size of about 60, black text, and make it bold. Center the text block on the Stage, making sure that it stays within the rectangle. Change the Text layer to a mask layer. The Gradient layer should automatically become a masked layer. Test your animation. The letters in FLASH should be green and appear to have a moving beam of light shining on them. Save this file as **Ch08FlashDP03** in the Projects folder for Chapter 8. Publish your movie for the Web using the default file names.

8

9

FIREWORKS: PART I

In this chapter you will:

- ♦ Create and edit bitmap and vector graphics using Fireworks
- ♦ Use the Fireworks tools, Optimize panel, Layers panel, and other panels to edit images
- ♦ Color and manipulate objects using the Property inspector
- ♦ Change fill, stroke, and effect attributes of objects and text
- ♦ Export and optimize a file for the Web

Macromedia Fireworks MX enables you to seamlessly integrate graphics into your Dreamweaver Web pages. The HTML and JavaScript code that is created by Fireworks is fully compatible with Dreamweaver. This lets you work on graphics and Web design in an integrated development environment. Fireworks offers in a single package various tools for creating and working with many different kinds of graphics files. For example, Fireworks allows you to create both bitmapped and vector graphics, and to scan and edit graphics, photographs, and files from many other graphics applications. In this chapter, you will learn to use the basic editing features of Fireworks. You will also learn about the tools and effects that are available in Fireworks.

Fireworks lets you edit bitmap and vector graphics. A **bitmap graphic** is an image defined as individual pixels of color that make the image. A photograph is a good example of a bitmap image. Photographs have complex variations of color. When digitized, the color is represented by a grid of pixels of complex color variations that make up the image. A **vector graphic** is one that uses mathematical formulas and vector paths to define shapes and figures. Because a vector graphic image is defined mathematically, you do not see the pixel variations as you do with a bitmap image. Fireworks lets you edit bitmap and vector images in one document.

FIREWORKS EDITING TOOLS

In this section, you will take a guided tour of the Fireworks workspace. But first, you need to start Fireworks.

To start Macromedia Fireworks MX:

1. Start **Macromedia Fireworks MX** from the Start menu. (If you are working on a Macintosh, start Macromedia Fireworks MX from the Applications folder.) Fireworks opens, and the interface looks similar to Figure 9-1.

2. If you do not see a blank canvas, as shown in Figure 9-1, click **File** on the menu bar, click **New**, and then click **OK** in the New Document dialog box.

 Your Fireworks screen might look different from Figure 9-1, depending on which tools and panels are currently open. If you are working on a Macintosh, the screen may not match the figure completely. For example, you will probably see the Dock at the bottom of your screen.

 The first time you start Fireworks, a dialog box appears, asking you to select Graphic Design, What's New, or Web Design. These options take you to tutorials that give you a quick overview of the Fireworks product. Close this window to begin using Fireworks.

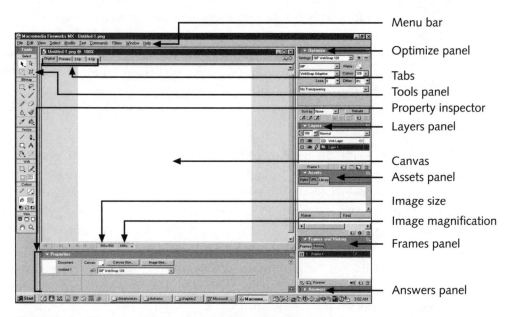

Figure 9-1   Macromedia Fireworks MX workspace

When you first start Fireworks, you may be a little intimidated by the number of elements displayed in the work area. If you have worked with another drawing tool, some of the icons you see may be familiar to you. For example, the Paint Bucket (used to fill a shape or area with a specific color) is a common icon used in many applications. As a rule, the toolbars and panels of the Fireworks interface work similar to those in other Macromedia products. Before proceeding with this chapter, you might find it helpful to review the material on manipulating the panels and tabs in the "Dreamweaver Workspace" section of Chapter 3.

Most of the icons in the Fireworks interface offer rollover text (screen tips) to indicate what happens when you click the icon. At the top of the screen, you see a menu bar. On the left-hand side of the work area, a two-column Tools panel provides drawing tools you can use to create and modify artwork. The center area of the screen is the Document window, or, more informally, the work area. The white rectangle in the center of the Document window is the **canvas** (sometimes called simply, a document). You create an image on the canvas.

At the top of the Document window are four tabs. The Original tab lets you view your original document; the Preview tab lets you see what your image will look like when it is loaded in a Web browser; and the other tabs help you to compare settings when you optimize a document for the Web. The image size (in pixels) appears at the bottom of the document. You can change the percentage to adjust the image's magnification in the work area. At the bottom of the Fireworks screen is the Property inspector. This is used to edit the size, color, and other attributes of objects you are using in the work area. As in Dreamweaver, the Property inspector shows the appropriate properties for the object selected in the work area.

The panels (located on the right side of the screen) contain tabs, each of which contain groups of settings that you can use to edit your images. You can minimize or expand the panels by clicking the expander to the left of the panel title. You can access the panels by clicking Window in the menu bar and then selecting the desired panel from the menu. Panels can be moved to other locations in the work area by dragging them with the gripper, located at the upper-left corner of the panel.

The Tools panel is essentially a toolbar with a variety of icons that you can click to perform specific tasks. It is divided into six categories: Select, Bitmap, Vector, Web, Colors, and View. You will learn more about these tools as you use them throughout the chapter. If you have used other drawing applications, these tools may be familiar to you. To use a tool, you click it and then apply it to the work area. If you see a small triangle at the lower-right corner of the tool, holding your mouse button down will reveal more tool options. If you are not sure of a tool's function, hold the mouse pointer over it to display a screen tip.

Every object you work with in the Fireworks work area has properties associated with it. For example, a simple rectangle has width, height, color, and placement properties that you can define and control. You can adjust an object's properties in the appropriate tab of the appropriate panel, or you can use the Property inspector, which displays the most important settings for the selected object. It is much easier to manipulate attributes of an object through the Property inspector rather than searching through panels for the correct setting. Figure 9-2 shows a Property inspector for a rectangle.

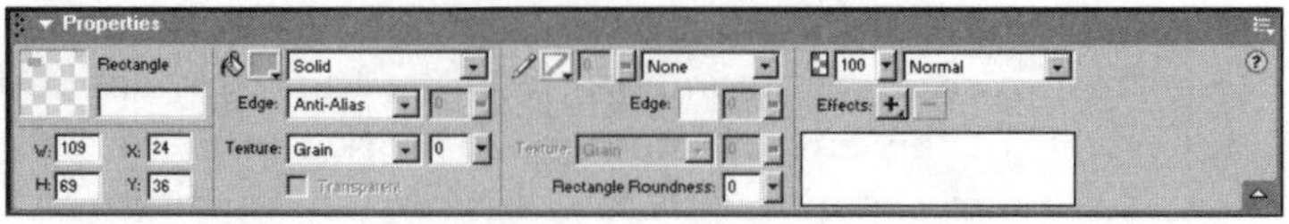

Figure 9-2   Property inspector for a rectangle

Creating a New Document

To create a new document, select the New command on the File menu. This displays the New Document dialog box (shown in Figure 9-3), where you must specify the canvas size and resolution, and select a canvas type. Most Web graphics are 72 dots per inch (dpi) because most monitors display graphics at this resolution. If you find working in inches or centimeters easier, you can click the list arrow next to the height and width text boxes.

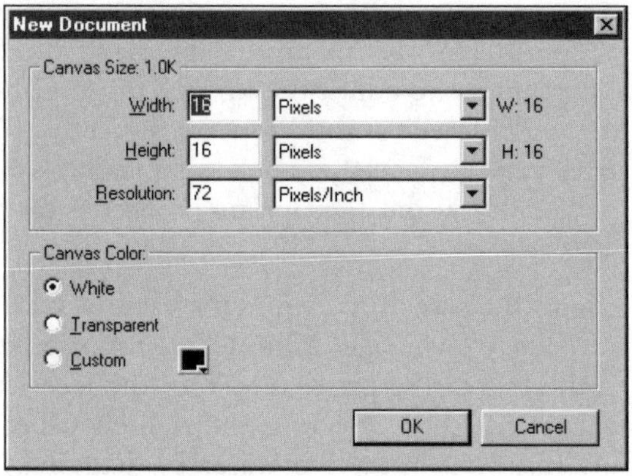

Figure 9-3   New Document dialog box

You can choose one of three options for canvas color: white, transparent, or custom. After you create your work area, you may decide that you need to modify the size of the canvas or image, or type of background you selected. To change any of these attributes, click Modify and then point to Canvas on the menu bar. Figure 9-4 shows the options for editing the canvas attributes. You can use the Image Size, Canvas Size, or Canvas Color options to edit the original settings for your document. Using the Trim Canvas option, you can crop a section of the canvas. Fit Canvas automatically resizes the canvas to the size of your image. This can eliminate unnecessary whitespace and create more efficient graphics by ensuring that extraneous whitespace is not saved with your drawing. The Rotate Canvas option allows you to rotate the entire work area by 180 degrees (flip it), 90 degrees clockwise, or 90 degrees counterclockwise.

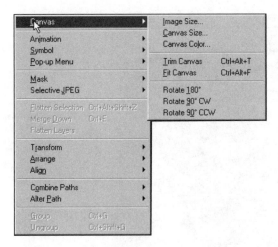

Figure 9-4 Modify Canvas attributes

To open an existing file, click Open on the File menu. Fireworks will open many file formats, including .png, .psd, .bmp, .gif, and .jpg. The graphic file formats most commonly used on the Internet are .gif and .jpg. Fireworks also maintains editable layers in files created with Adobe Photoshop (.psd). (To learn about using layers in Photoshop, see Chapters 5 and 6.)

Saving and Exporting Files

To save your work in Fireworks, click File on the menu bar, and then click Save or Save As. Fireworks will automatically save your file in **Portable Network Graphic (PNG)** format. Many Web browsers do not support .png graphics without the use of a plug-in. Saving your graphics file in .png format maintains all the file's editable features as well as the layers created as part of the graphic, so that you may continue editing the file in detail. To save the file in .gif or .jpg format to be used with your Dreamweaver application, you must export the file, not save it.

Before exporting a file in a given format, Fireworks helps you preview and optimize it so you see which format has optimal quality at minimal file size. You can use the 2-Up and 4-Up preview tabs to optimize your graphic. For example, the 4-Up tab will show you four different panels of your image. The first is the original image, the next three can be altered using the Optimize panel, and a direct comparison can be made between the different images. Once you have selected the optimal file, you can export the image or the image and html. You can also click Export Preview from the File menu to open the Export Preview dialog box, as shown in Figure 9-5. You can use this dialog box to preview changes to the file format, palette, transparency, and other formatting features.

9

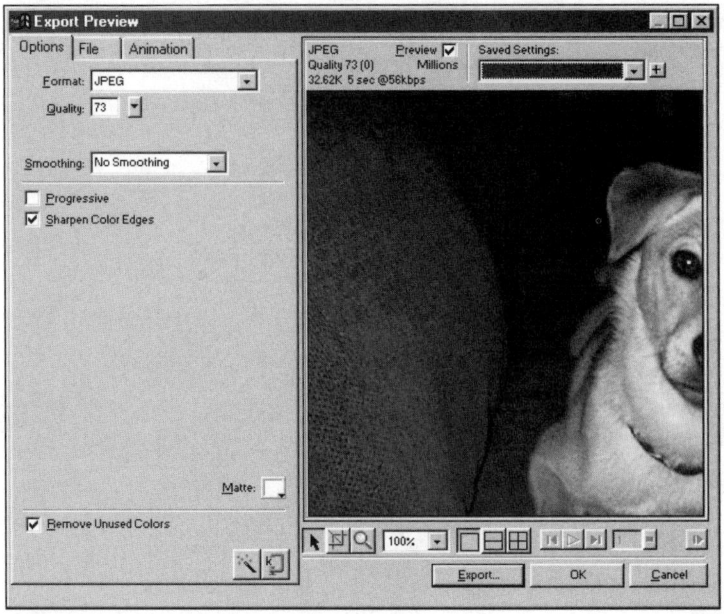

Figure 9-5   Export Preview dialog box

In the following steps, you will open, optimize, and save a Web graphic.

To open, optimize, and save a Web graphic:

1. Click **File** on the menu bar, and then click **Open**. In the Open dialog box, navigate to the Chapter folder for Chapter 9, select the file named **Ch09FW01.png**, and click **Open**. (Depending on how your computer is set up, you may not see file extensions displayed.)

2. Click the **2–Up** tab at the top of the document work area. As shown in Figure 9-6, two copies of your image appear—the original image and a preview image. When you optimize a graphic, you balance the need for high image quality with small file size. You can optimize images in the 2-Up and 4-Up tabs individually by using the Optimize panel. If the Optimize panel is not open (in the upper-right corner), open it now by selecting it from the Windows pull-down menu in the menu bar or by pressing the F6 key. Close any other open panels on the right side of the screen.

3. Look in the bottom left corner of the original image (on the left) to view its current size (94.83K).

4. Click the preview image, on the right of the screen. An outline around the image indicates that it is selected. The right-hand image shows you what the original image will look like when saved as a GIF file. Below the image, you see the projected size of the GIF file (11.17K), and the projected download time for a 56-kbps modem.

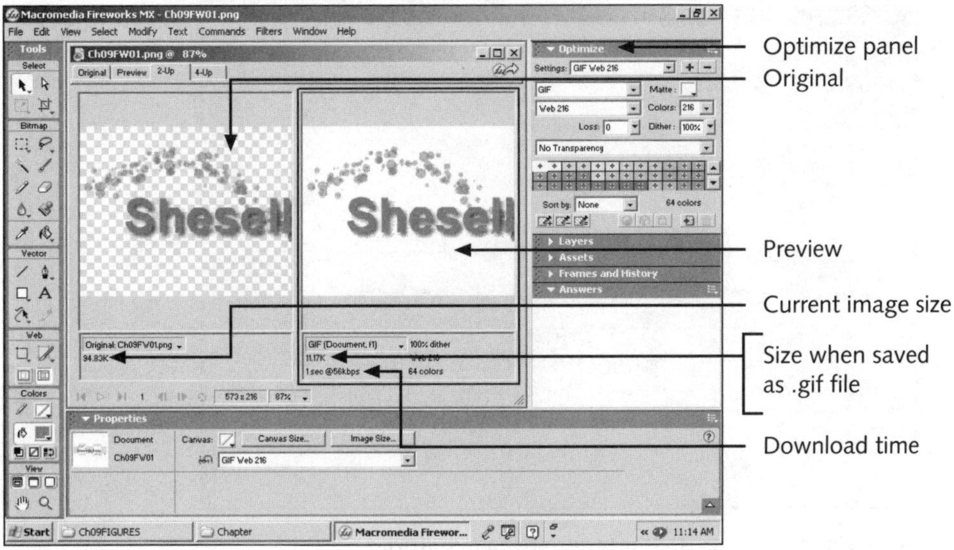

Figure 9-6   Ch09FW01.png displayed in 2-Up tab

5. Click the down arrow next to Optimize, if necessary, to display the Optimize panel, click the **Settings** list arrow at the very top of the Optimize panel and select **JPEG–Smaller File**. The file size and download time are reduced, but the image quality (as shown in the preview image) is somewhat degraded. (The image is not quite as clear.)

6. Click the **Settings** list arrow at the very top of the Optimize panel and select **GIF Web 216**. The file size and download time increase, and the image quality is better.

7. In the Optimize panel, click the list arrow next to the text box that reads No Transparency and click **Alpha Transparency**. A checkered background appears in the image preview, indicating it has a transparent background.

8. Click **File** on the menu bar and then click **Export**. The Export dialog box opens.

9. Open the Chapter folder for Chapter 9. In the File name text box, enter the file name **Ch09FW01SOL**.

10. Click the **Save as type** list arrow and click **HTML and Images**. This tells Fireworks to save your Fireworks document as an HTML file and a .gif file. The file name has changed to .htm file format, so you see "Ch09FW01SOL.htm" in the File name text box. See Figure 9-7.

9

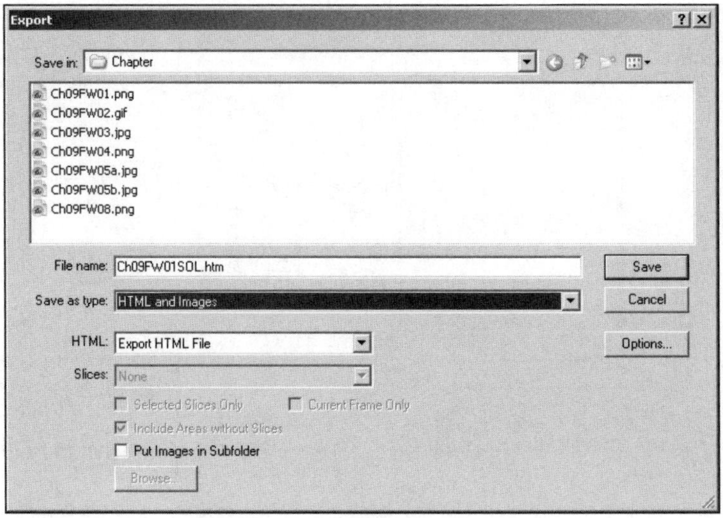

Figure 9-7   Export dialog box with new settings

11. Click **Save**. The Export dialog box closes.

12. Open your browser and then open the **Ch09FW01SOL.htm** file from the Chapter folder for Chapter 9. Close the browser and return to Fireworks. (If you are working on a Macintosh, you may need to click the application's icon in the Dock to display the entire Fireworks interface.)

13. Click **File** on the menu bar and then click **Close**. If you are asked if you want to save changes to the file, click **Yes** (or **Save** on a Macintosh).

SELECTION TOOLS

You use selection tools in any graphics application to manipulate the parts of an image. The ability to select shapes allows you to add colors to specific objects very precisely. The ability to select portions of drawings allows you to delete unneeded colors and backgrounds and to recolor photographs so they fit any color scheme. Graphics applications usually give you several different ways to select elements of the drawing. The Fireworks tools that allow you to select objects and areas of the page are located at the top of the Tools panel.

The following sections describe some essential Fireworks tools. As you read these descriptions, keep in mind that a small triangle at the bottom of a tool icon tells you that additional, related tools are available on a pop-up menu. To display such a pop-up menu, point to a tool with your mouse and press the mouse button. Continue holding down the mouse button while you drag the mouse pointer onto the pop-up menu, and then select the tool you need. If you cannot find a tool on your computer, look for it on one of these hidden, pop-up menus.

Pointer and Subselection Tools

The Pointer tool has two options: the Pointer tool and the Select Behind tool. (By default, you see the Pointer tool on the Tools panel. To see the Select Behind tool, press and hold the Ctrl key and click the black triangle on the Pointer tool.) Using the Pointer tool, you can select and reposition any object on the canvas. A selected object has an outline around it and has small, square handles on its edges. The Property inspector displays the properties of the selected object so that you can edit them if necessary. To deselect an object, click elsewhere on the canvas, or click the object while holding the Shift key down. Figure 9-8 shows a selected rectangle and a selected line. The Select Behind tool lets you perform the same action and more. If you have one object on top of another, you can use the Select Behind tool to select the bottom object (in which case the object on the bottom will have red selection handles). This is extremely useful for selecting and manipulating objects in a complex graphic.

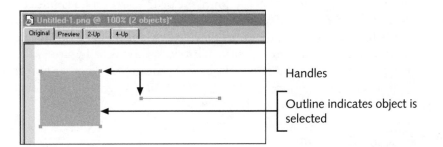

Figure 9-8   Selected rectangle and line

The Subselection tool is used to select an object for reshaping. When you select the tool and click an object, you will see several small squares—called **Bezier points**—around the object. With your mouse, you can drag these points into new positions, and thus create new shapes. Figure 9-9 shows how a Bezier point looks on the screen. In this figure, a polygon is being reshaped by dragging the point to another position.

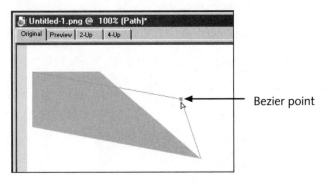

Figure 9-9   Reshaping a polygon using Bezier point

Pointer selection tools are useful for only shapes because they let you select an entire object and manipulate it. They are not useful for editing a photograph, because clicking on a photograph reveals no selectable shape, just a canvas of single colors.

To select multiple objects, hold the Shift key down and click each of the objects you want to select.

Scale and Cropping Tools

The Scale tool offers two additional tools in its pop-up menu: the Skew tool and the Distort tool. The Skew tool lets you stretch a selection along its vertical or horizontal axis, and the Distort tool lets you stretch a selection by dragging its sides with the mouse. All three tools let you rotate selections. To use these tools, you must first select the shape you wish to transform and then click the Scale (or Skew or Distort) tool. Handles then appear around the shape, including a small circle handle in the center of the selection, as shown in Figure 9-10. When you position the mouse anywhere in the canvas outside the selected object, the mouse pointer turns into a curved arrow, as shown in Figure 9-11. You click and drag this pointer to rotate the selected object. You can also scale an object by using the Property inspector. The inspector displays width and height settings that you can modify precisely by entering pixel measurements.

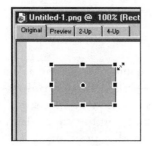

Figure 9-10   Handles shown during use of Scale tool

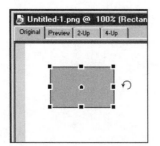

Figure 9-11   Rotating an object

Using Cropping Tools

The Crop tool is used to select a portion of the document you are working on and discard the remainder of the document. This is a quick way to select part of a photograph or graphic that you wish to use and immediately get rid of everything else. On the Crop tool's pop-up menu, you will find the Export Area tool, which you can use to select a smaller portion of a graphic by dragging your mouse over that area. Double-clicking that area opens the Export Preview dialog box, which you can use to export that portion of your graphic into another file. In the following steps, you will modify a photograph of a dog by using the Crop tool.

To modify a photograph by using the Crop tool:

1. Open the file named **Ch09FW04.jpg** from the Chapter folder for Chapter 9.

2. Click the **Crop** tool in the Tools panel. Move the mouse over the image of the dog. The mouse pointer changes shape to match the icon on the Crop tool in the Tools panel.

3. Click just above and to the left of the dog's left ear, and drag down to draw a rectangle around the dog's face, as shown in Figure 9-12. When the rectangle is the right shape, release the mouse button.

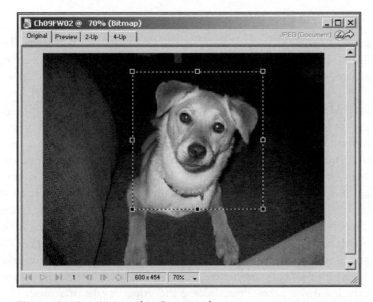

Figure 9-12   Using the Crop tool

4. You can fine-tune the area marked for cropping by using the Property inspector at the bottom of the work area. In the Property inspector, enter the following values in the W (width), H (height), and X and Y coordinate boxes.

- W: **250**
- H: **250**

- X: **220**
- Y: **40**

As you enter the values in the Property inspector, the selection rectangle alters to reflect the new settings.

5. Double-click the mouse in the middle of the selection. The area outside the cropping rectangle disappears. You have successfully cropped the image.

6. Click **File** and then click **Save** (or **Save as** on a Macintosh). In the Save dialog box, save the image as **Ch09FW02SOL.png** in the Chapter folder for Chapter 9.

BITMAP TOOLS

Bitmap images are defined by a grid of pixels. Each pixel has a color assigned to it. The combination of all the pixel colors make up the image. The Bitmap tools in the Tools panel are used to select and modify areas of pixels based upon selections of areas or selections of colors. The tools in the Bitmap area of the Tools panel are described in the following sections.

Marquee, Lasso, and Magic Wand Tools

The Marquee and Lasso tools allow you to select an area of the canvas by drawing a shape around it. Using the Marquee tool, you can draw a rectangular selection shape. You can use the Marquee tool's other option, the Oval Marquee tool, to draw an oval selection shape. You select an area of the canvas by clicking one of the Marquee tools and then dragging the Marquee pointer over the desired area. Once a marquee is drawn, you can reposition it to more accurately select an area by dragging it with your mouse. You can also resize it by using the Property inspector. Figure 9-13 shows a rectangular marquee drawn on a photograph to select a dog's face. The Property inspector for the marquee displays settings for width (W), height (H), X and Y locations on the canvas, Style, and Edge. The Style option lets you set constraints for the marquee, if desired. For example, if you only wish to select images that are 100 by 100 pixels, you can set Style to Fixed Size and then enter 100 in the two text boxes below the Style list box. Under the Edge option, Hard, Anti-Alias, and Feather are the possible options. The Hard setting creates a straight edge for the marquee, as if you cut it out of paper with a pair of scissors. The Anti-Alias option lets you create an edge that blends into the canvas color. The Feathered option creates a fuzzy effect along the edge of the marquee.

Using the Lasso tool, you can draw a customized selection shape. The Lasso tool has one additional option, the Polygon Lasso. To use the Lasso tool, simply drag the mouse around a desired area. Using the Polygon Lasso tool, you can select part of an image by clicking points around that area. The Lasso tool allows you to draw freely around a shape; the Polygon Lasso tool lets you select a shape by clicking the mouse to indicate angles and edges along the drawing. Figure 9-14 shows an area selected using the Polygon Lasso tool. The Property Inspector for the Lasso tool lets you change size and location options and Edge options just like the Marquee tool does.

Figure 9-13   Using a rectangular marquee to select an area

Figure 9-14   Selection using the Polygon Lasso tool

Once you create a marquee over a portion of a bitmap graphic, more selection alternatives become available on the Select menu. These options are useful when you need to alter a selection slightly to create a specific effect. For example, you may use the Lasso tool to roughly select a shape and then use the Contract Marquee command on the Select menu to shrink the selection so the background around the shape does not show.

Using the Magic Wand tool, you can select areas of a document that are all the same color. For example, if your photograph has a blue sky and you want a pink sky, you could use the Magic Wand tool to select all the blue parts of the image and recolor it to a shade of pink. Figure 9-15 shows a Magic Wand selection in the work area. In the Property inspector, you can set the tool's tolerance, and then select an edge that is Hard, Anti-Alias, or Feathered.

Figure 9-15   Selection using the Magic Wand tool

Creating a Feathered Edge

In the following steps, you will use the Oval Marquee tool to create a feathered edge on a photograph.

To create a feathered edge on a photograph:

1. Open the file named **Ch09FW03.jpg** from the Chapter folder for Chapter 9. You see an image of a baby in a white hat.

2. Point to the **Marquee** tool, hold down the mouse button to display the pop-up menu, drag the mouse to the **Oval Marquee** tool in the pop-up menu, and release the mouse button. The Marquee tool icon is now selected. The Property inspector displays settings related to the selected tool.

3. In the Marquee tool Property inspector, the two list arrows next to the word "Edge" control the kind of edge the Marquee tool creates and the thickness of the edge in pixels. Click the **Edge of selection** list arrow (the one next to the word "Edge") and and then click **Feather**. Click the **Amount of feather** box (to the right of the Edge of Selection list arrow) and change the setting from 10 to **20**.

4. Click above and to the left of the baby's face, and drag down and to the right to draw an oval marquee around the face. If you do not like your results, draw the oval again. Your new oval will replace the old one. You may have to draw the oval marquee a few times until you select the entire face. If necessary, move the marquee over the baby's face by clicking in the middle of the marquee and dragging it to a new location. When you are finished, your selection oval should look similar to the one in Figure 9-16.

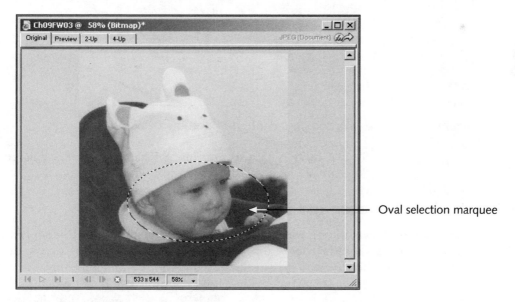

Oval selection marquee

Figure 9-16   Oval selection marquee

5. Press **Ctrl+X** to cut the selection out of the image. Next, you will create a new document and paste the selection into the new document.

Recall that, when working on a Macintosh, you need to press the Command Key whenever this book tells you to press the Ctrl Key.

6. Press **Ctrl+N**. The New Document dialog box opens. The size attributes are preset to make them appropriate for the size of the image you selected.

7. Click the **Transparent** option button to choose a transparent canvas and then click **OK**.

8. Press **Ctrl+V** to paste the image into the new document. Notice the feathered edges, as shown in Figure 9-17.

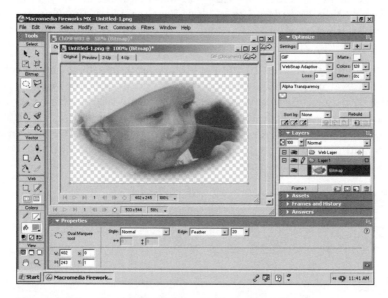

Figure 9-17   Oval selection pasted into new document

9. Save this file as **Ch09FW03SOL.png** in the Chapter folder for Chapter 9 and close it. Close the file named **Ch09FW03.jpg** without saving changes to it.

Brush, Pencil, Eraser and Blur Tools

The Brush tool, Pencil tool, and Eraser tool operate like the other Bitmap tools. To use them, you simply click the tool in the Tools panel and begin drawing on the document. You can use the Brush and Pencil tools to draw lines by dragging the mouse pointer across the canvas. To create a straight line, hold the Shift key down while dragging the brush or pencil in the desired direction. The Property inspector for the Brush tool, shown in Figure 9-18, provides you with many options for changing the brush stroke options. Using the Brush Property inspector, you can alter the brush color, the tip area of the brush, the stroke category, the brush edge, and the texture of the stroke. You can also control how strongly it is applied to the canvas. In addition, you can change the opacity of the brush application and control how it blends into the canvas. The Preserve Transparency option only lets you draw paths over existing pixels without drawing on transparent areas of the image.

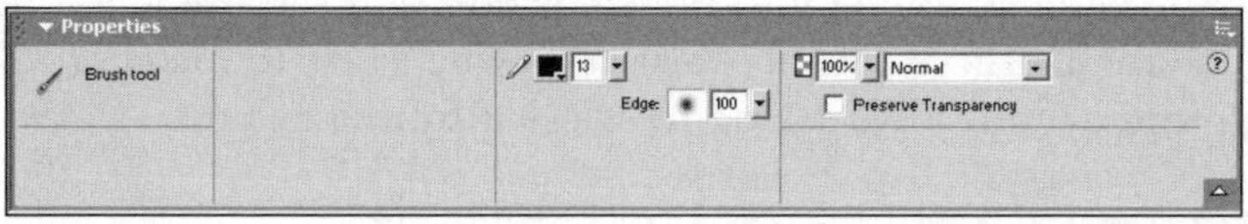

Figure 9-18   Brush tool Property inspector

Using the Property inspector for the Pencil tool, shown in Figure 9-19, you can control the tool's color and opacity. You can also control the way the pencil line blends into the surrounding image (that is, its blend mode). Selecting the anti-aliased check box creates a softer line that blends with the background color of the canvas.

Figure 9-19   Pencil tool Property inspector

The Eraser tool allows you to erase portions of your document by dragging the mouse pointer over the canvas. Using the Property inspector for the Eraser tool, you can control Size, Edge, Shape, and Opacity of the Eraser.

The Blur tool can distort the focus of selected areas of an image. By holding the mouse down and dragging the tool over the canvas, areas of a bitmapped image become less defined, in effect, blurred. The Blur tool offers four other options: the Sharpen tool, the Dodge tool, the Burn tool, and the Smudge tool. The Property inspectors for this group of tools are highly similar, allowing you to change size, edge, and shape of the effect. These tools are used to touch-up small portions of bitmapped images.

Rubber Stamp and Eyedropper Tools

Using the Rubber Stamp tool, you can copy a portion of a graphic and duplicate it over another area of the canvas. For example, if your graphic includes an airplane on a sky background, you can create a rubber stamp of the blue sky and stamp the airplane with the same sky texture to eliminate it from the picture. When you select the Rubber Stamp tool, you see a small indicator on the canvas. Clicking sets the beginning position for the rubber stamp. After you click, a blue circle appears on the canvas. Place the circle over the area you want to copy and then drag the circle. The Rubber Stamp tool copies the stamped area over the canvas. In Figure 9-20, the Rubber Stamp tool was used to give the dog a third eye. The Property inspector for the Rubber Stamp tool lets you modify size, edge, offset from cursor, source of pixels, opacity, and blend mode.

Sometimes when you edit a graphic or photograph, you may want to use an exact color from one portion of the photo and apply it to another area. The Eyedropper tool lets you change the fill color in the color box by clicking a pixel that contains the color you wish to use. Once the color is copied into the color box, you can use it as a fill color on other selections (like the Brush or Pencil tools). It may be easier to match a color exactly by using the eyedropper, rather than trying to select it from a palette.

Figure 9-20   Using the Rubber Stamp tool

Paint Bucket Tools

With the Paint Bucket tool, you can fill selections and areas with color. The Paint Bucket tool can be used in conjunction with the Colors tools at the bottom of the Tools panel. To apply that color, you simply move the Paint Bucket pointer over the area that you want to fill with color and click. The Paint Bucket tool Property inspector, shown in Figure 9-21, lets you change the tool's attributes, including edge, texture, tolerance, and opacity.

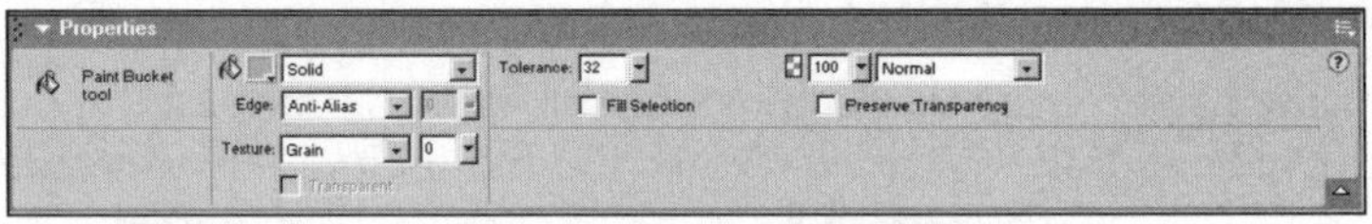

Figure 9-21   Paint Bucket tool Property inspector

The Paint Bucket tool offers another option, the Gradient tool. This tool enables you to fill selections with a gradient fill rather than a solid fill. To apply the gradient, click the Gradient tool and then click and drag your mouse in the fill area, in the direction you want the gradient to be applied.

Using Bitmap Tools

In the following steps, you will use the Bitmap tools to edit an image of a dog. First, you will eliminate the background by using the Polygon Lasso tool. Then you will use the Rubber Stamp tool to add a third eye, as shown earlier in Figure 9-20. You will rotate the image so the dog's head is not tilted.

To use Bitmap tools to edit an image:

1. Open the file named **Ch09FW04.png** from the Chapter folder for Chapter 9.

2. Select the **Polygon Lasso** tool. Place the mouse pointer at the top of the dog's head and click. Move the mouse to the right and click at the left edge of the dog's ear. Continue using the Polygon Lasso tool to draw a polygon around the dog's head. When you click the last time to close the polygon, the head becomes outlined with a flashing dotted line.

3. Click **Select** in the menu bar and choose **Smooth Marquee**. The Smooth Marquee dialog box opens. Enter a sample radius of **2** pixels and click **OK**.

4. Click **Select** in the menu bar and choose **Contract Marquee**. The Contract Marquee dialog box opens. Enter a Contract by **1** pixel and click **OK**.

5. Click **Select** in the menu bar and choose **Select Inverse**. A flashing outline surrounds the entire image, indicating that the area between that rectangle and the dog's head is now selected. Press the **Delete** key to eliminate this portion of the photograph, leaving only the dog's head.

6. Deselect the image by pressing the **Escape** key.

 To deselect an object, you can press the Escape key, or the Ctrl+D key combination. You can also click the Deselect command on the Select menu.

7. Click the Rubber Stamp tool in the Tools panel. In the Property inspector for the Rubber Stamp tool, change the Size setting to **50** and the Edge setting to **50** (if necessary).

8. Position the mouse pointer directly over the dog's eye on the left and click the mouse. A blue circle appears around the eye, as shown in Figure 9-22.

9. Drag the mouse to position the blue circle directly between the dog's eyes and click the mouse. A third eye is added to the dog's face, similar to the image shown earlier in Figure 9-20.

10. Click the Scale tool in the Select portion of the Tools panel. The image is automatically selected, as indicated by the black square with small black handles around the edge of the image. Place the mouse pointer outside the right, center edge of the selection border. The mouse pointer changes to a curved arrow, indicating that you can rotate the image.

11. Click the mouse and drag it up slightly to rotate the image. Continue rotating the image until the dog's face is no longer tilted.

12. Deselect the image.

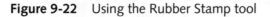

Blue circle

Figure 9-22   Using the Rubber Stamp tool

13. Click **Modify** on the menu bar, point to **Canvas**, and then click **Fit Canvas**. The canvas size contracts to accommodate the size of the image.

14. Save the image as **Ch09FW04SOL.png** in the Chapter folder for Chapter 9 and close it.

Editing an Image

In the following steps, you will edit an image to create a picture of a person dunking a basketball.

To edit an image:

1. Open the file named **Ch09FW05a.jpg** from the Chapter folder for Chapter 9, and then open the file named **Ch09FW05b.jpg** from the same folder.

To select among multiple open images, click Window on the menu bar, and then click the name of image you want to see (at the bottom of the Window menu).

2. Verify that the file named **Ch09FW05b.jpg** (a photograph of a basketball hoop) is currently displayed. First, you need to rotate the canvas 90 degrees counterclockwise.

3. Click **Modify** on the menu bar, point to **Canvas**, and then **Rotate 90° CCW**. (Note that "CCW" is short for "counterclockwise.")

4. Click **Window** on the menu bar, and then click **Ch09FW05a.jpg** at the bottom of the Window menu to display an image of a girl playing basketball.

5. Use the Polygon Lasso tool to select the girl and the basketball.

6. Press **Ctrl+X** to cut the girl from the photograph.

7. Use the Window menu to display the image named **Ch09FW05b.jpg**. Press **Ctrl+V** to paste the person into the photograph. The person is turned away from the basketball hoop.

8. Click **Modify** in the menu bar, point to **Transform**, and then choose **Flip Horizontal**. The girl now faces the basketball hoop. Next, you need to reduce the girl's size, so that she matches the scale of the basketball hoop.

9. Click the **Pointer** tool, select the image of the girl, press and hold the **Shift** key, and then drag the upper-right corner of the girl image down to shrink the image. Drag the mouse pointer until the girl is approximately the right size relative to the basketball hoop.

10. Drag the selected image of the girl to a new position, to make it look like she is dunking the basketball.

11. Deselect the image. Your completed image should look like Figure 9-23.

Figure 9-23   Image edited to include girl dunking basketball

12. Save this file as **Ch09FW05SOL.png** in the Chapter folder for Chapter 9. Close all open images without making any other changes.

VECTOR TOOLS

Vector images are defined by mathematical formulas and algorithms, rather than individual pixels. Codes that indicate color and scale, along with formulas for the shape or line, define the image. Vector lines and areas are often called "paths" and "fills." This terminology reflects the fact that the images are defined mathematically. The Vector tools in the Tools panel are used to draw, select, and modify lines and shapes on the canvas. Each shape consists of strokes and fills that can be solid or patterned colors. Although the Property inspector changes for each object you create, many attributes are common to all objects. For example, the attributes for most objects include width and height, X and Y coordinates, and fill and stroke color. You will see how these attributes are defined and modified in the sections that follow, as you learn about each tool in the Vector Tools panel.

Line and Pen Tools

To draw a line using the Line tool, you simply click the Line tool and then drag the pointer over the canvas. To draw a straight vertical or horizontal line, hold the Shift key down while you drag the mouse. You can alter the appearance of the line by changing its attributes in the Line tool Property inspector, shown in Figure 9-24. The Property inspectors for the Pen and Shape tools are very similar to this with only a few additional attributes for specific tools.

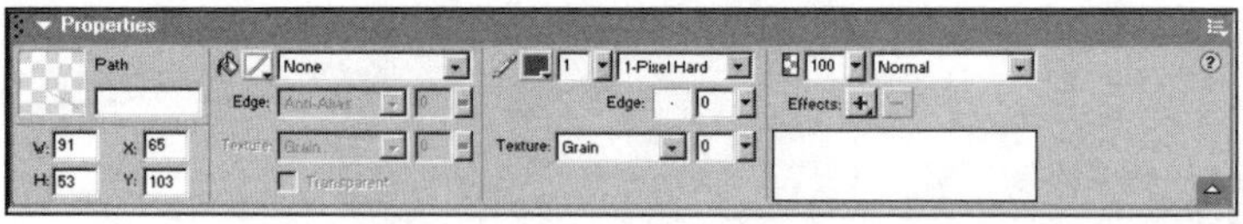

Figure 9-24   Line tool Property inspector

The Pen tool is a bit more complex to operate. This tool lets you define a path by using anchor points and segments. You can draw straight lines in a series of segments by clicking the mouse to create anchor points. You can also draw curved lines by creating an anchor point and then holding the mouse button down as you drag it to create the desired curve. It takes some practice to get used to drawing curves. The Property inspector for the Pen tool has identical options to those of the Pencil tool.

Shape Tools

The Rectangle tool in the Tools panel displays a menu with four tool options: Rectangle, Rounded Rectangle, Ellipse, and Polygon. Together these tools are referred to as the Shape tools. Because you can change the rounded rectangle and polygon shapes' attributes, the range of possible shapes you can create with the Shapes tools is actually larger.

To draw a rectangle, click the Rectangle tool, and then click and drag the mouse until the rectangle is the size you desire, as shown in Figure 9-25. Releasing the mouse button draws the rectangle on the page.

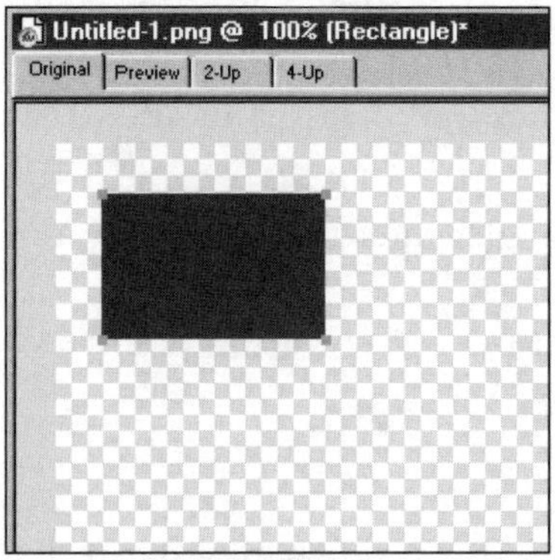

Figure 9-25   Drawing a rectangle

The Rectangle tool Property inspector is identical to the Line tool Property inspector shown in Figure 9-4, with one additional attribute, Rectangle Roundedness. For this setting, you can either enter a number between 0 and 100, or you can use the list arrow to open a slider bar and slide to the desired number. At 0%, the rectangle corners appear perfectly square; at 100%, the maximum angle, the corners will be completely rounded, so that the rectangle appears to be oval on the canvas. Instead of using this setting, you could use the Rounded Rectangle tool to draw your rectangle. When you use this tool, the default setting for Rectangle Roundedness is 30, though you can change this setting in the Property inspector. Setting Rectangle Roundedness to 0 will result in the object becoming a rectangle without round corners.

To draw a shape of equal height and width, hold down the Shift key as you drag the mouse over the canvas to create the shape.

You draw an ellipse much as you would a rectangle, only using the Ellipse tool. Hold down the Shift key as you drag the mouse to draw a circle. The Property inspector for the Ellipse tool is identical to that of the Line tool Property inspector.

The last Shape tool is the Polygon Shape tool. Using this tool, you can draw a multi-sided polygon or star.

Using the Shape Tool

The steps that follow will guide you through the creation of the four basic shapes that you can create by using the Shape tools.

To create shapes using the Shape tools:

1. Click **File** on the menu bar, and then click **New** to create a new document. In the New File dialog box, enter **350 pixels** for both the Width and Height settings, and set the Resolution to **79 Pixels/Inch**. Click the **White** radio button if it is not already selected and then click **OK**.

2. Click the **Rectangle** tool, and then click and drag the mouse to draw a rectangle in the center of the canvas.

3. In the Property inspector for the rectangle, enter the following values:
   - W: **100**
   - H: **100**
   - X: **30**
   - Y: **30**

4. Now you are ready to select a new fill color for the rectangle. With the rectangle still selected, click the color box next to the paint bucket in the Property inspector. (This color box, one of several in the Fireworks interface, is called the Fill color box.) A color palette opens. Click the text box at the top of the palette, delete its current contents, type **#FF00FF**, and press **Enter**. The rectangle is now a solid pink.

5. Click the **Stroke color** box (the box next to the pencil) in the Property inspector, click in the text box at the top of the palette, delete the current contents of the text box, type **#00FFFF**, and press **Enter**. The stroke (the outline of the rectangle) is now turquoise.

6. To change the thickness of the stroke, replace the current contents of the Tip Size box (next to the Stroke color box) with **4** and then press **Enter**. The rectangle outline is now somewhat thicker, as shown in Figure 9-26.

7. Select the **Rounded Rectangle** tool in the Shape tools' pop-up menu.

8. Draw a rounded rectangle in the upper-right corner of the canvas. The object should have the same attributes you set for the previous object, including the same pink fill and turquoise stroke. In the Property inspector for the rounded rectangle, enter the following values:
   - W: **100**
   - H: **100**
   - X: **200**
   - Y: **30**

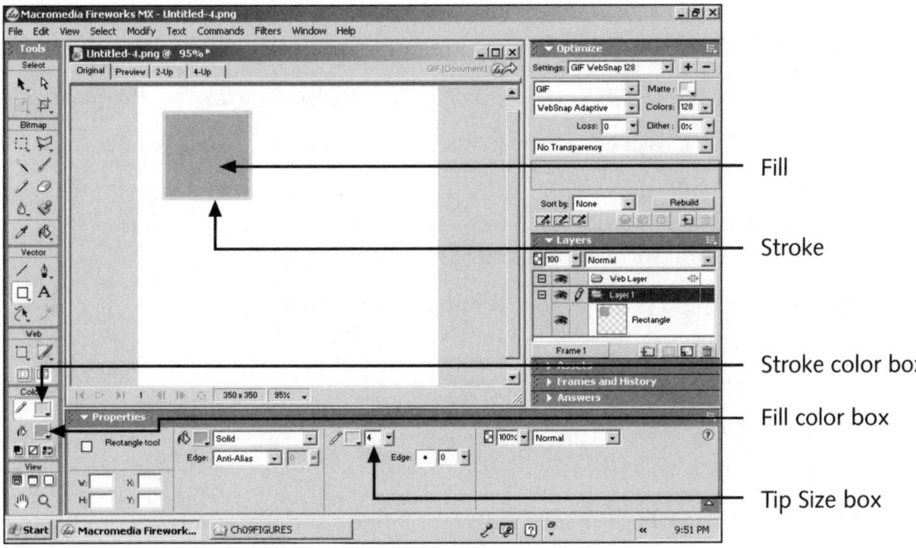

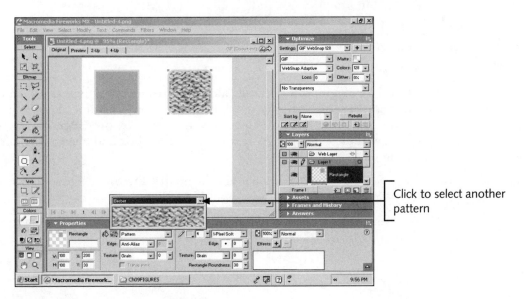

Figure 9-26   Rectangle with new settings

9

9. With the rounded rectangle still selected, Click the **Fill category** list arrow in the Property inspector (to the right of the Fill color box) and click **Pattern**. The rectangle is now filled with a black and white pattern. The Fill color box now gives you access to a selection of possible patterns.

10. Click the **Fill color** box. A pop-up menu appears containing a list arrow that you can use to select additional patterns. See Figure 9-27.

Figure 9-27   Selecting a new fill pattern

11. Click the list arrow, click **Grass–Large**, and then press **Enter**. The rectangle is now filled with the grass pattern.

12. Enter **50** for the Rectangle Roundedness setting in the Property inspector.

13. Select the **Ellipse** tool from the Shape tools pop-up menu.

14. To draw a circle in the lower left-hand corner of the canvas, press and hold the **Shift** key while you click and drag the mouse. The circle you draw has the same fill and stroke as the rounded rectangle.

15. In the Property inspector for the ellipse, enter the following values:
    - W: **100**
    - H: **100**
    - X: **30**
    - Y: **200**

16. Select the **Polygon** tool from the Shape tools pop-up menu. Note the Sides setting in the Property inspector, which controls the number of sides the polygon you draw will have. Verify that the Sides setting is currently 5.

17. Press and hold the **Alt** key and then drag the mouse to draw a polygon in the lower right-hand corner of the canvas. Use the Undo command if necessary to delete your polygon and try again. It is sometimes difficult to control the size and placement of a polygon. Holding the Alt key while you drag the mouse gives you more control over the process.

18. In the Property inspector for the polygon, enter the following values:
    - W: **100**
    - H: **100**
    - X: **200**
    - Y: **200**

19. With the polygon still selected, click the **Stroke color** box and then click the **Transparent** button (a white box with a diagonal line through it) in the palette. Immediately below the Fill color box, click the **Edge** list arrow and click **Feather**. Click the **Amount of feather** box and change the current setting to **20**.

20. Click **Select** on the menu bar and then click **Deselect**. The polygon is deselected. Your completed shapes should look like those in Figure 9-28.

21. Save your image as **Ch09FW06.png** in the Chapter folder for Chapter 9 and then close it.

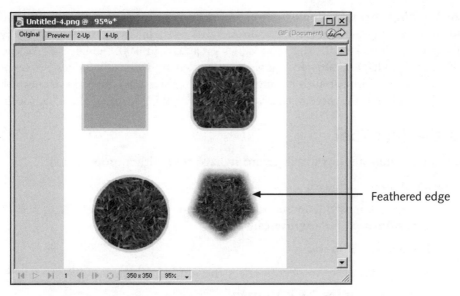

Feathered edge

Figure 9-28 Completed shapes

9

Text Tool

The Text tool is useful for adding labels and text to your graphics. For example, if you are creating buttons or rollovers, you can use the Text tool to add text indicating each link's destination. When you add text to a Fireworks canvas, you actually add a text box, and then type text in the text box similar to typing text in a word-processing document. The Text Property inspector, shown in Figure 9-29, lets you modify text characteristics.

Figure 9-29 Text Property inspector

Using the Text Property inspector, you can change your text's font type, size, color, and style. You can also control text alignment and flow. If you have edited text in a word processor, many of these text options are probably familiar to you. A few, however, may be new to you, such as Kerning, Leading, and Anti-Aliasing.

Kerning is a means of controlling the amount of space between the characters of the text. A negative kerning value brings the text closer together; a positive value adds more space. You can control the kerning value by using the slider, by typing a value directly into the text box, or by selecting the Auto Kerning check box.

The **Leading** attribute allows you to control the amount of space between multiple lines of text. Changing the Horizontal Scale stretches or shrinks your text horizontally. A value of less than 100% shrinks the text; values greater than 100% enlarge it. As you learned earlier in this chapter, anti-aliasing is a feature that smoothes the edges between the path and the canvas. Without anti-aliasing, text and graphics can sometimes appear block-like. You can choose from three varieties of anti-aliasing: Crisp, Strong, and Smooth.

Using the Text Tool

In the following steps, you will create stylized text with a drop shadow.

To create stylized text with a drop shadow:

1. Create a new document **500 pixels** wide and **100 pixels** high, with **79-pixel resolution** and a **white** canvas.

2. Click the Text tool.

3. In the Property inspector, select the following options:
   - Font: **Times New Roman**
   - Size: **40**
   - Color: **#FF0000** (red)
   - Anti-Alias Level: **Crisp Anti-Alias**

4. Click in the center of the canvas. A small text box appears, with a blinking cursor inside.

5. Type **Kids Reading Room**. The text box expands to accommodate the text. However, the text box is too far to the right.

6. Click the text box border to select the text box itself, rather than the text inside. (You should no longer see the blinking cursor inside the text box.)

7. In the Property inspector for the Text object, enter the following values in the coordinate boxes: X: **20** and Y: **20**.

8. With the text box still selected, click the **Add Effects or choose a preset** button (the plus sign next to the word "Effects") in the Properties inspector. (If you do not see the Effects setting, then the text box is not selected properly. Click the Pointer tool, click the text box border and try again.) In the pop-up menu, point to **Shadow and Glow**, and then click **Drop Shadow**. The Drop Shadow dialog box appears over the Effects section of the Property inspector, as shown in Figure 9-30.

9. Change the Distance setting to **8** and the color to **#000068** (blue). Verify that the opacity is to **65%**, softness is set to **4**, and the angle is **315** degrees. Press **Enter** to close the Drop Shadow dialog box. A blue drop shadow is added to the text, as shown in Figure 9-31. A Drop Shadow element is also added to the Property inspector. Note that you can click this element to reopen the

Drop Shadow dialog box and alter the drop shadow effect. Each time you add a new effect to the text, an additional element is added to this list.

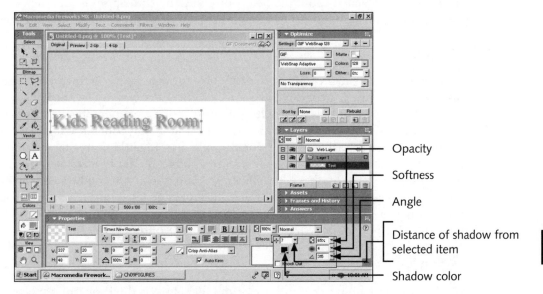

Figure 9-30   Drop Shadow dialog box

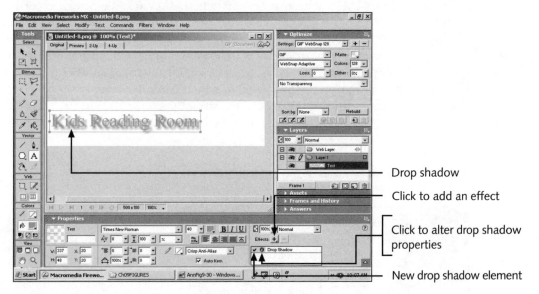

Figure 9-31   Drop shadow added to text

10. Save the image as **Ch09FW07.png** in the Chapter folder for Chapter 9 and close it.

OTHER TOOLS

So far, you have learned about the Selection tools, the Bitmap tools, and the Vector tools. The remaining tool categories in Fireworks are Web tools, Color tools, and View tools.

Web Tools

Use Web tools to create hotspots and slices. **Hotspots** are areas defined on a graphic that a user can click like a hyperlink to go to another Web page. The three Hotspot tools (Rectangle, Circle, and Polygon) help you create a shape on a graphic that users can click to link to a different Web page. The Slice tool and Polygon Slice tool let you cut a graphic into several smaller graphics or **slices** and arrange them in a table using HTML. Slices reduce the time needed to load a large graphic and let you attach different behaviors to specific areas of the table. Slices are also the most productive way to create rollovers. (To learn more about rollovers and slices, see Chapter 6.) The Hide Slices and Hotspots button lets you view your image free of hotspot or slice outlines. The Show Slices and Hotspots button displays hotspot or slice outlines for your image.

Color Tools

You already know how to control stroke and fill color via the Property inspector. You can also select stroke and fill colors using the Stroke tool and the Fill tool in the Tools panel. Figure 9-32 shows the palette that appears when you click the Stroke color box in the Tools panel. As with other palettes you have used in Fireworks, you can select a color by clicking a square on the palette or by entering a hexadecimal color code in the text box. Clicking the Transparent button makes the path invisible. Clicking the Sys color picker opens the Color panel where you can designate colors by using another method. Clicking the Stroke Options button opens a panel in which you can define attributes of the stroke, much like you did with the Line tool Property inspector earlier in the chapter.

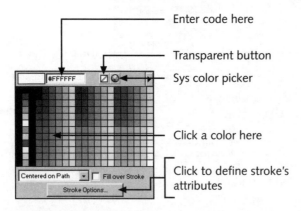

Figure 9-32   Stroke tool color palette

Beneath the Stroke and Fill tools are three smaller icons. The first icon, a black square over a clear square, is the Set Default Stroke/Fill Colors tool. Use this tool to select a default stroke and fill color (a color that is used by default until you specify another by using the Stroke and Fill tools). You can also use this tool to reselect (restore) the default colors, after you have selected alternatives using the Stroke and Fill tools.

The middle of the three small icons (a white square with a diagonal line) is the No Stroke or Fill tool. Click it once to change the Stroke color to transparent. Click it again to change the Fill color to transparent as well. The third of the three small icons (a double-sided, curved arrow) is the Swap Brush/Fill colors, which lets you instantly swap the color values for stroke and fill. For example, if the stroke color is blue and the fill color is red, clicking this tool would make the stroke color red and the fill color blue.

 Use the Eyedropper tool in the Tools panel to sample a color from an existing graphic. After you use the Eyedropper tool, eyedropper sample is added to the Fill color box in the Tools panel.

View Tools

View tools are located at the very bottom of the Fireworks Tools panel. The first three options let you quickly specify how you view the screen: Standard Screen mode, Full Screen with Menus mode, or Full Screen mode. The Hand tool is used to display items that have scrolled off the screen. To use the Hand tool, click it, and then click and drag the mouse on the canvas to drag the item you want to see back into view. The Zoom tool is used to magnify a document so that you can edit it more accurately. You can zoom into a graphic and edit it at the pixel level to achieve a perfect effect for your artwork. You can also use the View menu on the menu bar to zoom into or out of a drawing.

 As an alternative to the Zoom tool, you can click the Set Magnification list arrow at the bottom of the Document window and select a specific magnification percentage.

THE LAYERS PANEL

When you create a complex graphic, it is often necessary to work in layers. **Layers** are transparent canvases, stacked on top of one another. For example, suppose an image shows a boy with a ball playing in the grass under the text "Bright Start Daycare Center." That image could consist of a background layer containing the grass and sky, another layer containing the boy and the ball, and a third layer containing the text. Working in layers allows you to move the boy or the text or alter the background without affecting the other parts of the image. The graphic formats available on the Web (.gif and .jpg) do not display layers. When you complete your drawing, you must combine (or flatten) the layers or export your document so that the layers are flattened for you. Flattened layers cannot be separated again. The .png format in which you work in Fireworks preserves your layers. It is a good idea to keep a copy of the original .png file in case you decide later to change the document and need to alter the layers within it.

Figure 9-33 shows the Layers panel for a train graphic composed of several cropped images of various types of produce. Each object on the canvas occupies its own layer. In the Layers panel, you can see each layer of the document (indicted by a folder) and the images that layer contains. When an object is selected in the work area, the layer is highlighted in the Layers panel. A pencil icon indicates that the layer is ready for editing. If you want to lock the layer to prevent it from being edited, click the pencil icon; a lock appears indicating that the layer cannot be edited. Click the eye icon to turn a layer on or off in a graphic. (It is sometimes useful to turn off all the layers except the one you are currently working on, so you can focus on a specific part of a document.) To rename a layer, click twice on the layer name in the Layers panel and then type your own custom layer name. To reposition layers with respect to one another, drag them in the Layers panel to the desired position, below or above other layers. The small squares on the left-hand side of the panel let you fold sublayers into the main layer. (A square with a plus sign indicates that layer is currently contracted.) Clicking the list arrow at the upper right of the Layers panel opens a menu with a series of commands that you can use to add, delete, and edit layers, and perform other operations related to layers.

In the following steps, you will use layers to create a logo for a company named La Bonne Cuisine. In these steps, you reposition layers in the work area with respect to one another. You also add text to the file and create a drop shadow effect in all the layers.

To create a logo:

1. Open the file named **Ch09FW08.png** from the Chapter folder for Chapter 9. You see an image of a salad.

2. Open the Layers panel via the **Windows** menu, or by pressing the **F2** key. The layers in this file overlap, so you cannot see each image in each layer. You can, however, see miniature versions of the image in each layer in the Layers panel.

3. Use the **Pointer** tool to drag the bowl of salad to a corner of the canvas so that you can see the layer below it. When you first point to the salad bowl layer, a red selection outline appears around it. Drag the orange to another corner of the canvas. Do the same with the blue bowl of shrimp, so you can see the cabbage image below it.

4. Click the **cabbage** image and observe that the corresponding layer (Layer2) in the Layers panel is highlighted. Double-click the text **Layer 2** in the Layers panel, rename this layer **cabbage** and press **Enter**. Rename the other layers the same way by calling them **orange**, **shrimp**, and **salad**.

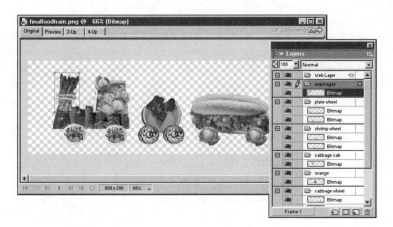

Figure 9-33   Layers panel

 The Web layer at the top of the Layers panel is used for hotspots and sliced images.

9

5. Select the **orange** with the **Pointer** tool. Slide it around on the canvas and observe that it moves on top of the cabbage and shrimp images, but behind the salad image. That is because the orange layer is located below the salad layer. Click the **orange** layer name in the Layers panel and drag it above the salad layer in the Layers panel. Drag the orange around the canvas to demonstrate that it now is on top of the salad layer.

6. Using the **Pointer** tool, click the **cabbage layer** on the canvas. In the Property inspector, enter the coordinates X: **4** and Y: **50**. Click the **salad layer** on the canvas. In the Property inspector, enter the coordinates X: **100** and Y: **4**. Click the **shrimp layer** on the canvas. In the Property inspector, enter the coordinates X: **10** and Y: **140**. Click the **orange layer** on the canvas. In the Property inspector, enter the coordinates X: **80** and Y: **115**.

7. Add a new layer to place text by clicking the **New/Duplicate Layer** icon (a folder) at the bottom of the Layers panel. A new layer, named Layer2, is added to the Layers panel. You cannot see the layer in the canvas because the new layer is currently blank.

8. Name the new layer **Text**.

9. Verify that the Text layer is still selected in the Layers panel, and then click the **Text** tool in the Tools panel. In the Property inspector, select the following attributes: **#0000FF (Blue)**, **Bold Text**, **50** point size, and **Arial** font. Click a blank area in the canvas and type the text **La Bonne Cuisine**. Enter position coordinates of X: **70** and Y: **100**.

10. Click the Pointer tool, then click **Select** from the menu bar and click **Select All**. All the layers are now selected. Click the **Add effects or choose a preset** button in the Property inspector (a black plus sign), point to **Shadow and Glow**, click **Drop Shadow**, and then press **Enter** to accept the Drop Shadow settings. A black shadow appears beneath the text and beneath the food images. The Drop Shadow effect is also added to the Effects panel.

11. Press **F12** to preview your image in your Web browser. Close the browser window.

12. Save this file as **Ch09FW08SOL.png** in the Chapter folder for Chapter 9.

CHAPTER SUMMARY

❑ Fireworks creates .png format files that you can export into other, more commonly supported Web formats such as .gif and .jpg.

❑ The Fireworks Tools panel allows you to create shapes and lines using a variety of colors, fills, and strokes.

❑ Selection tools include the Pointer, Subselection, and Scale and Crop tools, which you can use to select, reshape, and resize images.

❑ You can apply a wide variety of strokes and fills to paths and objects by using the Stroke and Fill options in the Property inspector for an object.

❑ Text tools are used to enter text on the canvas. You can alter text features, including font, size, color, and style. You can also adjust alignment, kerning, and anti-aliasing. You can also apply effects to text and other objects. Effects such as drop shadows and embossing can create appealing headlines and titles on a Web page.

❑ Paths, or lines, can be manipulated by using the Property inspector. A wide variety of strokes create different pen styles, pen tip widths, and textures.

❑ Solid, Web Dithered, and Pattern fills can be used to fill shapes and selected areas. Gradient fills can also add to the wide variety of effects you can apply to fill an area.

❑ The Optimize panel can be used with the preview of your graphic to experiment with different optimization properties.

❑ Layers are transparent, stacked canvases in one document. Using layers allows you to create a complex graphic with independent, editable elements on the different layers. The final graphic used on the Web must be flattened and exported as a .gif or .jpg file.

REVIEW QUESTIONS

1. What is the optimal resolution for a Web graphic?

    a. 72 dpi

    b. 100 dpi

    c. 200 dpi

    d. 350 dpi

2. What is the extension for the Fireworks default file type?

    a. .bmp

    b. .png

    c. .gif

    d. .jpg

3. What types of graphics can you edit in Fireworks?

    a. Bitmap

    b. Vector

    c. both Bitmap and Vector separately

    d. both Bitmap and Vector simultaneously

4. What is the difference between saving and exporting a file?

    a. Saving a file saves all your information (including layers) in .png format so you can still edit the image with all its detail.

    b. Saving a file makes it possible to view the file on the Web as .gif or .jpg.

    c. Exporting a file creates a .png file that is editable later.

    d. Exporting a file flattens all your layers into .png format.

5. What happens when you optimize an image for the Web?

    a. You create a .gif file.

    b. You create an image of less than 20k.

    c. You find a balance between image quality and file size.

    d. You export an image.

6. Which of the following tools is not used for selection?

    a. Lasso

    b. Marquee

    c. Magic Wand

    d. Line

9

7. Which of the following can you do with the Rubber Stamp tool?

   a. copy an image

   b. paste patterns onto an image

   c. copy a portion of an image and stamp it elsewhere on the image

   d. export areas of an image

8. What is a Bezier point?

   a. a handle on a rectangle that you can drag to resize the rectangle

   b. a point on a path that you use to reshape an image

   c. the point at the center of the image

   d. none of the above

9. What is a Bitmap graphic?

   a. a graphic in which individual pixels define colors in the image

   b. a graphic where color is defined by mathematical representations of paths and fills in the image

   c. a black and white image that includes only lines

   d. all of the above

10. What does kerning do?

    a. It controls the amount of space between different text characters.

    b. It controls the amount of space between different words.

    c. It controls line spacing.

    d. All of the above.

11. What is a fill?

    a. the color of the edge of an object

    b. the color of an object

    c. the amount of transparency applied to an object

    d. the color of a line

12. What does the Effects option in the Property inspector do?

    a. lets you display text along a nonlinear path

    b. lets you animate text

    c. allows you to create embellishments such as a drop shadow

    d. none of the above

13. Which of the following statements is true of layers?

    a. They can be displayed on the Web.

    b. Layers place objects together so they cannot be separated.

    c. They let you edit elements in a graphic document separately.

    d. Each layer of a file can have a different graphic format.

14. When you choose to use fewer colors in an image, which of the following is true?

    a. The file will be optimized.

    b. Your file size will be smaller.

    c. Areas of your image will be transparent.

    d. The file size will be larger.

15. A photograph is best saved as what file format for the Web?

    a. .gif

    b. .jpg

    c. .png

    d. .bmp

HANDS-ON EXERCISES

9

Exercise 9-1

In this exercise, you will use Fireworks to create a button.

1. Open a new document in Fireworks that is 90 pixels wide and 50 pixels high. Select a transparent canvas.

2. Draw a rounded rectangle on the canvas.

3. In the Property inspector for the rectangle, enter the following values: W: 80, H: 25, X: 6, and Y: 12. Set the Fill color to #0000FF (blue) and the Stroke color to Transparent. Set Rectangle Roundedness to 30, if necessary.

4. Add text on top of the rectangle you just created by clicking the Text tool in the Tools panel and clicking on the canvas. In the Property inspector, change the text color to #FFFF00 (yellow), size 16, bold, and font Arial. Type the text "Welcome". Enter the position coordinates X: 6 and Y: 13. Yellow text should appear on top of the blue rectangle.

5. Using the Pointer tool, select both the rectangle and the text by holding down the mouse button and dragging the mouse from the upper left of the canvas to the lower right.

6. Add a drop shadow to both items. Change the drop shadow attributes if necessary to Distance: 7, Color: black, Opacity: 65%, Softness: 4, and Angle: 315 degrees.

7. Save the file as **Ch09FWEX01.png** in the Exercises folder for Chapter 9.

8. Optimize the file for the Web and export it to an appropriate file type.

Exercise 9-2

In this exercise, you transform a photograph into a button the user can click.

1. Open the file named **Ch09FWEX02.jpg** from the Exercises folder for Chapter 9.
2. Using the Oval Marquee tool, draw an oval over the kiwi fruit shown in the photograph. In the Property inspector for the oval marquee, enter the following values: W: 145, H: 80, X: 55, and Y: 116.

   This selection will be the button background.
3. Cut the selected area out of the veggies photograph by selecting Cut from the Edit menu, or by pressing the Ctrl+X key combination.
4. Open a new canvas using the default dimensions and paste the cut oval into the new work area. Observe that the canvas is the size of the oval.
5. In the new canvas, select the oval image of the kiwi fruit by using the Pointer tool. A blue rectangle appears around the selected image. Click Add effects or choose a preset in the Property inspector, point to Bevel and Emboss, and then click Inner Bevel.

   Observe that an inner bevel is created on the button.
6. Use the Text tool to insert the text "Healthy Diet" over the button. Use text color #FF6633, text size 24, and the Arial font.
7. Save the file as **Ch09FWEX02SOL.png** in the Exercises folder for Chapter 9.
8. Optimize the file for the Web and export using an appropriate file type.

Exercise 9-3

In this exercise, you will create a textured background for a Web page.

1. Open a new document in Fireworks, using the pixel dimensions 500 by 500 and a transparent canvas.
2. Draw a rectangular marquee over the entire canvas.
3. Click the Paint Bucket tool in the Tools panel.
4. In the Property inspector, click the Fill color box, enter #33FF33 (green), and press Enter. Click the list arrow for texture and select Parchment texture, set to 100%, for your background. Click the canvas with the Paint Bucket tool to fill the marquee with the Parchment texture.
5. Save the file as **Ch09FWEX03.png** in the Exercises folder for Chapter 9. (To use this background on a Web page, set the image as a background in the body tag of your HTML.)
6. Optimize the file for the Web and export it using an appropriate file type.

Exercise 9-4

In this exercise, you will create an elliptical background for a side menu.

1. Open a new document that is 500 pixels wide and 700 pixels high. Use a transparent canvas.

2. Draw an oval marquee that exceeds the size of the canvas, leaving a curved background shape on the left side of the canvas. The top and bottom edges of this curved background should extend about 250 pixels from the left edge of the canvas.

   Your objective is to create a curved solid on the left-hand side of the work area. Using this graphic as wallpaper for a Web page provides a nice background for menu buttons.

3. After you are satisfied with the appearance of the oval over the canvas, click Select on the menu bar, and then click Select Inverse.

4. Select the color #0099FF (blue) for the Fill Color tool. Click inside the marquee to apply the fill color.

5. Use the Subselection tool and double-click the shape you created to select it. In the Property inspector, click Add effect or choose a preset button, point to Shadow and Glow and then click Drop Shadow. Change the drop shadow settings so the distance is 20 and the softness is 16. This will create the illusion that the swath of color is coming off the page.

6. Save this file as **Ch09FWEX04.png** in the Exercises folder for Chapter 9. (To use this background on a Web page, set the background to this image in the body tag of your HTML.)

7. Optimize the file for the Web and export it using an appropriate file type.

Exercise 9-5

In this exercise, you practice working with layers.

1. Open a new document that is 500 pixels wide by 250 pixels high.

2. Open the Layers panel. Verify that Layer1 is selected in the Layers panel, and draw a rounded rectangle in the upper-left corner of the canvas. Rename Layer1 "rounded rectangle" in the Layers panel.

3. Click the eye icon next to the layer name "rounded rectangle" in the Layers panel. The rounded rectangle on the canvas is no longer visible. (Take care to click the eye icon next to the layer name, rather than the eye icon next to the rectangle object within the layer.)

4. Add a new layer, select the Polygon tool, in the Property inspector change the Sides setting to 3, draw a triangle in the upper-left corner of the canvas, and edit the attributes of the triangle to make it a different color than the rounded rectangle you drew earlier. Rename the new layer "triangle" in the Layers panel.

5. Click the eye icon next to the layer named "triangle". The layer is no longer visible.

9

6. Click the box next to the rounded rectangle name in the Layers panel to redisplay the rounded rectangle layer. An eye icon reappears in the box, indicating that the layer is currently displayed.

7. Display the triangle layer. If you cannot see the triangle, check to see if the triangle layer is behind the rounded rectangle layer. If so, drag the triangle layer up to put it on top of the rounded rectangle layers.

8. Continue adding layers with various shapes to gain practice manipulating layers. Move layers above and below other layers.

9. Save the file as **Ch09FWEX05.png** in the Exercises folder for Chapter 9.

10. Optimize the file for the Web and export it using an appropriate file type.

WEB DESIGN PROJECTS

Project 9-1

The BuyMe.com Toy Company wants to create a Web site to market their products to children and their parents who shop online. They have asked you to create a button style for their site that uses primary colors and would be attractive to children. Use Shape, Fill, and Text Effect tools to create three buttons titled Stop, Go, and Play for a children's Web page. Save your files in the Projects folder for Chapter 9. Be sure to optimize your files and export them using an appropriate file type.

Project 9-2

The BuyMe.com Toy Company is so pleased with your button design that they hire you to create a company logo. Create a logo for BuyMe.com and export it as a .gif graphic. Insert it into a Dreamweaver Web page with a non-white background. Export and insert the buttons you created in the last project as well. Align them in the Dreamweaver work area by using a table. Save your files in the Projects folder for Chapter 9.

Project 9-3

The Sprinkles Cookies Company is working on its new Web site. They would like you to design several "cyber-cookies" to use as images on their site. Use the Shape tools to create rectangles, circles, and polygons for the Web site. Make sure to decorate the cookies. Create four basic cookies, and then use the drawing tools to create a cookie that looks like a gingerbread man. Save your files in the Projects folder for Chapter 9. Be sure to optimize your files and export them using an appropriate file type.

10

FIREWORKS: PART II

In this chapter you will:

♦ Create image maps to produce linkable hotspots on images
♦ Learn how to export images for use on the Web
♦ Learn how to slice an image
♦ Create symbols and use the library panel
♦ Create buttons with rollover effects
♦ Create menus, including pop-up memus
♦ Create animated graphics for the Web

In Chapter 9, you learned to use Fireworks tools to edit and manipulate images. In this chapter you use these skills to create image maps, buttons, rollovers, and animations, all of which can greatly enhance the visual appeal of a Web page and make it easier for users to navigate your Web site. You will create special objects called symbols which are stored in the document's library and are used to create menu bars and animations. You will learn how to create buttons, menus, and animations and how to export these graphics for use on Web pages.

CREATING AN IMAGE MAP

A graphic with several areas that are linked to URLs or other Web pages is called an **image map**. The areas on an image map that are linked are called **hotspots**. Image maps are most useful when they involve a graphic made up of distinct parts. One good example is a geographic map. A user looking at a geographic map intuitively understands where each hotspot in the image will take her. For instance, in a map labeled "Rainfall in North America" the user would expect that clicking on Kansas would display a page of rainfall statistics for that state.

In another example, you might create an image map of a class picture where you define each student's face as a hotspot. Clicking on a particular student's face can then take the user to that student's home page. You can also create a simple rectangular graphic that contains text links. You can create hotspots over each text area that represents a link to another page, thus creating a simple navigation bar. This navigation bar can then be placed on each page of your Web site. (Note that this kind of navigation bar is somewhat restrictive, because you cannot edit links individually without editing the entire image map.)

Creating Hotspots using the Hotspot Tool

The tools you will use most when creating an image map are found in the Web section of the Tools panel, as shown in Figure 10-1. To create an image map, you use the Hotspot tool to draw shapes on top of an existing image in the areas where you want to define the links. There are three Hotspot tools, the Rectangle Hotspot tool, the Circle Hotspot tool, and the Polygon Hotspot tool. These tools work similar to the Rectangle, Rounded Rectangle, Ellipse and Polygon tools you used in Chapter 9. You can also use the Hide slices and hotspots button and the Show slices and hotspots button to hide and display hotspots after you draw them. Hiding hotspots makes it easier to edit a graphic.

When you draw a hotspot on an image on the canvas, the shape you draw is overlaid on the image in a blue translucent color. The hotspots you create also appear under the Web layer in the Layers panel. Figure 10-2 shows a hotspot over an image, as well as the Property inspector associated with that hotspot.

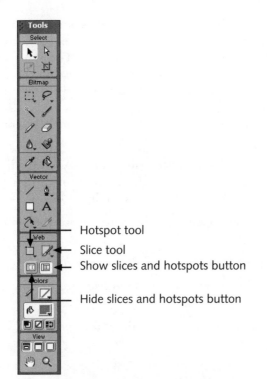

Figure 10-1   Web Tools in Tools panel

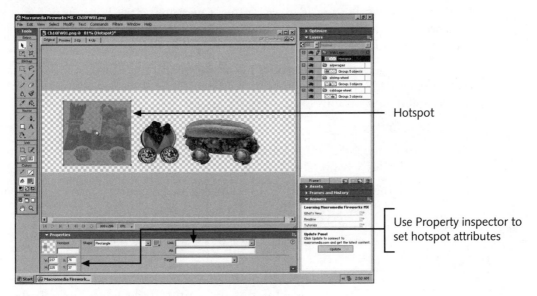

Figure 10-2   Hotspot Properties inspector

Using the Property inspector, you can modify a hotspot's attributes, including its width, height and location. You can also specify the URL or Web page the hotspot links to in the Link textbox and you can add alternate text in the Alt textbox. The link's alternate text appears over the hotspot when the user points at it with her mouse when viewed in a Web browser. If you leave this option blank, no text appears when the user moves the mouse over the hotspot, and the user may not realize that the hotspot exists. Alternate text can also provide the user with more information about the link's destination.

You can define several targeting options for the links on an image map. These options control how a Web page opens when the user clicks a link. You may be familiar with these options from working with frames in HTML. In the Property inspector, you can specify targeting options in the Target list box. The options are listed below.

- **None:** Results in the linked page opening in the current browser window, replacing the current Web page.

- **_blank:** Opens the linked page in a new browser window.

- **_self:** When using frames, this option opens the linked page in the same frame as the link.

- **_parent:** When using frames, this option opens the linked page in the parent frameset of the frame that contains the link.

- **_top:** When using frames, this option opens the linked page in a full browser window and removes all of the frames.

As you create hotspots on your Web graphics, be sure to use them carefully. Do not allow hotspots on an image to overlap each other. Overlapping the hotspots prevents the links from working properly. Also, note that very small hotspots or hotspots drawn too close together are difficult for users to identify and click.

In the following exercise, you will create an image map by editing a file with three train cars represented by pictures of food items. You will create a hotspot out of each car and use three different options for drawing hotspots.

To create an image map:

1. Start Fireworks and open the file named **Ch10FW01.png** from the Chapter folder for Chapter 10.

2. Save the file as **Ch10FW01SOLa.png** in the Chapter folder for Chapter 10.

 You use the letter "a" at the end of the file name in Step 2 to distinguish it from the version of the file you will create later in the chapter.

3. Select the **Rectangle Hotspot** tool in the Tools panel. Move the pointer over the canvas, and draw a rectangle over the left-most graphic representing

the train's engine. If you don't enclose the train engine entirely the first time, use the Undo command and try again. A blue translucent rectangle appears over the train. This delineates the area that will contain the active hyperlink.

4. In the Property inspector for the rectangle hotspot, enter **recipe1.htm** in the Link textbox. Also, enter **A main course** in the Alt text box and select **_blank** from the Target list as shown in Figure 10-3. Recall that _blank will cause the linked page to open in a new browser window. You have created a hotspot.

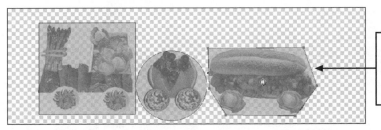

Hotspot link

Alternate text

Target set to _blank

Figure 10-3   Hotspot attributes in Property inspector

5. Click and hold the **Rectangle Hotspot** tool to display the hidden hotspot tools, and then select the **Circle Hotspot** tool.

6. Draw a circular hotspot over the middle graphic representing the first train car.

 After you draw a hotspot, you can move or resize it using the Pointer tool.

7. In the Property inspector for the circle hotspot, enter **http://www.salad.com** in the Link textbox, enter **A simple salad** in the Alt text box, and select **_blank** in the Target list box.

8. Select the **Polygon Hotspot** tool and click points around the right-most graphic representing the last train car. Each time you click, a handle appears. Completely enclose the train car to create the hotspot as shown in Figure 10-4.

Points clicked around image using the Polygon Hotspot tool to create hotspot

Figure 10-4   Polygon hotspot

9. In the Property inspector enter **recipe3.htm** in the Link box, enter **A sandwich** in the Alt text box, and select **_blank** in the Target list box.

10. Save the document and then press the **F12** key to preview the image map in your Web browser. Move your mouse over the three train cars to see that the recipe links are there and that the alternate text is displayed. The Salad train car is the only one created with an operating link. If your Internet connection is active, test the link to verify that the link opens a page in a new browser window.

11. Close the Web browser to return to Fireworks.

Exporting Fireworks Graphics

Once you create an image map or other graphic in Fireworks, you need to export it in order to add it to a Web page. You then use a program such as Macromedia Dreamweaver to insert the exported image in the appropriate place in your Web page. When you export an image map Fireworks creates an image file in either GIF or JPEG format according to the document's optimize settings. In addition to the image file, Fireworks also creates an HTML file with the code needed to make the hotspots work. You can then import this HTML into another Web page using Dreamweaver.

To export an image map:

1. Make sure the **Ch10FW01SOLa.png** file is still open in Fireworks.

2. Click **File** on the menu bar and then click **Export**. The Export dialog box opens.

3. Make sure that the **Save in** setting is set to the Chapter folder for Chapter 10 and that the File name is **Ch10FWSOLa.htm**. Also make sure that the **Save as type** setting is set to HTML and Images and that the **HTML** setting is set to Export HTML File. See Figure 10-5.

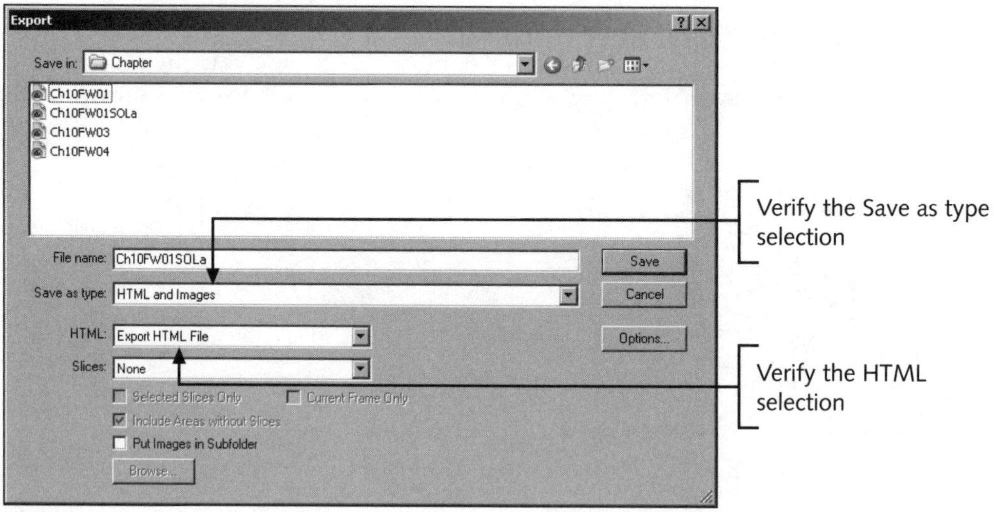

Figure 10-5 Export settings

4. Click the **Save** button to export the files to the Chapter folder.

5. Start Dreamweaver MX and if necessary create a new blank document. Save this document as **Ch10FW02.htm** in the Chapter folder for Chapter 10.

6. In Dreamweaver, click **Insert** on the menu bar, point to **Interactive Images**, and then click **Fireworks HTML**. The Insert Fireworks HTML dialog box opens.

7. Browse to the Chapter folder and select the Ch10FW01SOLa.htm file you exported in Step 4. Click the **Open** button in the Select the Fireworks HTML file dialog box. Then click the **OK** button to insert the HTML into the Web page. The image map displays in the Dreamweaver document.

8. Click **View** on the menu bar and then click **Code**. The HTML code created by Fireworks for the image map appears as shown in Figure 10-6.

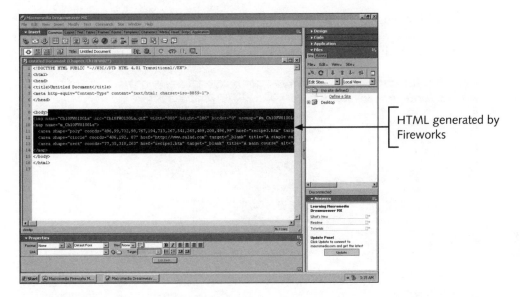

HTML generated by Fireworks

Figure 10-6   Image map HTML code

9. Close the Web page and exit Dreamweaver. You do not need to save the Web page.

10. In Fireworks, save the document, if necessary, and then close it.

Creating Hotspots using the Insert Hotspot Command

Another way to create hotspots is to have Fireworks automatically create them using the Insert Hotspot command in the Edit menu. Using this command, you can create a hotspot over one image at one time, or you can convert several images into multiple hotspots. If you select several images on the canvas and use the Insert Hotspot command, a dialog box prompts you for single or multiple hotspots. When you select multiple hotspots, Fireworks automatically creates rectangular hotspots for each image selected. Having Fireworks create hotspots for you is much quicker than drawing individual hotspots yourself. You can then add the links, alternate text, and targeting options for each hotspot using the Property inspector.

To have Fireworks create multiple hotspots:

1. Open the file named **Ch10FW01.png** from the Chapter folder for Chapter 10.

2. Save the file as **Ch10FW01SOLb.png** in the Chapter folder for Chapter 10.

3. Select the **Pointer** tool, press and hold the **Shift** key and click each of the three train car images to select all of them at the same time. Each graphic has four square handles indicating it is selected.

4. Click **Edit** on the menu bar, point to **Insert**, and then click **Hotspot**.

5. A dialog box appears asking if you want to create single or multiple hotspots. Click the **Multiple** button. Fireworks creates three rectangular hotspots automatically, one over each of the train cars as shown in Figure 10-7.

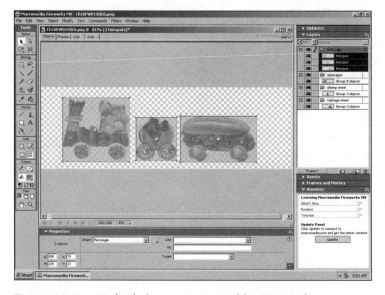

Figure 10-7   Multiple hotspots created by Fireworks

6. Press **Ctrl+D** to deselect the hotspots.

7. Select each hotspot individually with the Pointer tool and enter the data shown in Table 10-1 into the Property inspector:

Table 10-1   Property inspector data for hotspots

Car	Link text box	Alt text box	Target list box
Engine	recipe1.htm	A main course	_blank
Middle	http://www.salad.com	A simple salad	_blank
Right-most	recipe3.htm	A sandwich	_blank

8. Press **F12** to preview the image map in your Web browser. Move your mouse over each of the train cars to see that the hotspots are present.

9. Close your browser, save and close the file in Fireworks.

SLICING IMAGES FOR THE WEB

In some situations it's helpful to divide, or **slice**, an image into multiple graphics. Slicing an image means you divide the image into smaller pieces that are then arranged in a table when exported for use in a Web page. When the pieces (slices) of the image are loaded into a Web page, they are combined in a table to look like the single larger image.

There are two reasons to divide an image into slices. First, you can attach specific behaviors to individual slices. For example, you can link one slice to another Web page or you can have one slice change as part of a rollover effect when the mouse pointer is moved over another part of the image. The second reason to divide images into slices is so that you can then optimize slices individually. This means that you can apply different optimization and file formats to each individual slice. For example, one part of an image may be optimized as a JPEG image while at the same time another part of the image can be optimized as a GIF image. When the image is exported each slice is saved as a separate file using the optimization settings you specify. In addition to the files exported for each image slice, a file containing the HTML code is also exported. This HTML code is used to arrange the image slices back as one larger image on a Web page. Ultimately, the ability to optimize individual slices translates into faster download times for your graphics. When working with slices, you use the Property inspector to set any links, alternate text, and targeting options for each slice. You can also set the width and height attributes, as well as the position coordinates for each slice individually. And you can specify different export settings for each slice using the Slice export settings list box which includes preset optimization formats.

Creating Slices

Creating slices is similar to creating hotspots. You can draw slices yourself using the Slice tool on the Tools panel or you can use a menu command to have Fireworks create the slices for you. The sliced areas are shown as translucent green overlays on the canvas and, just like hotspots, the slices appear under the Web layer in the Layers panel.

10

To create slices you select the Slice tool on the Tools panel. You can either use the Slice tool or the Polygon Slice tool. With the Slice tool you click and drag the mouse pointer to draw rectangles over the images you want to include in a slice. With the Polygon Slice tool, you click points around the images you want to include in a slice. As you draw slices, Fireworks displays red lines over the canvas indicating how the document will be divided.

To have Fireworks create the slices for you, first select the images that you want to transform into slices, then click Edit on the menu bar, point to Insert and click Slice. When a dialog box appears asking if you want to create single or multiple slices, select the Multiple button to create individual slices for each image you selected. Fireworks then creates slices for each of the selected images. You can then set the properties for each of the slices in the Property inspector. Figure 10-8 shows the train image you used earlier, divided into slices via the Insert/Slice command on the Edit menu.

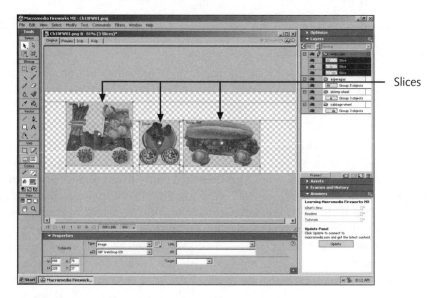

Figure 10-8   Image divided into slices

Note that if you prefer an uncluttered view of your image, you can use the Hide slices and hotspots button to hide the slices. To redisplay hidden slices, click the Show slices and hotspots button.

The following steps show you how to use the Slice tool to create slices for a navigation bar.

To slice an image:

1. Open the file named **Ch10FW03.png** from the Chapter folder for Chapter 10.

2. Save the file as **Ch10FW03SOL.png** in the Chapter folder for Chapter 10. The image consists of four words, each contained in a yellow tab that simulates the tabs at the top of a manila folder.

3. Select the **Slice** tool on the Tools panel. Click and drag the mouse pointer to draw a rectangle around the Toys tab. A green overlay covers the Toys tab, and red horizontal and vertical guidelines appear, allowing you to see the position of the slice. See Figure 10-9.

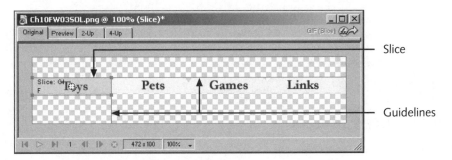

Slice

Guidelines

Figure 10-9   Slice created over Toys tab

4. In the Property inspector for the slice, enter the following values: W: **116**, H: **24**, X: **0**, Y: **30**, Link: **http://www.toys.com**, Alt: **Toys**, and Target: **_blank**. Notice that the guidelines readjust as you position the slice.

5. Create a second slice, this time over the Pets tab. Set the following values in the Property inspector for this slice. W: **116**, H: **24**, X: **116**, Y: **30**, Link: **http://www.pets.com**, Alt: **Pets**, and Target: **_blank**.

6. Repeat this process for the Games tab and set the following values in the Property inspector. W: **116**, H: **24**, X: **232**, Y: **30**, Link: **http://www.games.com**, Alt: **Games**, and Target: **_blank**.

7. Repeat this process once more for the Links tab and set the following values. W: **116**, H: **24**, X: **348**, Y: **30**, Link: **http://www.links.com**, Alt: **Links**, and Target: **_blank**. See Figure 10-10 to see how the image is sliced.

10

```
Ch10FW03SOL.png @ 100% (Slice)*          _ □ ×
Original | Preview | 2-Up | 4-Up                 GIF (Slice)

        Toys        Pets       Games    Slice: Sl...
                                        Links

◄ ▷ ▶| 1 ◄| |▷ ⊘   472 x 100   100%  ▾
```

Figure 10-10   Sliced image for navigation bar

8. Click the **Hide slices and hotspots** button in the Tools panel to make the slices transparent. Observe that your slices disappear. This can be very useful when you are editing an image and the slices become distracting. Now click the **Show slices and hotspots** button so you can see the slices again.

9. Click **File** on the menu bar, and then click **Save**.

10. Press **F12** to preview your page in your Web browser. If your Internet connection is active, you can test the links too. Notice that each hyperlink opens a new browser window.

11. Close your Web browser and return to Fireworks. Close the document.

Exporting a Sliced Image

Once you slice an image you need to export it so that you can add it to a Web page. The export process is similar to that used with hotspots. However, when you slice an image, Fireworks divides the canvas into rectangles based on the slices you create. These rectangular areas of the image are then saved as individual files which are automatically assigned filenames based on the original image's name plus row (r) and column (c) numbers (such as Ch10FW04_r1_c1.gif). If desired, you can assign individual names to each slice using the Property inspector before you export the slices. In addition to the individual slice files, Fireworks generates an HTML document that defines a table, with each of the slices assigned to a separate cell. This table brings all of the slices together on a Web page so that they appear as one whole image. If needed, Fireworks will also create a file named spacer.gif that is a one-pixel image file. This file is inserted in the table as a spacer to ensure that the image aligns properly. To export a sliced image, be sure to select Export Slices from the Slices list arrow in the Export dialog box.

Slicing an Image using the Slice Command

Instead of slicing each part of an image individually, you can let Fireworks do the work for you. You first select one or more objects on the image, and then you use the Edit, Insert, Slice command. Fireworks creates the slices necessary based on the selected objects on the canvas. This makes it easier to create slices and also ensures that slices do not overlap each other.

To slice an image using the Slice command:

1. Open the file named **Ch10FW04.png** from the Chapter folder for Chapter 10.

2. Save the file as **Ch10FW04SOL.png** in the Chapter folder for Chapter 10. The image contains several images of vegetables.

3. Click **Select** on the menu bar and then click **Select All**. All of the three vegetable pictures, as well as the text, are now selected at the same time.

4. Click **Edit** on the menu bar, point to **Insert**, and then click **Slice**. A dialog box prompts you to select single or multiple slices. Click the **Multiple** button. Fireworks creates slices based on the selected objects in your image as

shown in Figure 10-11. Note that each slice is covered in a green overlay and each one displays the words Slice: GIF. This indicates that when exported, each slice will be saved as a GIF image file. Also note that each of the image slices is shown under the Web layer in the Layers panel.

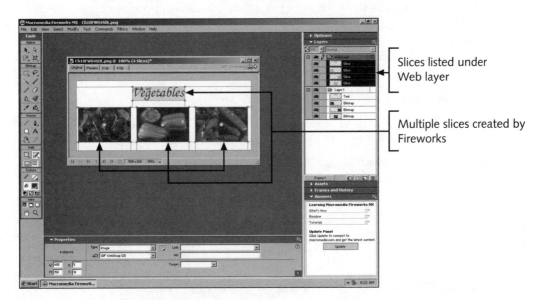

Slices listed under Web layer

Multiple slices created by Fireworks

Figure 10-11   Sliced vegetables image

5. Keep the file **Ch10FW04SOL.png** open in Fireworks so you can use it in the next section.

Creating a Rollover Effect on Slices

Once you have created slices on your image, you can then attach different behaviors to each slice. A **behavior** is a series of JavaScript statements that perform an action when the image is displayed in a Web browser and the user does something with the slice to which the behavior is attached. For example, if the user moves her mouse pointer over the slice, a behavior might cause the image to change or text to be displayed over the sliced image. This is an example of a simple rollover effect seen in many Web pages. Fireworks provides tools for adding behaviors to slices. A behavior's JavaScript code is generated by Fireworks when you export the image.

Adding behaviors to slices in Fireworks is a fairly straightforward process. You start by creating slices as discussed previously. Once you create a slice, a small circle with cross hairs appears at the center of the slice. Click this circle to display a menu of behaviors and then click the behavior you want. For example, to create a rollover, click Add Simple Rollover Behavior in the menu. Fireworks then adds the behavior to the slice. To view the behaviors attached to a slice, open the Behaviors panel.

Before you can create a rollover behavior, you need to understand one other Fireworks concept: frames. A **frame** represents the contents of the canvas. Every Fireworks document starts with one frame. To create a rollover effect (in which text is displayed over an image whenever the user points the mouse at the image) you need two frames. The first frame contains the image without the text. The second frame consists of two layers, and contains the image with the text. When the image is exported and displayed in a Web browser, the contents of the first frame are displayed initially. When the user moves her mouse pointer over the image slice, the contents of the second frame are displayed. You add and organize frames using the Frames panel.

To create a rollover effect:

1. Make sure you have the **Ch10FW04SOL.png** file open. This document should contain the sliced vegetables created in the previous section.

2. Select the **Pointer** tool on the Tools panel and click on an empty area of the canvas to deselect the slices.

3. Click the left-most slice with the vegetable picture to select it. Then click the small circle at the center of the slice and click **Add Simple Rollover Behavior** from the behaviors menu as shown in Figure 10-12. To see that the behavior has been added open the Behaviors panel.

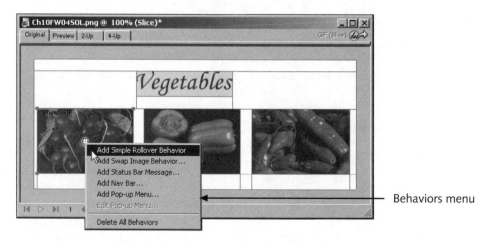

Figure 10-12   Adding a behavior to a slice

4. Repeat the previous step to add the same behavior to each of the other two slices with pictures of vegetables.

5. If necessary, open the Layers panel. Select Layer 1 and then click the Options menu icon to display the Options menu. Click **Share This Layer** to select this option. A small Share This Layer icon appears in Layer 1 as shown in Figure 10-13. This option needs to be on so that the contents of Layer 1 are shared with the frame you will add in Step 7.

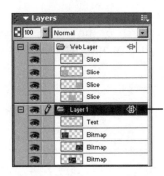

Share This Layer icon on Layer 1

Figure 10-13   Share This Layer option selected for Layer 1

6. Click the Options menu icon again and then click **New Layer**. Enter **Text** for the name of this layer in the New Layer dialog box. Make sure that Share Across Frames is not selected. Click **OK**. A new layer is added.

7. If necessary, click the **Frames** tab in the Frames and History panel. Click the panel's **Options menu** icon and then click **Add Frames**. In the Add Frames dialog box, enter **1**, if necessary, for the number of frames to be added and make sure that the After current frame radio button is selected. Click **OK**. A new frame is added and is named Frame 2.

8. Make sure that the Text layer is selected and that Frame 2 is selected.

9. Select the **Text** tool from the Tools panel. In the Property inspector select a font and font size of your choice. (The example in Figure 10-14 shows the Monotype Corsiva font with a font size of 20.) Make the text color white and select Bold and Left Alignment. Type **Enjoy fresh**, press **Enter**, then type **vegetables!** over the left-most slice with the radishes. Type **Eat vegetables**, press **Enter**, then type **with every meal!** over the middle slice with the bell peppers. And type **Make vegetables**, press **Enter**, then type **a daily habit!** over the right-most slice with the chili peppers.

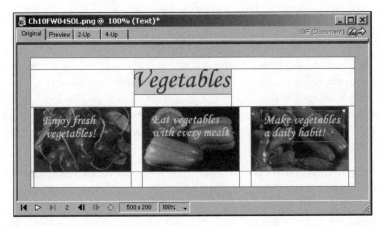

Figure 10-14   Text added to slices

10. To preview the rollover effect, press the **F12** key to open the image in your Web browser. Move your mouse pointer over each of the pictures to see the rollover effect. The text appears on a picture only when the mouse is over the picture.

11. Close the browser window to return to Fireworks.

12. Close the Behaviors panel and save and close the file.

SYMBOLS AND THE LIBRARY

Fireworks includes tools you can use to create buttons, menus, and animations. These features make use of **symbols**, which are special objects that can contain specific behaviors and characteristics and are stored in the document's library. The **library**, which is accessed from the Library tab in the Assets panel, is used to store and organize these symbols for use throughout your document. Each document has its own library. Once you create a symbol, you can create multiple copies of it in your document by dragging the symbol from the Library panel to the document's canvas. These copies are called **instances**. If you then change a symbol stored in the library, every instance of that symbol in your document is also changed. An example of how symbols can be useful is when you want to create a navigation bar. Suppose you want to create a navigation bar with five buttons and each of the five buttons will be the same size, shape, and color, but with different text. You can create one button as a symbol which is stored in the library. Then you can drag an instance of the button symbol from the Library panel to the canvas for each button in the navigation bar. Once you have the instances on the canvas, you can then add different text over each instance. If you then decide you need the navigation bar to be a different color, you only need to change the button symbol in the library and not each of the instances on the canvas.

To create a symbol you select an object on the canvas, click Modify on the menu bar, point to Symbol, and click Convert to Symbol. You then give the symbol a name and select the type of symbol you want to create. You can also click Edit on the menu bar, point to Insert, and click New Symbol. You can create three types of symbols in Fireworks: graphic, animation and button.

Graphic symbols are simple graphics that you can use throughout your Web site. For example, you may have a logo that you want to reuse together with other graphic documents you create in Fireworks. By creating a graphic symbol of the logo, you can create an instance of the logo when you need it instead of recreating it. More importantly, if you need to make a change to the logo, you only need to change the logo's symbol and all of the instances you created are changed automatically.

Animation symbols have special properties that make it easy to animate graphic objects over several frames. When you create an animation symbol, you set these properties which include the number of frames to use, the direction to move the object, as well as properties that change the size, opacity, and rotation of the object.

Button symbols contain several states that are used to create buttons with rollover effects. Buttons are discussed in more detail in the next section.

Fireworks also has a library of predefined symbols that include animations, bullets, buttons, and themes. You can incorporate these symbols into your documents by importing them into the document's library. For example, to import a predefined button, click Edit on the menu bar, then point to Libraries and click Buttons. The Import Symbols: Buttons dialog box opens as shown in Figure 10-15.

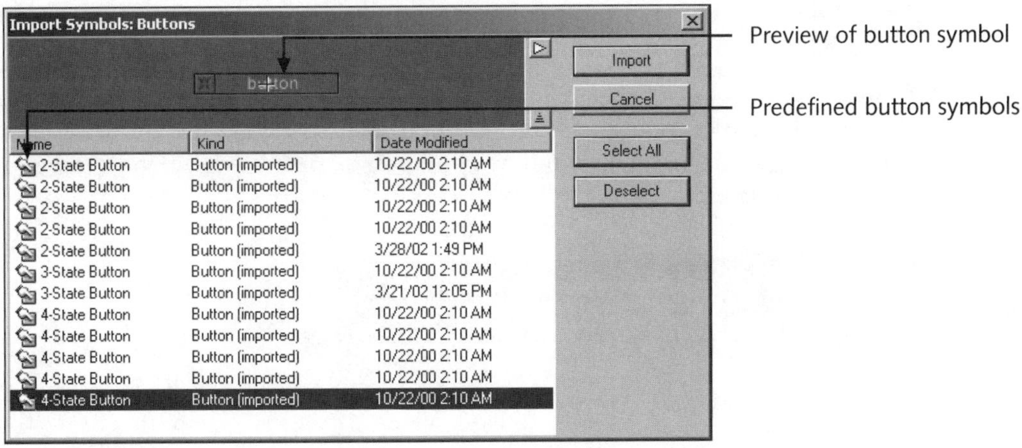

Figure 10-15 Import Symbols: Buttons dialog box

You can then select one, several, or all of the predefined buttons. When you click the Import button, the selected buttons are imported into the document's library.

BUTTONS AND MENUS

To make your Web pages easier for users to interact with, it's helpful to add buttons and menus. Fireworks makes it easy to create buttons with rollover effects so that the button changes when the user moves her mouse pointer over the button. You can also create navigation menu bars by placing several buttons together. With Fireworks you can also create pop-up menus. A pop-up menu is useful on a Web site with many links. A pop-up menu displays only when the user places the mouse pointer over the initial menu option. The user can then click one of the options in the pop-up menu to follow its link.

Creating New Buttons

Using buttons instead of static, blue, underscored text hyperlinks, helps give your Web application a much more dynamic look and feel. Buttons come in many forms. Some buttons are text on a geometrically shaped background with added 3-D effects which look like they can be physically pushed. Some buttons contain images that illustrate their purpose, and some incorporate graphics and text. Combining several buttons on a navigation bar allows you to give the user a high level view of the Web site without showing all its content.

A single button on a Web page often consists of multiple images. Each button image is associated with a different state. For example, you can define one image for the button's Up state (its normal state, when the user is not pointing at it, and the button is not selected). You can then define another image for the Over state (when the user points at the button with the mouse). This creates a rollover effect, so that the button changes when the user points at it with the mouse.

To insert a new button, click Edit on the menu bar, click Insert, then click New Button (you can also create a new symbol with button as its type). The Button Editor opens, as shown in Figure 10-16. This window contains five panels where you can define the button's various states.

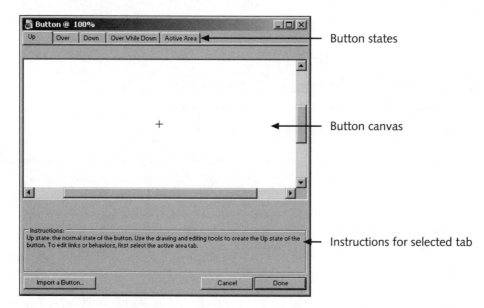

Figure 10-16 Button Editor

As you click the various tabs, instructions defining each button state appear at the bottom of the Button Editor. The Property inspector works the same as when you work on your document, so you can use it to change the attributes of the graphics you define for each state of the button.

The following list describes the Tabs in the Button Editor:

- **Up:** Displays the normal (mouse off) state of the button as it appears on the Web page.

- **Over:** Shows how the button looks when the user places the mouse over it. At the bottom right of the Over tab is a button labeled Copy Up Graphic. Clicking this button copies the graphic from the Up state to the Over state.

- **Down:** Shows the button when it is pressed in, or selected. The Down state image is often used on a navigation bar.

- **Over While Down:** Displays the button when the user points to a selected button. The Over While Down state is typically used in conjunction with a Down state image in a navigation bar. It is not used in simple rollovers.

- **Active Area:** Shows the part of the button that the user can click, also known as the hit area, or the clickable range. This image on this tab is never actually displayed. Select the Set Active Area Automatically check box to have Fireworks define the active area for you.

After you finish creating a button, click Done in the Button Editor to insert the button in the document's canvas. You can then create a link for the button by selecting the button in the canvas and specifying a link in the Property inspector. You can also specify the button's text, export options (GIF or JPG), link, alternate text and targeting options and add effects such as embossing or drop shadow.

In the following steps, you create a graphic for a button's Up state, then use a copy of the graphic to define the other four states of the button. You will create a button with a blue background and yellow text that blurs when the rollover state is activated. You will then use this button later in this chapter to create a menu bar.

To create a new button:

1. Open a new, blank canvas that is **500** pixels wide by **500** pixels high with a white canvas.

2. Save the document as **Ch10FW05.png** in the Chapter folder of Chapter 10.

3. Click **Edit** on the menu bar, point to **Insert** and then click **New Button**.

   The Button Editor opens. The plus sign at the center of the Button Editor's canvas defines the center of the canvas. You will create the graphic for the button's Up state.

4. Verify that the Up tab is selected, select the **Rectangle** tool on the Tools panel and draw a rectangle over the center point of the Button tab's canvas. In the Property inspector, enter the following values: W: **110**, H: **50**, X: **-55**, Y: **-25**. Click the Fill color box and select blue (**#0000FF**). Click the Stroke color box and then click the Transparent button, if necessary. See Figure 10-17.

5. Select the **Text** tool in the Tools panel.

10

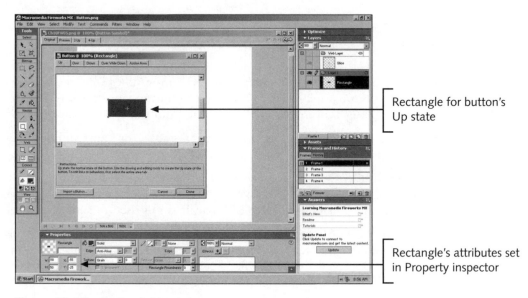

Rectangle for button's
Up state

Rectangle's attributes set
in Property inspector

Figure 10-17   Button's Up state

6. In the Property inspector, make the text **Arial**, size **16**, color yellow (**#FFFF00**), bold and centered. Click inside the button in the Up tab, type **Food**, press **Enter**, and then type **Consulting**. Use the **Pointer** tool to center the text on the button. Next, you will define a drop shadow for the button.

7. Click **Select** on the menu bar, and then click **Select All**. Selecting both the button and its text is the first step in creating a drop shadow.

8. To add a drop shadow effect to the text and button, click the **Add effects or choose a preset** icon (the plus sign) in the Property inspector, point to **Shadow and Glow**, and then click **Drop Shadow**. The Drop Shadow dialog box appears over the Effects section of the Property inspector.

9. In the Drop Shadow dialog box, change the distance to **6**, the color to **black** (if necessary), the opacity to **75%**, the softness to **2**, and the angle to **330**-degrees as shown in Figure 10-18. Then press **Enter**. The shadow appears beneath the text and button.

The Up state you just created determines how your button looks when your Web page first loads in the browser. Next, you need to define the button's other states.

To define additional states for the button:

1. Click the **Over** tab in the Button Editor, then click the **Copy Up Graphic** button. This copies the image from the Up tab onto the Over tab work area.

2. Using the **Pointer** tool select the blue rectangle. Make sure you do not select the text. Use the Fill color box in the Property inspector to change the color to orange (**#FF6600**). See Figure 10-19.

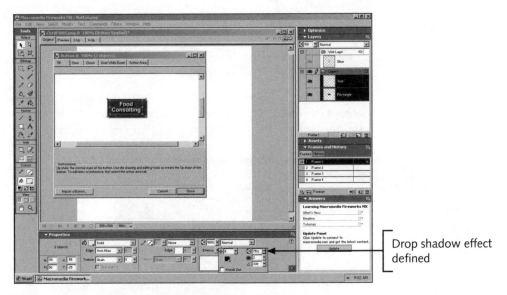

Figure 10-18   Settings for drop shadow effect

10

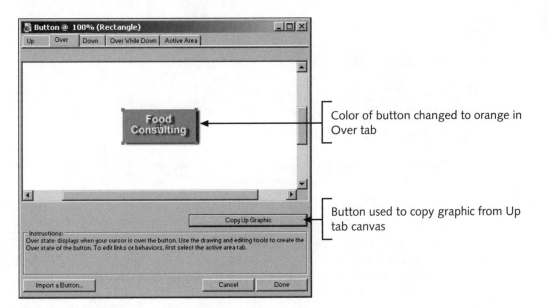

Figure 10-19   Button in Over tab defined

3. Click the **Down** tab, then click the **Copy Over Graphic** button.

4. Click the **Over While Down** tab, then click the **Copy Down Graphic** button. This button state is used when you create several buttons as part of a menu bar.

5. Click the **Active Area** tab, and make sure the Set Active Area Automatically check box is selected. This ensures that the hit area covers the entire button.

6. Click the **Done** button in the Button Editor. The Button Editor closes and the new button is inserted in the canvas.

7. On the Button Property inspector, click the **Button export options** list box, and select **Gif Web 216**. Use **consulting.htm** for the link, and **Consulting Services** for the alternate text as shown in Figure 10-20.

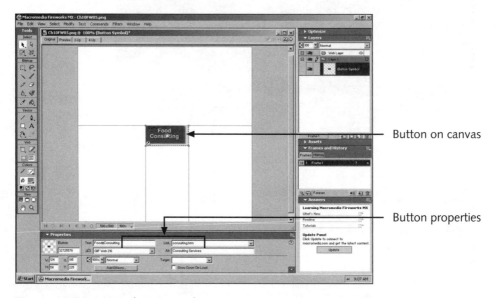

Button on canvas

Button properties

Figure 10-20   New button and its properties

8. Click the **Preview** tab on the canvas window and move your mouse over the button to see that it changes color.

9. If necessary, press **F11** to open the Library panel in the Assets panel group. The Library panel shows the button symbol you just created.

10. Be default, the button symbol is named Button. To rename the symbol, double-click **Button** under the Name column in the Library panel. The Symbol Properties dialog box opens. Type **Consulting** in the Name text box and then click **OK**.

11. Save the file.

Duplicating Buttons to Create a Menu Bar

Once you create a button, you can duplicate it to create more buttons with the same style and the same button states. In the following steps you will duplicate the Consulting button to create a menu bar.

To duplicate the Consulting button:

1. Verify that the file named **Ch10FW05.png** is still open in Fireworks. Verify that the Library panel is also visible.

2. If necessary, click the Frames and History panel's title bar to collapse it. Also, if necessary, click the Answers panel's title bar to collapse it.

3. Click the **Original** tab in the canvas window and then make sure the blue Consulting button is selected.

4. Click the **Options** menu icon in the upper-right corner of the Assets panel group to display the Options menu. Click **Duplicate**. A new button, named Consulting 1, is added to the list of symbols in the Library panel.

5. Double-click the **Consulting 1** symbol in the Library panel to open the Symbol Properties dialog box. Type **Excursions** in the Name text box and then click the **Edit** button. The Button Editor opens.

6. Verify that the Up tab is selected, select the **Text** tool in the Tools panel, and then click the button text to select the text box.

7. Drag the mouse to select the text **Food Consulting**. Type **Culinary**, press **Enter**, and then type **Explorations**. The text should be centered on the blue rectangle as shown in Figure 10-21. If it is not, you can use the Pointer tool to center it. Click on the white space outside the button to deselect it.

10

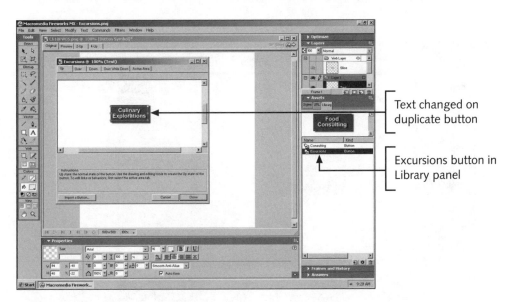

Figure 10-21 Duplicate button

Depending on how your computer is set up, you may see a Fireworks dialog box asking if you want to update the text in other buttons to match new text in the Up state tab.

8. If you do see the Fireworks dialog box, click **Yes**. The text in all the other button states is now "Culinary Explorations," just as it is in the Up tab. (If you do not see this dialog box, Fireworks will update the text in the other button states by default.)

9. Examine the other button states to verify that the text has been updated.

10. Click the **Done** button in the Button editing window. Your button, Excursions, is listed in the Library panel. Next, to make it part of the menu bar you need to add it to the canvas.

11. Click the **Excursions** button in the Library panel and drag it onto the canvas beneath the Consulting button. A rectangle appears while you drag the mouse to help you position the new button on the canvas.

Remember that you can maximize the canvas and move the Properties inspector to make it easier to see the objects you are currently working on.

12. Use the Pointer tool, if necessary, to align the Excursions button under the Consulting button.

13. In the Property inspector, set the link to **tour.htm** and the alternate text to **Come dine with us in exotic places**. Your screen should look similar to Figure 10-22.

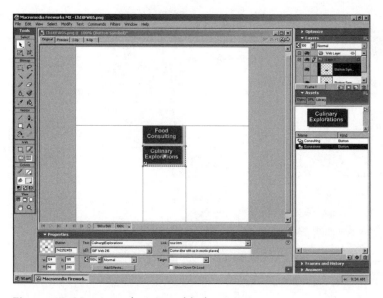

Figure 10-22   New button added to canvas

You successfully created another button in the same style as your previous one. Now you can create the remaining buttons for the menu bar using the techniques you have learned so far. You will create two more buttons, containing the text "Culinary Training" and "About Us" and add these buttons to the menu bar.

To create two more buttons for the menu bar:

1. Create a duplicate of the Consulting button and name it **Training**. Then change the button's text to read **Culinary Training** (with each word on a separate line).

2. Create another duplicate of the Consulting button and name it **About Us**. Then change the button's text to read **About Us** (with each word on a separate line).

3. Drag the Training button from the Library panel onto the canvas to place the button beneath the Culinary Explorations button. Use the Pointer tool to adjust the button with the other buttons on the canvas. In the Property inspector change the link to **training.htm**. Change the alternate text to **Learn to host a gala event**.

4. Drag the About Us button from the Library panel onto the canvas and position it above the Food Consulting button. Use the Pointer tool to adjust the button with the other buttons on the canvas. In the Property inspector change the link to **aboutlbc.htm**. Change the alternate text to **Learn about LBC**. Your screen should look similar to Figure 10-23. (The order of the buttons in your Library panel may differ.)

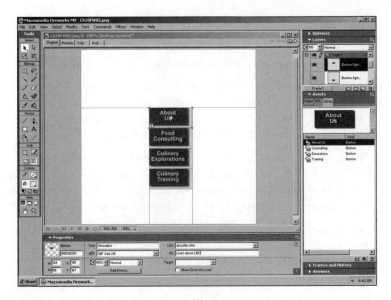

Figure 10-23   Four buttons added to canvas

5. To see how the buttons will work in a Web page, press the **F12** key. The buttons are displayed in a browser window. Move your mouse pointer over each button. You can also click the buttons to see that they are linked. The linked files do not exist so the browser will display a message that the page cannot be displayed.

6. Close the browser window to return to Fireworks. Save and close the document.

Creating a Pop-Up Menu

When a Web site has a large amount of information it is sometimes useful to use pop-up menus. Pop-up menus only display when the user points to the button or graphic to which the menu is attached. Using these types of menus reduces the number of links that must be visible on the page at one time. When the menu pops up, users can see what information is available in specific content areas. Users can then examine their options before they actually visit a new page of the site.

To create a pop-up menu in Fireworks, right-click on a slice and then click Add Pop-up Menu. This opens the Pop-up Menu Editor, which contains various tabs that you can use to define how the pop-up menu will work. Clicking the + and − icons on the Content tab of the Pop-up Menu Editor lets you add text, link and targeting information for your pop-up menu. You can use the other tabs to change the appearance of the buttons and to control how the menu is displayed.

The steps below show you how to create a simple pop-up menu that will allow the user to selection an option from a list of soft drinks.

To create a pop-up menu:

1. Open a new document that is **300** pixels wide and **300** pixels high with a white canvas.

2. Save this document as **Ch10FW06.png** in the Chapter folder for Chapter 10.

3. Click the **Rectangle** tool on the Tools panel and draw a rectangle on the canvas. In the Property inspector, enter the following values in the width, height, and coordinate boxes: W: **120**, H: **50**, X: **10**, Y: **10**. Click the Fill color box and select blue (**#0000FF**). Click the Stroke color box and click the transparent button.

4. Click the **Text** tool. In the Property inspector, make the text **Arial**, size **16**, color yellow (**#FFFF00**). Click inside the blue button and type **Pick a Soda**. To center the text on the button enter the following values in the coordinate boxes in the Property inspector: X: **18**, Y: **22**. Press **Enter**. See Figure 10-24.

5. Click the **Slice** tool and draw a slice over the rectangle. In the Property inspector for the slice, enter the following values in the width, height, and coordinate boxes: W: **120**, H: **50**, X: **10**, Y: **10**. Press **Enter**.

6. Right-click the slice (or Control-click on a Macintosh) and click **Add Pop-up Menu**. The Pop-up Menu Editor opens.

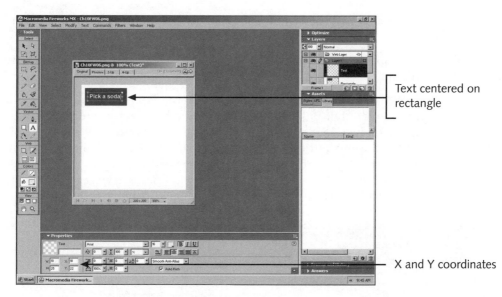

Figure 10-24   Text on rectangle

7. Double click in the space below the Text column in the Pop-up Menu Editor. A blank text area appears. Type **Coke** and then press **Tab**. In the Link column, type **http://www.coke.com**. Press **Tab** twice to advance to the next line as shown in Figure 10-25.

10

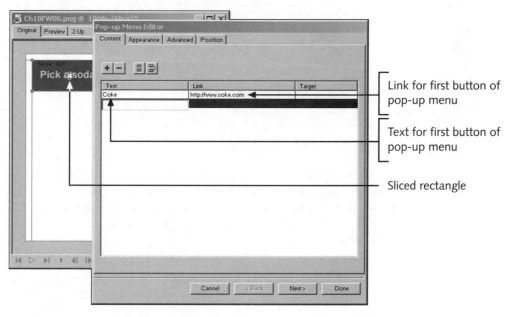

Link for first button of pop-up menu

Text for first button of pop-up menu

Sliced rectangle

Figure 10-25   Pop-up Menu Editor

8. Type **Pepsi** and then press **Tab**. Type **http://www.pepsi.com** in the Link column, and then press **Tab** twice to advance to the next line.

9. Type **Sprite**, press **Tab**, and then type **http://www.sprite.com** in the Link column.

10. Click the **Appearance** tab at the top of the Pop-up Menu Editor. Click the **Image** radio button. Vertical menu should be selected already. Set the Font to **Arial, Helvetica, sans-serif**. In the Up State section set the text color to red (**#FF0000**) and the cell color to light blue (**#00FFFF**). Also in the Up State section, click the upper-left preset style to select it. Notice the preview of your button. In the Over State section, if necessary, set the text color to white (**#FFFFFF**) and the cell color to blue (**#000084**). See Figure 10-26.

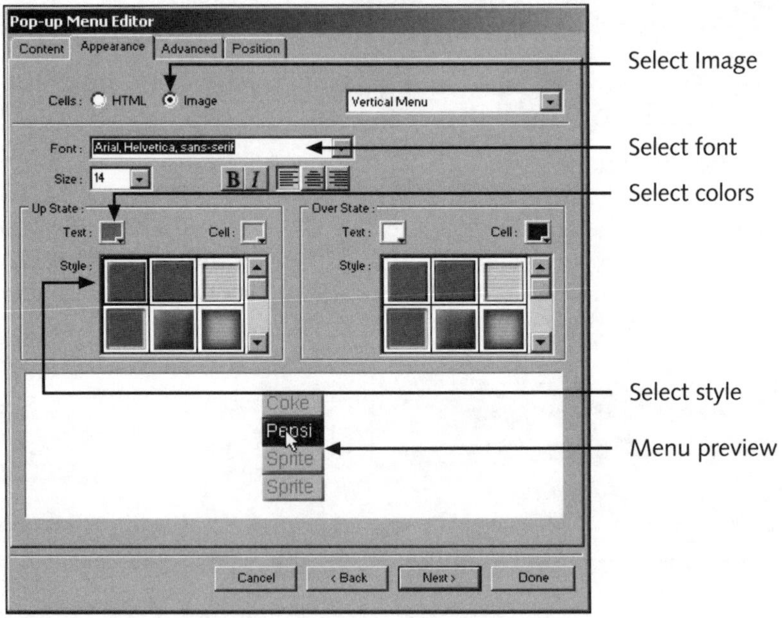

Figure 10-26   Appearance tab selections

11. Click the **Position** tab at the top of the Pop-up Menu Editor to advance to the Position panel. Under Menu position, click the fourth icon from the left so that your menu pops out of the top-right side of your button. Click **Done**. The blue outline of the menu displays on the canvas to show how the pop-up menu will display.

12. Press **F12** to preview the menu in your Web browser. Move your mouse pointer over the rectangle to see the pop-up menu display. When finished previewing the menu, close the browser window and return to Fireworks.

13. Save and close the document.

CREATING ANIMATIONS

You may have noticed small, animated graphics decorating many Web site pages. Animation can make a Web page more visually interesting and can persuade the user to perform a particular action. Perhaps you have seen banner advertisements that contain animation enticing you to click a box that, in fact, takes you to an advertisement for a product or service. You may have also noticed flashing stars or icons telling you where to find new information or encouraging you to participate in a contest. Animation can draw a visitor's eye to an important section of the Web page.

There are several ways to create animation on the Web. You can create JavaScript code that displays a series of images one after the other like a slide show. This code is added to the HTML code of the Web page and controls how the image files are loaded to be displayed. You can also create an animated GIF file in which a series of images contained in the file are displayed one after the other. This type of file does not require any special code in the HTML of the Web page. Animated GIF files are added to a Web page the same way as any other GIF or JPEG image file. Fireworks can create animated GIFs for use in Web pages.

To create an animation you create a series of images that are displayed in sequence. Fireworks uses separate frames to hold these images and plays the frames one after the other, thus creating an animation effect. You can create animations in Fireworks in two ways. First, you can create the images in each frame individually, through a process called **frame-by-frame animation**. Second, you can create the images for the beginning and ending frames and then let Fireworks fill in the frames between them, through a process called **tweening**.

Once you create your animations, you can preview them before exporting them as animated .gifs. To do this, use the controls at the bottom of the document's window. You are probably already familiar with the controls from playing media files on the Web, or from using your VCR or CD player. Using the controls, you can play and stop the animation, play it backward and forward, or advance frame-by-frame backward and forward.

Using Frames to Create Animation

To create a frame-by-frame animation, you need to use the Layers and Frames panels in unison to draw and distribute the animation as desired across the frames. In the Layers panel, layers of your image can be associated with specific frames. If you want an image to be visible throughout all of the animation sequence you need to create the image in a layer that is then shared across all frames. To share a layer across all frames you can double-click the layer in the Layers panel as if you were going to rename it and under the layer's name select the Share Across Frames check box. You can also click the Share This Layer option from the Layers panel Options menu. Any changes you make to that layer are propagated across all of your frames.

The Frames panel shows each frame with a frame number and a frame delay. The frame delay is displayed in increments of 1/100 second. For example, a frame delay of 50 means that each frame plays for one-half of a second. The default frame delay is 7. Double-clicking the frame delay allows you to change the value. You can also reorder frames by selecting them and dragging them to another position. Fireworks renumbers the frames and maintains the sequential order.

To create a simple text animation:

1. Open a new canvas in Fireworks that is **400** pixels wide by **200** pixels high with a white canvas.

2. Save this file as **Ch10FW07.png** in the chapter folder for Chapter 10.

3. Select the **Text** tool from the Tools panel. In the Property inspector, set Font to **Arial**, size to **28**, with the color red (**#FF0000**). Click the canvas and type the letter **B**.

4. Click the **Pointer** tool. Click the **B** and copy it (**Ctrl+C**). Paste it (**Ctrl+V**) onto your canvas four times to create four copies of the letter. The letters are on top of each other so it may not look like five B's until you move them. You must separate each letter so that you can alter it individually.

5. Use your Pointer tool to position the letters next to each other. Space them close enough together so they look like a single word rather than individual letters. You can use the Align options under the Modify menu to space the letters evenly on the canvas. See Figure 10-27.

Figure 10-27   Letters repositioned

6. Double-click the second B so you can edit the text. Change the B to an **o**, leaving all the letter characteristics the same. Repeat this process for all duplicated B's until you create the word **Bonne**. Next, you create more frames that use this same image.

7. If necessary, open the Layers panel. Double-click **Layer 1** to open the Layer Name dialog box (you may need to scroll the layers to see Layer 1). Make sure that the Share Across Frames option is not checked for Layer 1. Click **Layer 1** again to close the dialog box.

8. If necessary, open the Frames panel. In the Frames panel, click the Options menu icon in the upper-right corner, then click **Duplicate Frame** to open the Duplicate Frame dialog box. Type **5** in the Number text box, then click the **After current frame** radio button to select it if it is not already selected. See Figure 10-28. Click **OK**.

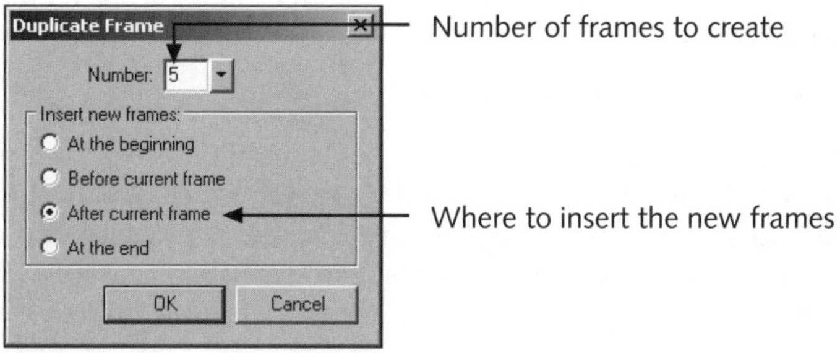

Number of frames to create

Where to insert the new frames

Figure 10-28   Duplicate Frame dialog box

Note that the Frames panel now contains six frames and each frame contains the five letters. To create the animation, you need to edit each frame individually.

9. Click **Frame 1** in the Frames panel to select it. Use the Pointer tool to click the **B** on the canvas. In the Property inspector, under **Effects**, click the **+** button to display a menu of effects. Point to **Shadow and Glow** and click the **Glow** effect. Change the glow color to yellow (**#FFFF00**). See Figure 10-29.

10

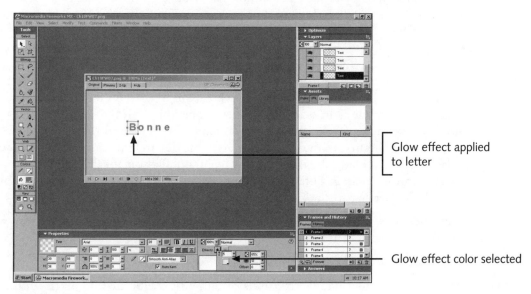

Glow effect applied to letter

Glow effect color selected

Figure 10-29   Glow effect selected

10. In the Frames panel, click **Frame 2**, select the letter **o** on the canvas by itself and apply the yellow glow effect as you did for the letter B in Step 9. Now the letter o will have the glow effect when Frame 2 is played.

11. Click **Frame 3**, select the first letter **n** by itself on the canvas, and apply the yellow glow effect. Repeat this process by clicking **Frame 4**, selecting the second letter **n** and applying the yellow glow effect to it. Repeat this once more for **Frame 5** and the letter **e**.

You are now ready to play the animation.

12. At the bottom of the document window, click the **Play/Stop** button to activate the animation. Notice that the glow effect scrolls through each of the letters. Click the **Play/Stop** button again to stop the animation. (To save this file as an animated .gif, you would use the Export Wizard in the File menu and select the Animated GIF option.)

13. Save and close this document.

Creating an Animation Using Tweening

Another way to create animated .gifs in Fireworks is to create instances of an image and have Fireworks create frames and fill in the animation in between the first and last frames. As mentioned earlier, this method is called tweening. To do this you first create a symbol for your document, then drag instances of the symbol from the library to the canvas, creating two or more instances of the symbol. To create an animation between the two images, you simply select the instances of that symbol on the canvas, click Modify on the menu bar, point to Symbol, then click Tween Instances. You are then prompted for the number of frames you want to create between the two instances. Selecting 5, for example, creates five frames between the two instances. The animation then consists of a total of seven frames: the first and last frames contain the original image, and Fireworks generates the five in between. You can also distribute the tweened images directly to frames by selecting the Distribute to Frames check box in the Tween Instances dialog box. The image in each frame is in a slightly different position than the image in the preceding frame. For example, if you start with an instance of a circle in the upper-left corner of the canvas for the first frame and an instance of the circle in the lower-right corner of the last frame, tweening the image across five frames automatically fills the intermediate frames with the circle in different positions. When you play the animation, it looks as if the circle is traveling to the right diagonally.

Follow the steps below to create a motion tween for a text symbol. The text will animate from one side of the canvas to the other.

To animate text using tweened instances:

1. Open a new Fireworks canvas of dimensions **500** by **200** pixels with a white canvas.

You need a wide canvas so that your animation can play across it.

2. Save the file as **Ch10FW08.png** in the Chapter folder for Chapter 10.

3. Using the **Text** tool, create the word **Cuisine** on the upper-left side of the canvas with text attributes of **Arial** font, size **28**, red color (**#FF0000**), and Left alignment.

   Now you need to convert the text into a symbol so that you can create instances of the symbol and activate tweening between the instances to create the animation.

4. Make sure that the text **Cuisine** is selected and press the **F8** key. When the Symbol Properties dialog box appears, name the symbol **Cuisine** and make sure the **Graphic** radio button is selected. Click **OK**. A symbol is created and stored in the library.

5. If necessary, open the Library panel to see the symbol you just created.

6. Drag and drop an instance of the **Cuisine** symbol from the Library panel to the lower-right side of the canvas. In the Property inspector, change the opacity to 0 as shown in Figure 10-30. The instance becomes transparent.

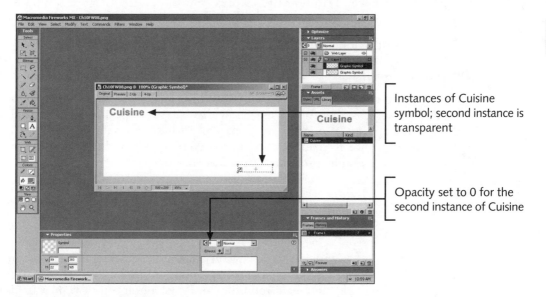

Figure 10-30 Instances of the Cuisine symbol

7. Click **Select** on the menu bar and click **Select All** to select both instances of Cuisine on the canvas.

8. Click **Modify** on the menu bar, point to **Symbol**, and then click **Tween Instances** to open the Tween Instances dialog box. Enter **10** to create 10 new instances. Click the **Distribute to Frames** check box to distribute the new instances onto separate frames. See Figure 10-31. Click **OK**.

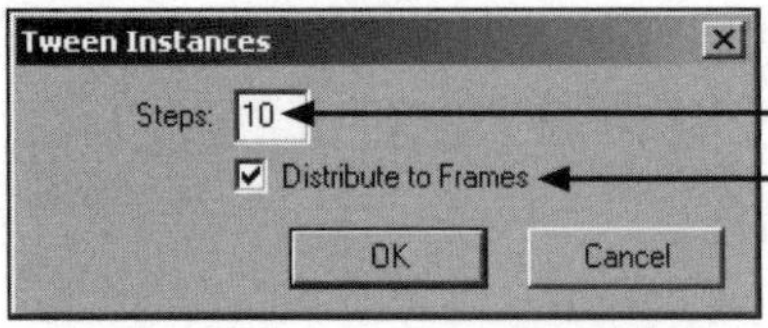

Figure 10-31   Tweened Instances dialog box

Individual frames are created for each tweened instance.

9. Play the animation by using the controls in the lower-left corner of your document's window. The animation shows the text moving diagonally from left to right on the canvas as it fades away.

10. Save this file and exit Fireworks.

CHAPTER SUMMARY

❑ Using the advanced features of Fireworks, you can create image maps, buttons, navigation bars, and animations that can easily be exported for use on Web pages.

❑ An image map is a graphic that has rectangle-, circle-, or polygon-shaped hotspots defined over specific areas. A user can click a hotspot on an image map and be taken to another Web page. You can define single or multiple hotspots on one image.

❑ Slicing is a technique for cutting a picture into pieces and loading the pieces as individual graphics on a Web page. Individual slices are positioned in a table so that the graphic appears as one image. Slicing an image is advantageous because you can optimize each slice to load quickly on the Web, thereby reducing the download time for a large graphic. You can also add behaviors such as rollover effects to individual slices.

❑ Fireworks provides two methods of slicing an image. You can draw the slices using the Slice tool or you can select objects and then let Fireworks create slices automatically based on the selections.

❑ Symbols are objects with special characteristics and are stored in the document's library. There are three types of symbols: graphic, animation, and button. Once you create a symbol, you can create multiple copies, or instances, of it in your documents. Making changes to the symbol changes every instance of that symbol.

❑ Each document has its own library which is used to store the document's symbols. The Library panel is used to access the symbols and to organize them.

❑ Buttons are symbols that have five states that can hold different content to create rollover effects. You create links on buttons and export them for use in your Web pages. You edit buttons using the Button Editor.

❑ A Pop-up menu can be created in Fireworks using slices and the Pop-up Menu Editor. Fireworks generates the JavaScript code needed to display the pop-up menu on a Web page.

❑ You can create animated .gifs using Fireworks, either by creating a frame-by-frame animation or by tweening images over frames. Animated .gifs are like simple cartoons that play a series of frames in logical sequence.

REVIEW QUESTIONS

1. A hotspot is
   a. an object that has been selected on the canvas.
   b. a group of objects selected on the canvas.
   c. a shape overlaid on an image on the canvas that links to a URL.
   d. the same as an image slice.

2. Fireworks generates _____ code when image maps are exported for use in Dreamweaver.
   a. JavaScript
   b. HTML
   c. text
   d. hotspot

3. Which target option on a hotspot causes the linked page to open in a new browser window?
   a. _self
   b. _parent
   c. _top
   d. _blank

4. Which is not a tool used to create hotspots on an image?
   a. Rectangle Hotspot tool
   b. Polygon Hotspot tool
   c. Circle Hotspot tool
   d. Square Hotspot tool

5. Slicing an image
   a. refers to dividing an image into several smaller images.
   b. is a technique for cropping an image.
   c. is a technique for creating an image map.
   d. converts segments of an image into symbols.

10

6. A spacer graphic is used to

    a. properly align sliced images in a table.

    b. separate objects selected on the canvas.

    c. reduce the size of exported images.

    d. identify hotspots on an image.

7. Slicing an image allows you to

    a. optimize individual slices of an image, creating a faster-loading graphic.

    b. attach behaviors to slices individually.

    c. provide the user with some image portions, or slices, while the remaining slices load to complete the full image.

    d. all of the above.

8. When slicing multiple images using the Slice command,

    a. the images must all be selected at the same time.

    b. you can have no more than 5 images.

    c. each image must be a hotspot.

    d. the images must be rectangular in shape.

9. Actions attached to slices such as a simple rollover effect are called

    a. HTML codes.

    b. graphic symbols.

    c. behaviors.

    d. frames.

10. Which list below represents the button states created in Fireworks?

    a. Up, Over, Down, Off, and Active Area

    b. Up, Over, Down, Over While Down, and Active Area

    c. Up, Over, Off, Hit Area, and On

    d. Off, Over, Down, Over While Down

11. Symbols are stored and organized in a document's

    a. Layers panel.

    b. Frames panel.

    c. Symbols panel.

    d. Library panel.

12. In Fireworks you can create the following types of symbols:

    a. Graphic, Movie, and Button

    b. Graphic, Button, and Hotspot

  c. Animation, Button, and Graphic

  d. Animation, Graphic, and Static

13. Copies of symbols placed in a document are called

  a. animations.

  b. slices.

  c. GIFs.

  d. instances.

14. Which file format is used by Fireworks to export an animation for use on a Web page?

  a. .png

  b. Animated .gif

  c. .gif

  d. .png and .gif

15. To have the contents of a layer visible on all frames of an animation, you

  a. make copies of the layer and place a copy in each frame.

  b. click Share This Layer in the Options menu for the selected layer.

  c. insert extra frames in the layer.

  d. move the layer into the Frames panel.

10

HANDS-ON EXERCISES

Exercise 10-1

In this exercise, you create an image map to serve as a navigation tool for a shopping Web site.

1. Open the file named **Ch10FWEX01.gif** from the Exercises folder for Chapter 10 and save it as **Ch10FWEX01SOL.png** in the same folder. This file contains an image with four stars and text.

2. Using the Circle Hotspot tool, draw hotspots over the each of the four navigation choices: Home, Email, Shop and Exit.

3. Use the Property inspector to enter the link and alternate text information for the hotspots as follows. Be sure to select the hotspot before entering its associated information.

Hotspot	Link	Alternate text
Home	home.htm	Shopping Home Page
Email	mailto:contactus@shop.com	Contact Us
Shop	shop.htm	Online Catalog
Exit	exit.htm	Bye Now

4. Preview the image map in your Web browser by pressing F12. Observe that the alternate text displays and that the link addresses show in the status bar of the browser when you move your mouse over the images.

5. Export your image map using the Export command to create the HTML and image files. Export **Ch10FWEX01SOL.htm** and **Ch10FWEX01SOL.gif**. Open the HTML file in your Web browser and observe the alternate text and link addresses in the status bar as you did in the previous step. Close your browser.

6. Save and close the document in Fireworks.

Exercise 10-2

In this exercise you create a new button with a simple rollover effect. You create content for the Up and Over states of the button.

1. Create a new Fireworks document with dimensions of 200 by 200 and a white canvas. Save this document as **Ch10FWEX02.png** in the Exercises folder for Chapter 10.

2. Click Edit on the menu bar and then click Insert and New Button. The Button Editor opens.

3. Use the Rectangle tool to draw a rectangle on the canvas for the button's Up state. In the Property inspector enter the following values for the width, height, and coordinates: W: 160, H: 30, X: -78, and Y: -14. Press Enter. Set the fill color to yellow (#FFFF00) and the stroke color to transparent.

4. Click the Text tool and create a text block on the rectangle. Set the text font to Arial, the size at 28 and the text color to red (#FF0000). Then type Welcome. You may need to use the Pointer tool to position the text in the center of the rectangle. You can also enter the following coordinates in the Property Inspector: X: -62, and Y: -16.

5. Click the Over tab and click the Copy Up Graphic button. This copies the button you created in the Up tab into the Over tab.

6. Select the rectangle using the Pointer tool and use the fill color box to color the rectangle blue (#0000FF). Click Done. Your button appears on the canvas.

7. With the button still selected, enter the link http://www.welcome.com, and the alternate text Welcome Button.

8. Press F12 to preview your button in your Web browser and observe the button's rollover effect. Close the Web browser window.

9. Save and close the document.

Exercise 10-3

In this exercise you import a button from the Fireworks button library and create a menu bar.

1. Create a new Fireworks document with dimensions of 150 by 400 and a white canvas. Save this document as **Ch10FWEX03.png** in the Exercises folder for Chapter 10.

2. Open the Library panel by selecting it from the Windows menu or pressing F11, if it is not already open.

3. Click Edit on the menu bar, point to Libraries and click Buttons. The Import Symbols: Buttons dialog box opens. Click the first button from the top of the list to select it. Click Import. The button appears in your document's library and on the canvas.

4. Double-click the button in the Library panel to open the Symbol Properties dialog box. Type Go to rename the button. Click OK.

5. In the Property inspector under Text, replace the text button with Go. Also, enter the following values in the coordinate boxes: X: 20, Y: 20. Set the Link to go.htm and the alternate text as Go Here.

6. In the Library panel, click Duplicate from the Library Options menu to create a copy of the button. Fireworks names the copy Go 1.

7. Double click the Go 1 button and rename it Stop. Click OK.

8. Drag the Stop button onto the canvas below the Go button. In the Property inspector for the Stop button, replace the text button with Stop and enter the following values in the coordinate boxes: X: 20, Y: 50. Set the Link to stop.htm and the alternate text Do Not Go Here.

9. Create one more copy of the Go button, rename the duplicate Wait, and drag the button to the canvas, placing it below the Stop button. In the Property inspector for the Wait button, replace the text button with Wait and enter the following values in the coordinate boxes: X: 20, Y: 80. Set the Link to wait.htm and the alternate text to Please Wait.

10. Preview the page in your Web browser by pressing F12. Move your mouse pointer over the buttons to see their rollover effect and to check the links and alternate text. Close your browser window when you are done.

11. Save and close the document.

10

Exercise 10-4

In this exercise, you create a pop-up menu with three buttons that link to three technology companies.

1. Create a new Fireworks document with dimensions of 300 by 300 and a white canvas. Save this document as **Ch10FWEX04.png** in the Exercises folder for Chapter 10.

2. Click the Rectangle tool on the Tools panel and draw a rectangle in the work area. In the Property inspector, enter the following values in the width, height, and coordinate boxes: W: 140, H: 40, X: 30, Y: 30. Click the fill color box and select red (#FF0000). Click the stroke color box and select transparent.

3. Click the Text tool. In the Property inspector, make the text Arial, size 18, and color white (#FFFFFF). Click on the red button on the canvas and type Technology, press Enter, and then type Companies. Enter the following values in the coordinate boxes: X: 42, Y: 29. Press Enter.

4. Click the Slice tool and draw a slice over the rectangle. In the Property inspector for the slice enter the following values in the width, height, and coordinate boxes: W: 140, H: 40, X: 30, Y: 30. Press Enter.

5. Right-click the slice (or Contol-click on a Macintosh) and then click Add Pop-up Menu from the menu. The Pop-up Menu Editor opens.

6. Double-click in the space below the Text column. A blank text area will appear. Type in Microsoft. Press Tab. Now you are below the Link column. Type http://www.microsoft.com. Press Tab twice to advance to the next line.

7. Type in Apple. Press Tab. Now you are below the Link column. Type http://www.apple.com. Press Tab twice to advance to the next line.

8. Type in Macromedia. Press Tab. Now you are below the Link column. Type http://www.macromedia.com.

9. Click the Appearance tab at the top of the Pop-up Menu Editor. If necessary, click the Appearance tab again to make it the active tab. Click the Image radio button to select it. The Vertical Menu option should already be selected. Set the Font to Arial, Helvetica, sans-serif. In the Up State section, set the text color to white (#FFFFFF) and the cell color to red (#FF0000). Select the upper-left style from the Style buttons. If necessary, in the Over State section set the text color to white (#FFFFFF) and the cell color to blue (#000084).

10. Click the Position tab at the top of the Pop-up Menu Editor. Under Menu Position, click the second icon from the left so your menu pops out of the bottom of your button. Click Done.

11. Press F12 to preview the menu in your Web browser. Move your mouse pointer over the graphic to see the pop-up menu. Test the buttons in the pop-up menu. Close your browser window when you are done.

12. Save and close your document.

Exercise 10-5

In this exercise, you create an animation of a circle and a text block that are first spaced apart and then come together as the animation plays.

1. Create a new Fireworks document with dimensions of 500 by 200 and a white canvas. Save this document as **Ch10FWEX05.png** in the Exercises folder for Chapter 10.

2. Click the Ellipse tool and draw a circle in the lower-right corner of the canvas. In the Property inspector, set the Fill color to red (#FF0000). Set the following values in the width, height, and coordinate boxes as follows: W: 60, H: 60, X: 425, Y: 130. Press Enter.

3. Click the Text tool, set the text color to black, its font to Arial, and its size to 28. Then type the text Hello in the upper-left corner of the canvas. Set the coordinates to X: 20 Y: 5 in the Property inspector. Press Enter.

   This is the first frame of your animation.

4. Open the Layers panel and double-click the layer you just created. Make sure that your layer is *not* shared across frames. And if necessary, press Ctrl+D to deselect the objects on the canvas.

5. Convert the circle to a symbol by selecting it with the Pointer tool and then pressing the F8 key. Name the symbol Circle and set Graphic as its type.

6. Also, convert the text to a symbol by selecting it with the Pointer tool and then press the F8 key. Name the symbol Text and use Graphic as its type.

7. Open the Library panel to see the symbols stored in the library.

8. Drag the Circle symbol from the Library panel onto the center of the canvas. In the Property inspector, set the coordinates to X: 215 and Y: 70. Press Enter.

9. Next drag the Text symbol from the Library panel onto the center of the canvas on top of the circle. Set the coordinates to X: 215 and Y: 90. Press Enter.

   The animation should float the text and the shape together, ending with the text on top of the shape in the center of the canvas.

10. Select both instances of the text at the same time, click Modify on the menu bar, point to Symbol, and then click Tween Instances. When the Tween Instances dialog box opens, enter 5 for Steps to create five tweened instances between your text instances. Click the Distribute to Frames check box to select it. Click OK.

11. Next select both instances of the circle at the same time, click Modify on the menu bar, point to Symbol, and then click Tween Instances. When the Tween Instances dialog box opens, enter 5 for the number of steps. Click the Distribute to Frames check box to select it and click OK.

12. Play the animation using the controls in the lower-left corner of the document window.

13. Save and close this file.

10

WEB DESIGN PROJECTS

Project 10-1

Create a new image in Fireworks that looks like a simple floor plan for a small house. The floor plan should have at least four rooms, such as the living room, kitchen, master bedroom, and guest bedroom. Add text to each room to identify it. Then create hotspots for each of the rooms. Add a link to each room (such as "living.htm" for the living room) and alternate text (such as "See the living room"). The end result should be an image map that allows a user to click a room to display more information about that room. Preview the image map in your browser to make sure each hotspot has a link and alternate text. Save the document as **Ch10FWDP01.png** in the Projects folder for Chapter 10.

Project 10-2

Open the Fireworks file **Ch10FWDP02.png** from the Projects folder for Chapter 10. Save this file as **Ch10FWDP02SOL.png** in the Projects folder. This document contains several images including pictures of rooms and text. You are to create a rollover effect where descriptive text appears over each picture when the mouse pointer is moved over the picture. Each picture will also have alternate text and a link to a Web page. To begin slice the document so that there is a slice for each picture and for the text. Add a link and alternate text to each picture slice. Add the Simple Rollover Behavior to each picture slice. Change Layer 1 so that its contents are shared across all frames. Add a new layer and name it Text. Also, add a new frame. Make Frame 2 the current frame and the Text layer the current layer. Then add a text block to each picture. Each text block should describe the associated picture with a short phrase. Preview the document in your Web browser to see the rollover effect on each picture slice. Save your Fireworks document.

Project 10-3

You are asked by a friend to create a navigation bar with two options (Sports and Hobbies) for his personal Web page. To keep his page uncluttered you will create pop-up menus for each of the two options. Start by creating a new document of 400 by 300 pixels. Save this file as **Ch10FWDP03.png** in the Projects folder for Chapter 10. Create two rectangles arranged horizontally across the top of the canvas. Make each rectangle about 100 pixels wide and 30 pixels high. Add the text Sports to the first rectangle and add the text Hobbies to the second rectangle. Then create slices for each rectangle. Add a pop-up menu to each slice. For the Sports slice add four choices in the Pop-up Menu Editor (such as Football, Baseball, Swimming, and Tennis). Make up the page names for the links (such as football.htm). Design the appearance of the pop-up menu as you like. Set the position of the pop-up menu so that it appears below the slice. For the Hobbies slice add four choices for the pop-up menu (such as Reading, Walking, Painting, and Photography). Make up the page names for the links. Design the appearance and position the same as the Sports menu. Preview your menus in your browser. Save your Fireworks document.

11

CASCADING STYLE SHEETS: PART I

In this chapter you will:

♦ Write your first style sheet
♦ Use basic CSS syntax
♦ Combine style rules with your HTML code
♦ Use CSS selectors to apply style rules
♦ Use the `<div>` and `<span>` elements with CSS style rules

In this chapter, you will learn about the need for Cascading Style Sheets (CSS) and how CSS is supported in the major browsers. You will learn basic CSS syntax and get a chance to write a variety of CSS style sheets.

INTRODUCING CASCADING STYLE SHEETS

When Tim Berners-Lee first proposed HTML in 1989, he wanted to make documents as portable as possible, so he decided to let the user's browser determine how the HTML pages should display. The first browser, Mosaic, had little support for any style characteristics, and most Web pages contained simple, left-justified documents.

As the Web evolved, its potential as a publishing medium became obvious. What Web developers needed was a way to have more control over the visual display of content. Users and publishers who were familiar with the visual display power of modern page layout and word-processing tools found HTML sorely lacking in its ability to handle even the most basic display characteristics, such as changing the color or typeface of text.

Berners-Lee and his colleagues realized early in the development of HTML that a style and display language, expressed separately from the structural HTML code, would let authors control the way material was displayed in a browser. In response to this need, the World Wide Web Consortium created a new style language called *Cascading Style Sheets (CSS)*. CSS is an easy-to-use style language that lets you use familiar desktop publishing terminology to control the appearance of Web pages. You can use CSS to control typography, colors, backgrounds, and other design characteristics.

Browser Support for Cascading Style Sheets

The only drawback to working with CSS is the lack of support in older browsers. To enjoy all the benefits of Web pages created with CSS, the user needs a newer browser. Netscape users need version 6.0 or above. Internet Explorer users need version 5.0 or above. The following figures illustrate the difference in support between browsers. Figure 11-1 shows an HTML file styled with CSS style rules in Microsoft Internet Explorer 6.0. This page includes a number of CSS properties, including specifying font characteristics, alignment, margins, and backgrounds.

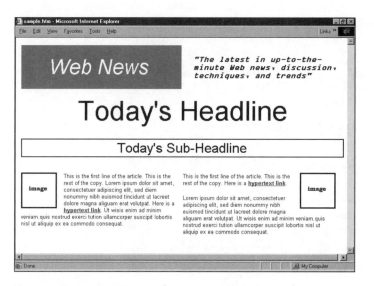

Figure 11-1   A CSS sample page in Internet Explorer 6.0

In contrast, Figure 11-2 illustrates the poor support for CSS in Netscape Navigator 4.7.

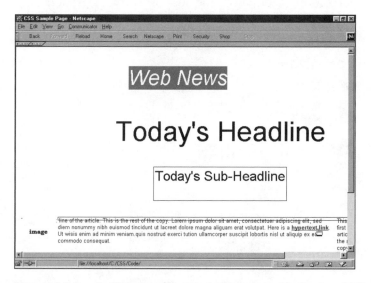

Figure 11-2   A CSS sample page in Netscape Navigator 4.75

Netscape 6 and above offer excellent support for CSS. Figure 11-3 shows the same page in Netscape Navigator 7.

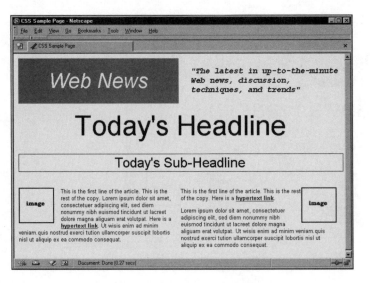

Figure 11-3   A CSS sample page in Netscape Navigator

Figure 11-4 shows the sample page in Opera, the popular browser from Norway. This browser, now in release 6.0, also contains good support for CSS properties.

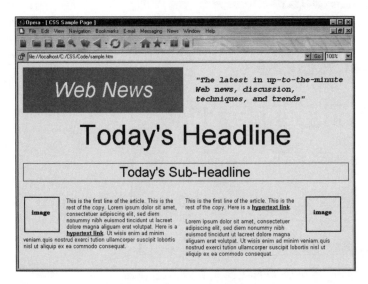

Figure 11-4   A CSS sample page in Opera 6.0

Understanding Style Rules

CSS syntax is designed to be easy to write and read. The main components of CSS syntax are `<style>` tags and their associated style rules. Briefly, CSS syntax works like this: You write style rules that select an HTML element and then declare style characteristics for the element.

The **style rule** expresses the style information for an element in the HTML document, and it is composed of two parts: a selector and a declaration. The **selector** determines the element to which the rule is applied. The **declaration** specifies the exact property values to be applied to the element. Figure 11-5 shows an example of a simple style rule that sets all `<h1>` headings to red.

Figure 11-5   Style rule syntax

As illustrated in Figure 11-5, the declaration contains a property and a value. The **property** is a quality or characteristic, such as color, font size, or margin, followed by a colon (:). The **value** is the precise specification of the property, such as `blue` for color, `12 pt` (point) for font size, or `30 px` (pixels) for margin, followed by a semicolon (;). CSS contains a wide variety of properties, each with a specific list of values.

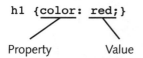

Figure 11-6   Property declaration syntax

The style rule in Figure 11-6 is a basic example of a style rule. As you will see later in this chapter, you can combine selectors and property declarations in a variety of ways.

The style rules you write are contained in a **style sheet**. An external style sheet is a stand-alone document that is shared by a number of Web pages; this is a convenient method of controlling styles throughout a Web site. Alternately, your style sheet can be contained within a single Web page, controlling the styles for that page only. You will read more about how to combine CSS style rules with your Web pages later in this chapter.

 The style sheets in this chapter use a variety of CSS style rules as examples. Although you have not yet learned about these properties in detail, you will see that the CSS property names express common desktop publishing characteristics such as font family, margin, text indent, and so on. The property values sometimes use abbreviations such as `px` for pixel and `pt` for point, percentages such as `200%`, or keywords such as `bold`.

Writing Your First Style Sheet

In this section, you will write a style sheet contained within an HTML document. The goal here is just to give you a taste of using CSS. You will learn more about basic CSS syntax in the following sections.

To write your first style sheet:

1. Start your text editor, and open the file **Ch11CSS01.htm** from the Chapter folder for Chapter 11.

2. Save the file as **Ch11CSS01SOL.htm** in the Chapter folder for Chapter 11. (In other words, add "SOL" to the file name.)

3. Start Internet Explorer, and open the file **Ch11CSS01SOL.htm**. When you open the file in the browser, it looks like Figure 11-7.

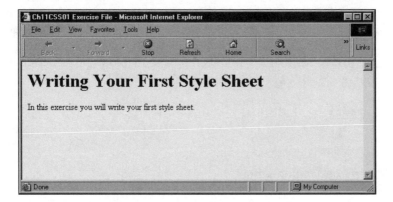

Figure 11-7   The original HTML document

4. In your text editor, examine the HTML code. The complete code for the page follows:

```
<html>
<head>
<title>11CSS01 Exercise File</title>
</head>
<body>
<h1>Writing Your First Style Sheet</h1>
<p>In this exercise you will write your first style sheet.</p>
</body>
</html>
```

5. Now you will add the **<style>** tags that will contain your style rules. Place your cursor after the opening **<head>** tag, and add opening and closing **<style>** tags as shown in the following code fragment. Also add the **type**

attribute as shown, which tells the browser that you are using the CSS style language. (In other words, type the code in boldface.)

```
<head>
<style type="text/css">
</style>
</head>
```

6. Now you will add a style rule for the `<h1>` element between the two `<style>` tags. This style rule uses the CSS `font-family` property to change the font of the page text to Arial. To create the style rule, add the code shown in bold.

```
<head>
<style type="text/css">
body {font-family: arial;}
</style>
</head>
```

7. Save your work, switch to your browser, and reload the page. The Web page's text is now displayed in the Arial font.

8. Return to your text editor.

9. Add the boldface style rule shown in the following code fragment. This style rule changes the color of the `<h1>` text to red.

```
<head>
<style type="text/css">
body {font-family: arial;}
h1 {color: red;}
</style>
</head>
```

10. Save your work, switch to your browser, and reload the page. The Web page's text is now displayed in the Arial font, and the color of the `<h1>` text is red, as shown Figure 11-8.

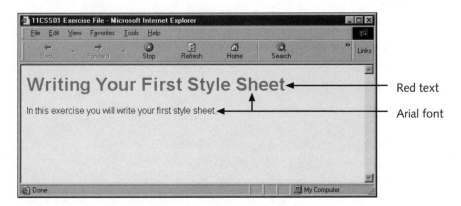

Figure 11-8   The document with CSS style rules

The formatting performed by the CSS style rules you just wrote is not possible using HTML alone.

COMBINING CSS RULES WITH HTML

You can combine CSS rules with HTML code in the following three ways.

- The `style` attribute
- The `<style>` element
- An external style sheet

Each method is discussed in detail in the following sections.

Using the `style` Attribute

The `style` attribute is an HTML attribute that can be used with any HTML element. You can define the style for a single element by using the `style` attribute. You generally use the `style` attribute to override a style that was specified at a higher level in the document, such as when you want a particular heading to be a different color from the rest of the headings on the page. The `style` attribute is also useful for testing styles during development. You will probably use this method of styling an element the least, because it affects only one instance of an element in a document. This is a different method of applying a style than the one you used in the "Writing Your First Style Sheet" section previously in this chapter.

In the following set of steps, you will add a style rule using the `style` attribute. Save your file, and test your work in the browser as you complete each step.

To use the `style` attribute:

1. In your text editor, open the file **Ch11CSS02.htm** from the Chapter folder for Chapter 11 and then save it as **Ch11CSS02SOL.htm** in the Chapter folder for Chapter 11.

2. In Internet Explorer, open the file **Ch11CSS02SOL.htm**. When you open the file, it looks like Figure 11-9.

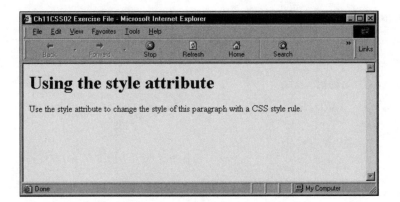

Figure 11-9   The original HTML document

3. Switch to your text editor, and examine the code. The complete code for the page follows:

```
<html>
<head>
<title>11CSS02 Exercise File</title>
</head>
<body>
<h1>Using the style attribute</h1>
<p>Use the style attribute to change the style of this
paragraph with a CSS style rule.</p>
</body>
</html>
```

4. Place your cursor after the **p** in the opening paragraph tag, enter a space, and add the **style** attribute with a style rule, as shown in the following code fragment. (Type only the boldface code.) This style rule uses the **font-weight** property to make the paragraph text bold.

```
</head>
<body>
<p style="font-weight: bold;">Use the style attribute to
change the style of this paragraph with a CSS style
rule.</p>
```

5. Save your work, switch to your browser, and reload the page. The <p> text is now displayed in bold, as shown Figure 11-10.

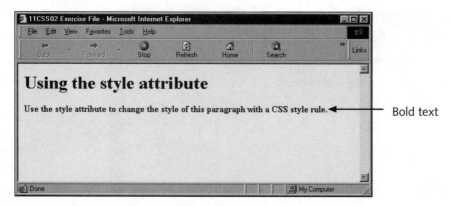

Bold text

Figure 11-10   The document with a CSS style rule

Using the <style> Element

The **<style>** element is always contained in the **<head>** section of the document. Style rules contained in the **<style>** element only affect the document in which they reside. In the "Writing Your First Style Sheet" section earlier in this chapter, you used style rules within a **<style>** element. The following code shows the **<style>** element and style rules from that exercise.

```
<style type="text/css">
body {font-family: arial;}
h1 {color: red;}
</style>
```

Linking to an External Style Sheet

So far, you have learned how to incorporate CSS code in an HTML document in order to alter the way that particular document is rendered by the browser. You can also create a style sheet as a separate file (called an **external style sheet**), and then make the style rules in that file apply to multiple HTML documents. This is a powerful way to use style sheets.

An external style sheet is simply a text document containing style rules. The advantage of the external style sheet is that you can create one external style sheet whose style rules affect all the pages on a Web site. When you want to update a style, you only have to change the style rule once in the external style sheet. External style sheets have a .css extension.

To create an external style sheet, simply create a new text document and type the style rules as explained earlier in this chapter. After you create the external style sheet, you need to link it to the HTML document (or documents) you want the style sheet to affect. In this set of steps, you will link an HTML file to an external style sheet that contains style rules. You can just as easily link multiple files to the same style sheet by using the syntax you will learn here.

To link an external style sheet to an HTML document:

1. In your text editor, open the file **Ch11CSS03.htm** from the Chapter folder for Chapter 11 and then save it as **Ch11CSS03SOL.htm** in the Chapter folder for Chapter 11.

2. In Internet Explorer, open the file **Ch11CSS03SOL.htm.** When you open the file, it looks like Figure 11-11.

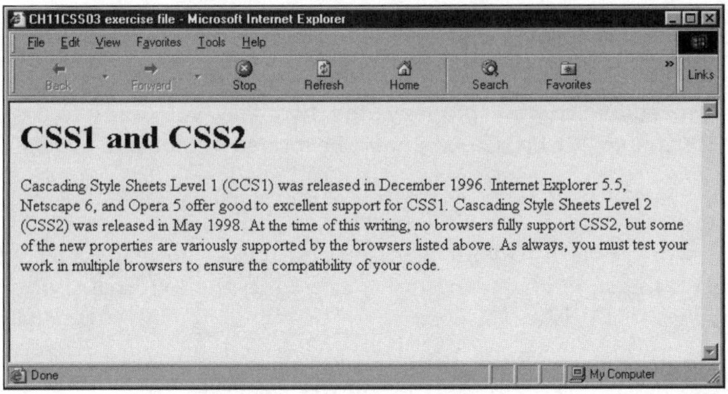

Figure 11-11   The original HTML document

3. Switch to your text editor, and examine the code. Notice that the file contains basic HTML code with no style information. The complete code for the page follows:

```
<html>
<head>
<title> Ch11CSS03 Exercise File </title>
</head>
<body>
<h1>CSS1 and CSS2</h1>
<p>Cascading Style Sheets Level 1 (CCS1) was released in
December 1996. Internet Explorer 5.5, Netscape 6, and Opera
5 offer good to excellent support for CSS1. Cascading Style
Sheets Level 2 (CSS2) was released in May 1998. At the time
of this writing, no browsers fully support CSS2, but some
of the new properties are variously supported by the
browsers listed above. As always, you must test your work
in multiple browsers to ensure the compatibility of your
code.</p>
</body>
</html>
```

4. Place your cursor before the closing **</head>** tag and press **Enter** to add a blank line in the code. (If you are working on a Macintosh, use the Return key whenever you are asked to use the Enter key.)

5. Add the `<link>` tag as shown in the following code. The `href` attribute contains the name of the external style sheet file. The `rel` attribute contains the relationship with the linked file, in this case a style sheet. The `type` attribute states the type of style sheet file.

```
<html>
<head>
<title>A Basic Document</title>
<link href="Ch11CSS03.css" rel="stylesheet"
type="text/css">
</head>
```

For this procedure to work properly, the two files you want to link, Ch11CSS03.htm and Ch11CSS03.css, must be located in the same folder.

6. Save your work, switch to your browser, and reload the page. The Web page now displays the style characteristics specified in the external style sheet, as shown in Figure 11-12.

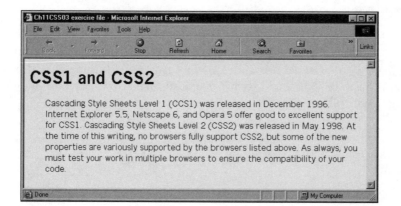

Figure 11-12   The HTML document linked to an external style sheet

7. In your text editor, open the style sheet file **Ch11CSS03.css** and examine the style rules. The complete style sheet code follows. Notice that the rule for the `<h1>` element uses the `font-family` property to set the font to a sans-serif typeface. The rule for the `<p>` element sets font family to sans-serif and uses the margin-left property to set a left margin of 30 pixels for each paragraph.

```
/* This is the style sheet for the Ch11CSS03.htm file */
h1 {font-family: sans-serif;}
p {font-family: sans-serif; margin-left: 30px;}
```

Adding Comments

CSS allows comments within the **<style>** element or in an external style sheet. CSS comments begin with the slash and asterisk characters (/*) and end with the asterisk and slash characters (*/). You can use comments in a variety of ways, as shown in the following code:

```
<style type="text/css">
/* This is the basic style sheet */
h1 {color: grey;} /* The headline color */
h2 {color: red;} /* The sub-head color */
</style>
```

Comments provide documentation for your style rules. Because they are embedded directly in the style sheet, they provide immediate information to anyone who needs to understand how the style rules work. Comments are always useful, and you should consider using them in all of your code, whether as a simple reminder to yourself or as an aid to others with whom you work.

Building a Basic Style Sheet

In the following set of steps, you will build and test a basic internal style sheet. Refer to Figure 11-13 as you progress through the steps to see the results you will achieve.

To build a basic style sheet:

1. In your text editor, open the file **Ch11CSS04.htm** from the Chapter folder for Chapter 11 and then save it as **Ch11CSS04SOL.htm** in the Chapter folder for Chapter 11.

2. In Internet Explorer, open the file **Ch11CSS04SOL.htm**. When you open the file, it looks like Figure 11-13.

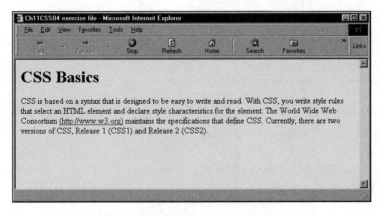

Figure 11-13   The original HTML document

3. Switch to your text editor, and examine the code. Notice that the file contains basic HTML code with no style information. The complete code for the page follows:

```
<html>
<head>
<title>ChCSS04 Exercise File</title>
</head>
<body>
<h1>CSS Basics</h1>
<p>CSS is based on a syntax that is designed to be easy to
write and read. With CSS, you write style rules that select
an HTML element and declare style characteristics for the
element. The World Wide Web Consortium <a
href="http://www.w3.org">(http://www.w3.org)</a> maintains
the specifications that define CSS. Currently, there are
two versions of CSS, Release 1 (CSS1) and Release 2
(CSS2).</p>
</body>
</html>
```

4. In the `<head>` section, add `<style>` tags with a **type** attribute to contain your style rules, as shown in the following code fragment. (Type only the boldface code.) Be sure to leave a few lines of white space between the `<style>` tags to contain the style rules.

```
<head>
<title>ChCSS04 exercise file</title>
<style type="text/css">

</style>
</head>
```

5. Add the boldface style rule for the `<h1>` element shown in the following code fragment. This style rule uses the **text-align** property to center the heading.

```
<head>
<title>ChCSS04 exercise file</title>
<style type="text/css">
h1 {text-align: center;}
</style>
</head>
```

6. Add a comment as shown in the following code:

```
<head>
<title>ChCSS04 exercise file</title>
<style type="text/css">
/* This rule centers the heading */
h1 {text-align: center;}
</style>
</head>
```

7. Save your work, switch to your browser, and reload the page. The `<h1>` element is now centered, as shown in Figure 11-14.

8. Switch back to your text editor. Add the boldface style rule for the `<p>` element, as shown in the following code fragment. This style rule uses the `font-family` property to specify a sans-serif font for the paragraph text.

```
<head>
<title>ChCSS04 exercise file</title>
<style type="text/css">
/* This rule centers the heading */
h1 {text-align: center;}
p {font-family: sans-serif;}
</style>
</head>
```

9. Add the boldface comment shown in the following code:

```
<head>
<title>ChCSS04 exercise file</title>
<style type="text/css">
/* This rule centers the heading */
h1 {text-align: center;}
/* This rule sets the paragraph font */
p {font-family: sans-serif;}
</style>
</head>
```

10. Save your work, switch to your browser, and reload the page. Figure 11-14 shows the finished Web page. Notice that the `<p>` element is now displayed in a sans-serif typeface.

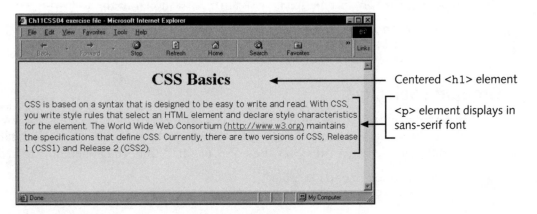

Figure 11-14   The HTML document styled with CSS

11

BASIC SELECTION TECHNIQUES

The power of CSS comes from the different methods of selecting elements, which allow an HTML author to apply style rules in a variety of ways. In this section, you will review style rule syntax and learn about the following basic selection techniques:

- Using type selectors
- Grouping selectors
- Combining declarations
- Using descendant selectors

Using Type Selectors

As you learned earlier in this chapter, the selector determines the element to which a style declaration is applied. To review, examine the syntax of the style rule shown in Figure 11-15. This rule selects the `<h1>` element in the document and sets the text color to red.

```
h1 {color: red;}
```

Selector   Declaration

Figure 11-15   Style rule syntax

This rule uses a **type selector**, a selector that applies the rule to every instance of the element in the document. This is the simplest type of selector, and many style sheets are composed primarily of type selector style rules, as shown in the following code:

```
body {color: gray;}
h2 {color: red;}
p {font-size: 10pt;}
```

Grouping Selectors

To make your style rules more concise, you can group type selectors for which the same rules apply. For example, the following style rules set the same declaration for two different elements—they set the color of `<h1>` and `<h2>` elements to red:

```
h1 {color: red;}
h2 {color: red;}
```

These two style rules can be expressed more simply by separating the selectors with commas:

```
h1, h2 {color: red;}
```

Combining Declarations

In many instances, you will want to state multiple property declarations for the same selector. The following style rules set the <p> element to 12-point blue text:

```
p {color: blue;}
p {font-size: 12pt;}
```

These two style rules can be expressed more simply by combining the declarations into one rule. The declarations are separated by semicolons:

```
p {color: blue; font-size: 12pt;}
```

Using Descendant Selectors

A **descendant selector** (sometimes known as a **contextual selector**) is based on the hierarchical structure of the elements in the document tree. This selector lets you select elements that are the descendants of other elements. For example, the following rule selects only <b> elements that are contained within <p> elements. All other <b> elements in the document will not be affected.

```
p b {color: blue;}
```

Notice that the selector contains multiple elements (the p and the b), separated only by white space. You can use more than two elements if you prefer to choose more specific selection characteristics. For example, the following rule selects <b> elements within <li> elements within <ul> elements only:

```
ul li b {color: blue;}
```

11

ADVANCED SELECTION TECHNIQUES

CSS's more advanced selection techniques allow a wider range of expression, making it possible to create custom-named style rules and offering more ways to zero in on the exact element you want to affect. In this section, you will learn about the following advanced selection techniques:

- Using the **class** selector
- Working with the <div> element
- Working with the <span> element

Using the class Selector

The **class selector** lets you write a style rule, assign it a name, and then apply that name to any elements you choose. To apply the style rule to an element, you add the **class** attribute to the element and set it to the name you have specified.

Rules with `class` selectors look very much like the rules you have been creating in this chapter, except they have a class name instead of an HTML element as the selector. Figure 11-16 shows a style rule with a `class` selector. Notice how the style rules (in brackets) appear on the same line, separated by a single space.

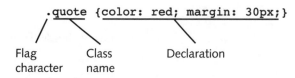

```
.quote {color: red; margin: 30px;}
```

Flag character   Class name   Declaration

Figure 11-16   Class syntax

The period at the beginning of the `class` attribute shown in Figure 11-16 is a special CSS character called a **flag character**. The period flag character indicates that what follows is a class name.

After you create a style rule containing a `class` selector, you add it to the document by using the `class` attribute, as shown in the following code fragment:

```
<p class="quote">This text will appear red with a 30 pixel
margin.</p>
```

The `class` attribute lets you select elements with greater precision than using basic selectors. For example, read the following style rule:

```
p {font-size: 10pt;}
```

This rule sets all `<p>` elements in the document to a font size of 10 points. Now suppose that you want one `<p>` element in your document in 10-point font like the others, but you also want the element to be boldface. To accomplish this, you need a way to specifically select that one paragraph. The most efficient way to do this is to use a `class` selector. You start by creating the style rule containing a `class` selector. The following style rule specifies the style for the class named `special`.

```
.special {font-size: 10pt; font-weight: bold;}
```

Note that you can name a `class` selector anything you choose. In this instance, the class name `special` denotes a special paragraph in the document. After you create the style rule, you need to apply the rule to the `<p>` element in the document by using the `class` attribute. The highlighted code in the following code fragment accomplishes this task:

```
<p class="special">This is the first paragraph of the
document. It has a different style based on the "special"
CLASS selector.</p>

<p>This is the second paragraph of text in the document. It
 is a standard paragraph without a CLASS attribute.</p>
```

Figure 11-17 shows the result of the style rule.

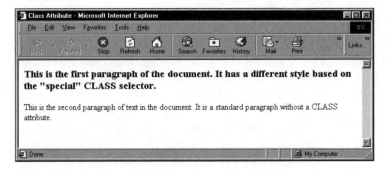

Figure 11-17   Styling with a `class` attribute

Making `class` Selectors More Specific

Using the `class` attribute is a powerful selection technique, because it allows you to write style rules with names that are meaningful to your organization or information type. The more specific your class names become, the greater control you need over the way they are applied. In the preceding example, you saw a style rule named `special` that was designed to be applied only to a particular `<p>` element. However, the `special` style could actually be applied to any element in the document, not just a `<p>` element. To solve this problem, you can restrict the use of the `class` attribute to a single element type.

For example, your organization might use a special style for a procedure heading. Suppose the style is based on an `<h1>` element, with a sans-serif font and left margin of 20 pixels. In conversation, everyone in your organization refers to this style "procedure." It would make sense, then, to use this same style name in your style sheet, as shown in the following style rule:

```
.procedure {font-family: sans-serif; margin-left: 20px;}
```

To use these rules in the document, you would apply the `class` attribute as shown in the following code fragment:

```
<h1 class="procedure">Procedure Heading</h1>
```

But, what happens if someone on your staff neglects to apply the classes properly? For the style rule to work, it can only be applied to an `<h1>` element. To restrict the use of the class to `<h1>` elements, you need to include a prefix indicating the element to which you want it applied:

```
h1.procedure {font-family: sans-serif; margin-left: 20px;}
```

This style rule restricts the use of the `procedure` style to `<h1>`.

11

Using the `<div>` and `<span>` Elements

The `<div>` (division) and `<span>` (span of words) elements in HTML are designed to be used with the CSS `class` selector. They let you specify logical divisions within a document that have their own class name and style properties. The difference between `<div>` and `<span>` is their element display type. `<div>` is a block-level element; `<span>` is its inline equivalent. Used with the `class` attribute, `<div>` and `<span>` let you effectively create your own element names for your HTML documents.

 A block-level element is an element that has a carriage return before and after, like `<p>`, `<h1>`, or `<blockquote>`. An inline element resides within a line of text, like a `<b>` or `<i>` element.

Working with `<div>`

You can use `<div>` with the `class` attribute to create customized block-level elements. Like other block-level elements, `<div>` contains a leading and trailing line break. However, unlike other block-level elements, `<div>` contains no additional white space around the element. You can set the margin or padding to any value that you wish.

To create a customized division, add a `div` prefix in front of the period flag character in the style rule. The following example selects a division with a class named `introduction` :

```
div.introduction {font-size: 14pt; margin: 24pt;
text-indent: 28pt;}
```

To apply this rule, use the `<div>` element in the document with a `class` attribute that specifies the class name. In the following example, the code defines the `<div>` element as the class named `introduction`.

```
<div class="introduction">This is the introduction to the
document.</div>
```

Working with `<span>`

The `<span>` element lets you specify inline elements within a document that have their own name and style properties. Inline elements reside within a line of text, like the `<b>` or `<em>` element. You can use `<span>` with the class to create customized inline elements.

To create a customized span, add a `span` prefix in front of the period flag character in the style rule. The following example selects a span with a class named `logo.`

```
span.logo {color: white; background-color: black;}
```

To apply this rule, use the `<span>` element in the document with a `class` attribute that specifies the class name. In the following example, the code defines the `<span>` element as the class named `logo`.

```
<p>Welcome to the <span class="logo">Wonder Software</span>
Web site.</p>
```

Figure 11-18 shows the result of the style rule.

Welcome to the Wonder Software Web site.

Figure 11-18   Using the `<span>` element

USING CSS SELECTION TECHNIQUES

In the following set of steps, you will build a style sheet that uses the basic selection techniques described in this chapter.

To build the style sheet:

1. In your text editor, open the file **Ch11CSS05.htm** from the Chapter folder for Chapter 11 and then save it as **Ch11CSS05SOL.htm** in the same folder.

2. In Internet Explorer, open the file **Ch11CSS05SOL.htm**. When you open the file, it looks like Figure 11-19.

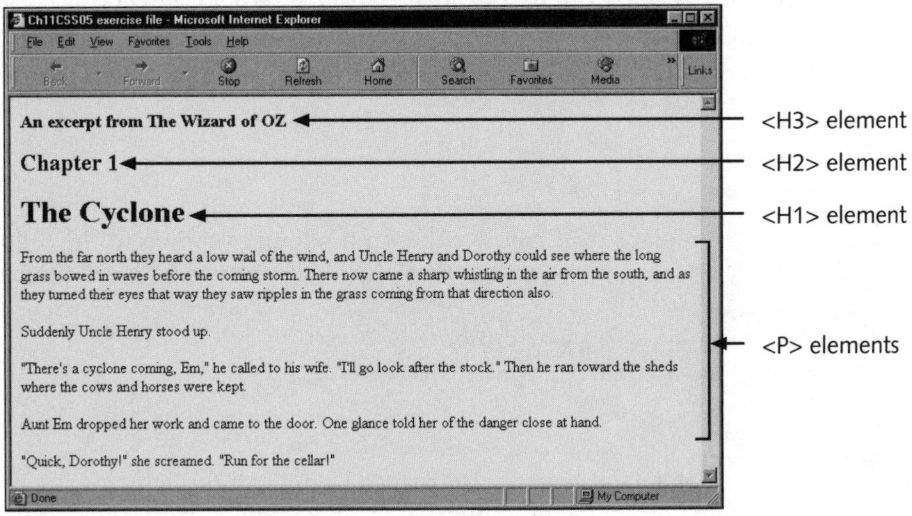

Figure 11-19   The original HTML document

3. Switch to your text editor. Notice that the file contains basic HTML code with no style information. The complete code for the page follows:

```
<html>
<head>
<title> Ch11CSS05 Exercise File </title>
</head>
<body >
<h3>An excerpt from The Wizard of OZ</h3>
<h2>Chapter 1</h2>
<h1>The Cyclone</h1>
<p>From the far north they heard a low wail of the wind,
and Uncle Henry and Dorothy could see where the long grass
bowed in waves before the coming storm. There now came a
sharp whistling in the air from the south, and as they
turned their eyes that way they saw ripples in the grass
coming from that direction also.</p>
<p>Suddenly Uncle Henry stood up.</p>
<p"There's a cyclone coming, Em," he called to his wife.
"I'll go look after the stock."  Then he ran toward the
sheds where the cows and horses were kept.</p>
<p>Aunt Em dropped her work and came to the door. One
glance told her of the danger close at hand.</p>
<p>"Quick, Dorothy!" she screamed. "Run for the
cellar!"</p>
</body>
</html>
```

4. In the `<head>` section, add the boldface `<style>` element shown in the following code fragment. Leave a few lines of white space between the `<style>` tags to contain the style rules, which you will add in a later step.

```
<head>
<title> Ch11CSS05 Exercise File </title>
<style type="text/css">

</style>
</head>
```

5. Add the boldface style rule for the `<h3>` element shown in the following code fragment. The requirements for this element are right-aligned gray text.

```
<head>
<style type="text/css">
h3 {text-align: right; color: gray;}
</style>
</head>
```

6. Add the boldface style rules for the `<h1>` and `<h2>` elements shown in the following code fragment. Note that these elements share some common

property values. Both have a left margin of 20 pixels (abbreviated as **px**) and a sans-serif font style. Because they share these properties, the two elements are grouped.

```
<head>
<style type="text/css">
h3 {text-align: right; color: gray;}
h1, h2 {margin-left: 20px; font-family: sans-serif;}
</style>
</head>
```

7. Write the boldface style rule for the <p> elements shown in the following code fragment. This style rule specifies a 20-pixel left margin (to ensure that the elements line up with the other elements on the page), a sans-serif font style, and a 14-point font size.

```
<head>
<style type="text/css">
h3 {text-align: right; color: gray;}
h1, h2 {margin-left: 20px; font-family: sans-serif;}
p {margin-left: 20px; font-family: serif; font-size: 14pt;}
</style>
</head>
```

8. Write the boldface style rule for a class named **firstparagraph** shown in the following code fragment. Note that this style rule sets the font weight to **bold**.

```
<head>
<style type="text/css">
h3 {text-align: right; color: gray;}
h1, h2 {margin-left: 20px; font-family: sans-serif;}
p {margin-left: 20px; font-family: serif; font-size: 14pt;}
.firstparagraph {font-weight: bold;}
</style>
</head>
```

11

9. Add the boldface **class** attribute shown in the following code fragment to apply the **firstparagraph** class to the first <p> element in the document:

```
<p class="firstparagraph">From the far north they heard a
low wail of the wind, and Uncle Henry and Dorothy could see
where the long grass bowed in waves before the coming
storm. There now came a sharp whistling in the air from the
south, and as they turned their eyes that way they saw
ripples in the grass coming from that direction also.</p>
```

10. Save your work, switch to your browser, and reload the page. Figure 11-20 shows the finished document with the style properties.

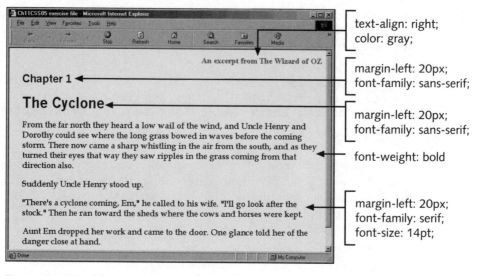

text-align: right;
color: gray;

margin-left: 20px;
font-family: sans-serif;

margin-left: 20px;
font-family: sans-serif;

font-weight: bold

margin-left: 20px;
font-family: serif;
font-size: 14pt;

Figure 11-20   The document styled with CSS rules

CHAPTER SUMMARY

❑ CSS is a style language that lets you gain visual control over the display of your Web content.

❑ CSS was poorly supported by browsers at first, but now it is becoming widely supported.

❑ A style sheet is a collection of style rules.

❑ A style rule defines style characteristics for an HTML element. It consists of a selector and a declaration. The declaration consists of a property and a value.

❑ You can combine CSS style rules with your HTML documents. To affect a single element in a document, use the `style` attribute. To affect the elements in a single document, use the `<style>` element to contain your style rules. To affect one or more HTML documents, use a separate CSS style sheet file to contain your style rules and link the file to your HTML document (or documents).

❑ The `class` selector lets you create naming conventions for styles that are meaningful to your organization or information type.

REVIEW QUESTIONS

1. What are the two parts of a style rule?

   a. the style and the rule

   b. the selector and the rule

   c. the element and the rule

   d. the selector and the declaration

2. What are the three ways to combine CSS rules with your HTML code?

   a. `style` attribute, internal style sheet, external style sheet

   b. in the `<head>` section, in the `<body>` section, in an attribute

   c. the `<type>` element, the `<link>` element, the `style` attribute

   d. the `style` attribute, the `<link>` element, the `<head>` section

3. What is the only drawback to working with CSS?

   a. The syntax of the rules is hard to understand.

   b. Older browsers do not support CSS.

   c. Newer browsers do not support CSS.

   d. You need special software to write CSS rules.

4. List two benefits of stating a style by using the `style` attribute.

   a. the ability to override a style and to test a style locally

   b. the ability to test a style and to cascade a style

   c. the ability to test a style and to force a style to affect an entire page

   d. the ability to override a style and to reset a style

5. What function does the attribute `type="text/css"` perform?

   a. It tells the browser that the style sheet language is CSS.

   b. It tells the browser which typeface to use.

   c. It sets the text for the `<type>` element.

   d. It sets the language of the document.

6. What element do you use to connect your HTML page to an external style sheet?

   a. the `<style>` element

   b. the `<head>` element

   c. the `<type>` element

   d. the `<link>` element

11

7. What type of file is an external style sheet?

   a. rules file

   b. html file

   c. text file

   d. programming file

8. Where does the `<style>` element reside in an HTML document?

   a. between the `<head>` tag pairs

   b. between the `<body>` tag pairs

   c. between the `<title>` tag pairs

   d. anywhere in the document

9. Which of the following basic style rules selects `<p>` elements and sets the color property to `red`?

   a. `paragraph {color: red;}`

   b. `p {color=red}`

   c. `p {color: red;}`

   d. `p {color; red:}`

10. Suppose you are asked to add the `<b>` element as an additional selector to the rule you chose as the correct answer in question 9. Which of the following is correct?

    a. `paragraph, b {color: red;}`

    b. `p, b {color=red}`

    c. `p, b {color: red;}`

    d. `p + b {color; red:}`

11. Suppose you are asked add a `font-size` property to the rule you chose as the correct answer in question 9. Suppose also that you were asked to set the size to `14 points`. Which of the following is correct?

    a. `paragraph, b {color: red; 14pt;}`

    b. `p, b {color: red; font-size: 14pt;}`

    c. `p, b {color=red, font=14pt}`

    d. `p + b {color; red: font-size: 14pt;}`

12. Which of the following is a style rule that selects `<ul>` elements only when they appear within `<p>` elements and sets the color property to `red`?

    a. `p, ul {color: red;}`

    b. `p ul {color: red;}`

    c. `p + ul {color: red;}`

    d. `p + ul {color; red:}`

13. Which of the following is a style rule for a **class** selector named **note** that sets the **font-weight** property to **bold**?

    a. `note {font-weight: bold;}`

    b. `class=note {font-weight: bold;}`

    c. `note {font-weight=bold;}`

    d. `.note {font-weight: bold;}`

14. Which of the following is a rule that has a **class** selector named **quote**, sets the font style to **italic**, and restricts the class so it can only be used with a `<p>` element?

    a. `quote {italic;}`

    b. `p.quote {font-style: italic;}`

    c. `quote.p {font-style=italic;}`

    d. `p.quote {font-style=italic;}`

15. Which of the following is a style rule for a `<div>` element that has a class name of **warning**, sets the color to **red,** and sets the **font-weight** property to **bold**?

    a. `div {italic;}`

    b. `div.warning {red, bold}`

    c. `div.warning {color: red; font-weight: bold;}`

    d. `div {color: red; font-weight: bold;}`

11

HANDS-ON EXERCISES

Exercise 11-1

In this exercise, you will have a chance to test a few simple style rules on a standard HTML document and view the results in your browser.

1. Start your text editor, and open the file **Ch11CSS01EX.htm** from the Exercises folder for Chapter 11 and save it as **Ch11CSS01EXSOL.htm** in the same folder.

2. Add a `<style>` element to the `<style>` section as shown in the following code.

```
<head>
<title>Ch11CSS01EX Exercise File</title>
<style type="text/css">

</style>
</head>
```

3. Add a style rule that uses **body** as a selector and sets the **color** property to **green**, as shown in the following code:

```
<style type="text/css">
body {color: green;}
</style>
```

4. Save your work.

5. Start your browser and open the file **Ch11CSS01EXSOL.htm**. All of the document text should now be green.

6. Switch to your text editor. Now add a style rule that sets **<h1>** elements to display in black:

```
<style type="text/css">
body {color: green;}
h1 {color: black;}
</style>
```

7. Save your work, switch to your browser, and reload the page to view the results.

8. Switch to your text editor. Add a style rule that sets a margin for **<p>** elements to **30 pixels**:

```
<style type="text/css">
body {color: green;}
h1 {color: black;}
p {margin: 30px;}
</style>
```

9. Save your work, switch to your browser, and reload the page to view the results.

Exercise 11-2

In this exercise, you will have a chance to test a few basic selection techniques on a standard HTML document and view the results in your browser. Save and view the file in your browser after completing each step.

1. Start your text editor, and open the file **Ch11CSS02EX.htm** in the Exercises folder for Chapter 11 and save it as **Ch11CSS02EXSOL.htm** in the Exercises folder for Chapter 11.

2. Add a **<style>** element to the **<head>** section as shown in the following code.

```
<head>
<title>Ch11CSS02EX Exercise File</title>
<style type="text/css">

</style>
</head>
```

3. Write a style rule that uses **body** as a selector and sets the **font-family** property to sans-serif.

4. Write a single style rule for both the `<h2>` and `<h3>` elements. Set the `color` property to `red` and the `margin` property to `20px`.

5. Write a style rule that selects `<p>` elements and sets the margin property to `20px.`

6. Save your work.

7. Start your browser, and open the file **Ch11CSS02EXSOL.htm** to view the result.

Exercise 11-3

In this exercise, you will have a chance to test a few advanced selection techniques on a standard HTML document and view the results in your browser.

1. Start your text editor, and open the file **Ch11CSS03EX.htm** in the Exercises folder for Chapter 11 and save it as **Ch11CSS03EXSOL.htm** in the Exercises folder for Chapter 11.

2. Add a `<style>` element to the `<head>` section.

3. Write a rule for a `class` selector named `heading`. Set the `color` property to `red` and the `font-size` property to `30pt`. Apply the heading class to an `<h2>` element in the document.

4. Write a rule for a `class` selector named `emphasis`. Set the `background-color` property to `yellow`. In the document, add a `<span>` element around the word `Camelot` that is contained in the `<h2>` element. Apply the `emphasis` class to the `<span>` element.

5. Start your browser, and open the file **Ch11CSS03EXSOL.htm** to view the result.

11

Exercise 11-4

In this exercise, you will have a chance to test a few basic selection techniques on a standard HTML document and view the results in your browser.

1. Start your text editor, and open the file **Ch11CSS04EX.htm** from the Exercises folder for Chapter 11 and save it as **Ch11CSS04EXSOL.htm** in the Exercises folder for Chapter 11.

2. Write a style rule that selects the `<h2>` element. Use the `text-align` property and set the value to `center`.

3. Write a style rule for the `<h3>` element. Set the `font-style` property to `italic` and the `text-align` property to `center`.

4. Write a style rule that selects `<p>` elements and sets the `font-family` property to `sans-serif`.

5. Save your work.

6. Start your browser, and open the file **Ch11CSS04EXSOL.htm** to view the result.

Exercise 11-5

In this exercise, you will have a chance to test a few basic selection techniques on a standard HTML document and view the results in your browser.

1. Start your text editor, and open the file **Ch11CSS05EX.htm** from the Exercises folder for Chapter 11 and save it as **Ch11CSS05EXSOL.htm** in the Exercises folder for Chapter 11.

2. Write a style rule that uses `body` as a selector and sets the `color` property to `blue`.

3. Write a style rule for the `<h2>` element. Set the `color` property to `white` and the `background-color` property to `blue`.

4. Continue working in the style rule for the `<h2>` element. Set the `font-family` property to `sans-serif` and the `padding` property to `20 px`.

5. Write a style rule that selects the `<h3>` element and sets the `font-family` property to `sans-serif`.

6. Write a style rule that selects the `<p>` elements and sets the `font-family` property to `sans-serif`.

7. Save your work.

8. Start your browser, and open the file **Ch11CSS05EXSOL.htm** to view the result.

WEB DESIGN PROJECTS

Project 11-1

View and copy the source code from a Web page of your choice into your HTML editor. Examine the code for existing display elements (such as `<FONT>`) and attributes (such as `BGCOLOR, ALIGN`). Write a paper describing how CSS properties could replace the existing display information, detailing the benefits of CSS. Refer to the CSS 2 Specification at www.w3.org/TR/REC-CSS2/ for a list of CSS properties. Include the HTML code from the Web page with your report. Save all files in the Projects folder for Chapter 11.

Project 11-2

Find an article from a magazine of your choice. Describe the style characteristics of the page. Does it use multiple heading styles? A different first paragraph style? A special footer style? Devise class names for the different elements. Indicate the class names on the magazine page. Save all files in the Projects folder for Chapter 11.

Project 11-3

Find a mainstream Web site and discuss how you would standardize the look and feel of the site by adding CSS style rules. Think about the different levels of information and how you would use CSS selectors to effectively select the different elements within the pages of the site. Save all files in the Projects folder for Chapter 11.

11

12

CASCADING STYLE SHEETS: PART II

In this chapter you will:

♦ Learn about CSS measurement values
♦ Format text with the CSS font properties
♦ Learn to use the CSS margin, padding, and border properties
♦ Add color with the CSS color properties

This chapter provides an introduction to the most commonly used CSS properties. First you will learn about the CSS measurement values, which are used with a variety of CSS properties. You will learn about the CSS font properties and how to control typography on your Web pages. You will also learn about the CSS box model and how to use the margin, padding, and border properties. Finally you will learn to use the CSS color properties to add color to your Web content.

UNDERSTANDING CSS MEASUREMENT UNITS

CSS offers a variety of measurement units, including **absolute units** (such as points), **relative units** (such as pixels), and **percentages** of the base font. The measurement values you choose depend on the destination medium for your content. For example, if you are designing a style sheet for printed media, you can use absolute units of measurement such as points or centimeters. When you are designing a style sheet for a Web page, you can use relative measurement values that adapt to the user's display type, such as ems or pixels. In this section, you will learn about the following CSS measurement units. These units are detailed in Table 12-1.

- Absolute units
- Relative units
- Percentage

Table 12-1   CSS measurement units

Unit	Unit Abbreviation	Description
Absolute Units		
Centimeter	cm	Standard metric centimeter
Inch	in	Standard U.S. inch
Millimeter	mm	Standard metric millimeter
Pica	pc	Standard publishing unit equal to 12 points
Point	pt	Standard publishing unit, with 72 points in an inch
Relative Units		
Em	em	The width of the capital M in the current font, usually the same as the font size
Ex	ex	The height of the letter x in the current font
Pixel	px	The size of a pixel on the current monitor
Percentage	For example: 150%	Sets a font size relative to the base font size. 150% equals one-and-one-half the base font size.

Absolute Units

CSS lets you use absolute measurement values that specify a fixed value. The measurement values require a number followed by one of the unit abbreviations listed in Table 12-1. The numeric value can be a positive value, negative value, or a fractional value. For example, the following rule sets margins to 1.25 inches:

```
p {margin: 1.25in;}
```

You generally want to avoid using absolute units for Web pages because they cannot be scaled to the individual user's display type. They are more suited for situations when you know the exact measurements of the destination medium. For example, if you know a document will be printed on 8.5 $\times$ 11-inch paper, you can plan your style rules accordingly because you know the physical dimensions of the finished document. Thus, absolute units are better suited to print destinations than Web destinations. Although the point (pt) is the standard unit of measurement for type sizes, it is not the best measurement value for the Web. This is because computer displays vary widely in size, lending themselves better to relative units of measurement that can adapt to different monitor sizes and screen resolutions.

Relative Units

The relative units are designed to let you build scalable Web pages that adapt to different display types and sizes. The designers of CSS2, Hakon Lie and Bert Bos, recommend that you always use relative sizes (specifically, the em value) to set font sizes on your Web pages. This practice ensures that your type sizes will display properly relative to each other or to the default font size set for the browser.

The em Unit

The **em** is a printing measurement, traditionally equal to the horizontal length of the capital letter M in any given font size. In CSS, it can be used for both horizontal and vertical measurement. In addition to stating font sizes, em is useful for padding and margins as well.

The size of the em in CSS is equivalent to the font size of the element. For example, if the default paragraph font size is 12 point, then one em equals 12 points. In that situation, a text size of 2 em creates 24-point text—two times the default size. This is useful because it means that measurements stated in em are always relative to their environment. For example, suppose that you want to include a heading on your page that is larger than the text in the other paragraphs. If you set the `<H1>` element to 24 points, the heading appears that size in all browsers. This means that if a user sets her default font size to 24 points, the headings will be the same size as the text. However, if you use the relative em unit, the heading size will adjust relative to the size of the default text. The following rule sets heading divisions to twice the size of the default text.

```
div.heading {font-size: 2 em;}
```

The ex Unit

The **ex** unit is equal to the height of the small letter x in any given font. As shown in Figure 12-1, the height of the small letter x varies widely from one typeface to another.

12

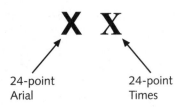

Figure 12-1   Differences in height of the ex unit

Ex is a less reliable unit of measurement than em because the size of the letter x changes in height from one font family to another, and the browser cannot always calculate the difference correctly. Most browsers simply set the ex value to one-half the value of the font's em size.

The px Unit

Pixels are the basic picture element of a computer display. The size of the pixel is determined by the display resolution. **Resolution** is the measure of how many pixels fit on a screen. The standard display resolutions are 640 × 480, 800 × 600, and 1024 × 768. As the resolutions grow in value, the individual pixel size gets smaller, making the pixel relative to the individual display settings. Pixel measurements work well for computer displays, but they are not so well-suited to other media, such as printing, because some printers cannot accurately determine the size of the pixel.

Percentages

Percentage values are always relative to another value. For example, the following rule sets the font size for the **<body>** element to one-and-one-half of the browser default:

```
body {font-size: 150%;}
```

Child elements inherit the percentage values of their parents. For example, the **<b>** text in the following example will be 125% larger than the **<p>** that contains it:

```
p {font-size: 12pt;}
p b {font-size: 125%;}
```

The first rule establishes the font size for the **<p>** element. The second rule selects any **<b>** elements within **<p>** elements. Because the **<p>** element has the font size set to 12 points, the **<b>** text will display at 15 points, or 125% larger than its parent.

Working with the CSS Measurement Units

In this exercise, you will experiment with some of the CSS measurement units.

To experiment with the measurement values:

    1. Start your text editor, and open the file named **Ch12CSS01.htm** from the Chapter folder for Chapter 12.

2. Save the file as **Ch12CSS01SOL.htm** in the Chapter folder for Chapter 12. (In other words, add "SOL" to the file name.)

3. In your text editor examine the HTML code. The complete code for the page follows:

```
<html>
<head>
<title>Ch12CSS01 Exercise File</title>
</head>
<body>
</body>
</html>
```

4. In the **<body>** section, add a **<p>** element with text as shown in the following code:

```
<p>The size of this text is 24 point.</p>
```

5. In the opening **<p>** tag, add the **style** attribute. Write a style rule that uses the **font-size** property to set the size of the text to 24 point, as shown in the following code.

```
<p style="font-size:24pt">The size of this text is 24
point.</p>
```

6. Save the file.

7. Start Internet Explorer and open the file named **Ch12CSS01SOL.htm**. When you open the file in the browser, it looks like Figure 12-2.

12

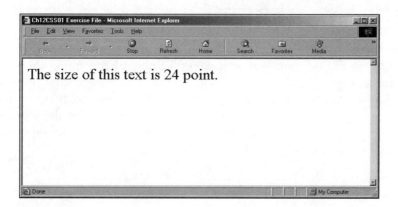

Figure 12-2   A paragraph with 24-point font size

8. In your text editor, add two more paragraphs, each with their own text.

```
<p>The size of this text is 2 em.</p>
<p>The size of this text is 24 pixels.</p>
```

9. Using a `style` attribute, set the font size of the first new paragraph to 2 em. Set the size of the second new paragraph to 24 pixels, as shown in the bold-face code in the following code fragment.

```
<p style="font-size:2em">The size of this text is 2 em.
</p>
<p style="font-size:24px">The size of this text is 24
pixels.</p>
```

10. Save your work, switch to your browser, and reload the page. The Web page now looks like Figure 12-3.

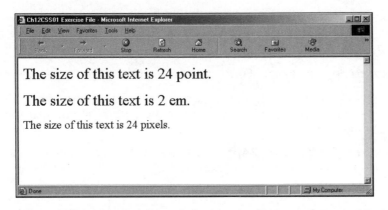

Figure 12-3   Paragraphs with font sizes of 24 point, 2 em, 24 pixels

USING THE CSS FONT PROPERTIES

Type is the basic building block of any Web page. You can use typography to enhance the display of information on your Web site, communicate relative importance of items, and guide the reader's eye. HTML offers only basic type controls, forcing many designers to use graphics to add interesting text effects to a Web page, with the unfortunate side-effect of increasing user download times. The CSS font properties allow you to control the appearance of your text. These properties describe how the letter forms look. You will learn about the following properties:

- font-family
- font-size
- line-height

When you are working with the font properties, keep in mind that the user's default settings can affect the display of your Web pages. If you do not specify font properties for an element, the element text will display in the user's default font. If the user sets a smaller default font size, the font sizes you specify may be affected. As you build your pages remember to test your work for user variations.

Specifying Font Families

The `font-family` property lets you state a generic font family name, such as sans-serif, or a specific font family name like Helvetica. You can also string together a list of substitute font families, separated by commas, supplying a selection of fonts that the browser can attempt to use instead of the default font

Using Generic Font Families

You can use the following generic names for font families:

- **Serif** fonts are the traditional letter form, with strokes (or serifs) that finish off the top and bottom of the letter. The most common serif font is Times.

- **Sans-serif** fonts have no serifs. They are block letters. The most common sans-serif fonts are Helvetica and Arial.

- **Monospace** fonts are fixed-width fonts. Every letter has the same horizontal width. Monospace is commonly used to mimic typewritten text, or for programming code. The style rules in this book are printed in a monospace font.

- **Cursive** fonts are designed to resemble handwriting. This is a less well-supported font family.

- **Fantasy** fonts are primarily decorative. Like cursive, fantasy is not a well-supported font family.

The ability to use generic names ensures greater portability across browsers and operating systems, because it does not rely on a specific font being installed on the user's computer. When you specify a generic font, the browser then substitutes the closest default version of that font on the user's machine.

The following rule sets `<p>` elements to the default sans-serif font:

```
p {font-family: sans-serif;}
```

Of course, if you do not specify any font family, the browser displays the default font, usually some version of Times.

Using Specific Font Families

The `font-family` property lets you declare a specific font family, such as Futura or Garamond. The user must have the font installed on his computer; otherwise, the browser uses the default font.

To make your pages display more consistently, think in terms of font families, such as serif and sans-serif typefaces, rather than specific styles. Because of the variable nature of fonts installed on different computers, you can never be sure that the user will see the exact font you have specified. You can, however, use font substitution to specify a variety of fonts within a font family, such as Arial or Helvetica, which are both common sans-serif fonts. Figure 12-4 shows the same paragraph in different fonts at the default browser size.

12

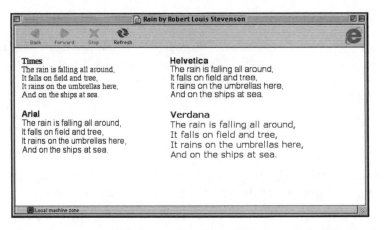

Figure 12-4   Default browser sizes in the common fonts

Table 12-2 lists the most common fonts on the PC, UNIX, and Macintosh systems.

Table 12-2   Common installed fonts

Common PC Fonts	Common UNIX Fonts	Common Macintosh Fonts
Arial	Helvetica	Helvetica
Courier New	Courier	Courier
Times New Roman	Times	Times
Verdana		Verdana
		Palatino
		Arial

This table shows that Times (Times Roman on the PC) is available on all three operating systems. It is the default browser font. Courier is the default monospace font. Arial or Helvetica are the default sans-serif fonts. Internet Explorer 4.0 and up comes with Arial and Verdana, so you can assume that many users, on both Macintoshes and PCs, have them installed. Some Macintosh users only have Helvetica, so it is a good idea to specify it as an alternate choice when you are using sans-serif fonts. (You will learn how to specify an alternate, or substitute, font in the next section.)

The following rule specifies Arial as the font family for the **<p>** element:

```
p {font-family: arial;}
```

Specifying Font Substitution

You can specify a list of **alternate fonts**, which are fonts the browser will attempt to use in place of the default font. When specifying alternate fonts, use commas as a separator. The browser will attempt to load each successive alternate font, one after the other.

If no fonts match, the browser uses its default font. The following code tells the browser to use Arial; if Arial is not present, it tells the browser to use Helvetica.

```
p {font-family: arial, helvetica;}
```

This rule uses a common font substitution string that produces a sans-serif font on both PCs that have Arial installed and Macintosh computers that have Helvetica installed. To further ensure the portability of this rule, you can add a generic font family name to the list as shown in the following rule:

```
p {font-family: arial, helvetica, sans-serif;}
```

This rule ensures that the <p> element will be displayed in some type of sans-serif font, even if it is not Arial or Helvetica.

Specifying Font Size

The font-size property gives you control over the specific sizing of your type. You can choose from length units, such as em or px, or a percentage value that is based on the parent element's font size.

The following rule sets the <blockquote> element to 18-point Arial:

```
blockquote {font-family: arial; font-size: 18pt;}
```

To specify a default size for a document, use body as the selector. This rule sets the text to 14-point Arial:

```
body {font-family: arial; font-size: 14pt;}
```

12

Specifying Line Height

CSS allows you to specify either a length or percentage value for the line height, which is more commonly called **leading**, the white space between lines of text. The percentage is based on the font size. Setting the value to 150% with a 12-point font size will result in a line height of 18 points. The following rule sets the line height to 150%:

```
p {line-height: 150%;}
```

Figure 12-5 shows the default line height and various adjustments in line height. A gray background color for the Web page and white background color for the text highlight the line box around each line. Notice that the line height is evenly divided between the top and bottom of the element.

The line height property can increase the legibility of your text. Adding to the default line height inserts additional white space between the lines of text. On a computer monitor, greater white space helps guide the user's eyes along the line of text and provides rest for the eye. Figure 12-6 shows two paragraphs—one with the standard line height and one with the line height set to 1.5 em. As you can see, the increased line height makes the text easier to read.

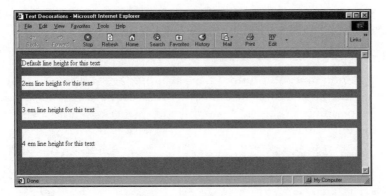

Figure 12-5   Line height

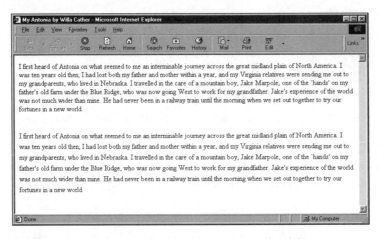

Figure 12-6   Adjusting line height increases legibility

Working with the Font Properties

In this exercise, you will use the CSS font properties you learned about in the preceding sections.

To work with the font properties:

1. In your text editor, open the file named **Ch12CSS02.htm** from the Chapter folder for Chapter 12.

2. Save the file as **Ch12CSS02SOL.htm** in the Chapter folder for Chapter 12.

3. Start Internet Explorer, and open the file named **Ch12CSS02SOL.htm**. When you open the file in the browser, it looks like Figure 12-7.

4. Close the browser, and examine the code in your text editor. Notice the `<style>` element in the `<head>` section. This is where you will enter your style rules.

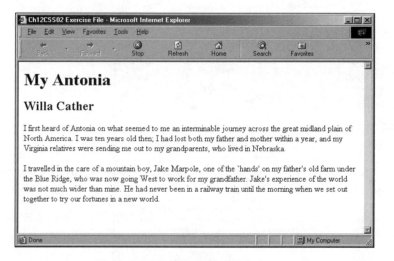

Figure 12-7   The original HTML document

5. Add a style rule that uses the `<body>` element as a selector. Use the `font-family` property to set the font to Arial, as shown in the boldface portion of the following code:

```
<style type="text/css">
body {font-family: arial;}
</style>
```

6. Use font substitution to add alternate fonts to the font-family declaration. Specify Helvetica and sans-serif as alternate fonts.

```
<style type="text/css">
body {font-family: arial, helvetica, sans-serif;}
</style>
```

7. Add a style rule that uses the `<p>` element as a selector. Use the `font-size` property to set the font size to 85 percent. This size will be slightly smaller than the browser's default font size.

```
<style type="text/css">
body {font-family: arial, helvetica, sans-serif;}
p {font-size: 85%;}
</style>
```

8. Add a second declaration to the rule for the `<p>` selector. Use the `line-height` property to set the line height to 150 percent.

```
<style type="text/css">
body {font-family: arial, helvetica, sans-serif;}
p {font-size: 85%; line-height: 150%;}
</style>
```

12

9. Save your work, switch to your browser, and reload the page. The Web page now looks like Figure 12-8.

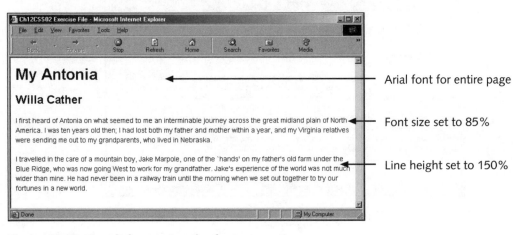

Arial font for entire page

Font size set to 85%

Line height set to 150%

Figure 12-8   Result from using the font properties

USING THE CSS MARGIN, PADDING, AND BORDER PROPERTIES

In this section, you will explore the CSS **box properties**, which let you control the margin, padding, and border characteristics of block-level elements. You will learn how to use these properties to enhance the display of content in the browser.

Understanding the CSS Box Model

The CSS **box model** describes the rectangular boxes that contain content on a Web page. Each block-level element you create is displayed as a box containing content in the browser window. Each content box can have margins, borders, and padding, as shown in Figure 12-9.

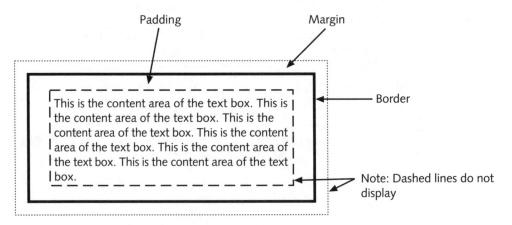

Padding   Margin

Border

Note: Dashed lines do not display

Figure 12-9   The CSS box model

As Figure 12-9 illustrates, the content box is the innermost box, surrounded by the padding, border, and margin areas. The padding area has the same background color as the content element, where the margin area is always transparent. The border separates the padding and margin areas.

Figure 12-10 shows the box model areas in a paragraph element. This paragraph has 2-em padding, a thin black border, and 2-em margins. Notice that the margin area is transparent.

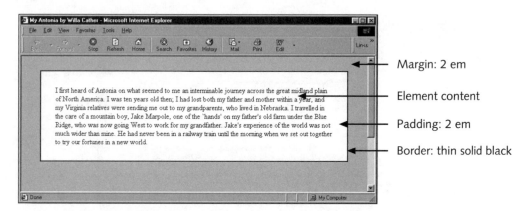

Figure 12-10   The CSS box model areas in a <p> element

The following code shows the style rule for the paragraph in Figure 12-10:

```
p {margin: 2 em;
   padding: 2 em;
   border: solid thin black;
   background: white;}
```

The margin and padding properties set the length to 2 em for all four sides of the box. The `border` property is a shorthand property that sets the `border-style` to solid; `border-weight` to thin, and `border-color` to black. The `background` property sets the paragraph background color to white.

Specifying Margins

The `margin` property lets you control the margin area of the box model. Margins are always transparent, showing the background of their containing element. You can use margins to enhance the legibility of text, create indented elements, and add whitespace around images.

The `margin` property is a shorthand property that lets you set all four individual margins with one property. You can specify either a length or a percentage value. The most commonly supported usage of the `margin` property is to state one value for all four margin sides, as shown in the following style rule:

```
p {margin: 2 em;}
```

Figure 12-11 shows two paragraph elements. The first paragraph has the margin set to 2 em; the second has the default margin setting.

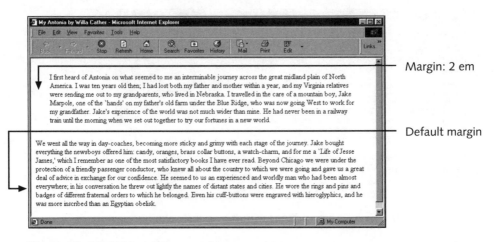

Figure 12-11 Using the `margin` property

Specifying Padding

The CSS padding properties let you control the padding area in the box model. The padding area is the space between the element content and the border. The padding area inherits the background color of the element, so if a `<p>` element has a white background, the padding area will be white as well. If you add a border to an element, you will almost always want to use padding to increase the whitespace between the content and the border, as shown in Figure 12-12.

The `padding` property is a shorthand property that lets you set all four individual padding values with one rule. You can specify either a length or a percentage value. The most common use of the `padding` property is to state one value for all four padding sides, as shown in the following style rule:

```
p {padding: 2 em;}
```

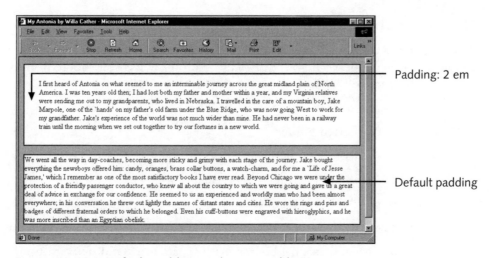

Figure 12-12   Default padding and 2-em padding

Specifying Borders

The **border** properties let you control the appearance of borders around elements. The border area is located between the margin and padding.

The **border** property lets you state three properties for all four borders of any element. You can state the **border-width**, **border-style**, and **border-color** in any order. **Border-style** must be included for the border to appear. If you do not include **border-width**, the width will default to medium. If you do not include **border-color**, the border will appear in the same color as the element. The following example rules show different uses of the **border** property.

The following rule sets the **border-style** to solid. The **border-weight** defaults to medium. The **border-color** will be the same as the color of the <p> element. Because no color is stated, the **border-color** will be black.

        p {border: solid;}

The following rule sets the **border-style** to solid. The **border-weight** is 1 pixel. The **border-color** will be red.

        p {border: solid 1px red;}

The following rule sets the **border-style** to double. The **border-weight** is thin. The **border-color** will be blue. Notice that the order of the values does not matter.

        p {border: double blue thin;}

Understanding Border Style

The border-style is the most important border property because it must be stated to make a border appear. The border-style property lets you choose from one of the following border style keywords:

- None - no border on the element. This is the default setting.
- Dotted - dotted border
- Dashed - dashed border
- Solid - solid line border
- Double - double line border
- Groove - 3-dimensional border that appears to be embossed into the page
- Ridge - 3-dimensional border that appears to extend outward from the page
- Inset - 3-dimensional border that appears to set the entire box into the page
- Outset - 3-dimensional border that appears to extend the entire box outward from the page

Figure 12-13 shows examples of the borders. The gray background for this page enhances the display of the 3-dimensional styles, which do not look the same on a white background. Not all borders are supported by all browsers, so test your work carefully. If you specify a border style that is not supported, the border will default to solid.

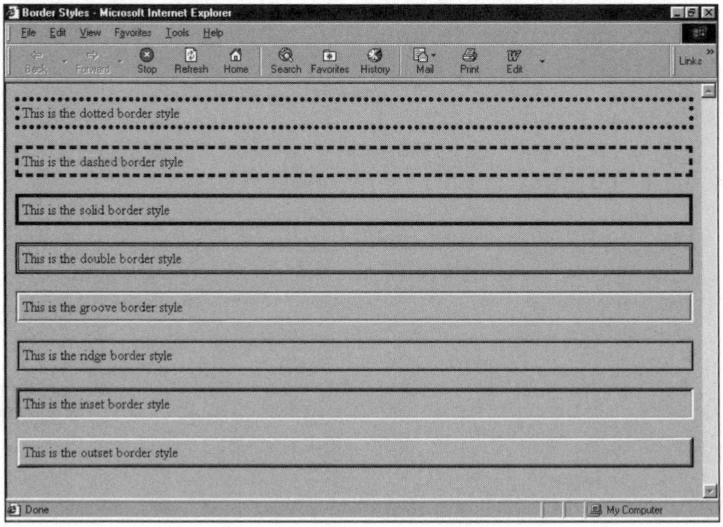

Figure 12-13 The different border styles

Understanding Border Width

The `border-width` property lets you state the width of the border with either a keyword or a length value. You can use the following keywords to express width:

- `thin`
- `medium` (default)
- `thick`

When you use these keywords, the width of the rule is based on the browser. The length values let you state an absolute or relative value for the border; percentages are not allowed. Using a length value lets you create anything from a hairline to a very thick border. Remember that the border will not display unless the `border-style` property is stated. Figure 12-14 shows examples of different border widths.

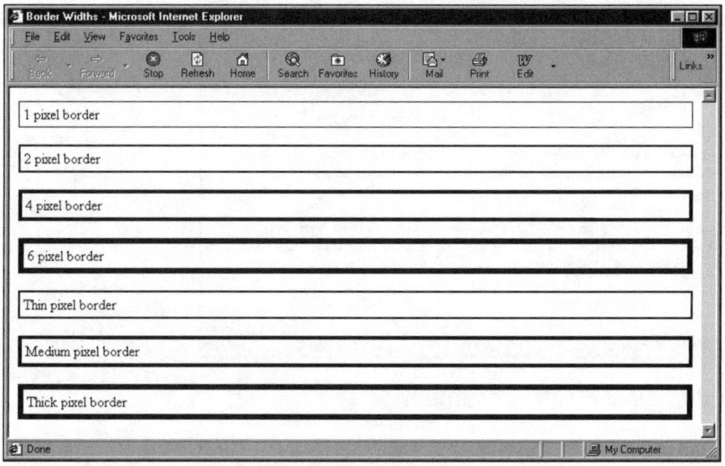

Figure 12-14   Different border widths

Understanding Border Color

The `border-color` property lets you set the color of the element border. The value can be either a hexadecimal value or one of the 16 predefined color names listed here:

- Aqua
- Black
- Blue
- Fuschia
- Gray
- Green
- Lime
- Maroon
- Navy
- Olive
- Purple
- Red
- Silver
- Teal
- White
- Yellow

12

Working with the Box Properties

In this exercise you will work with the CSS box model properties, including the `margin`, `padding`, and `border` properties.

To work with the box properties:

1. In your text editor, open the file named **Ch12CSS03.htm** from the Chapter folder for Chapter 12.

2. Save the file as **Ch12CSS03SOL.htm** in the Chapter folder for Chapter 12.

3. Start Internet Explorer and open the file named **Ch12CSS03SOL.htm**. When you open the file in the browser, it looks like Figure 12-15.

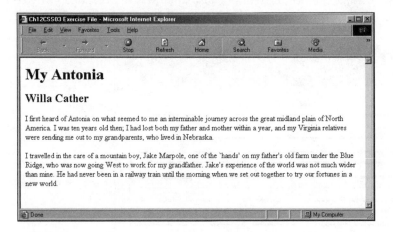

Figure 12-15 The original HTML document

4. In your text editor, examine the code. Notice that there is a `<style>` element in the `<head>` section. This is where you will enter your style rules.

5. Add a style rule that selects the `<h1>` element. Set the border to `solid thin` and the padding to 20 pixels (`20px`), as shown in the boldface portion of the following code:

```
<style type="text/css">
h1 {border: solid thin; padding: 20px;}
</style>
```

6. Add a style rule that selects the `<h2>` element. Set the margin to 20 pixels as shown in the following code:

```
<style type="text/css">
h1 {border: solid thin; padding: 20px;}
h2 {margin: 20px;}
</style>
```

7. Finally, add a style rule that selects the **<p>** element. Set the margin to 20 pixels as shown in the following code:

```
<style type="text/css">
h1 {border: solid thin; padding: 20px;}
h2 {margin: 20px;}
p {margin: 20px;}
</style>
```

8. Save your work, switch to your browser, and reload the page. The Web page now looks like Figure 12-16.

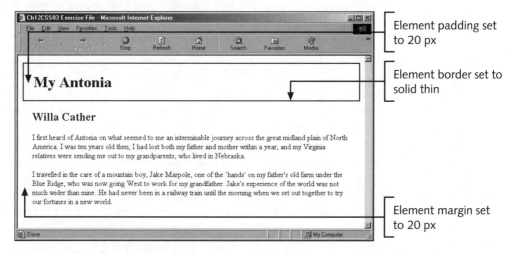

Figure 12-16   Result from using the box properties

WORKING WITH COLOR

In this section, you will explore the CSS color properties. These properties let you control the text color and background colors of any element on a Web page. The CSS **color** property replaces the obsolete **<font>** element in HTML, and gives you much more precise control over element by element color on your Web pages.

Color Basics

A computer monitor displays color by mixing three basic colors of light: red, green, and blue, which are called **RGB colors**. Each of these three basic colors is called a **color channel**. The monitor can express a range of intensity for each color channel, from 0 (absence of color) to 100% (full intensity of color). With the CSS color properties, you can select a specific color from the range of colors the monitor can display. Colors are relative to the specific environment in which they are viewed. What looks like red on one monitor can look orange on another monitor. Colors vary widely based on where a monitor is placed on the user's desk, the user's individual preferences, and equipment brand.

The range of colors a computer monitor can display is based on the color depth of the monitor. The **color depth** is the amount of data used to create the color. Most computer monitors can display 8-bit, 16-bit, and 24-bit color depths. The higher the color depth, the more colors the monitor can display. The problem when choosing colors for a Web page is that you never know the color depth of the user's monitor. If you specify a color that the monitor does not support, the browser will attempt to mix the color, which can create unreliable results. Therefore, you should use colors that will appear correctly at different color depths and on different monitor types. The palette of colors that will display faithfully is called the **browser-safe palette**. This palette contains 216 colors that display properly across both PC and Macintosh platforms at the lowest color depth setting.

Because of the variable nature of color on the Web, be sure to test the colors you choose, and use restraint when adding color to your design. Remember that colors will not look the same on different monitor brands and operating systems. When used properly, color can enhance the presentation of your information, providing structural and navigation cues to your user. Conversely, poor use of color distracts from your content and can annoy your users. Dark backgrounds, clashing colors, and unreadable links are just a few examples of the unrestrained use of the HTML color attributes that are common on the Web. Remember that many of your users might have accessibility issues that prevent them from seeing color the way you do. The user's ability to navigate, read, and interact with your content should always determine the choices and use of color in a Web site.

Specifying Color

The `color` property lets you specify the foreground color of any element on a Web page. This property sets the color for the both the text and the border of the element, unless you have specifically stated a border color with one of the border properties.

The value for the `color` property is a valid color keyword or numerical representation, either hexadecimal or a RGB value. The following style rules show the different methods of specifying a color:

```
p {color: blue;}    /* color name */
p {color: #0000ff;}    /* hexadecimal value */
p {color: rgb(0,0,255);}    /* RGB numbers */
p {color: rgb(0%,0%,100%);}    /* RGB percentages */
```

Figure 12-17 shows a `<p>` element with the color set to gray. By default, the element's border is the same color as the element content.

Here is the style rule for the paragraph. Notice that the border color is not specified, so the element's border is the same color as the content.

```
p {color: gray; border: solid thin; padding: 1em;}
```

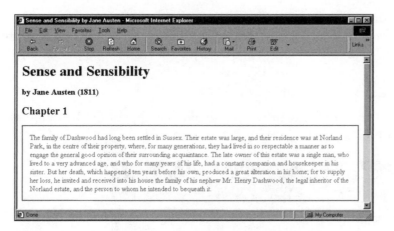

Figure 12-17   The element border defaults to the element color

If you set the color for **<body>**, all elements on the page will inherit their color from the **<body>** element, effectively setting the default text color for the entire Web page. The following rule sets the color for the **<body>** element.

```
body {color: #006633;}
```

Background Color

The **background-color** property lets you set the background color of any element on a Web page. The background color includes any padding area that you have defined for the element. Figure 12-18 shows **<p>** elements with background color and different padding values.

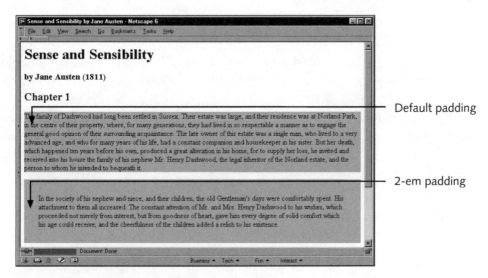

Figure 12-18   Background color and padding

The `background-color` property can be applied to both block-level and inline elements. The following style rule uses descendant selection (described in Chapter 11) to select **<b>** elements only when they reside within **<p>** elements and apply a background color:

```
p b {background-color: #cccccc;}
```

This rule selects the bold text in the paragraph and applies the background color, as shown in Figure 12-19.

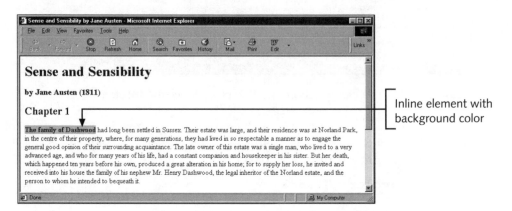

Figure 12-19   An inline element with a background color

To set the page background color, use the **<body>** element as the selector. This sets the background color for the content area of the Web page. By default, the background color of any element is transparent. Therefore, all elements will show the page background color unless a background color is specifically stated. The following rule sets a background color for the **<body>** element:

```
body {background-color: #cccccc;}
```

In Figure 12-20, notice that the first two headings have their background color set to white; the remainder of the elements shows the background color of the **<body>** element.

It is always a good practice to include a page background color, because some users might have a default background color that is different from the color you chose in your design. Even if you plan on a white page background, you can never be sure that all browsers will have their default set to white, so include the **background-color** property rather than relying on the user's settings.

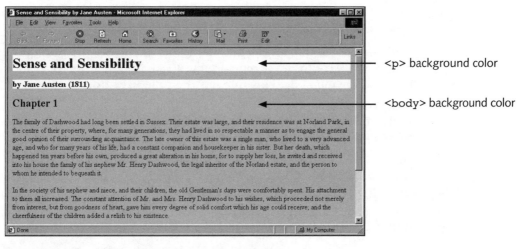

Figure 12-20   Setting the page background color

Working with the `Color` Properties

In this exercise, you will work with the CSS color properties, including the `color`, `background-color`, and `link` color properties.

To work with the color properties:

1. In your text editor, open the file named **Ch12CSS04.htm** from the Chapter folder for Chapter 12.

2. Save the file as **Ch12CSS04SOL.htm** in the Chapter folder for Chapter 12.

3. Start Internet Explorer and open the file named **Ch12CSS04SOL.htm**. When you open the file in the browser, it looks like Figure 12-21.

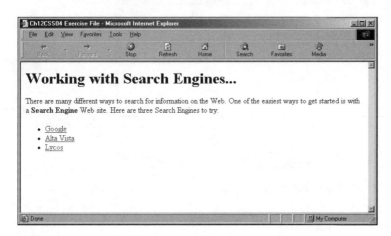

Figure 12-21   The original HTML document

4. In your text editor, examine the code. Notice that there is a `<style>` element in the `<head>` section. This is where you will enter your style rules.

5. Add a style rule that selects the `<body>` element. Set the `background-color` property to hexadecimal value `ffffcc` (a light beige color), as shown in the following code. This rule sets the page background color.

```
<style type="text/css">
body {background-color: #ffffcc;}
</style>
```

6. Add another declaration to the `<body>` style rule that sets the text color to maroon, as shown in the following code:

```
<style type="text/css">
body {background-color: #ffffcc; color: maroon;}
</style>
```

7. Add a style rule that selects `<b>` elements only when they occur within `<p>` elements. Use the `background-color` property and set the color to yellow. This will highlight the bold text within the paragraph with a yellow background.

```
<style type="text/css">
body {background-color: #ffffcc; color: maroon;}
p b {background-color: yellow;}
</style>
```

8. Save your work, switch to your browser, and reload the page. The Web page now looks like Figure 12-22.

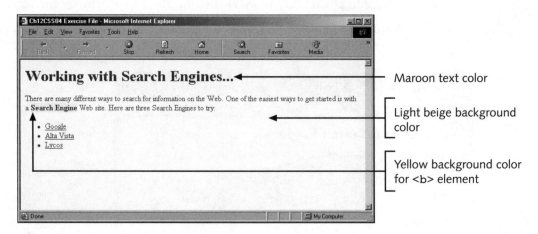

Figure 12-22   Results from using color properties

CHAPTER SUMMARY

- ❏ Choose the correct measurement unit based on the destination medium. For the computer screen, ems, pixels, or percentage measurements will scale to the user's preferences.

- ❏ Use the font properties to control the look of your letter forms. Specify font substitution values to ensure that your text displays properly across different platforms.

- ❏ The CSS box model lets you control the margin, padding, and border characteristics of HTML elements.

- ❏ Margins are transparent, showing the color of the containing element's background color. Padding takes on the color of the element to which it belongs.

- ❏ The border properties let you add borders to all individual sides or all four sides of an element. The three border characteristics are style, color, and width. Style must be stated to make the border appear.

- ❏ Color is widely variable on the Web. Different monitors and operating systems display colors differently.

- ❏ Use the `color` property to set foreground colors for elements. Remember that the element border defaults to the element color unless you specifically state a border color.

- ❏ Background colors affect any padding areas in the element. They can be applied to both block-level and inline elements.

12

REVIEW QUESTIONS

1. What is the default browser font?

   a. `times`

   b. `arial`

   c. `helvetica`

   d. `sans-serif`

2. Which of the following is not a valid CSS measurement unit?

   a. `pixel`

   b. `percentage`

   c. `em`

   d. `el`

3. What selector would you use to set default text properties for a document?

   a. `body`

   b. `p`

   c. `head`

   d. `text`

4. Write a font-family substitution string that selects Arial, Helvetica, or any sans-serif font for a `<p>` element.

   a. `p {arial, helvetica, sans-serif;}`

   b. `p {font-family: arial, helvetica, sans-serif;}`

   c. `p {font-family: "arial, helvetica, sans-serif";}`

   d. `p arial, helvetica, sans-serif`

5. What is the common printing term for line height?

   a. `l-height`

   b. `leading`

   c. `line-spacing`

   d. `lines`

6. Which of the following is not a valid space area in the box model?

   a. `padding`

   b. `leading`

   c. `margin`

   d. `background-area`

7. Which box model space area is transparent?

   a. `padding`

   b. `leading`

   c. `margin`

   d. `background-area`

8. What are the preferred length units for margins and padding?

   a. inches

   b. picas

   c. ems

   d. points

9. Where is the padding area located?

   a. outside the margin

   b. between the margin and border

c. between the text and border

d. within the text

10. What is the default border style?

    a. `solid`

    b. `double`

    c. `outline`

    d. `none`

11. What is the default border weight?

    a. `thin`

    b. `thick`

    c. `medium`

    d. `none`

12. What is the default border color?

    a. color of the element text

    b. color of the body text

    c. black

    d. none

13. Write a style rule for a `<p>` element that sets margins to 2 em, padding to 1 em, and creates a black solid 1 pixel border.

    a. `p {margin: 2 em; padding: 1em; border solid 1px;}`

    b. `p {margin, padding: 2 em; border solid 1px;}`

    c. `p {margin: "2 em;" padding: "1em;" border "solid 1px;"}`

    d. `p {margin=2 em; padding=1em; border=solid1px;}`

14. Which of the following is not a valid CSS color method?

    a. RGB

    b. CMYK

    c. hexadecimal

    d. color names

15. What selector would you use to set background color for a document?

    a. `head`

    b. `p`

    c. `body`

    d. `text`

12

HANDS-ON EXERCISES

Exercise 12-1

In this exercise, you will have a chance to test the font and text properties on paragraphs of text.

1. In your text editor, open the file named **Ch12CSS01EX.htm** from the Exercises folder for Chapter 12. Save it as **Ch12CSS01EXSOL.htm** in the same folder.

2. Start Internet Explorer and open the file named **Ch12CSS01EXSOL.htm.** When you open the file, it looks like Figure 12-23.

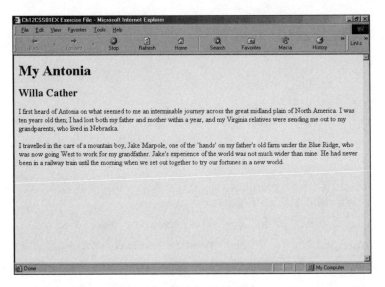

Figure 12-23 The beginning exercise file

3. In your text editor, add a **<style>** element to the **<head>** section, as shown in the boldface portion of the following code.

```
<head>
<title>CSS Test Document</title>
<style TYPE="text/css">
</style>
</head>
```

4. Write a style rule that uses **p** as a selector and sets the font family to Arial font.

5. Specify a list of alternate fonts, including Helvetica and sans-serif to ensure that your font choice will display properly across a range of computers.

6. Add the **line-height** property to the style rule. Set the line height to 1.5 times the default font size.

7. Save the file, and switch to your browser. The results should look like Figure 12-24.

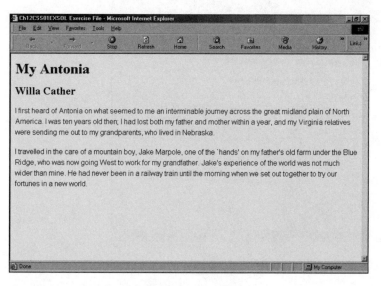

Figure 12-24 The finished exercise file

Exercise 12-2

In this exercise, you have a chance to apply some of the box properties you learned about in this chapter.

1. In your text editor, open the file named **Ch12CSS02EX.htm** from the Exercises folder for Chapter 12. Save it as **Ch12CSS02EXSOL.htm** in the same folder.

2. Start Internet Explorer and open the file named **Ch12CSS02EXSOL.htm.** When you open the file, it looks like Figure 12-25.

3. Switch to your text editor and examine the code. Notice the **<style>** section of the file. It contains three basic style rules that center the **<h1>**, **<h2>**, and **<h3>** element, as shown in the following code:

```
<style type="text/css">
h1 {text-align: center;}
h2 {text-align: center;}
h3 {text-align: center;}
</style>
```

4. Start by styling the **<h1>** element with a 1-em margin. Add the **margin** property to the existing **<h1>** style rule:

```
h1 {text-align: center; margin: 1em;}
```

12

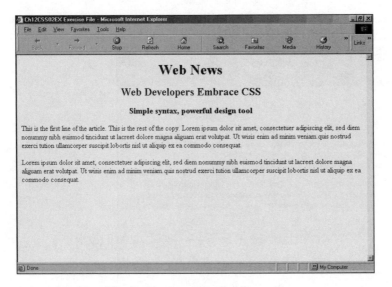

Figure 12-25   The beginning exercise file

5. The `<h2>` element has a margin bottom of 1 em. Add this property to the existing style rule:

   h2 {text-align: center; **margin-bottom: 1em;**}

6. The `<h3>` element has the most complex style effects, so break the style rule into separate lines. Start by adding .5 em of padding to the element. Add the `padding` property to the existing style rule:

   h3 { text-align: center;
       padding: .5em;
       }

7. Now add borders to the `<h3> element`. Set the style to solid and the weight to thin. Because the finished border is black, you do not have to state a color:

   h3 {text-align: center;
       padding: .5em;
       border:solid thin;
       }

8. Finish the `<h3>` element by setting the left and right margins to 40 pixels:

   h3 {text-align: center;
       padding: .5em;
       border:solid thin;
       margin:40px;
       }

9. Finish styling the document by setting the **<p>** margins to 40 pixels, to line up with the borders of the **<h3>**:

```
p {margin: 40px;}
```

10. Save the file, switch to your browser, and view the results, as shown in Figure 12-26.

Figure 12-26   The finished Web page

Exercise 12-3

In this exercise, you will experiment with color.

1. In your text editor, open the file named **Ch12CSS03EX.htm** from the Exercises folder for Chapter 12. Save it as **Ch12CSS03EXSOL.htm** in the same folder.

2. Start Internet Explorer and open the file named **Ch12CSS03EXSOL.htm.** When you open the file, it looks like Figure 12-27.

3. Switch to your text editor and examine the code, which contains the following style rules:

```
<style type="text/css">
p {margin-left: 40px;}
h1 {padding-left: 10px;}
h3 {padding-left: 10px;}
</style>
```

4. Edit the code, using the color and background color properties to achieve the results shown in Figure 12-28. You can use the hexadecimal color codes indicated in the figure, or try your own combinations.

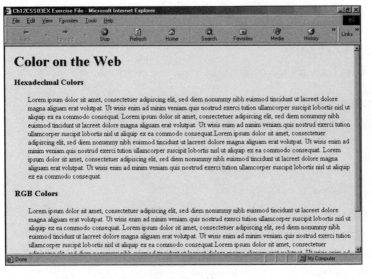

Figure 12-27   The original HTML file

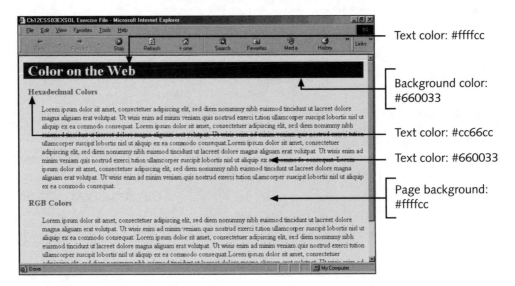

Figure 12-28   The finished HTML file

Exercise 12-4

In this exercise, you will apply styles using class names. Refer to Chapter 11 if you need help using class names.

1. In your text editor, open the file named **Ch12CSS04EX.htm** from the Exercises folder for Chapter 12. Save it as **Ch12CSS04EXSOL.htm** in the same folder.

2. Start Internet Explorer and open the file named **Ch12CSS04EXSOL.htm.**
   When you open the file, it looks like Figure 12-29.

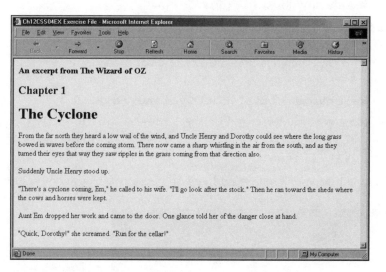

Figure 12-29   The original HTML file

3. Switch to your text editor and examine the code. Notice the `<style>` section of
   the file. This is where you will add your style rules.

4. Write a style rule for a class named `credit`. Set the `text-align` property to
   right and the color to gray, as shown in the following code:

   ```
   .credit {text-align: right; color: gray;}
   ```

5. Apply the style to the `<h3>` element using the `class` attribute, as shown in the
   following code:

   ```
   <h3 class="credit">An excerpt from The Wizard of OZ</h3>
   ```

6. Write a style rule for a class named `chapternumber`. Use the `font-family`
   property to specify font substitution using `arial`, `helvetica`, and `sans-serif`
   for values. The following code shows the new style rule:

   ```
   .chapternumber {font-family: arial, helvetica,
   sans-serif;}
   ```

7. Apply the style to the `<h2>` element using the `class` attribute as shown in the
   following code:

   ```
   <h2 class="chapternumber">Chapter 1</h2>
   ```

8. Write a style rule for a class named `chaptertitle`. Use the `font-family`
   property to specify font substitution using `arial`, `helvetica`, and `sans-serif`
   for values. The new style rule looks like the following:

   ```
   .chaptertitle {font-family: arial, helvetica, sans-
   serif;}
   ```

9. Continue working in the **chaptertitle** style rule. Add the **border** property and set the value to **solid 1px**. Add a **padding** property and set the value to **10px**. The style rule now looks like the following:

```
.chaptertitle {font-family: arial, helvetica, sans-serif;
border: solid 1px; padding: 10px;}
```

10. Apply the style to the **<h1>** element using the **class** attribute as shown in the following code:

```
<h1 class="chaptertitle">The Cyclone</h1>
```

11. Write a rule using **p** as the selector. Use the **line-height** property to set the line height of the paragraph text to **150%**, as shown in the following code:

```
p {line-height: 150%}
```

12. Save the file, switch to your browser, and view the results, as shown in Figure 12-30.

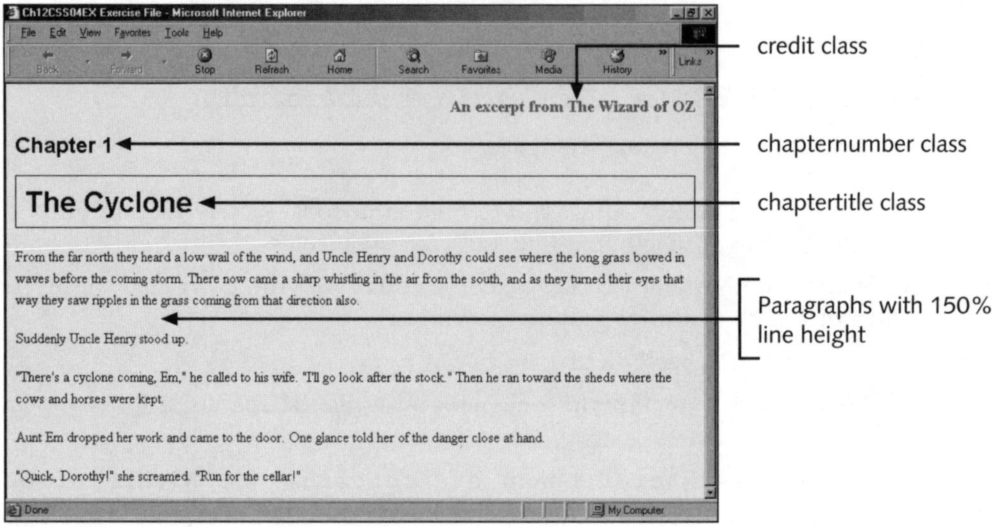

Figure 12-30 The finished HTML file

Exercise 12-5

In this exercise, you will apply styles to a Web page that already has a style sheet. You will have to choose which style properties to use and how to apply them.

1. In your text editor, open the file named **Ch12CSS05EX.htm** from the Exercises folder for Chapter 12. Save it as **Ch12CSS05EXSOL.htm** in the same folder.

2. Start Internet Explorer and open the file named **Ch12CSS05EXSOL.htm**. When you open the file it, looks like Figure 12-31.

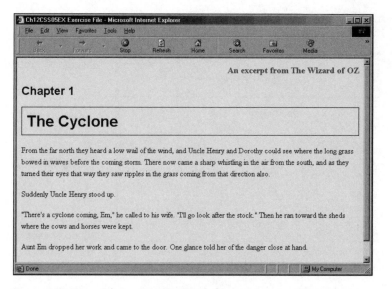

Figure 12-31 The original HTML file

3. Switch to your text editor and examine the code. Notice the existing `<style>` sheet, as shown in the following code:

```
<style type="text/css">
.credit {text-align: right; color: gray;}
.chapternumber {font-family: arial, helvetica,
sans-serif;}
.chaptertitle {font-family: arial, helvetica, sans-serif;
border: solid 1px; padding: 10px;}
p {line-height: 150%}
</style>
```

4. Add the following style characteristics to the file. You will have to either write new style rules, or add properties to the existing rules. Refer to Figure 12-32 to see the finished Web page.

- Change the color of the chapter number text to gray.

- Change the paragraph text to a sans-serif font.

- Change the background color of the entire page to beige.

- Add a margin of 40 pixels to the entire page.

5. When you are finished, save the file, switch to your browser, and view the results, as shown in Figure 12-32.

12

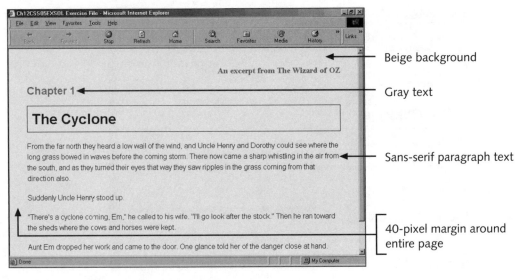

Figure 12-32   The finished HTML file

WEB DESIGN PROJECTS

Project 12-1

Browse the Web and choose a site that you feel exhibits positive use of color, both in content and backgrounds. Write a short design critique that describes how the use of color enhances the legibility of the site and improves user access to information. Save your work in the Projects folder for Chapter 12.

Project 12-2

Design a type properties style sheet for a fictitious Web site. Create a sample HTML page that shows examples of the different typefaces and sizes and how they will be used in the site. This page can be a mocked-up page that uses generic content but demonstrates the overall typographic scheme. Build the style sheet directly within the Web page. Save your work in the Projects folder for Chapter 12. Consider the following questions:

❑ What style will you use for the paragraph text?

❑ How many levels of headings are necessary?

❑ What are the different weights and sizes of the headings?

❑ Will you adjust the line height of the paragraph text?

❑ Will you use class names to differentiate styles?

❑ Will you use borders and any spacing in margins and padding areas?

❑ What colors will you use for text?

Project 12-3

Browse the Web and choose a site that can benefit from the box properties you learned about in this chapter. Print a copy of the site's pages and indicate where you would change the spacing and border properties. Write a short design essay that describes the changes you want to achieve and how they increase the legibility of the page content. Save your work in the Projects folder for Chapter 12.

13

JavaScript: Part I

The original purpose of the World Wide Web was locating and displaying information. However, once the Web grew beyond a small academic and scientific community, people began to recognize that greater interactivity would make the Web more useful. As commercial applications of the Web grew, the demand for more interactive and visually appealing Web sites also grew.

But how to respond to this demand? Web developers were hampered by the fact that documents created using basic HTML are static. After all, the main purpose of HTML is to tell a browser how the document should appear. You can think of an HTML document as being approximately equivalent to a document created in a word-processing or desktop publishing program; the only thing you can do with it is view or print it. Thus, to respond to the demand for greater interactivity, an entirely new Web programming language was needed. Netscape filled this need by developing the JavaScript programming language for use in Navigator Web browsers.

Although JavaScript is considered a programming language, it is in fact a critical part of Web page design. This is because the JavaScript language "lives" within a Web page's HTML code. JavaScript brings HTML to life and makes Web pages dynamic. JavaScript can turn static HTML documents into applications such as games or order forms. JavaScript code can change the contents of a Web page after the page has been rendered by a browser. JavaScript code can allow a Web page to interact with a user through forms and controls. It can also create visual effects such as animation, and it can control the Web browser window itself. None of this was possible before the creation of JavaScript.

In this chapter, you will learn the skills required to create basic JavaScript programs.

THE JAVASCRIPT PROGRAMMING LANGUAGE

JavaScript is a scripting language. The term **scripting language** refers to programming languages that are executed by an interpreter from within a Web browser. An **interpreter** is a program that executes scripting language code. A **scripting engine** is an interpreter that is part of the Web browser. When a scripting engine loads an HTML page, it interprets any programs written in scripting languages, such as JavaScript. A Web browser that contains a scripting engine is called a **scripting host**. Navigator and Internet Explorer are both examples of scripting hosts that can run JavaScript programs.

JavaScript was first introduced in Navigator and was originally called *LiveScript*. With the release of Navigator 2.0, the name was changed to *JavaScript 1.0*. Subsequently, Microsoft released its own version of JavaScript in Internet Explorer 4.0 and named it *JScript*. The most current versions of each implementation are JavaScript 1.5 in Navigator and JScript 5.5, which is available for Internet Explorer versions 4.0 and later.

 If you are using Internet Explorer 4.0 or higher, you can upgrade the scripting engine to interpret the most recent version of JavaScript. To do this, you need to install the most recent version of Windows Script from www.microsoft.com/msdownload/vbscript/scripting.asp.

When Microsoft released JScript, several major problems occurred. For example, the Netscape and Microsoft versions of the JavaScript language differed so greatly that programmers were required to write almost completely different JavaScript programs for Navigator and Internet Explorer. To avoid similar problems in the future, an international, standardized version of JavaScript (called **ECMAScript**) was created. The most recent version of ECMAScript is edition 3. Both Netscape JavaScript 1.5 and Microsoft JScript 5.5 conform to ECMAScript edition 3. Nevertheless, Netscape JavaScript and Microsoft JScript each include unique programming features that are not supported by the other language.

In this book, you will learn to create JavaScript programs that run on either Navigator or Internet Explorer. To allow for compatibility with both browsers, this chapter focuses on ECMAScript edition 3 code that is supported by Navigator 6 and higher and Internet Explorer 4 and higher. At the time of this writing, older versions of Navigator and Internet Explorer (which are not 100% compatible with ECMAScript edition 3) are widely used. This is particularly true for Netscape browsers. With Internet Explorer 4.0 and higher, you can upgrade the version of JScript that is interpreted by the browser. However, with Navigator, the JavaScript version is built directly into the browser. To update the version of JavaScript used by Navigator, you must update the browser itself. This book will list the necessary code changes, where appropriate, to provide backward-compatibility with older versions of Navigator.

Many people think that JavaScript is related to or is a simplified version of the Java programming language. However, the languages are entirely different. Java is an advanced programming language that was created by Sun Microsystems and is considerably more difficult to master than JavaScript. Although Java is often used to create programs that can run from a Web page, Java programs are external programs that execute independently of a browser. In contrast, JavaScript programs run within a Web page and control the browser.

ADDING JAVASCRIPT TO AN HTML DOCUMENT

JavaScript programs run from within an HTML document. JavaScript programs contained within HTML documents are also referred to simply as **scripts**. This section discusses the basic techniques for adding JavaScript code to an HTML document.

The `<script>` Element

The statements that make up a JavaScript program in an HTML document are contained within the `<script>` element. The `<script>` element is used to notify the Web browser that the commands it contains must be interpreted by a scripting engine. The **language** attribute of the `<script>` element tells the browser which scripting language and which version of the scripting language are being used. To tell the Web browser that the statements that follow must be interpreted by the JavaScript scripting engine, include the following code in your HTML document:

```
<script language="JavaScript">
JavaScript code;
</script>
```

13

Although this book covers JavaScript, you can also use other scripting languages with Web pages. Microsoft's VBScript, another kind of scripting language, is based on the Visual Basic programming language. To use VBScript in your HTML document, you would use the following code: `<script language="VBScript">`*VBScript code*`</script>`. Do not confuse JScript with VBScript. JScript is Microsoft's version of the JavaScript scripting language. To specify the JScript language, you specify JavaScript as the language attribute.

If you anticipate that your JavaScript programs will run only in Internet Explorer, then you can specify "JScript" as your scripting language by using the statement `<script language="JScript">`. However, few browsers other than Internet Explorer will recognize "JScript" as a valid language attribute for the `<script>` element; it is safer to always use "JavaScript".

Before you can actually use `<script>` elements to create a JavaScript program, you need to learn some basic terminology that is commonly used in JavaScript programming and in other kinds of programming languages. In addition to being an interpreted scripting language, JavaScript is considered an object-based programming language. An **object** is programming code and data that can be treated as an individual unit or component. Individual lines in a programming language are called **statements**. Individual statements used in a computer program are often grouped into logical units called **procedures**, which are used to perform specific tasks. The procedures associated with an object are called **methods**. JavaScript treats many things as objects. One of the most commonly used objects in JavaScript programming is the `Document` object. The **`Document object`** represents the content of a browser's window. Any text, graphics, or other information displayed in a Web page is part of the `Document` object. One of the most common uses of the `Document` object is to add new text to a Web page. You create new text on a Web page with the **`write()` method** or the **`writeln()` method** of the `Document` object.

Using the `write()` and `writeln()` Methods

At this point, you have become familiar with the elements of a JavaScript program, and you are ready to learn how to use the `write()` and `writeln()` methods in a short program. To execute an object's method, you append the method to the object with a period and include any required arguments between the method's parentheses. Executing an object method is also referred to as **calling** the method. To call a method, you write a statement that includes the function name followed by parentheses containing any variables or values, called **arguments**, that will be used by the method. Sending arguments to a method is known as **passing arguments**.

Different methods require different kinds of arguments. For example, the `write()` and `writeln()` methods of the `Document` object require a text string as an argument. A **text string**, or **literal string**, is text that is contained within double quotation marks. The text string argument of the `write()` and `writeln()` methods specifies the text that the `Document` object uses to create new text on a Web page. For example, `document.write ("this is a text string");` writes the text "this is a text string" to the HTML document. If you want the text in the HTML document to be surrounded by quotation marks, you must surround the quoted text with single quotation marks. For example, `document.write("this is a 'text' string");` writes the text "this is a 'text' string" to the HTML document. Note that literal strings must be on a single line. If you include a line break within a literal string, you will receive an error message.

The `write()` and `writeln()` methods perform essentially the same function that you perform when you manually add text to the body of a standard HTML document. Whether you add text to an HTML document by using standard HTML tags or by using the `write()` or `writeln()` methods, the text is added according to the order in which the statement appears in the HTML file.

The only difference between the `write()` and `writeln()` methods is that the `writeln()` method adds a carriage return after the line of text. Carriage returns, however, are only recognized inside a preformatted text container that you create with the

<pre> element. In other words, in order to use carriage returns with the writeln() method, you must place the method within a <pre> element. Figure 13-1 contains a script that prints "Hello World" in a Web browser using the writeln() method of the Document object. In this context, the term "print" refers to the rendering of information in a Web browser. Notice that the <script>...</script> tag pairs are enclosed in the <pre>...</pre> tag pairs. Figure 13-2 shows the output.

```
<pre>
<script language="JavaScript">
document.writeln("Hello World");
document.writeln("This line is printed below the 'Hello World' line.");
</script>
</pre>
```

Figure 13-1   Hello World script using the writeln() method of the Document object

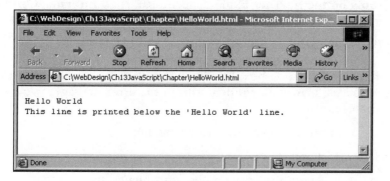

Figure 13-2   Output of the Hello World script using the writeln() method of the Document object

Although the two document.writeln() statements in Figure 13-1 appear on separate lines, you can include JavaScript statements on the same line if they are separated by semicolons. Because the statements in Figure 13-1 are on separate lines, the semicolons at the end of each statement are not actually necessary. However, it is considered good JavaScript programming practice to end any statement with a semicolon.

Case Sensitivity in JavaScript

Objects that are part of the JavaScript programming language itself, such as the Document object, are commonly referred to with an initial capital letter to distinguish them as "top-level" objects. However, unlike HTML, JavaScript is case-sensitive. Although we refer to the Document object in the course of this book with an uppercase *D*, you must use a lowercase *d* when referring to the Document object in a script. The statement Document.write ("Hello World"); will cause an error message because the

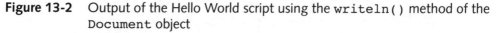

JavaScript interpreter will not recognize an object named `Document` with an uppercase *D*. Similarly, the following misspelled statements will cause errors:

```
DOCUMENT.write("Hello World");
Document.Write("Hello World");
document.WRITE("Hello World");
```

Creating a Simple JavaScript Program

In this section, you will create a simple JavaScript program. As you type your JavaScript code, you will probably make a few mistakes. Fortunately, when a JavaScript program contains errors, most Web browsers display a message informing you of the error. However, if you are using a version of Internet Explorer higher than version 4, you need to make sure error notification is turned on.

To verify that error notification is turned on:

1. Click **Tools** on the Internet Explorer menu bar, click **Internet Options**, and then click the **Advanced** tab.

2. In the Browsing category on the Advanced tab, make sure the "Display a notification about every script error" check box is selected, and click the **OK** button to close the dialog box. Depending on your browser version, the error messages you see may appear different from the error messages you see in the figures in this book.

You are now ready to create a simple JavaScript program.

To create a JavaScript document:

1. Open your text editor and create a new document.

2. Type the opening `<html>` and `<head>` tags:

```
<html>
<head>
```

3. Press **Enter** and add the title:

```
<title>My First JavaScript Program</title>
```

4. Press **Enter** and type `</head>` to close the `<head>...</head>` tag pair.

5. Press **Enter** and type the opening `<body>` tag.

6. Press **Enter** and type the following statements to start a preformatted text container and a JavaScript section:

```
<pre>
<script language="JavaScript">
```

7. Press **Enter** and type `document.writeln("This is the first line in my JavaScript file.");`.

The string in step 7 wraps to a second line due to space limitations in this book. Space limitations in this book often require that text strings wrap to the next line. However, remember that strings cannot be broken, or you will receive an error message. Wherever you see a broken string, be sure to type the entire string on a single line. Also, you should *not* type the period at the end of the step.

8. Press **Enter** again and type `document.writeln("This is the second line in my JavaScript file.");`.

9. Press **Enter** one more time and type these closing tags:

```
</script>
</pre>
</body>
</html>
```

10. Save the file as **Ch13JavaScript01.html** in the Chapter folder for Chapter 13.

11. Open the **Ch13JavaScript01.html** file in your Web browser. If you receive an error message, check the case of the object and the `writeln()` method in the `document.writeln()` statements. Figure 13-3 displays the MyFirstJavaScript.html file as it appears in Internet Explorer.

Figure 13-3   Ch13JavaScript01.html in Internet Explorer

12. Close the Web browser window.

Creating a JavaScript Source File

JavaScript is often incorporated directly into an HTML document. However, you can also save JavaScript code in an external file called a **JavaScript source file** that you can execute (or "call") from an HTML document. When you call a JavaScript source file, the HTML document looks in the JavaScript source file and executes the code only when necessary. A JavaScript source file is usually designated by the file extension .js and contains only JavaScript statements; it does not contain the `<script>` element tag pair.

Instead, the `<script>` element is located within the HTML document that calls the source file. To access JavaScript code that is saved in an external file, you use the **src** attribute of the `<script>` element. You assign to the **src attribute** a text string that specifies the URL or directory location of a JavaScript source file. For example, to call a JavaScript source file named *SampleSourceFile.js* that is located in the C:\javafiles directory, you would include the following code in an HTML document:

```
<script language="JavaScript"
src="c:\javafiles\samplesourcefile.js">
</script>
```

JavaScript source files cannot include HTML tags. If you include HTML tags in a JavaScript source file, you will receive an error message. Also, when you specify a source file in your HTML document using the **src** attribute, the browser will ignore any other JavaScript code located between the `<script>...</script>` tag pairs. For example, consider the following JavaScript code. In this case, the JavaScript source file specified by the **src** attribute of the `<script>` tag executes properly, but the `document.write()` statement is ignored.

```
<script language="JavaScript"
src="c:\javafiles\samplesourcefile.js">
document.write("this JavaScript statement will be ignored");
</script>
```

If the JavaScript code you intend to use in an HTML document is fairly short, then it is usually easier to include JavaScript code in an HTML document. However, for longer JavaScript code it is easier to include the code in a .js source file. There are several reasons you may want to use a .js source file instead of adding the code to an HTML document:

- Your HTML document will be neater. Lengthy JavaScript code in an HTML document can be confusing. You may not be able to tell at a glance where the HTML code ends and the JavaScript code begins.

- The JavaScript code can be shared among multiple HTML documents. For example, your Web site may contain pages that allow users to order an item. Each Web page displays a different item but uses the same JavaScript code to gather order information. Instead of recreating the JavaScript order information code within each HTML document, the Web pages can share a central JavaScript source file. Sharing a single source file among multiple HTML documents reduces disk space. In addition, when you share a source file among multiple HTML documents, a Web browser needs to keep only one copy of the file in memory, which reduces system overhead.

- JavaScript source files hide JavaScript code from incompatible browsers. If your HTML document contains JavaScript code, instead of calling an external JavaScript source file, an incompatible browser will display the code as if it were standard text.

You can use a combination of embedded JavaScript code and JavaScript source files in your HTML documents. The ability to combine embedded JavaScript code and JavaScript source files in a single HTML document is advantageous if you have multiple HTML documents, each of which requires individual JavaScript code statements, but all of which also share a single JavaScript source file.

Suppose you have a Web site with multiple Web pages. Each page displays a product that your company sells. You may have a JavaScript source file that collects order information, such as a person's name and address, that is shared by all the products you sell. Each individual product may also require other kinds of order information that you need to collect using JavaScript code. For example, one of your products may be a shirt, for which you need to collect size and color information. On another Web page, you may sell jellybeans, for which you need to collect quantity and flavor information. Each of these products can share a central JavaScript source file to collect standard information, but each may also include embedded JavaScript code to collect product-specific information.

When you include multiple JavaScript sections in an HTML document, you must include a `<script>` element for each section. Each JavaScript section in an HTML document is executed in the order in which it appears. Figure 13-4 displays an HTML document that calls an external source file and includes embedded JavaScript.

```
<html>
<head>
<title>HTML Document with Two JavaScript Sections</title>
</head>
<body>
<p>The following two lines call an external JavaScript source file.</p>
<script language="JavaScript"
src="c:\javafiles\samplesourcefile.js">
</script>
<pre>
<script language="JavaScript">
document.writeln("Your order has been confirmed.");
document.writeln("Thank you for your business.");
</script>
</pre>
</body>
</html>
```

Figure 13-4   HTML document that calls an external source file and includes embedded JavaScript

Next, you will create an HTML document that calls an external JavaScript source file and that includes embedded JavaScript. First, you will create the main HTML document.

To create the main HTML document:

1. Create a new document in your text editor.

2. Type the opening `<html>` and `<head>` tags:

```
<html>
<head>
```

3. Press **Enter** and add the title as follows: `<title>Multiple JavaScript Calls</title>`.

 Remember not to type the period at the end of step 3. Keep this in mind for similar steps throughout this chapter.

4. Press **Enter** and type `</head>` to close the `<head>...</head>` tag pair.

5. Press **Enter** and add the following code to begin the body of the HTML document and to call an external JavaScript source file:

```
<body>
<script language="JavaScript" src="Ch13JavaScript02.js">
</script>
```

6. Press **Enter** and type the following JavaScript code that executes from within the HTML document in a preformatted text container:

```
<pre>
<script language="JavaScript">
document.writeln(
"This line was created with embedded JavaScript code.");
document.writeln(
"This line was also created with embedded JavaScript code.");
</script>
</pre>
```

7. Press **Enter** and add the following code to close the `<html>` and `<body>` tags:

```
</body></html>
```

8. Save the file as **Ch13JavaScript02.html** in the Chapter folder for Chapter 13.

Next, you will create the JavaScript source file and then open Ch13JavaScript02.html.

To create the JavaScript source file and open Ch13JavaScript02.html:

1. Create a new document in your text editor.

2. Type `document.write("This line was printed from the JavaScript source file.")`. (Remember not to include a line break within the literal string or you will receive an error message.) This will be the only line in the document. Remember that you do not include the `<script>` element within a source file.

3. Save the file as **Ch13JavaScript02.js** in the Chapter folder for Chapter 13 and close your text editor. (Note that this file has the same number, 02, as the file you created in the preceding set of steps. This is to remind you that the two files work in conjunction with each other, one as the source file and one as the main HTML document. Note, however, that the files do have different file extensions.)

4. Open the **Ch13JavaScript02.html** file in your Web browser. Figure 13-5 displays the **Ch13JavaScript02.html** file as it appears in Internet Explorer.

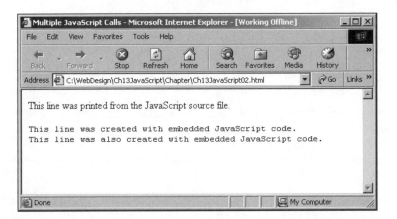

Figure 13-5   Ch13JavaScript02.html in Internet Explorer

5. Close the Web browser window.

Adding Comments to a JavaScript Program

When you create a program, whether in JavaScript or any other programming language, it is considered good programming practice to add comments to your code. In Chapter 2, you learned how to create HTML comments. In this section, you will learn how to create JavaScript comments.

JavaScript supports two kinds of comments: line comments and block comments. **Line comments** are created by adding two slashes // before the text you want to use as a comment. The // characters instruct the JavaScript interpreter to ignore all text immediately following slashes to the end of the line. You can place a line comment either at the end of a line of code or on its own line. **Block comments** span multiple lines and are created by adding /* to the first line that you want included in the block. You close a comment block by typing */ after the last character in the block. Any text or lines between the opening /* characters and the closing */ characters is ignored by the JavaScript interpreter.

Comments in JavaScript use the same syntax as comments created in C++ and Java.

Next, you will add comments to the Ch13JavaScript01.html file.

To add comments to the Ch13JavaScript01.html file:

1. Open the **Ch13JavaScript01.html** file in your text editor.

2. Place the insertion point at the end of the line containing the opening `<script>` tag, press **Enter**, and add the following comment block. Be sure to add the comment block after the opening `<script>` tag.

```
/*
JavaScript code for Ch13JavaScript01.html
your name
today's date
*/
```

When you create comments in your JavaScript programs, be sure to use a forward slash (/) and not a backward slash (\). People often confuse these two characters. If you include a backward slash instead of a forward slash when creating a comment, you will receive an error when you attempt to open the file in a Web browser.

3. Place the insertion point at the end of the line that reads `document.writeln` `("This is the first line in my JavaScript file.");`, press **Space**, then type **// Line 1**.

4. Place the insertion point at the end of the line that reads `document.writeln` `("This is the second line in my JavaScript file.");`, press **Space**, and type **// Line 2**.

5. Save the file and then open it in your Web browser to confirm that the comments are not displayed.

6. Close the Web browser window.

Hiding JavaScript from Incompatible Browsers

As you know, JavaScript is not compatible with all browsers. If your HTML document contains embedded JavaScript codes, then an incompatible browser will display the codes as if they were standard text. To avoid this problem, you can do one of two things. One option is to move your code into a source file, in which case the incompatible browser will simply ignore the lines that call the source file. Alternatively, if you prefer to keep the JavaScript code in the HTML document, you can enclose the code within the `<script>...</script>` tag pair in an HTML comment block. This will hide the embedded code from incompatible browsers. HTML comments are different from JavaScript comments. HTML comment blocks begin with `<!--` and end with `-->`. The browser does not render any text located between the opening and closing comment tags.

Most Web browsers do not display lines that are set off with an HTML comment tag. However, browsers compatible with JavaScript ignore the HTML comment tags and execute the JavaScript code normally. Remember that JavaScript-compatible browsers never display JavaScript code. Instead, the code is interpreted by the browser's scripting engine. Only JavaScript comment tags can be used to hide JavaScript code from the interpreter. Figure 13-6 shows an example of JavaScript code that is hidden from incompatible browsers (using HTML comments), but that would be executed by compatible browsers.

```
<script language="JavaScript">
<!--  This line starts the HTML comment block
document.writeln("Your order has been confirmed.");
document.writeln("Thank you for your business.");
// This line ends the HTML comment block -->
</script>
```

Figure 13-6   JavaScript code hidden from incompatible browsers, using HTML comments

Notice in Figure 13-6 that the line containing the closing HTML comment (**-->**) begins with a JavaScript line comment (**//**). The line comment instructs the JavaScript compiler to ignore the closing HTML comment and gives you an opportunity to leave a text comment that identifies the end of the HTML comment block. Incompatible browsers, however, will ignore the line comment and recognize the closing HTML comment as the end of the HTML comment block.

It is a good idea to design your scripts so that, when your HTML document is displayed by a browser that is incompatible with JavaScript or by a browser with JavaScript disabled, a message appears informing the user of the problem. You use the **<noscript> element** to display a message telling the user that his or her browser is not compatible with the JavaScript code in your program. The **<noscript>** element usually follows the **<script>...</script>** tag pair.

Next, you will modify the Ch13JavaScript01.html file so that it is hidden from incompatible browsers and displays an alternate message using the **<noscript>** element.

To modify the Ch13JavaScript01.html file so that it is hidden from incompatible browsers and displays an alternate message:

1. Return to the **Ch13JavaScript01.html** file in your text editor.

2. Place the insertion point at the end of the line containing the opening **<script>** tag, press **Enter**, and then type **<!-- This line starts the HTML comment block** to begin the HTML comment block. This HTML comment block will hide the JavaScript code from incompatible browsers.

3. Place the insertion point at the end of the line that reads document.writeln ("This is the second line in myJavaScriptfile.");// Line 2, press **Enter**, and then type **// This line ends the HTML comment block -->** to close the HTML comment block.

4. Place the insertion point at the end of the line that reads **</pre>**, press **Enter** to insert a new line, and type the following code to display a message that will appear in browsers that do not support JavaScript:

```
<noscript>
Your browser does not support JavaScript or JavaScript is
    disabled.<br>
</noscript>
```

13

5. Save the file and open it in your Web browser. Because you are using a recent version of Navigator or Internet Explorer, the JavaScript section executes normally. However, if you were using a browser that did not support JavaScript, or if JavaScript were disabled, you would see the message "Your browser does not support JavaScript."

6. Close the Web browser window.

Placing JavaScript in Head or Body Sections

A Web browser renders elements in an HTML document in the order in which they are encountered. When you have multiple JavaScript code sections in an HTML document, each section is also executed in the order in which it appears in the script. For example, the embedded JavaScript code in Figure 13-7 executes before the call to the JavaScript source file because the embedded code appears first.

```
<p>The following embedded JavaScript code executes first.</p>
<script language="JavaScript">
document.writeln(
    "First JavaScript code section in document");
</script>
<p>The following JavaScript source file executes after the
embedded JavaScript code.</p>
<script language="JavaScript" src="javascriptsource.js">
</script>
```

Figure 13-7   Execution of multiple JavaScript code sections

JavaScript code can be placed in either an HTML document's head section or its body section. Where you place your JavaScript code will vary, depending on the program you are writing. As a general rule, though, it is a good idea to place as much of your JavaScript code as possible in the head section, because the head section of an HTML document is rendered before the body section. When placed in the head section, JavaScript code will be processed before the main body of the HTML document is displayed. It is especially important to place JavaScript code in the head section when your code performs behind-the-scenes tasks that are required by JavaScript code sections located in the body section.

WORKING WITH VARIABLES

One of the most important aspects of programming is the ability to store values in computer memory and to manipulate those values. The values a program stores in computer memory are commonly called **variables**. Technically speaking, though, a variable is actually a specific location in the computer's memory. Data stored in a specific variable often changes. You can think of a variable as being similar to a storage locker: A program can put any value into it and then retrieve the value later for use in calculations. To use a variable in a program, you first have to write a statement that creates the variable and assigns it a name. For example, you may have a program that creates a variable named `Time` and then stores the current time in that variable. Each time the program runs, the current time is different, so the value will vary. Programmers often talk about "assigning a value to a variable," which is the same as storing a value in a variable. For example, a payroll program might assign employee names to a variable named `employeeName`. The variable `employeeName` might contain different values (a different value for every employee of the company) at different times.

Variable Names

The name you assign to a variable is called an **identifier**. Identifiers must begin with an uppercase or lowercase ASCII letter, dollar sign ($), or underscore (_). You can use numbers in an identifier, but not as the first character.

JavaScript does not allow you to use a number as the first character in an identifier.

You need to follow some rules and conventions when naming a variable. You cannot use reserved words for variable names. **Reserved words**, which are also called **keywords**, are special words that are part of the JavaScript language syntax. Also, you cannot include spaces within a variable name. It is common practice to use an underscore (_) character to separate individual words within a variable name, as in `my_variable_name`. Another option is to use a lowercase letter for the first letter of the first word in a variable name, with subsequent words starting with an initial cap, as in `myVariableName`.

13

Some versions of Web browsers, including Navigator 2.02 and Internet Explorer 3.02, do not recognize the dollar sign in variable names. If you want your JavaScript programs to interact seamlessly with older Web browsers, avoid using the dollar sign in variable names.

Variable names, like other JavaScript code, are case-sensitive. Therefore, the variable name `myVariable` is a completely different variable than one named `myvariable`, `MyVariable`, or `MYVARIABLE`. If you receive an error when running a JavaScript program, be sure that you are using the correct case when referring to any variables in your code.

Declaring Variables

Before you can use a variable in your code, you have to create it. In JavaScript, you usually use the reserved keyword `var` to create variables. For example, to create a variable named `myVariable`, you would use this statement: `var myVariable;`. Using a statement similar to `var myVariable;` to create a variable is called **declaring** the variable.

When you declare a variable, you can also assign a specific value to, or **initialize**, the variable using the syntax `var variable_name = value;`. The equal sign in a variable declaration assigns a value to the variable.

The value you assign to a variable can be a literal string or a numeric value. For example, the statement `var myVariable = "Hello";` assigns the literal string "Hello" to the variable `myVariable`. (Keep in mind that literal strings must be enclosed in quotation marks.) The statement `var myVariable = 100;` assigns the numeric value 100 to the variable `myVariable`.

You are not required to use the `var` keyword to declare a variable. However, omission of the `var` keyword affects where a variable can be used in a program. Regardless of where in your program you intend to use a variable, it is good programming practice to use the `var` keyword when declaring a variable.

Although you can assign a value when a variable is declared, you are not required to do so. Your program may assign the value later, or you may use a variable to store user input. When you declare a variable without assigning it a value, you must use the `var` keyword.

In addition to assigning literal strings and numeric values to a variable, you can also assign the value of one variable to another. For instance, in the following code, the first statement creates a variable named `firstNum` without assigning it an initial value. The second statement creates another variable named `secondNum` and assigns to it a numeric value of 100. The third statement then assigns the value of the `secondNum` variable to the `firstNum` variable. If you were to print the value of the `firstNum` variable after assigning to it the value of the `secondNum` variable, it would print a value of 100.

```
var firstNum;
var secondNum = 100;
firstNum = secondNum;
```

You can also perform arithmetic by using variables that contain numeric values. For instance, the following code declares two variables and assigns to them numeric values. The last statement declares another variable and assigns to it the sum of the values stored in the other variables. If you were to print the value of the sum variable after assigning to it the sum of the `firstNum` and `secondNum` variables, it would print a value of 300.

```
var firstNum = 100;
var secondNum = 200;
var sum = firstNum + secondNum;
```

Modifying Variables

Regardless of whether you assign a value to a variable when it is declared, you can change the variable's value at any point in a program by using a statement that includes the variable's name, followed by an equal sign, followed by the value you want to assign to the variable. The following code declares a variable named `myDog`, assigns it an initial value of "Golden Retriever", and prints it using the `document.writeln()`

method. The third statement changes the value of the `myDog` variable to `Irish Setter`, and the fourth statement prints the new value. Notice that it is only necessary to declare the `myDog` variable (using the `var` keyword) once.

```
var myDog = "Golden Retriever";
document.writeln(myDog);
myDog = "Irish Setter";
document.writeln(myDog);
```

It is a tradition among programmers to practice a new language by writing a program that prints or displays the text "Hello World!". Creating a Hello World program is surprisingly addictive. If you are an experienced programmer, then you have undoubtedly created Hello World programs in the past. If you are new to programming, then you will probably find yourself creating Hello World programs when you learn new programming languages. Earlier in this chapter, you examined a Hello World program written in JavaScript. Now, you will create your own Hello World program in JavaScript. You will create a simple program that prints the text "Hello World!" and says hello to the sun and the moon. Your program will also print a line of scientific information about each celestial body. You will use variables to store and print each piece of information.

To create the Hello World program:

1. Create a new document in your text editor.

2. Type the opening `<html>` and `<head>` tags. Also type the `<title>...` `</title>` tag pair and an opening `<pre>` tag, as follows:

   ```
   <html><head><title>Hello World</title><pre>
   ```

3. Type the opening `<script>` tag and HTML comments (to hide the code from incompatible browsers) as follows:

   ```
   <script language="JavaScript">
   <!-- HIDE FROM INCOMPATIBLE BROWSERS
   ```

4. Type the following statements, which declare variables containing the name of each celestial body and variables containing scientific information about each celestial body:

   ```
   var worldVar = "World";
   var sunVar = "Sun";
   var moonVar = "Moon";
   var worldInfo = 92897000;
   var sunInfo = 72000000;
   var moonInfo = 3456;
   ```

5. Next, add the following statements that print the values stored in each of the variables you declared and initialized in the last step. Notice that the `document.write()` and `document.writeln()` methods use a plus

13

sign (+) to combine literal strings with variables. (In the next chapter, you will learn more about performing similar operations in JavaScript.)

```
document.writeln("Hello " + worldVar + "!");
document.writeln("The " + worldVar + " is "
    + worldInfo + " miles from the " + sunVar + ".");
document.writeln("Hello " + sunVar + "!");
document.writeln("The " + sunVar
    + "'s core temperature is approximately "
    + sunInfo + " degrees Fahrenheit" + ".");
document.writeln("Hello " + moonVar + "!");
document.writeln("The " + moonVar + " is " + moonInfo
    + " miles in diameter.");
```

6. Add the following code to end the HTML comments and close the `<script>`, `<pre>`, `<body>`, and `<html>` tag pairs:

```
// STOP HIDING FROM INCOMPATIBLE BROWSERS -->
</script></pre></body></html>
```

7. Save the file as **Ch13JavaScript03.html** in the Chapter folder for Chapter 13. Open the **Ch13JavaScript03.html** file in your Web browser. Figure 13-8 shows how the HelloWorld.html file looks in a Web browser.

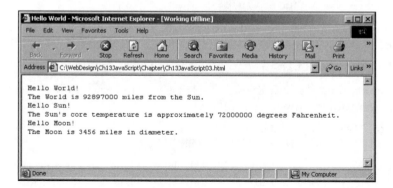

Figure 13-8   Output of Ch13JavaScript03.html

 If you receive error messages, make sure that all of your JavaScript code is in the correct case. (Remember that JavaScript is case-sensitive.) Also check to see that you have entered all of the opening and closing HTML tags.

8. Close the Web browser window.

WORKING WITH FUNCTIONS

Earlier in this chapter, you learned that procedures associated with an object are called methods. In JavaScript programming, you can write your own procedures, called **functions**, which are similar to the methods associated with an object. Functions are useful because they make it possible to treat a related group of JavaScript statements as a single unit. Functions, like all JavaScript code, must be contained within the `<script>`... `</script>` tag pair. In the following section, you will learn more about incorporating functions in your JavaScript code.

Defining Functions

Before you can use a function in a JavaScript program, you must first create, or define, it. Within an HTML document, the lines that make up a function are called the **function definition**. The syntax for defining a function is:

```
function name_of_function(parameters) {
statements;
}
```

Parameters are placed within the parentheses that follow a function name. A **parameter** is a variable that will be used within a function. Placing a parameter name within the parentheses of a function definition is the equivalent of declaring a new variable. However, you do not need to include the **var** keyword. For example, suppose that you want to write a function named `calculate_square_root()` that calculates the square root of a number contained in a parameter named **number**. The function name would then be written as `calculate_square_root(number)`. In this case, the function declaration is declaring a new parameter (which is a variable) named **number**. Functions can contain multiple parameters separated by commas. To add three separate number parameters to the `calculate_square_root()` function, you would write the function name as `calculate_square_root(number1, number2, number3)`. Note that parameters (such as `the number1`, `number2`, and `number3` parameters) receive their values when you call the function from elsewhere in your program. (You will learn how to call functions in the next section.)

 Functions do not have to contain parameters. Many functions only perform a task and do not require external data. For example, you might create a function that displays the same message each time a user visits your Web site; this kind of function only needs to be executed and does not require any other information.

Following the parentheses that contain the function parameters is a set of curly braces (called function braces) that contain the function statements. Function statements are the statements that do the actual work of the function (such as calculating the square root of the parameter or displaying a message on the screen), and they must be contained

13

within the function braces. The following is an example of a function that prints the names of multiple companies using the `writeln()` method of the `Document` object. (Recall that functions are very similar to the methods associated with an object.)

```
function print_company_name(company1, company2, company3) {
    document.writeln(company1);
    document.writeln(company2);
    document.writeln(company3);
}
```

Notice how the preceding function is structured. The opening curly brace is on the same line as the function name, and the closing curly brace is on its own line following the function statements. Each statement between the curly braces is indented one-half inch. This structure is the preferred format among many JavaScript programmers. However, for simple functions it is sometimes easier to include the function name, curly braces, and statements on the same line. Recall that JavaScript ignores line breaks, spaces, and tabs. The only syntax requirement for spacing in JavaScript is that a semicolon separate statements on the same line.

Calling Functions

A function definition does not execute automatically. Creating a function definition only names the function, specifies its parameters, and organizes the statements it will execute. To execute a function, you must invoke, or **call**, it from elsewhere in your program. The code that calls a function is referred to as a **function call** and consists of the function name followed by parentheses that contain any variables or values to be assigned to the function arguments. Sending arguments (variables or values) to the parameters of a called function is called **passing arguments**. When you pass arguments to a function, the value of each argument is then assigned to the value of the corresponding parameter in the function definition. (Again, remember that parameters are simply variables that are declared within a function definition.)

Always put your functions within the head section, and place calls to a function within the body section. As you will recall, the head section of an HTML document is always rendered before the body section. Thus, placing functions in the head section and function calls in the body section ensures that functions will be created before they are actually called. If your program does attempt to call a function before it has been created, you will receive an error. Figure 13-9 shows a JavaScript program that prints the name of a company. Figure 13-10 shows the output. Notice that the function is defined in the head section of the HTML document and is called from the body section.

In the program in Figure 13-10, the statement that calls the function passes the literal string "Course Technology" to the function. When the `print_company_name()` function receives the literal string, it assigns it to the `company_name` variable.

```
<html><head>
<title>Print Company Name Function</title>
<script language="JavaScript">
<!-- HIDE FROM INCOMPATIBLE BROWSERS
function print_company_name(company_name) {
     document.writeln(company_name);
}
// STOP HIDING FROM INCOMPATIBLE BROWSERS -->
</script></head><body>
<script language="JavaScript">
<!-- HIDE FROM INCOMPATIBLE BROWSERS
print_company_name("Course Technology");
// STOP HIDING FROM INCOMPATIBLE BROWSERS -->
</script></body></html>
```

Figure 13-9   JavaScript function being called from the body section

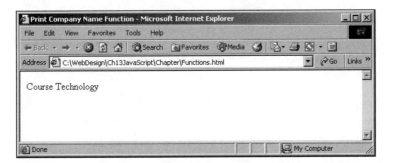

Figure 13-10   Output of JavaScript function being called from the body section

13

 A JavaScript program is composed of all the `<script>` sections within an HTML document; each individual `<script>` section is not necessarily its own individual JavaScript program (although it could be if there are no other `<script>` sections in the HTML document).

In many instances, you may want your program to receive the results from a called function and then use those results in other code. For instance, consider a function that calculates the average of a series of numbers that are passed to it as arguments. Such a function would be useless if your program could not print the result or use it elsewhere in your program. Plus, you may need to use the result elsewhere in your program. As another example, suppose you have created a function that simply prints the name of a company. Now suppose that you want to alter the program so that it uses the company name in another section of code. You can return a value from a function to a calling statement by assigning the calling statement to a variable. The following statement calls a function named **average_numbers()** and assigns the return value to a variable named **returnValue**. The statement also passes three literal values to the function.

```
var returnValue = average_numbers(1, 2, 3);
```

To actually return a value to a `returnValue` variable, the code must include a return statement within the `average_numbers()` function. A **return statement** is a statement that returns a value to the statement that called the function. The following code contains the `average_numbers()` function, which calculates the average of three numbers. The code also includes a return statement that returns the value (contained in the result variable) to the calling statement :

```
function average_numbers(a, b, c) {
    var sum_of_numbers = a + b + c;
    var result = sum_of_numbers / 3;
    return result;
}
```

You are not required to return a value from a function.

Next, you will create a JavaScript program that contains two functions. The first function will print a message when it is called; the second function will return a value that is printed after the calling statement.

To create a JavaScript program that contains two functions:

1. Create a new document in your text editor.

2. Type the opening `<html>` and `<head>` tags, and also type the `<title>...</title>` tag pair, as follows:

   `<html><head><title>Two Functions Program</title>`

3. Type the opening `<script>` tag and HTML comments to hide the code from incompatible browsers:

   ```
   <script language="JavaScript">
   <!-- HIDE FROM INCOMPATIBLE BROWSERS
   ```

4. Type the first function, which writes a message to the screen using an argument that will ultimately be passed to it from the calling statement:

   ```
   function print_message(first_message) {
       document.writeln(first_message);
   }
   ```

5. Type the second function, which displays a second message. In this case, the message ("This message was returned from a function") is defined within the function itself. The only purpose of this function is to return the literal string "This message was returned from a function" to the calling statement.

   ```
   function return_message(second_message) {
       return "This message was returned from a function.";
   }
   ```

6. Type the following lines to close the `<script>` and `<head>` elements:

```
// STOP HIDING FROM INCOMPATIBLE BROWSERS -->
</script></head>
```

7. Add the following code to begin the body of the HTML document and to create a preformatted text container. Also, type the opening statements for the JavaScript section that will call the functions in the head section:

```
<body><pre>
<script language="JavaScript">
<!-- HIDE FROM INCOMPATIBLE BROWSERS
```

8. Type the following three statements to call the functions in the head section. The first statement sends the text string "This message was printed from a function." This statement does not receive a return value. The second statement assigns the function call to a variable named `return_value`, but does not send any arguments to the function. The third statement writes the value of the `return_value` variable to the screen.

```
print_message("This message was printed from a function.");
var return_value = return_message();
document.writeln(return_value);
```

9. Add the following code to end the HTML comments and close the `<script>`, `<pre>`, `<body>`, and `<html>` tag pairs:

```
// STOP HIDING FROM INCOMPATIBLE BROWSERS -->
</script></pre></body></html>
```

10. Save the file as **Ch13JavaScript04.html** in the Chapter folder for Chapter 13. Open the **Ch13JavaScript04.html** file in your Web browser. Figure 13-11 shows how the Ch13JavaScript04.html file looks in a Web browser.

13

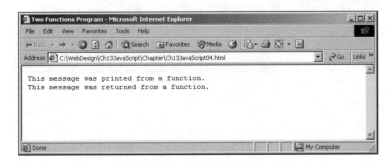

Figure 13-11   Output of Ch13JavaScript04.html

11. Close the Web browser window.

UNDERSTANDING EVENTS

One of the primary ways in which JavaScript makes HTML documents dynamic is through events. An **event** is a specific circumstance that is monitored by JavaScript. As you will see in this section, you can use JavaScript events to allow users to interact with your Web pages. The most common events are actions that users perform. For example, when a user clicks a button, a Click event is generated. You can think of an event as a trigger that fires specific JavaScript code in response to a given situation.

User-generated events, however, are not the only kinds of events monitored by JavaScript. Events that are not direct results of user actions, such as the Load event, are also monitored. The Load event, which is triggered automatically by a Web browser, occurs when an HTML document finishes loading in a Web browser. Table 13-1 lists some JavaScript events and explains what triggers them.

Table 13-1   JavaScript events

Event	Triggered When
Abort	The loading of an image is interrupted
Blur	An element, such as a radio button, becomes inactive
Click	The user clicks an element once
Change	The value of an element, such as text box, changes
Error	An error occurs when a document or image is being loaded
Focus	An element, such as a command button, becomes active
Load	A document or image loads
MouseOut	The mouse moves off an element
MouseOver	The mouse moves over an element
Reset	A form's fields are reset to its default values
Select	A user selects a field in a form
Submit	A user submits a form
Unload	A document unloads

HTML Tags and Events

The `<input>` tag is a commonly used HTML tag that allows users to generate events. As you learned in Chapter 2, the `<input>` tag creates input fields (such as text boxes and command buttons) that interact with users. The `<input>` tag has several attributes, including the type attribute. The basic syntax for the `<input>` tag is `<input type="input type">`. The type attribute is a required field and determines the kind of input field that the `<input>` tag generates. For example, the statement `<input type="radio">` creates a radio button, and the statement `<input type="text">` creates a text field. You will use the `<input>` tag throughout this text. The `<input>` tag is most often used with forms and is placed within the `<form>` element.

Event Handlers

When an event occurs, a program executes JavaScript code that responds to that particular event. Code that executes in response to a specific event is called an **event handler**. An event itself, such as a Click event, tells JavaScript to execute an event handler. You include event handler code as an attribute of the HTML tag that initiates the event. The syntax of an event handler within an HTML tag is:

```
<html_tag event_handler="JavaScript Code">
```

Event handler names are the same as the name of the event itself, but with a prefix of "on". For example, the event handler for the Click event is `onClick`, and the event handler for the Load event is `onLoad`. Recall that HTML tags are not case-sensitive, whereas JavaScript code is. Because event handlers are part of an HTML tag, they are not case-sensitive. Therefore, you could write the name of the `onClick` event handler as `ONCLICK`, `onclick`, or `ONclick`. However, capitalizing only the first letter of the event name itself is a standard convention.

The JavaScript code for an event handler is contained within the quotation marks following the name of the JavaScript event handler. The following code uses the `<input>` tag to create a Command button, which is similar to an OK or Cancel button. The tag also includes an `onClick` event handler that executes the JavaScript `alert()` method, in response to a Click event (which occurs when the button is clicked). The **alert() method** displays a pop-up dialog box with an OK button. You can pass a single literal string or a variable as an argument to the `alert()` method. The value of the literal string or variable is then displayed in the pop-up dialog box.

```
<input type="button" onClick="alert('You clicked a button!')">
```

Typically, the code executed by the `onClick` event handler—the `alert()` method—is contained within double quotation marks. In the preceding example, however, the literal string being passed is contained in single quotation marks. This is because the `alert()` method itself is already enclosed in double quotation marks.

The `alert()` method is the only statement being executed in the preceding event handler. You can, however, include multiple JavaScript statements in an event handler, as long as the statements are separated by semicolons. For example, to include two statements in the event handler example—a statement that creates a variable and another statement that uses the `alert()` method to display the variable—you would type the following:

```
<input type="button" onClick="var message='You clicked a
button'; alert(message)">
```

Another JavaScript function that responds to events is `prompt()`, which is similar to `alert()`. The **prompt() method** displays a dialog box with a message, a text box, an OK button, and a Cancel button. Any text that the user enters into a `prompt()` method text box can be assigned to a variable. The syntax for the `prompt()` method is `variable_name = prompt(message, default_text);`.

Next, you will create an HTML document that demonstrates JavaScript `onLoad`, `onUnload`, `onClick`, and `onChange` event handlers and uses both the `alert()` and the `prompt()` functions.

To create an HTML document that incorporates JavaScript event handlers:

1. Create a new document in your text editor. Then, type the opening `<html>` and `<head>` tags along with the title, the opening `<script>` tag, and the HTML comments that will hide the code from incompatible browsers:

```
<html><head><title>JavaScript Events</title>
<script language="JavaScript">
<!-- HIDE FROM INCOMPATIBLE BROWSERS
```

2. Type **var visitor_name = "";** on the next line to create a variable that will store the name of a visitor to the Web page.

3. Type **function greet_visitor() {** on the next line to begin the `greet_visitor()` function. You will call the `greet_visitor()` function with the `onLoad` event in the `<body>` tag.

4. Add the following statement, which prompts the user for his or her name and assigns the name to the `visitor_name` variable.

```
visitor_name = prompt("Please enter your name",
    "Enter your name here");
```

5. Type an `alert()` method that displays a personalized greeting to the visitor, followed by a closing brace for the function.

```
alert("Welcome, " + visitor_name + "!");
}
```

6. Next, add the following `farewell_visitor()` function, which will be called by the `onUnload` event in the `<body>` tag. The `farewell_visitor()` function also uses the `visitor_name` variable.

```
function farewell_visitor() {
    alert("Thanks, " + visitor_name +
        ", for visiting this Web page!");
}
```

7. Type the following lines to close the `<script>` and `<head>` sections.

```
// STOP HIDING FROM INCOMPATIBLE BROWSERS -->
</script></head>
```

8. Type the following `<body>` tag, which uses the `onLoad` and `onUnload` events to call the `greet_visitor()` and `farewell_visitor()` functions.

```
<body onLoad="greet_visitor();"
onUnload="farewell_visitor();">
```

9. Add the following form section, which includes two `<input>` tags. The first `<input>` tag creates a text field that includes an `onChange` event handler.

The onChange event handler displays an alert() dialog box whenever a user leaves the text field (by clicking elsewhere or by pressing Tab) after changing its contents. The second <input> tag creates a button that displays the contents of the text field by using its name attribute. Also, add the tags to close the <body> and <html> tags.

```
<form>
<input type="text" name="text_field" size="25"
      onChange="alert(
            'The value of the text_field has changed.');"><br>
<input type="button" value="Display Text Field Contents"
      onClick="alert(text_field.value);">
</form></body></html>
```

10. Save the file as **Ch13JavaScript05.html** in the Chapter folder for Chapter 13.

Next, open the Ch13JavaScript05.html file in your Web browser and test the JavaScript code.

To open the Ch13JavaScript05.html file in your Web browser and test the JavaScript code:

1. Open **Ch13JavaScript05.html** in your Web browser. The onLoad event handler is called, and the greet_visitor() function executes, displaying the prompt dialog box shown in Figure 13-12.

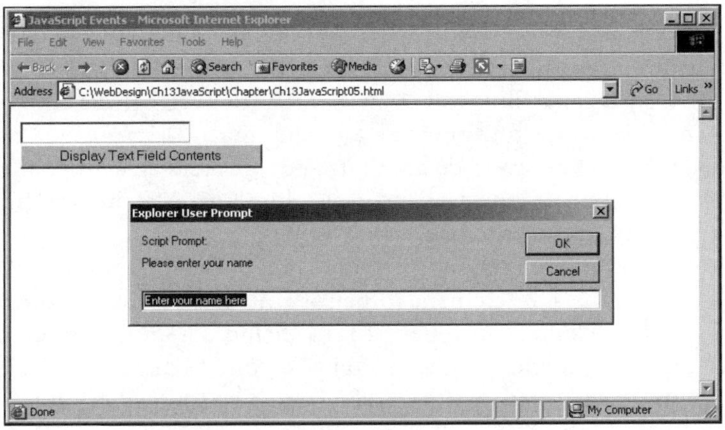

Figure 13-12   Example of the prompt() method

2. Enter your name into the dialog box and click the **OK** button. An alert dialog box displays the personalized greeting. Click the **OK** button in the alert dialog box.

3. Click in the text field, type **Sample Text**, and then press **Tab** to exit the field. Because you made a change in the text field, the onChange event handler is called, and another alert dialog box opens.

4. Click the **OK** button in the alert dialog box. Now click the **Display Text Field Contents** button to call the `onClick` event handler, which displays another alert dialog box with the contents of the text field (`Sample Text`). Click the **OK** button in the alert dialog box.

5. To demonstrate the `onUnload` event handler, open the file named **Ch13JavaScript03.html**, which you created earlier in this chapter named in the current Web browser window. Before your Web browser displays the file, the `onUnload` event handler executes and the `farewell_visitor()` function executes, displaying the last alert dialog box, which thanks you by name for visiting the Web page. Click **OK** to close the alert dialog box.

6. Close the Web browser window.

Link Events

Recall that HTML documents contain hypertext links, which are used to open files or to navigate to other documents on the Web. The primary event associated with links is the Click event. Clicking a link automatically executes the Click event, and the URL associated with the link opens. When a user clicks a link, execution of the Click event is handled automatically by the Web browser. You do not need to add an `onClick` event handler to the `<a>` element.

There may be times, however, when you want to override the automatic Click event with your own code. For instance, you may want to warn the user about the content of the HTML document that a particular link will open. In order to override the automatic Click event with your own code, you add to the `<a>` element an `onClick` event handler that executes custom code. When you override an internal event handler with your own code, your code must return a value of true or false, using the return statement. With the `<a>` element, a value of false indicates that you want the Web browser to perform its default event handling operation of opening the URL referenced in the link. A value of true indicates that you do *not* want the `<a>` element to perform its default event handling operation. For example, the `<a>` element in Figure 13-13 includes a custom `onClick` event handler. The `warn_user()` function that is called by the `onClick` event handler returns a value generated by the `confirm()` method. The **confirm()** method displays a dialog box that contains a Cancel button as well as an OK button. When a user clicks the OK button in the confirm dialog box, a value of `true` is returned. When a user clicks the Cancel button, a value of `false` is returned. Figure 13-14 shows how the program appears in Internet Explorer after you click the link.

Notice that there are two return statements in Figure 13-13. The return statement in the `warnUser()` function returns a value to the `onClick` event handler. The return statement in the `onClick` event handler returns the same value to the Web browser.

```
<html>
<head>
<title>Custom onClick Event Example</title>
<script language="JavaScript">
<!-- HIDE FROM INCOMPATIBLE BROWSERS
function warnUser() {
     return confirm(
"This link is only for people who love golden retrievers!");
}
// STOP HIDING FROM INCOMPATIBLE BROWSERS -->
</script>
</head>
<body>
<a href="GoldenRetrievers.html" onClick=
"return warnUser();">Golden Retriever Club Home Page</a>
</body>
</html>
```

Figure 13-13   Link with a custom `onClick` event handler

Figure 13-14   Output in Internet Explorer of program with a custom `onClick` event handler

Two other events associated with links are the `MouseOver` and `MouseOut` events. The **`MouseOver` event** occurs when the mouse is moved over a link. The **`MouseOut` event** occurs when the mouse is moved off a link. One of the most common uses of the `MouseOver` and `MouseOut` events is to change the text that appears in a Web browser status bar. By default, a link's URL appears in the status bar when the mouse passes over a link. If you prefer, you can use the `onMouseOver` event handler to display your own custom message for a link in the status bar. To make your custom message appear in the status bar, you use the JavaScript **status property**, which stores the text that will appear in the status bar.

The `onMouseOut` event handler is used to reset the text displayed in the status bar after the mouse is moved off a link. Most often, any text that is displayed in the status bar is cleared by using the statement `onMouseOut="status = ' ';"` to set the `status` property to an empty string. Here, the two single quotation marks specify an empty string. You use single quotation marks instead of double quotation marks because the statement is already contained within a pair of double quotation marks. (Remember that you cannot use double quotation marks inside another set of double quotation marks.) The semicolon marks the end of the JavaScript statement. If you prefer, instead of an empty string, you could use this statement to display another custom message in the status bar.

The following code uses the `onMouseOver` event handler to display the text "Golden Retriever Club Home Page" in the status bar instead of the link's URL, GoldenRetrievers.html. The `onMouseOut` event handler displays the text "You almost visited the Golden Retriever Home Page!" after the mouse moves off the link:

```
<a href = "GoldenRetrievers.html" onMouseOver = "status =
'Golden Retriever Club Home Page'; return true;" onMouseOut =
"status = 'You almost visited the Golden Retriever Club Home
Page'; return true;" >Golden Retriever Club Home Page</a>
```

 JavaScript also includes a `defaultStatus` property that you can use within a `<script>...</script>` tag pair to specify the default text that appears in the status bar whenever the mouse is not positioned over a link. The syntax for the `defaultStatus` property is `defaultStatus = "Enter default status text here.";`. Note that the `defaultStatus` property overrides any text specified by an `onMouseOut` event handler.

Next, you will create two HTML documents (one with a green background and one with a red background) that demonstrate the `Click`, `MouseOver`, and `MouseOut` events associated with a link.

To create an HTML document that demonstrates the Click, MouseOver, and MouseOut events associated with a link:

1. Create a new document in your text editor. Type the opening `<html>` and `<head>` tags along with the title, opening `<script>` tag, and HTML comments to hide the code from incompatible browsers:

```
<html><head>
<title>Red Page</title>
<script language="JavaScript">
<!-- HIDE FROM INCOMPATIBLE BROWSERS
```

2. Add the following function, which will ultimately be called from a link's `onClick` event handler. The function displays a dialog box that asks the user to confirm that he or she wants to open the link's URL.

```
function confirmPageChange() {
     return confirm
("Are you sure you want to display the green page?");
}
```

3. Type the following lines to close the `<script>` and head sections:

```
// STOP HIDING FROM INCOMPATIBLE BROWSERS -->
</script></head>
```

4. Type the opening `<body>` tag, including the BGCOLOR attribute, which determines the document background color:

```
<body bgcolor="red">
```

5. Create the following link that contains onClick, onMouseOver, and onMouseOut event handlers. Also, add the tags to close the `<body>` and `<html>` tags.

```
<a href="Ch13JavaScript06b.html"
onClick="return confirmPageChange();"
onMouseOver=
"status = 'This link opens the green page';
return true;"
onMouseOut=
"status = 'You did not open the green page!!';
return true;">
Click here to open the green page</a>
</body></html>
```

6. Save the file as **Ch13JavaScript06a.html** in the Chapter folder for Chapter 13. (Note the "a" after the "6".) Then immediately save the file again as **Ch13JavaScript06b.html**. (Note the "b" after the "6".)

7. Within the new **Ch13JavaScript06b.html** file, change the text in the `<title>` tag to **Green Page**. In the confirmPageChange() function, change the word **green** to **red** within the text string. Change the BGCOLOR attribute in the `<body>` tag to **green**.

8. Within the `<a>` tag, change the href from Ch13JavaScript06b.html to **Ch13JavaScript06a.html.** Also change the word **green** to **red** within the two event handlers in which it appears. Notice that you are using relative URLs because the Ch13JavaScript06a.html and Ch13JavaScript06b.html files are located within the same folder. Finally, change the descriptive text between the `<a>...</a>` tag pair from Click here to open the green page to **Click here to open the red page.**

9. Save the file and then open either **Ch13JavaScript06a.html** or **Ch13JavaScript06b.html** in your Web browser. Clicking the link in either file should display the Confirm dialog box, which in turn should open the other file when you click OK. Also check to see that the status bar text is being updated during the MouseOver and MouseOut events for each file. An example of Ch13JavaScript06b.html and the Confirm dialog box appears in Figure 13-15.

10. Close the Web browser window.

13

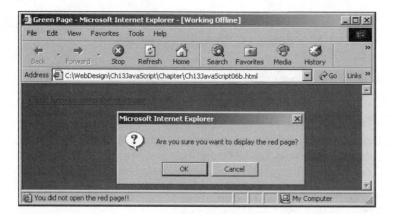

Figure 13-15   Ch13JavaScript06b.html and the Confirm dialog box

CHAPTER SUMMARY

◘ The term "scripting language" refers to programming languages that are executed by an interpreter from within a Web browser.

◘ The international, standardized version of JavaScript is called ECMAScript.

◘ The `<script>` tag is used to notify the Web browser that the commands that follow it need to be interpreted by a scripting engine.

◘ Comments are nonprinting lines that contain various kinds of remarks.

◘ To hide embedded JavaScript code from incompatible browsers, enclose the code between the `<script>...</script>` tag pair in an HTML comment block.

◘ In an HTML document with multiple JavaScript code sections, each section is executed in the order in which it appears.

◘ The values a program stores in computer memory are commonly called variables.

◘ The name you assign to a variable is called an identifier.

◘ Reserved words, which are also called keywords, are special words that are part of the JavaScript language syntax.

◘ In JavaScript programming, you can write your own procedures, called functions, which are similar to the methods associated with an object.

◘ Within an HTML document, the lines that compose a function are called the function definition.

◘ A parameter is a variable that will be used within a function.

◘ To execute a function, you must invoke, or call, it from elsewhere in your program. The call to a function is referred to as a function call.

❏ Sending arguments (variables or values) to the parameters of a called function is referred to as passing arguments.

❏ A return statement returns a value to the statement that called the function.

❏ An event is a specific circumstance that is monitored by JavaScript.

❏ Code that executes in response to a specific event is called an event handler.

REVIEW QUESTIONS

1. Scripting code in an HTML document is located _____.

   a. inside the closing bracket of the `<script>` tag

   b. between the `<script>...</script>` tag pairs

   c. before the opening `<script>` tag

   d. after the closing `<script>` tag

2. With JavaScript, new text is created on a Web page using the `write()` method or the _____ method.

   a. `output()`

   b. `writeln()`

   c. `print()`

   d. `println()`

3. Which of the following is the correct syntax for including a quoted string within a literal string?

   a. `"this is a ""quoted"" string"`

   b. `'this is a 'quoted' string'`

   c. `"this is a "quoted" string"`

   d. `"this is a 'quoted' string"`

4. When would you *not* use a JavaScript source file?

   a. when you will use the JavaScript code with incompatible browsers

   b. when the JavaScript source file is shared by multiple HTML documents

   c. when the JavaScript code is fairly short and is not shared

   d. when you do not want to share your code with other programmers

5. Block comments begin with /* and end with _____.

   a. `*/`

   b. `/*`

   c. `//`

   d. `**`

13

6. How are JavaScript code sections executed in an HTML document?

   a. All embedded JavaScript code is executed first.

   b. All JavaScript source files are executed first.

   c. Each JavaScript code section is executed according to the sequence in which you added it to the HTML document.

   d. Each JavaScript code section is executed in the order in which it appears.

7. Which is the correct syntax for declaring a variable and assigning it a string?

   a. `var myVariable = "Hello";`

   b. `var myVariable = Hello;`

   c. `"Hello" = var myVariable;`

   d. `var "Hello" = myVariable;`

8. A(n) _____ allows you to treat a related group of JavaScript commands as a single unit.

   a. statement

   b. variable

   c. function

   d. event

9. You use a _____ statement to return a value to the statement that called a function.

   a. return

   b. result

   c. reply

   d. send

10. The _____ event occurs when an HTML document finishes loading in a Web browser.

    a. Load

    b. Complete

    c. Display

    d. Click

11. Which of the following is correct?

    a. `onClick="alert('You clicked a button!');"`

    b. `onClick="alert("You clicked a button!");"`

    c. `onClick="alert(You clicked a button!);"`

    d. `onClick=alert('You clicked a button!');`

12. What is the second argument passed to the `prompt()` method used for?

    a. Default text in the prompt dialog text box

    b. As title bar text for the prompt dialog box

c. As a variable to which the value passed as the first argument to the **prompt()** method is assigned

d. You cannot pass a second argument to the **prompt()** method.

13. Which of the following is the correct syntax for printing "Welcome to My Home Page" in the status bar, using the **MouseOver** event?

a. `<a href="HomePage.html"`
`onMouseOver="status = 'Welcome to My Home Page; return`
`true;">`
`Welcome to My Home Page</A>`

b. `<a href="HomePage.html"`
`onMouseOver="status = true;">`
`Welcome to My Home Page</A>`

c. `<a href="HomePage.html"`
`onMouseOver="status = 'Welcome to My Home Page'; return`
`true;">`
`My Home Page</A>`

d. `<a href="HomePage.html"`
`onMouseOver="status = 'Welcome to My Home Page'; return`
`true;">`
`My Home Page</A>`

14. The _____ event handler is used to reset the text displayed in the status bar after the mouse is moved off a link.

a. `onMouseOff`

b. `onMouseLeave`

c. `onMouseOut`

d. `onMouseMove`

15. The default text that appears in the status bar whenever the mouse is not positioned over a link is controlled by the _____ property.

a. `originalStatus`

b. `onMouseOutDefault`

c. `defaultText`

d. `defaultStatus`

13

HANDS-ON EXERCISES

Exercise 13-1

In this exercise, you will create a simple HTML document that displays two text lines. The first text line will be displayed by embedded JavaScript code and the other by a JavaScript source file.

1. Create a new document in your text editor, and then create the document header using the appropriate HTML tags. Include a head section with a `<title>`; use **Exercise 13-1** for the title text.

2. Add code that displays the first text line of the Web page using embedded JavaScript code. Be sure to include the language attribute in the `<script>` element. Place the `<script>` element within a `<pre>` element.

3. Add code that displays the second text line of the Web page using a JavaScript source file. Be sure to include the language attribute in the `<script>` tags.

4. Add an HTML comment with your name and the date. Add the same comment information to the embedded JavaScript and the JavaScript source file, using JavaScript comments. Hide the JavaScript code from incompatible browsers by using HTML comment tags, and create a `<noscript>` section that says "Your browser does not support JavaScript or JavaScript is disabled."

5. Type the closing `</body>` and `</html>` tags.

6. Save the HTML document as **Ch13JavaScriptEX01.html** and the JavaScript source file as **Ch13JavaScriptEX01.js** in the Exercises folder for Chapter 13.

7. Open **Ch13JavaScriptEX01.html** in your browser. Figure 13-16 shows part of the document.

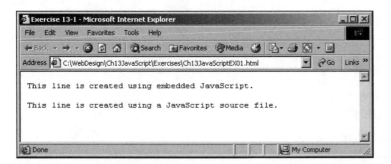

Figure 13-16   Output of Exercise 13-1

Exercise 13-2

In this exercise, you will create a JavaScript program that assigns values to several variables, and then prints the value of each variable using the `write()` and `writeln()` methods.

1. Create a new document in your text editor, and then create the document header using the appropriate HTML tags. Include a head section with a `<title>`; use **Exercise 13-2** for the title text.

2. Create a script section in the document body and declare five variables for holding the names of stocks. Declare each variable on its own line.

3. Following the variable declarations, add statements that assign a value to each of the stock variables.

4. Finally, write code that prints each of the variables using `writeln( )`methods, starting with your most preferred stock choice. Also, combine the `write( )` and the `writeln( )` methods to add descriptive text before the stock name. For example, if your most preferred stock choice is Microsoft, you should print "My first stock choice is Microsoft".

5. Type the closing `</body>` and `</html>` tags.

6. Save the HTML document as **Ch13JavaScriptEX02.html** in the Exercises folder for Chapter 13.

7. Open **Ch13JavaScriptEX02.html** in your browser. Your document should look similar to Figure 13-17.

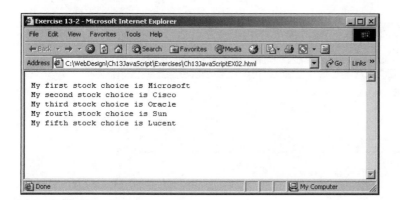

```
My first stock choice is Microsoft
My second stock choice is Cisco
My third stock choice is Oracle
My fourth stock choice is Sun
My fifth stock choice is Lucent
```

Figure 13-17   Output of Exercise 13-2

Exercise 13-3

13

In this exercise, you will create a JavaScript program with a function that returns a string value.

1. Create a new document in your text editor, and then type the following code:

```
<html>
<head>
<title>Exercise 13-3</title>
<pre>
<script language="JavaScript">
<!-- HIDE FROM INCOMPATIBLE BROWSERS
function getCompanyName() {
  var companyName = "Course Technology";
}
// STOP HIDING FROM INCOMPATIBLE BROWSERS -->
</script>
</pre>
</head>
<body>
</body>
</html>
```

2. Modify the `getCompanyName()` function so that it returns the company name to another calling function.

3. Add statements after the `getCompanyName()` function definition that call the `getCompanyName()` function and assign the return value to a variable named `retValue`.

4. Finally, write code that prints the contents of the `retValue` variable.

5. Save the program as **Ch13JavaScriptEX03.html** in the Exercises folder for Chapter 13.

6. Open **Ch13JavaScriptEX03.html** in your browser. Your document should look similar to Figure 13-18.

Figure 13-18   Output of Exercise 13-3

Exercise 13-4

In this exercise, you will correct errors in a simple JavaScript program.

1. Create a new document in your text editor, and then type the following code:

```
<html>
<head>
<title>Exercise 13-4</title>
<script language="JavaScript">
document.write(sampleScript());
</script>
</head>
<body>
<script language="JavaScript">
function sampleScript() {
    return "This line returned from the sampleScript() function."
}
</script>
</body>
</html>
```

2. The code you typed in the preceding step should print a single statement that reads "This line is returned from the sampleScript() function." However, the code actually contains a design error that generates error messages when you attempt to

open the program in a Web browser. Correct the error and make sure the program runs successfully in a browser. (*Hint:* The problem has to do with where the script sections are placed in the HTML document.)

3. Save the program as **Ch13JavaScriptEX04.html** in the Exercises folder for Chapter 13.

4. Open **Ch13JavaScriptEX04.html** in your browser. Your document should look similar to Figure 13-19.

Figure 13-19 Output of Exercise 13-4

Exercise 13-5

In this exercise, you will correct errors in the event handler code for an `<a>` element.

1. Create a new document in your text editor, and then create the document header using the appropriate HTML tags. Include a head section with a `<title>`; use **Exercise 13-5** for the title text.

2. Type the following body section, which contains a form section:

```
<body>
<form>
<a href = "Yahoo.html"
   onMouseOver = "status = 'Yahoo!'"
   onMouseOut = "status = 'You did not select Yahoo!'">
Yahoo!</A>
</form>
</body>
```

3. The event handlers in the form section should display "Yahoo!" when your mouse passes over the link and "You did not select Yahoo!" when your mouse moves off the link. However, only the `onMouseOut` event handler actually works correctly. Locate and fix the error.

4. Type the closing `</body>` and `</html>` tags.

5. Save the file as **Ch13JavaScriptEX05.html** in the Exercises folder for Chapter 13.

6. Open **Ch13JavaScriptEX05.html** in your browser and test the link. Figure 13-20 shows how the status bar should appear when you pass your mouse over the link and then move it off.

13

Figure 13-20   Output of Exercise 13-5

WEB DESIGN PROJECTS

Project 13-1

Create an HTML document with a function in the head section named `printPersonalInfo()`. Within the `printPersonalInfo()` function, use the `document.write()` and `document.writeln()` methods to print your name, address, date of birth, and Social Security number to the screen. Call the function from the body section of the document. Save the file as **Ch13JavaScriptDP01.html** in the Projects folder for Chapter 13.

Project 13-2

Create an HTML document containing a list of links to your favorite Web sites. Create a unique function for each link. Call the functions using each link's `onClick` event handler. Each function should display a confirm dialog box asking if the user really wants to visit the associated Web page. Save the file as **Ch13JavaScriptDP02.html** in the Projects folder for Chapter 13.

Project 13-3

Create a political survey as an HTML document. Create the survey using text fields in a form. Use fields that ask users for their political party affiliation, the state they live in, and which politician got their vote for president, governor, senator, and so on. Include an `onLoad` event handler that displays `"This is an online political survey"` in the status bar. As the user enters each field, an `onFocus` event handler should display helpful information in the status bar. As the user leaves a text field, an `onChange` event handler should display an alert dialog box containing the information entered by the user in that text field. Also include an `onUnload` event handler that displays an alert dialog box containing the text `"Thank you for filling out the survey."` Save the file as **Ch13JavaScriptDP03.html** in the Projects folder for Chapter 13.

14

JAVASCRIPT: PART II

In this chapter you will:

♦ Study data types
♦ Use expressions and arithmetic, assignment, comparison, conditional, and logical operators
♦ Work with strings

The values, or data, contained in JavaScript variables are classified into categories known as *data types*. The concept of data types is often difficult for beginning programmers to grasp; in real life, you do not often distinguish among different types of information. If someone asks your name, your age, or the current time, you do not usually stop to consider that your name is a text string or that your age and the current time are numbers. However, a variable's specific data type is very important in programming because the data type helps determine how much memory the computer will allocate for the data stored in the variable. The data type also governs the kinds of operations that can be performed on a variable.

In this chapter, you will learn about JavaScript data types and the operations that can be performed on them.

DATA TYPES

Variables can contain many different kinds of values—for example, the time of day, a dollar amount, or a person's name. A **data type** is the specific category of information that a variable contains. Data types that can be assigned only a single value are called **primitive types**. JavaScript supports six primitive data types: Integer numbers, Floating-point numbers, Boolean values, Strings, and the Undefined and Null values. You will learn about these data types in the following sections.

The JavaScript language also supports **reference**, or **composite**, data types. These data types can contain multiple values or complex types of information, as opposed to the single values stored in primitive data types. The three reference data types supported by the JavaScript language are Functions, Objects, and Arrays. You learned about Functions and Objects in Chapter 13. Arrays, which you will learn about later in this tutorial, are sets of data represented by a single variable name.

Table 14-1 describes the most commonly used data types in JavaScript.

Table 14-1   Primitive JavaScript data types

Data Type	Description
Integer numbers	Positive or negative numbers with no decimal places
Floating-point numbers	Positive or negative numbers with decimal places or numbers written using exponential notation
Boolean	A logical value of true or false
String	Text such as "Hello World"
Undefined	A variable that has never had a value assigned to it, has not been declared, or does not exist
Null	An empty value

The Null value is a data type as well as a value that can be assigned to a variable. Assigning the null value to a variable indicates that the variable does not contain a value. A variable with a value of null actually has a value assigned to it: Null is really the value "no value." In contrast, an undefined variable has never had a value assigned to it, has not been declared, or does not exist.

Many programming languages require you to declare the type of data that a variable contains. Programming languages that require you to declare the data types of variables are called **strongly-typed programming languages**. Strong typing is also known as **static typing**, because data types do not change after they have been declared. Programming languages that do not require you to declare the data types of variables are called **loosely-typed programming languages**. Loose typing is also known as **dynamic typing**, because data types can change after they have been declared.

JavaScript is a loosely-typed programming language. In JavaScript, you are not required to declare the data type of variables in JavaScript; in fact, you are not allowed to do so. Instead, the JavaScript interpreter automatically determines what type of data is stored in a variable and assigns the variable's data type accordingly. The following code demonstrates how a variable's data type changes automatically each time the variable is assigned a new literal value.

```
changingVariable = "Hello World";  // String
changingVariable = 8;              // Integer number
changingVariable = 5.367;          // Floating-point number
changingVariable = true;           // Boolean
changingVariable = null;           // null
```

The data type of variables can change during the course of program execution. This can cause problems if you attempt to perform an arithmetic operation and one of the variables is a string or the null value. JavaScript includes a `typeof()` operator that you can use to determine the data type of a variable. You will learn about operators later in this chapter. For now, you should understand that an operator is used for manipulating different parts of a statement. The syntax for the `typeof()` operator is `typeof(variablename);`. You should use the `typeof()` operator whenever you need to be sure that a variable is the correct data type. The values that can be returned by the `typeof()` operator are listed in Table 14-2.

Table 14-2   Values returned by the `typeof()` operator

Return Value	Returned for
Number	Integers and floating-point numbers
String	Text strings
Boolean	True or false
Object	Objects, arrays, and null variables
Function	Functions
Undefined	Undefined variables

14

Next, you will create a program that assigns different data types to a variable and prints the variable's data type. You will use the `typeof()` operator to determine the data type of each variable.

To create a program that assigns different data types to a variable and prints the variable data type:

1. Start your text editor and create a new document.

2. Type the `<html>`, `<head>`, and `<title>` sections of the document:

   `<html><head><title>Print Data Types</title></head>`

3. Add the following code to begin the body of the HTML document and create a preformatted text container:

```
<body><pre>
```

4. Add the opening statements for a JavaScript section:

```
<script language="JavaScript">
<!-- HIDE FROM INCOMPATIBLE BROWSERS
```

5. Declare a variable named differentType:

```
var differentType;`
```

6. Type the following, which prints the data type contained in the differentType variable. The data type is currently undefined, because differentType has not yet been assigned a value.

```
document.writeln("The differentType variable is "
    + typeof(differentType));
```

7. Add the following lines, which assign a string to the differentType variable and repeat the statement that prints the data type.

```
differentType = "This is a text string.";
document.writeln("The differentType variable is "
    + typeof(differentType));
```

8. Now add the following lines, which change the differentType variable to the Integer, Floating-point, Boolean, and Null data types. The statement that prints each data type repeats each time the variable's data type changes.

```
differentType = 100;
document.writeln("The differentType variable is "
    + typeof(differentType));
differentType = 3.679;
document.writeln("The differentType variable is "
    + typeof(differentType));
differentType = false;
document.writeln("The differentType variable is "
    + typeof(differentType));
differentType = null;
document.writeln("The differentType variable is "
    + typeof(differentType));
```

9. Add the following code to close the <script>, <pre>, <body>, and <html> tags:

```
// STOP HIDING FROM INCOMPATIBLE BROWSERS -->
</script></pre></body></html>
```

10. Save the file as **Ch14JavaScript01.html** in the Chapter folder for Chapter 14. Open the **Ch14JavaScript01.html** file in your Web browser. You should see the same lines as shown in Figure 14–1.

```
The differentType variable is undefined
The differentType variable is string
The differentType variable is number
The differentType variable is number
The differentType variable is boolean
The differentType variable is object
```

Figure 14-1   Ch14JavaScript01.html

11. Close the Web browser window.

Numeric Data Types

Numeric data types—an important part of any programming language—are particularly useful for arithmetic calculations. JavaScript supports two numeric data types: Integers and Floating-point numbers. An **Integer** is a positive or negative number with no decimal places. Integer values in JavaScript can range from −9007199254740990 (-2^{53}) to 9007199254740990 (2^{53}). The numbers −250, −13, 0, 2, 6, 10, 100, and 10,000 are examples of integers. The numbers −6.16, −4.4, 3.17, 0.52, 10.5, and 2.7541 are not integers; they are floating-point numbers because they contain decimal places. A **Floating-point number** is a number that contains decimal places or that is written in exponential notation. **Exponential notation**, or **scientific notation**, is a shortened format for writing very large numbers or numbers with many decimal places. Numbers written in exponential notation are represented by a value between 1 and 10 multiplied by 10 raised to some power. The value of 10 is written with an uppercase or lowercase E. For example, the number 200,000,000,000 can be written in exponential notation as 2.0e11, which means "two times 10 to the eleventh power." Floating-point values in JavaScript range from approximately $\pm 1.7976931348623157 \times 10^{308}$ to $\pm 5 \times 10^{-324}$.

> Floating-point values that exceed the largest positive value of $\pm 1.7976931348623157 \times 10^{308}$ result in a special value of Infinity. Floating-point values that exceed the smallest negative value of $\pm 5 \times 10^{-324}$ result in a value of −Infinity.

Next, you will create a program that assigns integers and exponential numbers to variables and prints the values.

14

To create a program that assigns integers and exponential numbers to variables and prints the values:

1. Create a new document in your text editor.

2. Type the `<html>`, `<head>`, and `<title>` sections of the document:

```
<html><head><title>Print Numbers</title></head>
```

3. Add the following code to begin the body of the HTML document and to create a preformatted text container:

```
<body><pre>
```

4. Add the opening statements for a JavaScript section.

```
<script language="JavaScript">
<!-- HIDE FROM INCOMPATIBLE BROWSERS
```

5. Add the following lines, which declare an `integer` variable and a `floating-point` variable:

```
var integerVar = 150;
var floatingPointVar = 3.0e7;
// floating-point number 30000000
```

6. Now add the following statements to print the variables:

```
document.writeln(integerVar);
document.writeln(floatingPointVar);
```

7. Add the following code to close the `<script>`, `<pre>`, `<body>`, and `<html>` tags:

```
// STOP HIDING FROM INCOMPATIBLE BROWSERS -->
</script></pre></body></html>
```

8. Save the file as **Ch14JavaScript02.html** in the Chapter folder for Chapter 14. Open the **Ch14JavaScript02.html** file in your Web browser. The integer `150` and the number `30000000` (for the exponential expression 3.0e7) should appear in your Web browser window.

9. Close the Web browser window.

Boolean Values

A **Boolean value** is a logical value of true or false. You can also think of a Boolean value as being yes or no, or on or off. Boolean values are most often used for deciding which parts of a program should execute and for comparing data. You used Boolean values in Chapter 13 to override an internal event handler with your own code. In that situation, you must use the return statement to return a value of true or false. You also used the Confirm dialog box to return a value of true or false to an event handler. When a user clicks the OK button in the Confirm dialog box, a value of true is returned. When a user clicks the Cancel button, a value of false is returned.

Arrays

An **array** contains a set of data represented by a single variable name. You can think of an array as a collection of variables contained within a single variable. You use arrays to store groups or lists of related information in a single, easily managed location. Lists of names, courses, test scores, and prices are typically stored in arrays. For example, Figure 14-2 shows that you can manage the lengthy and difficult-to-spell names of hospital departments by using a single array named `hospitalDepartments`. You can use the array to refer to each department without having to retype the names and possibly introduce syntax errors through misspellings.

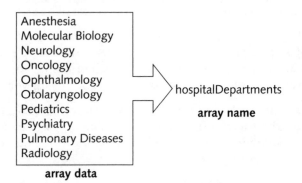

Figure 14-2   Conceptual example of an array

Arrays are represented in JavaScript by the `Array` object. The `Array` object contains a special constructor function named `Array()`. (A **constructor function** is a function that is used as the basis for creating variables of reference data types.) You create new arrays by using the keyword new and the `Array()` constructor function with the following syntax:

```
hospitalDepartments = new Array(number of elements);
```

Notice that the `Array()` function receives a single argument representing the number of elements to be contained in the array. Each piece of data contained in an array is called an **element**. The following code creates an array named `hospitalDepartments` that has 10 elements:

```
hospitalDepartments = new Array(10);
```

The numbering of elements within an array starts with an index number of zero (0). You refer to a specific element by enclosing its index number in brackets at the end of the array name. For example, the first element in the `hospitalDepartments` array is `hospitalDepartments[0]`, the second element is `hospitalDepartments[1]`, the third element is `hospitalDepartments[2]`, and so on. This also means that if you have an array consisting of 10 elements, then the tenth element in the array would be referred to by using an index number of 9. You assign values to individual array elements in the same fashion as you assign values to a standard variable, except that you

14

include the index for an individual element of the array. The following code assigns values to the 10 elements within the hospitalDepartments array:

```
hospitalDepartments[0] = "Anesthesia";   // first element
hospitalDepartments[1] = "Molecular Biology";   // second element
hospitalDepartments[2] = "Neurology";   // third element
```

You use an element in an array in the same manner that you use other types of variables. For example, the following code prints the values contained in the 10 elements of the hospitalDepartments array:

```
document.writeln(hospitalDepartments[0]); // prints "Anesthesia"
document.writeln(hospitalDepartments[1]); // prints "Molecular Biology"
document.writeln(hospitalDepartments[2]); // prints "Neurology"
```

Once you have assigned a value to an array element, you can change it later, just as you can change other variables in a program. To change the first array element in the hospitalDepartments array from "Anesthesia" to "Anesthesiology", you include the statement hospitalDepartments[0] = "Anesthesiology"; in your code.

Most programming languages require that all of the elements in an array be of the same data type. However, in JavaScript the values assigned to array elements can be of different data types. For example, the following code creates an array and stores values with different data types in the array elements:

```
multiple_types = new Array(5);
multiple_types[0] = "Hello World"; // string
multiple_types[1] = 10;            // integer
multiple_types[2] = 3.156;         // floating-point
multiple_types[3] = true;          // Boolean
multiple_types[4] = null;          // null
```

When you create a new array with the **Array()** constructor function, declaring the number of array elements is optional. You can create the array without any elements and add new elements to the array as necessary. The size of an array can change dynamically. If you assign a value to an element that has not yet been created, the element is created automatically, along with any elements that might precede it. For example, the first statement in the following code creates the hospitalDepartments array without any elements. The second statement then assigns "Anesthesia" to the third element, which also creates the first two elements (hospitalDepartments[0] and hospitalDepartments[1]) in the process. However, note that until you assign values to them, hospitalDepartments[0] and hospitalDepartments[1] will both contain undefined values.

```
hospitalDepartments = new Array();
hospitalDepartments[2] = "Anesthesia";
```

You can assign values to array elements when you first create the array. The following code assigns some values to the `hospitalDepartments` array when it is created and then prints each of the values, using the array element numbers:

```
hospitalDepartments = new Array("Anesthesia", "Molecular Biology",
    "Neurology");
document.writeln(hospitalDepartments[0]); // prints "Anesthesia"
document.writeln(hospitalDepartments[1]); // prints "Molecular Biology"
document.writeln(hospitalDepartments[2]); // prints "Neurology"
```

The `Array` object, which contains various methods for working with arrays, also contains a single property, called `length`. The `Array` object methods are somewhat advanced, so they will not be discussed in this book. However, the `Array` object's `length` property, which returns the number of elements in an array, is quite useful. You append the `length` property to an array name by using the syntax `arrayName.length`. The following code prints the value 3 by using the length property to return the number of elements in the `hospitalDepartments` array.

```
hospitalDepartments = new Array();
hospitalDepartments[0] = "Anesthesia";
hospitalDepartments[1] = "Molecular Biology";
hospitalDepartments[2] = "Neurology";
document.write(hospitalDepartments.length); // prints '3'
```

Next, you will create an array containing the months of the year and use the `length` property to print the number of array elements.

To create an array containing the months of the year:

1. Create a new document in your text editor.

2. Type the `<html>`, `<head>`, and `<title>` sections of the document:

   `<html><head><title>Months of the Year</title></head>`

3. Add the following code to begin the body of the HTML document and create a preformatted text container:

   `<body><pre>`

4. Add the opening statements for a JavaScript section:

   ```
   <script language="JavaScript">
   <!-- HIDE FROM INCOMPATIBLE BROWSERS
   ```

5. Type this statement to declare a new array containing 12 elements:
   `varmonthsOfYear = new Array(12);`

6. Assign the 12 months of the year to the 12 elements of the array. Remember that the first element in an array starts with 0. Therefore, the element in the array that will hold January is `monthsOfYear[0]`.

   ```
   monthsOfYear[0] = "January";
   monthsOfYear[1] = "February";
   ```

14

```
monthsOfYear[2] = "March";
monthsOfYear[3] = "April";
monthsOfYear[4] = "May";
monthsOfYear[5] = "June";
monthsOfYear[6] = "July";
monthsOfYear[7] = "August";
monthsOfYear[8] = "September";
monthsOfYear[9] = "October";
monthsOfYear[10] = "November";
monthsOfYear[11] = "December";
```

7. Next, add the following statements to print each element of the array:

```
document.writeln(monthsOfYear[0]);
document.writeln(monthsOfYear[1]);
document.writeln(monthsOfYear[2]);
document.writeln(monthsOfYear[3]);
document.writeln(monthsOfYear[4]);
document.writeln(monthsOfYear[5]);
document.writeln(monthsOfYear[6]);
document.writeln(monthsOfYear[7]);
document.writeln(monthsOfYear[8]);
document.writeln(monthsOfYear[9]);
document.writeln(monthsOfYear[10]);
document.writeln(monthsOfYear[11]);
```

 A looping statement is a more efficient way to print all the elements of an array. You will learn about looping statements in Chapter 15.

8. Add the following statement that uses the `length` property to return the number of elements in the array:

```
document.writeln("There are " + monthsOfYear.length
     + " months in a year.");
```

9. Add the following code to close the `<script>`, `<pre>`, `<body>`, and `<html>` tags:

```
// STOP HIDING FROM INCOMPATIBLE BROWSERS -->
</script></pre></body></html>
```

10. Save the file as **Ch14JavaScript03.html** in the Chapter folder for Chapter 14. Open the **Ch14JavaScript03.html** file in your Web browser. Figure 14-3 shows the output.

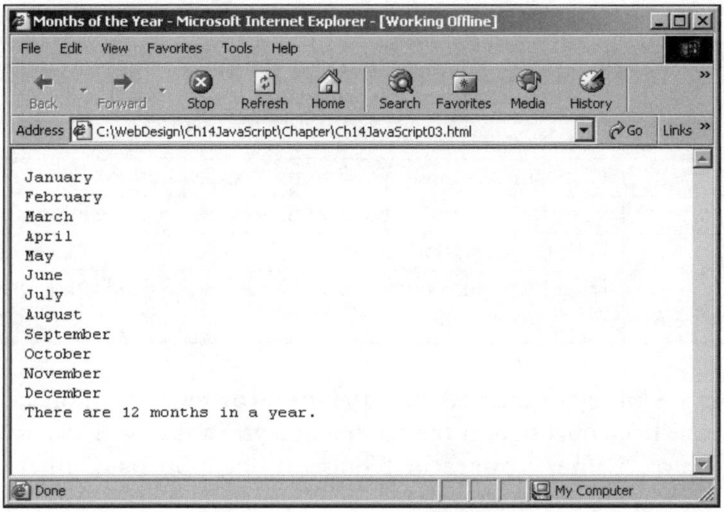

Figure 14-3   Output of Ch14JavaScript03.html

11. Close the Web browser window.

EXPRESSIONS AND OPERATORS

Variables and data become most useful when you use them in expressions. An **expression** is a combination of literal values, variables, operators, and other expressions that can be evaluated by the JavaScript interpreter to produce a result. You can use operands and operators to create more expressions in JavaScript. **Operands** are variables and literals contained in an expression. **Operators** are symbols, such as the addition operator (+) and multiplication operator (*), used in expressions to manipulate operands. You have worked with several simple expressions so far that combine operators and operands. Consider the following statement:

```
myNumber = 100;
```

This statement is an expression that results in the value 100 being assigned to myNumber. The operands in the expression are the myNumber variable name and the integer value 100. The operator is the equal sign (=) assignment operator. The equal sign operator is an assignment operator, because it *assigns* the value (100) on the right side of the expression to the variable (myNumber) on the left side of the expression. Table 14-3 lists the main types of JavaScript operators. You will learn more about specific operators in the following sections.

14

Table 14-3   JavaScript operator types

Operator Type	Description
Arithmetic	Used for performing mathematical calculations
Assignment	Assigns values to variables
Comparison	Compares operands and returns a Boolean value
Logical	Used for performing Boolean operations on Boolean operands
String	Performs operations on strings
Special	Used for various purposes and includes the conditional, instance of, in, delete, void, new, this, typeof, and comma operators

JavaScript operators are binary or unary. A **binary operator** requires an operand before and after the operator. The equal sign in the statement `myNumber = 100;` is an example of a binary operator. A **unary operator** requires a single operand either before or after the operator. For example, the increment operator (`++`), an arithmetic operator, is used for increasing an operand by a value of 1. The statement `myNumber++;` changes the value of the `myNumber` variable to 101.

 The operand to the left of an operator is known as the *left operand*; the operand to the right of an operator is known as the *right operand*.

Next, you will learn more about the different types of JavaScript operators.

Arithmetic Operators

Arithmetic operators are used to perform mathematical calculations, such as addition, subtraction, multiplication, and division, in JavaScript. You can also return the modulus of a calculation, which is the remainder when you divide one number by another number. JavaScript binary arithmetic operators and their descriptions are listed in Table 14-4.

Table 14-4   Arithmetic binary operators

Operator	Description
+ (addition)	Adds two operands
– (subtraction)	Subtracts one operand from another operand
* (multiplication)	Multiplies one operand by another operand
/ (division)	Divides one operand by another operand
% (modulus)	Divides one operand by another operand and returns the remainder

Arithmetic operations can also be performed on a single variable by using unary operators. Table 14-5 lists the unary arithmetic operators available in JavaScript.

Table 14-5   Arithmetic unary operators

Operator	Description
++ (increment)	Increases an operand by a value of 1
-- (decrement)	Decreases an operand by a value of 1
- (negation)	Returns the opposite value (negative or positive) of an operand

The increment (++) and decrement (--) unary operators can be used as prefix or postfix operators. A **prefix operator** is placed before a variable. A **postfix operator** is placed after a variable. The statements `++myVariable;` and `myVariable++;` both increase `myVariable` by one. However, the two statements return different values. When you use the increment operator as a prefix operator, the value of the operand is returned *after* it is increased by a value of one. When you use the increment operator as a postfix operator, the value of the operand is returned *before* it is increased by a value of one. Similarly, when you use the decrement operator as a prefix operator, the value of the operand is returned *after* it is decreased by a value of one; when you use the decrement operator as a postfix operator, the value of the operand is returned *before* it is decreased by a value of one.

Unlike the increment and decrement unary operators, the negation (-) unary operator cannot be used as a postfix operator. The negation (-) unary operator must be placed as a prefix in front of the operand that you want changed to a negative value.

Next, you will create a program that performs arithmetic calculations.

To create a program that performs arithmetic calculations:

1. Create a new document in your text editor.

2. Type the `<html>`, `<head>`, and `<title>` sections of the document:

   ```
   <html><head><title>Arithmetic Examples</title></head>
   ```

3. Add the following code to begin the body of the HTML document and to create a preformatted text container:

   ```
   <body><pre>
   ```

4. Add the opening statements for a JavaScript section:

   ```
   <script language="JavaScript">
   <!-- HIDE FROM INCOMPATIBLE BROWSERS
   ```

5. Type the following statements to declare two variables: a `number` variable to contain a number, which you will use in several arithmetic operations, and a `result` variable to contain the value of each arithmetic operation.

   ```
   var number = 100;
   var result;
   ```

6. Now add the following statements, which perform addition, subtraction, multiplication, and division operations on the `number` variable, and assign each

14

value to the `result` variable. The `result` variable is printed each time it changes.

```
result = number + 50;
document.writeln("Result after addition = " + result);
result = number / 4;
document.writeln("Result after division = " + result);
result = number - 25;
document.writeln("Result after subtraction = " + result);
result = number * 2;
document.writeln("Result after multiplication = " + result);
```

7. Next, add the following two statements. The first statement uses the increment operator to increase the value of the `number` variable by one and assigns the new value to the `result` variable. The second statement prints the `result` variable. Notice that the increment operator is used as a prefix, so the new value is assigned to the `result` variable. If you used the postfix increment operator, you would assign the old value of the `number` variable to the `result` variable, before the `number` variable is incremented by one.

```
result = ++number;
document.writeln("Result after increment = " + result);
```

8. Add the following code to close the `<script>`, `<pre>`, `<body>`, and `<html>` tags:

```
// STOP HIDING FROM INCOMPATIBLE BROWSERS -->
</script></pre></body></html>
```

9. Save the file as **Ch14JavaScript04.html** in the Chapter folder for Chapter 14. Open the **Ch14JavaScript04.html** file in your Web browser. Figure 14-4 shows the output.

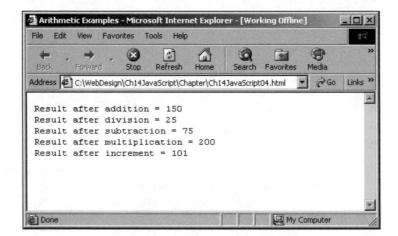

Figure 14-4   Output of Ch14JavaScript04.html

10. Close the Web browser window.

Assignment Operators

Assignment operators are used for assigning a value to a variable. You have already used the most common assignment operator, the equal sign (=), to assign values to variables you declared using the **var** statement. The equal sign assigns an initial value to a new variable or assigns a new value to an existing variable. For example, the following code creates a variable named **myCar**, uses the equal sign to assign it an initial value, then uses the equal sign again to assign it a new value.

```
var myCar = "Ford";
myCar = "Corvette";
```

JavaScript includes other assignment operators in addition to the equal sign. These additional assignment operators perform mathematical calculations on variables and literal values in an expression, and then assign a new value to the left operand. Table 14-6 displays a list of the common JavaScript assignment operators.

Table 14-6   JavaScript assignment operators

Operator	Description
=	Assigns the value of the right operand to the left operand
+=	Combines the value of the right operand with the value of the left operand or adds the value of the right operand to the value of the left operand and assigns the new value to the left operand
-=	Subtracts the value of the right operand from the value of the left operand and assigns the new value to the left operand
*=	Multiplies the value of the right operand by the value of the left operand and assigns the new value to the left operand
/=	Divides the value of the left operand by the value of the right operand and assigns the new value to the left operand
%=	Divides the value of the left operand by the value of the right operand and assigns the remainder to the left operand (modulus)

14

Next, you will create an HTML document that uses assignment operators.

To create an HTML document that uses assignment operators:

1. Create a new document in your text editor.

2. Type the `<html>`, `<head>`, and `<title>` sections of the document:

   ```
   <html><head><title>Assignment Examples</title></head>
   ```

3. Add the following code to begin the body of the HTML document and to create a preformatted text container:

   ```
   <body><pre>
   ```

4. Add the opening statements for a JavaScript section:

   ```
   <script language="JavaScript">
   <!-- HIDE FROM INCOMPATIBLE BROWSERS
   ```

5. Type the following statements that perform several assignment operations on a variable named `changingVar`. After each assignment operation, the result is printed.

```
var changingVar = "text string 1";
changingVar += " & text string 2";
document.writeln("Variable after addition assignment = "
     + changingVar);
changingVar = 100;
changingVar += 50;
document.writeln("Variable after addition assignment = "
     + changingVar);
changingVar -= 30;
document.writeln("Variable after subtraction assignment = "
     + changingVar);
changingVar /= 3;
document.writeln("Variable after division assignment = "
     + changingVar);
changingVar *= 8;
document.writeln("Variable after multiplication assignment = "
     + changingVar);
changingVar %= 300;
document.writeln("Variable after modulus assignment = "
     + changingVar);
```

6. Add the following code to close the `<script>`, `<pre>`, `<body>`, and `<html>` tags:

```
// STOP HIDING FROM INCOMPATIBLE BROWSERS -->
</script></pre></body></html>
```

7. Save the file as **Ch14JavaScript05.html** in the Chapter folder for Chapter 14. Open the **Ch14JavaScript05.html** file in your Web browser. Figure 14-5 shows the output.

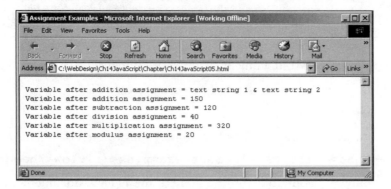

Figure 14-5   Output of Ch14JavaScript05.html

8. Close the Web browser window.

Comparison and Conditional Operators

Comparison operators are used to compare two operands and determine if one numeric value is greater than another. A Boolean value of true or false is returned after two operands are compared. For example, the statement 5 < 3 would return a Boolean value of false, because 5 is not less than 3. Table 14-7 lists the JavaScript comparison operators.

Table 14-7   JavaScript comparison operators

Operator	Name	Description
==	Equal	Returns true if the operands are equal
===	Strict equal	Returns true if the operands are equal and of the same type
!=	Not equal	Returns true if the operands are not equal
!==	Strict not equal	Returns true if the operands are not equal or not of the same type
>	Greater than	Returns true if the left operand is greater than the right operand
<	Less than	Returns true if the left operand is less than the right operand
>=	Greater than or equal	Returns true if the left operand is greater than or equal to the right operand
<=	Less than or equal	Returns true if the left operand is less than or equal to the right operand

The comparison operator (==) consists of two equal signs and performs a different function than the one performed by the assignment operator, which consists of a single equal sign (=). The comparison operator *compares* values; the assignment operator *assigns* values.

Comparison operators are often used with two kinds of special statements: conditional statements and looping statements. You will learn how to use comparison operators in such statements in Chapter 15.

14

The comparison operator is often used with another kind of operator, the conditional operator. The **conditional operator** executes one of two expressions, based on the results of a conditional expression. A **conditional expression** returns a Boolean value and determines whether to execute a conditional or looping statement. The syntax for the conditional operator is *conditional expression ? expression1: expression2;*. If the conditional expression evaluates to true, then **expression1** executes. If the conditional expression evaluates to false, then **expression2** executes.

The following code shows an example of the conditional operator. In the example, the conditional expression checks to see if the `intVariable` variable is greater than 100. If `intVariable` is greater than 100, then the text `"intVariable is greater than 100"` is assigned to the result variable. If intVariable is not greater than 100, then the text "intVariable is less than or equal to 100" is assigned to the result variable. Because intVariable is equal to 150, the conditional statement returns a value of true, *expression1* executes, and "intVariable is greater than 100" prints to the screen.

```
var intVariable = 150;
var result;
(intVariable > 100) ? result =
     "intVariable is greater than 100" : result =
     "intVariable is less than or equal to 100";
document.write(result);
```

Next, you will create an HTML document that uses comparison operators.

To create an HTML document that uses comparison operators:

1. Create a new document in your text editor.

2. Type the <html>, <head>, and <title> sections of the document:

   ```
   <html><head><title>Comparison Examples</title></head>
   ```

3. Add the following code to begin the body of the HTML document and to create a preformatted text container:

   ```
   <body><pre>
   ```

4. Add the opening statements for a JavaScript section:

   ```
   <script language="JavaScript">
   <!-- HIDE FROM INCOMPATIBLE BROWSERS
   ```

5. Type the following statements that perform various comparison operations on two variables. The result is assigned to the returnValue variable and printed. Notice that the first comparison is performed using the conditional operator.

   ```
   var returnValue;
   var value1 = "first text string";
   var value2 = "second text string";
   value1 == value2 ?  document.writeln(
        "value1 equal to value2: true")
        : document.writeln("value1 equal to value2: false");
   value1 = 50;
   value2 = 75;
   returnValue = value1 == value2;
   document.writeln("value1 equal to value2: "
        + returnValue);
   returnValue = value1 != value2;
   document.writeln("value1 not equal to value2: "
        + returnValue);
   returnValue = value1 > value2;
   document.writeln("value1 greater than value2: "
        + returnValue);
   ```

```
returnValue = value1 < value2;
document.writeln("value1 less than value2: "
    + returnValue);
returnValue = value1 >= value2;
document.writeln(
    "value1 greater than or equal to value2: "
    + returnValue);
returnValue = value1 <= value2;
document.writeln(
    "value1 less than or equal to value2: "
    + returnValue);
value1 = 25;
value2 = 25;
returnValue = value1 === value2;
document.writeln(
    "value1 equal to value2 AND the same data type: "
    + returnValue);
returnValue = value1 !== value2;
document.writeln(
    "value1 not equal to value2 AND not the same data type: "
    + returnValue);
```

6. Add the following code to close the `<script>`, `<pre>`, `<body>`, and `<html>` tags:

```
// STOP HIDING FROM INCOMPATIBLE BROWSERS -->

</script></pre></body></html>
```

7. Save the file as **Ch14JavaScript06.html** in the Chapter folder for Chapter 14. Open the **Ch14JavaScript06.html** file in your Web browser. Figure 14-6 shows the output.

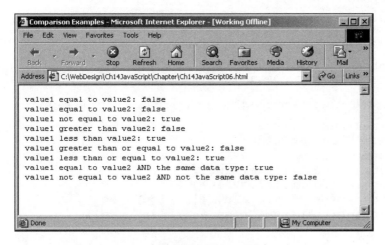

Figure 14-6   Output of Ch14JavaScript06.html

8. Close the Web browser window.

Logical Operators

Logical operators are used for comparing two Boolean operands for equality. As with comparison operators, a Boolean value of true or false is returned after two operands are compared. Table 14-8 lists the JavaScript logical operators.

Table 14-8   JavaScript logical operators

Operator	Name	Description
&&	And	Returns true if both the left operand and right operand return a value of true; otherwise, it returns a value of false
||	Or	Returns true if either the left operand or right operand returns a value of true; if neither operand returns a value of true, then the expression containing the || (or) operator returns a value of false
!	Not	Returns true if an expression is false and returns false if an expression is true

Next, you will create an HTML document that uses logical operators.

To create an HTML document that uses logical operators:

1. Create a new document in your text editor.

2. Type the `<html>`, `<head>`, and `<title>` sections of the document:

   ```
   <html><head><title>Logical Examples</title></head>
   ```

3. Add the following code to begin the body of the HTML document and to create a preformatted text container:

   ```
   <body><pre>
   ```

4. Add the opening statements for a JavaScript section:

   ```
   <script language="JavaScript">
   <!-- HIDE FROM INCOMPATIBLE BROWSERS
   ```

5. Type the following statements that use logical operators on two variables:

   ```
   var trueValue = true;
   var falseValue = false;
   var returnValue;
   document.writeln(!trueValue);
   document.writeln(!falseValue);
   document.writeln(trueValue || falseValue);
   document.writeln(trueValue && falseValue);
   ```

6. Add the following code to close the `<script>`, `<pre>`, `<body>`, and `<html>` tags:

   ```
   // STOP HIDING FROM INCOMPATIBLE BROWSERS -->
   </script></pre></body></html>
   ```

7. Save the file as **Ch14JavaScript07.html** in the Chapter folder for Chapter 14. Open the **Ch14JavaScript07.html** file in your Web browser. Figure 14-7 shows the output.

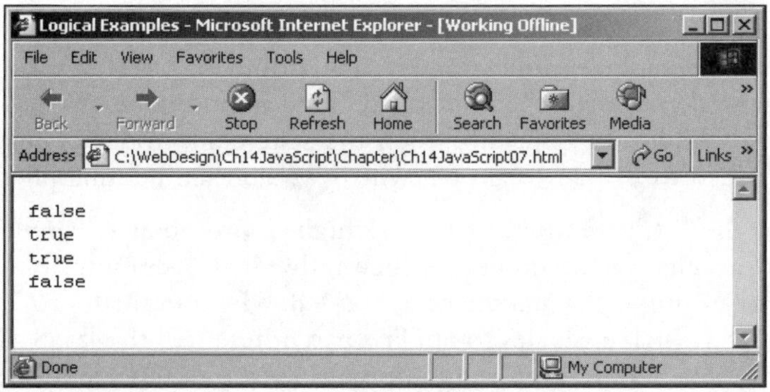

Figure 14-7   Output of Ch14JavaScript07.html

8. Close the Web browser window.

Operator Precedence

When using operators to create expressions in JavaScript, you need to be aware of the precedence of an operator. **Operator precedence** is the order of priority in which operations in an expression are evaluated. Expressions are evaluated from left to right, with the highest priority precedence evaluated first. In other words, when the JavaScript interpreter evaluates an expression, it first determines which operators have the highest priority of precedence. Operators with the highest priority of precedence are evaluated first. However, if all of the operators in the expression have the same priority of precedence, then the expression is evaluated from left to right. The following list shows JavaScript operators arranged in order of precedence. The operator at the top of the list has the highest precedence, with the lowest precedent operator at the bottom of the list.

- Parentheses/brackets/dot (() [] .)—*highest precedence*
- Negation/increment (! − ++ -- typeof void)
- Multiplication/division/modulus (* / %)
- Addition/subtraction (+ −)
- Comparison (< <= > >=)
- Equality (== !=)
- Logical and (&&)
- Logical or (||)
- Assignment operators (= += −= *= /= %=)
- Comma (,)—*lowest precedence*

14

The preceding list does not include all JavaScript operators. Only operators discussed in this book are included.

The statement 5 + 2 * 8 evaluates to 21 because the multiplication operator (*) has a higher precedence than the addition operator (+). The numbers 2 and 8 are multiplied first, for a total of 16, and then the number 5 is added. If the addition operator had a higher precedence than the multiplication operator, then the statement would evaluate to 56, because 5 would be added to 2, for a total of 7, which would then be multiplied by 8.

As you can see from the list, parentheses have the highest precedence. Parentheses are used with expressions to change the order in which individual operations in an expression are evaluated. For example, the statement 5 + 2 * 8, which evaluates to 21, can be rewritten to (5 + 2) * 8, which evaluates to 56. The parentheses tell the JavaScript interpreter to add the numbers 5 and 2 before multiplying by the number 8. Using parentheses forces the statement to evaluate to 56 instead of 21.

STRINGS

As you learned in Chapter 13, when you want to include a quoted string within a literal string surrounded by double quotation marks, you surround the quoted string with single quotation marks. When you want to include a quoted string within a literal string surrounded by single quotation marks, you surround the quoted string with double quotation marks. However, you need to use extra care when using single quotation marks with possessives and contractions in strings, because the JavaScript interpreter always looks for the first closing single or double quotation mark to match an opening single or double quotation mark. For example, consider the following statement:

```
document.writeln('My city's zip code is 01562.');
```

This statement will cause an error because the JavaScript interpreter will assume that the literal string ends with the apostrophe following `city` and, therefore, look for the closing parentheses for the `document.writeln()` function immediately following `city's`. To get around this problem, you include an escape character before the apostrophe in `city's`. An **escape character** is a special character that tells the compiler or interpreter that the character following it has a special purpose. In JavaScript, the escape character is the backslash (\). Placing a backslash in front of an apostrophe tells the JavaScript interpreter to treat the apostrophe as a regular keyboard character, such as a, b, 1, or 2, and not as part of a single quotation mark pair that encloses a text string. The backslash in the following statement tells the JavaScript interpreter to print the apostrophe following the word "city" as an apostrophe:

```
document.writeln('My city\'s zip code is 01562.');
```

You can also use the escape character in combination with other characters to insert a special character into a string. The combination of the escape character with other characters is called an **escape sequence**. The backslash followed by an apostrophe (\') and the backslash followed by a double quotation mark (\") are both examples of escape sequences. Most escape sequences carry out special functions. For example, the escape sequence \t inserts a tab into a string. Table 14-9 describes some of the escape sequences you can add to a string in JavaScript.

Table 14-9   JavaScript escape sequences

Escape Sequence	Character
\b	Backspace
\f	Form feed
\n	New line
\r	Carriage return
\t	Horizontal tab
\'	Single quotation mark
\"	Double quotation mark
\\	Backslash

The new line and carriage return escape sequences are only recognized inside a container element such as the <pre>...</pre> tag pair.

In addition to including escape sequences, you can also include HTML tags in strings. HTML tags within JavaScript strings must be located within a string's opening and closing quotation marks. For example, suppose you want to include the line break tag <br> in a string that will be printed by the `document.write()` function. To accomplish this, you would use the following statement: `document.write("There is a line break following this sentence.<br>");`. HTML tags cannot be used directly within JavaScript code. Therefore, the statement `document.write("There is a line break following this sentence."<br>);` would cause an error, because the <br> tag is located outside the literal string.

Next, you will create a program that displays a restaurant's daily menu by combining strings with escape characters and HTML tags. Note that you can create the same document more easily by using only HTML tags. The purpose of this exercise is to demonstrate how text strings can be combined with HTML tags and escape characters.

To create a file that combines strings with escape characters and HTML tags:

1. Create a new document in your text editor.

2. Type the `<html>`, `<head>`, and `<title>` sections of the document, along with the opening `<body>` tag:

```
<html><head><title>Daily Specials</title></head><body>
```

3. Add the opening statements for a JavaScript section:

```
<script language="JavaScript">
<!-- HIDE FROM INCOMPATIBLE BROWSERS
```

4. Declare the following variables and assign to them strings containing combinations of text, HTML tags, and escape characters:

```
var restaurant = "<h1>Small Town Restaurant</h1><br>";
var specials = "<h2>Daily Specials for Wednesday</h2>";
var prixfixe = "<i>Prix fixe:</i> <b>$9.95</b><hr>";
var appetizer = "<h3>Caesar Salad</h3>";
var entree = "<h3>Chef\'s \"Surprise\"</h3>";
var dessert = "<h3>Chocolate Cheesecake</h3><hr>";
```

5. Next, add the following statements to print the variables:

```
document.write(restaurant);
document.write(specials);
document.write(prixfixe);
document.write(appetizer);
document.write(entree);
document.write(dessert);
```

The preceding statements include the `write()` method instead of the `writeln()` method, because the heading-level styles contained in the string variables automatically force line breaks.

6. Add the following code to close the `<script>`, `<body>`, and `<html>` tags:

```
// STOP HIDING FROM INCOMPATIBLE BROWSERS -->
</script></body></html>
```

7. Save the file as **Ch14JavaScript08.html** in the Chapter folder for Chapter 14. Open the **Ch14JavaScript08.html file** in your Web browser. Figure 14-8 shows the output.

8. Close the Web browser window.

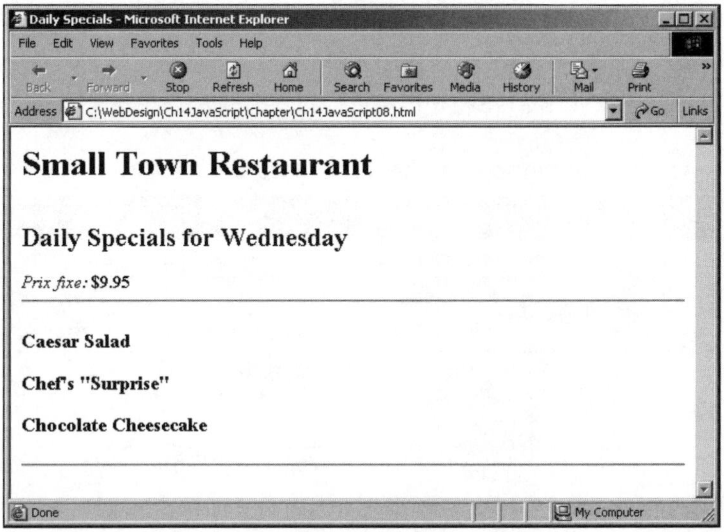

Figure 14-8   Output of Ch14JavaScript08.html

Working with Strings

JavaScript has two operators that can be used with strings: (+) and (+=). When used with strings, the plus sign is known as the concatenation operator. The **concatenation operator** (+) is used to combine two strings. The following code combines a string variable and a literal string, and assigns the new value to another variable:

```
var firstString = "Ernest Hemingway wrote ";
var newString;
newString = firstString + "<i>For Whom the Bell Tolls</i>";
```

The combined value of the `firstString` variable and the string literal that is assigned to the `newString` variable is "Ernest Hemingway wrote *For Whom the Bell Tolls*".

You can also use the (+=) assignment operator to combine two strings. The following code combines the two text strings, but without using the `newString` variable:

```
var firstString = "Ernest Hemingway wrote ";
firstString += "<i>For Whom the Bell Tolls</i>";
```

Note that the same symbol—a plus sign—serves as the concatenation operator and the addition operator. When used with numbers or variables containing numbers, expressions using the concatenation operator will return the sum of the two numbers. However, if you use the concatenation operator with a string value and a number value, the string value and the number value will be combined into a new string value, as in the following example:

```
var textString = "The legal voting age is ";
var votingAge = 18;
newString = textString + votingAge;
```

14

The String Object

The JavaScript **String object** contains methods for manipulating text strings. Table 14-10 lists commonly used methods of the `String` object.

Table 14-10   Commonly used methods of the `String` object

Method	Description
`big()`	Adds a `<big>...</big>` tag pair to a text string.
`blink()`	Adds a `<blink>...</blink>` tag pair to a text string.
`bold()`	Adds a `<b>...</b>` tag pair to a text string.
`charAt(index)`	Returns the character at the specified position in a text string. Returns nothing if the specified position is greater than the length of the string.
`fixed()`	Adds a `<tt>...</tt>` tag pair to a text string.
`fontcolor(color)`	Adds a `<font color=color>...</font>` tag pair to a text string.
`fontsize(size)`	Adds a `<font size=size>...</font>` tag pair to a text string.
`indexOf(text, index)`	Returns the position number in a string of the first character in the text argument. If the `index` argument is not included, then the `indexOf()` method starts searching at the beginning of the string. If the `index` argument is included, then the `indexOf()` method starts searching at that position within the string. Returns −1 if the text is not found.
`italics()`	Adds a `<i>...</i>` tag pair to a text string.
`lastIndexOf(text, index)`	Returns the position number in a string of the last instance of the first character in the `text` argument. If the `index` argument is not included, then the `lastIndexOf()` method starts searching at the end of the string. If the `index` argument is included, then the `lastIndexOf()` method starts searching at that position within the string. Returns −1 if the character or string is not found.
`link(href)`	Adds a `<a href=url>...</a>` tag pair to a text string.
`small()`	Adds a `<small>...</small>` tag pair to a text string.
`split(separator)`	Divides a text string into an array of substrings, based on the specified separator. The `separator` argument can be any character.
`strike()`	Adds a `<strike>...</strike>` tag pair to a text string.
`sub()`	Adds a `<sub>...</sub>` tag pair to a text string.

Table 14-10   Commonly used methods of the `string` object (continued)

Method	Description
`substring(starting index, ending index)`	Extracts text from a string starting with the position number specified by the `starting index` argument and ending with the position number specified by the `ending index` argument.
`sup()`	Adds a `<sup>...</sup>` tag pair to a text string.
`toLowerCase()`	Converts the specified text string to lowercase.
`toUpperCase()`	Converts the specified text string to uppercase.

The `String` object also contains a single property, the **length property**, which returns the number of characters in a string. The `length` property is quite useful if you need to manipulate the contents of a string, but you do not know how many characters it has. You use the methods and the `length` property of the `String` object by appending a period to a string variable or a literal string, followed by a `String` method or the `length` property. Note that you use an index number of zero to refer to the first character in text strings. For instance, the first character, J, in the string `JavaScript` has an index number of 0. The second character, *a*, has an index number of 1, and so on. To use the `charAt()` method to return the first character (*J*) in the literal string `JavaScript`, you use the statement `JavaScript".charAt(0);`.

To make information stored in long strings of text usable, the long strings usually must be parsed. When applied to text strings, the term **parsing** refers to the act of extracting characters or substrings from a larger string. This is essentially the same kind of parsing that occurs in a Web browser when the Web browser extracts the necessary formatting information from an HTML document before displaying it on-screen. For an HTML document, the document itself is one large text string from which the browser must extract formatting and other information. However, on a programming level, parsing usually refers to the extraction of information from string literals and variables.

14

Although understanding exactly when and why you would use parsing on a programming level requires a deeper understanding of JavaScript, one simple example has to do with an e-mail address that a user may enter into a form on a Web page. Often times, a Web page will require a user to enter his or her Web address to obtain certain kinds of information or to process an online transaction. To ensure that the user enters an e-mail address in a valid format, you could use JavaScript to parse the address. For instance, all e-mail addresses are required to include the ampersand (@) symbol along with a domain identifier such as .com or .org. You could write a JavaScript program that parses the address to check whether it includes the ampersand and a domain identifier. Although a simple JavaScript program could not detect whether an entered e-mail address is actually legitimate, it could be used to ensure that users enter their e-mail address in the correct format.

You use several `String` object methods and the `length` property to parse strings. For instance, the statement `newString = "JavaScript".substring(4,10);` (from the preceding example) uses the `substring()` method to parse the `newString` variable and extract the text `Script` from the `JavaScript` text string.

Next, you will create an HTML document that uses string operators and `String` object methods.

To create an HTML document that uses string operators:

1. Create a new document in your text editor.

2. Type the `<html>`, `<head>`, and `<title>` sections of the document:

   ```
   <html><head><title>String Examples</title></head>
   ```

3. Add the following code to begin the body of the HTML document and to create a preformatted text container:

   ```
   <body><pre>
   ```

4. Add the opening statements for a JavaScript section:

   ```
   <script language="JavaScript">
   <!-- HIDE FROM INCOMPATIBLE BROWSERS
   ```

5. Type the following statements containing examples of string operators. Use your own name and place of birth where indicated.

   ```
   var name;
   firstName = "your first name";
   lastName = "your last name";
   var placeOfBirth;
   name = firstName + " ";
   name += lastName;
   placeOfBirth = "city where you were born";
   placeOfBirth += ", state where you were born";
   ```

6. Type the following `print` and `String` method statements:

   ```
   nameArray = name.split(" ");
   document.writeln("My first name is: " + nameArray[0]);
   document.writeln("My last name is: " + nameArray[1]);
   document.writeln("There are " + firstName.length
       + " characters in my first name");
   document.writeln("I was born in " + placeOfBirth);
   document.writeln("My initials are: " + firstName.charAt(0)
       + lastName.charAt(0));
   ```

7. Add the following code to close the `<script>`, `<pre>`, `<body>`, and `<html>` tags:

   ```
   // STOP HIDING FROM INCOMPATIBLE BROWSERS -->
   </script></pre></body></html>
   ```

8. Save the file as **Ch14JavaScript09.html** in the Chapter folder for Chapter 14. Open the **Ch14JavaScript09.html** file in your Web browser. The output should appear similar to Figure 14-9.

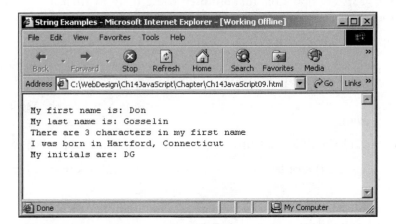

Figure 14-9   Output of Ch14JavaScript09.html

9. Close the Web browser window.

CHAPTER SUMMARY

❑ A data type is the specific category of information that a variable contains.

❑ Data types that can be assigned only a single value are called primitive types.

❑ Reference, or composite, data types can contain multiple values or complex types of information.

❑ Programming languages that require you to declare the data types of variables are called strongly-typed programming languages.

❑ Programming languages that do not require you to declare the data types of variables are called loosely-typed programming languages.

❑ An Integer is a positive or negative number with no decimal places.

❑ A Floating-point number is a number that contains decimal places or is written using exponential notation.

❑ A Boolean value is a logical value of true or false.

❑ An Array is a variable that contains a set of data represented by a single variable name.

❑ An expression is a combination of literal values, variables, operators, and other expressions that can be evaluated by the JavaScript interpreter to produce a result.

14

❑ Operands are variables and literals contained in an expression.

❑ Operators are symbols used in expressions to manipulate operands.

❑ Arithmetic operators are operators that are used to perform mathematical calculations, such as addition, subtraction, multiplication, and division, in JavaScript.

❑ Assignment operators are operators that are used for assigning a value to a variable.

❑ Comparison operators are operators that are used to compare two operands to determine if one numeric value is greater than another.

❑ The conditional operator executes one of two expressions based on the results of a conditional expression.

❑ Logical operators are used for comparing two Boolean operands for equality.

❑ Operator precedence is the order of priority in which operations in an expression are evaluated.

❑ An escape character is a special character that tells the compiler or interpreter that the character following it has a special purpose.

❑ Parsing refers to the act of extracting characters or substrings from a larger string.

❑ The JavaScript `String` object contains methods for manipulating text strings.

REVIEW QUESTIONS

1. A loosely-typed programming language _____.
   a. does not require data types of variables to be declared
   b. requires data types of variables to be declared
   c. does not have different data types
   d. does not have variables

2. You can determine the data type of a variable using the _____.
   a. `returnValue` function
   b. `typeof()` operator
   c. `parseFloat()` function
   d. `toString` operator

3. How many decimal places does an Integer store?
   a. 0
   b. 1
   c. 2
   d. as many as necessary

4. Which of the following is not a Floating-point number?

    a. –439.35

    b. 3.17

    c. 10

    d. –7e11

5. Which of the following is the correct syntax for including double quotation marks within a string that is already surrounded by double quotation marks?

    a. `"Some computers have \"artificial\" intelligence."`

    b. `"Some computers have "artificial" intelligence."`

    c. `"Some computers have /"artificial/" intelligence."`

    d. `"Some computers have ""artificial"" intelligence."`

6. Which of the following refers to the first element in an array named `employees[]`?

    a. `employees[0]`

    b. `employees[1]`

    c. `employees[first]`

    d. `employees[a]`

7. You return the number of elements in an array using the _____ property of the `Array` object.

    a. `size`

    b. `length`

    c. `elements`

    d. `dimension`

8. The modulus operator (%) _____.

    a. converts an operand to base 16 (hexadecimal) format

    b. returns the absolute value of an operand

    c. calculates the percentage of one operand compared to another

    d. divides two operands and returns the remainder

9. What value is assigned to the `returnValue` variable in the statement `returnValue = 100!= 200;`?

    a. first string

    b. second string

    c. true

    d. false

14

10. The `&&` (and) operator returns `true` if _____.

    a. the left operand returns a value of true

    b. the right operand returns a value of true

    c. the left operand and right operand both return a value of true

    d. the left operand and right operand both return a value of false

11. What value is assigned to the `returnValue` variable in the statement `returnValue = !x;`, assuming that `x` has a value of `true`?

    a. `true`

    b. `false`

    c. `null`

    d. `undefined`

12. _____ refers to the act of extracting characters or substrings from a larger string.

    a. Extrapolating

    b. Parsing

    c. Excerpting

    d. Concatenation

13. What is the correct syntax for returning the number of characters in a string?

    a. *text_string*`.length;`

    b. *text_string*`.characters();`

    c. *text_string*`.numChars();`

    d. *text_string*`.lastIndex;`

14. The order of priority in which operations in an expression are evaluated is known as _____.

    a. prerogative precedence

    b. operator precedence

    c. expression evaluation

    d. priority evaluation

15. What is the value of the expression `4 * (2 + 3)`?

    a. 11

    b. −11

    c. 20

    d. 14

HANDS-ON EXERCISES

Exercise 14-1

Identify the data types assigned to the result variable in each of the following statements:

1. `var result;`

2. `var result = 3e10;`

3. `var result = 10;`

4. `var result = null;`

5. `var result = 874.0;`

6. `var result = new Array();`

7. `var result = true;`

Exercise 14-2

In this exercise, you will create and modify a JavaScript program so that it uses escape sequences instead of `document.writeln()` statements.

1. Create a new document in your text editor, and then type the following code:

```
<html>
<head>
<title>Escape Sequences</title>
</head>
<body>
<pre>
<script language="JavaScript">
<!-- HIDE FROM INCOMPATIBLE BROWSERS
document.writeln("Line 1");
document.writeln("Line 2");
document.writeln("Line 3");
document.writeln("Line 4");
document.writeln("Line 5");
// STOP HIDING FROM INCOMPATIBLE BROWSERS -->
</script>
</pre>
</body>
</html>
```

2. Modify the program so that it uses escape sequences instead of `document.writeln()` statements to print each line of text on its own line.

3. Save the program as **Ch14JavaScriptEX02.html** in the Exercises folder for Chapter 14.

4. Open **Ch14JavaScriptEX02.html** in your browser. Your document should look similar to Figure 14-10.

14

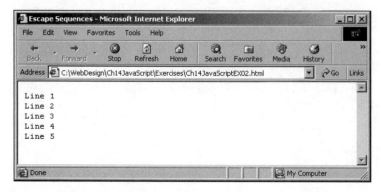

Figure 14-10   Output of Exercise 14-2

Exercise 14-3

In this exercise, you will create and modify a JavaScript program that builds a string variable using other string variables and string literals.

1. Create a new document in your text editor, and then type the following code:

```
<html>
<head>
<title>Phone Number</title>
</head>
<body>
<pre>
<script language="JavaScript">
<!-- HIDE FROM INCOMPATIBLE BROWSERS
var areaCode, exchange, number, phoneNumber;
areaCode = 212;
exchange = 555;
number = 1212;
// STOP HIDING FROM INCOMPATIBLE BROWSERS -->
</script>
</pre>
</body>
</html>
```

2. Add code to the program that assigns the **areaCode**, **exchange**, and **number** variables to the **phoneNumber** variable, separated by dashes. Your code should display the phone number using a **document.write()** statement.

3. Save the program as **Ch14JavaScriptEX03.html** in the Exercises folder for Chapter 14.

4. Open **Ch14JavaScriptEX03.html** in your browser. Your document should look similar to Figure 14-11.

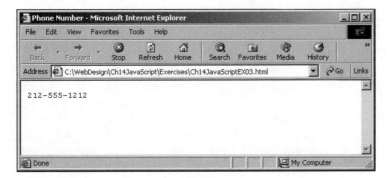

Figure 14-11   Output of Exercise 14-3

Exercise 14-4

What value is assigned to `returnValue` for each of the following expressions?

1. `returnValue = 2 == 3;`
2. `returnValue = "2" + "3";`
3. `returnValue = 2 >= 3;`
4. `returnValue = 2 <= 3;`
5. `returnValue = 2 + 3;`
6. `returnValue = (2 >= 3) && (2 > 3);`
7. `returnValue = (2 >= 3) || (2 > 3);`

Exercise 14-5

1. Use parentheses to modify the order of precedence of the following code so that the final result of **x** is **581.25**. (The result of **x** using the current syntax is **637.5**.)

   ```
   var  x  =  75;
   x =  x + 30 * x / 4;
   ```

2. Save the document as **Ch14JavaScriptEX05.html** in the Exercises folder for Chapter 14.

14

WEB DESIGN PROJECTS

Project 14-1

Create a temperature conversion calculator that converts Fahrenheit to Celsius and Celsius to Fahrenheit. To convert Fahrenheit to Celsius, you will need to write code that subtracts 32 from the Fahrenheit temperature, and then multiplies the remainder by .55. To convert Celsius to Fahrenheit, multiply the Celsius temperature by 1.8, and then add 32. Save the document as **Ch14JavaScriptDP01.html** in the Projects folder for Chapter 14.

Project 14-2

Create an HTML document that calculates the square feet of carpet required to carpet a room. Include three text boxes. Create one text box for the width of the room in linear feet and another for the length of the room in linear feet. Also create a text box for the cost per square foot of carpeting. When you calculate the cost, add 25% to the total number of square feet to account for closets and other features of the room. Display the total cost in an alert dialog box. Save the document as **Ch14JavaScriptDP02.html** in the Projects folder for Chapter 14.

Project 14-3

The JavaScript `Math` object contains advanced mathematical methods and constants. You can find a complete listing of `Math` object methods at www.w3schools.com/js/js_math.asp. Using some of the `Math` object methods, create a calculator that performs advanced calculations, including the `exp()` (exponential value) function and the `sqrt()` (square root) function. Allow users to type a number into a text field and then calculate the number directly by using individual buttons for each advanced math function. Save the program as **Ch14JavaScriptDP03.html** in the Projects folder for Chapter 14.

15

JAVASCRIPT: PART III

In this chapter you will:

♦ Use `if` statements and `if...else` statements to make decisions
♦ Nest one `if` statement in another
♦ Use `switch` statements to make decisions
♦ Use `while` and `do...while` statements to execute code repeatedly
♦ Use `for` statements to execute code repeatedly

So far, the code you have written has been linear in nature. In other words, your programs start at the beginning and end when the last statement in the program executes. Decision-making and flow-control statements allow you to determine the order in which statements execute in a program. The abilities to control the flow of code and to make decisions during program execution are two of the most fundamental skills required in programming. In this chapter, you will learn about both decision-making statements and flow-control statements.

DECISION MAKING

When you write a computer program, regardless of the programming language, you often need to execute different sets of statements, depending on some predetermined criteria. For example, you might create a program that needs to execute one set of code in the morning and another set of code at night. You might create another program that must execute one set of code when it is running in Windows Explorer and another when it runs in Netscape Navigator. Additionally, you might create a program that depends on user input to determine exactly what code to run. For instance, suppose you create a Web page through which users place online orders. If a user clicks an Add to Shopping Cart button, a set of statements that builds a list of items to be purchased must execute. However, if the user clicks a Checkout button, an entirely different set of statements, which complete the transaction, must execute. The process of determining the order in which statements execute in a program is called **decision making** or **flow control**. The special types of JavaScript statements used for making decisions are called **decision-making structures**. The most common type of decision-making statement is the `if` statement, which you will study first.

`if` Statements

The `if` statement is one of the more common ways to control program flow. The **`if` statement** is used to execute specific programming code if the evaluation of a conditional expression returns a value of true. The syntax for a simple `if` statement is as follows:

```
if (conditional expression)
    statement(s);
```

The `if` statement contains three parts: the keyword `if`, a conditional expression enclosed within parentheses, and executable statements. Note that the conditional expression must be enclosed within parentheses.

If the condition being evaluated returns a value of true, then the statement immediately following the conditional expression executes. After the `if` statement executes, any subsequent code executes normally. Consider the example in Figure 15-1. The `if` statement uses the equal (==) comparison operator to determine whether the variable `exampleVar` is equal to 5. (You learned about operators in Chapter 14.) Because the condition returns a value of true, two alert dialog boxes appear. The first alert dialog box is generated by the `if` statement when the condition returns a value of true, and the second alert dialog box executes after the `if` statement is completed.

```
var exampleVar = 5;
if (exampleVar == 5)      // CONDITION EVALUATES TO 'TRUE'
    alert("The variable is equal to '5'.");
alert("This dialog box is generated after the if statement.");
```

Figure 15-1   An `if` statement that evaluates to true

The statement immediately following the if statement in Figure 15-1 can be written on the same line as the if statement itself. However, using a line break and indentation makes the code easier to read.

In contrast, the code in Figure 15-2 displays only the second alert dialog box. The condition evaluates to false, because `exampleVar` is assigned the value 4 instead of 5.

```
var exampleVar = 4;
if (exampleVar == 5)      // CONDITION EVALUATES TO 'FALSE'
     alert("This dialog box will not appear.");
alert("This is the only dialog box that appears.");
```

Figure 15-2   An if statement that evaluates to false

You can use a command block to construct a decision-making structure using multiple if statements. A **command block** is a set of statements contained within a set of braces, similar to the way function statements are contained within a set of braces. Each command block must have an opening brace ({) and a closing brace (}). If a command block is missing either the opening or closing brace, an error will occur. Figure 15-3 shows a program that runs a command block if the conditional expression within the if statement evaluates to true.

When an if statement contains a command block, the statements in the command block execute when the if statement condition evaluates to true. After the command block executes, the code that follows executes normally. When the condition evaluates to false, the command block is skipped, and the statements that follow execute. If the conditional expression within the if statement in Figure 15-3 evaluates to false, then only the `document.writeln()` statement following the command block executes.

```
var exampleVar = 5;
if (exampleVar == 5) {    // CONDITION EVALUATES TO 'TRUE'
     document.writeln("The condition evaluates to true.");
     document.writeln("exampleVar is equal to 5.");
     document.writeln("Each of these lines will be printed.");
}
document.writeln(
     "This statement always executes after the if statement.");
```

Figure 15-3   An if statement with a command block

15

Next, you will create a Cartoon Quiz program. The program is set up so that users select answer alternatives by means of radio buttons created with the `<input>` tag.

In this quiz, each question will be scored immediately. You will create the form containing the radio buttons and then use a series of if statements to score each question. The following steps require you to type a great deal of code. If you prefer not to type so much code, you can open the Ch15JavaScript01.html file from the Chapter folder for Chapter 15 on your data disk. However, you should still take the time to read through the following steps in order to learn how the Ch15JavaScript01.html file is set up.

To create the Cartoon Quiz program and its form section:

1. Start your text editor and create a new document.

2. Type the `<html>` and `<head>` sections of the document. This section also includes a `<script>...</script>` tag pair. You will use the `<script>...</script>` tag pair later to create code that scores the quiz.

```
<html><head><title>Cartoon Quiz</title>
<script language="JavaScript">
<!--HIDE FROM INCOMPATIBLE BROWSERS
// ADD CODE HERE
// STOP HIDING FROM INCOMPATIBLE BROWSERS-->
</script></head>
```

3. Add the following lines, which contain the opening `<body>` tag, the text that will appear at the top of the quiz, and the opening `<form>` tag for the radio buttons:

```
<body>
<h1>Cartoon Quiz</h1>
<p>Answer all of the questions on the quiz, then select
     the Score button to grade the quiz. </p>
<form>
```

4. Next, add the following lines for the first question. The four radio buttons represent the answers. Because each button within a radio button group requires the same NAME attribute, these four radio buttons have the same name of "question1." Each radio button is also assigned a value corresponding to its answer number: *a*, *b*, *c*, or *d*. For each radio button group, the onClick event sends the button value to an individual function that scores the answer. Notice that the value for each button is sent to the function by using the this reference in the form of this.value. The this.value statement essentially says "Send the value of this button to the function."

```
<p><b>1. What is the name of Walt Disney's famous mouse?
     </b></p>
<p><input type=radio name=question1 value="a"
     onClick="scoreQuestion1(this.value)">Mighty Mouse
     <br>
<input type=radio name=question1 value="b"
     onClick="scoreQuestion1(this.value)">Mickey Mouse
     <br>
<input type=radio name=question1 value="c"
     onClick="scoreQuestion1(this.value)">Marty Mouse<br>
<input type=radio name=question1 value="d"
     onClick="scoreQuestion1(this.value)">Melvin Mouse
     </p>
```

You can build the program quickly by copying the input button code for the first question and pasting it for questions 2 through 5. If you use copy and paste to create the input buttons, make sure you change the question number for each input button name and the function it calls.

5. Add the lines for the second question. If you prefer, copy and paste the code you typed earlier, taking care to make the necessary edits.

```
<p><b>2. The character Buzz Lightyear was featured in
    which animated film?</b></p>
<p><input type=radio name=question2 value="a"
    onClick="scoreQuestion2(this.value)">Fantasia<br>
<input type=radio name=question2 value="b"
    onClick="scoreQuestion2(this.value)">Hercules<br>
<input type=radio name=question2 value="c"
    onClick="scoreQuestion2(this.value)">Toy Story<br>
<input type=radio name=question2 value="d"
    onClick="scoreQuestion2(this.value)">Mulan</p>
```

6. Add the lines for the third question, using copy and paste if you prefer:

```
<p><b>3. Pluto is a dog. What is Goofy?</b></p>
<p><input type=radio name=question3 value="a"
    onClick="scoreQuestion3(this.value)">A bear<br>
<input type=radio name=question3 value="b"
    onClick="scoreQuestion3(this.value)">A mule<br>
<input type=radio name=question3 value="c"
    onClick="scoreQuestion3(this.value)">A horse<br>
<input type=radio name=question3 value="d"
    onClick="scoreQuestion3(this.value)">Also a dog</p>
```

7. Add the lines for the fourth question:

```
<p><b>4. Who was always trying to eat Tweety Bird?</b>
    </p>
<p><input type=radio name=question4 value="a"
    onClick="scoreQuestion4(this.value)">Porky Pig<br>
<input type=radio name=question4 value="b"
    onClick="scoreQuestion4(this.value)">Yosemite Sam
    <br>
<input type=radio name=question4 value="c"
    onClick="scoreQuestion4(this.value)">Sylvester<br>
<input type=radio name=question4 value="d"
    onClick="scoreQuestion4(this.value)">
    Foghorn Leghorn</p>
```

8. Add the lines for the fifth question:

```
<p><b>5. What is Winnie the Pooh's favorite food?</b></p>
<p><input type=radio name=question5 value="a"
    onClick="scoreQuestion5(this.value)">Honey<br>
```

15

```
<input type=radio name=question5 value="b"
    onClick="scoreQuestion5(this.value)">Molasses<br>
<input type=radio name=question5 value="c"
    onClick="scoreQuestion5(this.value)">Peanut Butter
    <br>
<input type=radio name=question5 value="d"
    onClick="scoreQuestion5(this.value)">Yogurt</p>
```

9. Add the following code to close the `<form>`, `<body>`, and `<html>` tags:

```
</form></body></html>
```

10. Save the file as **Ch15JavaScript01.html** in the Chapter folder for Chapter 15.

Next, you will add the functions to score each of the questions. The functions contain `if` statements that evaluate each answer. (Note that you need to complete the following steps, whether you typed the code in the preceding set of steps or whether you started with the file from the Data Disk.)

To add JavaScript code to score each of the questions:

1. Replace the line `// ADD CODE HERE` with the following function that scores the first question. A response of `"Correct Answer"` appears if the user provides the correct answer. A response of `"Incorrect Answer"` appears if the user provides an incorrect answer.

```
function scoreQuestion1(answer) {
    if (answer == "a")
        alert("Incorrect Answer");
    if (answer == "b")
        alert("Correct Answer");
    if (answer == "c")
        alert("Incorrect Answer");
    if (answer == "d")
        alert("Incorrect Answer");
}
```

2. Add the `scoreQuestion2()` function after the `scoreQuestion1()` function:

```
function scoreQuestion2(answer) {
    if (answer == "a")
        alert("Incorrect Answer");
    if (answer == "b")
        alert("Incorrect Answer");
    if (answer == "c")
        alert("Correct Answer");
    if (answer == "d")
        alert("Incorrect Answer");
}
```

3. Add the scoreQuestion3() function after the scoreQuestion2() function:

```
function scoreQuestion3(answer) {
    if (answer == "a")
        alert("Incorrect Answer");
    if (answer == "b")
        alert("Incorrect Answer");
    if (answer == "c")
        alert("Incorrect Answer");
    if (answer == "d")
        alert("Correct Answer");
}
```

4. Add the scoreQuestion4() function after the scoreQuestion3() function:

```
function scoreQuestion4(answer) {
    if (answer == "a")
        alert("Incorrect Answer");
    if (answer == "b")
        alert("Incorrect Answer");
    if (answer == "c")
        alert("Correct Answer");
    if (answer == "d")
        alert("Incorrect Answer");
}
```

5. Add the scoreQuestion5() function after the scoreQuestion4() function:

```
function scoreQuestion5(answer) {
    if (answer == "a")
        alert("Correct Answer");
    if (answer == "b")
        alert("Incorrect Answer");
    if (answer == "c")
        alert("Incorrect Answer");
    if (answer == "d")
        alert("Incorrect Answer");
}
```

15

6. Save the file, and then open the **Ch15JavaScript01.html** file in your Web browser. As you select a response for each question, you will immediately learn whether the answer is correct. Figure 15-4 shows the output that appears if you select a wrong answer for question 1.

7. Close the Web browser window.

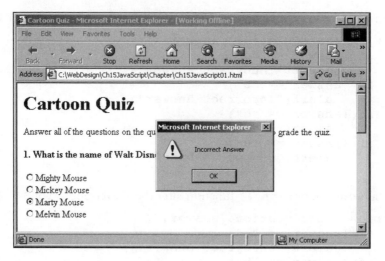

Figure 15-4   Output of Ch15JavaScript01.html

`if...else` **Statements**

So far, you have learned how to use an `if` statement to execute a statement (or statements) if a condition evaluates to true. In some situations, however, you may want to execute one set of statements when the condition evaluates to false and another set of statements when the condition evaluates to true. In that case, you need to add an `else` clause to your `if` statement. For instance, suppose you create a program that displays a confirm dialog box that asks users to indicate whether or not they invest in the stock market by clicking a Yes or No button. An `if` statement in the program might contain a conditional expression that evaluates the user's input. If the condition evaluates to true (the user clicked the Yes button), then the `if` statement would display a Web page on recommended stocks. If the condition evaluates to false (the user clicked the No button), then the statements in an `else` clause would display a Web page on other types of investment opportunities.

An `if` statement that includes an `else` clause is called an **`if...else` statement**. You can think of an `else` clause as being a backup plan that is implemented when the condition returns a value of false. The syntax for an `if...else` statement is as follows:

```
if (conditional expression)
      statement;
else
      statement;
```

You can use command blocks to construct an `if...else` statement as follows:

```
if (conditional expression) {
      statements;
}
```

```
    else {
         statements;
    }
```

An if statement can be constructed without the else clause. However, the else clause can only be used with an if statement.

Figure 15-5 shows an example of an **if...else** statement.

```
var today = "Tuesday"
if (today == "Monday")
     document.writeln("Today is Monday");
else
     document.writeln("Today is not Monday");
```

Figure 15-5   Example of an **if...else** statement

In Figure 15-5, the **today** variable is assigned a value of **Tuesday**. If the condition (**today == "Monday"**) evaluates to false, control of the program passes to the **else** clause, the statement **document.writeln("Today is not Monday");** executes, and the string **Today is not Monday** prints. If the **today** variable had been assigned a value of **Monday**, the condition (**today == "Monday"**) would have evaluated to true, and the statement **document.writeln("Today is Monday");** would have executed. Only one set of statements executes: either the statements following the **if** statement or the statements following the **else** clause. Once either set of statements executes, any code following the **if...else** statements executes normally.

The JavaScript code for the Ch15JavaScript01.html file you created earlier uses multiple **if** statements to evaluate the results of the quiz. Although the multiple **if** statements function properly, they can be simplified using an **if...else** statement. Next, you will simplify the Ch15JavaScript01.html program by replacing multiple **if** statements with one **if...else** statement.

15

To add **if...else** statements to the Cartoon Quiz program:

1. Return to the **Ch15JavaScript01.html** file in your text editor and immediately save it as **Ch15JavaScript02.html**.

2. Because you only need the **if** statement to test for the correct answer, you can group all the incorrect answers in the **else** clause. Modify each of the functions that scores a question so that the multiple **if** statements are replaced with an **if...else** statement. The following code shows how the statements for the **scoreQuestion1()** function should appear:

```
        if (answer == 'b')
              alert("Correct Answer");
        else
              alert("Incorrect Answer");
```

Keep in mind that the correct answer for question 2 is *c*, the correct answer for question 3 is *d*, the correct answer for question 4 is *c*, and the correct answer for question 5 is *a*. You will need to modify the preceding code accordingly for each question. Copy and paste code and then edit it to save on typing time.

3. Save the **Ch15JavaScript02.html** document and open it in your Web browser. The program should function the same as when it contained only `if` statements.

4. Close the Web browser window.

Nested `if` and `if...else` Statements

As you have seen, you can use a control structure such as an `if` or `if...else` statement to allow a program to make decisions about what statements to execute. In some cases, however, you may want the statements executed by the control structure to make other decisions. For instance, you may have a program that uses an `if` statement to ask users if they like sports. If users answer yes, you may want to run another `if` statement that asks users whether they like team sports or individual sports. You can include any code you like within the code block for an `if` statement or an `if...else` statement, and that includes other `if` or `if...else` statements.

When one decision-making statement is contained within another decision-making statement, they are referred to as **nested decision-making structures**. An `if` statement contained within an `if` statement or within an `if...else` statement is called a **nested if statement**. Similarly, an `if...else` statement contained within an `if` or `if...else` statement is called a **nested if...else statement**. You use nested `if` and `if...else` statements to perform conditional evaluations that must be executed after the original conditional evaluation. For example, the following code evaluates two conditional expressions before the `document.writeln()` statement executes:

```
var number = 7;
if (number > 5)
  if (number < 10)
    document.writeln("The number is between 5 and 10.");
  document.writeln("The number is not between 5 and 10.");
```

If either of the conditions in the preceding example evaluates to false, then the JavaScript interpreter skips the rest of the `if` statement and immediately executes the last statement, which prints "The number is not between 5 and 10".

The JavaScript code in the Ch15JavaScript02.html file is somewhat inefficient, because it contains multiple functions that perform essentially the same task of scoring the quiz. A more efficient method for scoring the quiz is to include nested decision-making structures within a single function. Next, you will modify the JavaScript code in the Ch15JavaScript02.html file so that it contains a single function that checks the correct answer for all the questions, using nested `if...else` statements.

To add nested `if...else` statements to the Cartoon Quiz program:

1. Return to the **Ch15JavaScript02.html** file in your text editor and immediately save it as **Ch15JavaScript03.html**.

2. Delete the five functions within the `<script>...</script>` tag pair, but be sure to leave the JavaScript comments that hide the code from incompatible browsers.

3. Add the first line for the single function that will check all the answers. The function will receive two arguments: the number argument, which represents the question number, and the answer argument, which will store the answer selected by the user. Code within the body of the function will use the number argument to determine which question to store and the answer argument to determine the answer selected by the user.

```
function scoreQuestions(number, answer) {
```

4. Press **Enter** and add the opening `if` statement, which will check to see if the question is equal to 1. If it is, the nested `if...else` statement in the following code will evaluate the response.

```
if (number == 1) {
    if (answer == 'b')
        alert("Correct Answer");
    else
        alert("Incorrect Answer");
}
```

5. Add an `if...else` statement for question number 2:

```
else if (number == 2) {
    if (answer == 'c')
        alert("Correct Answer");
    else
        alert("Incorrect Answer");
}
```

6. Add an `if...else` statement for question number 3:

```
else if (number == 3) {
    if (answer == 'd')
        alert("Correct Answer");
    else
        alert("Incorrect Answer");
}
```

7. Add an `if...else` statement for question number 4:

```
else if (number == 4) {
    if (answer == 'c')
        alert("Correct Answer");
    else
        alert("Incorrect Answer");
}
```

15

8. Add an `if...else` statement for question number 5:

```
else if (number == 5) {
     if (answer == 'a')
          alert("Correct Answer");
     else
          alert("Incorrect Answer");
}
```

9. Add a closing brace (}) for the `scoreQuestions()` function. The completed function should appear in your file as shown in Figure 15-6.

```
function scoreQuestions(number, answer) {
    if (number == 1) {
         if (answer == 'b')
              alert("Correct Answer");
         else
              alert("Incorrect Answer");
    }
    else if (number == 2) {
         if (answer == 'c')
              alert("Correct Answer");
         else
              alert("Incorrect Answer");
    }
    else if (number == 3) {
         if (answer == 'd')
              alert("Correct Answer");
         else
              alert("Incorrect Answer");
    }
    else if (number == 4) {
         if (answer == 'c')
              alert("Correct Answer");
         else
              alert("Incorrect Answer");
    }
    else if (number == 5) {
         if (answer == 'a')
              alert("Correct Answer");
         else
              alert("Incorrect Answer");
    }
}
```

Figure 15-6   Completed `scoreQuestions ()` function

10. Within each of the `<input>` tags, change the function called within the `onClick()` event handler to `scoreQuestions(number, this.value)`, changing the `number` argument to the appropriate question number. For

example, the event handler for question 1 should read:
`scoreQuestions(1, this.value)`. The modified `<input>` tags in your file should appear as shown in Figure 15-7.

```
<p><b>1. What is the name of Walt Disney's famous mouse?</b></p>
<p><input type=radio name=question1 value="a"
    onClick="scoreQuestions(1, this.value)">Mighty Mouse<br>
<input type=radio name=question1 value="b"
    onClick="scoreQuestions(1, this.value)">Mickey Mouse<br>
<input type=radio name=question1 value="c"
    onClick="scoreQuestions(1, this.value)">Marty Mouse<br>
<input type=radio name=question1 value="d"
    onClick="scoreQuestions(1, this.value)">Melvin Mouse</p>
<p><b>2. The character Buzz Lightyear was featured in which
animated film?</b></p>
<p><input type=radio name=question2 value="a"
    onClick="scoreQuestions(2, this.value)">Fantasia<br>
<input type=radio name=question2 value="b"
    onClick="scoreQuestions(2, this.value)">Hercules<br>
<input type=radio name=question2 value="c"
    onClick="scoreQuestions(2, this.value)">Toy Story<br>
<input type=radio name=question2 value="d"
    onClick="scoreQuestions(2, this.value)">Mulan</p>
<p><b>3. Pluto is a dog. What is Goofy?</b></p>
<p><input type=radio name=question3 value="a"
    onClick="scoreQuestions(3, this.value)">A bear<br>
<input type=radio name=question3 value="b"
    onClick="scoreQuestions(3, this.value)">A mule<br>
<input type=radio name=question3 value="c"
     onClick="scoreQuestions(3, this.value)">A horse<br>
<input type=radio name=question3 value="d"
    onClick="scoreQuestions(3, this.value)">Also a dog</p>
<p><b>4. Who was always trying to eat Tweety Bird?</b></p>
<p><input type=radio name=question4 value="a"
    onClick="scoreQuestions(4, this.value)">Porky Pig<br>
<input type=radio name=question4 value="b"
    onClick="scoreQuestions(4, this.value)">Yosemite Sam<br>
<input type=radio name=question4 value="c"
    onClick="scoreQuestions(4, this.value)">Sylvester<br>
<input type=radio name=question4 value="d"
    onClick="scoreQuestions(4, this.value)">Foghorn Leghorn</p>
<p><b>5. What is Winnie the Pooh's favorite food?</b></p>
<p><input type=radio name=question5 value="a"
    onClick="scoreQuestions(5, this.value)">Honey<br>
<input type=radio name=question5 value="b"
    onClick="scoreQuestions(5, this.value)">Molasses<br>
<input type=radio name=question5 value="c"
    onClick="scoreQuestions(5, this.value)">Peanut Butter<br>
<input type=radio name=question5 value="d"
    onClick="scoreQuestions(5, this.value)">Yogurt</p>
</form>
```

Figure 15-7   Completed `<input>` tags

15

11. Save the HTML document and open it in your Web browser. The program should function the same way that it did with the multiple `if` statements and the multiple functions.

12. Close the Web browser window.

`switch` **Statements**

Another JavaScript statement that is used for controlling program flow is the `switch` statement. The **`switch` statement** controls program flow by executing a specific set of statements, depending on the value of an expression. The `switch` statement compares the value of an expression to a value contained within a special statement called a *case label*. A **case label** in a `switch` statement represents a specific value and contains one or more statements that execute if the value of the case label matches the value of the `switch` statement's expression. For example, you may have a variable in your program named `favoriteMusic`. A `switch` statement can evaluate the variable and compare it to a case label within the `switch` construct. The `switch` statement may contain several case labels, such as `Jazz`, `Rock`, or `Gospel`. If the `favoriteMusic` variable is equal to `Rock`, then the statements that are part of the `Rock` case label execute. Although you could accomplish the same task using `if` or `if...else` statements, a `switch` statement makes it easier to organize the different branches of code that can be executed.

A `switch` statement consists of the following components: the keyword `switch`, an expression, an opening brace, a case label, executable statements, the keyword `break`, a default label, and a closing brace. The syntax for the `switch` statement is as follows:

```
switch (expression) {
    case label:
        statement(s);
        break;
    case label:
        statement(s);
        break;
    ...
    default:
        statement(s);
}
```

A case label consists of the keyword **case**, followed by a literal value or variable name, followed by a colon. JavaScript compares the value returned from the `switch` statement expression to the literal value or variable name following the **case** keyword. If a match is found, the case label statements execute. For example, the case label `case 3.17:` represents a floating-point integer value of 3.17. If the value of a `switch` statement expression equals 3.17, then the `case 3.17:` label statements execute. You can use a variety of data types as case labels within the same `switch` statement. Figure 15-8 shows examples of four case labels.

A case label can be followed by a single statement or multiple statements. However, unlike `if` statements, multiple statements for a case label do not need to be enclosed within a command block.

```
case exampleVar:          // variable name
     statement(s)
case "text string":       // string literal
     statement(s)
case 75:                  // integer literal
     statement(s)
case -273.4:              // floating-point literal
     statement(s)
```

Figure 15-8 Examples of case labels

Other programming languages, such as Java and C++, require all case labels within a `switch` statement to be of the same data type.

Another type of label used within `switch` statements is the default label. The **default label** contains statements that execute when the value returned by the `switch` statement conditional expression does not match a case label. A default label consists of the keyword `default` followed by a colon.

When a `switch` statement executes, the value returned by the conditional expression is compared to each case label in the order in which it is encountered. Once a matching label is found, its statements execute. Unlike the `if...else` statement, execution of a `switch` statement does not automatically stop after particular case label statements execute. Instead, the `switch` statement continues evaluating the rest of the case labels in the list. Once a matching case label is found, evaluation of additional case labels is unnecessary. If you are working with a large `switch` statement with many case labels, evaluation of additional case labels can potentially slow down your program.

To avoid slow performance, then, you need to give some thought as to how and when to end a `switch` statement. A `switch` statement ends automatically after the JavaScript interpreter encounters its closing brace (}). You can, however, use a special kind of statement, called a `break` statement, to end a `switch` statement once it has performed its required task. To end a `switch` statement once it has performed its required task, include a `break` statement within each case label.

A **break statement** is also used to exit other types of program control statements, such as the `while`, `do...while`, and `for` looping statements. You will learn about these statements later in this chapter.

15

Figure 15-9 shows a **switch** statement contained within a function. When the function is called, it is passed an argument named **americanCity**. The **switch** statement compares the contents of the **americanCity** argument to the case labels. If a match is found, the city's state is returned and a **break** statement ends the **switch** statement. If a match is not found, the value **United States** is returned from the default label.

```
function city_location(americanCity) {
    switch (americanCity) {
        case "Boston":
            return "Massachusetts";
            break;
        case "Chicago":
            return "Illinois";
            break;
        case "Los Angeles":
            return "California";
            break;
        case "Miami":
            return "Florida";
            break;
        case "New York":
            return "New York";
            break;
        default:
            return "United States";
    }
}
document.writeln(city_location("Boston"));
```

Figure 15-9   Function containing a **switch** statement

Next, you will modify the Cartoon Quiz program so that the **scoreAnswers()** function contains a **switch** statement instead of nested **if...else** statements. Each **case** statement in the modified program will check for the question number that is passed from the function's number argument. The **switch** statement makes better programming sense than the nested **if...else** statements, because it eliminates the need to check the question number multiple times.

To add a **switch** statement to the Cartoon Quiz program:

1. Return to the **Ch15JavaScript03.html** file and immediately save it as **Ch15JavaScript04.html**.

2. Change the **if...else** statements within the **scoreQuestions()** function to the following **switch** statement.

```
switch (number) {
  case 1:
        if (answer == 'b')
                alert("Correct Answer");
```

```
                else
                        alert("Incorrect Answer");
                break;
        case 2:
        if (answer == 'c')
                alert("Correct Answer");
        else
                alert("Incorrect Answer");
        break;
        case 3:
        if (answer == 'd')
                alert("Correct Answer");
        else
                alert("Incorrect Answer");
        break;
        case 4:
        if (answer == 'c')
                alert("Correct Answer");
        else
                alert("Incorrect Answer");
        break;
        case 5:
        if (answer == 'a')
                alert("Correct Answer");
        else
                alert("Incorrect Answer");
        break;
}
```

3. Save the HTML document and open it in your Web browser. The program should still function the same as it did with the nested if...else statements.

4. Close the Web browser window.

REPETITION

The statements you have worked with so far execute one after the other in a linear fashion. The if, if...else, and switch statements select only a single branch of code to execute and then continue to the statement that follows. But what if you want to repeat the same statement, function, or code section 5 times, 10 times, or 100 times? For example, you might want to perform the same calculation until a specific number is found. In that case, you would need to use a **loop statement**, a control structure that repeatedly executes a statement or a series of statements while a specific condition is true or until a specific condition becomes true. In this section, you will learn about three types of loop statements: while statements, do...while statements, and for statements.

while Statements

One of the simplest types of loop statements is the `while` statement. The **while statement** is used for repeating a statement or series of statements as long as a given conditional expression evaluates to true. The syntax for the `while` statement is as follows:

```
while (conditional expression) {
    statement(s);
}
```

Like the `if...else` and `switch` statements, the conditional expression that the `while` statement tests for is enclosed within parentheses following the keyword `while`. As long as the conditional expression evaluates to true, the statement or command block that follows will execute repeatedly. Each repetition of a looping statement is called an **iteration**. Once the conditional expression evaluates to false, the loop ends and the next statement following the `while` statement executes.

A `while` statement will keep repeating until its conditional expression evaluates to false. To ensure that the `while` statement ends after the desired tasks have been performed, you must include code that tracks the progress of the loop and changes the value produced by the conditional expression. You track the progress of a `while` statement, or any other loop, with a counter. A **counter** is a variable that increments or decrements with each iteration of a loop statement.

 Many programmers often name counter variables `count`, `counter`, or something similar. The letters `i`, `j`, `k`, and `l` are also commonly used as counter names. Using a name such as `count`, or the letter `i` (for increment) or a higher letter, helps you remember (and lets other programmers know) that the variable is being used as a counter.

The following code shows a simple program that includes a `while` statement. The program declares a variable named `count` and assigns it an initial value of 1. The `count` variable is then used in the `while` statement conditional expression (`count <= 5`). As long as the `count` variable is less than or equal to 5, the `while` statement will loop. Within the body of the `while` statement, the `document.writeln()` statement prints the value of the `count` variable and then the `count` variable increments by a value of 1. The `while` statement loops until the `count` variable increments to a value of 6.

```
var count = 1;
while (count <= 5) {
    document.writeln(count);
    ++count;
}
document.writeln("You have printed 5 numbers.");
```

The preceding code prints the numbers 1 to 5, with each number representing one iteration of the loop. Once the counter reaches 6, the message "You have printed 5 numbers" prints, thus demonstrating that the loop has ended. Figure 15-10 shows the output of this simple program.

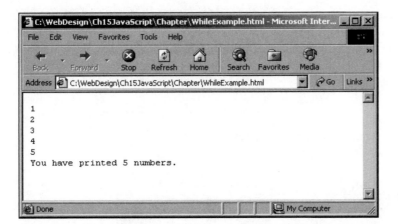

Figure 15-10   Output of a `while` statement using an increment operator

You can also control the repetitions in a **while** loop by decrementing (decreasing the value of) counter variables. Consider the following program code:

```
var count = 10;
while (count > 0) {
     document.writeln(count);
     --count;
}
document.writeln("We have liftoff.");
```

In this example, the initial value of the **count** variable is 10, and the decrement operator (--) is used to decrease **count** by one. While the **count** variable is greater than zero, the statement within the **while** loop prints the value of the **count** variable. When the value of **count** is equal to zero, the **while** loop ends, and the statement immediately following it prints. Figure 15-11 shows the program output.

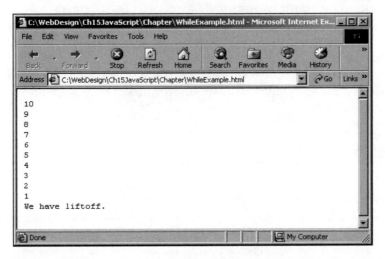

Figure 15-11   Output of a `while` statement using a decrement operator

15

There are many ways to change the value of a counter variable and to use a counter variable to control the repetitions of a `while` loop. The following example uses the `*=` assignment operator to multiply the value of the `count` variable by two. Once the `count` variable reaches a value of 128, the `while` statement ends. Figure 15-12 shows the program output.

```
var count = 1;
while (count <= 100) {
     document.writeln (count);
     count *= 2;
}
```

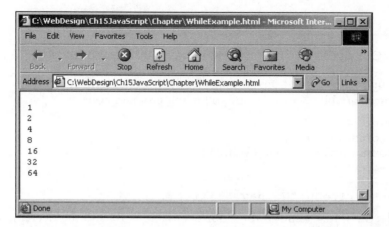

Figure 15-12   Output of a `while` statement using the `*=` assignment operator

It is important to include code within the body of the `while` statement that changes the value of the conditional expression in a way that ensures that the `while` statement will eventually end. For example, you may have a `while` statement that prints even numbers between 0 and 100. You need to include code within the body of the `while` statement that ends the loop once the last even number (100) prints. If you do not include code that changes the value used by the conditional expression, your program will be caught in an infinite loop. An **infinite loop** is a situation in which a loop statement never ends because its conditional expression is never false. Consider the following `while` statement:

```
var count = 1;
while (count <= 10) {
     alert("The number is " + count);
}
```

Although the `while` statement in the preceding example includes a conditional expression that checks the value of a `count` variable, there is no code within the body of the `while` statement that changes the `count` variable value. The `count` variable will continue to have a value of 1 through each iteration of the loop. That means an alert dialog box containing the text string "The number is 1" will appear over and over again, no matter how many times the user clicks the OK button.

 In most cases, you must force a Web browser that is caught in an infinite loop to close. The method for forcing an application to close varies from one operating system to another. For Windows operating systems, you can force an application to close by pressing Ctrl+Alt+Delete to access Task List or Task Manager.

Next, you will create a program that demonstrates the use of the `while` statement. The program asks the user to enter a speed measurement (in miles per hour) in a prompt dialog box. The speed is then assigned to a counter variable that is used by a `while` statement. As long as the user enters a speed that is under 65 mph, the user will continue to see prompt dialog boxes asking for new speeds. If the user enters a speed over 65, or less than or equal to 0, the `while` loop will end.

To create the Speed Limit program:

1. Create a new document in your text editor.

2. Type the opening `<html>` tag, the opening lines of a `<head>` section, and a new `<script>` section:

```
<html><head><title>Speed Limit</title>
<script language="JavaScript">
<!-- HIDE FROM INCOMPATIBLE BROWSERS
```

3. Type the opening constructor for a function that accepts a single `speed` argument:

```
function speedLimit(speed) {
```

4. Add the opening constructor for a `while` statement that keeps looping as long as the speed variable is less than or equal to 65:

```
while(speed <= 65) {
```

5. Add the following line that assigns the input from a prompt dialog box to a variable named `newSpeed`:

```
var newSpeed = prompt("Your speed is " + speed
    + ". Please enter a new speed.", "");
```

6. Add an `if...else` statement to determine if the speed entered by the user is over 65. If the speed is greater than 65, this code will make an alert dialog box appear, and it will call the `break` statement.

```
if (newSpeed > 65) {
    alert("You are speeding!");
    break;
}
```

15

7. Add an `if...else` statement to determine if the speed entered by the user is less than or equal to 0. If the speed is less than or equal to 0, this code will display an alert dialog box, and it will call the `break` statement.

```
else if (newSpeed <= 0) {
    alert("You are stopped!");
    break;
}
```

8. Next, add a final `else` clause that continues the `while` statement:

```
else {
    speed = newSpeed;
}
```

9. Add the following code to close the `while` statement, function, `<script>` section, and `<head>` section:

```
    }
}
// STOP HIDING FROM INCOMPATIBLE BROWSERS -->
</script></head>
```

10. Type the following lines for the opening `<body>` tag, along with an `<h1>` tag. The `<body>` tag uses an onLoad event to call the `speedLimit()` function in the `<head>`. The `speedLimit()` function is sent a starting speed of 55.

```
<body onLoad= "speedLimit(55);">
<h1>Select Reload or Refresh to restart the SpeedLimit
program.</h1>
```

11. Add the following code to close the `<body>` and `<html>` tags:

```
</body></html>
```

12. Save the file as **Ch15JavaScript05.html** in the Chapter folder for Chapter 15 and then open it and test it in your browser by entering a speed in the prompt dialog box. If you enter any number between 1 and 55, then the prompt dialog box reappears with the speed you entered and prompts you to enter another number. If you enter a number over 55, then you see an alert dialog box telling you that you are speeding. If you enter 0, then an alert dialog box tells you that you are stopped. If you select Reload or Refresh, then the onLoad event in the `<body>` element is called again, which restarts the program. Figure 15-13 shows an example of the output of Ch15JavaScript05.html.

13. Close the Web browser window.

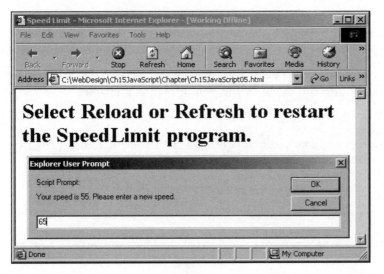

Figure 15-13   Output of Ch15JavaScript05.html

do...while **Statements**

Another JavaScript looping statement, similar to the while statement, is the do...while statement. The do...while **statement** executes a statement or a group of statements once and then repeats the execution for as long as a given conditional expression evaluates to true. The syntax for the do...while statement is as follows:

```
do {
     statement(s);
} while (conditional expression);
```

As you can see in the syntax description, the statements execute before a conditional expression is evaluated. Unlike the simpler while statement, the statements in a do...while statement always execute once, before a conditional expression is evaluated.

The following do...while statement executes once before the conditional expression evaluates the count variable. Therefore, a single line that reads "The count is equal to 2" prints. After the conditional expression (count < 2) executes, the count variable is equal to 2. This causes the conditional expression to return a value of false, and the do...while statement ends.

```
var count = 2;
do {
     document.writeln("The count is equal to " + count);
     ++count;
} while (count < 2);
```

15

Note that this `do...while` example includes a counter within the body of the `do...while` statement. As with the `while` statement, you need to include code that changes the conditional expression in order to prevent an infinite loop from occurring.

In the following example, the `while` statement never executes, because the `count` variable does not fall within the range of the conditional expression:

```
var count = 2;
while (count > 2) {
     document.writeln("The count is equal to " + count);
     ++count;
}
```

Figure 15-14 shows an example of a `do...while` statement that prints the days of the week, using an array.

```
<pre>
<script>
var daysOfWeek = new Array();
daysOfWeek[0] = "Monday"; daysOfWeek[1] = "Tuesday";
daysOfWeek[2] = "Wednesday"; daysOfWeek[3] = "Thursday";
daysOfWeek[4] = "Friday"; daysOfWeek[5] = "Saturday";
daysOfWeek[6] = "Sunday";
var count = 0;
do {
     document.writeln(daysOfWeek[count]);
     ++count;
} while (count < daysOfWeek.length);
</script>
</pre>
```

Figure 15-14   Example of a `do...while` statement

In the example in Figure 15-14, an array is created containing the days of the week. A variable named `count` is declared and initialized to zero. Remember, the first subscript or index in an array is zero. Therefore, in the example, the statement `daysOfWeek[0];` refers to Monday. The first iteration of the `do...while` statement prints "Monday" and then increments the `count` variable by one. The conditional expression in the `while` statement then checks the `Array` object length property to determine when the last element of the array has been printed. As long as the count is less than the `Array` object length property (which is one number higher than the largest element in the `daysOfWeek[]` array), the loop continues. Figure 15-15 shows the output of the Days of Week program in a Web browser.

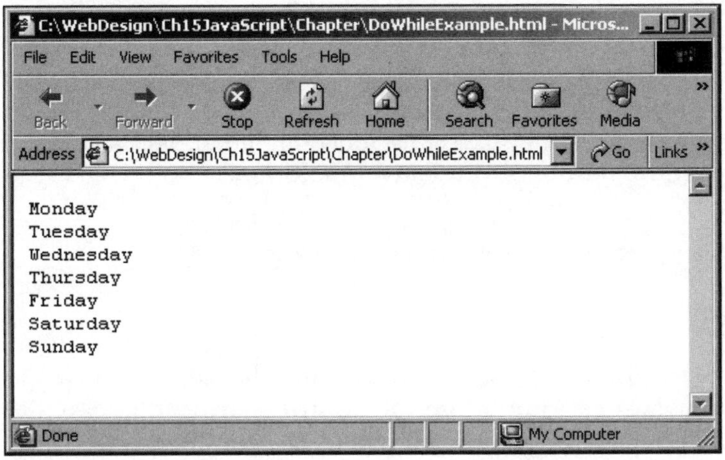

Figure 15-15   Days of Week program in a Web browser

Next, you will modify the Speed Limit program to incorporate a **do...while** statement instead of a **while** statement. Using a **do...while** statement eliminates the need to send an initial speed argument to the **speedLimit()** function. Instead, the **speed** variable is initialized during the first pass of the **do** statement. The **while** statement then checks the **speed** variable to see if the loop should continue.

To add a **do...while** statement to the Speed Limit program:

1. Return to the **Ch15JavaScript05.html** file and immediately save it as **Ch15JavaScript06.html**.

2. Delete the **speed** argument in the **speedLimit()** function.

3. Replace the **while** statement in the **speedLimit()** function with the following **do...while** statement. Notice that you no longer need the **newSpeed** variable. Also notice that you no longer need the final **else** clause to assign the value of the **newSpeed** variable to the **speed** variable.

```
do {
    var speed = prompt("Your speed is " + speed
        + ". Please enter a new speed", "");
    if (speed > 65) {
        alert("You are speeding!");
        break;
    }
    else if (speed <= 0) {
        alert("You are stopped!");
        break;
    }
} while(speed <= 65)
```

4. Delete the **55** in the statement that calls the **speedLimit()** function.

15

5. Save the file and then open it in your Web browser. When you first open it, the message in the dialog box reads "Your speed is undefined". Remember that when a variable is declared, it contains an initial value of `undefined` until you explicitly assign a value to it. Because you removed the `speed` argument from the `speedLimit()` function, the `speed` variable contains a value of `undefined` until you enter a speed limit into the dialog box and press **Enter**.

6. Click **OK** and close the Web browser window.

for Statements

So far, you have learned how to use the `while` and the `do...while` statements to repeat, or loop through, code. You can also use the `for` statement to loop through code. The **for statement** is used for repeating a statement or series of statements as long as a given conditional expression evaluates to true. The `for` statement performs essentially the same function as the `while` statement: If a conditional expression within the `for` statement evaluates to true, then the `for` statement executes and will continue to execute repeatedly until the conditional expression evaluates to false. One of the primary differences between the `while` statement and the `for` statement is that in addition to a conditional expression, the `for` statement can also include code to initialize a counter and change its value with each iteration. This is useful because it provides a specific place for you to declare and initialize a counter, and to update its value, which helps prevent infinite loops. The syntax of the `for` statement is as follows:

```
for (counter declaration and initialization; condition;
    update statement) {
    statement(s);
}
```

When the JavaScript interpreter encounters a `for` loop, the following steps occur:

1. The counter variable is declared and initialized. For example, if the initialization expression in a `for` loop is `var count = 1;`, then a variable named `count` is declared and assigned an initial value of 1. The initialization expression is only started once, when the `for` loop is first encountered.

2. The `for` loop condition is evaluated.

3. If the condition evaluation in step 2 returns a value of true, then the `for` loop statements execute, step 4 occurs, and the process starts over again with step 2. If the condition evaluation in step 2 returns a value of false, then the `for` statement ends and the next statement following the `for` statement executes.

4. The `update` statement in the `for` statement constructor is executed. For example, the count variable may increment by one.

You can omit any of the three parts of the `for` statement constructor, but you must include the semicolons that separate each section. If you omit a section of the constructor, be sure you include code within the body that will end the `for` statement or your program may get caught in an infinite loop.

Figure 15-16 shows a `for` statement that prints the contents of an array.

```
var fastFoods = new Array();
fastFoods[0] = "pizza"; fastFoods[1] = "burgers";
fastFoods[2] = "french fries"; fastFoods[3] = "tacos";
fastFoods[4] = "fried chicken";
for (var count = 0; count < fastFoods.length; ++count) {
    document.writeln(fastFoods[count]);
}
```

Figure 15-16   A `for` statement that displays the contents of an array

As you can see in this example, the counter is initialized, evaluated, and incremented within the constructor. You do not need to include a declaration for the **count** variable before the `for` statement, nor do you need to increment the **count** variable within the body of the `for` statement. Figure 15-17 shows the output of the Fast Foods program.

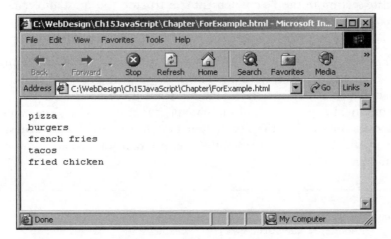

Figure 15-17   Output of Fast Foods program

Using a `for` statement is more efficient because you do not need as many lines of code. Consider the following `while` statement:

```
var count = 1;
while (count <= 5) {
    document.writeln(count);
    ++count;
}
```

You could achieve the same flow control more efficiently by using a **for** statement as follows:

```
for (var count = 1; count <= 5; ++count) {
    document.writeln(count);
}
```

There are times, however, when using a **while** statement is preferable to using a **for** statement, especially for looping statements that do need to declare, initialize, or update a counter variable. The following code relies on a Boolean value returned from a confirm dialog box, rather than a counter, for program control.

```
var i = true;
while (i == true)
    i = confirm(
        "Do you want to redisplay this dialog box?");
```

You could accomplish the same task using a **for** statement, but in this case, the third part of the **for** statement constructor, which updates the counter, would be unnecessary. This is because the counter is updated by the value returned from the **confirm()** method; a value of true would cause the loop to reiterate, while a value of false would cause the loop to exit. Therefore, this code is better written using a **while** statement. If you use a **for** statement instead of a **while** statement in the preceding example, you must not include the update section in the **for** statement constructor. You must also remember to retain the semicolon that separates the conditional section from the update section. If you include the update section in the constructor, you could create an infinite loop.

Figure 15-18 shows an example of the Days of Week program you saw in Figure 15-14 (that prints the contents of an array). This time, however, the program includes a **for** statement instead of a **do...while** statement. Notice that the declaration of the **count** variable, the conditional expression, and the statement that increments the **count** variable are now all contained within the **for** statement constructor. Using a **for** statement instead of a **do...while** statement simplifies the program somewhat, because you do not need as many lines of code.

```
<pre><script>
var daysOfWeek = new Array();
daysOfWeek[0] = "Monday"; daysOfWeek[1] = "Tuesday";
daysOfWeek[2] = "Wednesday"; daysOfWeek[3] = "Thursday";
daysOfWeek[4] = "Friday"; daysOfWeek[5] = "Saturday";
daysOfWeek[6] = "Sunday";
for (var count = 0; count < daysOfWeek.length; ++count) {
    document.writeln(daysOfWeek[count]);
}
</script></pre>
```

Figure 15-18   Example of a `for` statement

Next, you will create a final version of the Cartoon Quiz program. In this version, the quiz will be scored by a single `for` statement containing a nested `if` statement. Although this `for` statement is somewhat more complicated than the `if`, `if...else`, and `switch` statements you created previously, it takes up considerably fewer lines of code. You will also include a Score button that grades the entire quiz after a user is finished. (Remember that the earlier version of the program graded the quiz answer by answer.)

To create the final version of the Cartoon Quiz program:

1. Open the **Ch15JavaScript04.html** file from the Chapter folder for Chapter 15 and immediately save it as **Ch15JavaScript07.html**.

2. Delete the entire `scoreQuestions()` function from the `<head>` section and then add the following lines to create two arrays named `answers[ ]` and `correctAnswers[ ]`. The `answers[ ]` array will hold the answers selected each time the quiz runs; the `correctAnswers[ ]` array will hold the correct response for each of the questions. The code also assigns the correct responses to each element of the `correctAnswers[ ]` array.

```
var answers = new Array(5);
var correctAnswers = new Array(5);
correctAnswers[0] = "b"; correctAnswers[1] = "c";
correctAnswers[2] = "d"; correctAnswers[3] = "c";
correctAnswers[4] = "a";
```

3. Add the following function, which assigns the response from each question to the appropriate element in the `answers[ ]` array. The program sends the actual question number (1-5) to the function using the onClick event of each radio button. To assign question responses to the correct element, 1 must be subtracted from the `question` variable, because the elements in an array start with 0.

```
function recordAnswer(question, answer) {
     answers[question-1] = answer;
}
```

4. Type the opening constructor for the function that scores the quiz. You will call this function from a new Score button.

```
function scoreQuiz() {
```

5. Type **var totalCorrect = 0;** to declare a new variable and assign to it an initial value of 0. The `totalCorrect` variable holds the number of correct answers.

6. Press **Enter** and type the opening constructor for a `for` loop that will score the quiz:

```
for(var count = 0; count < correctAnswers.length;
   ++count) {
```

In this code, a counter named `count` is initialized to a value of 0, because 0 is the starting index of an array. The conditional expression checks to see if

15

count is less than or equal to the number of elements in the `answers[]` array. Finally, the `count` variable increments by one with each iteration of the loop.

7. Add the following `if` statement within the `for` loop. This `if` statement compares each element within the `answers[]` array to each corresponding element within the `correctAnswers[]` array. If the elements match, the `totalCorrect` variable increments by one.

```
if (answers[count] == correctAnswers[count])
    ++totalCorrect;
```

8. Add the closing brace for the `for` loop. Then add the code for an alert dialog box that shows how many questions were answered correctly:

```
}
alert("You scored " + totalCorrect
    + " out of 5 answers correctly!");
```

9. Add a closing brace (}) for the `scoreQuiz()` function.

10. In the `onClick` event handlers for each radio button, change the name of the called function from `scoreQuestions()` to **recordAnswer()**, but use the same arguments that you used for the `scoreQuestions()` function. For example, the `onClick` event handlers for the question 1 radio buttons should now read `onClick="recordAnswer(1, this.value)"`.

11. Finally, add the following `<input>` tag immediately after the last radio button for question 5. The `<input>` tag creates a command button whose `onClick` event handler calls the `scoreQuiz()` function.

```
<input type=button value="Score" onClick =
"scoreQuiz();"><p>
```

12. Save the file. Figure 15-19 shows how your file should look.

```
<html>
<head>
<title>Cartoon Quiz</title>
<script language="JavaScript">
<!-- HIDE FROM INCOMPATIBLE BROWSERS
var answers = new Array(5);
var correctAnswers = new Array(5);
correctAnswers[0] = "b";
correctAnswers[1] = "c";
correctAnswers[2] = "d";
correctAnswers[3] = "c";
correctAnswers[4] = "a";
```

Figure 15-19 The completed Ch15JavaScript07.html file

```
function recordAnswer(question, answer) {
    answers[question-1] = answer;
}
function scoreQuiz() {
var totalCorrect = 0;
for(var count = 0; count < correctAnswers.length; ++count) {
if (answers[count] == correctAnswers[count])
    ++totalCorrect;
}
alert("You scored " + totalCorrect
    + " out of 5 answers correctly!");
}
// STOP HIDING FROM INCOMPATIBLE BROWSERS -->
</script>
</head>
<body>
<h1>Cartoon Quiz</h1>
<p>Answer all of the questions on the quiz, then select the Score button to
    grade the quiz.</p>
<form>
<p><b>1. What is the name of Walt Disney's famous mouse?</b></p>
<p><input type=radio name=question1 value="a"
    onClick="recordAnswer(1, this.value)">Mighty Mouse<br>
<input type=radio name=question1 value="b"
    onClick="recordAnswer(1, this.value)">Mickey Mouse<br>
<input type=radio name=question1 value="c"
    onClick="recordAnswer(1, this.value)">Marty Mouse<br>
<input type=radio name=question1 value="d"
    onClick="recordAnswer(1, this.value)">Melvin Mouse</p>
<p><b>2. The character Buzz Lightyear was featured in which animated
    film?</b></p>
<p><input type=radio name=question2 value="a"
    onClick="recordAnswer(2, this.value)">Fantasia<br>
<input type=radio name=question2 value="b"
    onClick="recordAnswer(2, this.value)">Hercules<br>
<input type=radio name=question2 value="c"
    onClick="recordAnswer(2, this.value)">Toy Story<br>
<input type=radio name=question2 value="d"
    onClick="recordAnswer(2, this.value)">Mulan</p>
<p><b>3. Pluto is a dog. What is Goofy?</b></p>
<p><input type=radio name=question3 value="a"
    onClick="recordAnswer(3, this.value)">A bear<br>
<input type=radio name=question3 value="b"
    onClick="recordAnswer(3, this.value)">A mule<br>
<input type=radio name=question3 value="c"
    onClick="recordAnswer(3, this.value)">A horse<br>
<input type=radio name=question3 value="d"
    onClick="recordAnswer(3, this.value)">Also a dog</p>
<p><b>4. Who was always trying to eat Tweety Bird?</b></p>
```

15

Figure 15-19   The completed Ch15JavaScript07.html file (continued)

```
<p><input type=radio name=question4 value="a"
    onClick="recordAnswer(4, this.value)">Porky Pig<br>
<input type=radio name=question4 value="b"
    onClick="recordAnswer(4, this.value)">Yosemite Sam<br>
<input type=radio name=question4 value="c"
    onClick="recordAnswer(4, this.value)">Sylvester<br>
<input type=radio name=question4 value="d"
    onClick="recordAnswer(4, this.value)">Foghorn Leghorn</p>
<p><b>5. What is Winnie the Pooh's favorite food?</b></p>
<p><input type=radio name=question5 value="a"
    onClick="recordAnswer(5, this.value)">Honey<br>
<input type=radio name=question5 value="b"
    onClick="recordAnswer(5, this.value)">Molasses<br>
<input type=radio name=question5 value="c"
    onClick="recordAnswer(5, this.value)">Peanut Butter<br>
<input type=radio name=question5 value="d"
    onClick="recordAnswer(5, this.value)">Yogurt</p>
<p><input type=button value="Score" onClick="scoreQuiz();"></p>
</form>
</body>
</html>
```

Figure 15-19   The completed Ch15JavaScript07.html file (continued)

13. Open the **Ch15JavaScript07.html** file in your Web browser window. Test the program by answering all five questions and clicking the Score button. Figure 15-20 shows how the program appears in Internet Explorer.

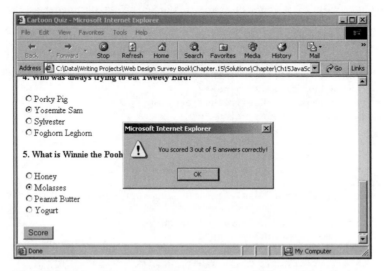

Figure 15-20   Ch15JavaScript07.html in Internet Explorer

14. Close the Web browser window and your text editor.

CHAPTER SUMMARY

❐ Flow control is the process of determining the order in which statements execute in a program.

❐ The `if` statement is used to execute specific programming code if the evaluation of a conditional expression returns true.

❐ A command block is a set of statements contained within a set of braces, similar to the way function statements are contained within a set of braces.

❐ `If...else` statements execute an alternate set of code if the conditional expression evaluated by an `if` statement returns a value of false.

❐ The `switch` statement controls program flow by executing a specific set of statements, depending on the value returned by an expression.

❐ A `loop` statement repeatedly executes a statement or a series of statements as long as a specific condition is true or until a specific condition becomes true.

❐ The `while` statement is used for repeating a statement or series of statements as long as a given conditional expression evaluates to true.

❐ The `do...while` statement executes a statement or statements once and then repeats the execution as long as a given conditional expression evaluates to true.

❐ The `for` statement repeats a statement or series of statements as long as a given conditional expression evaluates to true.

REVIEW QUESTIONS

1. Which of the following is the correct syntax for an `if` statement?

   a. `if (myVariable == 10);`
      `alert("Your variable is equal to 10.");`

   b. `if myVariable == 10`
      `alert("Your variable is equal to 10.");`

   c. `if (myVariable == 10)`
      `alert("Your variable is equal to 10.");`

   d. `if (myVariable == 10),`
      `alert("Your variable is equal to 10.");`

2. An `if` statement can include multiple statements provided that they
   _____.

   a. execute after the `if` statement closing semicolon

   b. are not contained within a command block

   c. do not include other `if` statements

   d. are contained within a command block

15

3. Which operators can you use with an `if` statement?

    a. only comparison operators

    b. only logical operators

    c. both comparison and logical operators

    d. You cannot use operators with an `if` statement.

4. Which is the correct syntax for an `else` clause?

    a. `else(document.write("Printed from an else clause.");`

    b. `else document.write("Printed from an else clause.");`

    c. `else "document.write('Printed from an else clause.')";`

    d. `else; document.write("Printed from an else clause.");`

5. The `switch` statement controls program flow by executing a specific set of statements, depending on _____.

    a. the result of an `if...else` statement

    b. the version of JavaScript being executed

    c. whether an `if` statement executes from within a function

    d. the value returned by a conditional expression

6. When the value returned by a `switch` statement conditional expression does not match a case label, then the statements within the _____ label execute.

    a. exception

    b. else

    c. error

    d. default

7. You can exit a `switch` statement using a(n) _____ statement.

    a. `break`

    b. `end`

    c. `quit`

    d. `complete`

8. Each repetition of a looping statement is called a(n) _____.

    a. recurrence

    b. iteration

    c. duplication

    d. re-execution

9. Which of the following is the correct syntax for a `while` statement?

   a. ```
while (i <= 5, ++i) {
        document.writeln(i);
   }
```

   b. ```
while (i <= 5) {
        document.writeln(i);
        ++i;
   }
```

   c. ```
while (i <= 5);
        document.writeln(i);
        ++i;
```

   d. ```
while (i <= 5; document.writeln(i)) {
        ++i;
   }
```

10. Counter variables _____.

    a. can only be incremented

    b. can only be decremented

    c. can be changed using any conditional expression

    d. do not change

11. An infinite loop is caused _____.

    a. when you omit the closing brace for a decision-making structure

    b. when a conditional expression never evaluates to false

    c. when a conditional expression never evaluates to true

    d. whenever you execute a `while` statement

12. If a `do...while` statement conditional expression evaluates to false, how many times will the `do...while` statement execute?

    a. never

    b. once

    c. twice

    d. Repeatedly—this conditional expression causes an infinite loop.

15

13. Which of the following is the correct syntax for a **do...while** statement?

    a. ```
       do while (i < 10) {
            alert("Printed from a do...while loop.");
       }
       ```

    b. ```
       do { while (i < 10)
            alert("Printed from a do...while loop.");
       }
       ```

    c. ```
       do {
            alert("Printed from a do...while loop.");
            while (i < 10)
       }
       ```

    d. ```
       do {
            alert("Printed from a do...while loop.");
       } while (i < 10);
       ```

14. Which of the following is the correct syntax for a **for** statement?

    a. ```
       for (var i = 0; i < 10; ++i)
            alert("Printed from a for statement.");
       ```

    b. ```
       for (var i = 0, i < 10, ++i)
            alert("Printed from a for statement.");
       ```

    c. ```
       for {
            alert("Printed from a for statement.");
       } while (var i = 0; i < 10; ++i)
       ```

    d. ```
       for (var i = 0; i < 10);
            alert("Printed from a for statement.");
            ++i;
       ```

15. When is a **for** statement initialization expression executed?

    a. when the **for** statement begins executing

    b. with each repetition of the **for** statement

    c. when the counter variable increments

    d. when the **for** statement ends

HANDS-ON EXERCISES

Exercise 15-1

In this exercise, you will create a simple HTML document that contains an **if** statement with a command block.

1. Create a new document in your text editor, and then create the document header using the appropriate HTML tags. Include a head section with a **<title>**; use **Exercise 15-1** for the title text.

2. Type the opening **\<body>** tag.

3. Create a script section in the document body that includes the following **if** statement:

```
if (boolValue == true)
    document.writeln("The condition is equal to 'true'");
```

4. Modify the **if** statement so that it can contain multiple statements.

5. Add a second statement to the **if** statement that prints the value of the **boolValue** variable.

6. Type the closing **\</body>** and **\</html>** tags.

7. Save the HTML document as **Ch15JavaScriptEX01.html** in the Exercises folder for Chapter 15.

8. Open **Ch15JavaScriptEX01.html** in your browser. Your document should look similar to Figure 15-21.

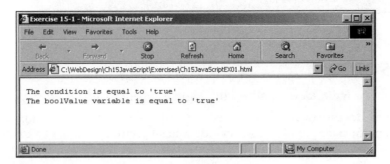

Figure 15-21 Output of Exercise 15-1

Exercise 15-2

In this exercise, you will create a simple HTML document containing a conditional operator that you will rewrite into an **if...else** statement.

1. Create a new document in your text editor, and then create the document header using the appropriate HTML tags. Include a head section with a **\<title>**; use **Exercise 15-2** for the title text.

2. Type the opening **\<body>** tag.

3. Create a script section in the document body that includes the following code, but replace the conditional expression statement with an **if...else** statement:

```
var intVariable = 75;
var result;
(intVariable > 100) ?
result = "intVariable is greater than 100"
: result =  "intVariable is less than or equal to 100";
document.write(result);
```

15

4. Type the closing **</body>** and **</html>** tags.

5. Save the HTML document as **Ch15JavaScriptEX02.html** in the Exercises folder for Chapter 15.

6. Open **Ch15JavaScriptEX02.html** in your browser. Your document should look similar to Figure 15-22.

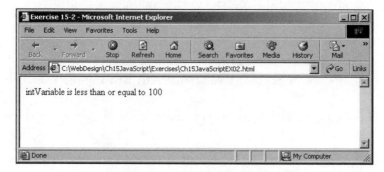

Figure 15-22 Output of Exercise 15-2

Exercise 15-3

In this exercise, you will identify and fix the logic flaws in an **if** statement.

1. Create a new document in your text editor, and then create the document header using the appropriate HTML tags. Include a head section with a **<title>**; use **Exercise 15-3** for the title text.

2. Type the opening **<body>** tag.

3. Examine the following code and note any logic flaws in the **if** statement. Create a script section in the document body that includes a corrected version of the following code:

```
var num = 100;
if (num >= 100);
    document.write("The variable is greater than ");
    document.write("or equal to '100.'");
```

4. Type the closing **</body>** and **</html>** tags.

5. Save the HTML document as **Ch15JavaScriptEX03.html** in the Exercises folder for Chapter 15.

6. Open **Ch15JavaScriptEX03.html** in your browser. Your document should look similar to Figure 15-23.

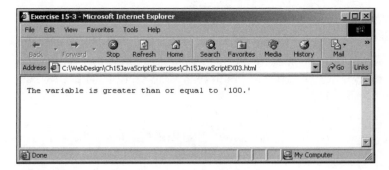

Figure 15-23   Output of Exercise 15-3

Exercise 15-4

In this exercise, you will write a `while` statement that prints all odd numbers between 1 and 100 to the screen.

1. Create a new document in your text editor, and then create the document header using the appropriate HTML tags. Include a head section with a `<title>`; use `Exercise 15-4` for the title text.

2. Type the opening `<body>` tag.

3. Create a script section with a `while` statement that prints all odd numbers between 1 and 100 to the screen.

4. Type the closing `</body>` and `</html>` tags.

5. Save the HTML document as **Ch15JavaScriptEX04.html** in the Exercises folder for Chapter 15.

6. Open **Ch15JavaScriptEX04.html** in your browser. Your document should look similar to Figure 15-24. (Figure 15-24 shows only a portion of the Web browser window due to space limitations.)

15

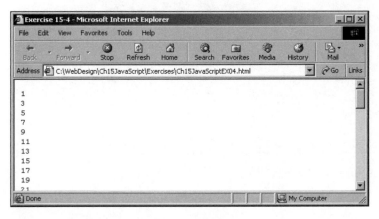

Figure 15-24   Output of Exercise 15-4

Exercise 15-5

In this exercise, you will identify and fix the logic flaws in a `while` statement.

1. Create a new document in your text editor, and then create the document header using the appropriate HTML tags. Include a head section with a `<title>`; use `Exercise 15-5` for the title text.

2. Type the opening `<body>` tag.

3. Create a script section in the document body that includes the following code:
   ```
   var count = 0;
   var numbers = new Array(100);
   while (count > 100) {
     numbers[count] = count;
     ++count;
   }
   while (count > 100) {
     document.writeln(numbers[count]);
     ++count;
   }
   ```

4. The code you typed in the preceding step contains several logic flaws that prevent it from running correctly. Identify and correct the logic flaws.

5. Type the closing `</body>` and `</html>` tags.

6. Save the HTML document as **Ch15JavaScriptEX05.html** in the Exercises folder for Chapter 15.

7. Open **Ch15JavaScriptEX05.html** in your browser. Your document should look similar to Figure 15-25. (Figure 15-25 shows only a portion of the Web browser window due to space limitations.)

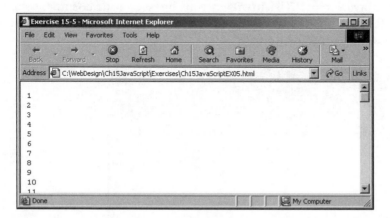

Figure 15-25 Output of Exercise 15-5

WEB DESIGN PROJECTS

Project 15-1

Create a program that calculates an employee's weekly gross salary, based on the number of hours worked and an hourly wage that you choose. Compute any hours over 40 as time-and-a-half. Use the appropriate decision structure to create the program. Save the HTML document as **Ch15JavaScriptDP01.html** in the Projects folder for Chapter 15.

Project 15-2

Write a program that calculates a 15% return on an investment of $10,000. Calculate how many years it will take for a single $10,000 investment to reach $1 million at an average annual return of 15%. Use a looping statement and assume that each iteration is equivalent to one year. Save the HTML document as **Ch15JavaScriptDP02.html** in the Projects folder for Chapter 15.

Project 15-3

Use an appropriate looping statement to write a program that prints a list of the Celsius equivalents of zero degrees Fahrenheit through 100 degrees Fahrenheit. To convert Fahrenheit to Celsius, subtract 32 from the Fahrenheit temperature, and then multiply the remainder by .55. To convert Celsius to Fahrenheit, multiply the Celsius temperature by 1.8, and then add 32. Save the HTML document as **Ch15JavaScriptDP03.html** in the Projects folder for Chapter 15.

15

CHAPTER

16

DYNAMIC HTML AND ANIMATION

> **In this chapter you will:**
>
> ♦ Study the Document Object Model
> ♦ Work with the `Image` object
> ♦ Use image caching
> ♦ Use JavaScript with CSS styles
> ♦ Use CSS positioning in Netscape and Internet Explorer
> ♦ Study cross-browser compatibility

More and more businesses today want their Web sites to include formatting and images that can be updated without the user having to reload an HTML document from the server. These businesses also want innovative ways to use animation and interactivity to attract and retain visitors and to make their Web sites effective and easy to navigate. Standard HTML cannot create these kinds of effects; instead, you need to use dynamic HTML (DHTML). In this chapter, you will become acquainted with DHTML techniques by creating two animations: a rocking horse and the Earth revolving around the sun. Both animation sequences are examples that could be used for advertising purposes or as visually appealing effects to draw visitors to a Web page.

Introduction

As you have probably realized by now, HTML would be much more useful if it were dynamic. In Internet terminology, the word "dynamic" means several things. Primarily, it refers to Web pages that respond to user requests through buttons or other kinds of controls. For example, a dynamic Web page may allow a user to change the document background color, process a query when a user submits a form, or interact with a user in other ways, such as through an online game or quiz. The term "dynamic" also refers to various kinds of effects, such as animation, that appear automatically in a Web browser.

To make Web pages dynamic, you need to use DHTML, which is actually a combination of JavaScript, HTML, CSS, and the Document Object Model. You should already be familiar with JavaScript, HTML, and CSS. Before you begin creating your animations, you will investigate the Document Object Model.

Document Object Model

Traditional programming languages, such as C++ and Java, are said to be object-oriented programming languages because they incorporate objects that are used for providing much of a program's functionality. (The actual work of a program is done by the methods and properties of the various objects.) JavaScript is not a true object-oriented programming language, although it does include many characteristics commonly associated with object-oriented languages. For instance, one common characteristic of object-oriented programming is **inheritance**, a way of relating objects to each other in which one object can be based on another object. Objects based on another object are said to descend from that object. An object from which another object is descended is called an **ancestor object**. An object that descends from another object inherits the methods and properties of the object from which it descends. Collections of objects that descend from one another are referred to as **object models**. Object models are assembled in a hierarchy similar to a family tree, in which all of the objects in the model descend from one common top-level ancestor object. The reason that the concepts of inheritance and object models are important to JavaScript programming has to do with the browser object model, which you use in your JavaScript code to control the Web browser window or the HTML document it displays.

At the core of DHTML is the Document Object Model. Within a DHTML page, the **Document Object Model**, or **DOM**, represents the Web page displayed in a window. Each HTML element on a Web page is represented in the DOM by its own object. With the DOM, you can use JavaScript to access and manipulate HTML elements through various events, properties, and methods. At the top of the DOM hierarchy is the `Document` object. Whenever you have used images and forms or have referred to the `Document` object, you have used the DOM. You have used two methods of the `Document` object, `write()` and `writeln()`, extensively. Figure 16-1 shows the object model of the HTML elements that make up the DOM.

The Document object refers not only to HTML documents, but also to other file types that are displayed in a Web browser, such as .jpg, .gif, and .xml. The file format .xml is used in structured documents that contain tags similar to HTML.

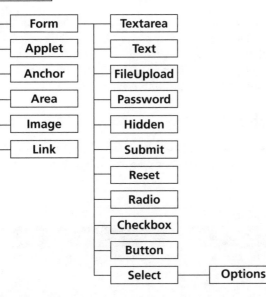

Figure 16-1   Document Object Model

The DOM lets you change individual HTML elements dynamically after a page has been rendered, without having to reload the page from the server.

Although the individual technologies that make up DHTML have been accepted standards for some time, the implementation of DHTML has evolved slowly. One of the main reasons for the slow implementation of DHTML has to do with the DOM. Earlier versions of Internet Explorer and Navigator included document object models that were almost completely incompatible with each other. In one of the most important battles of the so-called browser wars, Microsoft and Netscape each wanted their version of the DOM to become the industry standard. To settle the argument, the World Wide Web Consortium (W3C) set out to create a platform-independent and browser-neutral version of the DOM. The W3C's first standardized DOM effort, a primitive version known as *Level 0*, was first supported by versions 3 of both Internet Explorer and Navigator. However, versions 4 of both Internet Explorer and Navigator added a number of proprietary DOM objects that were completely incompatible with the other browser. These incompatibilities meant that for advanced DHTML techniques, such as animation, you had to write a different set of JavaScript code for each browser type. Subsequent releases of each browser have become more compatible with each other as they provide greater support for the W3C specification.

16

Currently, there are two levels to the W3C DOM. DOM Level 1 first defined basic document functionality, such as navigation and HTML element manipulation. DOM Level 2 introduced style sheet functionality and event handling. You need to keep in mind that earlier versions of each browser were not 100 percent compliant with the W3C DOM. Throughout this chapter, it will be noted which DOM technique function is used with which browser types and versions.

 This chapter discusses only methods and properties of the `Document` object that conform to the W3C DOM specifications. Even though later versions of Internet Explorer and Navigator conform to the W3C DOM specification, both browsers also support additional `Document` object methods and properties that may or may not be compatible with each other.

`Document` Object Properties

The `Document` object contains various properties used for manipulating HTML objects. Table 16-1 lists the properties of the `Document` object that are specified in the W3C DOM.

Table 16-1   `Document` object properties

Property	Description
`anchors[]`	An array referring to document anchors created with the `<a>` element
`applets[]`	An array referring to document applets, which are Java programs that run within a Web page
`body`	The element that contains the content for the document
`cookie`	The current document cookie string, which contains small pieces of information about a user that are stored by a Web server in text files on the user's computer
`domain`	The domain name of the server where the current document is located
`forms[]`	An array referring to document forms
`images[]`	An array referring to document images
`links[]`	An array referring to document links
`referrer`	The URL of the document that provided a link to the current document
`title`	The title of the document as specified by the `<title>` element in the document `<head>` section
`URL`	The URL of the current document

If you decide to dynamically change properties of the `Document` object, keep in mind that JavaScript programs that dynamically change `Document` object properties may not function with older browsers (such as Navigator 4) that do not support DOM Level 1.

Document Object Methods

In some situations, you may want your Web page to dynamically create a new HTML document. For example, after your Web page runs a CGI script that processes an online order, you may want the page to dynamically generate a new HTML document that confirms the order. The DOM methods listed in Table 16-2 can be used for dynamically generating and manipulating Web pages.

Table 16-2   Document object methods for dynamically generating Web pages

Method	Description
close()	Closes a new document that was created with the open() method
open()	Opens a new document in a window or frame
write()	Adds new text to a document
writeln()	Adds new text to a document, followed by a line break

You have used the write() and writeln() methods throughout this book to add content to a new Web page as it is being rendered. A limitation of the write() and writeln() methods is that they cannot be used to change content after a Web page has been rendered. You can write code that will execute the write() and writeln() methods in the current document after it is rendered, but in that case the write() and writeln() methods will overwrite the existing content.

THE IMAGE OBJECT

One of the most visually pleasing parts of a Web page is its images. At this point, you should be able to include images in a Web page. You simply include an <img> element with the src attribute set to the URL of the image you want to display. Each <img> element in an HTML document is represented in the DOM images[] array by an Image object. An Image object represents images created using the <img> element. If you want to change an image on the basis of a user's selection, as part of a timed advertising routine, or for simple animation, you must use JavaScript with an Image object.

16

Table 16-3 lists frequently used Image object properties, and Table 16-4 lists frequently used Image object events.

Table 16-3   Image object properties

Property	Description
border	A read-only property containing the border width, in pixels, as specified by the BORDER attribute of the <img> element
complete	A Boolean value that returns true when an image is completely loaded
height	A read-only property containing the height of the image as specified by the HEIGHT attribute of the <img> element

Table 16-3 Image object properties (continued)

Property	Description
hspace	A read-only property containing the amount of horizontal space, in pixels, to the left and right of the image, as specified by the HSPACE attribute of the <img> element
lowsrc	The URL of an alternate image to display at low resolution
name	A name assigned to the element
src	The URL of the displayed image
vspace	A read-only property containing the amount of vertical space, in pixels, above and below the image, as specified by the VSPACE attribute of the <img> element
width	A read-only property containing the width of the image as specified by the WIDTH attribute of the <img> element

Table 16-4 Image object events

Event	Description
onLoad	Executes after an image is loaded
onAbort	Executes when the user cancels the loading of an image, usually by clicking the Stop button
onError	Executes when an error occurs while an image is loading

One of the most important parts of the **Image** object is the **src** property, which allows JavaScript to change an image dynamically. The **src** property of the **Image** object represents the **src** attribute of an **<img>** element. Changing the value of the **src** property also changes the **src** attribute associated with an **<img>** element, which dynamically changes an image displayed on a Web page.

Next, you will create a document that allows users to dynamically change the image displayed with an **<img>** element. You will create three buttons that allow users to display differently sized versions of the same image. The JPEG images you will use (named *smallbird, mediumbird,* and *largebird*) are located in the Chapter folder for Chapter 16. As the file names suggest, one image is of a small bird, one of a medium-sized bird, and one of a large bird.

To create a document that allows users to dynamically change the image displayed with an **<img>** element:

1. Start your text editor and create a new document.

2. Type the **<html>** and **<head>** sections of the document:

   <html><head><title>Image Options</title></head>

3. Add **<body>** to start the body section, and then type **<form>** to start a form.

4. Create the following **\<input\>** elements that will allow the user to click a button in order to select a small bird, a medium bird, or a large bird. The elements use the **onClick** event handler to change the height and width properties of the **Image** object.

```
<input type="button" VALUE=" Small Bird "
    onClick="document.bird.src='smallbird.gif';">
<input type="button" VALUE=" Medium Bird "
    onClick="document.bird.src='mediumbird.gif';">
<input type="button" VALUE=" Big Bird "
    onClick="document.bird.src='largebird.gif';">
```

5. Type the closing **\</form\>** tag.

6. Next, add the following line, which adds the **\<img\>** element. The image is initially set to **smallbird.gif**.

```
<img src="smallbird.gif" name="bird">
```

7. Type the closing **\</body\>** and **\</html\>** tags.

8. Save the file as **Ch16DHTML01.html** in the Chapter folder for Chapter 16. Open the **Ch16DHTML01.html** file in your Web browser. The page first displays the small bird image.

9. Click the **Medium Bird** button. Your document should look like the one in Figure 16-2.

Figure 16-2   Ch16DHTML01.html

10. Test the **Big Bird** and then the **Small Bird** buttons. The image changes size each time you click a button. When you are finished, close the Web browser window.

16

Working with Timeouts and Intervals

As you develop Web pages, you may need to have some JavaScript code execute repeatedly, without user intervention. Alternately, you may want to create animation or allow for some kind of repetitive task that needs to execute automatically. You use JavaScript's timeout and interval methods to create code that executes automatically. The **setTimeout() method** is used in JavaScript to execute code after a specific amount of time has elapsed. Code executed with the setTimeout() method executes only once. The syntax for the setTimeout() method is var *variable* = setTimeout("*code*", *milliseconds*);. This variable declaration assigns a reference for the setTimeout() method to a variable. The code argument must be enclosed in double or single quotation marks and can be a single JavaScript statement, a series of JavaScript statements, or a function call. The amount of time the Web browser should wait before executing the code argument of the setTimeout() method is expressed in milliseconds. A millisecond is one thousandth of a second; there are 1,000 milliseconds in a second. For example, five seconds is equal to 5,000 milliseconds. The **clearTimeout() method** is used to cancel a setTimeout() method before its code executes. The clearTimeout() method receives a single argument, which is the variable that represents a setTimeout() method call.

Two other JavaScript methods that create code that executes automatically are the setInterval() **method** and the clearInterval() method. The **setInterval() method** is similar to the setTimeout() method, except that it repeatedly executes the same code after being called only once. The **clearInterval() method** is used to clear a setInterval() method call in the same fashion that the clearTimeout() method clears a setTimeout() method call. The setInterval() and clearInterval() methods are most often used for starting animation code that executes repeatedly. The syntax for the setInterval() method is the same as the syntax for the setTimeout() method: var *variable* = setInterval("*code*", *milliseconds*);. As with the clearTimeout() method, the clearInterval() method receives a single argument, which is the variable that represents a setInterval() method call.

Animation with the Image Object

By combining the src attribute of the Image object with the setTimeout() or setInterval() methods, you can create simple animation in an HTML document. In this context, "animation" does not necessarily mean a complex cartoon character, but any situation in which a sequence of images changes automatically. However, Web animation can also include traditional animation involving cartoons and movement. Examples of JavaScript programs that use animation include a simple advertisement in which two images change every few seconds and the ticking hands of an online clock (each position of the clock hands requires a separate image). Figure 16-3 contains a program that uses the setInterval() method to automatically swap two advertising images every couple of seconds. Figure 16-4 shows the two images displayed in a browser.

```
<html><head><title>Advertisement</title>
<script language="JavaScript">
<!-- HIDE FROM INCOMPATIBLE BROWSERS
var qa = "q";
function changeImage() {
    if (qa == "q") {
            document.animation.src = "answer.jpg";
            qa = "a";
    }
    else {
            document.animation.src = "question.jpg";
            qa = "q";
    }
}
// STOP HIDING FROM INCOMPATIBLE BROWSERS -->
</script></head>
<body onLoad="var begin=setInterval('changeImage()',2000);">
<p><img src="question.jpg" name="animation"></p>
</body></html>
```

Figure 16-3   Changing images program

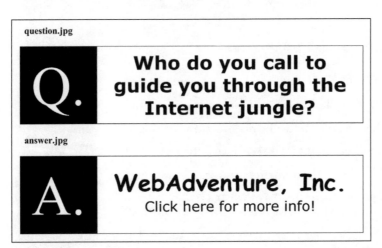

Figure 16-4   Advertising images

 If you would like to try out the flashing advertising program for yourself, you will find a copy of the document (named *Advertisement.html*) in the Chapter folder for Chapter 16.

True animation requires a different graphic, or frame, for each movement that a character or object makes. This book does not teach the artistic skills necessary for creating frames in an animation sequence. Instead, the goal is to show how to use JavaScript and the `Image` object to perform simple animation by swapping frames displayed by an `<img>` element.

Do not confuse animation frames with frames created with the `<frameset>` and `<frame>` elements.

Next, you will create an animated rocking horse. The six images required for the animation are located in the Chapter folder for Chapter 16. Figure 16-5 shows the figures.

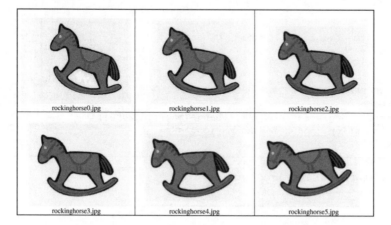

Figure 16-5   Rocking horse frames

To create the rocking horse animation:

1. Create a new document in your your text editor.

2. Type the `<html>` and `<head>` sections of the document:

   ```
   <html><head><title>Rocking Horse</title>
   ```

3. Add the opening statements for a JavaScript section:

   ```
   <script language="JavaScript">
   <!-- HIDE FROM INCOMPATIBLE BROWSERS
   ```

4. Type the following four variable declarations. The `horses` variable will contain the names of the six image files. The `curHorse` variable will be used in an `if` statement as a counter. (Counters are described in Chapter 15.) The `direction` variable will be used to determine if the horse should "rock" right or left. The `begin` variable will be assigned to the `setInterval()` method that starts the animation.

   ```
   var horses = new Array(5);
   var curHorse = 0;
   var direction;
   var begin;
   ```

5. Assign the image files to the corresponding elements in the horses array:

```
horses[0] = "rockinghorse0.jpg"; horses[1] =
"rockinghorse1.jpg";
horses[2] = "rockinghorse2.jpg"; horses[3] =
"rockinghorse3.jpg";
horses[4] = "rockinghorse4.jpg"; horses[5] =
"rockinghorse5.jpg";
```

6. The following function actually performs the animation. The first `if` statement checks the `curHorse` variable to see if it is equal to 0 or 5. If the variable is equal to 0, the `direction` variable is set to `right`; if it is equal to 5, the direction variable is set to `left`. The next `if` statement then checks the `direction` variable to determine whether to increment or decrement the `curHorse` variable. The final statement in the function changes the image displayed by an `<img>` element named `animation` to the image that corresponds to the element in the `horses[]` array that matches index specified by the `curHorse` variable. You will create the animation `<img>` element in step 9.

```
function rockHorse() {
    if (curHorse == 0)
        direction = "right";
    else if (curHorse == 5)
        direction = "left";
    if (direction == "right")
        ++curHorse;
    else if (direction == "left")
        --curHorse;
    document.animation.src = horses[curHorse];
}
```

7. Next, add the following function, which will be called whenever the user clicks the Start Rocking button in the body of the document. The `if` statement checks whether the animation is already running. Notice that the `if` statement conditional expression includes only the name of the `begin` variable, without any other operators. This technique enables the program to quickly check whether an object exists or if a variable has been initialized. If the `setInterval()` method has been called and assigned to the `begin` variable, then the conditional expression returns a value of `true`, which causes the `if` statement to execute the `clearInterval()` method to cancel the animation. If you did not include the `if` statement, the user could click the Start Rocking button several times, which would cause multiple instances of the `setInterval()` method to occur. This would then cause the browser to execute as many animation sequences as there are instances of the `setInterval()` method, which in turn could make the animation appear to run faster than desired or function erratically. The last statement in

16

the function is the `setInterval()` method, which runs the `rockHorse()` function you created in step 6.

```
function startRocking() {
  if (begin)
      clearInterval(begin);
  begin = setInterval('rockHorse()',100);
}
```

8. Add the following code to close the `<script>` and `<head>` elements:

```
// STOP HIDING FROM INCOMPATIBLE BROWSERS -->
</script></head>
```

9. Add the following body section to the document. The `<img>` element, named `animation`, opens the first frame in the animation, rockinghorse0.jpg. The Start Rocking button uses the `onClick` event handler to execute the `startRocking()` function, and the Stop Rocking button stops the `setInterval()` method executed by the `startRocking()` function.

```
<body><h1>Rocking Horse Toys, Inc.</h1>
<p><img src="rockinghorse0.jpg" name="animation"></p>
<form><input type="button" name="run"
VALUE=" Start Rocking " onClick="startRocking();">
<input type="button" name="stop"
VALUE=" Stop Rocking " onClick="clearInterval(begin);">
</form></body>
```

10. Type a closing `</html>` tag.

11. Save the file as **Ch16DHTML02.html** in the Chapter folder for Chapter 16. Open the **Ch16DHTML02.html** file in your Web browser and verify that the Start Rocking and Stop Rocking buttons work correctly.

12. Close the Web browser window.

Image Caching

In the rocking horse program, you may have noticed that the loading of each image appears to be jerky, erratic, or slow, and that the URL for each image flickers in the status bar each time the image changes. This occurs because JavaScript does not save a copy of the image in memory to be used whenever necessary. Instead, each time a different image is loaded by an `<img>` element, JavaScript must physically open or reopen the image from its source. You probably accessed the rocking horse image files directly from the data disk on your local computer. If you have a particularly fast computer, you may not have noticed a loading problem. If you did experience erratic loading of the images, then you can imagine how erratic and slow the animation would appear if you had to download the images from the Web server *each time they were loaded*. To eliminate multiple downloads of the same file, you can use a technique called *image caching*. **Image caching** is the process of temporarily storing image files in memory on a local computer. This technique allows JavaScript to store and retrieve an image from memory rather than download the image each time it is needed.

You cache images using the Image() constructor of the Image object. The Image() constructor creates a new Image object. There are three steps for caching an image in JavaScript:

- Create a new object using the Image() constructor
- Assign a graphic file to the src property of the new Image object
- Assign the src property of the new Image object to the src property of an <img> element

In the following code, the src attribute of the <img> element named myImage is initially set to an empty string (""). In the <script> section, a new Image object named newImage is created. The newImage object is used to save and access the memory cache containing the image file. A file named *graphic.jpg* is assigned to the src property of the newImage object. The src property of the newImage object is then assigned to the src property of the <img> element.

```
<body><img name="myImage" src="">
<script language="JavaScript">
<!-- HIDE FROM INCOMPATIBLE BROWSERS
newImage = new Image()
newImage.src = "graphic.jpg"
document.myImage.src = newImage.src
// STOP HIDING FROM INCOMPATIBLE BROWSERS -->
</script></body>
```

Keep in mind that in the preceding code, the graphic.jpg file is *not* assigned directly to the src property of the <img> element. Instead, the newImage object is assigned to the src property of the <img> element. If you assigned the graphic.jpg file directly to the src property of the <img> element using the statement document.myImage.src = "graphic.jpg"; then the file would reload from its source each time it was needed. By contrast, the newImage object opens the file once and saves it to a memory cache.

Next, you will modify the rocking horse program to incorporate image caching.

To add image caching to the Ch16DHTML02.html document:

1. Return to the **Ch16DHTML02.html** file in your text editor and then save it as a new file named **Ch16DHTML03.html** in the Chapter folder for Chapter 16.

2. Locate the following six statements that assign each rocking horse frame to the horses[] array:

```
horses[0] = "rockinghorse0.jpg"; horses[1] =
"rockinghorse1.jpg";
horses[2] = "rockinghorse2.jpg"; horses[3] =
"rockinghorse3.jpg";
horses[4] = "rockinghorse4.jpg"; horses[5] =
"rockinghorse5.jpg";
```

16

3. Replace the preceding statements with the following for statement. The for statement creates a new **Image** object within each element of the **horses[ ]** array. Each object in the **horses[ ]** array is then assigned an image file using the **src** property.

```
for(var i = 0; i < 6; ++i) {
    horses[i] = new Image();
    horses[i].src = "rockinghorse" + i + ".jpg";
}
```

4. Add the **src** property to the **document.animation.src = horses[curHorse];** statement in the **rockHorse( )** function so that it reads **document.animation.src = horses[curHorse].src;**.

5. Save the document and open it in your Web browser. If you previously experienced erratic animation, the new animation should appear much smoother.

6. Close the Web browser window.

Even when you use image caching, the images must all be loaded into an **Image** object before the animation will function correctly. Often, you will want animation to start as soon as a page finishes loading. (The rocking horse animation, for example, is designed to start as soon as the page finishes loading.) However, even if a page has finished loading, all the images may not have finished downloading and may not be stored in image caches. This means that if you run the rocking horse program across a slow Internet connection, the **onLoad** event handler of the **<body>** element may execute the animation sequence before all the frames are transferred and assigned to **Image** objects. The animation will still function, but it will be erratic until all the images have been successfully stored in **Image** objects. To avoid such problems, you can use the **onLoad** event handler of the **Image** object, which ensures that all images are downloaded into a cache before commencing an animation sequence.

Next, you will add to the rocking horse program an image **onLoad** event that executes the animation after all the images load. You will also modify the program so that the animation executes as soon as all the images load.

To add an image **onLoad** event to the rocking horse program and to modify it so that the animation executes as soon as all the images load:

1. Return to the **Ch16DHTML03.html** file in your text editor and then save it as a new file named **Ch16DHTML04.html** in the Chapter folder for Chapter 16.

2. Add **var imagesLoaded = 0;** on a new line below the **var begin;** statement. The **imagesLoaded** variable will keep a count of the number of images loaded.

3. Add the statement **horses[i].onload = loadImages;** on a new, blank line just before the closing brace in the **for** loop that assigns each rocking horse image file to the **horses[ ]** array. As each image is loaded, its **onLoad** event calls the **loadImages( )** function.

4. After the `for` loop, create the following `loadImages()` function, which is called from the `horses[i].onload = loadImages;` statement you added in step 3. The function increments the `imagesLoaded` variable each time it is called. After the `imagesLoaded` variable equals 6, a `setInterval()` method executes the `rockHorse()` function.

```
function loadImages() {
    ++imagesLoaded;
    if (imagesLoaded == 6)
        begin = setInterval('rockHorse()',100);
}
```

5. Delete the `startRocking()` function from the `<script>` section, and delete the form from the body of the document.

6. Save the document and open it in your Web browser. The animation should begin as soon as all the images load.

7. Close the Web browser window.

USING JAVASCRIPT WITH CSS STYLES

As you learned in Chapter 11, CSS styles determine the formatting of HTML document elements. You use JavaScript to modify CSS styles after a Web browser renders a document. As mentioned earlier, prior to the release of the W3C standardized DOM specifications, there was no compatible DHTML standard that worked with both Internet Explorer and Netscape Navigator. This incompatibility was particularly evident when using JavaScript to manipulate CSS styles. Earlier versions of Internet Explorer and Navigator supported incompatible `Document` object properties and methods. Because JavaScript uses `Document` object properties and methods to access CSS styles, if you wanted to use JavaScript code to manipulate CSS in older browsers, you had three options:

- Write code that functioned only in Navigator
- Write code that functioned only in Internet Explorer
- Write both sets of code and execute the correct set depending on which Web browser was in use

This section briefly explains how to use JavaScript to refer to CSS styles and presents some techniques for writing DHTML code that functions in older versions of each browser and current versions of each browser that support the W3C DOM Level 2.

Using JavaScript and Styles in Older Versions of Navigator

The Navigator Document Object Model in older versions of Navigator accesses the styles for selectors using the `tags`, `classes`, and `ID` properties of the `Document`

16

object. The **tags property** provides access to the styles of elements in an HTML document. The **classes property** provides access to the styles of classes in an HTML document. The **ID property** provides access to the styles of ID attributes in an HTML document.

The tags, classes, and ID properties of the Document object are available only in Navigator 4.7 and earlier.

To refer to a CSS style in older versions of Navigator, you append the **tags**, **classes**, or **ID** property to the **Document** object with a period. For the **tags** and **ID** properties, you then append the name of a CSS selector, followed by another period and a CSS property. For example, to change the font color for the <h1> element to blue, you use the statement **document.tags.h1.fontColor = "blue";**. To modify the font color for the ID named **bigGreenLine** to blue, you use the statement **document.ids.bigGreenLine.fontColor = "blue";**. For the **classes** property, you must append either the **all** property to modify all instances of the class or the name of a CSS selector, followed by another period and a CSS property. For example, to change the font color for all HTML elements that include the **level1** class attribute, you use the statement **document.classes.level1.all.fontColor = "blue";**. To change just the <h1> elements that include the **level1** class attribute, you use the statement **document.classes.level1.h1.fontColor = "blue";**. Notice that when you refer to a CSS property containing a hyphen in JavaScript code, you remove the hyphen, convert the first word to lowercase, and convert the first letter of subsequent words to uppercase. CSS properties without hyphens are referred to with all lowercase letters. **Border** is referred to as **border**, **border-color** is referred to as **borderColor**, **font-size** is referred to as **fontSize**, and so on. For example, to modify the font size of the <h1> element to **18pt**, you use the statement **document.tags.h1.fontSize = "18pt";**.

You can use JavaScript code to change the value of a style after it has been rendered by Navigator, but the change does not appear until the user resizes the screen.

Using JavaScript and Styles in Older Versions of Internet Explorer

The Internet Explorer Document Object Model in older versions of Internet Explorer accesses the styles for selectors by using the **all** property of the **Document** object. The **all property** is an array of all the elements in an HTML document. The **all** property is appended with a period to the **Document** object. If you want to modify the styles for a CSS selector, you then append another period and the name of a specific CSS selector. You then append a period and the **style** property, followed by a period and a specific

CSS property. The **style property** represents the CSS styles for a particular `tag` or `ID` attribute. When you refer to a CSS property in JavaScript code in older versions of Internet Explorer, you remove the hyphen from the property name and convert the property to mixed case. (In other words, you follow the same rule as for older versions of Navigator.) For example, to modify the font size for the `ID` attribute named `bigGreenLine` to `36pt`, you use the statement `document.all.bigGreenLine.style.fontSize = "36pt";`. To modify the styles for a specific HTML element, you must first gain access to the styles using the `tags(tag name)` method. The **tags(*tag name*) method** returns an array of HTML elements represented by *tag name*. You append the `tags()` method to the `all` property (which is appended to the `Document` object) with a period, and then pass the tag name enclosed in quotation marks to the `tags()` method.

 The `all` and `style` properties and the `tags()` method are available only in Internet Explorer. Unlike the Navigator Document Object Model, which is only available in Navigator versions 4.7 and earlier, the Internet Explorer Document Object Model is available in all versions of Internet Explorer, including version 6. However, keep in mind that if you use the `all` and `style` properties in your JavaScript programs, they will not be compatible with the W3C DOM, and therefore, they are not cross-browser compatible.

With the `tags()` method, the HTML tags that match a specific tag name are assigned to the elements of an array in the order in which they are encountered in a document. The following code shows how to use the `tags()` method to return all of the `<h1>` elements in a document to an array named `allh1Tags[]`. Text placed within the `<h1>` element shows the element number that each `<h1>` element is assigned to the `allh1Tags[]` array.

```
<body><h1>Assign to allh1Tags[0]</h1>
<h1>Assign to allh1Tags[1]</h1>
<h1>Assign to allh1Tags[2]</h1>
<h1>Assign to allh1Tags[3]</h1>
<script language="JavaScript">
<!-- HIDE FROM INCOMPATIBLE BROWSERS
var allh1Tags = document.all.tags("h1");
// STOP HIDING FROM INCOMPATIBLE BROWSERS -->
</script></body>
```

16

You append a period and the `style` property to the array returned by the `tags()` method, followed by a period and a specific CSS property, just as when you modify an `ID` attribute. However, you must use the element number to access a specific element in the returned array. For example, the following code shows how to modify the `color` CSS property for the third `<h1>` element found in a document using the `allh1Tags[]` array:

```
allh1Tags[2].style.color = "red";
```

You can also use the `Document` object with the `tags()` method directly in a statement that modifies a CSS style, just as you can with an `ID` attribute. However, the statement may get somewhat cumbersome, as shown in the following statement:

```
document.all.tags("h1")[2].style.color = "red";
```

In order to change `style` properties for all of the elements in an array returned by the `tags()` method at the same time, you must use a looping statement, such as the following `for` statement:

```
var allh1Tags = document.all.tags("h1");
for (var i = 0; i < allh1Tags.length; ++i) {
    allh1Tags[i].style.color = "red";
    allh1Tags[i].style.fontFamily = "arial";
    allh1Tags[i].style.fontSize = "24pt";
}
```

One of the advantages to the Internet Explorer Document Object Model is that you can use JavaScript to dynamically change styles in Internet Explorer. When you change a style in Internet Explorer using JavaScript, the changes appear immediately in the browser; in Navigator, you must resize the window.

 Modifying the CSS styles for a particular class with JavaScript in older versions of Internet Explorer is somewhat advanced for our purposes, so these techniques will not be discussed here. If you would like to learn how to use JavaScript to modify CSS styles for a particular class in older versions of Internet Explorer see the topic "Dynamic Styles" and its subtopics in the MSDN Library at msdn.microsoft.com/ library/default.asp?url=/workshop/author/dynstyle/ changing.asp. Also see the MSDN Library article "Scripting with Elements and Collections" at msdn.microsoft.com/library/default.asp?url=/workshop/author/ om/scripting_elements_collections.asp.

Using JavaScript and Styles with the W3C DOM

In order to manipulate CSS styles with the W3C DOM, you must first gain access to the styles by using either the `getElementByID(ID)` method or the `getElementsByTagName(tag name)` method. The **getElementByID(ID) method** returns the HTML element represented by ID. The **getElementsByTagName(tag name) method** returns an array of HTML elements represented by *tag name*. You append each of the methods to the `Document` object with a period, and then pass the appropriate argument to the method you are using. The following statement shows how to use the `getElementByID()` method to access the tag with an ID of `bigGreenLine` and assign it to a variable named `curStyle`:

```
var curStyle = document.getElementByID("bigGreenLine");
```

After using the `getElementByID()` method to assign a tag to a variable, you then append a period and the `style` property to the variable, followed by a period and a specific CSS property. The `style` property represents the CSS styles for a particular tag, class, or ID, the same as in the Internet Explorer Document Object Model. The following code shows how to modify CSS properties by using the `curStyle` variable, which contains the tag returned by the `getElementByID()` method for the `bigGreenLine` ID.

```
curStyle.style.color = "green";
curStyle.style.fontFamily = "arial";
curStyle.style.fontSize = "36pt";
```

Instead of assigning the tag returned by the `getElementByID()` method to a variable, you can use the `Document` object and `getElementByID()` method directly in a statement that modifies a CSS style, as follows:

```
document.getElementById("bigGreenLine").style.color = "green";
document.getElementById("bigGreenLine").style.fontFamily = "arial";
document.getElementById("bigGreenLine").style.fontSize = "36pt";
```

With the `getElementsByTagName()` method, the HTML tags that match a specific element name are assigned to the elements of an array in the order in which they are encountered in a document. The following code shows how to use the `getElementsByTagName()` method to return all of the `<h1>` elements in a document to an array named `allh1Tags[]`. Text placed within the `<h1>` element shows the element number that each `<h1>` element is assigned to in the `allh1Tags[]` array.

```
<body><h1>Assign to allh1Tags[0]</h1>
<h1>Assign to allh1Tags[1]</h1>
<h1>Assign to allh1Tags[2]</h1>
<h1>Assign to allh1Tags[3]</h1>
<script language="JavaScript">
<!-- HIDE FROM INCOMPATIBLE BROWSERS
var allh1Tags = document.getElementsByTagName("h1");
// STOP HIDING FROM INCOMPATIBLE BROWSERS -->
</script></body>
```

You append a period and the `style` property to the array returned by the `getElementsByTagName()` method, followed by a period and a specific CSS property, just as when you use a variable returned with the `getElementByID()` method. However, you must use the element number to access a specific element in the returned array. For example, the following code shows how to modify the `color` CSS property for the third `<h1>` element found in a document using the `allh1Tags[]` array:

```
allh1Tags[2].style.color = "red";
```

You can also use the `Document` object with the `getElementsByTagName()` method directly in a statement that modifies a CSS style, just as you can with the `getElementByID()` method. However, the statement may get somewhat cumbersome, as shown in the following statement:

```
document.getElementsByTagName("h1")[2].style.color = "red";
```

16

In order to change `style` properties for all of the elements in an array returned by the `getElementsByTagName()` method at the same time, you must use a looping statement, such as the following `for` statement:

```
var allh1Tags = document.getElementsByTagName("h1");
for (var i = 0; i < allh1Tags.length; ++i) {
    allh1Tags[i].style.color = "red";
    allh1Tags[i].style.fontFamily = "arial";
    allh1Tags[i].style.fontSize = "24pt";
}
```

 Modifying the CSS styles for a particular class with JavaScript and the W3C DOM is somewhat advanced for our purposes, so these techniques will not be discussed here. If you would like to learn how to use JavaScript to modify CSS styles for a particular class in the W3C DOM, see the article "How to Dynamically Change an Element's Style by Its Class Attribute" at the Markup for Hand Coders Web site at www.markup.co.nz/dom/styleClass_with_dom.htm.

CSS POSITIONING

Earlier in this chapter, you used the `<img>` element to create simple animations with JavaScript. The `<img>` element is limited, however, because the only kind of animation you can perform with it is stationary. That is, an animation created with the `<img>` element does not travel across the screen. To reposition an image on a Web page, you need to use **CSS positioning**, a specialized DHTML technique. CSS positioning is supported in W3C DOM–compliant browsers as well as older versions of both Navigator and Internet Explorer. Because of `Document` object incompatibilities between the two older browsers, however, you cannot write JavaScript code that works in both older browsers and in W3C DOM–compliant browsers. You must design your program for either older versions of Navigator, older versions of Internet Explorer, or W3C DOM–compliant browsers, or write three sets of code and execute the correct set depending on which Web browser is in use.

There are two types of CSS positioning: relative and absolute. **Relative positioning** places an element according to other elements on a Web page. **Absolute positioning** places elements in a specific location on a Web page. Relative positioning is mainly used for the design and layout of Web pages and is beyond the scope of this text. Absolute positioning is used with JavaScript to create full animation, among other things.

You usually add positioning to elements with inline styles. You can also use CSS positioning in a document-level style sheet. However, if you apply positioning to an element, such as `<h1>`, in a document-level style sheet, then all instances of the `<h1>` element in the document will be positioned in exactly the same place. In contrast, using positioning for IDs in document-level style sheets works fine. It is usually easier, however, to add positioning directly to an element as an inline style.

Several common CSS positioning properties are listed in Table 16-5.

Table 16-5 Common CSS positioning properties

Property	Description	Values
position	Determines how an element is to be positioned	Absolute or relative
Left	The horizontal distance from the upper-left corner of the window	A value in pixels
Top	The vertical distance from the upper-left corner of the window	A value in pixels
width	The width of the boundary box	A value in pixels
height	The height of the boundary box	A value in pixels
visibility	Determines if an element is visible	Visible or hidden

Older Navigator versions do not recognize CSS positioning for empty elements—that is, elements without a closing tag. For instance, you cannot use CSS positioning on an **<img>** element, because it does not include a closing tag. To maintain cross-browser compatibility, elements that are to be positioned are usually placed within **<span>** or **<div>** elements. The **<span>** element is used for applying formatting to sections of an HTML document; the **<div>** element breaks a document into distinct sections. Specific CSS positioning properties are placed inside the closing bracket of an opening **<span>** or **<div>** tag.

The following code absolutely positions an image contained within a **<span>** element. The resulting image is displayed in a Web browser in Figure 16-6.

```
<span style="position:absolute; left:150; top:165">
<img src="sun.gif"></span>
```

Next, you will position two images in an HTML document. The images, named *up.gif* and *down.gif*, are located in the Chapter folder for Chapter 16. The up.gif file contains an image of a bird with its wings lifted, and the down.gif file contains an image of the same bird with its wings down. The Web page you create will contain the up.gif image twice and the down.gif image once. You will position the three images so the bird appears to be taking off.

16

To position two images in an HTML document:

1. Create a new document in your text editor.

2. Type the **<html>** and **<head>** sections of the document:

   <html><head><title>Three Birds</title></head>

3. Type **<body>** to start the body section.

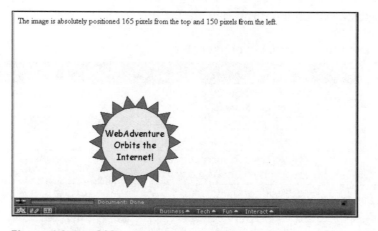

The image is absolutely positioned 165 pixels from the top and 150 pixels from the left.

WebAdventure
Orbits the
Internet!

Figure 16-6   CSS positioning

4. Add the following lines to create the first absolutely positioned image. The image, up.gif, is contained within a **<span>** element. You use the **style** attribute to absolutely position the image at 40 pixels from the left and 200 pixels from the top.

```
<span style="position:absolute; left:40; top:200">
<img src="up.gif"></span>
```

5. Add the following lines to create the second absolutely positioned image. The image, down.gif, is also contained within a **<span>** element. You use the **style** attribute to absolutely position the image at 250 pixels from the left and 80 pixels from the top.

```
<span style="position:absolute; left:250; top:80">
<img src="down.gif"></span>
```

6. Now add the following lines to create the third absolutely positioned image. The up.gif image is used again and is absolutely positioned at 480 pixels from the left and 10 pixels from the top.

```
<span style="position:absolute; left:480; top:10">
<img src="up.gif"></span>
```

7. Add the following code to close the **<body>** and **<html>** elements:

```
</body></html>
```

8. Save the file as **Ch16DHTML05.html** in the Chapter folder for Chapter 16. Open the **Ch16DHTML05.html** file in your Web browser. Figure 16-7 shows the output.

Figure 16-7   Output of Three Birds Web page

  9. Close the Web browser window.

Next, you will learn how to create traveling images by dynamically positioning images with JavaScript. Because of the incompatibilities between older versions of Navigator and Internet Explorer, you will learn how to achieve dynamic positioning for each older browser, as well as how to perform dynamic positioning in W3C DOM–compatible browsers. First, you will learn about dynamic positioning in older versions of Internet Explorer.

Dynamic Positioning in Older Versions of Internet Explorer

As you learned earlier, older versions of Internet Explorer allow you to use JavaScript to dynamically change CSS styles. In this situation, changes to the document's appearance are displayed immediately. You dynamically position an element in Internet Explorer by appending the `all` property to the `Document` object, followed by a period and the name of a specific CSS selector, followed by the `style` property. Finally, you append another period and the `left` or `top` CSS properties. For example, the statement `document.all.sampleimage.style.left = "3.00in";` moves an element with an ID of `sampleimage` three inches to the right by changing its `left` property to `"3.00in"`. Combining the `left` and `top` CSS properties with a `setTimeout()` or `setInterval()` method allows you to create traveling animation.

Next, to practice creating traveling animation, you will create an animation of the Earth revolving around the sun; this animation will be for older versions of Internet Explorer. The images you need, named *earth.gif* and *sun.gif*, are located in the Chapter folder for Chapter 16. The coordinates of the orbit that the Earth will take are plotted in Figure 16-8. Note that the positions around the sun are not exact. To calculate exact

16

positions, you would need a complicated formula to calculate the radius of the orbit. Also, note that smoother animation can be created by using more positions in the Earth's orbit.

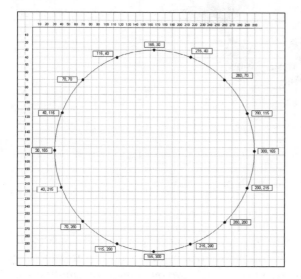

Figure 16-8   Orbit animation coordinates

 Create the program even if you do not have a copy of Internet Explorer, because you will use the program later in this section when you learn about cross-browser compatibility.

To create the orbit animation for Internet Explorer:

1. Create a new document in your text editor.

2. Type the \<html> and \<head> sections of the document, along with the opening statements for a JavaScript section:

```
<html><head><title>Orbit</title>
<script language="JavaScript">
<!-- HIDE FROM INCOMPATIBLE BROWSERS
```

3. To create a variable to track which of the 16 orbit positions are current, add the statement **var position = 0;**.

4. Create the following array to hold the 16 positions corresponding to the left position of the image. The positions correspond to the first position in each set of positions plotted in Figure 16-8.

```
var leftEarth = new Array(16);
leftEarth[0] = 165; leftEarth[1] = 215; leftEarth[2] = 260;
leftEarth[3] = 290; leftEarth[4] = 300; leftEarth[5] = 290;
leftEarth[6] = 260; leftEarth[7] = 215; leftEarth[8] = 165;
```

```
leftEarth[9] = 115; leftEarth[10] = 70; leftEarth[11] = 40;
leftEarth[12] = 30; leftEarth[13] = 40; leftEarth[14] = 70;
leftEarth[15] = 115;
```

5. Create the following array to hold the 16 positions corresponding to the top position of the image. The positions correspond to the second position in each set of positions plotted in Figure 16-8.

```
topEarth = new Array(16);
topEarth[0]  = 30;  topEarth[1]  = 40;  topEarth[2]  = 70;
topEarth[3]  = 115; topEarth[4]  = 165; topEarth[5]  = 215;
topEarth[6]  = 260; topEarth[7]  = 290; topEarth[8]  = 300;
topEarth[9]  = 290; topEarth[10] = 260; topEarth[11] = 215;
topEarth[12] = 165; topEarth[13] = 115; topEarth[14] = 70;
topEarth[15] = 40;
```

6. Add the following orbit() function, which cycles the image of the Earth through the 16 positions of the leftEarth and topEarth arrays. Each position is tracked by the position variable. The orbit() function will be called by using a setInterval() method from the onLoad event handler in the <body> element.

```
function orbit() {
    document.all.earth.style.left = leftEarth[position];
    document.all.earth.style.top = topEarth[position];
    ++position;
    if (position == 16)
        position = 0;
}
```

7. Add the following code to close the <script> and <head> sections:

```
// STOP HIDING FROM INCOMPATIBLE BROWSERS -->
</script></head>
```

8. Add the following opening <body> tag, which uses the setInterval() method to execute the orbit() function with the onLoad event handler:

```
<body onLoad="setInterval('orbit()',200)">
```

9. Type the following two <span> sections. The first section contains and positions the image of the sun. The second section contains and initially positions the image of the Earth. Because you will be animating the Earth using CSS positioning, the <span> section is given an ID of earth.

```
<span style="position:absolute; left:95; top:95">
<img src="sun.gif"></span>
<span ID="earth" style="position:absolute; left:165;
        top:30"><img src="earth.gif"></span>
```

10. Type the closing </body> and </html> tags.

16

11. Save the file as **Ch16DHTML06.html** in the Chapter folder for Chapter 16. If you have a copy of Internet Explorer, open the file and see if the animation functions properly. Figure 16-9 shows the program output in Internet Explorer as it appears before the animation begins.

Figure 16-9 Orbit document in Internet Explorer

12. Close the Web browser window.

Dynamic Positioning in Navigator

Older versions of Navigator do not use CSS positioning for dynamic animation. Instead, you must use layers. **Layers** are Web page elements that are used in Navigator for positioning other elements. You can still use CSS positioning with Navigator, but not for traveling animation. Although layering is not part of the CSS protocol, you need to understand layers to be able to create animation that functions in Navigator. Layering is a large topic that deals not only with animation, but also with other HTML design issues in Navigator. However, you will learn only the aspects of layering that relate to animation.

You create a layer in an HTML document by using a `<layer>` element. You use `left` and `top` attributes of the `<layer>` element to specify an initial position for a layer. You can also include the `name` attribute in a `<layer>` element.

JavaScript accesses each `<layer>` element by using a `Layer` object. The **Layer object** contains several properties and methods for manipulating layers in JavaScript. The two methods of the `Layer` object that create traveling animation in Navigator are the `moveTo()` method and the `offset()` method. The **moveTo() method** moves a layer to a specified position, and it accepts two arguments. The first argument represents the number of pixels from the left side of the window, and the second argument represents the number of pixels from the top of the window. The **offset() method** moves a layer a specified number of pixels horizontally and vertically from its current position. The **offset()** method also accepts two arguments. The first argument represents the number of pixels to move horizontally, and the second argument represents the number of pixels to move vertically.

You refer to a specific layer in JavaScript by using its position in the **layers[]** array or by using the value assigned to the **<layer>** element's name attribute. As with other arrays in JavaScript, such as the **forms[]** array, layers are assigned to the array in the order in which they are encountered by the JavaScript interpreter. To refer to the first layer in a document, you use the statement **document.layers[0];**. However, it is usually easier to refer to a layer by using the value assigned to its name attribute. For example, to refer to an array named "animation", you would use the statement **document.animation;**. Each layer contains its own **Document** object that you must also include in order to refer to layer elements. Therefore, you use the **Document** object twice. For example, to change the **src** property of an image named **myImage** on a layer named **animation**, you use the statement **document.animation.document.myImage. src = "new_image.jpg";**.

Next, you will modify the orbit program so that it functions in Navigator. As with the Internet Explorer version, create the program even if you do not have a copy of Navigator; you will need it when you learn about cross-browser compatibility.

To modify the orbit animation program so that it functions in Navigator:

1. Return to the **Ch16DHTML06.html** file in your text editor and immediately save it as **Ch16DHTML07.html** in the Chapter folder for Chapter 16.

2. In the **orbit()** function, replace the two statements that modify the **left** and **top** properties of the **<span>** element for the Earth image with the following single statement. The new statement uses the Navigator **moveTo()** method to change the position of the Earth layer, which you will add next:

```
document.earth.moveTo(leftEarth[position],
topEarth[position]);
```

3. Replace the **<span>** section for the Earth image with the following **<layer>** element:

```
<layer name="earth" LEFT=165 TOP=30>
<img src="earth.gif"></layer>
```

4. Save the document. If you have a copy of Navigator 4.7 or earlier, open the document and see if it functions correctly. Figure 16-10 shows the program output as it appears in Navigator before the animation begins.

5. Close the Web browser window.

16

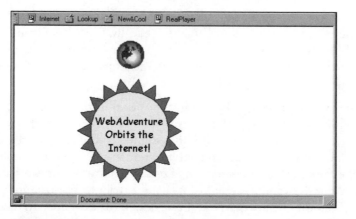

Figure 16-10   Orbit document in Navigator

Dynamic Positioning with W3C DOM–Compliant Browsers

Dynamic positioning with JavaScript in W3C DOM–compliant browsers is quite similar to positioning with JavaScript in the Internet Explorer Document Object Model. You move an element using the `style` property and the `left` and `top` CSS properties. The only difference is that you replace the Internet Explorer `all` property with a call to the `getElementByID()` or `getElementsByTagName()` methods, or with a variable that has been assigned the return value from one of those methods. For example, the statement `document.getElementByID("sampleimage").style.left = "3.00in";` moves an element with an ID of `sampleimage` three inches to the right by changing its left property to `3.00in`.

Next, you will modify the orbit program so that it functions in W3C DOM–compliant browsers.

To modify the orbit animation program so that it functions in W3C DOM–compliant browsers:

1. Open the **Ch16DHTML06.html** file in your text editor and immediately save it as **Ch16DHTML08.html** in the Chapter folder for Chapter 16.

2. In the `orbit()` function, replace the two statements that modify the `left` and `top` properties of the `<span>` element for the Earth image with the following statements. The new statements use the `getElementByID()` method to access the `<span>` element with the `earth` ID attribute.

```
document.getElementById("earth").style.left = leftEarth[position];
document.getElementById("earth").style.top = topEarth[position];
```

3. Save the document, open it in a W3C-compliant browser, and verify that it functions correctly.

4. Close the Web browser window.

CROSS-BROWSER COMPATIBILITY

People and companies want to attract visitors to their Web pages, and they want their Web pages to be as appealing and interesting as possible. However, both Navigator and Internet Explorer are widely used, along with other browsers such as Opera and HotJava. If developers were forced to choose a single Web browser, then a significant portion of Internet users would not be able to visit their Web sites. The best solution is to create DHTML code for each Document Object Model in which you expect your program will run. You could place all of this code in the same document; however, that could make your program difficult to work with because you would need to write numerous conditional expressions for each browser type.

An easier solution is to create separate documents for each Document Object Model: one for older Netscape browsers, one for older Internet Explorer browsers, and one for W3C DOM–compliant browsers. You can then use a "master" document that checks which browser is running when users open the file. After the master document determines which browser is running, it opens the appropriate Web page. A JavaScript program that checks which type of browser is running is commonly called a **browser sniffer**.

Although there are several ways to check which browser is running, including using properties of the Navigator `Document` object, many JavaScript programmers prefer to test which DOM is being used. You can test which DOM is being used by checking whether the `Document` object has a `layers` property (for older Navigator versions), an `all` property (for older Internet Explorer versions), or the `getElementByID()` method (for W3C DOM–compliant browsers). You can check for the `layers` property, the `all` property, and the `getElementByID()` method using conditional statements such as `if (document. layers)`, `if (document.all)`, and `if (getElementByID)`. If the property or method is available in the browser, then a value of `true` is returned. For example, because only the Navigator `Document` object includes a `Layers` object, the statement `if (document.layers)` checks if the object exists and returns `true` if executed in an older version of Navigator or `false` if executed in Internet Explorer or a W3C DOM–compliant browser. Similarly, because only W3C DOM–compliant browsers support the `getElementByID()` method, the statement `if (document.getElementByID)` returns `true` only if executed in a W3C DOM–compliant browser and `false` if executed in earlier versions of Internet Explorer or Navigator. Note that when checking for the existence of a method, you do not include the method parentheses in the conditional expression.

Next, you will create a browser sniffer that opens a browser-specific version of the orbit program.

16

To create a browser sniffer that opens a browser-specific version of the orbit program:

1. Create a new document in your text editor.

2. Type the opening `<html>`, `<head>`, and `<title>` sections of the document:

```
<html><head><title>Orbit</title>
```

3. Add the opening statements for a JavaScript section within the `<head>` section:

```
<script language="JavaScript">
<!-- HIDE FROM INCOMPATIBLE BROWSERS
```

4. Create the following function to check which browser is being used. The function will be called from the `onLoad` event in the `<body>` element:

```
function checkBrowser() {
    if (document.all)
        document.location.href = "Ch16DHTML06.html";
    else if (document.layers)
        document.location.href = "Ch16DHTML07.html";
    else if (document.getElementById)
        document.location.href = "Ch16DHTML08.html";
    else
        document.write("Sorry! Your browser type is not
supported.")
    }
```

5. Add the following code to close the `<script>` and `<head>` sections:

```
// STOP HIDING FROM INCOMPATIBLE BROWSERS -->
</script></head>
```

6. Type the following `<body>` tag that includes an `onLoad` event, which calls the `checkBrowser()` function:

```
<body onLoad="checkBrowser()">
```

7. Add the closing `</body>` and `</html>` tags.

8. Save the file as **Ch16DHTML09.html** in the Chapter folder for Chapter 16. Open the **Ch16DHTML09.html** file. If you are working with a recent browser, then the W3C version of the program should open. The name of the document that opens appears in the Address box in Internet Explorer, in the Location box in Navigator, or in the Search box in Netscape.

9. Close the Web browser window and your text editor.

CHAPTER SUMMARY

❑ The Document Object Model (DOM) represents the HTML document displayed in a window and provides programmatic access to document elements.

❑ The World Wide Web Consortium (W3C) is responsible for defining a platform-independent and browser-neutral version of the DOM.

❑ An `Image` object represents images created using the `<img>` element.

❑ By combining the `src` attribute of the `Image` object with the `setTimeout()` or `setInterval()` methods, you can create simple animation in an HTML document.

❑ Image caching, which temporarily stores image files in memory, is a technique for eliminating multiple downloads of the same file.

❑ The Netscape Document Object Model accesses the styles for selectors using the `tags`, `classes`, and `ID` properties of the `Document` object in older versions of Navigator.

❑ The Internet Explorer Document Object Model accesses the styles for selectors using the `all` and `style` properties and the `tags()` method of the `Document` object in older versions of Internet Explorer.

❑ In order to manipulate CSS styles with the W3C DOM, you must first gain access to the styles using either the `getElementByID(ID)` method or the `getElementsByTagName(tag name)` method.

❑ CSS positioning is used to position or lay out elements on a Web page.

❑ You dynamically position an element in older versions of Internet Explorer by appending the `all` property to the `Document` object, followed by a period and the name of a specific CSS selector, followed by the `style` property. Finally, you append another period and the `left` or `top` CSS properties.

❑ Layers are Web page elements that are used in Navigator for positioning other elements.

❑ You use the `moveTo()` and `offset()` methods of the `Layer` object to dynamically position elements in older versions of Navigator.

❑ You dynamically position an element with JavaScript in W3C DOM–compliant browsers by accessing a tag using the `getElementByID()` or `getElementsByTagName()` methods, and then by using the `style` property and the `left` and `top` CSS properties.

❑ A JavaScript program that checks which type of browser is running is commonly known as a browser sniffer. After a master document learns which browser is running, it opens the appropriate Web page.

16

REVIEW QUESTIONS

1. Which version of the DOM is supported by both Navigator 3 and Internet Explorer 3?

   a. Level 0

   b. Level 1

   c. Level 2

   d. none of the above

2. The _____ method opens a window or frame other than the current window or frame, in order to update its contents with the `write()` and `writeln()` methods.

   a. `draw()`

   b. `get()`

   c. `update()`

   d. `open()`

3. The _____ method notifies the Web browser that you are finished writing to the window or frame and that the document should be displayed.

   a. `complete()`

   b. `close()`

   c. `update()`

   d. `refresh()`

4. The _____ array contains all of an HTML document's images.

   a. `images[]`

   b. `pictures[]`

   c. `graphics[]`

   d. `figures[]`

5. Each image in an HTML page is represented in JavaScript by the _____ object.

   a. `Picture`

   b. `Graphic`

   c. `Image`

   d. `Figure`

6. The speed of animation in JavaScript depends on:

   a. the animation speed option, which is set in the Options dialog box in Internet Explorer or the Preferences dialog box in Navigator.

   b. the speed of a computer's microprocessor.

   c. how many frames are used in the animation sequence.

   d. how many milliseconds are passed as an argument to the `setInterval()` or `setTimeout()` methods.

7. Which of the following is an unnecessary step in image caching?

   a. Create a new object using the `Image()` constructor.

   b. Assign a graphic file to the `src` property of the new `Image` object.

   c. Assign the `src` property of the new `Image` object to the `src` property of an `<img>` element.

   d. Download a copy of an image file to a local hard drive.

8. To be certain that all images are downloaded into a cache before commencing an animation sequence, you use the _____ of the `Image` object.

    a. `onLoad` event handler

    b. `animation` property

    c. `loadImages()` method

    d. `images[]` array

9. When does a change to a style value using JavaScript code appear in older versions of Navigator?

    a. immediately

    b. after the HTML document is reloaded from the server

    c. after the user resizes the window

    d. You cannot use JavaScript to change style values in Navigator.

10. How do you change the `color` style for the `companyLogo` ID using JavaScript code in older versions of Internet Explorer?

    a. `document.companyLogo.style.color = "red";`

    b. `document.all.companyLogo.style.color = "red";`

    c. `document.all.companyLogo.color = "red";`

    d. `document.companyLogo.color = "red";`

11. Which W3C DOM method do you use for manipulating HTML elements that are represented by an `ID` attribute?

    a. `getElement()`

    b. `getElementID()`

    c. `getElementById()`

    d. `getElementByID()`

12. Which W3C DOM method returns an array of HTML elements that represents all instances of a particular element in a document?

    a. `getElementName()`

    b. `getElementTagName()`

    c. `getElementByTag ()`

    d. `getElementByTagName()`

13. Which properties are used with the `style` attribute of inline styles for CSS positioning?

    a. `left` and `top`

    b. `x` and `y`

    c. `horizontal` and `vertical`

    d. `x-axis` and `y-axis`

16

14. Which HTML element is used exclusively by older versions of Navigator for positioning?

  a. `<span>`

  b. `<div>`

  c. `<layers>`

  d. `<position>`

15. A JavaScript program that checks which type of browser is running is commonly referred to as a:

  a. browser sniffer

  b. browser rooter

  c. Web check routine

  d. branching browser program

HANDS-ON EXERCISES

Exercise 16-1

In this exercise, you will complete an animated program showing a stick figure performing jumping jacks.

  1. Use Paint or another graphics program to create a series of frames in which a stick figure performs jumping jacks. In each frame, position the stick figure in one step or stage of performing jumping jacks.

  2. Create a new HTML document and write the code necessary to animate the images you created in step 1. Add two buttons, Jump and Stop, that control the animation.

  3. Save the HTML document as **Ch16DHTMLEX01.html** in the Exercises folder for Chapter 16 and then test it in your browser window. Your document should look similar to Figure 16-11.

Figure 16-11   Output of Exercise 16-1

Exercise 16-2

In this exercise, you will complete an animated program of a fat cat dancing.

1. Create a new document in your text editor. Then enter the following code, which
   is a partially completed animation program of a fat cat dancing. The three images
   required for the program, fatcat0.gif, fatcat1.gif, and fatcat2.gif, are found in the
   Exercises folder for Chapter 16.

```html
<html>
<head>
<title>Fat Cat Dancing</title>
<script language="JavaScript">
<!-- HIDE FROM INCOMPATIBLE BROWSERS
var cats = new Array(3);
var fatCat = 0;
var direction;
var begin;
cats[0] = "fatcat0.gif";
cats[1] = "fatcat1.gif";
cats[2] = "fatcat2.gif";
function dance() {
    if (fatCat == 0)
                direction = "right";
    else if (fatCat == 2)
                direction = "left";
    if (direction == "right")
                ++fatCat;
    else if (direction == "left")
                --fatCat;
```

16

```
        document.animation.src = cats[fatCat];
}
// STOP HIDING FROM INCOMPATIBLE BROWSERS -->
</script>
</head>
<body>
<h1>Fat Cat Dancing</h1>
<p><img src="fatcat1.gif" name="animation"></p>
<form>
<input type="button" name="run" VALUE=" Start Dancing "
onClick="startDancing();>
<input type="button" name="stop" VALUE=" Stop Dancing "
onClick="clearInterval(begin);">
</form>
</body>
</html>
```

2. Complete the program so that the fat cat images change every 200 milliseconds.

3. Save the HTML document as **Ch16DHTMLEX02.html** in the Exercises folder for Chapter 16 and test it in your browser window. Your document should look similar to Figure 16-12.

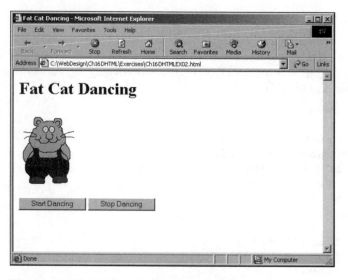

Figure 16-12 Output of Exercise 16-2

Exercise 16-3

In this exercise, you will add image caching to the Fat Cat Dancing program.

1. Add image caching to the Fat Cat Dancing program.

2. Delete the control buttons and modify the program so that the cat starts dancing as soon as the images finish loading.

3. Save the modified HTML document as **Ch16DHTMLEX03.html** in the Exercises folder for Chapter 16 and test it in your browser window.

Exercise 16-4

In this exercise, you will complete an animated program of a turning windmill.

1. Create a new HTML document and use JavaScript to animate the windmill images (windmill0.gif through windmill5.gif) in the Exercises folder for Chapter 16. Add two buttons, Turn and Stop, that control the animation.

2. Save the document as **Ch16DHTMLEX04.html** in the Exercises folder for Chapter 16 and test it in your browser window. Your document should look similar to Figure 16-13.

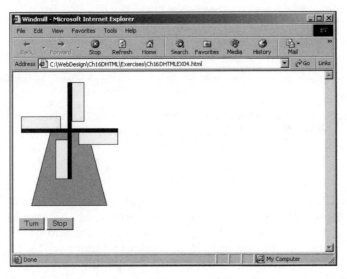

Figure 16-13 Output of Exercise 16-4

Exercise 16-5

16

In this exercise, you will complete an animated program of a basketball bouncing up and down on the screen.

1. Create a new HTML document and use JavaScript to animate the basketball images (basketball0.gif through basketball4.gif) in the Exercises folder for Chapter 16. Animate the images so that the basketball appears to bounce up and down on the screen. Add two buttons, Dribble and Stop, that control the animation.

2. Save the document as **Ch16DHTMLEX05.html** in the Exercises folder for Chapter 16 and test it in your browser window. Your document should look similar to Figure 16-14.

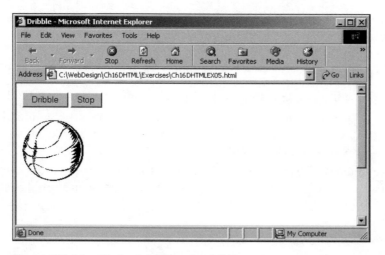

Figure 16-14   Output of Exercise 16-5

WEB DESIGN PROJECTS

In the following projects, create documents for older versions of Navigator and Internet Explorer as well as for the W3C DOM. Also create a browser sniffer for each program. Save all files you create in the Projects folder for Chapter 16.

Project 16-1

The Projects folder for Chapter 16 contains three images of snowflakes: **snowflake1.gif**, **snowflake2.gif**, and **snowflake3.gif**. Use each image as many times as you like to create a snowstorm effect on a Web page. It should "snow" from the top of the browser screen to the bottom. Your document should look similar to Figure 16-15. Name your documents Ch16DHTMLP01a.html, Ch16DHTMLDP01b.html, and so on, and save them in the Projects folder for Chapter 16.

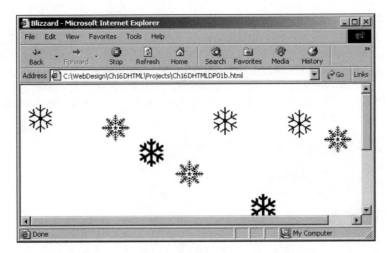

Figure 16-15   Output of Project 16-1

Project 16-2

The Projects folder for Chapter 16 contains an image of a kangaroo, **kangaroo.gif**. Animate the image so that the kangaroo appears to hop up and down and across the browser screen. Your document should look similar to Figure 16-16. Name your documents Ch16DHTMLDP02a.html, Ch16DHTMLDP02b.html, and so on, and save them in the Projects folder for Chapter 16.

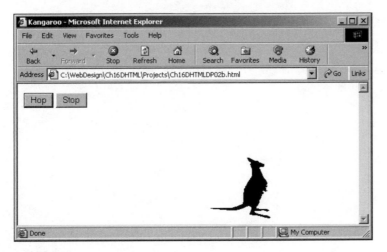

Figure 16-16   Output of Project 16-2

16

Project 16-3

The Projects folder for Chapter 16 contains three images of fish: **fish1.gif**, **fish2.gif**, and **fish3.gif**. Use the fish images to create a fish tank on a Web page. The fish should swim across the browser screen from both directions. Use as many copies of the images as you think necessary. Your document should look similar to Figure 16-17. Name your documents Ch16DHTMLDP03a.html, Ch16DHTMLDP03b.html, and so on, and save them in the Projects folder for Chapter 16.

Figure 16-17   Output of Project 16-3

Glossary

<!DOCTYPE> Declaration — The first line of an XHTML document. This line determines the XHTML document type definition with which the document complies.

Absolute URL — A URL that refers to a specific drive and directory or to the full Web address of a Web page. (*See also* Relative URL.)

Aliasing — An effect that causes the edges of text in Web images to appear jagged when rendered in a Web browser. (*See also* Anti-Aliasing.)

Anchor — The text or image used to represent a link on a Web page.

Anti-Aliasing — A technique that slightly blurs the edges of text in Web images in order to create a smooth edge. (*See also* Aliasing.)

Attributes — Special parameters used to configure the elements that compose a Web page.

Banding — A side effect of reducing the number of colors in an image, in which smooth gradations of colors are marred by stripes. (*See also* Dithering.)

Bitmap Image — An image format defined using individual pixels of color.

Block-Level Elements — Elements that give a Web page its structure.

Browser Wars — Term used to refer to controversy regarding the way browsers work with DHTML, which allows a Web page to change after it has been rendered by a browser. Earlier versions of Internet Explorer and Navigator included DHTML tags that were completely incompatible with each other. Furthermore, Microsoft and Netscape each wanted its version of DHTML to become the industry standard. To settle the argument, the W3C set out to create a platform-independent and browser-neutral version of DHTML.

Browser-Safe Palette — *See* Web Palette.

Cascading Style Sheets — A standard set by the W3C for managing the formatting information of Web pages. Commonly referred to as "CSS" or "style sheets."

Character Entity Reference — A sequence of characters used to display special individual characters on a Web page. You display a character entity reference by using a descriptive name preceded by an ampersand (&) and followed by a semicolon. For instance, the descriptive name for the copyright symbol is "copy." Also known as "character entities."

Client-Side Scripting Language — A programming language included in Web pages to control the Web page itself and the Web browser window. The most popular client-side scripting language is JavaScript. (*See also* JavaScript.)

Color-Reduction — An image optimization method that reduces an image's colors in order to reduce its file size. Color-reduction is appropriate for simple images that contain few colors, such as line graphs.

Common Attributes — *See* Standard Attributes.

Compression — An image optimization method that reduces an image's size by removing portions of the image not visible to the human eye. Compression is appropriate for complex images that contain many colors, such as photographs.

Content — The information contained within an element's opening and closing tags.

Core Attributes — *See* Standard Attributes.

CSS — An acronym for "Cascading Style Sheets."

Definition List — A list of terms and their definitions.

Deprecated — A term used to describe elements and attributes that are considered obsolete and that will eventually be eliminated.

DHTML — An acronym for "Dynamic Hypertext Markup Language."

Dithering — A technique for reducing banding in which pixels are added to an image to break up the boundaries between different colors. (*See also* Banding.)

Document Body — A term used to describe a Web page's <body> element and the text and elements it contains.

Document Head — A term used to describe a Web page's <head> element and the elements it contains.

Document Type Definition — Defines the tags and attributes that can be used in an XHTML document, along with the rules that a document must follow when it includes them. Commonly referred to as a "DTD."

Domain Identifier — The last part of a domain name that identifies the type of institution or organization. Common domain identifiers include .biz, .com, .edu, .info, .net, .org, .gov, .mil, or .int. Each domain identifier briefly describes the type of business or organization it represents. For instance, com (for "company") represents private companies, gov (for "government") represents government agencies, and edu (for "educational") represents educational institutions.

Domain Name — A unique address used for identifying a computer, often a Web server, on the Internet.

Dreamweaver — A Web page authoring tool sold by Macromedia.

DTD — An acronym for "Document Type Definition."

Dynamic Hypertext Markup Language — A combination of HTML, Cascading Style Sheets, and JavaScript used to create dynamic Web pages that a user can interact with. Commonly referred to as "DHTML."

Element — A tag pair and the information it contains.

Empty Element — An element that does not include a closing tag.

Extensible Hypertext Markup Language — A combination of XML and HTML that is used to create Web pages that appear on the Web. Extensible hypertext markup language, or XHTML, will eventually replace HTML as the preferred language for creating Web pages.

Extensible Markup Language — A simple language based on SGML that is used for creating Web pages and for defining and transmitting data between applications. Commonly referred to as "XML."

External Style Sheets — Separate files that contain lists of style rules that can be called from multiple Web pages, making it easier to maintain a common look and feel for an entire Web site. (*See also* Cascading Style Sheets.)

Field — Any form element into which a user can enter data, such as a text box, or that a user can select or change, such as a radio button.

File Transfer Protocol — A protocol used for transferring files across the Internet.

Fireworks — An image creation and editing tool sold by Macromedia.

Flash — A Web page animation tool sold by Macromedia.

Formatting Elements — Elements that provide specific instructions as to how their contents should be displayed. The <b> element, for instance, instructs user agents to display its contents as boldface text.

Forms — A means of collecting information from users on a Web site and transmitting that information to a Web server for processing.

Frames — Independent, scrollable portions of a Web browser window, each of which is capable of containing its own URL.

Frameset DTD — An XHTML DTD that is identical to the Transitional DTD, except that it includes the `<frameset>` and `<frame>` elements, which allow you to split the browser window into two or more frames.

FTP — An acronym for "File Transfer Protocol."

GIF — An acronym for "Graphic Interchange Format."

Graphic Interchange Format — An image format with an extension of .gif that can contain a maximum of 256 colors, optimized through color-reduction. Commonly referred to as "GIF images." GIF images can contain transparent pixels that allow background colors to show through and also can be animated. (*See also* Color-Reduction and Optimization.)

Heading-Level Elements — Block-level elements that are used for emphasizing a document's headings and subheadings. There are six heading-level elements, `<h1>` through `<h6>`. The highest level of importance is `<h1>`; the lowest level of importance is `<h6>`. Also known as "headings."

Headings — *See* Heading-Level Elements.

Home Page — The primary Web page for any given Web site.

Hotspot — A hypertext link defined on an image map that a user can click to go to another Web page. (*See also* Hypertext Link and Image Map.)

HTML — An acronym for "Hypertext Markup Language."

HTTP — An acronym for "Hypertext Transport Protocol."

Hyperlink — *See* Hypertext Link.

Hypertext Link — Text or graphics that the user can click to open files or to navigate to other documents on the Web. A hypertext link on a Web page is underlined and is often displayed in a vivid color. The target of a link can be another location on the same Web page, an external Web page, an image, or some other type of document. Other types of elements, such as images, can also be hypertext links to other Web pages, images, or files. Commonly referred to as "links" or "hyperlinks."

Hypertext Markup Language — A simple language used to design the pages that appear on the World Wide Web. Commonly referred to as "HTML."

Hypertext Transfer Protocol — A protocol that manages the hypertext links that are used to navigate the Web. HTTP ensures that Web browsers correctly process and display the various types of information contained in Web pages (text, graphics, audio, and so on).

Image Map — An image on a Web page that allows users to navigate to different Web pages by clicking on an area of an image known as a hotspot. (*See also* Hotspot.)

Image Rollover — An effect in which an image changes when the user moves his or her mouse pointer over it. Image rollovers are created using JavaScript. (*See also* JavaScript.)

ImageReady — An image animation tool sold by Adobe.

Inline Elements — Elements that describe the individual data that appears on a Web page. Also known as text-level elements.

Inline Styles — Styles used to format specific elements within a document. (*See also* Cascading Style Sheets.)

Internal Style Sheets — A group of style definitions in the header of an HTML document that apply to the entire document. (*See also* Cascading Style Sheets.)

Internet — A vast network that connects computers all over the world. (*See also* World Wide Web.)

Invalid — Term that describes an XHTML document that does not conform to an associated DTD. (*See also* Valid.)

JavaScript — A client-side scripting language included in Web pages to control the Web page itself and the Web browser window.

Joint Photographic Experts Group — An image format with an extension of .jpg that can contain over 16 million colors, optimized through compression. Also known as "JPEG" or "JPG images." JPEG images cannot include transparent pixels and cannot be animated. (*See also* Compression and Optimization.)

JPEG — An acronym for "Joint Photographic Experts Group."

Kerning — The amount of space between characters.

Leading — The amount of whitespace between lines of text.

Link — *See* Hypertext Link.

Markup Language — A set of characters or symbols that define a document's logical structure or how a document should be printed or displayed.

Metadata — A term that means "information about information." In the case of a Web page, you use metadata to provide information to search engines and Web servers about the information in your Web page.

Nesting — A technique in which elements are placed inside of other elements.

Optimization — A technique in which an image's file sized is reduced while its quality is maintained. You optimize images with one of two methods: color-reduction or compression. (*See also* Color-Reduction and Compression.)

Ordered List — A list of numbered items. (*See also* Unordered List.)

Parsing — The process of assembling and formatting a Web page in order for it to be displayed in a Web browser. Also known as "rendering."

Photoshop — An image creation and editing tool sold by Adobe.

Phrase Elements — Elements that primarily describe their contents. For instance, the `<em>` element is an emphasized piece of information, similar to a quotation.

Pixel — A single point on a computer screen. You can think of pixels as millions of tiny dots arranged in columns and rows on your monitor.

The number of pixels available depends on a computer monitor's resolution. Short for *picture element*. (*See also* Resolution.)

PNG — An acronym for "Portable Network Graphics."

Portable Network Graphics — An image format with an extension of .png that is similar to the GIF format. Also known as "PNG images." PNG images are a relatively new format that allows both kinds of optimization (color-reduction or compression) and can contain transparent pixels. Only the newest browsers are able to display PNG images, so this format is rarely used. (*See also* Graphic Interchange Format, Color-Reduction, Compression, and Optimization.)

Relative URL — A URL that specifies the location of a file according to the location of the currently loaded Web page. (*See also* Absolute URL.)

Rendering — The process of assembling and formatting a Web page in order for it to be displayed in a Web browser. Also known as "parsing."

Request — The process that occurs when a Web browser asks a Web server for a Web page after a user either enters the Web page's URL in a browser's address box or clicks a link to the Web page. (*See also* Response.)

Resolution — The number of pixels that can be displayed on a monitor. (*See also* Pixels.)

Response — The Web page (or other type of file or information) that a Web server returns after a request from a Web browser. (*See also* Request.)

Rollover — *See* Image Rollover.

Scripts — Programs that are written using client-side or server-side scripting languages.

Search Engines — Web sites that use software to "crawl" or "spider" their way through the Web and automatically compile an index of Web sites.

Server-Side Scripting Language — A programming language used for writing programs that execute on a Web server. Some of the more popular server-side scripting languages include Common Gateway Interface (CGI), Active Server Pages (ASP), and Java Server Pages (JSP).

Slicing — A technique in which multiple graphics are positioned on a Web page so as to look like a single larger image. Individual image slices can contain their own animations or rollover effects. (*See also* Image Rollover.)

Standard Attributes — Attributes available to almost every element on a Web page (with a few exceptions). Also known as "common attributes" and "core attributes."

Standard Generalized Markup Language — An older language upon which HTML and XHTML are based that defines the data in a document independent of how the data will be displayed.

Strict DTD — An XHTML DTD that eliminates the elements that were deprecated in the Transitional DTD and Frameset DTD.

Style Rule — The style characteristics for a Web page element. (*See also* Cascading Style Sheets.)

Style Sheets — *See* Cascading Style Sheets.

Tables — Collections of rows and columns used to organize and display data on Web pages.

Tag — The starting or ending portion of an element. Most elements consist of a starting and ending tag, known as a "tag pair," that contains text or other elements.

Target Output Format — The medium in which a document will be displayed, such as a Web page or an online help system.

Text-Level Elements — *See* Inline Elements.

Transitional DTD — An XHTML DTD that allows you to continue using deprecated style tags in your XHTML documents.

Uniform Resource Identifier — A generic term for many types of names and addresses on the World Wide Web.

Uniform Resource Locator — A unique address that identifies a Web page. A Uniform Resource Locator, or URL, is also commonly referred to as a "Web address." A URL is a type of Uniform Resource Identifier.

Unordered List — A list of bulleted items. (*See also* Ordered List.)

URI — An acronym for "Uniform Resource Identifier."

URL — An acronym for "Uniform Resource Locator."

User Agent — A device that is capable of retrieving and processing XHTML; it can take the form of a traditional Web browser or be a device such as a mobile phone or personal digital assistant (PDA).

Valid — Term that describes an XHTML document that conforms to an associated DTD.

Validating Parser — A program that checks whether an XHTML document is well formed and whether the document conforms to a specific DTD.

Validation — The process of verifying that an XHTML document is well formed and checking that the elements in your document are correctly written according to the element definitions in a specific DTD.

Vector Image — An image format that uses mathematical formulas and vector paths to define shapes and figures.

W3C — An acronym for "World Wide Web Consortium."

W3C Markup Validation Service — A free service that validates both HTML and XHTML documents. The W3C Markup Validation Service is located at *http://validator.w3.org/*.

Web Address — A common term for "Uniform Resource Locator" or "URL."

Web Browser — A program used to display a Web page on your computer screen.

Web Directories — Lists of Web sites that have been compiled by humans.

Web Hosting — The process by which a Web site is published, making it available for public access.

Web Page — A document written in HTML or XHTML that appears on the World Wide Web.

Web Page Authoring — The creation and assembly of the tags, attributes, and data that make up a Web page. (*See also* Web Page Design.)

Web Page Design — The visual design and creation of the documents that appear on the World Wide Web. (*See also* Web Page Authoring.)

Web Palette — A palette of 216 colors that display properly across both PC and Macintosh platforms at the lowest color depth setting. Also known as the "browser-safe palette."

Web Server — A special type of computer that delivers Web pages to a requesting Web browser.

Web Site — The location on the Internet where Web pages and related files (such as graphic files) that belong to a company, organization, or individual are located.

Well Formed — A term used to describe a document that conforms to the rules and requirements of XHTML.

Whitespace — An empty area on a page. Whitespace is an important design element that can make a page visually pleasing and easy to read.

World Wide Web — A part of the Internet that allows users to easily access Web pages through the use of hypertext links. Also known as "the Web." (*See also* Internet.)

World Wide Web Consortium — An organization that oversees the development of Web technology standards. Commonly referred to as "the W3C."

XHTML — An acronym for "Extensible Hypertext Markup Language."

Index